MW01106049

Social, Health, and Environmental Infrastructures for Economic Growth

Ramesh Chandra Das
Katwa College, India

A volume in the Advances in Finance, Accounting, and Economics (AFAE) Book Series

www.igi-global.com

Published in the United States of America by
IGI Global
Business Science Reference (an imprint of IGI Global)
701 E. Chocolate Avenue
Hershey PA, USA 17033
Tel: 717-533-8845
Fax: 717-533-8661
E-mail: cust@igi-global.com
Web site: http://www.igi-global.com

Library of Congress Cataloging-in-Publication Data

Names: Das, Ramesh Chandra, 1973- editor.
Title: Social, health, and environmental infrastructures for economic growth / Ramesh Chandra Das, editor.
Description: Hershey : Business Science Reference, [2017]
Identifiers: LCCN 2016059803| ISBN 9781522523642 (hardcover) | ISBN 9781522523659 (ebook)
Subjects: LCSH: Infrastructure (Economics)--Developing countries | Economic development--Developing countries.
Classification: LCC HC79.C3 S633 2017 | DDC 338.9009172/4--dc23 LC record available at https://lccn.loc.gov/2016059803

This book is published in the IGI Global book series Advances in Finance, Accounting, and Economics (AFAE) (ISSN: 2327-5677; eISSN: 2327-5685)

British Cataloguing in Publication Data
A Cataloguing in Publication record for this book is available from the British Library.

All work contributed to this book is new, previously-unpublished material. The views expressed in this book are those of the authors, but not necessarily of the publisher.

For electronic access to this publication, please contact: eresources@igi-global.com.

Editorial Advisory Board

Table of Contents

Foreword xiii

Preface xv

Acknowledgment xx

Chapter 1
Infrastructure, Education, and Economic Development in India: A State Level Analysis 1
Sebak K. Jana, Vidyasagar University, India
Asim K. Karmakar, Jadavpur University, India

Chapter 2
Changes in Infrastructural Condition of Slums in India: A State Level Analysis 14
Somenath Ghosh, Visva Bharati University, India

Chapter 3
Role of Infrastructure Development to Empower Women: An Over-Determined View 39
Indrani Basu, Berhampore College, India

Chapter 4
MGNREGS of India: Complementarities Between Employment and Infrastructure 57
Pratip Kumar Datta, Rajatpur Indranarayan Vidyapith, India
Harsha Tiwary, Visva Bharati University, India
Saumya Chakrabarti, Visva Bharati University, India

Chapter 5
Health Infrastructure and Economic Growth in Sub-Saharan Africa 82
Samuel Adams, Ghana Institute of Management and Public Administration, Ghana
Edem Kwame Mensah Klobodu, Ghana Institute of Management and Public Administration, Ghana
Richmond Odartey Lamptey, Ghana Institute of Management and Public Administration, Ghana

Detailed Table of Contents

Foreword xiii

Preface xv

Acknowledgment xx

Chapter 1
Infrastructure, Education, and Economic Development in India: A State Level Analysis 1
Sebak K. Jana, Vidyasagar University, India
Asim K. Karmakar, Jadavpur University, India

A large number of studies reveal that regions with larger stocks of physical infrastructure and human capital often are associated higher level of economic development. The present chapter attempts to find whether this is valid for India. Factor Analysis has been used to find the index of scores of infrastructure of the selected 20 major states of India. We have then used regression analysis to find the impact of infrastructure and education on economic development of the states. The results indicate that there is huge variation of infrastructure development across the states in India. The findings also indicate the significant impact of infrastructure development and education on economic development of the state, measured in terms of Per Capita Net State Domestic Product (PCNSDP).

Chapter 2
Changes in Infrastructural Condition of Slums in India: A State Level Analysis 14
Somenath Ghosh, Visva Bharati University, India

Addressing the importance of infrastructure development towards inclusive city, the study aims to see the change in the condition of housing, road, latrine, drainage, sewerage, etc. within the slums across states and over time in India. The study has been done with the help of three rounds (49th, 58th and 69th) of NSSO data on slum. Though the condition of slums seems to have improved over time, but it is not satisfactory. However, it seems the improvement of one infrastructural aspect in slum is very much associated with the improvement of others. The factors like 'Workforce Participation Rate of slums' and overall infrastructure of the state have a positive influence on the infrastructural condition of slums, whereas, per capita NSDP is affecting it negatively. The 'associations made by the residents of slum for improvement' within the slums seems to have played no role to improve it.

A modern economy is market focused. It is held that when a woman becomes a participant in the market on her own term as a rational economic agent she is empowered in an economic sense. It does not take into account the other spectrums of empowerment viz. gender political, cultural and like. A nation's infrastructure provides the basic scaffolding for development. The differences in how men and women use infrastructure services have important implications for sector policies, investment priorities, and program designs. This chapter will analyse how the infrastructure development programme as an economic process assist women to enhance capability of them within society and how its actual impact is mutually constituted by other non-economic social processes and make it an over determined matter. Our study has shown that adequate access of the social infrastructure services has fetched benefits for women and ensures empowerment of women.

Controlling surplus population, on the one hand and use of underutilized resources on the other, have induced governments of the developing world to adopt measures so that, poverty, underdevelopment and social insecurity are managed outside the sphere of core sector, especially through rural employment generation. MGNREGS of India is one such programme. Many researchers suggested the need for government intervention in job creation. On the other hand, some researchers have criticized such policies on the ground that these programmes misallocate resources towards relatively less productive frontiers. We propose theoretically that, the problem is not so much with the revenue expenditure, rather the bottleneck lies on the supply-side and can be mitigated by introducing infrastructural factors. Moreover in this chapter, we have tried to criticize the quality of jobs done and types of infrastructure generated through MGNREGS as it seems that both fail to increase food production and thus create some conflicts between rural and urban sectors.

In this study, we examine the effect of health infrastructure on economic growth in 30 Sub-Saharan Africa (SSA) countries over the period 1990-2014. Using modern econometric techniques that account for cross-sectional dependence in panel data, we find that health infrastructure (measured by mortality rate) does not have robust impact on economic growth. Gross fixed capital formation, however, is positively associated with economic growth while labor force and polity variables exhibit significant association with economic growth. The results provide sufficient evidence that although capital investment is adequate, the labor force and political environment have not facilitated the health infrastructure in increasing the GDP per capita level in SSA.

The chapter examines different aspects of health care service facilities and health infrastructure available in India. Major health outcomes like Life expectancy at birth and infant mortality rate depend on available health facilities like hospitals, beds and health trained personnel. Life expectancy in India has increased and IMR declines over the years, except few states like Bihar, Jharkhand, Madhya Pradesh, Uttar Pradesh. India has achieved a considerable progress in providing health infrastructure and its access to health care services to the mass population. However, less developed states like Uttar Pradesh and Bihar need more attention to improve health infrastructure and distribution of health facilities. In this context, we also highlight the department of Ayurveda, Yoga and Naturopathy, Unani, Siddha and Homoeopathy, abbreviated as AYUSH which is a Governmental body in India purposed with developing, education and research in Ayurveda, which mostly prevails in under-developed state like Bihar. Our empirical results provide the evidence of strong association between health infrastructure and economic development in India.

The objective of this chapter is to take a closer look at the liaison between the two focus variables viz. growth and public healthcare expenditure, and the associated implications for public health infrastructure development. Initially, a theoretical model has been proposed which brings out the link between the focus variables. Panel cointegration and causality are the techniques applied in a Vector Error Correction Mechanism (VECM) set-up using panel data from 1980-2015. Next, a health infrastructure index has been constructed using the Euclidean distance function approach for India for two time points i.e. 2005-06 and 2014-15, to evaluate the interstate performance in public healthcare infrastructure. The findings validate the existence of a cointegrated relationship between health expenditure and economic growth coupled with a bidirectional causality linking the focus variables in this model. It comes to a close by highlighting the policy implications and the future research possibilities in this regard.

Infrastructure investments can have long term consequences for the economy and environment of a country. Some notable public infrastructure projects include energy, transportation, water, and waste disposal systems. There are strong financial, environmental, and social change drivers that are forcing immediate changes. We need to rethink our infrastructure investments and develop sustainable, resilient, and affordable infrastructure systems for vital services of our society. These systems will be able to support the healthy and prosperous communities in future. The objective of this chapter is to review the current state of sustainable infrastructures and provide suggestions to policy makers responsible for infrastructure development how to develop sustainable infrastructures.

The present chapter seeks to analyze the trend and growth of energy production, supply, growth, consumption and trade in South Asian countries based on data from 1971 to 2011 collected from World Bank data base, South Asia Development reports, Energy Outlook, ADB database. While India, Pakistan, and Bangladesh account for the major natural gas and coal resources, Bhutan and Nepal have large hydropower resources. The study suggests that South Asian countries need enhanced regional energy transfer to leverage economies of scale through a more vibrant intra and inter regional energy trade structure. Mobilizing financial resources to develop the necessary energy infrastructure is a major challenge to enhance energy security in the region. Therefore, South Asian countries need to develop policies that will attract investment in the region.

This chapter examines the implications of projects abandonment with test of the Ricardian Equivalence on the failed Lagos metro line project in Nigeria as case study. The main variables used are Rail and Pipeline Output, Budget Deficit, Interest Rate, Corruption Index, Savings and some others. The study results on the Ricardian Equivalence hypothesis on deficit financing of projects using Vector auto-regression model from 1980-2012 indicate that no causal influence holds in Nigeria. Results show that poor planning, corruption, political factors, poor support infrastructures, poor quality of local resources, etc. were attributable. The results of the Impulse Response tests reveal that Rail and Pipeline output and a few others responded positively to shocks in the short run (years 1-2), and negatively to others. The result affirms that Government should privatize the railway system, legislate against project abandonment and ensure that projects are adequately planned, funded, insured and insulated against corruption.

This study examined the effect of electric power transmission and distribution losses (ETL) on economic growth over the period of 1971 to 2012 in Ghana. Using bounds testing approach to cointegration and Bai-Perron test in ordinary least squares framework, we find long-run relationship between ETL, gross capital formation, inflation, trade openness and economic growth. Secondly, while ETL do not have robust impact on economic growth, trade openness exerts a positive impact on economic growth in the long-run. Inflation and gross capital formation, however, have mixed relationships with economic growth. Furthermore, ETL yield a threshold value of 2.07. Finally, controlling for the urban population reveals that ETL moderates the relationship between urbanization and economic growth; higher ETL associates with an increasing negative effect on GDP per capita.

The present chapter focuses on the importance of infrastructure in the dryland areas of West Bengal, India, covering four districts, namely, Purulia, Bankura, West Midnapore and Birbhum. The importance and necessity of having good infrastructure is a well-known phenomenon but it carries a special significance for the drylands, where good infrastructure can open various avenues of earning, communication, better life standard as well as management and nourishment of all types of natural resources in these areas. Sustainable use of natural resources occur utmost importance because it is the only source of livelihood for the people of these areas. Through this study, we have tried to make an assessment of the existing infrastructure scenarios in these four districts for the period 2003-04 to 2012-13. Doing the SWOT analysis amongst the districts, the results show that West Midnapur and Bankura are in a better position than Purulia and Birbhum, although, Birbhum is in a good position in few indicators.

In recent years, Indian rural market has been gaining increasing attention from researchers in view of its growing importance in huge potential marketing for various consumer durables such as white goods, brown goods and consumer electronics. India has a vast rural market, which consists of around 833 million potential consumers constituting 68.84% of the total population spread over 6.40 Lac villages. Rural India is now exhibiting changing living standard with higher income, modern education and infrastructure development. This is leading to higher demand for several consumer durables such as colour television, refrigerator, two wheelers etc. The urban consumer's durable market is growing annually 10% to 20%. The corresponding rural market is zooming ahead 20% to 40% annually. Thus, this chapter attempts to investigate the changing market penetration of consumer durables in rural India during 1995-96 to 2009-10. This work also finds out the role of per capita income, rural infrastructure in market penetration of consumer durables.

The chapter tries to find out the relationship between public expenditures on infrastructure related to agriculture and allied factors and agricultural sustainability in Indian context. India has been suffering from appalling chronic poverty and to reduce the same, we need to focus on rural development, particularly in agriculture as it is unavoidable relation with economic development. Gini index of India is 33.9 (2011)

Foreword

Infrastructure is the system of public works typically providing essential services to the people. It has both economic and social dimensions, therefore, there are subdivisions such as economic infrastructure and social infrastructure. While economic infrastructure includes financial infrastructure, energy, transport, utilities (energy distribution networks, power generation, water, dam, irrigation, sewage, waste) and communication; social infrastructure includes schools, hospitals, courts, prisons, stadiums, etc.

According to the OECD estimations, global infrastructure requirements will amount to US$50 tn until 2030. The International Energy Agency also estimates that adapting to and mitigating the effects of climate change will require US$45 tn ofinfrastructure expenditures until 2050 (approx. US$1 tn a year).

Infrastructure expenditure typically adds to the productive capacity in an economy, like other investments. Infrastructure investment can have direct effects on the one hand. These effects can occur through a number of different channels, such as facilitating trade and the division of labour, optimum allocation of resources and economic activities across regions, the diffusion of technology and the adoption of new organisational models. On the other hand, they can also have indirect effects by creating some positive externalities by increasing the productivity of human capital, and life quality of society through education, health, and safety services.

The aim of this publication titled *Social, Health, and Environmental Infrastructures for Economic Growth* edited by Dr. Ramesh Chandra Das is to provide further information on the economic and social dimension of infrastructure investments by distinguished scholars from several countries. Since each country has her own (mostly unique) experience in infrastructure investments, such a collection will absolutely make remarkable contribution to the literature.

It firstly focuses on its economic importance by analysing its effects on economic growth across countries and regions (including SAARC Countries, developing countries, Latin America and East Asia in general, and Ghana and India specifically). In the second section, it analyzes the relationship between financial infrastructure and growth, taking foreign direct investment into account in theory and in practice (in India and China, Mexico). Finally, it studies social infrastructure including health and environmental infrastructures in India, Sub-Saharan Africa, South Asia, Nigeria, Ghana, West Bengal, and Mexico) by making reference to rural development.

With its 15 original chapters, I believe that this comprehensive book will be very useful for the readers, and a very important reference fort he researchers in the field.

Yaşar Bülbül
İstanbul University, Turkey

Yaşar Bülbül *is a Professor of Economics at İstanbul University, Faculty of Economics, Istanbul-Turkey. He graduated from İstanbul University, Faculty of Economics in 1991. Dr. Bülbül has BAs in Economic History (1993). He received his PhD in Economics with his thesis entitled as "Accounting Order of the Ottoman Empire: 1300-1600". Economic history, history of economic thought, history of technology and innovation, history of finance, development, and entrepreneurship are the main pillars of his interdisciplinary studies.*

Preface

Infrastructure development in general and its specification with respect to social, health and environment is widely accepted in all schools of economic thoughts, particularly in the modern economics, as one of the most important factors of production, growth and development of an economy in a sustainable way. It also helps in developing the productivity of the usual factors of production and leads the economy to obtain the frontier of efficiency. In a competitive market economy with nearly absence of excess capacity, the infrastructure development plays the role as a catalyst to the overall production system of an economy. All classes of economies in the world are benefitted by the development of infrastructure. But the magnitudes of the impact of this development upon the different economies are subject to the way of appropriation of this infrastructure technology by the existing other factors of production.

The financing of infrastructural inputs are done by public and private initiatives. Again, a major part of these financing are done by the domestic sources of the economy. But, after almost all countries entering into the umbrella of *globalization* the situation has changed in a larger extent. Mostly, the infrastructure projects are financed by the outsourcing from the foreign direct investors who enters into the territory of a domestic economy by means of favorable economic and political conditions. Sometimes, the foreign investors change their investment avenues to an economy whose domestic demand capacity is so sound to absorb any short of economic shocks. For example, the investors from the western world travelled to the Asian, African and Latin Zone, particularly to the Asian Giants China and India, and Latin hub, Brazil, and African mine, Nigeria, South Africa and Ethiopia, to protect themselves from the heats of *global financial crisis* that ruined the US and European economy. In spite of weak governance and poor human quality in these zones, the foreign investors invested upon these economies since the magnitude of loss under the financial crisis was much larger compared to the economies with lax governance and low human development and poverty.

The recent trends in the output of the WTO meetings in different locations have pin pointed that the improper economic policies and capitalistic development in the West have made worsening the distributional results of global output and the policy makers and diplomats of different countries into the meets have shown their desire to work with hand in hand of all classes of economies together. The magnitudes of associations among the rich and poor nations become proactive by the so called developed zones of the world when they are unable to manage the crisis and protect their own economies. Hence, it has now been a pertinent issue on my part as editor of exploring the roles of infrastructure development upon the sustainable world economic development. The present book titled *Social, Health, and Environmental Infrastructures for Economic Growth* thus, has tried to explore the roles of infrastructure developments in World Economic development taking into account of different economic and political shocks and dimensions of governance.

After invitation to the potential authors through the official website of the IGI Global and my personal networks for contributions to the said mission through chapter submission on the recommended topics a number of chapters has been singled out. All the chapters have attempted to justify their positions in terms of standard quantitative analysis at per their capabilities. After a double blind peer review system and additional review by me, as editor, the number of chapters in revised form ultimately turned out to be 15 with a standard volume. The entire book has been arranged by chapters in the content to cover the basic themes as addressed in the title.

The book capturing Chapters 1 to 15 encompasses the issues of social, health and environmental perspectives of infrastructure developments of a country in general and rural developments in particular. It highlights the infrastructural issues of education, health, women empowerment, forestry, among others, and their roles of development of rural economy of a country as well as global economy. Most of the chapters have tried heavily on empirical foundations with modern tools of quantitative economics to have concrete research outputs. A brief outcome of the chapter contributions are addressed below sequentially.

Chapter 1 attempts to find whether revelation that 'regions with larger stocks of physical infrastructure and human capital often are associated higher level of economic development' is valid for India. Factor Analysis has been used to find the index of scores of infrastructure of the selected 20 major states of India. After that the study uses regression analysis to find the impact of infrastructure and education on economic development of the states. The results indicate that there is huge variation of infrastructure development across the states in India. The findings also indicate the significant impact of infrastructure development and education on economic development of the state, measured in terms of per capita net state domestic product.

Chapter 2 takes attempt to see the changes in the conditions of housing, road, latrine, drainage, sewerage, like livelihood infrastructure within the slums across different states in India over time addressing the importance of infrastructure development towards inclusive city. The study has been done with the help of three rounds (49th, 58th and 69th) of National Sample Survey Organization data on slum. Though the condition of slums seems to have improved over time, but it is not satisfactory. However, it seems the improvement of one infrastructural aspect in slum is very much associated with the improvement of others. The factors like 'Workforce Participation Rate of slums' and overall infrastructure of the state have a positive influence on the infrastructural condition of slums, whereas, per capita net state domestic product is affecting it negatively. The 'associations made by the residents of slum for improvement' within the slums seems to have played no role to improve it.

Chapter 3 analyses theoretically how the infrastructure development programme as an economic process assists women to enhance capability of them within society and how its actual impact is mutually constituted by other non-economic social processes and make it an over determined matter. The study has shown that adequate access of the social infrastructure services has fetched benefits for women and ensures empowerment of women.

Chapter 4 throws light on the aspects of popular public programme in India under the caption of Mahatma Gandhi National Rural Employment Guarantee Scheme (MGNREGS) to find whether there is any complementary relation between rural infrastructure and employment generation. The study also proposes theoretically that, the problem is not so much with the revenue expenditure, rather the bottleneck lies on the supply-side and can be mitigated by introducing infrastructural factors. The results show that, with the rise in MGNREGS expenditure, rural non-farm employment has been generated as also some rural non-farm works have been done possibly targeted towards employment generation. Moreover the study has censured the quality of jobs done and types of infrastructure generated through MGNREGS as it seems that both fail to increase food production and thus create some conflicts between rural and urban sectors.

Chapter 5 examines the effect of health infrastructure on economic growth in 30 Sub-Saharan African (SSA) countries over the period 1990-2014. Using modern econometric techniques that account for cross-sectional dependence in panel data, the study observes that health infrastructure as measured by mortality rate does not have robust impact on economic growth. Gross fixed capital formation, however, is positively associated with economic growth while labor force and polity variables exhibiting significant association with economic growth. The results additionally provide sufficient evidence that although capital investment is adequate, the labor force and political environment have not facilitated the health infrastructure in increasing the GDP per capita level in SSA.

Chapter 6 elucidates different aspects of health care service facilities and health infrastructure available in India including the department of Ayurveda, Yoga and Naturopathy, Unani, Siddha and Homoeopathy, abbreviated as AYUSH. Major health outcomes like Life expectancy at birth and infant mortality rate depend on available health facilities like hospitals, beds and health trained personnel. Life expectancy in India has increased and IMR declines over the years, except few states like Bihar, Jharkhand, Madhya Pradesh, Uttar Pradesh. India has achieved a considerable progress in providing health infrastructure and its access to health care services to the mass population. The study provides the evidence of strong association between health infrastructure and economic development in India. It suggests that the less developed states like Uttar Pradesh and Bihar need more attention to improve health infrastructure and distribution of health facilities.

Chapter 7 concentrates on looking at the liaison between the two, growth and public healthcare expenditure, and the associated implications for public health infrastructure development in Indian states. Initially, a theoretical model has been proposed which brings out the link between the focus variables and then the study applies panel cointegration and causality techniques in a Vector Error Correction Mechanism set-up using panel data from 1980-2015. Besides, it a health infrastructure index has been constructed using the Euclidean distance function approach for India for two time points i.e. 2005-06 and 2014-15, to evaluate the interstate performance in public healthcare infrastructure. The findings validate the existence of a cointegrated relationship between health expenditure and economic growth coupled with a bidirectional causality linking the focus variables in this model.

Chapter 8 reviews the current state of sustainable infrastructures and provide suggestions to leaders policy makers responsible for infrastructure development how to develop sustainable infrastructures. The study is recommends that infrastructure planners should realize the critical significance of these infrastructures for providing greater financial, social and economic benefits and plan ahead to develop these infrastructures in a manner that benefits all stakeholders.

Chapter 9 seeks to analyze the trend and growth of energy production, supply, growth, consumption and trade in South Asian countries based on data from 1971 to 2011. While India, Pakistan, and Bangladesh account for the major natural gas and coal resources, Bhutan and Nepal have large hydropower resources. The study suggests that South Asian countries need enhanced regional energy transfer to leverage economies of scale through a more vibrant intra and inter regional energy trade structure. Additionally it shows concern that mobilizing financial resources to develop the necessary energy infrastructure is a major challenge to enhance energy security in the region.

Chapter 10 examines the implications of projects abandonment with test of the Ricardian Equivalence on the failed Lagos metro line project in Nigeria with respect to the variables, Rail and Pipeline Output, Budget Deficit, Interest Rate, Corruption Index, Savings and some others. The study results on the Ricardian Equivalence hypothesis on deficit financing of projects using Vector auto-regression model from 1980-2012 indicate that no causal influence holds in Nigeria and it blames that poor planning, corruption, political factors, poor support infrastructures, poor quality of local resources, etc, were attributable. Moreover, the results of the Impulse Response tests reveal that Rail and Pipeline output and a few others responded positively to shocks in the short run, and negatively to others. The study thus suggests that Government should privatize the railway system, legislate against project abandonment and ensure that projects are adequately planned, funded, insured and insulated against corruption.

Chapter 11 sheds light on the examination of the effect of electric power transmission and distribution losses (ETL) on economic growth over the period of 1971 to 2012 in Ghana. Using bounds testing approach to cointegration and Bai-Perrontest in ordinary least squares framework, it observes long-run relationship between ETL, gross capital formation, inflation, trade openness and economic growth. Moreover, while ETL do not have robust impact on economic growth, trade openness exerts a positive impact on economic growth in the long-run. Inflation and gross capital formation, however, have mixed relationships with economic growth. The study also reveals that ETL moderates the relationship between urbanization and economic growth; higher ETL associates with an increasing negative effect on GDP per capita.

Chapter 12 focuses on the importance of infrastructure in the dryland areas of West Bengal, India, covering four districts, namely, Purulia, Bankura, West Midnapore and Birbhum and tries to make an assessment of the existing infrastructure scenarios in these four districts for the period 2003-04 to 2012-13. Doing the SWOT analysis amongst the districts, the results show that West Midnapur and Bankura are in a better position than Purulia and Birbhum, although, Birbhum is in a good position in few indicators.

Chapter 13 attempts to investigate the changing market penetration of consumer durables in rural India during 1995-96 to 2009-10. This work also finds out the role of per capita income, rural infrastructure in market penetration of consumer durables. As the rural infrastructure is improving and helping in the aggravation of the economy of the belt, the study reveals that the urban consumer's durable market is growing annually 10% to 20% whereas the corresponding rural market is zooming ahead 20% to 40% annually.

Chapter 14 tries to explore the relationship between public expenditures on infrastructure related to agriculture and allied factors and agricultural sustainability in Indian context. It contributes a new dimension to the study of sustainable rural development through agrarian reforms by investigating the impact of public expenditure on agriculture in terms of production and export empirically in India for a long period from 1970-71 to 2014-15. The findings, by applying cointegration tests on the basis of unit root test results, imply that there is at least one co-integrating equation as suggested by both trace and maximum eigen value statistics. So there may have a long run equilibrium relationship among variables. The results of vector error correction mechanism model to find the long run dynamics show that growth of agricultural output is significantly influenced by public expenditures on agricultural and allied sectors with one period lag. The study suggest that Adopting bottom-up agricultural development approaches which emphasize the involvement of the rural people in the implementations of different development programmes may escalate agrarian reforms.

Finally Chapter 15 analyzes Manzanillo's harbor from the perspective of theories based on the Industry, the Dynamic Resources and Institutions, around the Mexican port system based on a review into an updated literature about the port's status and its global environment. It reveals that the port's competitiveness is based on its resources VRIO, its generic strategies and how it has handled the institutions that affect the port and commercial operation of the port at local, national and international level.

The outcome of the covered studies in the book offers positive roles of infrastructure related to education, environmental resources, health, etc. on rural as well as cross country developments. In some studies, the negative effects of project abandonment and electricity transmission loss upon income of the countries like Nigeria and Ghana are observed.

Hence, in overall sense, the studies covered in the present book strongly justify the roles of different types of sustainable infrastructures as the engine of world economic growth and it also supports that infrastructure development can usher the economies to recover themselves from any kind of economic shocks or recession. Hence, the corollary of this entire work suggests that '*develop infrastructural base and keep the present as well as future generation protected*'.

It is now become news that the proposed project has drawn closer to reality. I expect that the said research outcome will help out to the academicians, policy makers and environmentalists and social workers all around the world to have a better understanding of the importance of sustainable infrastructure on development in general that the book addressed to.

Ramesh Chandra Das
Katwa College, India

Acknowledgment

There was a long journey from planning to execution of the proposed title of the book, *Social, Health, and Environmental Infrastructures for Economic Growth*, edited by me. It is now an inexplicable delight to announce that the proposed book on the said title has been in due course uncovered. The ultimate success in budding such a huge volume of the edited book could not be consummated if the contributions of the concerned foams of academicians all around the world were conglomerated particularly when the entire work was controlled and managed from a rural belt of Indian subcontinent. Hence, it would be culpable if I do not acknowledge the contributions of the concerned academicians and other members of the society associated to the project.

At first, I must recognize the IGI Global Team for approving the proposal and continuously guiding me at all stages of impediments by means of their congenial and corroborative suggestions. I did not face any kind of non mutual aid from their parts and hence their sincere efforts were always laudable. Secondly, I should be grateful to my research guides Professor Soumyen Sikdar of Indian Institute of Management, Calcutta, India and Professor Sarmila Banerjee of Calcutta University, India for persistently encouraging me to undergo such a project and circulating the message to the potential chapter contributors of the said field. Thirdly, I must express gratitude to Dr. Amaresh Das, Dr. Igwe, E. Udeh and Dr. Frank Martin of College of Business, Southern University at New Orleans, USA, and Dr. Soumyananda Dinda, Dr. Maniklal Adhikary and Dr. Arindam Laha of The University of Burdwan, India, Dr. Kamal Ray of Katwa College, India and Dr. Chiranjib Neogi of (formerly) Indian Statistical Institute, Calcutta, India, for their incessant efforts in helping review works in higher masses and editing the texts of the book besides added encouragements to me. Fourthly, I should acknowledge the efforts of the editorial advisory board members for reviewing the chapters with greater genuineness and providing me suggestions in a ceaseless manner even though their busy academic schedules. Fifthly, I must be grateful to Dr. Hasan Dincer of Istanbul Medipol University, Turkey for his sincere participation in editing a major part of the book with bubbles of good suggestions and recommendations. Sixthly, I should tribute to all the contributing authors for their valuable chapter contributions and showing their patience for such a long duration project coming into reality. I must acknowledge the values they added to the existing literature through this edited volume.

Last but not the least I must be indebted to my parents, wife and daughter and other members of the family for their continuous persuading, supports and sacrifice in carrying out the long lasting project. Of course, no one other than me, as the editor, discloses to remain utterly responsible for any errors still appear in the book.

Ramesh Chandra Das
Katwa College, India

Chapter 1
Infrastructure, Education, and Economic Development in India:
A State Level Analysis

Sebak K. Jana
Vidyasagar University, India

Asim K. Karmakar
Jadavpur University, India

ABSTRACT

A large number of studies reveal that regions with larger stocks of physical infrastructure and human capital often are associated higher level of economic development. The present chapter attempts to find whether this is valid for India. Factor Analysis has been used to find the index of scores of infrastructure of the selected 20 major states of India. We have then used regression analysis to find the impact of infrastructure and education on economic development of the states. The results indicate that there is huge variation of infrastructure development across the states in India. The findings also indicate the significant impact of infrastructure development and education on economic development of the state, measured in terms of Per Capita Net State Domestic Product (PCNSDP).

INTRODUCTION

Development and economic growth of a region depends very much on its infrastructure including physical and human capital. Sound infrastructure of a region plays a key role in the economic development of a region. Infrastructure facilities may be of various types like physical (like power, irrigation, transport and communications), social (education and health) and economic (like banks). All these are important for the pursuit of the country's development goals. On the contrary, inadequate infrastructure and services result in increased costs of production and transaction, which reduce competitiveness and make it more difficult to achieve overall development goals. Infrastructure has various effects on the economy (Yoshino and Nakahigashi, 2000). Infrastructure affects growth in a complex way because the effects are both direct and indirect (Ghosh & De, 2004). Several studies have examined the role of infrastructure

DOI: 10.4018/978-1-5225-2364-2.ch001

and an educated workforce in regional economic development such as Fullerton et al (2010), Almada et al. (2006), Wang (2002), Aboudou (2011), Das (2012), Montgomery (2008), Novianti (2014), Owolabi-Merus (2015), Sawada (2015), De (2008), Bhandari and Gupta, (2011), Jana et al., (2012), Jana (2014).

Infrastructure determines directly and indirectly economic development. On the demand side, it opens up possibilities of investment by making available a number of necessary inputs and services, opening up the size of the market as well as increasing the supply elasticity and efficiency of factors of production. On the supply side, the development of infrastructure helps in mobilizing potential saving and channelizing them into productive investment. Adequate quantity, quality and reliability of infrastructure are keys to the growth of any economy (Mohan, 2003, 2016). It has been found that interstate disparities in physical, social and economic infrastructure facilities have high impact on productivity. The 11th five year plan in India laid special emphasis on the development of infrastructure and proposed strategies for better investment in infrastructure. With a projected GDP growth averaging 9% per year for the Eleventh Plan, the plan document estimated almost doubling infrastructure spending from 5% of GDP in 2006-07 to 9% by 2011-12.

The importance of access to electricity to economic and human development has been well documented in a large number of studies across regions. Most of these studies on developing countries find a positive impact of energy infrastructure on output/growth (Estache & Garsous, 2012). Laxmi and Sahoo (2013) described health infrastructure index as a "weighted average of various components". They have taken the number of hospitals and dispensaries, the number of beds and number of doctors etc. for constructing index using Principal Component Analysis (PCA). Hati and Majumder (2013) constructed a health infrastructure index by combining three components of healthcare namely preventive, curative and promotional health infrastructure. Kumari and Raman (2011) used Maher's methodology to standardize 8 indicators for the health attainment and 13 for educational attainment and then applied principal component analysis to compute the composite indices and found wide disparity among the districts in Uttar Pradesh. The objective of this study by Lyngdoh (2015) was to understand the rural public health care system in North East India. Walke et al (2015) used Aggregate production functions in order to analyze the determinants of economic performance across Mexican states and their results indicate that regional-level investments in transportation infrastructure and education facilitate economic growth in Mexico.

OBJECTIVE OF THE STUDY

The major objectives of the present study are as follows:

1. Status of infrastructure development across different states in India.
2. Ranking of States in respect of infrastructure development.
3. Impact of education and infrastructure on economic development of the states in India.

STATUS OF INFRASTRUCTURE DEVELOPMENT IN INDIA

The present study is based on secondary information collected from different sources. At present there are 29 states and 7 union territories in India. We have selected 20 major states for our study. These are Andhra Pradesh (A.P.), Bihar, Chhattisgarh, Gujarat, Haryana, Himachal Pradesh (H.P.), Jammu &

Kashmir (J & K), Jharkhand, Karnataka, Kerala, Madhya Pradesh (M. P.), Maharashtra, Odisha, Punjab, Rajasthan, Tamil Nadu, Tripura, Uttar Pradesh (U.P.), Uttarakhand and West Bengal (W.B.).

Infrastructure may be of different kinds and may be classified in different ways like Economic Infrastructure, Finance Infrastructure and Social Infrastructure. We have grouped the infrastructure variables in four groups: (i) Transport sector consisting of road density (per 1000 sq. km), road density (per 1000 population), registered motor vehicles (per 1000 population), rail density (per 1000 sq. km), rail density (per 1000 population), number of airports (per crore population, (ii) Agriculture, Industry and Energy sector consisting of irrigated land per capita (ha), fixed capital/lakh population, invested capital/lakh population number of LPG distributors (per lakh population) and electricity installed generating capacity (gwh) per lakh population, (iii) Banks, Telecommunication and Post Offices consisting of banks branches per lakh population, deposit (Rs. Crore) per lakh population, credit (Rs. Crore), tele density, post offices per lakh population and (iv) Health infrastructure consisting of number of hospitals, hospital beds and toilet facilities per lakh population.

Transport infrastructure facilitates the transportation of people and goods and provides them access to markets, employment and investment opportunities. An efficient transportation system in a country is likely to have a multiplier effect on the economy whereas a deficient transportation system can result in economic loss (GoI, 2014). Transportation can be provided by various modes depending on the surface over which one has to travel – land (road, rail, and pipelines), water (shipping) and air. Heavy industries are often linked by rail transportation. State-wise infrastructure development for the transport sector in India is presented in Table 1. As Table 1 reveals the road density (per 1000 sq. km.) is highest in Kerala (5543.52) and lowest in Jammu & Kashmir (163.58). Registered Motor vehicles (per1000 population) is highest in Tamil Nadu (256.58) and lowest in Bihar (31.44). Rail Density (per 1000 sq. km) is highest in Uttarakhand (165.00) and lowest in Jammu & Kashmir (1.00). Air transportation has unlimited routes but are constrained by site for landing and takeoff of planes, climate, fog and aerial currents. Air transportation is especially useful in long distance mobility of people and has been one of the most important factors in the globalization era. As an important component, infrastructure segment has played vital role in facilitating the growth of business and economy in India. A robust civil aviation set-up is crucial for seamless flow of investment, trade and tourism, with significant multiplier effects through the economy. This sector not only provides air transport for passengers and goods, but also is a strategic element for employment generation. Total number of airport per crore of population is highest in Andhra Pradesh and Gujarat (10.00) and lowest in Haryana (0.00) for the states under consideration.

The second component includes agriculture, industry and energy. Irrigation is an essential component of agriculture in India as the rains occur only for three to four Months. During rest of the year irrigation is the only source of water for agriculture. Access to good irrigation allows people to increase their productivity. They can also diversify to other crops. Irrigation reduces the vulnerability of farmers to unpredicted rains and other external shocks, thus enhancing their chances of higher productivity and better incomes. Availability of irrigation facilities encourages farmers to switch from low value subsistence production to high valued market oriented production. They can substitute low yielding crops with high yielding and more profitable crops. Irrigation through canals, wells and other sources is considered as a catalyst of economic development of a country. We have taken fixed capital and invested capital in industry as industrial infrastructure. An effective energy infrastructure is the backbone of every modern economy. Economic development cannot go ahead if there is not sufficient energy to fuel it and no headway can be made with living conditions either. Growing economies like India need to have stable and sustainable sources of energy supply as it is an important input in the production

Table 1. State-wise Indicators Transport Sector in India, 2012

	State	Road Density (Per 1000 sq. km)	Road Density (Per 1000 Population)	Registered Motor vehicles (Per1000 Population)	Rail Density (Per 1000 sq. km)	Rail Density (per 1000 Population)	Total Airport/ crore Population
1	A.P.	932.39	3.00	145.33	19.00	0.060	10.00
2	Bihar	1471.03	1.40	31.44	38.00	0.040	6.00
3	Chhattisgarh	560.26	3.08	126.26	9.00	0.050	2.00
4	Gujarat	832.29	2.73	241.03	27.00	0.090	10.00
5	Haryana	964.40	1.65	231.23	35.00	0.060	0.00
6	H.P.	906.17	7.36	107.44	5.00	0.040	4.00
7	J&K	163.58	3.06	77.28	1.00	0.020	3.00
8	Jharkhand	329.64	0.82	98.98	26.00	0.060	1.00
9	Karnataka	1580.51	5.05	181.75	16.00	0.050	5.00
10	Kerala	5543.52	6.19	198.07	27.00	0.030	3.00
11	M.P.	652.93	2.74	111.04	16.00	0.070	8.00
12	Maharashtra	1289.14	3.47	170.18	18.00	0.050	8.00
13	Odisha	1635.82	6.20	91.44	16.00	0.060	2.00
14	Punjab	1863.93	3.35	223.83	43.00	0.080	3.00
15	Rajasthan	726.40	3.61	130.43	17.00	0.080	6.00
16	Tamil Nadu	1769.98	3.39	256.58	30.00	0.060	7.00
17	Tripura	2789.24	8.00	55.62	14.00	0.040	4.00
18	U.P.	1673.12	1.97	75.62	1.00	0.001	8.00
19	Uttarakhand	984.01	5.22	123.37	165.00	0.870	2.00
20	West Bengal	3553.77	3.49	42.75	45.00	0.040	7.00

Source: GOI (2014)

process. Indirectly, it also affects the health and education system of the country. Affordable energy directly contributes to reducing poverty, increasing productivity and improving quality of life. An efficient energy system provides better opportunities for industries and production processes. A number of energy sources are used in India. In rural India, the main source is biomass. Most electricity supplies are generated by fossil fuels. The most visible form of energy, which is often identified with progress in modern civilization, is power, commonly called electricity. It is a critical component of infrastructure that determines the economic development of a country. To increase the availability of electricity, India has adopted a blend of thermal, hydel and nuclear resources. State-wise indicators of Agriculture, Industry and Energy in India are presented in Table 2. As Table 2 reveals the Irrigated per capita (ha) is highest in Punjab (0.143) and lowest in Jharkhand (0.007). Fixed Capital per lakh population is highest in Himachal Pradesh (H.P.) (64887.70) and lowest in Bihar (727.05). Invested Capital (Rs. lakhs) per lakh Population is highest in Himachal Pradesh (80511.04) and lowest in Bihar (1174.96). Number of LPG distribution (per lakh population) is highest in Himachal Pradesh (1.94) and lowest in Bihar (0.50). Installed generating capacity of electricity (GWH) per lakh population is highest in Himachal Pradesh (37.91) and lowest in Bihar (0.49).

Table 2. State-wise Indicators of Agriculture, Industry and Energy, 2012

		Agriculture	Industry		Energy	
	State	Irrigated Land Per Capita (ha)	Fixed Capital/ Lakh Population (Rs. lakhs)	Invested Capital/Lakh Population (Rs. lakhs)	Number of LPG Distributors (Per Lakh Population)	Electricity Installed Generating Capacity (GWh) Per lakh Population
1	A.P.	0.058	29993.20	38497.62	1.40	15.35
2	Bihar	0.034	727.05	1174.96	0.50	0.49
3	Chhattisgarh	0.033	19824.59	26260.01	0.75	15.69
4	Gujarat	0.053	51793.24	75690.78	0.94	31.46
5	Haryana	0.129	21242.34	36410.33	1.20	19.15
6	H.P.	0.016	64887.70	80511.04	1.94	37.91
7	J&K	0.029	3507.41	5958.52	1.31	8.72
8	Jharkhand	0.007	20452.98	25721.95	0.65	5.12
9	Karnataka	0.039	21580.23	30037.32	0.93	19.30
10	Kerala	0.012	4630.71	8579.40	1.26	7.77
11	M.P.	0.058	6874.36	11002.47	0.91	6.87
12	Maharashtra	0.030	23223.17	36697.26	1.10	18.11
13	Odisha	0.030	38335.02	43734.39	0.62	10.44
14	Punjab	0.143	13480.07	24489.02	1.69	18.91
15	Rajasthan	0.075	7725.95	11529.83	0.93	11.59
16	Tamil Nadu	0.037	22380.65	35997.13	1.13	19.41
17	Tripura	0.019	956.00	1382.99	0.95	4.60
18	U.P.	0.073	4541.88	7371.36	0.73	4.17
19	Uttarakhand	0.035	50083.89	70616.02	1.79	18.17
20	West Bengal	0.033	7849.06	11960.56	0.63	8.34

Source: Based on GOI (2014)

The third Communication is an important part of economic development. It facilitates exchange of commercial activities and integrates the nation economically and socially. Communication system connects a place to rest of the world and provides facilities to trade both nationally and internationally. Telecommunication and posts are the two main constituents of communication system. Postal communication system had been the main method of communication in India for nearly a century and half. It is viewed as the most dependable means of written communication. Postal services have provided other services as well in addition to delivery of letters. These are: delivery of letter and other mail, savings bank operations, money transfer and provision of life insurance. The telecommunications sector plays an increasingly important role in the Indian economy. It contributes to economic growth and generates revenue for the government and creates employment. The increase in tele-density has mainly been driven by the increase in mobile phones. State-wise status of Banks, Telecommunication and post offices in India is presented in Table 3. As Table 3 reveals the bank branches per lakh population is highest in Himachal Pradesh (13.96) and lowest in Bihar (2.89). Deposit (Rs. Croe 2012) per lakh population is highest in Maharashtra (1080072.00) and lowest in Tripura (7407.00). Credit (Rs. Crore) is highest in

Table 3. State-wise Status of Banks, Telecommunication and Post Offices, 2012

State	Banks Branches per Lakh Pop	Deposit (Rs. Crore 2012) Per Lakh Pop	Credit (Rs. Crore Per Lakh Population)	Tele Density	Post Offices Per Lakh Population
A.P.	6.93	269846.00	305304.00	8.09	18.88
Bihar	2.89	120685.00	32964.00	4.89	9.14
Chhattisgarh	3.95	59044.00	31468.00	5.38	12.72
Gujarat	7.12	254678.00	170750.00	9.11	15.02
Haryana	8.53	101661.00	128213.00	8.94	10.30
H.P.	13.96	34826.00	13132.00	12.07	40.52
J&K	3.05	14042.00	3746.00	5.48	14.29
Jharkhand	5.04	79960.00	25990.00	4.89	99.21
Karnataka	7.76	286645.00	213433.00	9.72	16.17
Kerala	8.59	124665.00	98690.00	10.66	14.56
M.P.	4.63	146229.00	79878.00	5.38	11.34
Maharashtra	6.38	1080072.00	947948.00	7.72	11.26
Odisha	5.23	102346.00	48564.00	6.58	19.86
Punjab	12.67	150215.00	126875.00	11.31	13.76
Rajasthan	4.61	117748.00	111772.00	7.30	14.99
Tamil Nadu	7.43	278058.00	322799.00	11.66	17.78
Tripura	3.84	7407.00	1957.00	6.57	6.58
U.P.	4.10	358016.00	157545.00	6.09	8.65
Uttarakhand	10.88	50736.00	17231.00	6.09	26.95
West Bengal	5.07	304305.00	196191.00	6.15	10.03

Source: GOI (2014), GOI (2015), GOI (2013)

Maharashtra (947948.00) and lowest in Jammu & Kashmir (3746.00). Tele Density is highest in Himachal Pradesh (12.07) and lowest in Jharkhand (4.89). Number of Post Offices per lakh Population is highest in Jharkhand (99.21) and lowest in Tripura (6.58).

The term physical infrastructure in health, according to Bhandari and Dutta (2007), has a much broader meaning. It includes not only healthcare centres, dispensaries, or hospitals, but also well trained staff with a service perspective. Healthcare infrastructure is also looked upon as an important indicator in order to understand the provisioning and the working of any health system. Thus the aim of a health care system is to provide healthcare facilities to the people, thereby improving their health status. Demographic indicators such as infant mortality rate, death rate and birth rate are dependent to a large extent on the availability of healthcare facilities. State-wise Development of Health and Toilet Facilities in India is presented in Table 4. As the Table 4 reveals the Hospital per lakh population is highest in Jammu & Kashmir (15.69) and lowest in Uttar Pradesh (0.43). Hospital bed per lakh Population is highest in Himachal Pradesh (123.75) and lowest in Bihar (12.75). Toilet facilities 2011-12 (in lakh numbers) per lakh population are highest in Himachal Pradesh (0.19) and lowest in Bihar (0.05).

Table 4. State-wise Development of Health Infrastructure, 2012

	State	Number of Hospitals Per Lakh Population	Number of hospital beds Per Lakh Population	Toilet facilities (In Lakh Numbers) Per Lakh Population
1	A.P.	0.54	44.84	0.12
2	Bihar	0.65	12.75	0.05
3	Chhattisgarh	7.92	42.17	0.08
4	Gujarat	2.57	58.74	0.09
5	Haryana	0.61	31.08	0.11
6	H.P.	2.20	123.75	0.19
7	J&K	15.69	58.32	0.07
8	Jharkhand	1.67	16.42	0.06
9	Karnataka	1.25	85.04	0.09
10	Kerala	3.76	110.88	0.15
11	M.P.	2.12	41.74	0.10
12	Maharashtra	1.04	42.02	0.08
13	Odisha	4.17	39.77	0.10
14	Punjab	0.88	41.22	0.07
15	Rajasthan	3.66	56.28	0.08
16	Tamil Nadu	2.77	86.26	0.11
17	Tripura	1.06	94.93	0.28
18	U.P.	0.43	28.25	0.11
19	Uttarakhand	6.87	78.73	0.11
20	West Bengal	1.71	84.52	0.12

Source: Source: GOI (2014)

RANKING OF STATES ON INFRASTRUCTURE DEVELOPMENT

We have used Principal Component Analysis (PCA) to derive the index of Infrastructure development for different states in India. The important factors have been extracted using PCA. Therefore, the importance of the factors in measuring infrastructure development is not the same. Using the proportion of these percentages as weights on the factor score coefficients, a Non- standardized Index (NSI) have been developed using the formula:

$$\text{Infrastructure Index} = w_1 * f_1 + w_2 * f_2 + \ldots\ldots\ldots\ldots + w_k * f_k$$

where, w_i is the weight of the factor i and f_i stands for i^{th} factor.

To determine the infrastructure index, we have considered the following 19 infrastructure variables. We have already presented the state-wise details for those in the earlier tables. In Table 5, we have presented the maximum, minimum and average values of all the 19 variables taken for consideration. As the range suggests, there is huge variation among the states in the development of infrastructure.

Table 5. Summary of the Infrastructure Variables, 2012

	Variable	Units	Code	Max	Min	Average
1	Road Density	Km. per 1000 sq. km	roadsqm	5543.52	163.58	1511.11
2	Road Density	Km. per 1000 population)	roadpop	8.00	0.82	3.79
3	Registered Motor vehicles	Nos. per1000 population)	motorv	256.58	31.44	135.98
4	Rail Density	Nos. per 1000 sq. km	raildkm	165.00	1.00	28.40
5	Rail Density	Nos. per 1000 population	raildpop	0.87	0.00	0.09
6	Total Airpor	Nos. Crore population	airp	10.00	0.00	4.95
7	Teledensity	Nos. per 1000 pop	Teledensity	12.07	4.89	7.70
8	Post offices	Nos. per lakh pop	postoff	99.21	6.58	19.60
9	Irrigated per capita	Hector		0.14	0.01	0.05
10	Fixed Capital	Rs. lakh /lakh pop	CapF	64887.70	727.05	20704.47
11	Invested Capital	/lakh pop	CapI	80511.04	1174.96	29181.15
12	Number of Distributors	Nos. per lakh pop	Elecdist	1.94	0.50	1.07
13	Electricity installed generating capacity	GWh	Elecgen	37.91	0.49	14.08
14	Banks bracnhes	Nos. per lakh pop	BankB	13.96	2.89	6.63
15	Deposit	Rs. crore 2012 per lakh pop	BankD	1080072.00	7407.00	197059.20
16	Credit	Rs. crore 2012) per lakh pop	BankC	947948.00	1957.00	151722.50
17	Hospital	Nos. per lakh pop	HOSN	15.69	0.43	3.08
18	Hospital beds	Nos. per lakh pop	HOSB	123.75	12.75	58.89
19	Toilet facilities 2011-12	Nos. (in lakh numbers) per lakh pop	Toilet	0.28	0.05	0.11

Source: Source: GOI (2014), GOI(2014a), GOI(2014,b)

With the 19 infrastructure variables for 20 states in India, we have conducted factor analysis to find the factors with eigen value greater than one. The scree plot derived from the factor analysis (Figure 1) reveals that there are seven factors with eigen value greater than one and they together explain about 90% variation of the variables as revealed from factor analysis.

After obtaining the factor scores, we have used the following formula to find the index value of infrastructure for each state.

$$\text{INFI} = \left(Index\ -\ (-0.7217547\ )\right) / \left(0.970583\ -\ (-0.7217547\ )\right)$$

The average value of infrastructure index was calculated to 0.4265 with standard deviation 0.275. Table 6 presents the derived values for infrastructure index and the ranks of the states in infrastructure development.

Figure 1. Scree Plot of Eigen Values

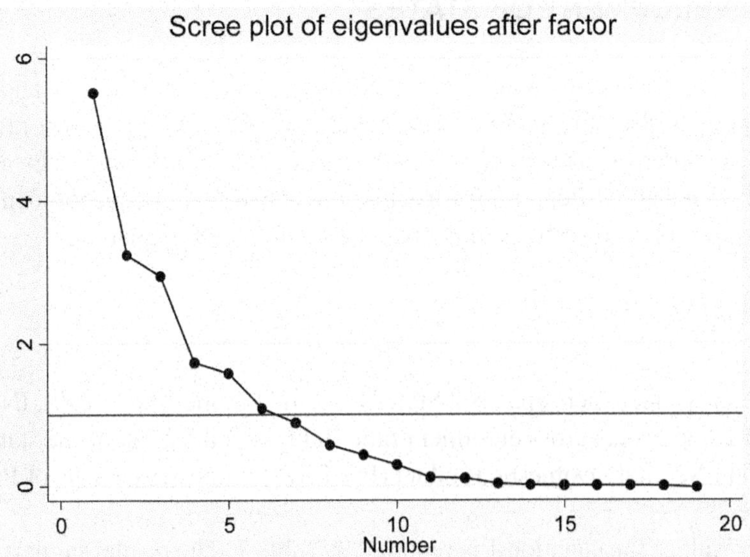

Table 6. Raking of States According to Infrastructure Development, 2012

	State	INFI (Infrastructure Index)	Rank in Infrastructure Development	Gross Enrolment Ratio (GER)
1	Andhra Pradesh	0.5808	6	29.90
2	Bihar	0.0000	20	12.50
3	Chhattisgarh	0.1725	17	10.50
4	Gujarat	0.7326	4	16.50
5	Haryana	0.3881	10	28.00
6	Himachal Pradesh	1.0000	1	24.80
7	Jammu & Kashmir	0.0218	19	22.80
8	Jharkhand	0.1317	18	9.90
9	Karnataka	0.5743	7	23.80
10	Kerala	0.5103	8	21.80
11	madhya Pradesh	0.2093	16	18.50
12	Maharashtra	0.8071	2	26.30
13	Odisha	0.3568	12	16.60
14	Punjab	0.4729	9	23.00
15	Rajasthan	0.2396	14	18.20
16	Tamil Nadu	0.6588	5	40.00
17	Tripura	0.3159	13	12.40
18	Uttar Pradesh	0.2101	15	17.40
19	Uttarakhand	0.7654	3	31.10
20	West Bengal	0.3818	11	13.60

Source: GOI (2014) and GOI (2014,b)

IMPACT OF INFRASTRUCTURE AND EDUCATION ON ECONOMIC DEVELOPMENT OF STATES

Various studies suggest that regions with larger stocks of physical infrastructure and human capital often exhibit comparatively robust economic performance. We shall use aggregate production functions (Walke et al, 2015) in order to analyze the determinants of economic performance across Indian states Explanatory variables include different infrastructure index and higher education enrolment.

The regression equation to be estimated is given by the following equation

$$PCNSDP_i = bo + b_1 INFIi + b_2 GERi + u_i \tag{1}$$

$PCNSDP_i$ represents annual per capita Net State Domestic Product (PCNSDP), INFI stands for infrastructure index, GER represents gross enrolment ratio in higher education of the states. The dependent variable is Per Capita Net State Domestic Product (PCNSDP). State-wise status of PCNSDP in 2012 is presented in Figure 2.

The regression result of the equation 1 is reported in Table 7. The results suggest that infrastructure and education have significant impact on economic development of the state which is measured by PCNSDP. The adjusted R^2 is found as 0.646 and the F value is significant at 1% level.

Figure 2. Per Capita Net State Domestic Product (PCNSDP) for States in India (Rs.), 2012
Source: GOI, Economic Survey

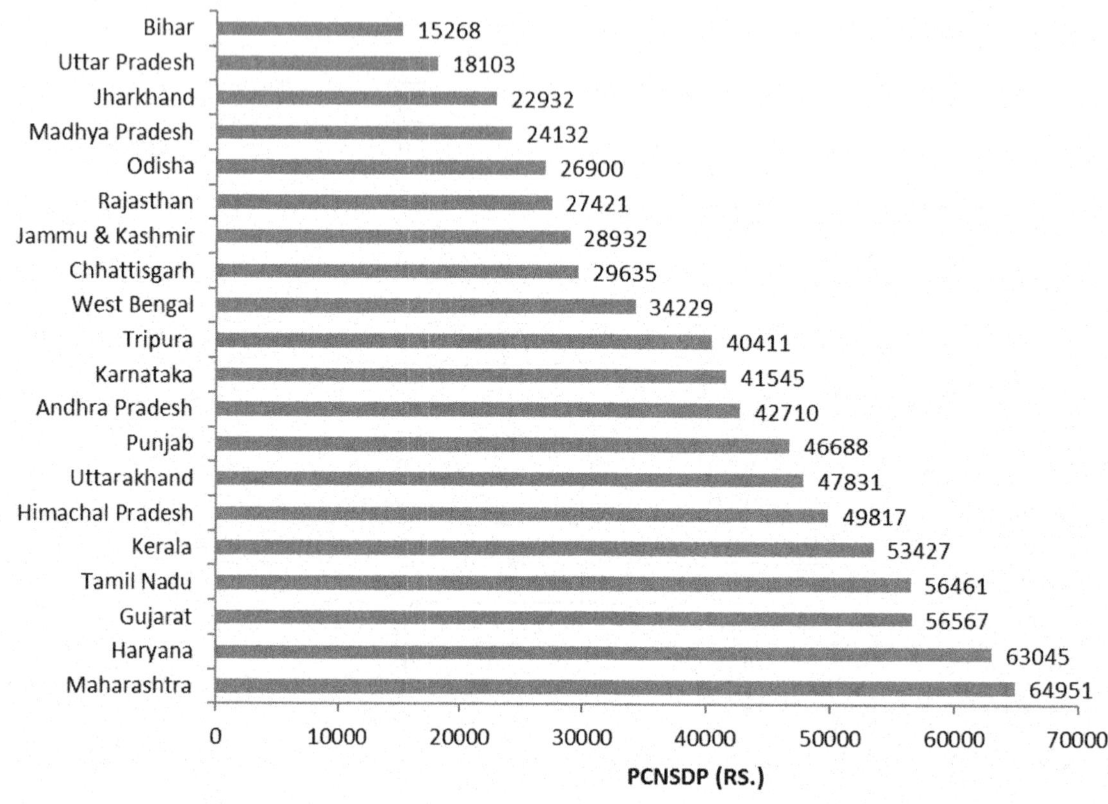

Table 7. Regression Results

.	*Coefficients*	*t Stat*	*P-value*
Intercept	19159.04	2.092012	0.051753
INFI	46151.11	3.152833	0.005808
GER	1143.408	2.209514	0.041147

Adjusted $R^2 = 0.646$, F= 18.3 (Significance level =0.0)

CONCLUSION

The present study attempts to look at the status of infrastructure development of the states in India. We have employed the methodology of factor analysis to construct the index of infrastructure development of the states in India. The results suggest there is huge variation in the infrastructure development of the states in India with poor infrastructure development in some states like Bihar, J&K, Jharkhand, Chhattisgarh, M.P., UP and Rajasthan. We have also attempted to check whether infrastructure development and education determines the economic development of the states. The regression results suggest there is significant positive impact of infrastructure development and education on economic development of the states. So, to accelerate the growth rate, efforts should be made to improve the infrastructure and education level in India.

REFERENCES

Aboudou, M. T. (2011). Infrastructure Development and Economic Growth in Togo. *International Journal of Economics and Finance, 3*(3). Retrieved from www.ccsenet.org/ijef

Almada, C., Gonzalez, L. B., Eason, P., & Fullerton, T. M. Jr. (2006). Econometric Evidence Regarding Education and Border Income Performance. *Mountains Plains Journal of Business and Economics, 7*, 11–24.

Bhandari, L., & Dutta, S. (2007). Health Infrastructure in Rural India. In P. Kalra & A. Rastogi (Eds.), *India Infrastructure Report* (pp. 265–285). New Delhi: Oxford University Press.

Bhandari, L., & Gupta, S. (2011). *The Indicus Handbook 2011: Indian Economy, Markets and Consumers*. Pearson.

Das, D., & Mahnta, R. (2012). Role of Infrastructure in Developing Countries: A Case Study of Assam. In R. P. Pradhan (Ed.), *Inclusive Financial Infrastructure*. Blumsbury.

De, P. (2008). Infrastructure Development in India. In N. Kumar (Ed.), *International Infrastructure Development in East Asia – Towards Balanced Regional Development and Integration, ERIA Research Project Report 2007-2* (pp. 105–130). Chiba: IDE-JETRO.

Estache, A. & Grégoire, G. (2012). The Impact of Infrastructure on growth in developing countries. *IFC Economic Notes*, 2012.

Fullerton, T. Jr, Licerio, E., & Wangmo, P. (2010). Education, infrastructure, and regional income performance in Arkansas. *Regional and Sectoral Economic Studies*, *10*(1), 5–22.

Ghosh, B., & De, P. (2004). How do Different Categories of Infrastructure affect Development? Evidence from Indian States. *EPW*, *39*(42), 4645–4657.

Government of India. (2012). *Statistics of School Education, 2011-12*. Ministry of Human Resource Development, Govt. of India.

Government of India. (2013). *Annual Report, 2012-13*. Department of Telecommunications, Ministry of Communication & Information Technology, Govt. of India. Retrieved from www.mospi.nic.in

Government of India. (2014a). *Annual Survey of Industries, 2011-12*. Ministry of Statistics and Programme Implementation, Govt. of India.

Government of India. (2014b). *Educational Statistics at a Glance*. MHRD, Govt. of India.

Government of India. (2015). *Annual Report, Indian Post, 2014-15*. Department of Post, Ministry of Communications and Information Technology, Govt. of India.

Hati, K. K., & Majumder, R. (2013). *Health Infrastructure, Health Outcome and Economic Wellbeing- A District Level Study in India*. Retrieved from https://mpra.ub.uni-muenchen.de/53363/

Jana, S. K. (2014). *Tank Irrigation in the Dry Zones in India*. New Delhi: Concept Publishing Co.

Jana, S. K., Palanisami, K. & Das, A. (2012). A Study on Tank Irrigation in the Dry Zones of West Bengal. *Indian Journal of Agricultural Economics*, *67*(2).

Kumari, R., & Raman, R. (2011). Inter- District Disparity in Health Care Facility and Education: A Case of Uttar Pradesh. *Journal of Education and Practice*, *2*(1), 38–56.

Lasara, M. L. (2015). Inter-State Variations in Rural Healthcare Infrastructure in North-East India. *The NEHU Journal, 13*(2), 31-48.

Mohan, R. (2003). Infrastructure Development in India: Emerging Challenges. *World Bank Annual Bank Conference on Development Economics*, Bangalore, India.

Mohan, R. (2016). *Infrastructure and Economic Development - A Conceptual Clarification*. Accessed on July 7, 2016. http://shodhganga.inflibnet.ac.in/bitstream/10603/8497/12/12_chapter%202.pdf

Montgomery, E. (2008). *Infrastructure in India: A vast land of construction opportunity*. Available to download at www.pwc.com

Naoyuki, Y., & Nakahigashi, M. (2000). *The Role of Infrastructure in Economic Development*. Retrieved from http://econ.keio.ac.jp/staff/dikamiya/pdf00/seminar/1205.pdf

Novianti, T., Amzul, R., Dian, V. P., & Retno, W. (2014). The Infrastructure's Influence on the ASEAN Countries' Economic Growth. *Journal of Economics and Development Studies*, *2*(4).

Owolabi-Merus, O. (2015). Infrastructure Development and Economic Growth Nexus in Nigeria. *International Journal of Academic Research in Business and Social Sciences, 5*(1).

Sawada, Y. (2015). *The Impacts of Infrastructure in Development: A Selective Survey.* ADBI Working Paper Series, No. 511.

Stewart, R., & Moslares, C. (2014). Regional Disparities Across Indian States: Are the Trends Reversing? *Journal of Economics*, *2*(3), 95–111.

Walke, A., Thomas, G., Fullerton, M. Jr, & Martha, P. (2015, December). An Empirical Analysis of Education, Infrastructure, and Regional Growth in Mexico. *Journal of Economics and Development Studies*, *3*(4), 1–12. doi:10.15640/jeds.v3n4a1

Wang, E. C. (2002). Public Infrastructure and Economic Growth: A New Applied to East Asian Economies. *Journal of Policy Modeling*, 24.

KEY TERMS AND DEFINITIONS

Economic Development: It is defined as the increase in the economic wealth of a country or a particular region, for the welfare of its residents.

Gross Enrolment Ratio (GER): Gross enrolment ratio in higher education is defined as the total enrolment of students in higher education regardless of age, expressed as a percentage of the corresponding eligible age group population.

Human Capital: It constitutes the skills, knowledge, and experience possessed by an individual or population.

Infrastructure: Infrastructure is the basic physical systems of a nation that are vital to a country's economic development.

Infrastructure Index: An indicator of the infrastructure development of a country or a region.

Net State Domestic Product: Value of all goods and services produced within the boundaries of the State during a given period of time after deducting the wear and tear or depreciation, accounted without duplication.

Principal Component Analysis (PCA): A method of analysis which involves finding the linear combination of a set of variables that has maximum variance and removing its effect, repeating this successively.

Chapter 2
Changes in Infrastructural Condition of Slums in India:
A State Level Analysis

Somenath Ghosh
Visva Bharati University, India

ABSTRACT

Addressing the importance of infrastructure development towards inclusive city, the study aims to see the change in the condition of housing, road, latrine, drainage, sewerage, etc. within the slums across states and over time in India. The study has been done with the help of three rounds (49th, 58th and 69th) of NSSO data on slum. Though the condition of slums seems to have improved over time, but it is not satisfactory. However, it seems the improvement of one infrastructural aspect in slum is very much associated with the improvement of others. The factors like 'Workforce Participation Rate of slums' and overall infrastructure of the state have a positive influence on the infrastructural condition of slums, whereas, per capita NSDP is affecting it negatively. The 'associations made by the residents of slum for improvement' within the slums seems to have played no role to improve it.

INTRODUCTION

The world is now experiencing a rapid expansion of urban areas with growing urban population[1]. One among the main reasons behind the rapid growth of urban population is migration from rural to the urban areas either due to pull Lewis (1954), Harris-Todaro (1969) or push Davis (2004) and Harvey (2008) of the population and among those migrants, most of them are poor and take shelter in slums. This phenomenon has created an over congestion toward the slum as well as non-slum areas, which is putting pressure on infrastructure facilities available to the cities[2].

Like most other developing countries, urban and slum population in India has grown rapidly. Census data has revealed that the share of slum population out of the urban population and the share of urban population out of total population have increased over time (see Table 1). Moreover, it is found that the rate of growth of slum population is higher than the growth rate of urban population. This situation has added up pressure on civic infrastructure[3].

DOI: 10.4018/978-1-5225-2364-2.ch002

Table 1. Share of slum and urban population

Year	% of Urban Population Out Total Population	% of Slum Population Out of Urban Population
2001	27.81%	14.88%
2011	31.16%	17.37%

Source. Author's calculation with census data of 2001 and 2011

Table 2. Percentage of comprehensive or good housing in urban areas

Year	% of Proper Housing in Urban Areas with Proper Facilities
2001	64.2%
2011	68.4%

Source. Author's calculation with census data of 2001 and 2011

But in contrast with the growth of slum and urban population in India, housing with all proper facilities together (like latrine, electricity, etc.) have not improved accordingly (see Table 2). This may indicate the inadequacy of infrastructural facilities in urban areas. In recent future, urban population in India is estimated to increase to a large extent and will be excess than the capacity of the cities. Compared to this, infrastructure has to grow at a higher rate than the rate the population will increase[4].

Besides, the government's attention towards slum and urban development in India has been limited to its capacity and the deficiency in comprehensive urban planning has fostered the problem of infrastructure inadequacy to the slum dwellers.

However, it is true that adequate infrastructure plays an important role behind the economic growth of the urban areas, but the concept of modern city is sometimes built upon dispossession and displacement of the urban poor[5]. In India, building of new roads, modern houses, office spaces, etc. within the cities has required free and enclosed spaces which occasionally have been expropriated through eviction or dislocation of slums[6]. This had worsened the infrastructure condition within slums as there was high chance that these evicted slum dwellers would be shifted to other slum locations; in turn it created added pressure on the infrastructure of those slums. Development with eviction gave rise to social and economic exclusion and comprehensive urban development with growth would fail to achieve.

So, to cope with the problem of urban poverty and to make an inclusive urban development, one of the most vital instruments can be development of slum infrastructure and sustainable infrastructure development to reduce the gaps between the slums and non slum areas within the urban areas. Subsequently, infrastructure development in slums will increase the productive capacity and standard of living of the slum dwellers. Here the search is not intended to explore how infrastructure performs as an engine of modern sector growth but the search will be directed to see whether the improvement in infrastructure is performed for the development of slums to make the cities an inclusive one. This chapter will focus to see the change in the infrastructural condition over time within the slums in India and the factors that have influenced the infrastructural development of slums.

LITERATURE REVIEW

Notion Regarding the Concept of Inclusive City

The UN-Habitat report, 2003 has described slum, is a place where there is *'insecurity of tenure, lack of basic services,... hazardous land, etc'* and the report has opined that *'development management'* can remove difficulties within the slum with *'Up-scaling'* and *'Up-grading'* the slums through infrastructure development to make the cities an inclusive one (UN-Habitat, 2003, Introduction).

Then the era comes when the idea of achieving the targets of inclusive city is not restricted alone with the development of slums. The concept of comprehensive urban planning is generated, which means wholeness of development through proper chain of planning that can make a city more inclusive UN-Habitat, (2009) and the cities would be changed into prosperous city UN-Habitat, (2012).

Some Propositions of Urban Planning for Inclusive City

Beltrao (2014) suggested that inclusive cities could be promoted through proper 'urban planning and land management'. He advised the planner to rethink about the spatial design, physical planning, infrastructure, etc of the city and provided two keys for development i.e. *'Transit Oriented Development' (TOD)* and *'Complete Community Development' (CCD).*

Dowall & Ellis (2014) discussed about three main ingredients behind the sustainable urban *planning those are a) managing urban expansion, b) renewal of existing urban areas and c) coordinating urban planning and infrastructure across different lines of development in urban areas.*

Roy (2014) had argued that the urban infrastructure projects in India were designed for 'open up economy' which aimed of a 'world class city' but had been built upon dispossession of urban poor. She suggested that there would be a) direct cash transfer to the poor, b) involvement of local government for buying and selling of land and c) philosophy of right to city Roy. (2014). She found out the condition of the slum was ranked somewhere between that of rural and non slum areas.

A study made by Bouddha et al (2014) aimed to see prevailing approaches to tackle the socio-economic and physical problem of slums. Concern of the study was to see inclusive aspects of the city. They observed the approaches for the improvement of the slum can be of three types that is 1) Punitive approach, 2) Curative approach and 3) Preventive approach. Among the three, they found out curative and preventive approaches were better. The study suggested that curative approach will be taken through development of infrastructure which has impact on socio-economic condition of slums.

Mitra (2015) had emphasised on slum improvement models of Thailand (Ban Mankong) and Nicaragua (PRODEL) which served as the basis for selecting the model for slum improvement in India. He found both of these models were "whole city whole slum". In the similar way JNNURM and RAY were adopted for development of clean city, infrastructure for credit facilities for housing. The author gave the view that JNNURM and RAY are upgrading the cities like Ban Mankong and PRODEL respectively for providing financial support.

Condition of Urban and Slum Infrastructure from Empiric Perspective

A FICCI's report on *'Urban Infrastructure in India'* in October 2014 has demonstrated that supply of water is only available for 2.9 hour per day across cities and towns, 50% households in cities and towns do not have sewerage connections, more than 80% waste water is not treated and 26% of the household on average in cities do not have latrine facilities. The report has also stated that besides the gaps between availability and requirement of infrastructure, there is shortfall of funds for improving urban infrastructure. This study is made with the help of NSSO data of 54th round.

Another report has been submitted by PRIA (Society for Participatory Research) in 2014 on infrastructure condition of slums across India with the help of primary survey in 50 cities of India, which has included 5350 households and about 24500 individuals. The study show that only about 50% of households in slum have access to tap water in their home and which is treated tap water. It also revealed that 82% of households have latrine facility within their home.

Chandrashekhar (2005) has seen the demographic, MPCE and infrastructure condition in slum in India and compared those with the condition of rural and non slum population with the help of NSSO data on slum of 58th round.

However, a detailed 'statistical compendium' has been prepared by Ministry of Housing and Urban Poverty Alleviation on the slum of India with the help of all the available indicators covered by census and NSSO so far in its report *'State of Slum in India'*, 2013.

In spite of macro level studies there are many micro level studies regarding the infrastructural condition of slums. Likewise a study done by Rusling (2007) has assessed a slum upgrading programme which has been implemented in 2005 through partnership approach among Municipal corporations, international organisations, slum residents and local NGOs in 45 slums of Ahmadabad. The objective of the study was to see improvement of the household in slums in basic infrastructure like water connections, underground sewerage, toilets to individual households, road system and solid waste management. This study has been done with the help of primary survey of 285 women and she found that the program was successful in improving the life of slum households in above aspects.

Limited studies have been done regarding the infrastructural condition of slum across states and over time. Moreover, reviewed studies have not focused to see the condition of various infrastructural aspects together. Perhaps, the time change incorporated in this study has not been studied in other literatures except in the statistical compendium of Ministry of Housing and Poverty Alleviation, Government of India, (2014). But this compendium is far behind in searching the factors which can affect the infrastructural condition of slums. Our study will mainly concentrate to see to what extent the condition of infrastructure of slums has improved and what the probable reasons for its improvement are.

OBJECTIVES OF THE STUDY

- To see the housing condition within the slum across states and over time.
- To see the condition of road within and approaching towards the slum across states and over time.
- To see the condition of drainage, sewerage, latrine and garbage disposal facilities across states and over time.
- Probable factors that are affecting the infrastructural development of slums.

DATA COLLECTION

Data has been collected from the reports of National Sample Survey Organization (NSSO) on slums (i.e. 49th, 58th and 69th round). The study has been done at all India level and across its major 19 states at three time periods (i.e. 1992, 2002, and 2012). The data of independent variables have been collected from other sources like CSO, Census, NSSO etc. The census data of slum population, WPR in slums, literacy rate in slums, total WPR, total literacy rate of the states, number of households having electricity in a state, total population, etc. have been collected for the year 2001 and 2011. The data of Net State Domestic Product (NSDP) has been collected from the data base of RBI. The data of number of slums have association for improvement has been collected from NSSO 58th and 69th round.

METHODOLOGY

The study has three parts. In the first part the study dealt with the condition of various infrastructural aspects in slums which has been seen with the help of Indicators, given in Table 3.

Dimensions and Indicators

The results or performances of those indicators for 19 states (the data of Bihar & Jharkhand; Madhya Pradesh & Chhattisgarh; Uttar Pradesh & Uttarakhand are taken together) have been explained with the help of bar diagrams. Then the relationship among the indicators has been seen with the help of pairwise correlation. This has been done to observe the degree of association of particular infrastructural aspects with the other aspects in slums.

The second part reveals the relationship among the indicators of known infrastructural aspects within the slum. The relationships have been seen with the help of line diagrams and correlations

In the third part, the exogenous factors which can influence the infrastructural condition of the slums have been drawn to see its effect.

The aspects that have been considered to see the effects on the infrastructural condition are:

- **Overall Development of the States:** Socio-economic development of a state may improve the Infrastructural condition of the slums in that state.
- **Socio-Economic Condition of the Slums Across States:** The social and economical progress within the slum may have also improved the Infrastructural condition of slums. This is because capacity to improve the infrastructure in slums will rise due to increase in employment within the slum. Increasing literacy rate in slums may generate awareness and develop understanding among the slum dwellers about the necessity of good infrastructure which may increase the condition of slums.

Table 3. Dimensions and Indicators of Infrastructural condition of slums

SL. No.	Dimensions	Indicators/Variables
1.	Housing Condition	% of slums having majority of its houses made up with permanent materials
2.	Road Connectivity	% of slums having metal road within the slums
		% of slums having motorable metal road approaching to the slums
3.	Drinking Water	% of Slums having tap water as the major source of drinking water
4.	Sanitation	% of slums own latrine facilities by most of the residents
		% of slums having underground sewerage system
		% of slums having underground drainage facilities
		% of slums having garbage disposal facilities arranged by the Govt.

- **Better Monitoring by the Slum Dwellers:** Better monitoring by the slum dwellers may positively change the infrastructural condition of the slums. Because through better monitoring slum dwellers may improve their own infrastructure within the slum.

So, the variables of the stated aspects are given in Table 4.

The data of independent variables have been collected for two years, i.e. 2001 and 2011 for same 22 states (as the data of Bihar & Jharkhand; Madhya Pradesh & Chhattisgarh; Uttar Pradesh & Uttarakhand for both dependent and independent variables are considered separately).

The degree of association between the exogenous aspects and infrastructural condition of slums with respective variables has been seen with the help of line diagrams & correlations. Regression has been done to see whether the probable factors are really affecting the condition of slums. While doing the regression, time dummy has been taken to see the effect of time change on Infrastructural condition of slums. For some regressions we have considered the log value of the actual variables and the author has also taken robust standard error to avert hetroscedasticity problems.

ANALYSIS AND RESULTS

Infrastructural Condition of Slums: Bar Diagrams

This part of the chapter illustrates bar diagrams showing the condition of various infrastructural aspects within the slums across states and over time.

Housing Condition

Figure 1 shows that the 'percentage of slums having majority of its houses made up with permanent material' have increased over time for over all India and in many states. It has increased from 30% in 1991 to 60% in 2011 for overall India and the average of the states has increased from 23.72% in 1991 to 57.51% in 2011. The states like Andhra Pradesh, Punjab, Karnataka, Gujarat, Tamil Nadu, etc. have shown an increasing trend, but the states Delhi, Bihar & Jharkhand, Maharashtra, and Kerala are showing a decreasing trend. Though the average of the states has increased, but it has not crossed 60%.

Table 4. Factors of the Infrastructural Condition of Slums

Exogenous Aspects	Indicators/Variables (Independent)
Overall development of the states	Per capita Net State Domestic Product (NSDP)
	Total Work Force Participation Rate (WPR)
	Total Literacy rate
	Total road density
	Percentage household having access to electricity
Socio-economic development of the slums	Workforce participation rate (WPR) in slums
	Literacy rate in slums
Better monitoring by the slum dwellers	Percentage of slums having association for improvement

Figure 1. Percentage of Slums having majority of its houses made up with Permanent Material
Source. Author's figure using NSSO Data of 49th, 58th and 69th rounds

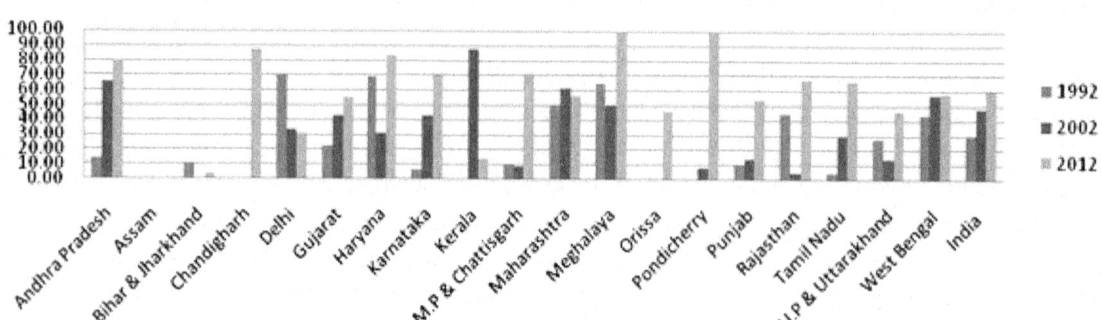

It may reveal that the developed states except Delhi, Maharashtra and Kerala have shown better housing condition within the slum over time.

Road Connectivity

Figure 2 reveals an increasing trend for the 'percentage of slums having puccka road within the slums' from 46.50% in 1991 to 66.13% in 2011 for overall India. The states like Andhra Pradesh, Bihar & Jharkhand, Gujarat, Kerela, M.P & Chattisgarh, Punjab and Tamil Nadu have increased from 1992 to 2012. But other states like Assam, Delhi, Karnataka, Maharashtra, Orissa, Pondicherry and West Bengal have decreased from 1992. For all states average has increased from 34.44% in 1992 to 66.13% in 2012.

Figure 3 shows 'percentage of slums having motorable puccka road approaching to the slums' has increased a little from 65.30% in 1992 to 68.71% in 2012 for overall India. All state average has increased from 68.30% in 1992 to 71.37% in 2012. The states like Chandigarh, Delhi, Haryana, Maharashtra, Meghalaya, Rajasthan, UP & Uttrakhand and West Bengal have decreased over time.

This reveals that the condition of road connectivity within and approaching to the slum in developed states like Chandigarh, Delhi, Maharashtra, West Bengal etc have deteriorated.

Figure 2. Percentage of Slums having Puccka Road within the Slums
Source. Author's figure using NSSO Data of 49th, 58th and 69th rounds.

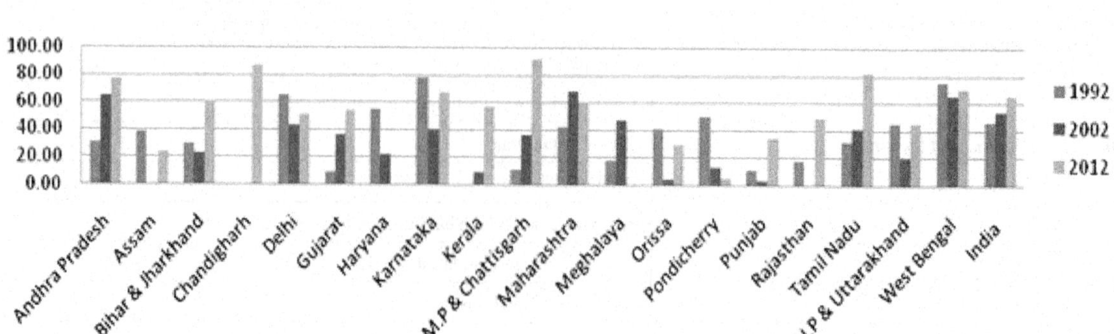

Figure 3. Percentage of slums having motorable puccka road approaching the slums
Source. Author's figure using NSSO Data of 49th, 58th and 69th rounds.

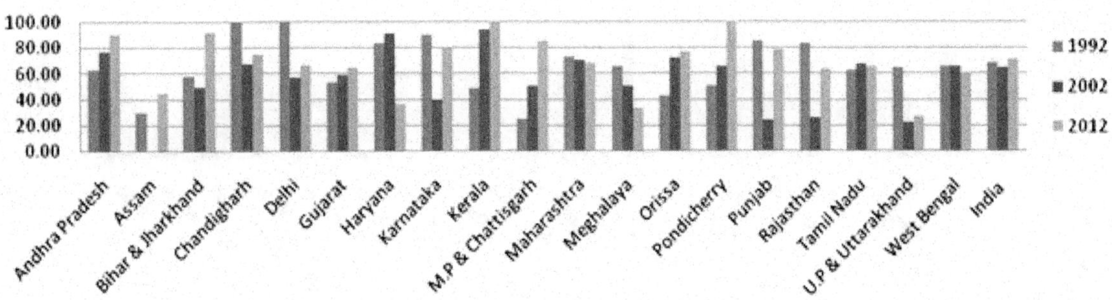

Figure 4. Percentage of Slums having tap water as the major source of drinking water facility
Source. Author's figure using NSSO Data of 49th, 58th and 69th rounds

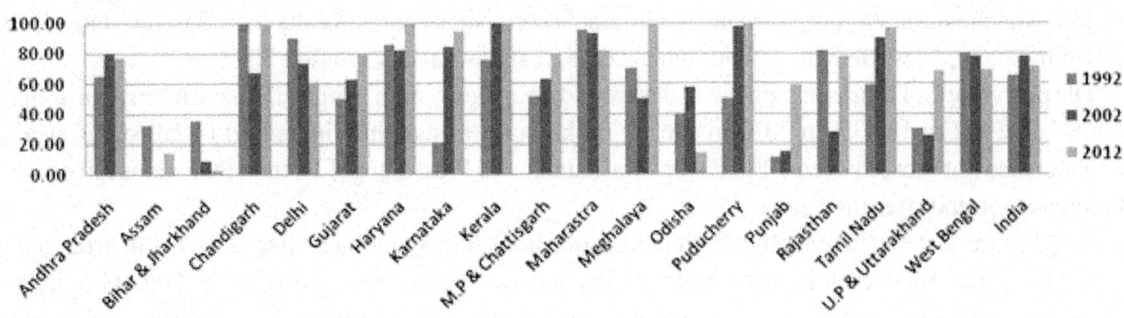

Drinking Water Facility

The above figure shows that the 'percentage of Slums having tap water as the major source of drinking water facility' have increased in the first decade and later decreased at all India level. While some states (Chandigarh, Haryana, Kerela and Pondicherry) were 100% successful and some (Assam, Bihar & Jharkhand and Orissa) were not even successful in providing 20% of tap water as the major source of drinking water facility to slums. The states like Gujarat, Haryana, Pondicherry, Tamil Nadu, M.P. & Chhattisgarh, etc though have not attained 100% but increased from its first decades. However, in the states like Delhi, Andhra Pradesh, Maharashtra, West Bengal, etc. it has deteriorated from first decades. This may divulge that the condition of drinking water in the most developed states like Delhi, Maharashtra, etc. got worse over the decades.

Sanitation Condition

Although the 'percentage of slums where most of the residents own the latrine facility' (Figure 5) have increased by more than double in overall India as well as for all the state average, but it has not crossed 35%. Only Kerala has attained 100% of slums where 'most of the residents own the latrine facility'.

Figure 5. Percentage of Slums have Owned Latrine Facility by most the Residents
SSource. Author's figure using NSSO Data of 49th, 58th and 69th rounds

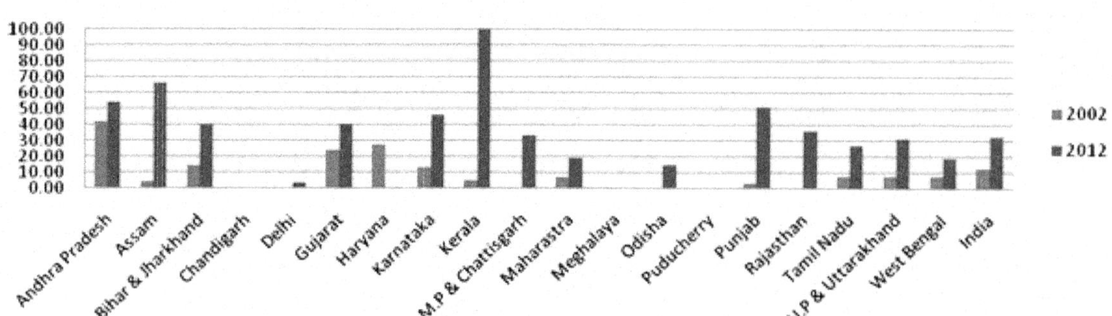

'The percentage of slums having underground sewerage facility' (Figure 6) have increased for overall India as well as for all the states average, but not more than 30% during the specified time period. Though the 'Percentage of slums having underground sewerage facility' have increased in some states (Andhra Pradesh, Maharashtra, Punjab, Karnataka, Gujarat, Tamil Nadu) and have decreased in the states Delhi, UP, Uttarakhand, West Bengal, etc. but the average of states has not crossed 30%.

'The percentage of Slums having the underground drainage system' (Figure 7) have more than doubled from 8% in 1992 to 18,63% in 2012 in overall India, but it has slightly increased for all states average and which has not crossed even 10%. Except Karnataka and West Bengal all the other states have shown an increasing trend over the years.

From Figure 8, it can be seen that 'percentage of Slums having garbage disposal system arranged by the Govt.' is more for overall India than that of all state average, but not crossed 65%. Only Pondicherry has attained 100% garbage disposal system arranged by the government, while Odhisha and Bihar & Jharkhand have not even attained 10% in 2011.

The analysis reveals that sewerage system in slums has deteriorated in developed states like Delhi and West Bengal and in the slums of Karnataka, Delhi and West Bengal the drainage system has deteriorated. The garbage disposal system has worsened in the developed states like Delhi and Maharashtra.

Figure 6. Percentage of Slums having underground sewerage facility
Source. Author's figure using NSSO Data of 49th, 58th and 69th rounds

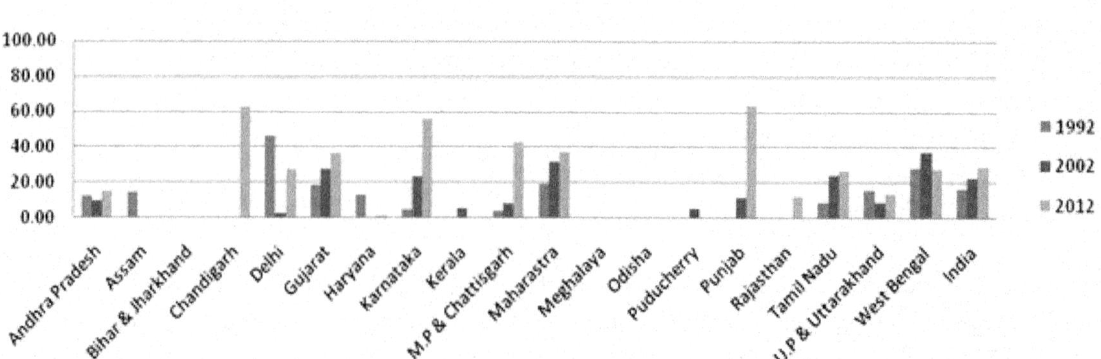

Figure 7. Percentage of Slums having Underground Drainage System
Source. Author's figure using NSSO Data of 49th, 58th and 69th rounds.

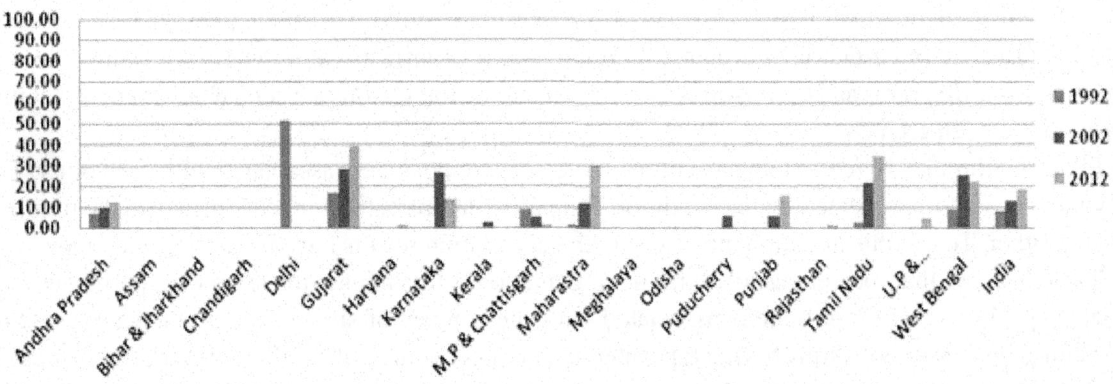

Figure 8. Percentage of Slums having Garbage Disposal Facility Arranged by the Govt.
Source. Author's figure using NSSO Data of 49th, 58th and 69th rounds.

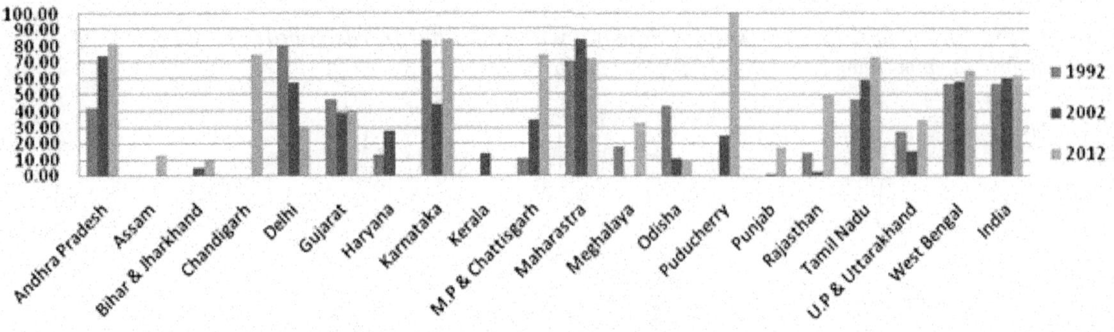

Key Findings and Some Abstract Observations

It can be summarized from the above result that the infrastructural condition in slums has improved for overall India and across some states in all the aspects stated above, but the condition of infrastructure in slums have not improved over 60% of slums. Sanitation facilities like the latrine, drainage and sewerage; improvement of those has not even crossed over 30% of slums. The result also showed that the condition of infrastructure in slums in developed states like Delhi, Maharashtra, West Bengal, Karnataka, etc. has deteriorated over the decades. In some cases, the condition of poor states like Bihar, Jharkhand and Orissa is even worst. This may be because the economic development in this states are pulling the population from the rural as well as from other urban areas at a higher rate than the rate at which the infrastructure is built. Or the other way round, infrastructure facilities provided by the government of these states might have failed to cope with the massive expansion of the urban area due to economic and social pull. Moreover, infrastructure development might have encountered the obstruction due to dislocation of slums Harvey, (2008).

Relationship Between the Infrastructural Aspects of the Slums: Line Diagrams and Correlations

The relationship among the various aspects of infrastructure within the slums perhaps will reveal the level of influence of certain infrastructure on other aspect of infrastructure within the slums. So with the help of line diagrams and correlations association among the various aspects of infrastructure within the slum has been seen.

Figures 9 through 16 reveal that most of the indicators are positively associated with each other. This may indicate that improvement in the condition of a particular infrastructure can influence the improvement of other. To see this in a more precise way the correlation results have been analyzed below.

Table 5 shows that 'percentage of slums having majority of its houses made up with permanent material' is positively and significantly associated with 'percentage of slums having puccka road within the slum', 'percentage of slums having tap water as the major source of drinking water', 'percentage of slums having underground sewerage facility' and 'percentage of slums have garbage disposal system arranged by the government'. This may reveal that housing condition in slums is being influenced by other infrastructure in slums. This may imply that housing condition in slum will improve if other infrastructures are improved as well.

Figure 9. Line Diagrams. Relationship of housing with the other infrastructure in slums
Source. Author's diagrams using NSSO Data of 49th, 58th and 69th rounds.

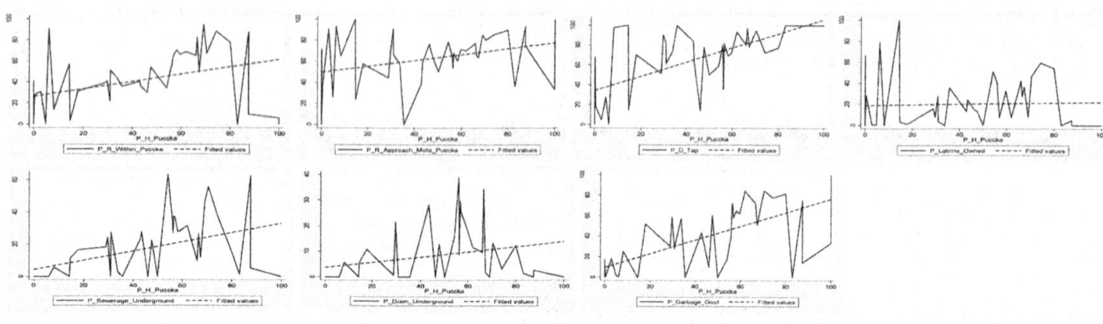

Figure 10. Line Diagram. Relationship of road with the other infrastructure in slums
Source. Author's diagrams using NSSO Data of 49th, 58th and 69th rounds.

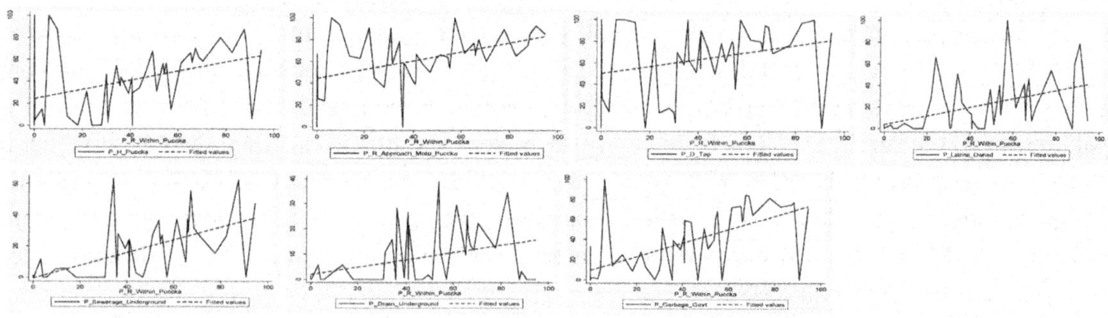

Figure 11. Line Diagram. Relationship of approaching road with the other infrastructure in slums
Source. Author's diagrams using NSSO Data of 49th, 58th and 69th rounds.

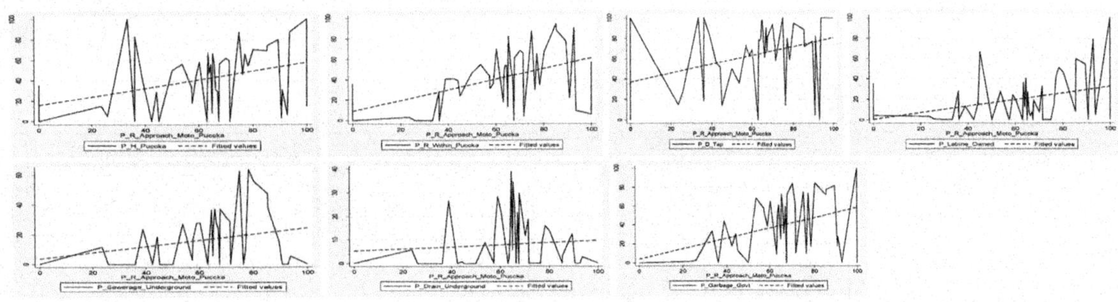

Figure 12. Line Diagram. Relationship of drinking water facility with the other infrastructure in slums
Source. Author's diagrams using NSSO Data of 49th, 58th and 69th rounds.

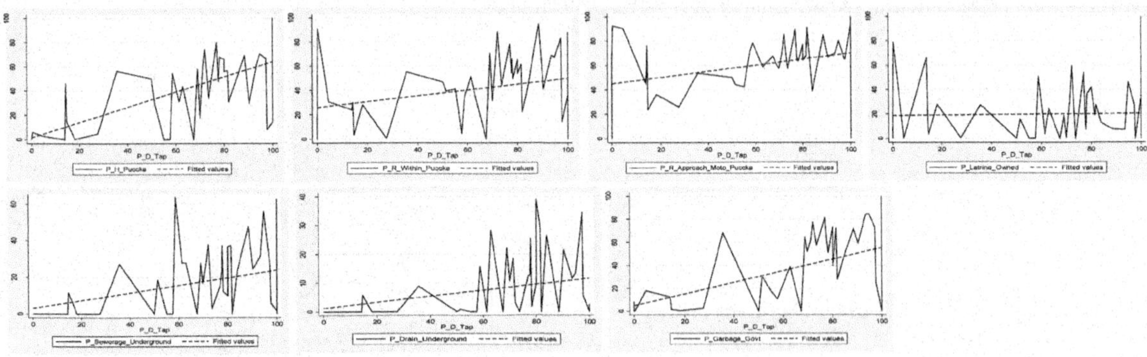

Figure 13. Line Diagram. Relationship of latrine facility with the other infrastructure in slums
Source. Author's diagrams using NSSO Data of 49th, 58th and 69th rounds.

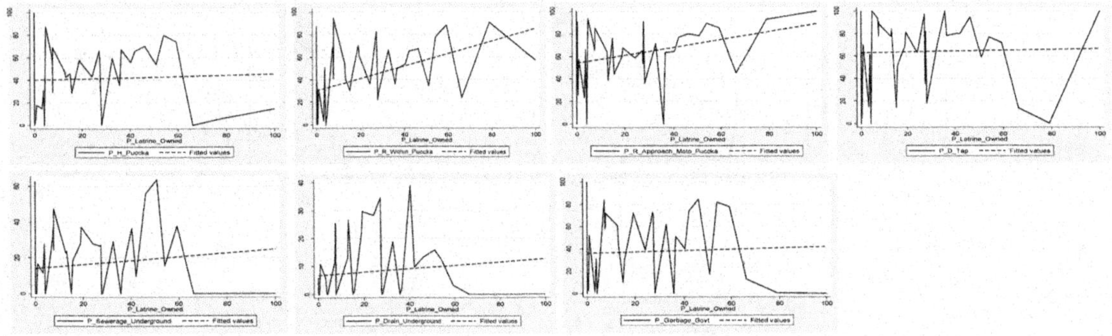

'Percentage of slums having puccka road within the slum' is positively associated with 'percentage of slums having motorable puccka road approaching to the slums', 'percentage of Slums have owned latrine facility by most the residents', 'percentage of slums having underground sewerage facility' and 'percentage of slums have garbage disposal system arranged by the government'. This may reveal that

Figure 14. Line Diagram. Relationship of sewerage facility with the other infrastructure in slums
Source. Author's diagrams using NSSO Data of 49th, 58th and 69th rounds.

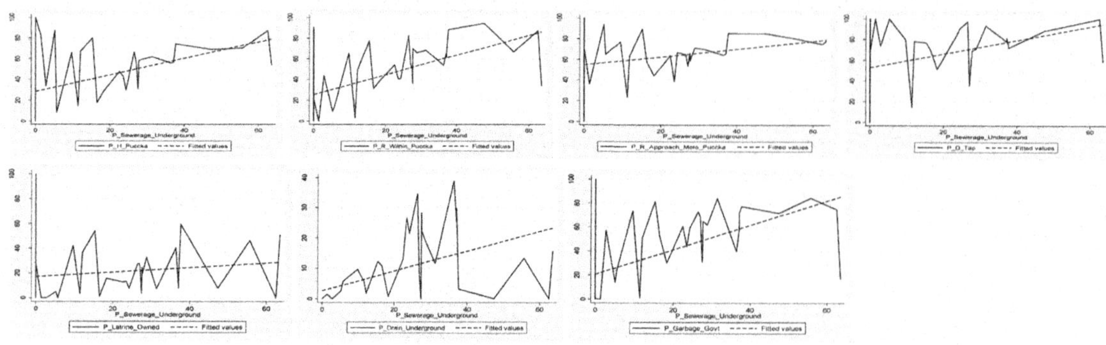

Figure 15. Line Diagram. Relationship of drainage facility with the other infrastructure in slums
Source. Author's diagrams using NSSO Data of 49th, 58th and 69th rounds.

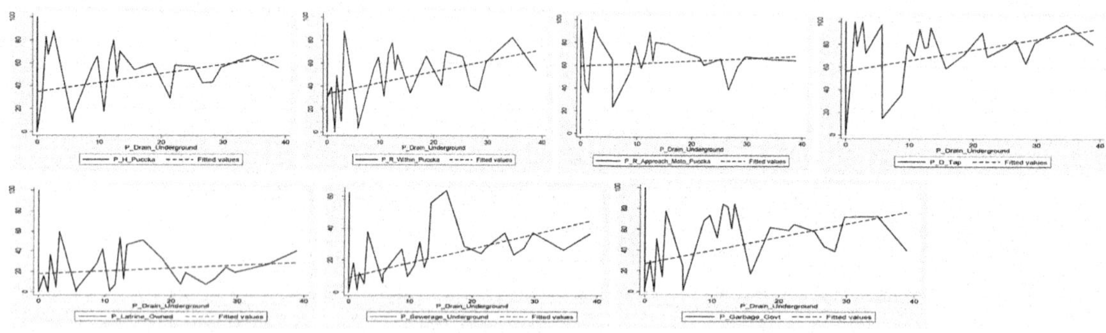

Figure 16. Line Diagram. Relationship of garbage disposal facility with the other infrastructure in slums
Source. Author's diagrams using NSSO Data of 49th, 58th and 69th rounds.

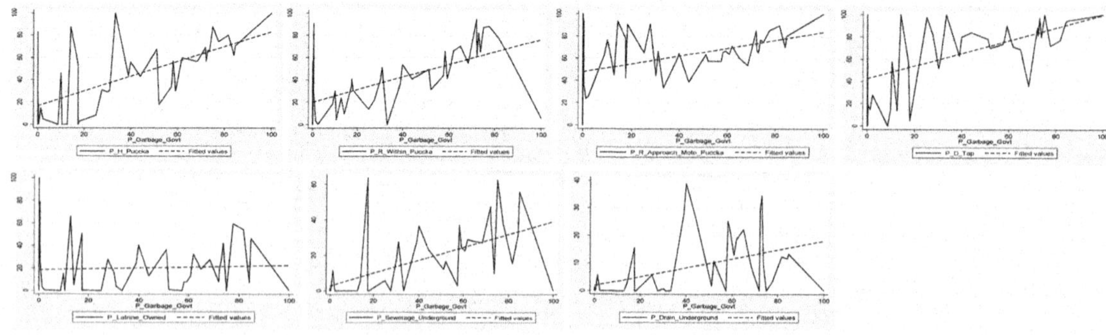

the condition of roads within the slum depends on the road approaching to the slum and the development in the condition of road within the slum may develop the condition of other infrastructure in slum. This may be because the road is the basic infrastructure required to access for the improvement of other infrastructure.

'Percentage of slum having motorable puccka road approaching to the slums' is positively and significantly associated with *'percentage of slums have garbage disposal system arranged by the government'*. The explanation is similar same like the above.

'Percentage of slum having underground sewerage facility' is positively and significantly associated with *'percentage of slums having underground drainage facility'* and *'percentage of slums have garbage disposal system arranged by the government'*. Even there is a positive correlation between the *'percentage of slums having underground drainage system'* and *'percentage of slums having garbage disposal system arranged by the government'*. This reveals that there is a strong association among different indicators of sanitation. This may be because good sewerage facility can improve the drainage as well as the latrine facility in slums.

Table 5. Correlation Matrix shows the relation among the indicators

Correlations								
INDEPENDENT / DEPENDENT	P_H_ Puccka	P_R_ Within_ Puccka	P_R_ Approach_ Moto_ Puccka	P_D_ Tap	P_ Latrine_ Owned	P_Sewerage_ Underground	P_Drain_ Underground	P_Garbage_ Govt
% of slums having majority of its houses made up with permanent material								
%of slums having puccka road within the slum	.381**							
%of slums having motorable puccka road approaching to the slums	.343*	.464**						
% of Slums have tap water as the major source of drinking water facilities	.668**	.278	.332*					
% of slums have owned latrine facilities by most of the residents	.041	.469**	.334*	.025				
% of slums having underground sewerage facilities	.480**	.624**	.281	.368*	.139			
% of slum having underground drainage system	.284	.373*	.099	.315*	.130	.546**		
%of slums having garbage disposal facilities arranged by the government	.664**	.617**	.443**	.538**	.046	.611**	.454**	

**. Correlation is significant at the 0.01 level (2-tailed).

*. Correlation is significant at the 0.05 level (2-tailed).

Source. Author's calculation using NSSO Data of 49th, 58th and 69th rounds

Note: Both dependent and independent variables are same, so the short-forms are used for the independent variables and dependent are used in full-form

Factors Influencing the Infrastructural Condition of Slums: Line Diagrams, Correlations and Regression

The influence of the exogenous factors behind the infrastructural condition of slums has been seen in this section. First the line diagrams correlations have been done to show the degree of association with the exogenous factors. In both the dependent and independent axis of Figures 17 though 24 are in percentage terms.

Both by line diagrams and from correlation results in Table 6, it can be seen that 'WPR of slums' is significantly and positively associated with the infrastructural condition of the slums except the latrine facility. However, unlike the line diagrams, the correlation result shows 'literacy rate in slum' has a significant positive association with a few of the indicators like the 'housing condition' and 'drinking water facility'. This indicates that social and economic development within the slum may have improved the condition of infrastructure within the slums. 7

The correlation shows that 'WPR', 'Literacy rate', and 'per capita NSDP' of the state have significantly positive relation with very few infrastructures of slums. This may indicate that more development of a state is influencing little improvement of infrastructure within the slum.

Figure 17. Line Diagram. Relation between Infrastructural condition of the slums and the WPR of the slums
Source. Author's diagrams based on 49th, 58th and 69th rounds of NSSO for infrastructure conditions & WPR of slums from Census 2001 & 2011

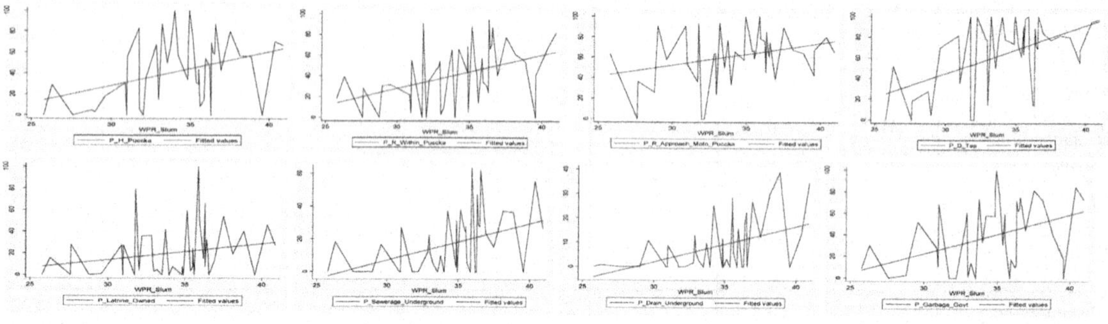

Figure 18. Line Diagram. Relation between Infrastructural condition of the slums and the literacy rate in slum
Source. Author's diagrams based on 49th, 58th and 69th rounds of NSSO for infrastructure conditions & literacy of slum from Census 2001 & 2011

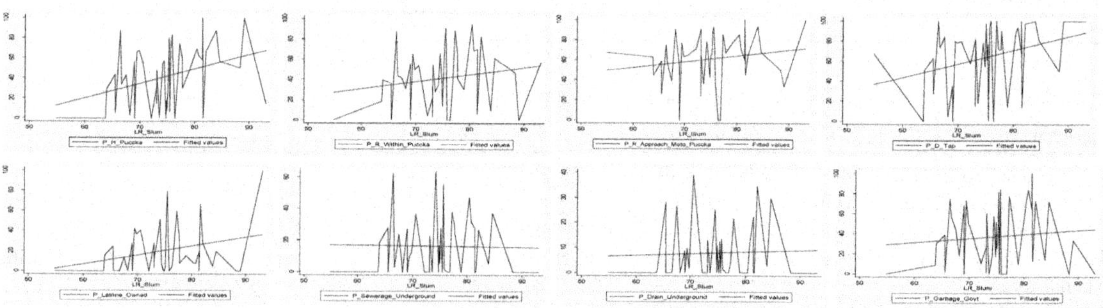

Figure 19. Line Diagram. Relation between Infrastructural condition of the slums and the total literacy rate
Source. Author's diagrams based on 49th, 58th and 69th rounds of NSSO for infrastructure conditions & total literacy Census 2001 & 2011

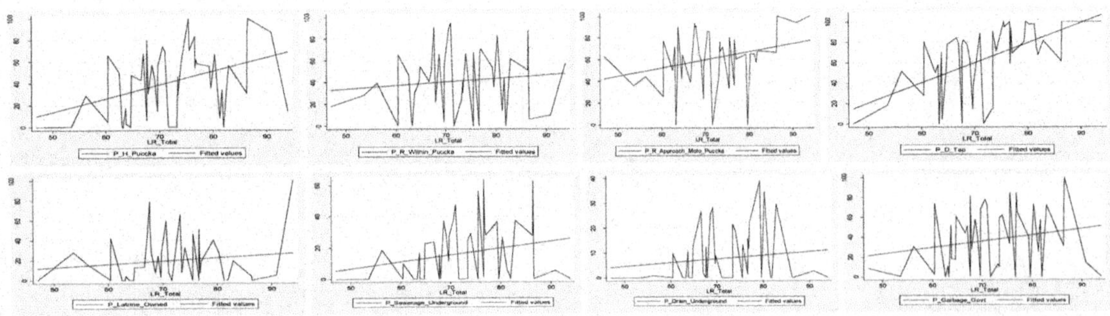

Figure 20. Line Diagram. Relation between Infrastructural condition of the slums and the Total WPR
Source. Author's diagrams based on 49th, 58th and 69th rounds of NSSO for infrastructure conditions & Total WPR Census 2001 & 2011

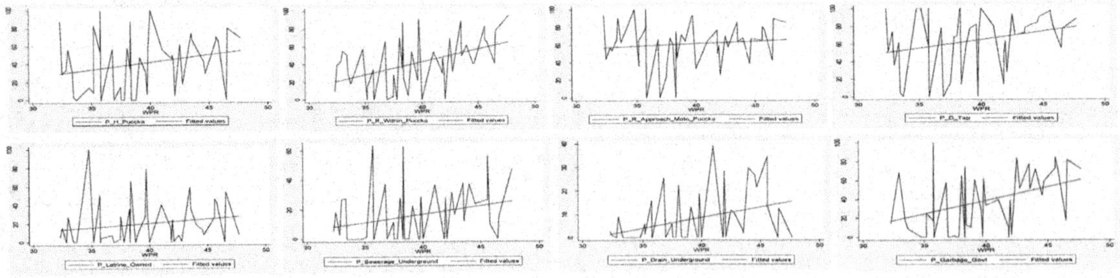

Figure 21. Line Diagram. Relation between Infrastructural condition of the slums and the per capita NSDP
Source. Author's diagrams based on 49th, 58th and 69th rounds of NSSO for infrastructure conditions & NSDP from RBI

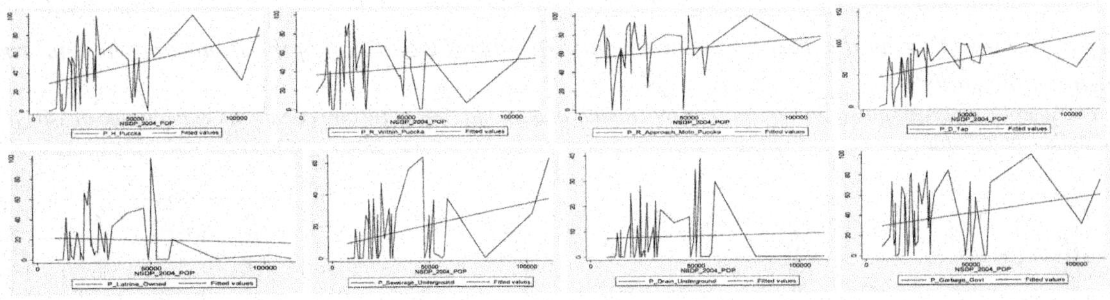

The Table 6 reveals that 'association for the improvement of slums' has no significant relationship with the infrastructure of slums. This may be because associations in slums are not working properly for the infrastructure improvement in slums. These 'associations' may be mostly politically influenced.

The 'electricity' facilities across states have significant and positive relation with some of the infrastructure of the slums. However, 'Total road density' of the state has shown no significant relation

Figure 22. Line Diagram. Relation between Infrastructural condition of the slums and the percentage of slums having association

Source. Author's diagrams based on 49th, 58th and 69th rounds of NSSO

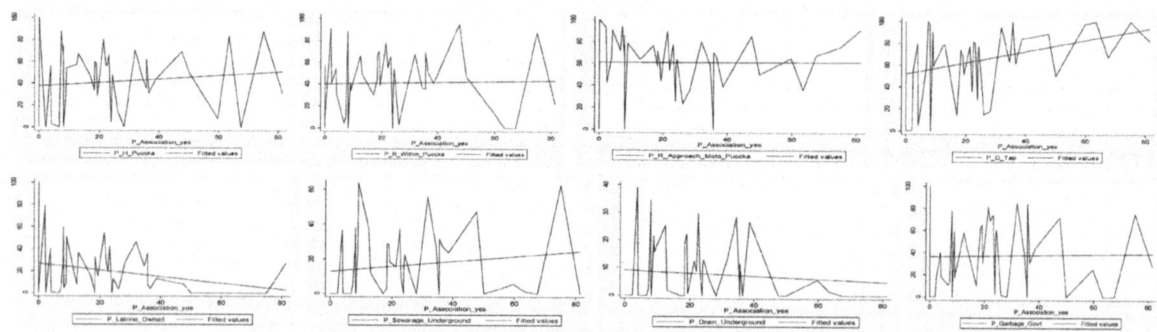

Figure 23. Line Diagram. Relation between the Infrastructural condition of the slums and the percentage of households having electricity

Source. Author's diagrams based on 49th, 58th and 69th rounds of NSSO for infrastructure conditions & percentage of households having electricity from Census 2001 & 2011

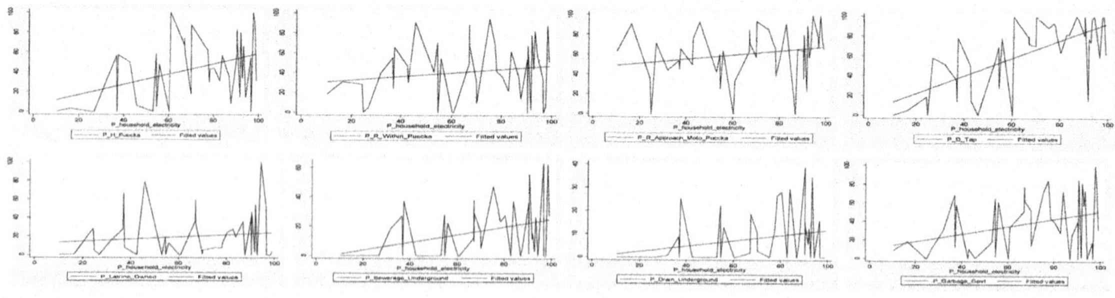

Figure 24. Line Diagram 16. Relation between Infrastructural Condition of the slums and the total road density of the states

Source. Author's diagrams based on 49th, 58th and 69th rounds of NSSO for infrastructure conditions & total road density from road authority of India

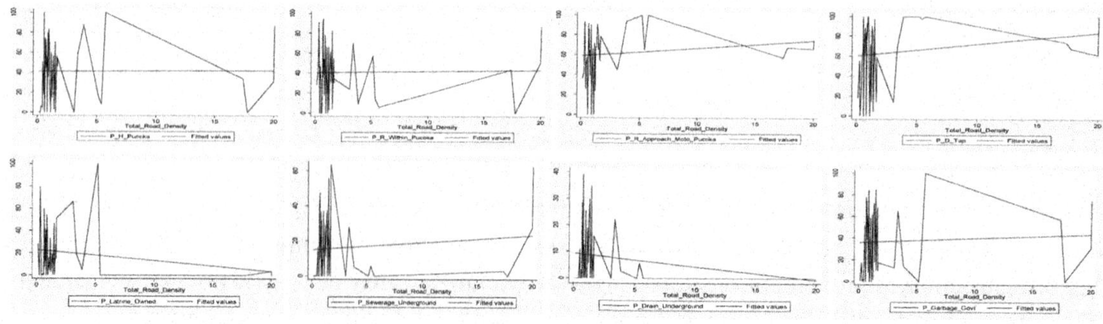

Table 6. Correlations results with the exogenous factors

Independent Variables → / Dependent Variables ↓	WPR of Slum	Literacy Rate of Slum	Total WPR	Total Literacy Rate	NSDP per Population	% of Slums Having Association for Improvements yes	% of Households Have Access to Electricity for Lighting	Total Road Density
% of slums having majority of its houses made up with permanent material	0.383*	0.342*	0.233	0.397*	0.346*	0.1102	0.4304*	0.006
%of slums having puccka road within the slum	0.417*	0.1813	0.443*	0.109	0.125	0.0251	0.1645	0.024
%of slums having motorablepuccka road approaching to the slums	0.317*	0.1703	0.099	0.290	0.191	0.003	0.2161	0.158
% of Slums have tap water as the major source of drinking water facilities	0.514*	0.301*	0.253	0.578*	0.470*	0.3318*	0.6847*	0.182
% of slums have owned latrine facilities by most of the residents	0.225	0.2708	0.168	0.134	-0.054	-0.2631	0.1239	-0.207
% of slums having underground sewerage facilities	0.443*	-0.017	0.271	0.232	0.329*	0.161	0.3651*	0.113
% of slum having underground drainage system	0.479*	0.0439	0.366*	0.130	0.037	-0.102	0.2665	-0.233
%of slums having garbage disposal facilities arranged by the government	0.422*	0.0965	0.408*	0.199	0.214	0.0201	0.3312*	0.061

Correlations (* implies 5% level of significance)
Source. Author's estimates

with the infrastructure condition of slums. This may be because the electricity facility is the necessary infrastructure for the improvement of infrastructure in slums.

In the subsequent section to confirm the above relations the regressions have been done. Before doing the regression, a hypothetical effect of factors has been anticipated in another table is given below.

It is anticipated that the effect of 'WPR' and 'Literacy rate' of slums is positive on the infrastructure of the slums as a rise in 'WPR' and 'Literacy rate' within the slums increases the economic capacity and idea about good infrastructure among the slum dwellers which in turn will increase the infrastructural condition within the slum.

The sign of the development of a state is depending on the indicators 'per capita NSDP', 'Total WPR' and 'Total Literacy rate'. So, the increase of those in turn will possibly improve the infrastructural condition within the slum.

The overall infrastructure of the state like 'electricity facilities' and 'roads' will possibly have influence to improve the infrastructure of the slums.

The 'association for improvement' in slums has no influence to improve the infrastructure condition of slums. This may be because the 'associations' are mostly inactive.

The condition of 'puccka road within the slums' has been taken for regression to see its' impact on the 'condition of houses' within the slum as an improvement of road connectivity with the slums has a positive connection with the improvement of slum infrastructure.

REGRESSION RESULTS

Table 8 explains the regression results of eight equations. The table shows the independent variable 'Total literacy rate' has been dropped due to multi-co- linearity problem. Except for the two equations

Table 7. Hypothetical effect of the factors

Table of Regression Equation with logic (tentative signs)								
Dependent → Independent ↓	% of Slums Having Majority of Its Houses Made Up with Permanent Material	% of Slums Having Puccka Road Within the Slum	% of Slums Having Motorablepuccka Road Approaching to the Slums	% of Slums Have Tap Water as the Major Source of Drinking Water Facilities	% of Slums Have Owned Latrine Facilities by Most of the Residents	% of Slums Having Underground Sewerage Facilities	% of Slum Having Underground Drainage System	% of Slums Having Garbage Disposal Facilities Arranged by the Government
Equations No.	1	2	3	4	5	6	7	8
WPR of Slum	+ve	+ve	+ve	+ve	+ve	+ve	+ve	+ve
Literacy Rate of Slum	+ve	+ve	+ve	+ve	+ve	+ve	+ve	+ve
Total WPR	+ve	+ve	+ve	+ve	+ve	+ve	+ve	+ve
Total Literacy Rate	+ve	+ve	+ve	+ve	+ve	+ve	+ve	+ve
NSDP_2004 at cont prices	+ve	+ve	+ve	+ve	+ve	+ve	+ve	+ve
% of Slums have association for improvements yes								
% of households have access to electricity for lighting	+ve	+ve	+ve	+ve	+ve	+ve	+ve	+ve
Total Road Density	+ve	+ve	+ve	+ve	+ve	+ve	+ve	+ve
%of slums having puccka road within the slum	+ve							
Time dummy of 2011	+ve	+ve	+ve	+ve	+ve	+ve	+ve	+ve

Table 8. Regression Results

Dependent Variables → / Independent Variables ↓	% of Slums Having Majority of Its Houses Made Up with Permanent Material	% of Slums Having Puccka Road Within the Slum	% of Slums Having Motorablepuccka Road Approaching to the Slums	% of Slums Have Tap Water as the Major Source of Drinking Water Facilities	% of Slums Have Owned Latrine Facilities by Most of the Residents	% of Slums Having Underground Sewerage Facilities	% of Slum Having Underground Drainage System	% of Slums Having Garbage Disposal Facilities Arranged by the Government
Equations No.s	1+	2	3+	4	5	6	7	8+
Constant	-2.732 (9.921)	-117.746 (51.894)	0.097 (2.631)	-116.716 (56.295)	0.113 (44.630)	-15.013 (40.423)	-12.276*** (18.661)	-5.436 (15.513)
WPR of Slum	4.299 (2.895)	0.597 (1.754)	0.089 (1.016)	1.242** (1.538)	0.361 (1.135)	1.748 (1.238)	2.311*** (.763)	7.10544* (3.82044)
Literacy Rate of Slum	1.359 (1.746)	0.229 (.621)	0.866 (.514)	1.111 (.508)	0.170 (.715)	-0.725 (.371)	-0.582 (.167)	-1.022 (2.519)
Total WPR	-1.835 (2.005)	3.000** (1.120)	0.692 (.767)	0.129 (1.158)	-0.580 (1.009)	0.420 (1.019)	-0.327 (.383)	1.410 (2.818)
Total Literacy Rate								
Per Capita NSDP_2004	-1.813** (.712)	-0.000 (.000)	-0.269** (.154)	0.000 (.000)	-0.001** (.000)	0.000 (.000)	0.000* (.000)	-2.262*** (.766)
% of Slums have association for improvements yes	0.175 (.191)	0.092 (.181)	-0.055 (.066)	0.267 (.160)	-0.115 (.174)	0.051 (.157)	-0.098 (.0736)	.4706 (.3064)
% of households have access to electricity for lighting	2.059** (.819)	-0.112 (.225)	0.047 (.182)	0.659** (.302)	0.459* (.229)	-0.036 (.179)	-0.015 (.088)	.9728 (.909)
Total Road Density	0.347 (.283)	1.905 (1.388)	0.199** (.067)	-0.875 (1.017)	0.536 (1.134)	-1.212 (1.049)	-2.031*** (.498)	0.862** (.320)
%of slums having puccka road within the slum	0.291** (.130)							
Time dummy of 2011	0.567 (.380)	24.915* (9.094)	0.233** (.098)	-7.017 (8.947)	29.900*** (8.008)	5.888 (6.996)	-5.926 (3.895)	0.478 (.489)
F significance value	0.0024	0.0006	0.0075	0.0000	0.0001	0.0084	0.0001	0.0154
Adjusted R^2	0.6475	0.4005	0.3514	0.5646	0.4140	0.3263	0.5354	0.5218
N	35	46	38	46	46	46	46	35
VIF mean values	3.26	3.06	3.30	3.06	3.06	3.06	3.06	3.33

*, ** & *** imply 10%, 5% & 1% levels of significance respectively.

Source. Author's Estimates

Note: + these equations are taken log on both side to eliminate dispersion

(i.e. equation 3 & 6) adjusted R-squares are above.40 which means the independent variables can explain the models more than 40%. Time dummy is positively significant for few cases which implying that with time some indicators of infrastructure have improved. The eight equations have been explained separately have been stated below.

Equation 1: Shows 'per capita NSDP' has a significant and negative effect on the 'housing condition' of slums at 5% level, whereas 'percentage of household having electricity' and 'condition of road within the slum' have significant and positive effects on the 'housing condition' of slums at 5% level.

Equation 2: Shows 'WPR' and 'time dummy' have significant and positive impact on the 'condition of road within' the slum at 5% and 10% respectively. But the 'per capita NSDP' is affecting negatively but not significant.

Equation 3: Shows 'per capita NSDP' has a significant and negative effect on the 'condition of road approaching' to the slums at 5% level. Whereas 'total road density' and 'time dummy have significant and positive impact on the same at 5% level.

Equation 4: Shows that 'WPR' of slums and 'percentage of household is having electricity' have significant and positive effect on the 'drinking water facility' in slums at 5% level. The 'per capita NSDP' has no influence on the 'drinking water facility' in slums.

Equation 5: Shows that 'per capita NSDP' has a negative effect on 'latrine facility' in slum at 5% level of significance. Whereas 'percentage of household is having electricity' and 'time dummy' have a positive effect on the same at the 5% level of significance.

Equation 6: Shows the factors have no significant effect on the 'sewerage facility' of slums.

Equation 7: Shows 'WPR of slums' has a significant and positive effect on the 'drainage facility' of slum at 1% level. Whereas the effect of 'per capita NSDP' on the 'drainage facility' is significantly zero. The 'total road density' is significantly and negatively effecting at 1% level.

Equation 8: Shows 'WPR of slums' and 'total road density' have significant and positive effect on 'garbage disposal system' in slums at 10% and 5% level respectively. However, 'per capita NSDP' is significantly and negatively affecting the 'garbage disposal system' of slums.

Summary Findings of the Regressions and Probable Implications

As per the information provided, the regression results reveal that in most of the cases 'per capita NSDP' is significantly and negatively affecting the 'condition of infrastructures' of slums. This may imply that with the growth of the economic condition of a state, infrastructure within the slum is deteriorating. Since the expropriation through growth might have deteriorated the condition of slums.

It has been noticed that WPR in slums has positive significant impact on some indicators of infrastructure condition of slums. This may imply that improvement in the economic conditions of the slum dwellers can improve the infrastructural condition in slum as well.

However, 'total road density' and 'percentage of households having electricity' have a significant and positive impact on the condition of most of the infrastructures in slums. This perhaps implies that the improvement of infrastructures in slums requires basic infrastructure facilities like electricity and road connectivity of the states.

The 'association for the improvement' of slums has no such impact on development of infrastructure in slums. The association in slums possibly does not have any active role towards the development of slums.

DISCUSSION AND CONCLUDING REMARKS

- **Government Initiatives:** It has been noticed that the condition of infrastructure in slums has improved over time, but at a slower pace and only 60% of slums have experienced improvement. In some cases not even 30% of slums have improved over time. This is perhaps that the Government has very skewed attention towards the improvement of slum infrastructure. The programs taken so far for the slum development (like VAMBAY, NSDP, IAY, etc.) have done satisfactorily but have many drawbacks Buckley et al, (2007). But some apparent facts of government schemes gave a different perception of the government initiative. Under National Slum Development Program (NSDP), total amount granted for 8 years was 685.36 lakhs in which 544 lakhs was released. Now if 42.6 million slum population as per census 2001 is considered same for 8 years then under the scheme per slum dweller has received only 72 rupees. After 2006, Integrated Housing and Slum Development Program (IHSDP) has been launched under JNNURM. Within this scheme about 4.8 lakhs dwelling unit was approved from 2006 to 2011. Out of that, 1.2 lakhs were completed and allotted to the slum dwellers which is a mere share as the total household of slum increased from 82.8 lakhs in 2001 to 1.39 crore in 2011 in India. Rajiv Awas Yojna (RAY) which was introduced in 2009 also showed a negligible performance. The total amount sanctioned under this scheme was Rs. 147.16 crore in 2009 in which 55.26 crore was released and only 20.54 crore was the expenditure. In 2010-11, the performance was more striking. The total amount sanctioned was Rs. 61.08 crore, out of it 55.26 crore has been released and only 1.08 crore was the expenditure[7].

- **Over Burden of Slums and Its Displacement:** Moreover, overburden with the slum population and displacement of slums has restricted the pace of the slum improvement. In some cases even the developed states like Delhi, Maharashtra, Karnataka, West Bengal, etc. have shown a deteriorating trend towards the development of slum infrastructure. This may be due to the economic development of those states centering around the urban areas are pulling the population from rural or urban areas of other states at a higher rate than the rate at which infrastructure is built for slum development. However, the story of 'expropriation' is also existed behind the deterioration of infrastructure development in slums Harvey (2008). Since one of the key results, i.e. the significant and negative effect of 'per capita NSDP' on the 'infrastructure condition' of slums perhaps is approving the fact that expropriation through growth has displaced slums and deteriorated development.
- **Comprehensive Infrastructure Development:** The result showed the overall infrastructure development like better electricity and road facility in the state have a positive impact on the infrastructure condition of slums. This conceivably implies the improvement of infrastructures in slums requires basic infrastructure development of the state. Overall development in infrastructure results to an inclusive development of slum infrastructure. Additionally, the finding shows the various aspects of infrastructure in slums are positively associated among themselves. This probably reflects the improvement in the condition of one infrastructure is associated with the improvement of other. This indicates the comprehensive planning that is required for the improvement of slum infrastructure.
- **Performance of Associations Towards Infrastructure Development:** The associations within the slum can be a positive factor behind the development of slums. But with the provided data, the result signifies the associations in slums have no impact towards the improvement in the infrastructure condition of slums, may reveal that associations are inactive towards slum development. This may be because the associations within the slums are either inactive or weakly organized to perform development in slums. Too much political influence in slum might have also made the associations dysfunctional. At the rudimentary level, the NGOs, CBOs and local bodies have effective roles and responsibilities to build up active group within the slums for its development.

Slum infrastructure is not only important for the betterment of slum life, but it may also have serious positive externalities for overall life of the city. It has the spillover effect within the slum itself; on the city as a whole, and most importantly on the concept of Inclusive city or 'Smart City' as a part of general doctrine of inclusive growth. Hence the concept of an inclusive city must address up-gradation and improvement of slums through its infrastructure development.

REFERENCES

Beltrao, G. (2013). *Urban Planning and Land Management for Promoting Inclusive Cities. Inclusive urban Planning*. Oxford University Press.

Bouddha, C., Dhote, K. K., & Sharma, A. (2014). Slum Redevelopment Strategy: A Way forward to Urban Environment Management through Inclusive Approach: Evidence from a review paper. *Research Journal of Engineering Sciences*, *3*(7), 28–37.

Buckley, R.M., et al. (2007). Strategizing Slum Improvement in India: A Method to Monitor and Refocus Slum Development Programs. *Global Urban Development Magazine, 3*(1), 3.

Chandrashekhar, S. (2005). *Growth of Slums, Availability of Infrastructure and Demographic Outcomes in Slums: Evidence from India*. Paper to be presented during the session on urbanization in developing countries at population association of America*Annual Meeting*, Philadelphia, PA.

Conditions of Urban Slums. NSS 58th Round July- December, 2002; NSSO Report no. 486 by Government of India.

David, E., & Ellis, P. (2013). *Urban Planning and Land Management for Promoting Inclusive Cities, Inclusive urban Planning*. Oxford University Press.

Davis, M. (2004). The Planets of Slums. *New Left Review*.

Harvey, D. (2008). The Right to the City. *New Left Review, 53*.

Jingan, M. L. (2009). The Economics of Development and Planning (39th ed.). Vrinda Publications.

Kolkata Study Report. (2014). Society for Participatory Research in Asia.

Marx, B., Stoker, T., & Suri, T. (2013). The Economics of Slums in the Developing World. *The Journal of Economic Perspectives*, *27*(4), 187–210. doi:10.1257/jep.27.4.187

Mitra, I. (2015). *Sustainable Slum Improvement Models, Terra Green, Planning Sustainable Cities*. Earth Scan Publications UN-Habitat, Ltd.

Population, Slum population, Literacy rate, slum literacy rate, WPR, Slum WPR from Census 2011. (n. d.). Retrieved from http://www.censusindia.gov.in/2011census/population_enumeration.html

Population, Slum population, Literacy rate, slum literacy rate, WPR, Slum WPR from Census 2001. (n. d.). Retrieved from http://www.censusindia.gov.in/Census_Data_2001/Census_Data_Online/Census-DataOnline_Login.aspx

Roy, A. (2013). *Urban Planning and Land Management for Promoting Inclusive Cities, Inclusive urban Planning*. Oxford University Press.

Rusling, S (2010). *Approaches to Basic Service Delivery for the Working Poor: Assessing the Impact of Mahila Housing Trust's Parivartan Slum Upgrading Programme in Ahmedabad, India*. WIEGO Policy Brief (Urban Policies) No.1.

Slums in India. NSS 49th Round January- June 1993; NSSO Report no. 417. Government of India State of Slums in India, A Statistical Compendium. (2013). MoHUPA, Government of India.

State of the World's Cities. (2012). UN-Habitat.

The Challenges of Slums: Earth Scan. (2003). UN-Habitat, Ltd.

Urban Infrastructure in India. (2011). FICCI.

KEY TERMS AND DEFINITIONS

Development: Here the development refers to the infrastructural development of slums.

Displacement: Here 'displacement' means the dislocation or displacement of slums from one place to another within the city.

Inclusive City: Persistence of inequality in many respects among the population within the cities signifies large chunk of excluded population. The concept of inclusive city can reframe the scope of inclusion to those who are poor or excluded from the growth process of the city.

Infrastructure: Here the 'Infrastructure' is mainly denoted to slum infrastructure i.e. type of housing, condition of road, condition of sanitation & drinking water facilities with the slum.

Sanitation: Here sanitation refers to own latrine facilities by most of the residents, underground sewerage system, underground drainage facilities and garbage disposal facilities arranged by the Govt for the slum.

Slum: Slum is an environmentally degradable place in urban areas with improper houses, low basic infrastructure and the place of living for most of the poor people.

Urbanization: Urbanisation and urban growth are the same. A country is said to be urbanised when the population share in cities increases rapidly and it becomes more than the rural counterpart. This happens mainly due to unequal economic and social condition between rural and urban.

ENDNOTES

1 Mike Davis has noticed that in 2004 the world wide urban population was 400, it has reached near about 550 million in 2015 and it would achieve 10 billion in 2050 (Davis, 2004, Planet of Slums, pp-1). According to census 2011 the urban population in India has increased to 377 million which is near about 31% of the total population.

2 A report on 'Urban Infrastructure in India' by FICCI in 2011 revealed with the help of NSS data of 66th round that the demographic surge towards urban in India is due to the economic disparity between rural and urban and this has created tremendous pressure on civic infrastructure.

3 The civic infrastructure signifies improved water and sanitation facilities, sufficient availability of power supply, efficient roads and communication networks, etc. *(UN-Habitat report, 2012).*

4 A report published by FICCI on 'Urban Infrastructure in India' in 2011 showed that urban population will be 534 million by 2026 against the capacity of the cities, which has to grow nearly 400% to cope with the growing urban population. This data is taken from the report on 'Urban Infrastructure in India' by FICCI in 2011, pp-3, ficci.in/spdocument/20122/Urban_infra.pdf

5 David Harvey in his article "Right to the City" has pointed out that "A process of displacement what I call 'accumulation by dispossession' lie at the core of urbanization under capitalism. It is the mirror image of capital absorption through urban redevelopment…" (Harvey, 2008; Pp- 34).

6 *'Vision Mumbai'* has been introduced for re-modification of Mumbai to make it an international standard city which aimed to build upon evicting the slums *(A Report by Calcutta Research Group on the condition of slum dwellers, 2014; discussed in a local newspaper – i.e. Anandabazzar Partika, Calcutta edition, 4th August, 2016)*

7 The related data of the government schemes have been collected from www.indiastat.com. In respect of international scale measurement 10 lakhs = 1 million; 100 lakhs = 1 crore = 10 million.

Chapter 3
Role of Infrastructure Development to Empower Women:
An Over-Determined View

Indrani Basu
Berhampore College, India

ABSTRACT

A modern economy is market focused. It is held that when a woman becomes a participant in the market on her own term as a rational economic agent she is empowered in an economic sense. It does not take into account the other spectrums of empowerment viz. gender political, cultural and like. A nation's infrastructure provides the basic scaffolding for development. The differences in how men and women use infrastructure services have important implications for sector policies, investment priorities, and program designs. This chapter will analyse how the infrastructure development programme as an economic process assist women to enhance capability of them within society and how its actual impact is mutually constituted by other non-economic social processes and make it an over determined matter. Our study has shown that adequate access of the social infrastructure services has fetched benefits for women and ensures empowerment of women.

INTRODUCTION

Gender equality stands as a key of Millennium Development Goal (MDG) and it is well recognised that poor infrastructure can act as an obstacle to meet this goal. Indeed, it is the first time when importance of women's contributions to development has received such high-level attention from the world's global leaders and institutions. The Gender Action Plan (GAP), launched in 2006, commits more than $65 million over 4 years to catalyze activities that strengthen women's economic empowerment (World Bank, 2010). This includes infrastructure that meets women's as well as men's needs. Before evaluating how infrastructure projects can and do transform people's lives, and especially those of women, we

DOI: 10.4018/978-1-5225-2364-2.ch003

need to realise why such integration of women into infrastructure development become a needful to ensure women's empowerment. Kabeer (1996) defines women's empowerment as the "ability to make strategic life choices in a context where this ability was previously denied to them." The global financial and economic crises have highlighted the need for greater gender equality in the society to counter vulnerability to economic shocks. Simultaneously these efforts support recovery and poverty reduction. Investing in women's full economic potential is critical to increasing productivity and economic growth, and supporting the move towards a more balanced and sustainable development. Not doing so is an under-utilization of available human resources and hampering of productive diversity (World Bank, 2010). Women continue to disproportionately face a range of multiple challenges relating to access to employment, choice of work, working conditions, employment security, wage parity, discrimination, and balancing the competing burdens of work and family responsibilities. To promote gender equality and empowerment of women, one useful weapon may be the gendering in infrastructure development.

REVIEW OF RELATED LITERATURE

There exists a two-way link between infrastructure development, and women empowerment. Women may be a part of infrastructure development programme by rendering their services as an employee. Here they are acting as a productive labour of an economic process. This process may be exploitative or non- exploitative depending on nature of fundamental and subsumed class process. On the other side one level lack of infrastructural development facilities (which is attached with other non-economic processes) exacerbated gender oppression. Inequalities between girls and boys in access to schooling, adequate health care and less accessibility of sanitation, safe drinking water, and adequate uses of electricity make the women less efficient. These less efficient women fail to achieve such opportunities that they can derive from the participation as a productive labour in infrastructure development programme (World Bank, 2010). Inadequate infrastructure also affects women more than men, because women are often responsible for a larger share of, and often more time consuming, household activities (World Bank, 2013). This lack of aforesaid facilities could be influenced by several non- economic processes such as gender, cultural, political and legal processes. While disparities in basic rights, access to schooling, credit and jobs, and the ability to participate in public life took their most direct toll on women and girls, the adequacy in infrastructural services may reduce the burden of domestic chores of women and allow them more time to be spent on marketing activities. Evidence has shown that gender inequality ultimately hindered economic growth.

According to the OECD Development Assistance Committee, the process of gendering infrastructural services requires a shift in mindsets from seeing gender as "requiring attention" to consider women and girls as the "primary clients". This effort is a critical factor in ensuring the project's success and sustainability. When gender equality issues are not taken into account, women can become worse off—both absolutely and in relation to men" (World Bank, 2010).

It is argued that as economic development proceeds, quality of life for all will improve. Quality of life includes freedom to make choices. The concept of empowerment can be explained in several ways. It may be economic empowerment, political empowerment and cultural empowerment. In gross, we can say that a person becomes empowered only if she would take spontaneous decision according her own choice that relates to different spheres of her life and also regarding the lives associated with her.

Considering women as a 'primary clients' of economic development, we have to go details to understand how their status has been determining within society.

There are several views to understand the women's status within a social arena. Keeping all the views those are used to analyse the women's' status within society, we can classifies these views into two categories. One is Essentialist theory and other is Anti-essentialism. Analysing Essentialist theories we have found that they organize their field of research into opposing and watertight binaries of cause and effect and subsequently see them as mutually exclusive. Whereas, Anti-essentialism, has rejected any presumption that complexities are reducible to simplicities of unidirectional causality. Every cause is itself also an effect and vice versa (Resnick & Wolff, 1987).

According to essentialist like orthodox Marxian, has considered economy as base of the social structure and this economy is influenced by politico-legal system, ideology, philosophy, religion and culture of a particular society. But the mode of production is causally prior to all other aspects of society. To ensure a stable society, relations of production should not impede the development of forces of production in any manner. If they do create barriers to the free development of forces of production, a condition of social crisis will emerge. Then through a class struggle this problem will be solved and advent of a new relation of production will take place. The rest of the social elements adjust to the shift in the mode of production. In orthodox Marxist theory, this way of looking which is 'historicism' is the undisputed logic of transition and economic essentialism is the undisputed logic for social transformation. Because the mode of production or the economy are the key to the understanding of society and its evolution, such a rendition of society has been described as driven by economics or economic essentialism which in turn determines the political and cultural. So, class process which is an economic process dictates the other non-class non-economic process.

Challenging these views, class-focused Marxist approach is based on the Althuserian logic of over-determination is premised on the understanding that no element can exist on its own. Thus, over-deterministic logic has rejected the logic of unidirectional causality. Mutual constitutively, unlike the logic of causality, does not simply affect the state of being that is presumed to exist but it makes possible the very existence of the being (Chakrabarti, Dhar & Cullenberg, 2012). This way of looking at the world marks a departure from the orthodox Marxist rendition of economic as the base of the society. In this over-deterministic logic economic, political, cultural and natural mutually constitute each other. In this way, a society and its institutions are disaggregated and decentred space of heterogeneous social processes which are mutually interrelated in complex over determined manner (Chakrabarti, Dhar & Cullenberg, 2012).

Following Anti-essentialism, We have observed that status of women within society is determined by different social processes which are prevalent in the society. Any society is a web of social relationships which are social processes, social patterns and social interactions. These relationships are also subject to change. The term 'social change' is used to describe variation of any aspect of social processes, social patterns, social interactions, or social organizations. Whenever a large number of persons is engaged in activities that differ from those which their immediate forefathers were engaged in some time before a social change is said to have occurred (Sharma, 1989). Within society we have several economic and non-economic processes. And these processes are subject to change.

Society is not a fixed and constant site. Rather, it is a perpetually on-going fabrication, a set of interacting and living and dynamic social processes. The contradictions between the persistently household-oriented practices of gendering and the challenges posed by a rapidly modernizing economy have made women increasingly vulnerable to degradation and violence (Banerjee 2002). It is also argued that tradition has, to a large extent, been responsible for many women's handicaps in the labour market.

However, in globalised economy, under a changed economic scenario, women's lives are changing. Women now work hard for survival. Thrown out into the competitive world; they have discover their potential to earn, to survive, and to protect their family from crisis. Simultaneously, condition of women is at severe disadvantage both at home and labours market (Banerjee, 2002). Society is a site where all type of social processes like, economic, political, legal, cultural, gender processes co-exists. Both public and private domain shapes one's life. They determine how does an individual behave, act, learn and communicate. As society changes, the relevance of such institutions also alter.

In 2009, the regions those have demonstrated their concern for gender in at least 50 per cent of their infrastructure projects were East Asia and the Pacific, Middle East and North Africa, South Asia, and Africa. The review of infrastructure operations from 1995 to 2009 reveals significant progress on the integration of gender into the portfolio. Yet, this progress was uneven across time, across the different regions and infrastructure sectors, and between the two lending windows for the middle- and low-income countries (World Bank, 2010).

OBJECTIVE

At the backdrop of above analysis our objectives are to see:

1. How infrastructure development programme assists to enhance the women's' capability within society.
2. Whether the success of gendering development process is mutually constituted by the other non-economic social processes and make it an over determined matter.

DATA AND METHODOLOGY

There is an ever present need for methodological work at all stages of survey process. To proceed our entire work we have used data published by World Bank on different gender development indicator its member economies for the period 2005. Countries are divided according to 2010 GNI per capita, calculated using the World Bank Atlas method. These economies are low income (LIC), lower middle income (LMC), upper middle income (UMC), and high income. However, these data do not provide trend data on key indicators of women empowerment. Data on decision making about women's own health care, household purchase, visiting their own family or relatives and data on gender role attitude are not provided by this source. Due to this shortage of information, we have used India's National Family Health Survey (NFHS-4) to analyse the over-determined pattern of gendering infrastructure process. Apart from that we have used secondary data collected from review of World Bank infrastructure development project during 1995-2009. Data published by Industrial Labour Organisation are also consulted to make an analysis.

FINDINGS AND DISCUSSION

Findings

Before penetrating into central analysis we have made a short analysis on the review of World Bank infrastructure development project during 1995-2009. Generally, it is accepted that poor women among other vulnerable social groups are suffering from receiving less wages due to lack of skills.Therefore, there were often strong demands from women to have greater economic opportunities to enter formal labour markets through infrastructure programs. On the other side the World Bank (2010) estimated 884 million people in developing countries are without safe water; 1.6 billion are without electricity; 2.5 billion have no sanitary facilities; and nearly 1 billion lack accesses to an all-weather road. The heaviest burdens of poor infrastructure fall on the shoulders of women and girls due to gender inequalities within society in accessing assets and opportunities and their responsibilities to the domestic chores.

To respond to these concerns, many projects included gender targeted actions such as skill development training, affirmative action measures to improve access to formal employment, and revolving loan funds or credit schemes, such as microcredit institutions, to foster entrepreneurship have been adopted. Initiatives have also been taken to make such infrastructure projects become gender specific (World Bank, 2010). Measures like gender analysis and consultations that recognize women's contributions and amplify the value and importance of addressing their needs; gender targeted actions such as quotas that provide paid jobs in construction works, and that position them alongside men in infrastructure user and maintenance groups; diverse enterprise development and asset-building activities; and social mobilization that buttresses women's awareness, solidarity, and collective voice haven adopted. Efforts like investment on road project carried by small and medium enterprises in formal sector, investment in complementary services that promote savings and provide information on markets, or management and financial training, constructing some projects to build daycare or recreation centers that ease women's childcare needs, urban programs with joint property which are helping women to gain control over a substantial asset and access to formal banking system loans, and evaluations for the rural water and sanitation project indicate that investing in infrastructure project may ensure women's economic empowerment (World Bank,2010).

Such project provided not only improved women's and men's access to markets, but also ensured women's equal participation in employment and market opportunities created by the new road and market. This was accomplished by applying quotas for women's participation in construction and maintenance jobs, promoting the formation of women's labor contracting agencies, reserving 30% of the shops for women in the market, requiring 30% women's participation in the market management committee, and establishing separate toilets for women and men in the marketplace (World Bank,2010). These measures enabled women to enter the formal labour force market and earn an equal income. In addition, female micro entrepreneurs were able to go to the marketplace themselves to buy inputs and trade openly, obtain market information on new and emerging demands, and expand to small and medium enterprises. A major social transformation had taken place, as not only are women now visible in the marketplace, but they have now become the major traders (World Bank, 2010). Now we represent the Table 1 to understand the performances of world –wise economies on some key indicators those are stressing on gender issues.

Table 1. World wise performances of economies on key indicator of development

Indicator	Region					
	Upper Middle Income(UMC)	**Middle Income(MIC)**	**Lower Middle Income(LMC)**	**Low Income(LIC)**	**High Income(HI)**	**World**
Population, female (% of total)	49.55	49.31	**49.08**	**50.32**	50.59	49.61
GDP growth (annual%)	**7.19**	7.05	6.6	6.16	**2.72**	3.82
Labor force participation rate, female (modeled ILO estimate)[1]	63.44	54.35	**44.61**	**73.12**	62.69	51.99
Literacy rate, adult female.[2]	91.57	78.72	66.01	**48.99**	**98.46**	81.32(10)
Literacy rate, adult male[3]	95.93	88.14	80.46	**66.46**	**98.89**	89.14(10)
[5]Employment in industry, female[5]	**32.6**	26.56	13.95		**12.88**	22.96 (05)
Region Indicator	Upper middle income(UMC)	Middle income(MIC)	Lower middle income(LMC)	Low income(LIC)	High income(HI)	World
Employment in service, female[6]	56.76	46.17	**24.02**		**83.74**	54.04(05)
Proportion of seats held by women in national parliaments (%)	15.84	13.96	**11.48**	17.88	**20.43**	16.48
Improved sanitation facilities [7]	71.41	57.2	43.83	**23.29**	**98.96**	61.86
Improved water source[8]	88.77	85.27	81.98	**56.69**	**99.19**	85.55
Pregnant women receiving prenatal care (%)	**95.66**	84.21	78.46	**78.03**		83.33
Used an account at a financial institution to receive government transfers, female (% age 15+) [9]	7.95	5.72	**3.61**	3.80	**36.73**	12.29
Used the Internet to pay bills or buy things, female (% age 15+)[10](2014)	15.94	9.37	1.74	**0.93**	**45.03**	16.06

note: [1]*(% of female population ages 15-64),* [2]*(% of females ages 15 and above),* [3]*(% of males ages 15 and above),* [4]*(% of total non -agricultural employment),* [5]*(% of female employment)* ,[6]*(% of female employment),*[7]*(% of population with access),* [8]*(% of population with access),*[9] *data are available for the year 2011 and*[10] *data are available for the year 2014.*

Figures in bold black represent lowest value and that in bold maroon represent highest value of corresponding variable

Source: Data of World Bank

The above table classifies all World Bank member economies and all other economies with populations of more than 30,000. Countries are divided according to 2010 GNI per capita, calculated using the World Bank Atlas method. These economies are low income (LIC), $ 1.005 or less, lower middle income (LMC), $1,006-$3,975, upper middle income (UMC), $ 3,976-$12,275, and high income, $12,276 or more. Almost all economies under East Asia and Pacific region are lower middle income countries, whereas economies in Latin American and the Caribbean belong to upper middle income group. Majority of Countries of Europe and Central Asia, South Asia and Middle East and North Africa are belongs to LMC and UMC category. Economies of Sub-Saharan Africa are mainly economies with low income. Apart from these countries remaining economies are the high-income countries. From the table, it is clear that economies with high income are performing efficiently in providing social infrastructural (like education, health, water, sanitation) facilities to their citizens as per as general expectation. With a high female literacy rate, women of these countries are capable to use those opportunities (like holding account, using internet) which can be treated as the indicator of women empowerment. Their political participation is also quite higher than the same in remaining region. A large share of their female employment in service sector and industrial sector is reflecting the fact that having high access of social infrastructural facilities enables the women to perform efficiently in labour market.

On the other hand, economies of low income with high population and high female labour force participation (Table 2) are suffering from poor social infrastructural facilities. This scenario has led to their poor performance in using modern technologies which are treated as an indicator of empowerment. Notwithstanding, having higher annual growth rate (i.e.; 4.69 in 2015) as compared to 1.91 in high income countries, LIC are suffering from poor accessibilities of social infrastructural development. Major of South and East Asian countries are belong to LMC, The following table shows that inspite of having high female labour force within economy, the penetration of female labour force in service sector is quite low than the same in developed economies in Asia. This events illustrates misery of female labour within economy.

Therefore, economic factors are not only the sole indicator of social infrastructural development. Other non-economic factors are also playing an important role for the development of this sector.

From our previous analysis we have seen that the economies of Europe and Central Asia are standing behind the economies of other region regarding their performances in gendering infrastructure. Surprisingly economies of Europe and Central asia belongs to upper middle income group whereas the South Asia and sub-Saharan African countries are mainly low income countries which are performing better in gender issues. This scenario has supported the view that not only income is the main determining factor of women empowerment. Other non-economic factors are playing determining role.

Table 2. Distribution of total employment by sector of employment (%), Asia and Sub regions, by sex, 2009

	Agriculture	Industry	Services
	Female		
ASIA-PACIFIC	48.2	18.2	33.6
Central Asia	50.3	15.0	34.7
Developed economies in Asia	3.9	15.3	80.8
East Asia	41.5	22.2	36.3
Pacific Islands	75.0	4.5	20.6
South East Asia	43.7	14.4	41.9
South Asia	71.0	13.6	15.5
	Male		
ASIA-PACIFIC	38.9	26.2	35.0
Central Asia	33.6	24.6	41.9
Developed economies in Asia	4.4	34.2	61.4
East Asia	33.6	31.8	34.6
Pacific Islands	64.4	7.0	28.6
South East Asia	44.1	20.4	35.5
South Asia	46.4	21.4	32.2

Source: ILO, Trends econometric models, October 2010.

Now such effort of gendering infrastructure programme an average of 14 percent of infrastructure projects applied some attention to gender concerns in 1995, this climbed to 36 percent by 2009 (World Bank, 2010). Project appraisal documents (PADs) and implementation completion reports (ICRs) made by World Bank review team has assessed all 1,246 projects systematically about their contributions to empower women. They have used six methods for integrating gender into projects.

Reviews of these projects have revealed that Consultation is the most widely used method. It covered in 211 projects, or 17 percent of all projects. The next most frequently applied method is targeted gender activities, which cover 13 percent of projects. Monitoring and evaluation and gender analysis were used in 5 and 6 percent of projects respectively. There was limited attention to gender in project development objectives and budgets. The trends in the use of gender methods provide a more promising picture. Projects those were using at least one gender method grew from 14 percent of the infrastructure portfolio in 1995 to 39 percent in 2008 and 36 percent in 2009.The highest peak in infrastructure projects with gender followed the "Gender Action Plan (GAP) launched to provide over $65 million in grants for mainstreaming gender in the economic sectors. However, infrastructure sector received only 4 percent of GAP funds (World Bank, 2010).

There was large variation in the extent to which the different regions incorporated gender into their infrastructure operations. With an average gender coverage of 43 percent over the review period, the performance South Asia region outpaces the others overall. Other regions, however, made major strides over the review period. Review in 2009 stated that by the final year East Asia and the Pacific, Middle East and North Africa, South Asia, and Africa were all incorporating gender into at least half of their projects. Latin America and the Caribbean have achieved some progress as well, reaching 20 percent of projects in 2009. Eastern Europe and Central Asia were the weaker regions who have failed to incorporate gender into their infrastructure operation. Some staff stressed in interviews that gender issues were more obvious in South Asia and Sub-Saharan Africa, and thus easier to make a case with client governments for gender approaches (World Bank, 2010).

The World Bank's infrastructure lending portfolio is organized into five sectors i.e., water, sanitation, transport, energy and urban development. Water and sanitation is a clear leader on gender. Report in

Table 3. Detail description of gender methods used in gendering infrastructure development programme

Sl. No	Type	Description
1	Consultation	Refers to a public meeting held with local women and men directly affected by an infrastructure project. The method is most often applied during project preparation and appraisal phases.
2	Gender analysis	Is conducted in the context of social or environmental assessments, in resettlement action planning, or reported as separate studies
3	Project development objectives	Gender equality goals in indicating gender-based results that the project will aim to achieve at completion.
4	Gender activities	Either gender-responsive or specific gender targeted activities designed in the projects to reduce potential gender based inequalities in access to services, risks, benefits and opportunities, and in some cases, to empower women directly to better their lives
5	Budget	Refers to the presence of a line item in the project documents indicating that resources have been earmarked for targeted gender activities.
6	Monitoring and evaluation (M&E)	Requires early planning to include gender responsive indicators to monitor progress towards gender equality of benefits in project outcomes and to collect gender-disaggregated data.

Source: combined by author herself.

2009 stated that water and sanitation sectors were using at least one gender method in 57 percent of its projects, and large gains could also be found in transport (48 percent) and energy (30 percent). Urban development incorporated gender methods by 27 percent over the review period. Increasingly, transport, energy, mining, and ICT projects are designed with a better understanding of gender differences. Traditionally, men have been more likely to be employed in sectors and occupations with stronger physical requirements than women (men have an advantage in brawn). ICT related activities are deemphasizing physical skills, should favour women, even if women have no advantage over men in using a computer or acquiring computer skills (World Bank, 2012). Evidence from the United states and Germany show that sustained increase in the demand for brain versus brawn associated with ICT and computerization of the workplace explain most of the observed rise in demand for female workers, female labour force participation, and female employment in these countries over few decades(Black and Spitz-Oener 2010;).Evidence from Brazil, India, Mexico, and Thailand during 1990-2005 show that brain requirement increased and brawn requirement decreased for both men and women(World Bank, 2012). ICTs can improve access to markets and increase participation in market works by reducing transaction costs associated with time and mobility constraints. They facilitate the gathering and transmission of price and other information and increase the flexibility in where and when economic activities can occur. Beyond access to services, mobile phones and the internet allow women to be more connected to each other and their communities and to have stronger social and political voices. Cell phone and the internet are the most useful devices among the ICTs. Cell phone access enables women by increasing the ability to coordinate their family and work lives, (Comfort and Dada, 2009; GSMA Development Fund, 2010). About 41 percent of women interviewed in Bolivia, The Arab Republic of Egypt, India and Kenya declared that owing a mobile phone had increased their income and their access to economic opportunities (World Bank, 2012). Though the mobile phone access is very high in developed countries, its uses in developing countries have grown substantially in the recent past in the developing world. Among the low-income countries gender differences in cell phone access and uses are still larger, where a woman is 21 percent less likely than a man to own a mobile phone (GSMA Development Fund,2010). The picture is quite different for the uses of internet. Low access in the developing world, as shown in Table 1 has severely limited its impact on access to economic opportunities. In high income countries, (where 45.30% of female population in 2014 are using internet to pay bills or buy things) ICTs allow people to work from different locations and on different schedules-in other words, to work in more flexible ways,. Whereas less uses of internet in low income countries (0.93%) creates a barrier to attain empowerment by increasing the transportation cost in marketing work. This time constraints are more binding for women, particularly those in families with children, tele-work can have big gender impacts. New ICT-enabled jobs in services-particularly information processing in banking, insurance, printing, and publishing –were mainly taken up by the women, but not the same women who lost their manufacturing jobs and agricultural employment.

Studies have also shown a variation in the performances of financing institution regarding integration of gendering into infrastructure development programmes. The 1,246 projects in the portfolio review amounted to $113.6 billion in loans and grants between 1995 and 2009. The IBRD (International Bank for Reconstruction and Development) which is the lending window for middle income borrowers has allocated 70 percent of this financing, but the smaller IDA (International Development Association) has delivered many more projects with gender. There are several reasons why the gap in gender focus between IDA and IBRD may exist. IBRD loans are for middle income countries, and for large infrastructure projects, e.g. trade corridors, electricity generation/transmission, and water treatment plants, where the immediate relevance of gender responsive design may be less clear (World Bank, 2010). IDA covered 34 percent lending for all of the economic sectors, in which infrastructure figures prominently in both 2008 and 2009. The central gender unit of the World Bank, found a much higher rate (76 percent) of gender integration in IDA's social and related sectors. The social sectors, which include health, education, and social protection, have been integrating gender concerns in most of their projects for many years, partly because these services interact so closely and continuously with beneficiaries (Wieczorek, 2009). On the other side, over the 15 years, IBRD has allocated 17 percent of its financing to infrastructure projects with gender, compared to 41 percent for IDA.

Discussion

After analysing entire report, it is clear that while important progress has taken place, there remains important scope for continued improvement in both the coverage and quality of gender inclusion in infrastructure projects. We have noticed how this integration has assisted local women and men to participate in infrastructure development programmes and to improve efficiency, effectiveness and ensure sustainability. Yet, this progress was uneven across gender oriented methods, across the different regions and infrastructure sectors, and between the two lending windows for the middle- and low-income countries.

1. We have seen that among the six methods, the most usable method has scored only 17% of the entire projects, followed by targeted gender activities whose contribution was13%. Share of Monitoring and evaluation, gender analysis, gender in project development objectives and budgets are so meagre that cannot be considerable. Project development objectives which includes gender equality is highly understated and budget, monitoring and evaluation which must be used to ensure gendering into infrastructure development programmes are highly under-estimated. This steps creates doubt about willingness of authority to ensure empowerment for women through these development project. Though they are uttering for changes in mind set, but their steps seem not matched with their statements. Still our society is used to ready seeing gender as "requiring attention" rather to viewing women and girls as the "primary clients".
2. Next, we have seen that there is a lot of variation in implementation of these projects across the region. The regions which have performed comparatively worse in human development index are stands behind of those countries whose performance in said category are better than them. From World Bank Infrastructure Development Program, we have seen that the economies of Europe and Central Asia are standing behind the economies of other region regarding their performances in gendering infrastructure. Surprisingly economies of Europe and Central Asia belongs to upper middle income group whereas the South Asia and sub-Saharan African countries are mainly low income countries which are performing better in gender issues. From Table 1, it is clear that performance of middle income countries in attaining female literacy is much higher than low income countries. Having a higher level of income, their performances in providing social infrastructural facilities and in uses of ICTs related measures are better than low income countries. Surprisingly, percentages of female participation in parliamentary seats are higher for low income group compared to middle income groups.
3. Further, a lot of variations have observed in using gender methods across sector. Projects that are related to water and sanitation have performed better in using this method whereas transport sector, energy and urban development sectors are still reluctant to apply gender methods. However,

it is well established fact that projects related to water and sanitation need less amount of capital compare to remaining three.

4. We have noticed that among the ICT enabled jobs, women are less interested in using internet compare to their uses of cell phone. This matter can be explained as low private access especially in rural areas (absence of tele centre for public uses that enhance the basic ICT services among the underserved populations), lack of technical education and finally lack of time that can be spent to enhance their productivities. However, it is the women who have experienced faster growth in telework in the past few years but failed to continue their job due to caring and responsibilities in household. Therefore, women's opportunity to get ICT education has influenced by several other factors that relates to the different social processes other than the economic opportunities. Such, social processes are gender, political, cultural and traditional in nature. The position occupied that occupied women in labour market depend upon and shape the definition of gender. Gender is also a set of processes that are cultural or ideological processes (Barrett1980) that involve the production and distribution of meanings which are attached to primary and secondary sex characteristics.
5. Finally. There is a significant variation in performances among the lending windows- IBRD and IDA. Though IBRD are financing majority of the infrastructure development programme (almost 70%), IDA finances relatively small portion but with gender. IDA's projects are mainly concentrated on promoting social infrastructure which includes health; education and social protection which are enable women to become efficient so that they can adopt the opportunities that they may get in infrastructure development programmes.

Now we take recourse of Althuserian theory of over determination to understand the logic behind above mentioned variations. The status of women within society is determined by different social processes which are prevalent in the society. Any society is a web of social relationships which are social processes, social patterns and social interactions. A single indicator is insufficient and incomplete to realize women's empowerment, which is considered as a multidimensional concept in multiple domains in which a woman generally functions and discharges her duties. As there are several social processes within society, therefore we have diversified knowledge on women's empowerment. Each space defines women's empowerment using their discipline. So, the conception also varies across the spaces. Now to evaluate the process of gendering into infrastructure development programmes, we have to understand the pattern of the social process (which includes both economic and non-economic processes) and their relevance to judge the efficacy of such project that has adopted within society. Here we opt the class focused Marxist approach.

Class focused Marxist approach is based on the Althuserian logic of over-determination where two variables X and Y mutually constitute each other each being cause and effect of the other. Hence, it cannot be said which one is before and which one is later. The concept of over-determination is premised on the understanding that no element can exist on its own. Thus, over-deterministic logic has rejected the logic of unidirectional causality. Mutual constitutive, unlike the logic of causality, does not simply affect the state of being that is presumed to exist but it makes possible the very existence of the being (Chakrabarti, Dhar & Cullenberg, 2012).

This way of looking at the world marks a departure from the orthodox Marxist rendition of economic as the base of the society. First, in this over-deterministic logic economic, political, cultural and natural mutually constitute each other. Second, the linear progression of society as claimed by historical materialism breaks down. Society does not follow the linear transition from primitive communism to socialism/

communism via feudalism and capitalism (Chakrabarti, Dhar & Cullenberg, 2012). Following Class Focused Marxist Approach we can say economic and non-economic processes mutually constitute each other and none is more significant than the other. Society' is not a thing, fixed and constant. Rather, it is a perpetually ongoing fabrication, a set of interacting and living process. Previously, theorist represents social formation as closed totalities. Resnick and Wolff do not reject the notion of 'totality.' But their totality has no closure. They believe that social theorist's perspective is always limited, partial, and fragmentary. This acknowledgement of the partial perspective of the theorist leads to their epistemological assertion: "Truth is not absolute, but rather relative" (Cassano, 2009).

Resnick and Wolff (1987) generate a unique definition of 'class'. Before, the political economists used the word – 'class' - as a category or group of similar things. A 'class' of social actors is defined based upon their possession of power or property or means of production or some composite of these elements. Resnick and Wolff furnish a new definition of 'class' which describes processes of performance, appropriation, distribution and receipt of surplus labour as indicated by Marx in his *Das Capital*. An individual can at the same time belongs to different class processes. Hence, this negates the concept of homogeneous class groups as propounded by the orthodox Marxist theory.

While class process is an economic process non-economic processes include political, cultural and natural processes including gender process, which is a non-class non-economic process. The Marxian category of exploitation is applicable in the case of class-process while oppression as category is associated with non-class processes including gender process.

While exploitation signifies appropriation of surplus labour by non-performers of surplus labour, 'oppression' signifies basically a political process of dominating other persons by directing and controlling their mind, body and labour power. Fradd, Resnick and Wolff (2009) refuse to give priority of one process on other processes. Economic and non-economic processes over determine one another. The point is to analyze the differences and varying interrelationships between political, cultural and economic processes. Therefore, it is very much essential to explore the interaction between class and other non-economic processes.

The concept of gender has been shaped by the economic and political power, social dominance and cultural authority. Society as a heterogeneous space does not furnish equal benefits in terms of resources, training, opportunities and entitlements. Such type of socialization ensures separate gender processes that explain the relationship between male and female members within society. Such gender processes teach the members what role she/he should play within society.

Along with gender process, a related concept is of entitlements. These are defined as ——the ideas, norms, and customs that govern resource allocation in a particular group of society. Thus, even a cursory observation informs that there is a gender difference in education, health services, inheritance of property and also access to information (Dube, 1986). In continuation of this concept, we can say that gender process is a strong determinant of the prevailing structure of class, political processes, cultural processes, legal processes within family. The ideal, norms and customs dictate that whether women are able to appropriate their surplus labour or not that means whether they will belong to exploited class or to non-exploited class. These ideologies further determine whether women can take of their own decision of their lives or not and whether they are entitled to inherit family property rights or not. The class position occupied within households depend upon and shape the definition of gender lived by the member of such household. Gender is also a set of processes that are cultural or ideological processes (Barrett 1980). As these gender processes are cultural and ideological, therefore, these processes have left deep impression within minds of members of family.

A gender process that deprived women from entitlement of all types of resource allocation and making decision of their own life make a women 'non empower'.An oppressed sex-gender process may be attached with exploitative class process and lead the women deprived from gaining control over her own decisions and make the women 'non-empowered'. Further, a gender process can help women gain control over all type of resources and over all decision of their own lives, may make the women as 'empowered.'

Cultural processes mean the processes of producing and disseminating meanings in society (Fradd, et al 2009). Traditionally society exerts the ideology that women should do the domestic chores as women are unfit physically and psychologically for the outside world. Whereas, family must provide her sustenance and security.So, proper womanhood means caring for family and its members while adopting a sub-ordinate, exploited and oppressed position in relationship to the 'master' of the family. This ideology however determines the gender processes that helped to sustain feudal family class structures inside the family. Ideologies of love and responsibility have illustrated the particular definition of male and female. Under such ideologies feudal surplus labour production appears as a 'natural' outgrowth and this helps to impose on women their servile status and on men their lordly position and facilitate class exploitation within the family.

By political conditions of existence, we mean processes of establishing and enforcing rules of family behaviour and adjudicating disputes over those rules. Generally, laws punish physical or sexual assault in the market while treating such assault within family more leniently or not at all. Now the political process of establishing and differentially enforcing laws helps to maintain exploitative and oppressive status for women within society. At the same time if laws fail to punish physical and sexual assault in the market widely, then these steps not only encourage the gender-discriminated exploitative class process in the market, it further strengthen the roots of feudal class processes within family. On the other hand, if the woman faces favourable political and legal processes in the market, then it may help her to resist exploitation and oppression within family and also, to transform the existing exploitative and oppressive family structure into non-exploitative and non-oppressive one.

Further, surplus labour performed by women in feudal family is determined by the access to property. Being property-less may push women more into feudal class process-based family. Women face discrimination in markets or societal institutions that prevent them from completing their education, entering certain occupations and earning the same income as men. When women farmers lack security of land tenure, the result is lower access to credit and inefficient land use, reducing yields.

If laws and economic condition help women to hold property, then this effort becomes conducive to reduce and/or eliminate exploitative and oppressive surroundings for women. This is by no means that political process of ownership itself undermines feudal family. Whether and to what extent it does so depend on all other processes that produce such family. If gender and cultural processes are such that women have to undertake stress for housework and became pride to do so, then she will perform such chores and produce surplus labour and strengthen the root of exploitation. Here women accept the gender notion of their own incapacity for financial management and free control over their property by male.

Sometimes they have done it less willingly out of fear of psychological or physical retaliation from the members of the family. Family exploits her feudally without making any payment from her property. Under such ideology of love of living being, responsibility, self-sacrifice, co-operation, universal brotherhood has been consciously and unconsciously make her unthinkable to use her political power to withhold property or to demand subsumed class payments for access to it. This ideology constrains the family from making payment to women. This may help to understand why in spite of having joint property ownership, feudal structure of family has not altered.

Following the perspective of theory of over determination, we can found that the process of gendering into infrastructure development programme which seeks to ensure economic empowerment of women should not be evaluate by ignoring the other non-economic processes. Less uses of gender methods reflects a non-cooperative gender process within the society. Lack of budget, neglecting gender in project development objectives and lack of monitoring and evaluation are the outcomes of oppressive political process that prevent women from the access of property.Here women face discrimination in markets or societal institutions that prevent them from entering certain occupations and earning the same Income as men. Along with these lacks of gendering into transport, energy and urban development ensure the existence of not only oppressive political process but oppressive cultural and gender processes which created differences in the outlook of male and female with respect to risk aversion, social preferences, attitude and choices. Unavailability of finance made by IDA reflects the discrimination in markets or societal institutions. If political and economic conditions prevent women to have an access of financial resources, then this effort becomes conducive to enhance and/or sustain exploitative and oppressive surroundings for women.

Next we are trying to identify the importance of social infrastructure services to ensure the empowerment of women. Simultaneously we are trying to observe the multidimensional characteristics of women empowerment. Due to lack of data on empowerment indicator across the regions at world level as mentioned before, we have used data of National Family Health Survey-4 across the states of India. By using such data, we can illustrates our theoretical background. Here we get the information on women empowerment indicator, social infrastructure indicator, etc., for 14 states of India. In Table 4 we consider data on 7 variables which are, -

1. Percentage of Women owning a house and/or land (alone or jointly with others).
2. Percentage of Women having a bank or savings account that they themselves use.
3. Average value of a & b are considered as the indicator of women empowerment. This is because opportunity to own a house and a bank account is possible when a woman faces non-exploitative economic process and non-oppressive non-economic process.
4. Sex ratio.
5. Female literacy rate.
6. Male literacy rate.
7. Average value of services of social infrastructure which includes: i) Household with electricity, ii) Household with drinking water, iii) Household with sanitation, iv) Household with clean fuel for cooking and v) Household under health scheme. Among the several infrastructure measures we have considered these variables because women are main beneficiaries of such services.

Next we make a data analysis and have tried to get the pattern of relationship among the variable. Here we have seen that women empowerment indicator is positively related with the social infrastructural services, favourable sex ration for women, female literacy rate, and male literacy rate. Notably, the relationship between female literacy and favourable sex ratio for female are negatively related. This relationship actually represents the oppressive cultural process of society where males have taken the decision about family planning. So, it is very rare that women taken the decision. Even educated male

Table 4. Key indicators of women empowerment and family health

State	A	B	C	D	E	F	G
Andhra Pradesh	44.7	66.3	55.5	1020	62.9	79.4	72.34
BIHAR	58.8	26.4	85.2	1062	49.6	77.8	32.12
GOA	33.9	82.8	116.7	1018	89	94.7	62.88
HARYANA	35.8	45.6	81.4	876	75.4	90.6	53.84
KARNATAKA	51.8	59.4	111.2	979	71.7	85.1	53.26
MP	43.5	37.3	80.8	948	59.4	81.8	40.06
MEGHALAYA	57.3	54.4	111.7	1005	82.8	84	45.36
PODUCHERRY	40.3	68.2	108.5	1068	85	91.9	75.52
SIKKIM	24.8	63.5	88.3	942	86.6	91.5	60.64
TAMIL NADU	36.2	77.6	113.8	1033	79.4	89.1	59.58
TELENGANA	50.5	59.7	110.2	1007	65.2	83.4	71.84
TRIPURA	57.3	59.2	116.5	998	80.4	89.5	66.26
UTTARAKHAND	29.2	58.5	87.7	1015	76.5	90.7	65.08

Source: National Family Health Survey-4, 2015 -16

are not out of this traditional and cultural taboos. Lastly we can see that services of social infrastructure is positively related with women empowerment, sex ratio, female literacy rate and male literacy rate. As these services benefit all the member of family, we have such relation.

States performing better in ensuring women empowerment (like, Goa, Tripura, Telengana, Meghalaya, Karnataka, Telengana and Poduchery) have better performances in getting infrastructural facilties. These regions are also performing better in educating male and female also. However, region like (Uttarakhand, Bihar, West Bengal and Andhra Pradesh) having a favourable sex ration for women, are performing poorer in ensuring women empowerment. First group of region have matriarchal cultural processes that help them to perform better on women issues. Second group of regions are patriarchal society so their performances are poorer in achieving success on women issues. So here oppressive gender, cultural processes are active with exploitative class processes. Regional differences are also the outcome of traditional cultural believes.

Table 5. Correlation results

	Column 1(C)	Column 2(D)	Column 3(E)	Column 4(F)	Column 5(G)
Column 1(c)	1				
Column2(d)	0.211883	1			
Column3(e)	0.521599	-0.0895	1		
Column 4(f)	0.520288	-0.18591	0.864332	1	
Column5(g)	0.104966	0.191512	0.473227	0.439889	1

CONCLUSION AND POLICY SUGGESTIONS

To encourage more equitable economic participation and growth, better access to infrastructure is needed. Due to the nature of household responsibilities, inadequate infrastructure often affects women. In our analysis we are reaching two findings that emerged from the gender coverage of infrastructure project. The first is the evidence that how the access to services of social infrastructure has positive impact on empowerment of women. Another finding is that how this gender coverage of infrastructure project is influences by both economic and non economic social processes.

Different studies have shown that how a transport project is enabling women to access the formal banking system with their own collateral, how inclusion of women in rural water supply project has reduced women's and girl's time of fetching water by at least half, and increased school enrolment for girls. A water project has found that women are more effective in providing quality work in a timely manner. Investment in local transport infrastructure may thus directly alleviate a major constraint to female entrepreneurs. Several projects have also included direct measures to empower women, often by working with or mobilizing local women's organizations. All these effort suggest that these measures enhance women's earnings as well as their social status and participation in making decision in their communities. Our study has shown that how adequate access of the social infrastructure services fetch benefits for women and ensure empowerment of women. Indeed, the inclusion of gender issue in to investment is not only to reach women. Though gender equality plays as a key millennium development goal (MDG) and inadequate services of social infrastructure is recognised as a significant barrier to meet MDGs, but there is a need to reach all beneficiaries that are targeted by this project.

In conclusion, when women and men do not have equal chances to be socially and politically active and to influence laws, politics, and policy making, then institutions and policies are more likely to systematically favour the interest of those with more influence. Family constraint and market failures that feed gender inequalities are less likely to be addresses and corrected, leading to their persistence. This creates an inequality trap which prevents women to resist producing surplus labour both domestic and public sphere and simultaneously make an obstacle to take up economic opportunities which enhance their potential as individual, prevail within society. It must be kept in mind that the gain of this infrastructure development programme ought to be reached to the targeted beneficiaries. As we have observed that society is a multidimensional space, therefore it is difficult to get homogeneity within any space and site. Therefore, consideration of the influences of existing social processes should keep it mind to make the design and implementation of infrastructure programme become successful. Knowing this over determined significance of social processes helps to plan and implement projects that better match client preferences and needs, and thus projects can be more effective and sustainable.

The design of activities that foster meaningful participation of women and men from different social groups requires an understanding of the local social, institutional, and cultural context, and the relevant gender-related social patterns. Projects with gender dimensions need close monitoring. Measures such as social and gender assessments, inclusive consultations, participatory project activities, and strong monitoring and evaluation systems provide second-best alternatives for getting services delivered successful. In addition, government should increase more public funding in adoption of gender methods in infrastructure development projects, carry out pilot projects to better understand what works, stress on outcome –oriented norms while defining minimum standards and develop strategy for recruitment and retention of women.

REFERENCES

Banerjee, N. (2002). Between the Devil and Deep Sea - Shrinking Options for Women in Contemporary India. In K. Kapadia (Ed.), *The Violence of Development: The Politics of Identity - Gender and Social Inequalities in India*. New Delhi: Kali for Women.

Barrett, M. (1980). *Women"s Oppression Today*. London: Verso.

Black, S. E., & Spitz-Oener, A. (2010). Explaining Women's Success: Technological Change and Skill Content of Women's Work. *The Review of Economics and Statistics*, 92.

Cassano, G. (Ed.). (2009). Class Struggle on the Home Front: Work, Conflict and Exploitation in the Household. Palgrave-Macmillan.

Chakrabarti, A., Dhar, A., & Cullenberg, S. (2012). *World of the Third and Global Capitalism*. Delhi: Worldview Publications.

Chakravarti, U. (1993). Conceptualizing Brahminical Patriarchy in Early India, Gender, Caste, Class and State. *Economic and Political Weekly*, *28*(14), 3.

Chakravarti, U. (2009). Gendering Caste - Through a Feminist Lens. STREE.

Comfort, K., & Dada, J. (2009). 'Rural Women's Use of Cell Phones to Meet Their Communication Needs: A Study from Northern Nigeria. In I. Buskens & A. Webb (Eds.), *African Women and ICTs: Investigating Technology, gender and Empowerment*. London: Zed Books.

Dube, L. (1986). *Seed and Earth: Symbolism of Biological Reproduction and Sexual Relations of Production. In Visibility and Power: Essays on Women in Society and Development*. Delhi: Oxford University Press.

Fraad, H., Resnick, S. A., & Wolff, R. D. (2009). For Every Knight in Shining Armour, There's a Castle Waiting to be Cleaned. In Class Struggle on the Home Front: Work, Conflict and Exploitation in the Household. Palgrave-Macmillan.

Government of India. (2016). National family health survey, 2015-2016. In *Ministry of Health and Family welfare*. New Delhi: Author.

GSMA Development Fund. (2010). *Women and Mobile: A Global Opportunity: A study on the Mobile Phone Gender Gap in Low and Middle Income Countries*. London: GSMA and the Cherie Blair Foundation for Women.

ILO. (2011). Women and labour market in Asia-Rebalancing for gender equality. International Labour Organisation and Asian Development Bank.

Kabeer, N. (1996). Agency, Well-Being & Inequality: Reflections on the Gender Dimensions of Poverty. IDS Bulletin, 27(1), 11-21.

Mandal, K. (2012). *Gender and Empowerment- A comparative Analysis of India and USA*. Levant Book.

Resnick, S. A., & Wolff, R. D. (1987). *Knowledge and Class: A Marxist Critique of Political Economy*. Chicago: University of Chicago Press.

Sharma, R. N. (1989). *Principles of Sociology*. Bombay: Media Promoters & Publishers Private Limited.

Wieczorek-Zuel & Heidemaria. (2009). IDA 16 and Gender Equality: Is a Breakthrough Possible? Gender Equality as Smart Economics: A World Bank Group Action Plan Newsletter.

KEY TERMS AND DEFINITIONS

Economic Process: Economic process is the class process which is a process of performance, appropriation, distribution and receipt of surplus labour non-economic process.

Exploitation: Exploitation is an economic term which relates to fundamental class process. It occurs when the surplus labour is not appropriated by direct producer.

Fundamental Class Process: The fundamental class process refers to the performance and appropriation of surplus labour.

Mode of Production: It is defined as the articulation of forces of production and relations of production. The forces of production show the fundamental way in which humans relate.

Non-Economic Process: It is non-class process social process which is mutually constituted by the political, cultural, economic and natural processes in a social space at a time.

Subsumed Class Process: Subsumed class process refers to the distribution and receipt of the surplus labour. Fundamental class process and subsumed class process mutually constitute each other in over determined manner. We cannot say which one is more important.

Theory of Over Determination: It is Althuserian logic of over-determination where two variables X and Y mutually constitute each other each being cause and effect of the other. Hence, it cannot be said which one is before and which one is later. The concept of over-determination is premised on the understanding that no element can exist on its own. Thus, over-deterministic logic has rejected the logic of unidirectional causality to non-human nature via production of basic necessities such as food and shelter. The relations of production reflect the social relations in which humans actually engage with each other to constitute a society's non-material base in the production process. Actually relations of production refer to the class relations between the direct producers and non-producers.

Women Empowerment: Women's empowerment indicates a situation where women gain autonomy over their own lives to improve their personal, social, economic, political and legal conditions so as to achieve greater self-respect in family, society and market including economic self-confidence.

Chapter 4
MGNREGS of India:
Complementarities Between Employment and Infrastructure

Pratip Kumar Datta
Rajatpur Indranarayan Vidyapith, India

Harsha Tiwary
Visva Bharati University, India

Saumya Chakrabarti
Visva Bharati University, India

ABSTRACT

Controlling surplus population, on the one hand and use of underutilized resources on the other, have induced governments of the developing world to adopt measures so that, poverty, underdevelopment and social insecurity are managed outside the sphere of core sector, especially through rural employment generation. MGNREGS of India is one such programme. Many researchers suggested the need for government intervention in job creation. On the other hand, some researchers have criticized such policies on the ground that these programmes misallocate resources towards relatively less productive frontiers. We propose theoretically that, the problem is not so much with the revenue expenditure, rather the bottleneck lies on the supply-side and can be mitigated by introducing infrastructural factors. Moreover in this chapter, we have tried to criticize the quality of jobs done and types of infrastructure generated through MGNREGS as it seems that both fail to increase food production and thus create some conflicts between rural and urban sectors.

INTRODUCTION

Today's globalized world often identifies growth as development. Since early 90's India is attempting to be a part of globalized world and in many fields she has done it successfully. The success story of globalization has been reflected in the growth rate data (sometimes it is estimated over 7% per annum). But there is a flip side of the coin. Market economy, by its very nature, excludes a portion of the popu-

DOI: 10.4018/978-1-5225-2364-2.ch004

lation of a country. Unfortunately, in case of India, the excluded portion of the population is too large. According to RBI, there was approximately 26.4 crore persons lying below the poverty line in 2015. Rehabilitation and utilization of the large surplus population, on the one hand and deployment of some underutilized resources on the other, have induced the government of India and governments of some other developing countries to take up measures so that, poverty, underdevelopment and social insecurity are managed outside the sphere of market economy, especially through rural/peripheral employment generation. Thus, "development management" by the State aiming at the excluded population outside the dynamics of accumulation has become the dominant developmental strategy Sanyal (2007), Sanyal and Bhattacharya (2009) and Chakrabarti (2011). Even the international funding and regulating agencies are advocating for such direct policies.

In 1662, Sir William Petty argued in support of "publicly employing the unemployed for building infrastructure", and the need for government intervention for employment generation was first felt way back in the seventeenth century, just after the Industrial Revolution Kaboub (2007). After the failure of the US government's policy, War on Poverty, Hyman Minsky (1965) suggested employment guarantee schemes for the US economy. During the last few decades, following the footsteps of their developed counterparts, different developing countries started introducing employment guarantee programmes. Argentina's the *Plan Jefes y Jefas de Hogar Desocupados* (Program for Unemployed Male and Female Heads of Households), South Africa's Expanded Public Works Programmes (EPWP), India's Mahatma Gandhi National Rural Employment Guarantee Scheme (MGNREGS), etc., are a few well-known programmes which are intended towards employment guarantee to the excluded mass of people.

In September 2005, India's parliament endorsed a significant legislation – the National Rural Employment Guarantee Act (NREGA), presently known as Mahatma Gandhi National Rural Employment Guarantee Act (MGNREGA). The Act, in one hand, recognized employment as a right and on the other hand, defines a compulsion for the government to provide, in each year, 100 days of wage employment along with rural asset generation at a predetermined minimum wage to all rural households whose members are looking for or eager to do unskilled manual work. Government of India has allotted approximately 8.6 percent of its total planned expenditure in the FY 2015-16 (http://indiabudget.nic.in).

Programmes like MGNREGS have faced severe criticisms on the grounds of misallocation and inefficient distribution of resources. Researchers like Murgai and Ravallion (2005), Marjit and Maiti (2007), Kostzer (2008), Sjoblom and Farrington (2008) have criticized such policies on the ground that these programmes misallocate resources towards relatively less productive frontiers by channelizing government finance from the so-called efficient urban/capitalist/modern sectors. Government budget constraint is proposed to be a crucial hurdle for these types of development management policies. On the other hand, many other researchers like Dreze & Sen (1989), Dreze (2004), Patnaik (2005), and Dev (2006) argued in favour of government's intervention in job creation outside the domain of core capitalist sector.

In India, started from 2006-07 since 2014-15, MGNREGS employment is showing an increasing trend as can be seen from Table 1. Although, there exists a very high degree of variations in performances among states/UTs, but the MGNREGS employment has been increased from 3% to 12% on an average while considering the all India figures.

From Table 1, we can see that states like Meghalaya, Mizoram, Nagaland, and Tripura perform extremely well in comparison with other states. There may be distinction in priorities among different dimensions of capacities and political commitments of MGNREGS, it is also visible from the table that most of the states fail to touch even the double-digit figure. Later, in this paper, we have tried to study empirically the MGNREGS performance incorporating its expenditure side also.

Table 1. MGNREGS Employment and Rural Population of Different States ant UTs of India

State / UT	Total Rural population[a]		No. of Persons Employed[b]		% of Rural Population Employed in MGNREGS[c]	
	2006-07	2014-15	2006-07	2014-15	2006-07	2014-15
Andaman and Nicobar	242183	245748		16328		6.6
Andhra Pradesh	55856428	56585004	2161395	5552399	3.9	9.8
Arunachal Pradesh	969626	1128888		140105		12.4
Assam	24998402	27849784	792270	1224039	3.2	4.4
Bihar	83195869	97402524	1688899	1246237	2	1.3
Chhattisgarh	18125857	20490339	1375802	3258555	7.6	15.9
Dadra & Nagar Haveli	176526	186923				
Daman & Diu	80594	48174				
Goa	614253	513711		7500		1.5
Gujarat	33205792	35549832	226269	917270	0.7	2.6
Haryana	15780377	16982163	50765	325944	0.3	1.9
Himachal Pradesh	5825062	6373451	109417	576160	1.9	9
Jammu and Kashmir	8380941	9587147	121328	429258	1.4	4.5
Jharkhand	22994517	26262403	1394108	1572430	6.1	6
Karnataka	36220781	38351578	1011021	3012990	2.8	7.9
Kerala	20514978	15619823	99107	1513167	0.5	9.7
Lakshadweep	23902	8252		493		6
Madhya Pradesh	48459389	54985005	2866349	5814206	5.9	10.6
Maharashtra	58661544	63275779		2155626		3.4
Manipur	1745222	1992265	18568	498833	1.1	25
Meghalaya	**2116841**	**2520249**	**96627**	**463164**	**4.6**	**18.4**
Mizoram	**488302**	**553478**	**50998**	**266606**	**10.4**	**48.2**
Nagaland	**1527055**	**1334745**	**27884**	**475122**	**1.8**	**35.6**
Odisha	33119328	36050378	1394169	2125008	4.2	5.9
Puducherry	360034	414926		31671		7.6
Punjab	16706644	17682894	31648	337560	0.2	1.9
Rajasthan	47416525	54014463	1175172	5140300	2.5	9.5
Sikkim	468472	448456	4107	68015	0.9	15.2
Tamil nadu	36055455	37869493	683481	6913415	1.9	18.3
Tripura	2681752	2727030	74335	1101480	**2.8**	**40.4**
Uttar pradesh	143384681	162146827	2573245	4718127	1.8	2.9
Uttarakhand	6667929	7240175	134312	543152	2	7.5
West bengal	59981311	63553095	3083757	7354471	5.1	11.6
Mean	**23849896**	**26060455**	**849801**	**1864504**	**3**	**12**
Sd	**31062239**	**34891791**	**983681**	**2220942**	**2**	**11**
Cv	**130.24**	**133.89**	**115.75**	**119.12**	**82.4**	**98.49**

Source: www.nrega.nic.in; Authors estimation

In the subsequent stage, we shall try to examine both theoretically as well as empirically that government's budget constraint is not the actual problem, but the problem lies within supply side constraint and quality of job creation through MGNREGS.

In this chapter we have suggested that financing in such employment generating programmes is not wastage as argued by many researchers though these programmes may lead to price hike of food (generic) if not address the problem of supply side constraint by developing infrastructure. Next section deals with a very brief literature review. Next section provides a model economy where MGNREG like CFW programme has been introduced. This section tries to illustrate the inflationary effect of the MGNREGS programme and also tries to find out the possible solution through infrastructure development. Then we try to assess MGNREGS empirically while the final section provides fundamental conclusions drawn out of this paper.

REVIEW OF LITERATURE

Economic literatures suggest *a priori* as well as *a posteriori* relationship between infrastructure development and economic growth. Although, rural infrastructure development is inherent within the policy objectives of MGNREGS like CFW programmes, as discussed earlier, such employment guarantee programmes are at the focal point of academic as well as political debate. Historically, in 1662, Sir Willium Petty first argued in favour of "publicly employing the unemployed for building infrastructure" Kaboub (2007). The US government's policy named War on Poverty had failed to prove its efficacy and as a consequence Hyman Minsky (1965) suggested employment guarantee schemes for the US economy, but he also opined in this connection that such an employment generating strategy should not be inflationary in nature. In this context, Mitchell (1998) suggested a policy where government would be the market maker for labour so that it buys all unemployed workers at a fixed wage and sell it at a higher wage to the private sector. In other words, government would maintain a buffer stock of labour. He argued that, such strategy would ensure a full employment in the economy with price stability. Papadimitriou (2008) in this connection analyses the basic features of the less developed countries (with special emphasizes on Argentina and India) and suggested that such employment guarantee programmes must be directed towards the production of necessary commodities and infrastructure.

While analyzing the *Plan Jefes y Jefas de Hogar Desocupados* (Program for Unemployed Male and Female Heads of Households) of Argentina, introduced after 2001 economic crisis, Kostzer (2008) cautioned that, "The state can always perform the role of employer of last resort in the framework of an aggregate demand (shortage) type of unemployment. When the problem is more of the type of structural unemployment, i.e., due to a lack of investment and *no excess capacity*, the selection of projects and the destination of the money involved should be thought through in a different way" (authors' emphasis).

Chakrabarti & Mukherjee (2013) assert the need for programmes like MGNREGS in order to include the excluded surplus population. They have tried to point out the possibility of 'elite capture' of the programme. But along with that they established that neither the government's budget constraint nor the demand driven tradeoff between MGNREGS and non – MGNREGS employment is important but the problem of supply-rigidities is the prime factor behind inflationary effect of MGNREGS programme. In this connection, Sanyal & Bhattacharya (2009) blamed on the factory production system for the emergence of 'surplus population'.

Chakrabarti (2011) has made an attempt on determination of optimum level of resource allocation in "Food for Work" programmes, which is very much similar to "Cash for Work" programme, where government procure food-grain from agricultural sector and use it to generate rural non-farm employment and to create rural infrastructure. He argued that, at the time of bumper harvest government could avoid the conflict between rural – urban employment through 'partial procurement' of food-grain. He also argued that, equilibrium amount of procurement has to be determined in such a way that, the resulting rise in demand for food owing to procurement expenditure injected into the economy is just compatible with the portion of aggregate food supply left out in the open market (after procurement). According to his proposition, "When an attempt is made to raise the level of rural non-agricultural employment through procurement, a conflict between urban and rural employment arises. However, this conflict is partially mitigated through a policy of partial procurement. This partial relaxation of the conflict in essence occurs due to relaxation in the food supply constraint, and appropriate allocation of this increased food-supply between rural and urban sectors through a suitably designed procurement policy" (Chakrabarti, 2011, pp. 191).

Ghosh (2011) also pointed out towards inflationary effect of MGNREGS programme in absence of supply flexibility. He opined that although; MGNREGS redistributes income from the non-poor to the poor, and increases money income of the poor to a large extend, but increased food demand due to MGNREGS income with a rigid supply restricts rural poverty to fall. He also questioned the quality of work done under MGNREGS.

Different studies in Sameeksha-II (2014) have also questioned the quality of asset created and number of works completed under, as both of these depend on political motivation and political environment as in many cases, local power holders try to hide their incompetency by criticizing the state government. While assessing the MGNREGS, existing literature suggest that local authority, monitoring the programme, focuses more on supply side of the work generation rather on its demand (ESID 2014). Due to its supply side nature, MGNREGS effectively turns into a welfare project instead of being an employment guarantee scheme or a rural infrastructure building programme.

The main proposition of this paper is quite similar with that of Chakrabarti (2011). But beyond the purview of Chakrabarti (2011), we consider MGNREGS, which is essentially Cash for Work programme. The way we address the problem of supply side constraint claims fundamentality.

THE MODEL

Assumptions

The basic assumptions of this paper are reserved similar to those of Chakrabarti (2011), with necessary additions and modifications[1]. The assumptions are:

1. We have assumed a closed economy with three sectors – a vertically integrated capitalistic modern industrial sector or the urban/core sector, a traditional agricultural or "food" sector, and the government sector.
2. The industrial sector is categorized by excess capacity, unemployment and industrial price is cost-determined (via a mark-up). On the other hand, industrial output is demand-determined. Thus, in

this model, industrial output and price determination methods are distinctly diverse as suggested by industrial organization literatures.

3. For the sake of simplification, it is assumed that all profits in the industrial sector are saved while all wages are consumed. A portion of wage-income is used for food-purchase so that there is a possibility of industry facing an agricultural supply-constraint.
4. Marketable surplus of food-grain is assumed to be unchanging (in the short-run, although not in the medium-run, as seen afterwards) and determines the agricultural supply-constraint for industry. Consequently, food price is determined by its demand. This food constraint is, in effect, the Kaleckian 'wage-good constraint'. This assumption will be relaxed afterwards – in a medium-run set-up.
5. Farmers earn their income only by selling food to industrial sector and their income is spent entirely on the purchase of industrial goods, so that, there is agriculture-industry balanced trade (again this is a simplifying assumption, discussed in detail along with its extensions in Chakrabarti, 2001 and 2011). Relaxation of this assumption will give us quantitative changes in the subsequent results without any substantive insight.
6. Industrial products are purchased by the government through money creation. Thus, this 'domestic export' Kalecki (1934) provides the 'home market' for industrial product.
7. Income distribution among different classes of the country is exogenously determined. Any attempt towards radical alteration in this distribution pattern is resisted by equally powerful lobbies formed by the capitalist producers, workers of industrial sector and the farmers. Consequently, we have rigid industrial real-wage and product-wage, and hence a rigid agriculture-industry terms of trade (t-o-t). This assumption is especially relevant for our following medium-run analysis. Although, in the short-run, there could be distributional fluctuations, in the medium-run, the lobbies bargain for their targeted shares. For details, we could refer to Skarstein (1997, chapter 8 on Kaldor) and to Chakrabarti (2014). Furthermore, in our subsequent analysis we will relax this assumption.
8. We consider a medium run scenario. By this, we have allowed some changes/flexibilities in the economy due to change in government policies. However, we are not considering the long-run phenomena like capital-accumulation, population-dynamics etc. In fact, we consider some comparative static exercises consistent with a medium-run situation.

Working of the Model[2]

Following Chakrabarti (2011), Labour-output ratio in industry (l) is given, as we have assumed excess capacity in industrial sector. Let us consider $l = 1$ by appropriate choice of unit, so that

$$L = Y \tag{1}$$

Where L: total industrial employment and Y: aggregate industrial output.

Therefore, mark-up pricing on unit wage-cost in industry is expressed as

$$P_i = (1+\tau)\, w_m \tag{2}$$

Where P_i: price of industrial output, τ: constant positive mark-up over prime cost in industry and w_m: money wage rate in industry.

Workers' targeted real wage is

$$\frac{w_m}{P_f} = \beta \tag{3}$$

Where, P_f: open market food price and β: positive constant.

Consider the assumption of exogenous nature of income distribution (especially, in a medium-run scenario). Equation (2) and (3) capture this exogenous nature of income distribution.

From Equation (2), we can have real wage in terms of industrial output as:

$$\frac{w_m}{P_i} = \frac{1}{(1+\ \tau)} = \alpha \ = \ constant \tag{3.1}$$

Terms of trade between agriculture and industry can also be obtained from Equations (2) and (3) as:

$$\frac{P_f}{P_i} = \frac{1}{\beta.(1+\ \tau)} = \ \theta \ = \ constant \tag{3.2}$$

Both α and θ are exogenously determined constants.

Assumption (v) implies that workers' food-expenditure is spent indirectly on industrial goods. Since workers do not save by assumption (iii), the other part of wage bill is directly spent on industrial goods. Thus, the industrial workers' total wage bill is spent fully (either directly or indirectly via agriculture) on industrial commodities. So, assumptions (iii), (v) and (vi) together lead us to the basic income – expenditure accounting equation as:

Total industry output = (Total industrial wage-bill in terms of industry output) + (Total industrial investment in terms of industry output) + (Total government expenditure on industry in terms of industry output) (4)

So,

$$Y = W + I^0 + \frac{G^0}{P_i} \tag{5}$$

Where, W stands for total wage bill in industry measured in terms of industrial output and I^0 is the real autonomous investment in industry and G^0 is the *nominal* government expenditure (government *budget*) on industrial output. Both I^0 and G^0 are exogenously determined.

Therefore,

$$Y = W + I^0 + \frac{G^0}{P_i} = \frac{w_m}{P_i}.L + I^0 + \frac{P_f}{P_i}.\frac{G^0}{P_f} \tag{6}$$

Substituting from Equations (1), (3.1) and (3.2) in (6) we have:

$$Y = \alpha.Y + I^0 + \theta.\frac{G^0}{P_f} \tag{6.1}$$

And also

$$L = \alpha.L + I^0 + \theta.\frac{G^0}{P_f} \tag{6.2}$$

Solving (6.2), we get,

$$L^* = \frac{\left[I^0 + \theta.\frac{G^0}{P_f}\right]}{(1-\alpha)} \tag{7}$$

Let us assume that, a_f = food demand per industry worker = $f\left(\frac{w_m}{P_i}, \frac{w_m}{P_f}\right)$ with $a_{f1} > 0, a_{f2} > 0$.

Equations (3) and (3.1) imply: $a_f = a_f^{\,0}$ (a positive constant)[3].

Now, going back to distributional rigidity, for the time being:

$$D_f = a_f^{\,0}.L \tag{8}$$

Substituting from Equation (7),

$$D_f = a_f^{\,0}.\frac{\left[I^0 + \theta.\frac{G^0}{P_f}\right]}{(1-\alpha)} \tag{8.1}$$

So, we have an inverse relation between food price and aggregate food demand from industry.

Now let us assume a fixed marketable surplus of food as:

$$F = F^0 \tag{9}$$

Where F stands for aggregate supply of marketable surplus of food to industry
So, food-market equilibrium-condition can be written as:

$$F^0 = D_f = a_f{}^0.\frac{\left[I^0 + \theta.\frac{G^0}{P_f}\right]}{(1-\alpha)} \tag{10}$$

From Equation (10), we can obtain equilibrium food price P_f^* as:

$$P_f^* = \frac{\left(a_f{}^0.\theta.G^0\right)}{\left\{\left(1-\alpha\right).F^0 - \left(a_f{}^0.I^0\right)\right\}} \tag{11}$$

Figure 1 depicts the equilibrium situation analysed above. It is a simple food market equilibrium situation (but, most crucially, balancing the demand as well as supply side constraints/ factors pertaining to industry). Here it is necessary to mention two more points: first, equilibrium food price is set to be directly proportional with nominal government expenditure on industrial output and secondly, P_f^* determines equilibrium industrial money wage (w_m^*) and this w_m^*, in turn, determines the equilibrium price of industrial output (P_i^*). Consequently, the equilibrium size of real domestic exports will be endogenously determined as:

Figure 1. Food Market Equilibrium

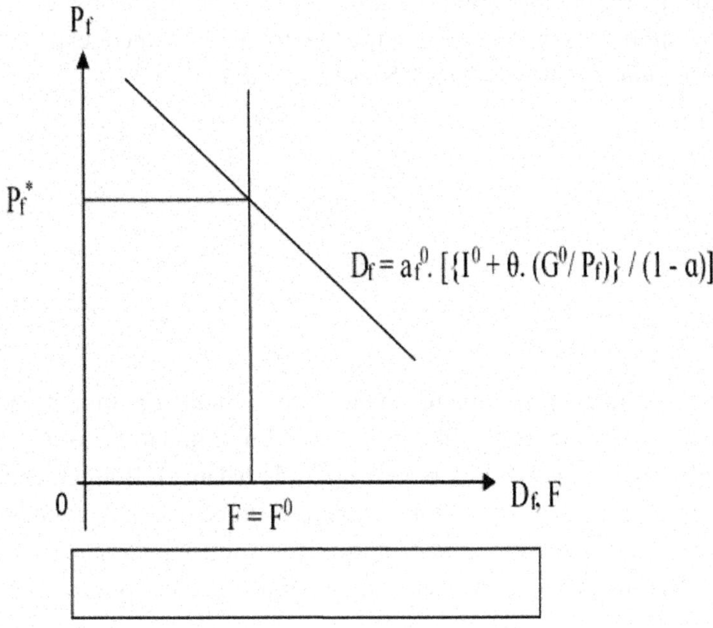

$$g^* = \frac{G^0}{P_f^*} \tag{11a}$$

Where g: real government expenditure on industry measured in terms of industrial output. Crucially, we could easily extend this equilibrium analysis by endogenising investment as well. Thus, the food-market equilibrium condition (Equation 10) changes to:

$$F^0 = D_f = a_f^{\ 0}.\frac{\left\{\theta.\frac{I^0}{P_f}+\theta.\frac{G^0}{P_f}\right\}}{(1-\alpha)}$$

Where I^0 represents autonomous investment in *nominal* terms. P_f* is solved from this equation, which determines $i^* = \frac{I^0}{P_f^*}$.

Suppose in the model economy, government decides to introduce a MGNREGS like project (which is basically 'cash for work' (CFW) programme) as a part of its development management agenda. In such a situation, we argue theoretically that, any ad hoc financing of such a programme may become macro-economically inconsistent. Simple economic logic states that, if total demand for food increases due to a cash transfer under MGNREGS like programme, given the food supply-constraint, food price will increase. This may constrict the industrial/urban employment and output through a reduction in the endogenously determined real domestic exports (as designed above). Thus we have a rural (or periphery) and urban (or core) conflict in terms of employment (given the food-supply constraint).

Given this background, let us assume that total non-agricultural labour force (L) of the country is divided into two parts, first urban labour force (L_u), engaged in modern-industrial production (core sector production) and secondly, rural/peripheral non-farm labour force (L_r) who are targeted to engage in a MGNREGS like programme. Further, let us assume that total government expenditure G is distributed between urban/modern industry and MGNREGS like programme.

$$G = G^0 + G^N \tag{A}$$

And also,

$$L = L_u + L_r \tag{B}$$

Where, G^0 stands for nominal government expenditure on industrial output and G^N are the amount spent by the government on MGNREGS like programme in nominal terms. G^N amount of money is financed through new money printing or by borrowing (idle balance). Both G^0 and G^N are *exogenously* determined. Government's nominal expenditure is assumed to be decided by budget-constraint as well as politically (given the political-economic discourse on government intervention in a market-economy). This is quite a realistic assumption in the sense that, government usually restricts itself from changing its nominal expenditures apprehending public reaction and an enhanced budget deficit. Thus, we assume that our government maintains a rule rather than following a discretionary policy.

Case 1

We assume (although a simplifying assumption) that, rural/peripheral non-farm labour force (engaged through MGNREGS like programme) does not save and spends the entire amount of money received from MGNREGS on food. However, this payment of rural/peripheral non-farm labour force is received by the farmers and they save this extra income entirely as idle balance.

Now, per-capita food-demand of urban/industrial worker (a_f^u) is constant. Therefore, using Equation (10) of section IIIB, aggregate food demand by (urban) industry is,

$$D_f^{\,u} = a_f^{\,u}.L_u = a_f^{\,u}.\frac{\left[I^0 + \theta.\frac{G^0}{P_f}\right]}{(1-\alpha)} \tag{i}$$

Next, per-capita food-demand function of peripheral labour is assumed to be: $a_f^{\,r} = a_f^{\,r}\left(\frac{w}{P_f}\right)$, with $a_f^{\,r\prime} < 0$. Here w is the MGNREGS programme-wage. Hence, aggregate food-demand by peripheral labour force:

$$D_f^{\,r} = a_f^{\,r}\left(\frac{w}{P_f}\right).L_r \tag{ii}$$

Let us suppose that, $w=w_0$ is the legally/policy determined minimum wage. So, we can write:

$$G^N = w_0.L_r \tag{iii}$$

Hence:

$$L_r = \frac{G^N}{w_0} \tag{iv}$$

Here, we have a policy determined peripheral employment as G^N and w_0 both are fixed. It is also assumed that, the administrative and other institutional costs of the MGNREGS like programme are zero (a simplifying assumption).

Now, per-capita food demand of peripheral non-farm labour force is an inverse function of P_f; thus:

$$a_f^{\,r} = a_f^{\,r}\left(\frac{w}{P_f}\right) = a_f^{\,r}\left(P_f\right),\text{ with } a_f^{\,r\prime} < 0 \tag{iva}$$

So, from equation (ii and iv):

$$D_f^{\,r} = a_f^{\,r}\left(P_f\right).L_r = a_f^{\,r}\left(P_f\right).\left(\frac{G^N}{w_0}\right) \quad \text{(v)}$$

Next, clubbing equations (i) and (v) together we can have total demand for food as:

$$(via)\ D_f = a_f^{\,u}.\frac{\left[I^0 + \theta.\frac{G^0}{P_f}\right]}{(1-\alpha)} + a_f^{\,r}\left(P_f\right).\left(\frac{G^N}{w_0}\right) \quad \text{(via)}$$

Assuming (for the time being) a fixed marketable food surplus F^0, food-market equilibrium condition is:

$$F^0 = a_f^{\,u}.\frac{\left[I^0 + \theta.\frac{G^0}{P_f}\right]}{(1-\alpha)} + a_f^{\,r}\left(P_f\right).\left(\frac{G^N}{w_0}\right) \quad \text{(viia)}$$

Further, rearranging equation (viia), we get:

$$G^N* = \frac{\left\{F^0(1-\alpha) - a_f^{\,u}.\frac{\left[I^0 + \theta.\frac{G^0}{P_f}\right]}{(1-\alpha)}\right\}.w_0}{\left\{(1-\alpha).a_f^{\,r}\left(P_f\right)\right\}} \quad \text{(viii)}$$

Equation (viia), in turn, gives us the equilibrium food-price, $P_f{}^{*2}{}_M$ (as in Figure 2).

Equilibrium point E_0 shows the equilibrium situation in absence of MGNREGS. As MGNREGS is introduced, increased food-demand due to MGNREGS -employment, shifts the food-demand curve from D_0D_0 to D_2D_2 and hence, equilibrium food-price also rises from P_f* to $P_f{}^{*2}{}_M$.

Now, this food price hike initiates some crucial macroeconomic effects: First, increased food price brings down real domestic-exports of industry, which in turn decreases industrial employment/output. Thus, a rural-urban employment-conflict or in other words, core-periphery employment-conflict arises. This also indicates at a policy-conflict between domestic exports and MGNREGS. Secondly, as a result of this food-price rise, real wage of the MGNREGS worker $\left(\frac{w_0}{P_f}\right)$ declines (from a targeted real wage set in a pre-MGNREGS situation) and hence, per-capita food-consumption of these workers declines (vis-a-vis the pre-MGNREGS target level). This indicates at another conflict between policy-target and policy-outcome. MGNREGS programme is targeted towards peripheral employment generation and improvement of their standard of living; but effectively, the programme reduces their (per-capita) pur-

Figure 2. Effect of MGNREGS on Food Market

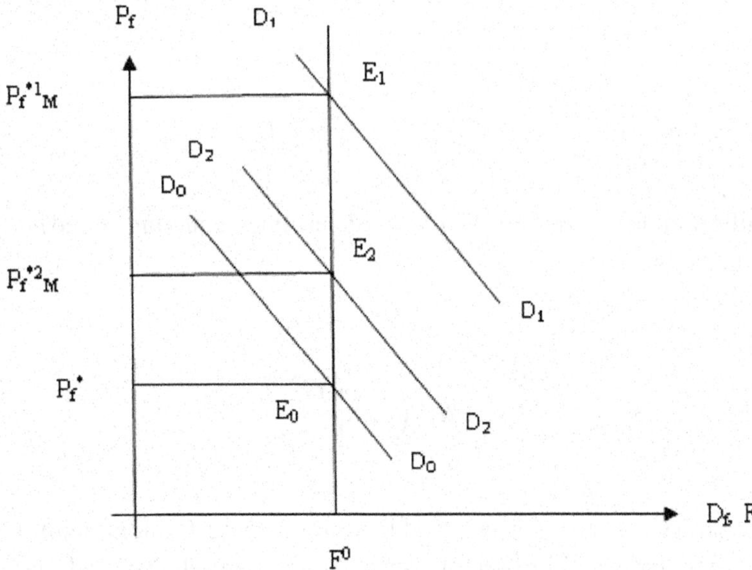

chasing power in terms of food (vis-a-vis an initial target-level). Thirdly, even if urban-employment contracts due to MGNREGS, as a whole, (post-MGNREGS) aggregate employment rises (due to a more than proportionate rise in peripheral/rural employment) having serious political-economic implications/conflicts, given that, usually, $a_f^u > a_f^r$ and $F = F^0$. Food (a part of F^0) diverted to MGNREGS creates peripheral employment, usually, which is more than the volume of employment-reduction in modern-industry, as $a_f^u > a_f^r$. Lastly, given the lower bounds for a_f^r (set biologically as also culturally) and L_u (set through political-economic bargaining), there has to be an upper bound for P_f (as per equations i and iva). Hence, following Equation (viii), G^{N*} has to have a maximum admissible limit; if G^N rises beyond it, the situation/policy becomes unsustainable.

Fundamentally, all these occur because of the basic constraint posed by food-supply. Development management by the government, in fact, intensifies this constraint. Thus, it is a supply-side problem, rather than a demand-driven one; government budget is not the main issue here.

Case 2

This case is almost similar to the earlier one with the only difference that, now the farmers' earnings from MGNREGS -workers are fully spent back on industrial product and hence, industry derives a demand-expansion and MGNREGS expenditure is not a problem for modern-industry – rather, it's a boon. So, the output Equation (6.1) can be rewritten as:

$$Y = \alpha.Y + I^0 + \theta.\frac{G^0}{P_f} + \theta.\frac{G^N}{P_f} \Rightarrow Y^* = \frac{\left(I^0 + \theta.\left(G^0 + G^N\right)\right)\Big/ P_f}{(1-\alpha)}$$

So, modifying equation (via) of case I, the total post-MGNREGS food-demand is:

$$(vib)\, D_f = a_f^{\,u}.\frac{\left(I^0 + \theta.\left(G^0 + G^N\right)\right) \big/ P_f}{(1-\alpha)} + a_f^{\,r}\left(P_f\right).\left(\frac{G^N}{w_0}\right)$$

Once again, equilibrium food-price ($P_{f\ M}^{*1}$) can be determined equating (fixed) food-supply with its demand (Figure 1), i.e. with:

$$(viib)\, F^0 = a_f^{\,u}.\frac{\left(I^0 + \theta.\left(G^0 + G^N\right)\right) \big/ P_f}{(1-\alpha)} + a_f^{\,r}\left(P_f\right).\left(\frac{G^N}{w_0}\right)$$

Comparing equations (viia) and (viib) we find that, in this case-II, along with the food-demand of rural/peripheral workers, industry/core-sector demands more food than before (than case-I). So, $P_{f\ M}^{*1} > P_{f\ M}^{*2} > P_f^{*}$. But, here a question may arise: from where this extra urban food-demand is acquired, as food-supply is still constant. The answer lies in that, with a further rise in food-price ($P_{f\ M}^{*1} > P_{f\ M}^{*2}$) the rural/peripheral workers are forced to consume less food (per-capita) compared to case-I and the industry/core sector absorbs this squeezed out food.

Industrial employment and food-demand are the highest in pre-MGNREGS situation. With MGNREGS, as food-price rises, real domestic exports shrink and hence, industrial employment and food-demand fall drastically (case-I, with farmers saving all of their incomes received by selling food to MGNREGS -workers). Again, when farmers fully spend back their MGNREGS -driven income to industry (case-II), these industrial/urban employment and food-demand components rise partially; however, still these are less than the pre-MGNREGS situation, as the food-supply is still distributed across core and periphery. Further, this partial gain for modern/urban industry, under case-II vis-a-vis case-I, comes at the cost of reduction of per-capita food-consumption of the MGNREGS workers.

Comparing cases I and II, we could address the other crucial issue. A strand of literature argues that, development management siphons off crucial government finance away from modern/urban industry and thereby creates inefficiencies. However, the problem is not so much with government expenditure/finance/demand; rather it is mainly a supply-side issue – as is clear from case-II. Even if, additional expenditure (G^N) is devoted to industry (over and above the pre-MGNREGS amount – G^0), industry contracts vis-a-vis the pre-MGNREGS situation! It is apparently a great paradox: here, government expenditure expansion on industry (via MGNREGS workers and then farmers) is rather reducing urban employment! In fact, the modern-sector contracts, as MGNREGS project siphons off (food) supply away from industry, even if there is an initial demand expansion in nominal terms. This will be clearer from the subsequent analysis. Furthermore, the inflation-effects of this supply-side problem can be neutralized by an adequate increase in food-supply.

Role of Infrastructure: Possible Solution to the Problem

Let us now discuss a (complementary) policy suggestion to handle the food-supply problem mentioned several times in our above analysis. Two major goals of the MGNREGS like programmes are eradication of poverty through cash transfer and also (mostly) rural infrastructure formation. Rural infrastructure formation would transform traditional agriculture and lead to a rise in agricultural productivity/production.

Let us suppose, t is the infrastructure (output) to labour (input) ratio[4] and η is the ratio of marketable surplus of food (output) with respect to infrastructure (input)[5]. Quite reasonably, it can be assumed that government's allotment on CFW programme develops rural/peripheral infrastructure (e.g. in MGNREGP in India or EPWP in South Africa) so that marketable surplus of agricultural product is raised by an amount: $\eta.t.\left(\frac{G^N}{w_0}\right)$. So, post-CFW:

$$F = F^0 + \eta.t.\left(\frac{G^N}{w_0}\right)$$

(G^N/w_0) is the rural/peripheral employment assuming away other (institutional) costs of CFW.

Now, following previous analysis, urban/industrial employment can be written as:

$$L_u = \alpha.L_u + I^0 + \theta.\frac{G^0}{P_f} \Rightarrow L_u^* = \frac{I^0 + \theta.\left(\frac{G^0}{P_f}\right)}{(1-\alpha)}$$

Further, food-demand by industry is:

$$D_f^{\,u} = a_f^{\,u}.L_u = a_f^{\,u}.\frac{I^0 + \theta.\left(\frac{G^0}{P_f}\right)}{(1-\alpha)}$$

This D_f^u varies inversely with P_f.

We assume that the (revised) targets of MGNREGS-programme are to increase peripheral employment and also to keep a_f^r fixed (at the pre-CFW targeted level); this actually requires a MGNREGS-expansion *without any change in* P_f (along with a policy-designed w_0). Further, MGNREGS-finance comes from outside (money-printing or borrowing idle cash). Now, as before, aggregate food demand by rural/peripheral non-farm labour force is:

$$D_f^{\,r} = a_f^{\,r}.L_r = a_f^{\,r}.\left(\frac{G^N}{w_0}\right) = D_f^{\,r0} \text{ [this is a constant]}$$

So, aggregate food-demand is:

$$D_f = a_f{}^u.\frac{I^0 + \theta.\left(\dfrac{G^0}{P_f}\right)}{(1-\alpha)} + a_f{}^r.\left(\frac{G^N}{w_0}\right)$$

In equilibrium, food-price cannot change (as targeted above, so that a_f^r becomes fixed) and hence, the following equality has to be satisfied (always):

$$F^0 + \eta.t.\left(\frac{G^N}{w_0}\right) = a_f{}^u.\frac{I^0 + \theta.\left(\dfrac{G^0}{P_f}\right)}{(1-\alpha)} + a_f{}^r.\left(\frac{G^N}{w_0}\right)$$

Thus, ceteris paribus, the government has to depend only on η and t. Government has to monitor the MGNREGS-programme in such a (comprehensive) way that η and t are adequately adjusted, when MGNREGS-employment changes influencing food-demand. These η and t are technological factors, but also can be improved by rational and far-sited planning along with strict supervision (and also institutional modifications/corrections). On the other hand, if η and t are influenced adequately along with an expansionary MGNREGS-expenditure, P_f could be maintained at the pre-MGNREGS level and hence, modern-industrial employment does not change – this is a crucial outcome. Thus, the periphery-core conflict could be mitigated only if MGNREGS-programme is complemented with adequate policy-design so that food-supply expands appropriately.

The effects of MGNREGS inducing peripheral/rural employment as well as peripheral/rural infrastructure and hence, aggregate food-supply, without any change in industrial output/employment and real income and without any change in per-capita food-consumption for the MGNREGS-worker (vis-a-vis the planned level), could be captured through Figure 2, as below. It shows that, with a rightward shift of the food-demand curve (with the introduction of MGNREGS – as in Figure 1 above), if food-supply curve can also be shifted rightward appropriately (which means we are able to relax the supply constraint adequately via infrastructure development), then the food-price can be stabilized at the pre-MGNREGS level (P_f*) itself. Thereby, peripheral employment expands with unchanging peripheral food-consumption per-capita and unchanging urban/core employment and real-income.

With the introduction of MGNREGS, initially (in the short-run), the food-demand curve shifts up, pushing up the food-price to P_f*/, as, initially $F = F^0$. But, gradually, in the medium-run, the MGNREGS develops infrastructure and thereby relaxes the food-supply-constraint. If food-supply could be relaxed adequately/proportionately (given the specificities of the parameters – η and t, as mentioned above), equilibrium food-price could return to the pre-MGNREGS level. Therefore, if η and t can be set/adjusted suitably (through policy-manoeuvres), then food-price can be stabilized at P_f* or even can be lowered than that (see Figure 3).

We know, from Equation (10), that the pre-MGNREGS equilibrium food-price can be derived from:

Figure 3. Effect of MGNREGS relaxing the Supply Constraint

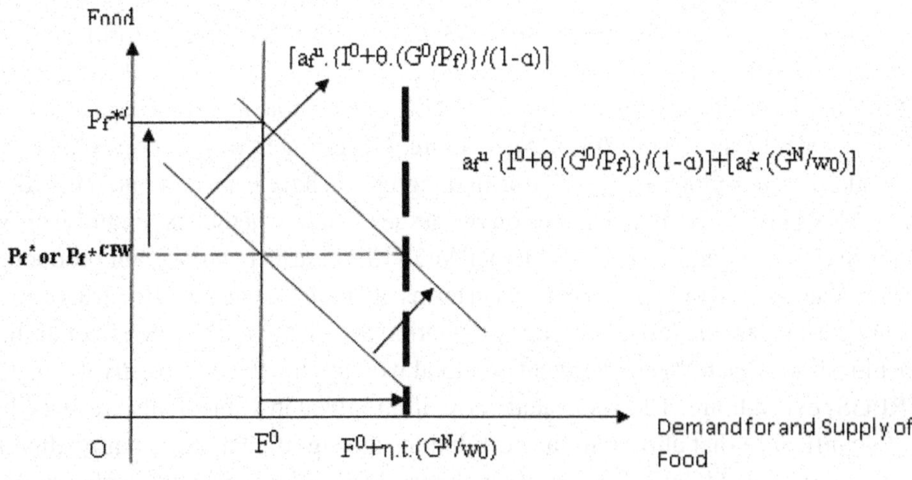

$$F^0 = a_f^{\ u}.\frac{I^0 + \theta.\left(\frac{G^0}{P_f}\right)}{(1-\alpha)}$$

Now, to maintain this pre-MGNREGS food-price, even with CFW-project, the following condition has to be satisfied:

Food-supply increase due to MGNREGS= Food-demand increase due to MGNREGS

Hence, we need to have: $\eta.t.\left(\frac{G^N}{w_0}\right) = a_f^{\ r}.\left(\frac{G^N}{w_0}\right)$

Therefore, the condition for unchanging equilibrium food-price is: $\eta.t. = a_f^{\ r}$. Hence, availability of per-capita food intake by rural non-farm labour-force must be guaranteed by an efficient application of the MGNREGS-programme. If, however, $(\eta.t) >$ or $< a_f^{\ r}$, post-MGNREGS equilibrium food-price $P_f^{*M} <$ or $>$ pre-MGNREGS equilibrium food-price P_f^*.

The merit of this exercise is that, it shows the way of overcoming the problem of supply-constraint discussed in the earlier sections. Furthermore, if food price can be lowered (via an increase in G^N and through appropriate inducements to η and t), then real government expenditure on industry will be raised, given the constant terms of trade between agriculture and industry. So, eventually urban employment may also rise. This is a very striking result, as, here, developmental expenses is inducing an expansion of the modern sectors! Further, η and t both depend upon the efficiency of governance and the performance of the social institutions. Thus, not only the determination of an appropriate level of expenditure in MGNREGS programme is necessary, but also well-monitored governance and a strong build up of social institutions are important.

DESCRIPTIVE STATISTICS ON MGNREGS PERFORMANCE

In this section we attempt some descriptive statistics to judge MGNREGS performance. In this study we consider those variables which have been shown in Table 2. We have used three data sources, viz. (a) Census 2001 and 2011, (b) official data of MGNREGA (available at www.nrega.nic.in) and (c) Agricultural Statistics at a Glance, Ministry of Agriculture, Government of India (available at http://dbie.rbi.org.in). Standard scatter-plots and correlation and regression have been computed in order to analyze performance of MGNREGS. We mainly focus on two issues – first, whether expenditure on MGNREGS really generate employment and secondly, whether MGNREGS affects food-grain production.

Figure 4 shows the MGNREGS performances in terms of employment and infrastructure creation. All the variables are deflated by the respective state population in order to nullify the effect of the size of the state. Scatter-plot shows that both employment and total work completed are positively related with real total (MGNREGS) expenditure. The associated correlation (given in Table 3) also reveals the same fact at 1% level of significance that almost all the correlations are significant. Apparently, this figure along with Table 3 suggests that MGNREGS increases demand for food (log number of persons employed divided by rural population can be treated as a good proxy of food demand) and also relaxes supply constraint by creating infrastructure log of total number of work completed divided by rural population in lakhs (logtotwkcomp_rlpoplac) can be taken for the time being one of the proxies of infrastructure creation through MGNREGS.

Figure 5 shows that log person-days and log total number of works completed are directly related. The result seems to be obvious but keeping in mind one of the main objections against MGNREGS that, it misallocates resources, the result seems to be crucial. Anyway, this figure also suggests that MGNREGS work attempts to relax supply side constraint as suggested by our model by generating rural infrastructure.

Table 4 onwards we put forward a few regression results closely associated with the propositions of our model. In Table 4 we regress log person-days by log real_tot_exp and control the regression by

Figure 4. MGNREGS Performance in terms of Employment and creating infrastructure
Source. Author's calculation with MGNREGA data and census data of 2001 and 2011

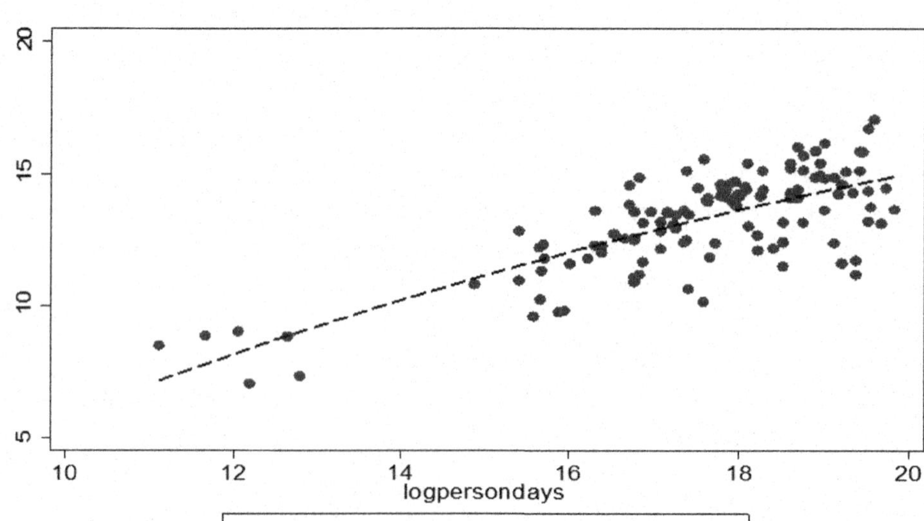

Table 2. List of Variables and their Descriptions

Sl.	Variable	Description	Unit
1	State	Name of states and UTs	-
2	state_code		-
3	year_code	2=2006-07, 3=2007-08 4=2008-09, 5=2009-10	-
		6=2010-11, 7=2011-12	
		8=2012-13, 9=2013-14 10=2014-15	
4	tot_wrk_compl	Total Work Completed	-
5	no_person_empl	No. Of Person Employed	-
6	real_exp_lab	Real Expenditure on Labour	-
7	real_exp_mat	Real Expenditure on Material	-
8	real_tot_exp	Real Total Expenditure	-
9	Persondays	No. Of Persondays Created	-
10	hh_emp	No. Of Household Employed	-
11	foodgrain_prod	State-wise production of Foodgrains	'000 tonnes
Dec-19	logfoodgrain_prod	Logarithmic values of the above variables	-
	loghh_emp		
	logpersondays		
	logreal_tot_exp		
	logreal_exp_mat		
	logreal_exp_lab		
	logno_person_empl		
	logtot_wrk_comlp		
20	twkcom_persnemp	Total Work Completed / No. Of Person Employed	-
21	food_persnemp	State-wise production of Foodgrains / No. Of Person Employed	-
22	logtwkcom_persnemp	logTotal Work Completed / No. Of Person Employed	-
23	logfood_persnemp	logState-wise production of Foodgrains / No. Of Person Employed	-
24	twkcom_persnds	Total Work Completed / No. Of Persondays Created	-
25	food_persnds	State-wise production of Foodgrains / No. Of Persondays Created	-
26	logfood_persnds	logState-wise production of Foodgrains / No. Of Persondays Created	-
27	logtwkcom_persnds	logTotal Work Completed / No. Of Persondays Created	-
28	Statedummy	=1, if major state	-
		=0, otherwise	
29	food_wkcomp	State-wise production of Foodgrains / Total Work Completed	-
30	logfood_wkcomp	log State-wise production of Foodgrains / Total Work Completed	-
31	twrkcom_pop	Total Work Completed / Total Rural Population (State-wise)	-
32	Pop	Total Rural Population (State-wise)	-
33	noperemp_pop	No. Of Person Employed / Total Rural Population (State-wise)	-
34	rlexplab_pop	Real Expenditure on Labour / Total Rural Population (State-wise)	-
35	rlexpmat_pop	Real Expenditure on Material / Total Rural Population (State-wise)	-
36	rltexp_pop	Real Total Expenditure / Total Rural Population (State-wise)	-
37	Rpoplac	Total Rural Population (State-wise) in lacs	-

Table 3. Correlations between logrealexptot_rlpop, logprsnemp_rlpop, logprsnds_rlpop and logtotwkcomp_rlpop at 1% significance of level for Major States (with state dummy = 1)

	logrealexptot_rlpop	logprsnemp_rlpop	logprsnds_rlpop	logtotwkcomp_rlpoplac
logrealexptot_rlpop	1.0000			
logprsnemp_rlpop	0.8934*	1.0000		
logprsnds_rlpop	0.8227*	0.8645*	1.0000	
logtotwkcomp_rlpoplac	0.6079*	0.6984*	0.4070*	1.0000

Source. Author's calculation with MGNREGA data and census data of 2001 and 2011

Table 4. Regression Results

Dependent Variables / Independent Variables	Person-Days Created Under MGNREGS	Values of Robust Standard Errors
Equations No.	**1**	
Constant	**-2.7000**	**1.2502**
Real total Expenditure	**0.5083*****	**0.1435**
Total rural population	**0.6591*****	**0.1902**
F significance value	**0.0000**	
R^2	**0.8006**	
N	**123**	
VIF mean values	**2.16**	

*, ** & *** imply 10%, 5% & 1% levels of significance respectively.
Source. Author's calculation with MGNREGA data and census data of 2001 and 2011

Figure 5. MGNREGS Performance in terms of Work Completion
Source. Author's calculation with MGNREGA data

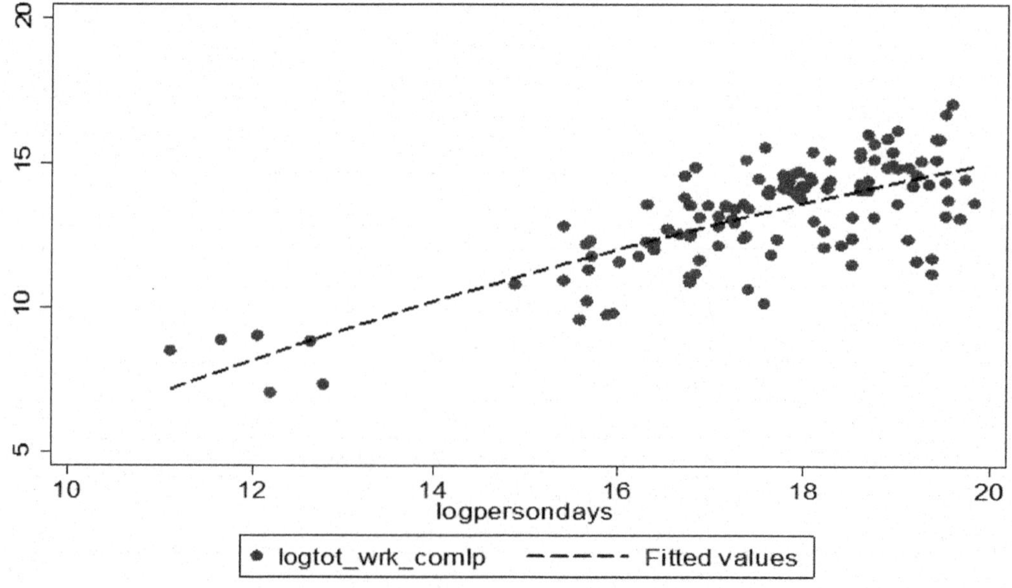

total rural population. Table 3.2 shows that real total expenditure on MGNREGS significantly explains the person-days created through the programme. This shows that, rural non-farm employment has been generated through MGNREGS thus supposed to increase food demand.

So what we have from the above analysis is that MGNREGS programme expenditure is supposed to enhance food demand and along with it the same possibly generates some rural infrastructure. Now let us address the questions that whether the generated infrastructure further increases food supply in order to relax supply constraint or not. To deal with this question we put forward Table 5.

Regression Table 5 shows that, food-grain production is positively associated with total number of works completed but weakly and negatively associated with person-days when controlled by total rural population.

So from the above analysis we may conclude that MGNREGS expenditure definitely enhance rural employment. The government has achieved successes to some extend while playing the role of "employer of the last resort." Moreover, MGNREGS expenditure is supposed to generate some rural infrastructure as well. But the generated infrastructure seems not to be able to enhance food production.

CONCLUSION

This paper explicitly analyses the effects of MGNREGS (as parts of the broader paradigm of 'development management') on the economy using a (medium run) post-Keynesian (Kaleckian) framework. Our theoretical model suggests that:

Table 5. Regression Results

Dependent Variables		
Independent Variables	**Food Grains Production**	**Values of Standard Errors**
Equations No.	**1**	
Constant	**2057.2170**	**1003.1590**
Total works completed under MGNREGS	**0.0002**	**0.0002**
Person-days created under MGNREGS	**0.0000**	**0.0000**
Total rural population	**0.0002*** **	**0.0000**
F significance value	**0.0000**	
Adjusted R^2	**0.6023**	
N	**123**	
VIF mean values	**1.41**	
Hettest		
chi2(1)	**0.05**	
Prob > chi2	**0.8269**	

*, ** & *** imply 10%, 5% & 1% levels of significance respectively.

Source. Author's calculation with MGNREGA data and census data of 2001 and 2011

1. The MGNREGS programme squeezes the volume of the industrial sector of the economy in terms of output and employment with a fixed food-supply. We argue that, this is a supply-side issue and not a problem of government budget constraint as suggested by many researchers. The MGNREGS is argued to redirect crucial (generic) resources away from the industrial sector and thereby prompts its contraction; this also decreases the (per-capita) real-income derived from the MGNREGS by the rural/peripheral labour, vis-a-vis the policy-target. Essentially, government intervention via CFW project only induces a diversion of resources (away from industry) towards the surplus/peripheral labour employed through MGNREGS.
2. However, infrastructure can be generated through MGNREGS (by employing labour in basic-infrastructure building activities), which, in turn, can loosen up the above-mentioned (food/generic) supply-constraint. If food-supply rises, simultaneously, along with MGNREGS, rural/peripheral employment can be created in such a way that industry employment remains unchanged and the economy is not exposed to changing prices; further, the targeted/planned real-income of MGNREGS worker also remains intact.
3. The supply-side constraint can be overcome, through infrastructural expansions and technological and institutional innovations, which can be influenced positively by rational and far-sited planning and institutional modifications along with strict supervision. Our empirical results show that:
    a. With the rise in MGNREGS expenditure, rural non-farm employment has been generated as also some rural non-farm works have been done possibly targeted towards employment generation. So, the arguments of resource misallocation which has been put forward cannot be supported. Along with the increase in MGNREGS employment rural non-farm food demand is supposed to increase.
    b. The problem lies in the fact that works done through MGNREGS or the generated rural infrastructure possibly cannot relax the food supply constraint. This result seems to question the quality of work done through MGNREGS. Somehow it seems that the work done through MGNREGS may not be related with agricultural infrastructure generation. Here comes the question of technology used, importance of proper supervision and governance as also proposed in our theoretical framework.

Therefore, with an increased food demand through MGNREGS and supply side (food) constraint is supposed to generate rural – urban employment conflict.

REFERENCE

Bhaduri, A., & Skarstein, R. (2003). Effective demand and the terms of trade in a dual economy: A Kaldorian perspective. *Cambridge Journal of Economics*, *27*(4), 583–595. doi:10.1093/cje/27.4.583

Chakrabarti, S. (2011). A macroeconomic structure of employment: Rural-urban conflict in a Kaleckian framework. *The Review of Radical Political Economics*, *43*(2), 172–197. doi:10.1177/0486613410391404

Chakrabarti, S. (2014). Agriculture-industry relation and the question of 'home market': Towards closing a centuries old debate. *Indian Journal of Agricultural Economics*, *69*(2), 183–210.

Chakrabarti, S., & Mukherjee, A. (2013). National Rural Employment Guarantee Scheme of India: Some Conceptual Problem. *International Critical Thought*, *3*(1), 1–19. doi:10.1080/21598282.2013.761441

Dev, S. M. (2006). Policies and programmes for employment. *Economic and Political Weekly*, (April): 1511–1516.

Dreze, J. (2004, November 22). Employment as a social responsibility. *The Hindu*. Retrieved from http://www.hindu.com/ 2004/11/22/stories/2004112205071000.htm

Dreze, J., & Sen, A. A. (1989). Hunger and public action. Oxford, UK: Oxford University Press.

Dutt, A. K. (2001). Demand and wage-goods constraints in agriculture-industry interaction in less-developed countries: a theoretical analysis. In A. Bose, D. Ray, & A. Sarkar (Eds.), *Contemporary Macroeconomics*. New Delhi: Oxford University Press.

ESED. (2014). *Success and failure in MGNREGA implementation in India* (Briefing No. 1). Retrieved from www.effective-states.org

Ghose, A. (2011). *Addressing the employment challenge: India's MGNREGA* (Employment Sector Employment Working Paper No. 105). International Labour Office (ILO).

Kaboub, F. (2007). *Employment Guarantee Programs: A Survey of Theories and Policy Experiences*. Working Paper No. 498. Annandale-on-Hudson, NY: The Levy Economics Institute of Bard College.

Kaldor, N. (1976). Inflation and recession in the world economy. *The Economic Journal*, *86*(December), 703–714. doi:10.2307/2231447

Kaldor, N. (1984). The problem of inter sectoral balance. In *Causes of growth and stagnation in the world economy*. Cambridge, UK: Cambridge University Press.

Kalecki, M. (1971). On foreign trade and domestic exports. In *Selected essays on the dynamics of the capitalist economy*. Cambridge, UK: Cambridge University Press. (Original work published 1934)

Kalecki, M. (1993). The problem of financing economic development. In J. Osiatynski (Ed.), *Collected works of Michał Kalecki* (Vol. 5). Oxford, UK: Clarendon Press. (Original work published 1954)

Kostzer, D. (2008). *Argentina: A Case Study on the Plan Jefes y Jefas de Hogar Desocupados, or the Employment Road to Economic Recovery*. The Levy Economics Institute of Bard College, Working Paper No. 534.

Marjit, S., & Maiti, D. S. (2007). Politics and contemporary macro economy of India. In *India macro-economics annual 2006*. Sage.

Minsky, H. P. (1965). The Role of Employment Policy. In M. S. Gordon (Ed.), *Poverty in America*. Chandler.

Mitchell, W. (1998). The Buffer Stock Employment Model and the NAIRU: The Path to Full Employment. *Journal of Economic Issues*, *39*(1), 235–244. doi:10.1080/00213624.2005.11506788

MNREGA Sameeksha-II. (2015). *An Anthology of Research Studies*. UNDP India.

Murgai, R., & Ravallion, M. (2005). Employment guarantee in rural India. *Economic and Political Weekly*, (July): 3, 450–455.

Papadimitriou, D. B. (2008). *Promoting Equality Through an Employment of Last Resort Policy*. Working papers, The Levy Economics Institute, No. 545. Available at www.econstor.eu

Patnaik, P. (2005). On the need for providing employment guarantee. *Economic and Political Weekly*, 203-7. Retrieved from http://www.censusindia.gov.in/Census_Data_2001/Census_Data_Online/CensusDataOnline_Login.aspx

Sanyal, K. (2007). *Rethinking capitalist development: Primitive accumulation, governmentality and post colonial capitalism*. New Delhi: Routledge.

Sanyal, K., & Bhattacharyya, R. (2009). Beyond the Factory: Globalisation, Informalisation of Production and the New Locations of Labour. Economic and Political Weekly, 44(22).

Sjoblom, D., & Farrington, J. (2008). *The Indian national rural employment guarantee act*. Retrieved from http://www.odi.org.uk

Taylor, L. (1983). *Structuralist Macroeconomics*. New York: Basic Books.

KEY TERMS AND DEFINITIONS

Balancing Demand- and Supply-Side Constraint: For growth of the modern sectors along with an expansion of employment via public works programmes, balancing of the macro-economic constraints are essential.

Cash for Work: Surplus labour is engaged in public infrastructure development project against a stipulated wage rate.

Food/Supply-Constraint: Constraint restricting the process of industrialization in a developing economy.

Growth-Employment Conflict: Employment generation via public works programmes may restrict modern industrial growth due to demand and supply side constraints.

Structuralist-Macroeconomics: Branch of macroeconomics that builds a macro-model on the basis of some structural features of the economy under consideration.

Urban/Core vs. Rural/Peripheral Employment-Conflict: If rural/peripheral employment is created via public works programme, it may affect the urban/core/modern-industrial employment through the interaction of demand and supply side factors.

ENDNOTES

1 The basic framework fundamentally derives from Kalecki (1934, 1954), Kaldor (1976, 1984), Taylor (1983), Bose (1989), Dutt (2001), Bhaduri and Skarstein (2003).

2 This basic model is based on Chakrabarti (2011); but, it will be substantially extended.

3 However, in another paper of Chakrabarti and Datta, this assumption has been relaxed with the supposition that, w_m/P_f is not a constant and thereby generate a new function: $a_f = f(P_f)$, with $f' < 0$. This does not alter the results derived here substantially.

4 How much of infrastructure is created with one unit of labour (via CFW-programme)

5 How much of agricultural output, i.e. food is generated from a unit of infrastructure created through CFW.

Chapter 5
Health Infrastructure and Economic Growth in Sub-Saharan Africa

Samuel Adams
Ghana Institute of Management and Public Administration, Ghana

Edem Kwame Mensah Klobodu
Ghana Institute of Management and Public Administration, Ghana

Richmond Odartey Lamptey
Ghana Institute of Management and Public Administration, Ghana

ABSTRACT

In this study, we examine the effect of health infrastructure on economic growth in 30 Sub-Saharan Africa (SSA) countries over the period 1990-2014. Using modern econometric techniques that account for cross-sectional dependence in panel data, we find that health infrastructure (measured by mortality rate) does not have robust impact on economic growth. Gross fixed capital formation, however, is positively associated with economic growth while labor force and polity variables exhibit significant association with economic growth. The results provide sufficient evidence that although capital investment is adequate, the labor force and political environment have not facilitated the health infrastructure in increasing the GDP per capita level in SSA.

INTRODUCTION

For more than three decades, many Sub-Saharan African economies have experienced stunted life expectancy as a result of rampant communicable and parasitical diseases (The Economist Intelligence Unit, 2012). These low life expectancies have further been worsened by the inability of several communities in Africa to provide portable drinking water, good sanitation and inadequate nutrition. Coupled with these problems are the lack of adequate financing for the improvement and expansion of health care infrastructure in the region. According to the International Finance Corporation (IFC) (2007), although

DOI: 10.4018/978-1-5225-2364-2.ch005

Sub-Saharan Africa (SSA) constitutes 11% of the world population, it accounts for 24% of the global disease burden. Further, the report notes that the region commands less than 1% of the global health expenditure creating a huge finance deficit in healthcare infrastructure and delivery. The result is that the region has not been able to achieve the Millennium Development Goals (MDGs) and the Abuja declaration.

Infant mortality rate per 1000 live births in 1960 was very high (160) in SSA compared to Latin America and East Asia which recorded 103 and133 respectively. Adult mortality rates per 1000 persons (male) that same year for SSA (547)was higher than Latin America (304) and a bit lower than East Africa (650).Total life expectancy at birth, in the 60's for SSA was 41 years while East Asia and Latin America stood at 39 years and 56 years respectively. By 2015, infant mortality rate per 1000 live births in SSA stood at 56.3 while Latin America and East Asia reduced drastically to 15.9 and 14.9 respectively. Concerning adult mortality rates per 1000,SSA documented 333 in 2013 while East Asia and Latin America documented 135 and 181 respectively. Turning to total life expectancy at birth, SSA improved to about 58 years in 2013 whereas Latin America and East Asia improved to 74 and 73 years respectively[1].Similarly, health expenditure, hospital beds and physician density have been relatively low in the region compared to other regions (see Appendix 1); Liberia had physician density (i.e. physicians per 1000 population) of 0.01 and South Africa had 0.78 in South Africa whiles advanced economies such as Switzerland and United Kingdom had 4.05 and 2.81 correspondingly. These deteriorating health indicators amidst the region's quest for improved economic conditions makes this study interesting case for empirical examination. Consequently, the World Bank's Global Economic Prospects (2015) report note that economic growth has been fairly constant in the region. The question then is whether the declining health indicators are linked to economic growth. Equally important is the effects of declining health indicators in SSA relative to global indicators on economic growth.

It is worth mentioning that amidst these poor conditions, however, some African countries have made remarkable strides; For example, Ghana, Rwanda and South Africa have established a health coverage system which promises universal health coverage. Nonetheless, life expectancy continues to increase steadily each year in OECD countries. Life expectancy at birth averaged 80.5 years in 2013, an increase of over ten years since 1970 (OECD, 2016). According to the OECD (2016) report OECD nations such as Japan, Spain and Switzerland have life expectancy above 80 years. This is not surprising because there are more than two specialist doctors for every generalist on average across the OECD. Likewise, student enrolment into domestic nursing and medical schools have increased substantially over the past two decades.

Generally, a good health infrastructure is crucial to economic development. Theoretically, a good health infrastructure is known to increase human capital levels as well as economic productivity of individuals in a country. Additionally, a good health infrastructure helps improve education levels by increasing the levels of schooling and scholastic performance. This affects economic growth by raising income levels and also decreasing poverty levels, ceteris paribus. This study measures health infrastructure with the number of infant deaths and the number of deaths under-five. The underlining logic behind the use of these measures is that good health infrastructure equates to low number of infant deaths in the region whereas high number of infant death denote a poor health infrastructure.

Many studies have examined health and economic growth but usually pertaining to developed economies. On the whole it is found that health is positively related to economic growth. For instance, Bloom, Canning, and Sevilla (2004) find that good health has a positive effect on aggregate output after controlling workforce experience. Gong, Li and Wang (2012) conclude that economic growth is related to both the health growth rate and the health level. Further, the authors find that while growth in health capital always facilitates economic growth, the gross effect of health level on the rate of economic growth is contingent on physical capital accumulation. On the contrary, Ashraf, Lester and Weil (2008) demonstrate that the effects of health improvements (measured by life expectancy and prevalence of malaria and tuberculosis) on income per capita are substantially lower than those that are often quoted by policy-makers. In SSA, Gyimah-Brempong and Wilson (2004) find a positive quadratic relationship between growth rate per capita and health human investment capital after controlling for endogeneity bias.

We contribute to the literature by using recently developed panel models that account for heterogeneity in the estimation of the slope coefficient and cross-sectional dependence to investigate the relationship between health infrastructure and economic growth in Sub-Saharan Africa from 1990 to 2014. Specifically, the mean group (MG) estimator of Pesaran and Smith (1995), Pesaran's (2006) Common Correlated Effects Mean Group (CCEMG) estimator and Eberhardt and Teal (2010)'s Augmented Mean group (AMG) estimators are used. Moreover, our model captures the political economy environment of various countries in SSA over the period 1970 to 2015 by measuring their regime type.

LITERATURE REVIEW

The ultimate goal of an effective health infrastructure in every country is improvement in the health status of the population (Organization for Economic Cooperation and Development (OECD), 2015; Bloom and Canning, 2008). Such improvements are measured by various quality care indicators (Kelley & Hurst, 2006). Key determinants of health infrastructure consist of internal and external indicators not limited to physical environment in which people live but also individual lifestyle and behaviours (World Health Organization (WHO), 2012; OECD, 2015).

For the purpose of this theoretical and empirical review of the health infrastructure-growth nexus, we define Infrastructures as "the basic services or social capital of a country, or part of it, which make economic and social activities possible" (Rutherford, 2002). The elements of public health infrastructure that tend to be easiest to recognise and to describe are those concerned with areas such as communicable disease control (including the safety of food), the protection of the health of mothers and children and the control of environmental contamination (Powles & Comim, 2003).

Theoretically, the neoclassical and endogenous growth theories provide a framework for an insight into the health infrastructure-growth nexus. Neoclassical growth theory pioneered by Solow (1956) assumes that output is a function of capital, labour and technical knowledge. Besides, these factors are assumed to be inputs just similar to raw materials for production and therefore not considered very important per the neoclassical growth model. The key assumption of the Solow (1956) model is that technology is free; it is publicly available as a non-excludable, non-rival good. Capital accumulation is deemed as the key determinants of growth per the neoclassical growth theory. However, the shortcomings of this model especially applying to the US economy led to the identification of omitted variables. Subsequently other growth variables were identified other than physical capital resulting in the human capital theory (Shultz, 1959).

In contrast, the endogenous growth model assumes that human capital (e.g. health and education), innovation and knowledge are the key drivers of growth (Romer, 1986; Lucas, 1988). Furthermore, the endogenous growth theory assumes a production function that exhibits non-decreasing returns to scale, i.e., constant or increasing returns, (Romer, 1986). This is because human capital improvement is catalytic to an efficient and effective resource use occasioned by technology, research and development.

Empirically, the growth-enhancing effects of health have been investigated by a number of researchers. For instance, Bloom, Canning and Sevilla (2004), Gyimah-Brempong and Wilson (2004), Jamison, Lau and Wang (2005), and Weil (2007) assert that good health systems improve human welfare as well as labor productivity, and positively affects economic growth in both developing and industrial countries. Additionally, some researches (Zhang, Zhang, & Lee, 2003; Miguel & Kremer, 2004;Soares, 2006; Jayachandran &Lleras-Muney, 2009) have sought to explain that longer life expectancy as a result of improved health conditions increases the propensity to save and become more productive, reflecting growth-enhancing effect. Bloom and Canning (2003) indicates four channels of positive effects of quality healthcare on growth; (1) increased productivity earns higher incomes, (2) spend more time in the labour force, (3) enhanced educational investment that increases their productivity and (4) save more.

Still focusing on the growth-enhancing effect of health infrastructure, Bhargava, Jamison, Lau and Murray (2001) adopted a panel data approach and studied the effects of health indicators, such as adult survival rates on GDP growth rates at 5-year intervals for a number of countries. The authors find that adult survival rates have a positive impact on GDP growth rates in low-income countries. Earlier, Rivera and Currais (1999) used an extended version of the Solow model and a log-linear equation which is estimated using Ordinary Least Square (OLS) for OECD countries over the period 1960-1990. The results support the fact that health has a positive impact on economic growth. Alsan, Bloom, Canning and Jamison, (2006) examine economic growth rates over the period 1960–2000 for countries grouped by initial income and life expectancy. The authors find health to be a significant predictor of economic growth. This particular study confirm earlier studies that the initial levels of population health are a significant predictor of future economic growth (Bloom, Canning, & Sevilla, 2004)

Gyimah-Brempong and Wilson (2004) find that investment in health and the stock of health capital have a positive and significant effect on growth of per capita income. The authors conclude that investment in health increases economic growth in the short run. Furthermore, the investment in health increases the per capita income of individuals in the long run arising from increase in stock of human capital. Interestingly, the findings from Acemoglu and Johnson (2007) suggest that improvement in health conditions reduces per capita income or GDP. The authors premise their argument on growth in population exceeding GDP growth which contrasts Gyimah-Brempong and Wilson (2004).

Another revelation in literature is the role of moderating variables that influence the health-growth nexus. Cooray (2013) using both Ordinary Least Squares (OLS) and Generalized Method of Moments (GMM), examine the differential effects of health on economic growth for a sample of 210 countries using panel data over the period 1990-2008. The author's findings show absence of robust relationship between health capital and economic growth in the long-run unless through an interaction effects of health expenditure and education. Similarly, Tang (2013) examined the relationship between health care spending, economic growth, relative prices and life expectancy in Malaysia for the period 1970 to 2010 using cointegration test proposed by Bayer and Hanck (2013). The author concludes that health care expenditure does not stimulate economic growth directly but through its impact on improved health status as reflected by the life expectancy.

With respect to the growth-decreasing effects of health studies, numerous studies have been conducted indicating the negative impact of poor health systems on growth. For example, UNAIDS (2004), United

Nations (UN) (2005), McDonald and Roberts (2006), and WHO (2007), have documented the negative effects of particular diseases such as malaria, HIV/AIDS and influenza pandemic which is the case especially in low-income countries. Likewise, poor nutrition or malnutrition, inadequate consumption of protein, energy and vitamin, smoking, and drinking, inter-linked to child and adult mortality, may cause poor health, which results in low level of labor productivity and shortens life expectancy, and therefore have an adverse, indirect effect on economic growth (see Strauss & Thomas, 1998; Wang & Taniguchi, 2003; Hoddinott, Alderman, & Behrman, 2005; Jensen & Lleras-Muney, 2012). Arora (2001) also admit that poor health, as seen in high rate of disease prevalence and deaths, is the major cause of poor growth in developing countries. Similar findings from Lorentzen, McMillan and Wacziarg, (2008) provide evidence that high mortality rate reduce the size of the labour force thus negatively affecting economic growth.

In a recent study in Nigeria, Usman, Muktarb and Inuwaa (2015) examined the long run relationship between health outcomes and economic growth in Nigeria for the period 1961 to 2012.Using annual time series data, the authors conducted Augmented Dickey-Fuller (ADF) test to check the stochastic properties of the variables. Also, Johansen Multivariate Cointegration approach and Vector Error Correction Mechanism (VECM) were applied to check the long run and short run dynamics respectively. Additionally, Granger causality test is employed to examine the direction of causality among the variables. The authors find that health outcomes (life expectancy and crude death rate) in the long run negatively and significantly affect economic growth rate.

On the issue of causality, numerous studies conclude that there is a bi-directional causality in the health-growth nexus. However, the verdict from other research works indicates uni-directional causality. Usman, Muktarb and Inuwaa (2015) examining the health outcomes and growth in Nigeria finds the existence of uni-directional causality running from life expectancy and crude death rate to economic growth. Sen, Kaya, and Alpaslan (2015) analysing the possible existence of Granger causality among three variables; education expenditure, health expenditure, and economic growth for the selected eight developing countries over the period 1995-2012 find a uni-directional causality from health expenditure to growth in Indonesia. Tang (2013) also finds a uni-directional causality running from life expectancy to economic growth.

Bloom and Canning (2008) assert the existence of two way causality between the health-growth nexus because health is partly due to income. Preston (1975) demonstrated a positive correlation between national income levels and life expectancy. Therefore, Bloom and Canning (2008) using recent data with the adoption of the "Preston Curve", conclude that higher income levels allow greater access to inputs that improve health, such as food, clean water and sanitation, education, and medical care. The outbreak and negative impact of Ebola clearly depicts the state of health infrastructure in SSA. According to Dalberg (2014),the Ebola outbreak exposed deep vulnerabilities and disparities in the health systems of the hardest-hit West African countries. Earlier, KPMG (2012) notes that Africa is not a healthy continent with the reason that examining all indicators of health, Africa lags behind the rest of the world, and behind poor countries of South-East and South Asia that were behind Africa when measured on these metrics a few decades ago. Widespread and rapacious corruption, health budgets gone missing, infrastructure problems, have made it difficult to provide services to many people in more remote areas (KPMG, 2012). Healthcare delivery infrastructure is insufficient; skilled healthcare workers and crucial medicines are in short supply; and poor procurement and distribution systems are leading to unequal access to treatment resulting in high out-of-pocket burden on individuals (WHO, 2011; The Economic Intelligent Unit (EIU), 2012). In addition to these difficulties, the EIU (2012) notes that public spending on health is insufficient, and international donor funding is becoming uncertain in the current global economic climate. The net effect is that in the absence of public health coverage, the poor have little or no access to care including lack of access to the fundamental prerequisites of health: clean water, sanitation and adequate nutrition. Interestingly, Sub-Saharan Africa makes up 11% of the world's population but accounts for 24% of the global disease burden and regrettably commands less than 1% of global health expenditure (EIU, 2012). In spite of this current state of health infrastructure in SSA, pragmatic efforts made in certain specific areas of intervention will ensure an improvement in the health of the population.

In summary, literature indicates both bi-directional and uni-directional causality in the health-growth nexus. Moreover some studies shows that direct effect of health on growth occur through moderating variables such as education and life expectancy.

OBJECTIVE OF THE CHAPTER

The objective of the present chapter is to examine the effect of health infrastructure on economic growth over the period 1990-2014 for a cross section of 30 Sub-Saharan African (SSA) countries.

DATA AND METHODOLOGY

Due to the ambiguities associated with first generation econometric techniques, we resort to panel heterogeneous techniques in explaining the association between health infrastructure and economic growth. Typically, we rely on the conventional neo-classical one-sector aggregate production framework in demonstrating this association. To obviate the inconsistencies associated with growth theories we adopt a conservative approach by treating capital, labour and health infrastructure as distinct factors of production given as;

$$Y_{it} = f(K_{it}, L_{it}, H_{it}) \tag{1}$$

Where the subscript i and t denote country and time (years) respectively; Y is output or real GDP; K is real gross capital formation as a proxy of capital stock, and H is health infrastructure. Taking the natural log of (1) we obtain:

$$\ln Y_{it} = \beta_i + \beta_{1i} \ln K_{it} + \beta_{2i} \ln L_{it} + \beta_{3i} \ln H_{it} + \varepsilon_{it} \tag{2}$$

β_i and ε_{it} in specification (2) represent country specific effects and random error (which allows the inclusion of other variables) respectively. Augmenting Equation (2) with our political economy variable (to capture moderation effect) we obtain:

$$\ln Y_{it} = \beta_i + \beta_{1i} \ln K_{it} + \beta_{2i} \ln L_{it} + \beta_{3i} \ln H_{it} + \beta_{4i} POL_{it} + \beta_{5i} \ln H_{it} * POL_{it} + \varepsilon_{it} \tag{3}$$

Recent developments in econometrics involve estimating panel models with heterogeneous slopes (with large cross-section and time series component). In this study our panel data is subjected to two main techniques; Pesaran's (2006) Common Correlated Effects Mean Group (CCEMG) estimator and Eberhardt and Teal (2010)'s Augmented Mean group (AMG) estimator.

The CCEMG is known for its ability to model heterogeneity by augmenting group-specific regression equation. This process involves the inclusion of the cross-section averages of dependent and independent variables as a means of accounting for unobserved common factors (see Eberhardt, 2012). Similarly, the AMG method averages the group-specific parameters across panel. However, unobservable common factors in the AMG approach are treated as a common dynamic process. Advantages of the CCEMG include robustness to structural breaks and spill over effects. Both the CCEMG and AMG methods perform well in the presence of cross-sectional dependence and in non stationary panel setting. We employ the MG estimator, which are affected by cross-sectional dependency to enable us to compare our results to previous studies.

The data is sourced from the World Bank's World Development Indicators [WDI] (2016) and Polity IV database over the period 1990 to 2014 for 30 Sub-Saharan African (SSA) countries. To achieve a stationary variance, we take natural logarithms of all variables except the political economy variable which takes on negative values at some instances. Real GDP ($\ln Y_{it}$) and real gross fixed capital formation ($\ln K_{it}$) are in constant US dollars (2005=100). Labor ($\ln L_{it}$) is the total Labor force and Health infrastructure ($\ln H_{it}$) constitute two measures; (1) Mortality rate, infant (per 1,000 live births) and (2) Mortality rate, under-5 (per 1,000). Polity2 (POL_{it}) captures democratic nature of the government (i.e. our political economy variable). Polity2 varies from -10 to 10, with negative scores are associated with autocracy and positive scores indicate democratic government which allows for fair elections and political freedoms for its citizens. The interaction variable ($\ln H_{it} * POL_{it}$) captures the complementary or the substitution effect of polity2. All the variables are from the WDI except Polity2 which was obtained from the PolityIV[2] database. It is worth mentioning that the time period of 1990 to 2014 was chosen due to outburst of democratization in Africa in the 90's (Ndulu & O'Connell, 1999; Hall & Jones, 1999; Rodrik & Wacziarg, 2005). Consequently, the use of panel data results in 750 (30*25) or 715 (attributable to our Polity2 variable which covers the period of 1990 to 2013) observations.

Table 1 presents the average annual growth of each variable for the 30 SSA economies. The differences in the statistics presented reflect the degree of heterogeneity across the countries. The annual average growth rate in GDP (income) per capita ranges from a high of 8.883 (Gabon) to a low of 5.123 (Liberia), with a sample average of 6.609.South Africa documents the highest share in capital (24.355) while Gambia has the lowest (18.752). Concerning Labor, Nigeria has the highest (17.521) while Equatorial Guinea has the lowest (12.570). The mean of mortality rate, infant (per 1,000 live births) ranges from a high of 4.871 (Sierra Leone) to a low of 2.750 (Mauritius). Equally, Sierra Leone experiences the highest mortality rate, under-5 per 1,000 (5.337) and Mauritius the lowest (2.882). There was wide variation in the mean of polity2 variable, precisely the mean (0.523) ranges from a high of 10 (Mauritius) to a low of -9.125 (Swaziland). In other words, Mauritius is more democratic than Swaziland over the period of 1990 to 2013.

Table 1. Average annual growth rates

Country	lnY	lnK	lnL	lnH	lnH2	POL
Benin	6.347	20.673	14.904	4.435	4.909	6.083
Botswana	8.522	21.522	13.632	3.815	4.165	7.708
Burkina Faso	5.915	20.598	15.518	4.463	5.062	-2.167
Cameroon	6.797	21.677	15.665	4.381	4.856	-4.333
Congo, DR	5.551	21.027	16.803	4.606	4.984	1.333
Congo, Rep	7.463	20.949	14.075	4.064	4.482	-2.542
Equatorial Guinea	8.332	21.220	12.570	4.580	4.944	-5.250
Eritrea	5.535	18.997	14.379	4.006	4.412	-6.619
Gabon	8.883	21.486	13.052	3.931	4.345	-2.625
Gambia	6.063	18.752	13.214	4.114	4.699	-3.042
Kenya	6.299	21.916	16.337	4.035	4.473	1.958
Lesotho	6.536	19.998	13.575	4.366	4.657	5.292
Liberia	5.123	18.908	13.820	4.643	5.007	2.375
Madagascar	5.639	20.672	15.900	4.120	4.544	5.625
Malawi	5.409	20.618	15.457	4.445	4.942	3.333
Mali	5.983	20.446	15.061	4.643	5.232	5.542
Mauritania	6.556	19.910	13.637	4.303	4.679	-4.583
Mauritius	8.455	20.981	13.170	2.750	2.882	10.000
Mozambique	5.727	20.698	15.999	4.628	5.015	3.083
Namibia	8.133	20.998	13.405	3.790	4.187	6.000
Nigeria	6.555	22.905	17.521	4.623	5.121	0.500
Rwanda	5.613	19.650	15.196	4.333	4.822	-4.667
Senegal	6.584	21.277	15.289	4.081	4.624	3.958
Sierra Leone	5.812	18.815	14.348	4.871	5.337	1.625
South Africa	8.568	24.355	16.584	3.843	4.147	8.500
Sudan	6.443	21.937	15.974	4.156	4.591	-5.727
Swaziland	7.719	19.758	12.738	4.221	4.607	-9.125
Tanzania	6.022	22.035	16.686	4.195	4.647	-1.917
Togo	5.977	19.597	14.636	4.270	4.722	-2.792
Uganda	5.699	21.227	16.161	4.301	4.774	-3.250
Full Sample	6.609	20.787	14.844	4.234	4.662	0.523

Correlations are presented in Table 2. The highest correlation in the sample is between the health indicators (mortality rates) (0.985). This informs us to use health indicators in separate regression equations to avoid multicollinearity, which usually inflates t-statistics giving rise to biased estimates. Health indicators, however, were negatively correlated with GDP per capita (-0.561 and -0.576). This indicates a possible negative association between health indicators and income per capita.

Table 2. Correlation Matrix

	lnY	lnK	lnL	lnH	lnH2	POL
lnY	1.000					
lnK	0.487	1.000				
lnL	-0.425	0.515	1.000			
lnH	-0.561	-0.333	0.185	1.000		
lnH2	-0.576	-0.336	0.206	0.985	1.000	
POL	0.166	0.286	0.131	-0.316	-0.332	1.000

Further, we investigate the time series properties of our variables by subjecting them to Pesaran's (2004) cross-sectional dependence test (CD test) and unit root test (Cross-sectional IPS test) that accounts for cross-sectional correlation. As can be seen from Table 3, CD test rejects the null hypothesis of no cross-sectional correlation in all the variables. Additionally, CIPS test demonstrates that only two variables ($\ln Y_{it}$, $\ln K_{it}$) are stationary at first difference and the rest are stationary at levels.

Our MG, CCEMG and AMG specifications (models) are presented in Tables 4, 5 and 6 respectively. Each model is distinguished by health indicators, polity2 and interaction variable. For instance, MG [1] represents the base model without mortality rate, infant (per 1,000 live births), MG [2] represent base model (i.e. Equation 1 with mortality rate, infant (per 1,000 live births) and MG [3] includes interaction variable (i.e. between mortality rate, infant (per 1,000 live births) and polity2). Afterwards, we replicate the order of specifications MG [1], MG [2] and MG [3] for MG [4], MG [5] and MG [6] using mortality rate, under-5 (per 1,000) as health indicator. The same applies to CCEMG and AMG models.

The estimated coefficients of capital ($\ln K_{it}$) range between 0.07 and 0.09. They are statistically significant at the specified levels (1%, 5% and 10%). Second, labor($\ln L_{it}$) exhibit negative elasticities but are not significant throughout the regression specifications (Table 4). Coefficients of health infrastructure provide mixed results. All but one specification are negative. Three out of the six MG specifications have negative coefficients statistically significant at 1% (see MG [2], MG[3] and MG[5]). Polity coefficients and interaction variables are mixed throughout all the regressions. Afterwards, we test the residuals for cross-sectional dependence using the Pesaran (2004) CD test. Results from CD test indicate that MG specifications are plunged with cross-sectional dependence. On the contrary, Wald test indicate a good model fit.

Table 3. Cross-sectional dependence and unit root test

Variables	lnY	lnK	lnL	lnH	lnH2	POL
Pesaran CD test	50.152	58.193	101.768	87.161	83.605	20.487
p-value	0.000	0.000	0.000	0.000	0.000	0.000
CIPS (Accounts for Cross-Sectional Dependence)						
Level	-1.862	-1.934	-1.711	-1.412	-1.328	-1.661
1st Difference	2.954***	-2.635*	-2.112	-1.926	-1.551	-2.013

Note: ***, **,* denote significance at 1%, 5% and 10% respectively

Table 4. Mean group (MG) Heterogeneous estimates

Dep: lnY	MG[1]	MG[2]	MG[3]	MG[4]	MG[5]	MG[6]
lnK	0.080***	0.076***	0.073***	0.083***	0.080***	0.073***
	(0.027)	(0.025)	(0.024)	(0.026)	(0.025)	(0.023)
lnL	-0.559	-0.581	-0.507	-0.569*	-0.465	-0.881
	(0.444)	(0.455)	(0.456)	(0.328)	(0.291)	(0.451)
lnH	-0.512	-0.478***	-0.221			
	(0.177)	(0.183)	(0.372)			
lnH2				-0.222**	-0.208***	-0.006
				(0.102)	(0.102)	(0.298)
POL		0.001	0.176*		0.001	0.193**
		(0.011)	(0.099)		(0.014)	(0.098)
lnH*POL			-0.017			
			(0.022)			
lnH2*POL						-0.041*
						(0.022)
_cons	15.540**	15.582***	12.586**	14.740***	15.186***	15.843***
	(6.676)	(5.640)	(5.202)	(4.784)	(4.174)	(5.055)
RMSE	0.040	0.038	0.036	0.041	0.039	0.037
Obs	750	715	715	750	715	715
Wald Test	19.08***	19.04***	16.44***	17.71**	17.49***	20.22***
CD Test	6.156***	4.208***	2.433**	6.089***	3.860***	2.196**

***, **,* denote significance at 1%, 5% and 10% respectively

As a result of issues related to specifications in Table 4, we implement CCEMG and AMG (see Tables 5 and 6) which perform well under cross-sectional dependence. Results from Table 5 and 6, confirm that capital is an important determinant of economic growth. The coefficients are statistically significant at 1% and range between 0.05 and 0.07 (See Table 5).

Similarly, the AMG specification indicates the capital coefficients are significant at specified levels and range between 0.07 and 0.08 (See Table 6). Labor, Health infrastructure, polity and interaction variable are not robust in all both CCEMG and AMG specifications. Pesaran (2004) CD test indicate absence of cross-sectional dependence with RMSE (root mean square error) values lower than MG specifications in both CCEMG and AMG specifications. Accordingly, the lower the RMSE value the better the model. Thus, CCEMG and AMG models are preferred. Overall, our results add to the literature that emphasize the importance of health or health infrastructure on economic growth (Gyimah-Brempong & Wilson, 2004; Cooray, 2013; Rivera & Currais, 1999; Jamison, Lau, & Wang; Weil, 2007) and further, corrects problems associated with heterogeneity in previous panel studies.

Table 5. Common Correlated Effects Mean Group (CCEMG) Heterogeneous estimates

Dep: lnY	CCEMG[1]	CCEMG[2]	CCEMG[3]	CCEMG[4]	CCEMG[5]	CCEMG[6]
lnK	0.065***	0.053**	0.051**	0.061***	0.058**	0.064***
	(0.021)	(0.025)	(0.023)	(0.022)	(0.023)	(0.022)
lnL	-0.105	0.504	1.083	-0.321	0.428	0.638
	(0.865)	(0.739)	(1.211)	(0.798)	(0.583)	(0.978)
lnH	0.299	-0.014	4.096			
	(1.064)	(0.894)	(3.893)			
lnH2				0.100	-0.074	2.795
				(0.712)	(0.437)	(2.607)
POL		0.005	-2.578		0.004	-2.163
		(0.006)	(2.640)		(0.005)	(2.028)
lnH*POL			0.530			
			(0.552)			
lnH2*POL						0.414
						(0.392)
_cons	-4.932	-4.293	-29.828	-2.316	-3.314	-24.580
	(19.825)	(16.095)	(37.075)	(16.856)	(12.053)	(28.981)
RMSE	0.030	0.028	0.024	0.029	0.028	0.025
Obs	750	715	715	750	715	715
Wald Test	10.32*	8.04*	10.56*	8.57**	11.55**	12.46**
CD Test	0.238	-0.671	-1.003	0.914	-0.441	-0.500

***, **,* denote significance at 1%, 5% and 10% respectively

CONCLUSION

We examine the effect of health infrastructure on economic growth in Sub-Saharan Africa (SSA). Using modern econometric techniques that account for cross-sectional dependence in our panel data, we find that health infrastructure (measured by mortality rate) does not have robust impact on economic growth. Gross fixed capital formation (gfcf), however, is positively associated with economic growth while labor force and polity variables exhibit insignificant association with economic growth. The results provide sufficient evidence that although capital investment is adequate, the labor force and political environment have not facilitated the health infrastructure in increasing the GDP per capita level in SSA.

The main implication of our results is that although investment in physical infrastructure is good, it is not sufficient for a transformation of health care system in SSA. Nonetheless, a complete health infrastructure must include infrastructure for sanitation, potable water, transportation, communication, education, and energy (i.e. all of which are important ingredients in providing and accessing quality

Table 6. Augmented Mean Group (AMG) Heterogeneous estimates

Dep: lnY	AMG[1]	AMG[2]	AMG[3]	AMG[4]	AMG[5]	AMG[6]
lnK	0.081***	0.076***	0.076***	0.076***	0.073*	0.070*
	(0.021)	(0.021)	(0.020)	(0.021)	(0.021)	(0.020)
lnL	0.142	0.053	-0.133	-0.088	-0.140	-0.116
	(0.836)	(0.770)	(0.864)	(0.840)	(0.748)	(0.812)
lnH	0.443	0.417	1.851			
	(1.201)	(1.089)	(1.797)			
lnH2				-0.357	0.351	1.277
				(0.955)	(0.842)	(1.351)
POL		0.001	-0.861		0.001	-0.811
		(0.003)	(0.840)		(0.003)	(0.665
lnH*POL			0.172			
			(0.179)			
lnH2*POL						0.155
						(0.130
_cons	2.092	3.598	0.346	5.452	6.338	2.167
	(15.51)	(14.050)	(18.405)	(14.703)	(12.977)	(16.018)
RMSE	0.035	0.032	0.029	0.035	0.032	0.029
Obs	750	715	715	750	715	715
Wald Test	14.75**	12.92**	20.88***	13.35**	12.60**	18.76***
CD Test	-0.621	-0.946	-1.749	-0.875	-1.161	-1.717

***, **,* denote significance at 1%, 5% and 10% respectively

health care). Consequently, a horizontal health transformation is now imperative for countries in SSA, as Bloom (2014) points out that the capacity and reach of health systems must also be expanded. In addition to the accessibility of health care delivery, new models for conducting epidemiological surveillance and for the efficient deployment of physicians, nurses, pharmacologists, community health workers, and counsellors must be developed.

REFERENCES

Acemoglu, D., & Johnson, S. (2007). Disease and Development: The Effect of Life Expectancy on Economic Growth. *Journal of Political Economy*, *115*(6), 699–749. doi:10.1086/529000

Alsan, M., Bloom, D. E., Canning, D., & Jamison, D. (2006). The consequences of population health for economic performance. In S. Mills, L. Gibson & A. Mills (Eds.), Health, Economic Development and Household Poverty (pp. 21–39). Oxford, UK: Routledge.

Arora, S. (2001). Health, human productivity, and long-term economic growth. *The Journal of Economic History*, *61*(03), 699–749.

Ashraf, Q. H., Lester, A., & Weil, D. N. (2008). *When does improving health raise GDP?* (NBER Working Paper No. 14449). Cambridge, MA: National Bureau of Economic Research.

Bayer, C., & Hanck, C. (2013). Combining non-cointegration tests. *Journal of Time Series Analysis, 34*(1), 83–95. doi:10.1111/j.1467-9892.2012.00814.x

Bhargava, A., Jamison, D. T., Lau, L. J., & Murray, C. J. (2001). Modeling the effects of health on economic growth. *Journal of Health Economics, 20*(3), 423–440. doi:10.1016/S0167-6296(01)00073-X PMID:11373839

Bloom, D. E. (2014). *The world has come a long way, but still has a long way to go*. Retrieved from http://www.imf.org/external/pubs/ft/fandd/2014/12/bloom.htm

Bloom, D. E., & Canning, D. (2008). Population Health and Economic Growth. In M. Spence & M. A. Lewis (Eds.), Health and Growth (pp. 53-75). Washington, DC: World Bank.

Bloom, D. E., Canning, D., & Graham, B. (2003). Longevity and life-cycle savings. *The Scandinavian Journal of Economics, 105*(3), 319–338. doi:10.1111/1467-9442.t01-1-00001

Bloom, D. E., Canning, D., & Sevilla, J. (2004). The effect of health on economic growth: A production function approach. *World Development, 32*(1), 1–13. doi:10.1016/j.worlddev.2003.07.002

Cooray, A. (2013). Does health capital have differential effects on economic growth? *Applied Economics Letters, 20*(3), 244–249. doi:10.1080/13504851.2012.690844

Dalberg Group. (2015). *From Response to Recovery in the Ebola Crisis. Revitalizing Health Systems And Economies, Ebola Report*. Retrieved fromhttp://www.dalberg.com/wp-content/uploads/2015/04/Dalberg_Ebola_Report.pdf

Eberhardt, M., & Teal, F. (2010). *Productivity analysis in global manufacturing production* (Discussion Paper Number 515). Oxford, UK: University of Oxford, Department of Economics.

Gong, L., Li, H., & Wang, D. (2012). Health investment, physical capital accumulation, and economic growth. *China Economic Review, 23*(4), 1104–1119. doi:10.1016/j.chieco.2012.07.002

Gyimah-Brempong, K., & Wilson, M. (2004). Health human capital and economic growth in Sub-Saharan African and OECD countries. *The Quarterly Review of Economics and Finance, 44*(2), 296–320. doi:10.1016/j.qref.2003.07.002

Hall, R. E., & Jones, C. I. (1999). Why Do Some Countries Produce So Much More Output per Worker than Others. *The Quarterly Journal of Economics, 114*(1), 83–116. doi:10.1162/003355399555954

Hoddinott, J., Alderman, H., & Behrman, J. (2005). Nutrition, Malnutrition and Economic Growth. In G. López-Casasnovas, B. Rivera, & L. Currais (Eds.), *Health and Economic Growth: Findings and Policy Implications* (pp. 164–194). Cambridge, MA: MIT Press.

International Finance Corporation (IFC). (2007). *The Business of Health in Africa; Partnering with the Private Sector to Improve People's Lives*. Washington, DC: IFC.

Jamison, D. T., Lau, L. J., & Wang, J. (2005). Health's Contribution to Economic Growth in an Environment of Partially Endogenous Technical Progress. In G. López-Casasnovas, B. Rivera, & L. Currais (Eds.), *Health and Economic Growth: Findings and Policy Implications* (pp. 67–91). Cambridge, MA: MIT Press.

Lleras-Muney, A., & Jayachandran, S. (2009). Longevity and human capital investments: Evidence from maternal mortality declines in Sri Lanka. *The Quarterly Journal of Economics*, *124*(1), 349–397.

Jensen, R., & Lleras-Muney, A. (2012). Does staying in school (and not working) prevent teen smoking and drinking? *Journal of Health Economics*, *31*(4), 644–657.

Kelley, E., & Hurst, J. (2006). *Health care quality indicators project. Conceptual framework paper* (OECD Health Working Papers No. 23). Paris: Organisation for Economic Co-operation and Development.

KPMG. (2012). *The State of Health Care in Africa*. Retrieved from https://www.kpmg.com/Africa/en/IssuesAndInsights/Articles-Publications/Documents/The-State-of-Healthcare-in-Africa.pdf

Lorentzen, P., McMillan, J., & Wacziarg, R. (2008). Death and development. *Journal of Economic Growth*, *13*(2), 81–124. doi:10.1007/s10887-008-9029-3

Lucas, R. E. Jr. (1988). On the mechanics of economic development. *Journal of Monetary Economics*, *22*(1), 3–42. doi:10.1016/0304-3932(88)90168-7

McDonald, S., & Roberts, J. (2006). AIDS and economic growth: A human capital approach. *Journal of Development Economics*, *80*(1), 228–250. doi:10.1016/j.jdeveco.2005.01.004

Miguel, E., & Kremer, M. (2004). Worms: Identifying impacts on education and health in the presence of treatment externalities. *Econometrica*, *72*(1), 159–217. doi:10.1111/j.1468-0262.2004.00481.x

Ndulu, B. J., & OConnell, S. A. (1999). Governance and growth in sub-Saharan Africa. *The Journal of Economic Perspectives*, *13*(3), 41–66. doi:10.1257/jep.13.3.41

Organisation for Economic Co-operation and Development (OECD). (2015). *Health at a Glance 2015: OECD Indicators*. Paris: OECD Publishing.

Pesaran, M. H. (2004). *General Diagnostic Tests for Cross Section Dependence in Panels* (IZA Discussion Paper No. 1240). Bonn: IZA.

Pesaran, M. H. (2006). Estimation and inference in large heterogeneous panels with a multifactor error structure. *Econometrica*, *74*(4), 967–1012. doi:10.1111/j.1468-0262.2006.00692.x

Pesaran, M. H., & Smith, R. (1995). Estimating long-run relationships from dynamic heterogeneous panels. *Journal of Econometrics*, *68*(1), 79–113. doi:10.1016/0304-4076(94)01644-F

Powles, J., & Comim, F. (2003). Public health infrastructure and knowledge. *Global public health goods for health: Health economics and public health perspectives*, 159-176.

Preston, S. H. (1975). The changing relation between mortality and level of economic development. *Population Studies*, *29*(2), 231–248. doi:10.1080/00324728.1975.10410201 PMID:11630494

Rivera, I. V. B. IV, & Currais, L. (1999). Economic growth and health: Direct impact or reverse causation? *Applied Economics Letters*, *6*(11), 761–764. doi:10.1080/135048599352367

Rodrik, D., & Wacziarg, R. (2005). Do democratic transitions produce bad economic outcomes? *The American Economic Review*, *95*(2), 50–55. doi:10.1257/000282805774670059

Romer, P. M. (1986). Increasing returns and long-run growth. *Journal of Political Economy*, *94*(5), 1002–1037. doi:10.1086/261420

Rutherford, D. (2002). *Routledge Dictionary of Economics*. London: Routledge. doi:10.4324/9780203000540

Schultz, T. W. (1959). Investment in man: An economists view. *The Social Service Review*, *33*(2), 109–117. doi:10.1086/640656

Şen, H., Kaya, A., & Alpaslan, B. (2015). *Education, Health, and Economic Growth Nexus: A Bootstrap Panel Granger Causality Analysis for Developing Countries* (The University of Manchester, Discussion Paper Series EDP-1502). Manchester, UK: The University of Manchester.

Soares, R. R. (2006). The effect of longevity on schooling and fertility: Evidence from the Brazilian Demographic and Health Survey. *Journal of Population Economics*, *19*(1), 71–97. doi:10.1007/s00148-005-0018-y

Solow, R. M. (1956). A contribution to the theory of economic growth. *The Quarterly Journal of Economics*, *70*(1), 65–94. doi:10.2307/1884513

Strauss, J., & Thomas, D. (1998). Health, nutrition, and economic development. *Journal of Economic Literature*, *36*(2), 766–817.

Tang, C. F. (2013). A Note on the Health-Growth Nexus in Malaysia. *Journal of Health Management*, *15*(3), 345–352. doi:10.1177/0972063413491872

The Economist Intelligence Unit (EIU). (2012). *The future of healthcare in Africa*. Switzerland: EIU.

UNAIDS. (2004). *Report on the Global AIDS Epidemic*. Geneva: UNAIDS.

United Nations (UN). (2005). The Millennium Development Goals Report 2005. New York: United Nations.

Usman, H. M., Muktarb, M., & Inuwaa, N. (2015). Health Outcomes and Economic Growth Nexus: Testing for Long Run Relationship and Causal Links in Nigeria. *International Journal of Economics and Empirical Research*, *3*(4), 176–183.

Wang, X., & Taniguchi, K. (2003). *Does better nutrition enhance economic growth? The economic cost of hunger.* Retrieved from http://www.fao.org/3/a-y4850e/y4850e04.htm

Weil, D. N. (2007). Accounting for the Effect of Health on Economic Growth. *The Quarterly Journal of Economics*, *122*(3), 1265–1305. doi:10.1162/qjec.122.3.1265

World Bank. (2015). *Global Economic Prospects*. Washington, DC: World Bank.

World Bank. (2016). *World Development Indicators 2016*. Washington, DC: World Bank.

World Health Organization. (2007). *World Health Statistics 2007*. Geneva: World Health Organization.

Zhang, J., Zhang, J., & Lee, R. (2003). Rising longevity, education, savings, and growth. *Journal of Development Economics*, *70*(1), 83–101. doi:10.1016/S0304-3878(02)00088-3

KEY TERMS AND DEFINITIONS

Cross-Sectional Dependence: Occurs when errors are of cross-sections are correlated in a panel data due to due to omitted common effects or spatial effects.

Economic Growth: It is an increase in a country's productive capacity or output.

Gross Fixed Capital Formation: according to the World Bank, gross fixed capital formation includes land improvements, plant, machinery, and equipment purchases; and the construction of roads, railways.

Health Infrastructure: The basic services or social capital or structures of a country concerned with areas such as communicable disease control (including the safety of food), the protection of the health of mothers and children and the control of environmental contamination.

Heterogeneity: It refers to differences across cross-sections (countries) being studied.

Infant Mortality Rate: Infant mortality rate is the number of infants dying before reaching one year of age, per 1,000 live births in a given year or the probability per 1,000 that a new-born baby will die before reaching age five, if subject to age-specific mortality rates of the specified year according to the World Bank.

Panel Data: It is a dataset with time and cross-sectional component.

ENDNOTES

1 Statistics are obtained from the World Bank (2016).

2 Available at: http://www.systemicpeace.org/inscrdata.html

3 https://www.cia.gov/library/publications/resources/the-world-factbook/fields/2225.html#103

4 https://www.cia.gov/library/publications/the-world-factbook/fields/2227.html

5 https://www.cia.gov/library/publications/the-world-factbook/fields/2226.html

APPENDIX

Table 7.

Country	Health Expenditures (% of GDP)[3]	Hospital Bed Density (Beds/1,000 Population)[4]	Physicians Density (Physicians/1,000 Population)[5]
Benin	4.6% of GDP (2014)	0.5 beds/1,000 population (2010)	0.06 physicians/1,000 population (2008)
Botswana	5.4% of GDP (2014)	1.8 beds/1,000 population (2010)	0.4 physicians/1,000 population (2009)
Burkina Faso	5% of GDP (2014)	0.4 beds/1,000 population (2010)	0.05 physicians/1,000 population (2010)
Cameroon	4.1% of GDP (2014)	1.3 beds/1,000 population (2010)	0.08 physicians/1,000 population (2009)
Congo, DR	4.3% of GDP (2014)	0.8 beds/1,000 population (2006)	-
Congo, Rep	5.2% of GDP (2014)	-	0.1 physicians/1,000 population (2007)
Cote D'Ivoire	5.7% of GDP (2014)	0.4 beds/1,000 population (2006)	0.14 physicians/1,000 population (2008)
Equatorial Guinea	3.8% of GDP (2014)	2.1 beds/1,000 population (2010)	-
Eritrea	3.3% of GDP (2014)	0.7 beds/1,000 population (2011)	-
Gabon	3.4% of GDP (2014)	6.3 beds/1,000 population (2010)	-
Gambia	7.3% of GDP (2014)	1.1 beds/1,000 population (2011)	0.11 physicians/1,000 population (2008)
Ghana	3.6% of GDP (2014)	0.9 beds/1,000 population (2011)	0.1 physicians/1,000 population (2010)
Kenya	5.7% of GDP (2014)	1.4 beds/1,000 population (2010)	0.2 physicians/1,000 population (2013)
Lesotho	10.6% of GDP (2014)	1.3 beds/1,000 population (2006)	-
Liberia	10% of GDP (2014)	0.8 beds/1,000 population (2010)	0.01 physicians/1,000 population (2008)
Madagascar	3% of GDP (2014)	0.2 beds/1,000 population (2010)	0.16 physicians/1,000 population (2007)
Malawi	11.4% of GDP (2014)	1.3 beds/1,000 population (2011)	0.02 physicians/1,000 population (2009)
Mali	6.9% of GDP (2014)	0.1 beds/1,000 population (2010)	0.08 physicians/1,000 population (2010)
Mauritania	3.8% of GDP (2014)	0.4 beds/1,000 population (2006)	0.13 physicians/1,000 population (2009)
Mauritius	4.8% of GDP (2014)	3.4 beds/1,000 population (2011)	1.62 physicians/1,000 population (2013)
Mozambique	7% of GDP (2014)	0.7 beds/1,000 population (2011)	0.04 physicians/1,000 population (2012)
Namibia	8.9% of GDP (2014)	2.7 beds/1,000 population (2009)	0.37 physicians/1,000 population (2007)
Nigeria	3.7% of GDP (2014)	-	0.41 physicians/1,000 population (2009)
Rwanda	7.5% of GDP (2014)	1.6 beds/1,000 population (2007)	0.06 physicians/1,000 population (2010)
Senegal	4.7% of GDP (2014)	0.3 beds/1,000 population (2008)	0.06 physicians/1,000 population (2008)
Sierra Leone	11.1% of GDP (2014)	0.4 beds/1,000 population (2006)	0.02 physicians/1,000 population (2010)
South Africa	8.8% of GDP (2014)	-	0.78 physicians/1,000 population (2013)
Sudan	8.4% of GDP (2014)	0.8 beds/1,000 population (2012)	0.28 physicians/1,000 population (2008)
Swaziland	9.3% of GDP (2014)	2.1 beds/1,000 population (2011)	0.17 physicians/1,000 population (2009)
Tanzania	5.6% of GDP (2014)	0.7 beds/1,000 population (2010)	0.03 physicians/1,000 population (2012)
Togo	5.2% of GDP (2014)	0.7 beds/1,000 population (2011)	0.05 physicians/1,000 population (2008)
Uganda	7.2% of GDP (2014)	0.5 beds/1,000 population (2010)	0.12 physicians/1,000 population (2005)

Chapter 6
Health Infrastructure and Economic Development in India

Dibyendu Ghosh
The University of Burdwan, India

Soumyananda Dinda
The University of Burdwan, India

ABSTRACT

The chapter examines different aspects of health care service facilities and health infrastructure available in India. Major health outcomes like Life expectancy at birth and infant mortality rate depend on available health facilities like hospitals, beds and health trained personnel. Life expectancy in India has increased and IMR declines over the years, except few states like Bihar, Jharkhand, Madhya Pradesh, Uttar Pradesh. India has achieved a considerable progress in providing health infrastructure and its access to health care services to the mass population. However, less developed states like Uttar Pradesh and Bihar need more attention to improve health infrastructure and distribution of health facilities. In this context, we also highlight the department of Ayurveda, Yoga and Naturopathy, Unani, Siddha and Homoeopathy, abbreviated as AYUSH which is a Governmental body in India purposed with developing, education and research in Ayurveda, which mostly prevails in under-developed state like Bihar. Our empirical results provide the evidence of strong association between health infrastructure and economic development in India.

INTRODUCTION

Good health is a state of physical and mental wellbeing necessary to live a meaningful and productive life. Long healthy life is the basic aspiration of human development. Hence, health has become an important indicator of human development. It is true that a healthy person is an asset for himself and for the economy also. To achieve 'good health for all' the country should promote health care services, prevent diseases and help people to make their healthy choices. In a society, 'good health for all' ensures economic progress. Good health promotes efficiency in workforce, enhances their skills and aptitude and is necessary for high life expectancy. Good health is absence of disease and also it represents both

DOI: 10.4018/978-1-5225-2364-2.ch006

physical and mental capability to enjoy life. Good health is achievable under the condition of deliverable effective health care services which is possible only if available good health infrastructures.

Health infrastructures are "the basic services or social capital of a country, or part of it, which make economic and social activities possible" structures that support public health, having both tangible and intangible aspects and existing inside and outside the government sector. Health infrastructure is an important indicator for understanding the health care policy and welfare mechanism in a country.

Health care is a social determinant which is influenced by social policies. To achieve good health for people, especially the poor and the under privileged, the Government of India has focused on improving primary health services and ready to provide more accessibility and affordable to the poor people. In last few decades, India has achieved considerable progress in providing access to health care services to the people. Recently, the health infrastructure of country has expanded manifold. Now, the question arises whether health infrastructure is sufficient and properly distributed in India. So, the basic research question is on distribution of health infrastructure in India.

1. Is this health infrastructure adequate in India?
2. How is it distributed across India?
3. How does it affect economic development in India?

Disparity in health exists in India because of uneven distribution of health infrastructure across Indian States. Now we examine the disparity in health infrastructure in India focusing on three major channels – a) Institution, b) Knowledge capacity and c) health care service. All these connect the issues of economic development – with special focus on India.

This study is organized as follows: next section provides a brief review of literature. After spell out of the objective of the study, Data and methodology section describe data and provide primary observations. Analysis section explains the results and finally this study concludes with remarks.

BRIEF REVIEW OF LITERATURE

Literature mainly highlights the relationship between human health capital and economic development, health care service and labour productivity, etc.; however, a few have focused on health infrastructure (and particularly its distribution) and development. Effective health care service truly depends on allocating or distributing proper health infrastructure.

Colgrove, Fried, Mary, Northridge and Rosner (2010) investigated the public health and infrastructure for the US economy in 21st-Century. They highlighted that health infrastructure is crucial for public health care and services. In this paper, they argued that schools of public health (SPHs) are also essential to the nation's health, security, and well-being.

Ademiluyi and Aluko-Arowolo (2009) studied the infrastructural distribution of healthcare services in Nigeria. They examine the biomedical or western orthodox health care with its expansive bureaucratic ethos within the concept of hospitals structure in Nigeria. They observed that distribution of medical care delivery in Nigeria is biased towards urban area. Medical care services are favoured to the urban population at the cost of rural settlers. Infrastructure distribution of health care in rural areas of Nigeria are neglected to satisfy the urban areas, where the educated, the rich and Government functionaries reside.

Banerjee, Duflo and Deaton (2004) examined health care delivery in Rajasthan, India. They observe that the quality of public service is extremely low. The supply of quality of health care serviceis scare and the gap is filled up by unqualified private service providers. These unqualified private providers account for the bulk of health care provision of rural Rajasthan. Banerjee, Duflo and Deaton (2004) conducted a survey at Udaipur district of Rajasthan. Udaipur is one of the poorest districts in India. Based on primary survey of Udaipur district, they observe that the low quality of public facilities has also had an adverse influence on the people's health. In such an environment where people's expectations of health care providers seem to be generally low. In this context, they suggest that the state has to take up the task of being the provider and regulator and that definitely improve the public health care services.

Laxmi and Sahoo (2013) examine the relation between health infrastructure and health indicators of Andhra Pradesh for the period of 1980-2010. They develop a health infrastructure index focusing on hospitals, nursing home, beds, doctors and government hospitals etc. They investigate health sensitivity in response of health infrastructure estimating its elasticity coefficient.

Bhandari and Dutta (2007) study the health infrastructure in rural India, focusing on family welfare, medical education, and control of drugs, prevention and control of major diseases. Bhandari and Dutta (2007) consider physical infrastructure in terms of considering health centers, dispensaries hospitals etc. This paper includes medical and trained staff in discussion on rural health infrastructure and identifies the critical gaps between requirement of infrastructure and services.

Patil, Somasundaram and Goyal (2002) examine the health scenario in rural India and observed regional and gender disparities. They find main reason of disparities in the available health infrastructure. About 75 percent of health infrastructure, medical trained staff and other health resources are concentrated in urban areas where only 27 percent to 29 percent people live. They suggest that a paradigm shift from biomedical model to a social cultural model which should bridge the gap and quality of life.

Majumder (2005) examined empirically the inter-linkage between infrastructure and regional development in India. Using Multidimensional approach and composite index the paper found a significant relation between infrastructural and development, which is different for regions at different stages of development. His findings also suggest that identification of specific requirements of different regions and infrastructural expansion are major requirement of balanced regional development.

In this context we also study several Human Development Reports (HDRs) (Human Development Report Hooghly 2011, Human Development Report Burdwan 2015), which mainly emphasis on improvement of health and education. The HDRs highlight health issues focusing on birth rate to death rate, child bearing motherhood to child care service, vector borne disease to HIV/AIDs etc. The HDRs cover three important indicators for examining the health status of the people - these are preventive health care indicator, curative health care indicator and promotional health care indicator. Index of Curative Health care facilities has been constructed using the indicator like (i)No. of Bed per 1000 Population, (ii)No. of Doctors per 1000 Population. Preventive Health care index has been constructed using indicators like (i) Percentage of Households having Latrine facility, (ii)Percentage of Households having Separate Bathroom, (iii)Percentage of Households having Safe Drinking Water facility. The Promotional Health care index has been constructed using indicators of (i) Percentage of Institutional delivery, (ii) Percentage of Mother facilitated with 3 times Ante-Natal Care (i.e. ANC-3), and (iii) percentage of immunized children. Using Principal Component method the reports have utilized the data driven weights for the construction of Curative health care index, Preventive health care index, and Promotional health care indices.

Sen, Iyer and Gorge (2002) consider the structural reforms and health equity in India, using NSS Survey data, 1986-87 and 1995-96. They find a gender inequality in health services particularly in untreated morbidity that is due to limited access to health services for the poor.

HEALTH INFRASTRUCTURE AND DEVELOPMENT

Human health is important for economic growth and development. Importance of health for socio-economic development has gained recognition in recent time. There is a strong relation between population, health and development. According to Banerjee, Duflo and Deaton (2004) better provision of health care is the key to improve health condition and also economic growth and development in poor countries like India. India's health challenges are not only huge in magnitude due to its large population but they are complex due to its diversity and the chronic poverty and inequality. There is little information available regarding the quality of health care delivery in developing countries. However, health care services are improving slowly with developing health infrastructure which is not properly recorded. Health infrastructure in the most of the developing economy is poor and so society need for the betterment of health service. Health care service providers could be either private or government; otherwise, jointly they can serve for betterment of the society. However, only the government can provide proportionately health infrastructure for whole population in poor country like India. Creation and distribution of health infrastructure is the first priority in a developing economy that it ensures good health.

IMPORTANCE OF HEALTH INFRASTRUCTURE IN INDIA

India is at the point of an exciting and challenging period in its history. India today enjoys as never before, a sophisticated arsenal of interventions, technologies and knowledge required for providing health care to her people. Yet the gaps in health outcomes continue to widen. On the face of it, much of the ill health, disease, premature death, and suffering we observed on such a large scale are needless, given the availability of effective and affordable interventions for prevention and treatment. Making healthcare affordable and accessible for all its citizens is one of the key focus areas of the country today. Health infrastructure is an important indicator to understand the health care delivery provisions and signify the investment and priority accorded to creating the infrastructure in a region.

OBJECTIVE OF THE STUDY

The main objective of this study is to examine at the provincial characteristic of distribution of health infrastructural facility in Indian States. This study investigates the disparity in health across India in three different areas, namely a) Institutional capacity building provision b) Skilled or trained personals c) Service providers. How are components of these health infrastructures distributed across states of India? This study examines state wise distribution of health infrastructure and availability of health care services in India.

DATA SOURCES AND METHODOLOGY

The present study is exclusively based on secondary data. For the analysis of health infrastructural distribution twenty-eight major states have been studied for interstate comparisons. Institutions are built up for creation of medical trained personals. The state wise numbers of Medical Colleges and MBBS Seats in India for the year 2015-2016 have been taken from Medical Council of India, AIIMS- All India Institute of Medical Science and Jawaharlal Institute of Postgraduate Medical Education and Research. The State wise data on Under Graduate Colleges and Post Graduate Colleges of AYUSH Hospital are collected from State Governments & concerned agencies of Government of India. This study broadly covers 25 state of India. The data for ANM and LHV Training School, (HFWTC) and Multipurpose Health Worker (M) Training Centre has been collected from Training Division, Ministry of Health & Family Welfare, Government of India. Similarly, the data for total number of Nursing Staff, Laboratory Technicians and Pharmacists at Public Health Centre and Community Health Centre of different states in India has been compiled from Rural Health Statistics 2014-15, Government of India. The statistics for Rural and Urban Hospitals, Beds are collected from Directorate General of State Health Services. Again the data of Licensed Blood Bank in India December was collected from Drug Controller General (I), Ministry of Health and Family Welfare, Govt. of India. Simple statistical tools are used in this study. Table and graph are used for presenting primary observation.

PRIMARY OBSERVATION

India has made a good progress in last few decades in health sector. Medical education infrastructures in the country have shown rapid growth in last 10 years. There are currently 420 medical colleges in the country that offer 56,838 MBBS seats between Government and private medical colleges. That makes India is the largest producer of doctors in the World. In comparison, the United States only produce 18,000 doctors a year. According to the Medical Council of India (MCI), the total number of registered doctors in the country is 936,488 and Auxiliary nurses' midwives are 756,937 & registered nurses are 1,673,338 as on December, 2014.There are 153,655 Sub Centres in a country which is the most peripheral institution. There are 25,308 Public Health Centres and 5396 Community Health Centres in India to provide integrated curative and preventive healthcare to the rural population.

INSTITUTIONS

Health infrastructures in terms of Government and private Colleges, ANM and LHV Training School, Health & Family Welfare Training Centre (HFWTC) and Multipurpose Health Worker (M) Training Centre, doctors, nurses, etc. have a major direct and positive contribution to health outcomes of any country.

INFRASTRUCTURE AVAILABLE FOR CREATING HEALTH SERVICES PROVIDERS

Table 1 provides state wise distribution of Medical Colleges and seats of MBBS in India in the current year. In terms of medical institution infrastructure the country has total 420 Government and private medical college with total admission of 56,838 during the year 2015-2016. The national distribution

Table 1. State wise details of medical colleges and MBBS seats in India for the year 2015-16 (as on 22.09.15)

	Government College		Private College	
State	Number	Seats	Number	Seats
Andhra Pradesh	17	2700	30	4450
Assam	6	726		
Bihar	9	950	4	400
Chhattisgarh	5	550	1	150
Goa	1	150		
Gujarat	11	1830	13	1400
Haryana	4	500	4	400
Himachal Pradesh	2	200	1	150
Jammu & Kashmir	3	400	1	100
Jharkhand	3	350		
Karnataka	15	1850	35	5405
Kerala	9	1250	21	2400
Madhya Pradesh	6	800	7	1050
Maharashtra	21	2950	27	3645
Manipur	2	200		
Meghalaya	1	50		
Orissa	3	550	5	600
Punjab	3	450	7	845
Rajasthan	8	1400	5	750
Sikkim			1	100
Tamil Nadu	22	2915	24	3300
Tripura	2	200		
Uttar Pradesh	15	1949	20	2600
Uttarakhand	2	200	2	300
West Bengal	14	2050	3	400
AIIMS*	7	673		
JIPMER*	1	150		
TOTAL	**200**	**27143**	**220**	**29695**

Source: Medical Council of India. * Outside the ambit of MCI.

between Government and private colleges is almost 50 percent. Looking at the breakup across states, the states with more than 20 colleges are biased towards private entities. On the cheeky side, states that possess less than 20 colleges tend to be heavily biased towards the Government institutions.

From Table 1, it is clear that Tamil Nadu state has the highest number of Government medical Colleges (22) and the admission capacity is 2915 seats. Whereas in Maharashtra has the second highest number of Government medical colleges (21) with admission seat capacity is 2950 and Andhra Pradesh has 17 medical colleges with 2700 admission capacity. But the interesting think, private medical college is highest in Karnataka with 35 colleges having 5405 seats and Andhra Pradesh is holding second rank in number of private medical college having 30 with admission capacity of 4450 seats. On the other hand, states like Meghalaya and Goa have a few numbers of Government colleges, and seat capacity is also very low which are 50 and 150, respectively. From Table 1 it is clear that the North-Eastern reason (states like Assam, Jharkhand, Manipur, Meghalaya and Tripura) and Goa have no private medical colleges.

Apart from western medical system, Indian traditional AYUSH medical colleges and hospitals are also available and spread all over India (see Table 2). AYUSH is the ellipsis of the medical systems that are being practiced in India such as Ayurveda, Yoga & Naturopathy, Unani, Siddha and Homeopathy.

Table 2. State wise details of the Undergraduate Colleges and Post Graduate Colleges of AYUSH Hospital in India for the Year 2015

State Name	UG Colleges	UG Adm. Capacity	PG Colleges	PG Adm. Capacity
Andhra Pradesh	15	680	4	74
Arunachal Pradesh	1	50		
Assam	4	190	1	12
Bihar	30	1280	2	95
Chhattisgarh	8	470	1	17
Goa	2	90		
Gujarat	28	2060	5	151
Haryana	7	380		
Himachal Pradesh	2	125	1	24
Jammu & Kashmir	3	130	1	15
Jharkhand	3	140		
Karnataka	76	3835	22	395
Kerala	22	1050	6	118
Madhya Pradesh	42	2725	4	24
Maharashtra	116	7065	35	835
Odisha	12	340	2	30
Punjab	16	880	2	53
Rajasthan	16	927	3	120
Tamil Nadu	28	1231	4	156
Uttarakhand	6	310	1	14
Uttar Pradesh	35	1605	6	203
West Bengal	16	843	3	30

Source: Medical Council of India

Under the department of AYUSH, there are 488 under graduate colleges with admission of 26,406 in India. Looking at the Table 2, the state Maharashtra has the highest number 116 of UG colleges with admission capacity is also highest 7065 and Karnataka has second highest 76 number of UG colleges and UG admission volume is 3835. On the other hand, states that possess lesser UG colleges in Arunachal Pradesh, Himachal Pradesh tend to be one and two UG institutions and also admission capacity is 50 and 125 respectively. However under the AYUSH department there are 103 Post graduate colleges in India with 2366 admission capacity. Maharashtra state has more numbers of PG medical colleges with admission seat capacity is highest 835 and Karnataka has 22 PG medical colleges with 395 admission capacity. Most interesting think is state like Jharkhand and Goa has no PG medical college.

Table 1 and Table 2 display the distribution of medical infrastructure for capacity building of medical personals. The Southern Indian states have more medical colleges and hospitals compared to the rest of India, and least in the North-Eastern part of India. Thus, there is asymmetric distribution of capacity building medical infrastructure in India. Now we also examine the second layer of medical trained staff and nurses who provide services for pregnant women in different stages of their child bearing period and care for new born child under different schemes like popular family welfare programme (see Table 3 and Table 4).

The health status of the people is judged by examining certain health indicators such as preventive and promotional health care services. There are several parameters are judged for preventive and promotional health care and construct simple index for curative health care indicator and preventive health care indicator. Number of medical qualified doctors and number of Beds available for citizens are used to construct the Index of Curative Health care facilities. Whereas Percentage of Households having Latrine facility, Percentage of Households having Separate Bathroom, and Percentage of Households having Safe Drinking Water facility are used for constructing Preventive Health care index.The Promotional Health care index has been constructed using indicators of Percentage of Institutional delivery, Percentage of Mother facilitated with 3 times Ante-Natal Care (i.e. ANC-3), and percentage of immunized children. For the construction of Curative health care index, Preventive health care index, and Promotional health care index. Ante-Natal Care (ANC) is the most important care service to the pregnant women. Table 3 and Table 4 display the state wise distribution of training schools for ANM and MPW, Family welfare trained staff and multipurpose health workers, respectively.

Table 5 provides the state wise distribution of trained supporting health staff and population in India. Normalizing number of trained supporting health staff across India we find that top rank holding states are Arunachal Pradesh, Mizoram and Nagaland, and their trained supporting health workers are 35.412, 30.168 and 27.849 per one lakh population, respectively. However, these states have less training institutions. Bottom three rank holding states are Maharashtra, Uttar Pradesh and Bihar with staff of 5.359, 4.133 and 2.495 per one lakh population, respectively. Uttar Pradesh and Bihar are high density population states with less trained health personnel, so quality of health care service is also low and probably health inequality arises due to lack of trained health staff. South Indian states like Tamil Nadu, Karnataka, Kerala and Andhra Pradesh are more developed compare to North Indian States (like Uttar Pradesh, Bihar, Assam). Average NSDP of South Indian states is around 50,000 and that of North Indian states is near about 22,000. So, comparatively developed states belong to South and afford to build up and improve institutions while less developed States in North India unable to do so.

Table 3. Auxiliary Nurse Midwife (ANM) and Lady Health Assistant (LHV) Training School

State Name	ANM/HW[F]	LHV/HA[F]
Andhra Pradesh*	14	3
Arunachal Pradesh	1	1
Assam	18	1
Bihar	21	0
Chhattisgarh	13	0
Goa	1	0
Gujarat	26	4
Haryana	8	0
Himachal Pradesh	0	0
Jammu & Kashmir	12	0
Jharkhand	10	0
Karnataka	28	4
Kerala	9	2
Madhya Pradesh	32	2
Maharashtra	29	5
Manipur	3	0
Meghalaya	2	0
Mizoram	1	0
Nagaland	1	0
Odisha	16	1
Punjab	6	0
Rajasthan	27	0
Sikkim	1	0
Tamil Nadu	6	1
Tripura	2	0
Uttarakhand	5	0
Uttar Pradesh	40	4
West Bengal	18	1

Source: Training Division, Ministry of Health & Family Welfare, Govt. of India.

Notes: *Data includes Telangana State.

Table 4. Health and Family Welfare Training Centre (HFWTC) and Multipurpose Health Worker (M) Training Centre

State Name	HFWTC	MPW(M)
Andhra Pradesh*	4	10
Arunachal Pradesh	1	1
Assam	1	0
Bihar	3	0
Chhattisgarh	0	3
Goa	0	0
Gujarat	1	0
Haryana	1	2
Himachal Pradesh	0	0
Jammu & Kashmir	2	0
Jharkhand	1	0
Karnataka	4	1
Kerala	2	1
Madhya Pradesh	3	7
Maharashtra	7	7
Manipur	1	0
Meghalaya	1	0
Mizoram	0	1
Nagaland	0	0
Odisha	3	3
Punjab	1	3
Rajasthan		0
Sikkim	0	0
Tamil Nadu	3	12
Tripura	0	1
Uttarakhand	0	0
Uttar Pradesh	11	0
West Bengal	3	2

Source: Training Division, Ministry of Health & Family Welfare, Govt. of India.

Notes: *Data includes Telangana State.

HEALTH CARE SERVICE

Health care service can be measured in terms of different parameters like available hospitals and number of beds in rural and urban areas. Table 6 shows the state wise distribution of Government Hospitals and available beds per one lakh population in rural and urban areas in India. Jammu and Kashmir,

Table 5. State wise total trained health staff served per one lakh population in India

State	Total Trained Health Staff	Population	Available Trained Health Staff (Per Lakh Population)	Rank
Andhra Pradesh	6443	84580777	7.618	21
Arunachal Pradesh	490	1383727	35.412	1
Assam	5628	31205576	18.035	8
Bihar	2597	104099452	2.495	27
Chhattisgarh	3012	25545198	11.791	14
Goa	116	1458545	7.953	19
Gujarat	4985	60439692	8.248	18
Haryana	2630	25351462	10.374	17
Himachal Pradesh	1248	6864602	18.18	7
Jammu & Kashmir	2819	12541302	22.478	6
Jharkhand	1836	32988134	5.566	24
Karnataka	6991	61095297	11.443	16
Kerala	5436	33406061	16.272	11
Madhya Pradesh	5544	72626809	7.634	20
Maharashtra	6022	112374333	5.359	25
Manipur	675	2855794	23.636	4
Meghalaya	673	2966889	22.684	5
Mizoram	331	1097206	30.168	2
Nagaland	551	1978502	27.849	3
Odisha	3137	41974218	7.474	22
Punjab	3195	27743338	11.516	15
Rajasthan	11847	68548437	17.283	9
Sikkim	86	610577	14.085	13
Tamil Nadu	10189	72147030	14.123	12
Tripura	619	3673917	16.849	10
Uttar Pradesh	8258	199812341	4.133	26
Uttarakhand	713	10086292	7.069	23
West Bengal	8461	91276115	9.27	28

Source: Training Division, Ministry of Health & Family Welfare, Govt. of India.

Uttarakhand and Kerala are top three states having 15.4, 9.5 and 6.5 rural hospitals per one lakh rural population, respectively; and the least 0.33 hospital is available for rural population in Uttar Pradesh. Now, 289.5 and 270 beds are available per one lakh rural population in Goa and Mizoram, respectively. It should be noted that 5.69, 7.76 and 9.95 number of beds are available for one lakh rural people in Bihar, Chhattisgarh and Uttar Pradesh, respectively. Medical facilities are mostly available in urban areas. From Table 6 it is clear that Jammu and Kashmir, Himachal Pradesh, and Sikkim have 16.5, 7.7 and 5.9 urban hospitals per one lakh urban population, respectively. Jharkhand has the least 0.05 hospital per lakh urban population and second least is Madhya Pradesh. Sikkim, Himachal Pradesh and Meghalaya are top three states having 846.5, 809.5 and 367.3 beds per lakh urban population, respectively; while Jharkhand has 6.7 beds per one lakh urban people.

Table 6 shows among the Indian States Percentage of per lakh rural population as well as urban population served by Govt. Hospital & Govt. Bed in Rural and Urban areas. This Table 6 displays the conditions of health service infrastructure in India.

There are 28 states in India among which Jammu & Kashmir served the highest 15.39 percentage of rural population in rural hospitals. From Table 6, the percentage of rural Population served per Government Hospital bed is highest in Goa with 289.453 and the percentage of urban Population served per Government Hospital is highest in Jammu & Kashmir. From the above table we find that Jammu & Kashmir served the highest percentage of population in rural and urban Government hospital among Indian States.

INFRASTRUCTURE IS CREATED FOR PROVIDING HEALTH SERVICES

As is shown in Table 6, there is large disparity in the healthcare infrastructure indicators across the Indian states when compared to the national average. Table 6 shows the comparison of different infrastructure indicators between India, with respect to its best performing state and a poorly performing state. Performance of health care service depends on the distribution of unit level health institution across India. Table 7 displays state wise distribution of health centre (normalized per lakh population) in India and the ranks of states in terms of number of available health centre per lakh. Top five rank holding states are Mizoram, Himachal Pradesh, Arunachal Pradesh, Tripura and Sikkim; and bottom five states are Bihar, Maharashtra, Haryana, Uttar Pradesh and Punjab.

Table 8 describes state wise AYUSH hospitals, Beds and dispensaries available for each ten lakh population in India. AYUSH systems are based on definite medical philosophies and represent a way of healthy living. The basic approach of all these systems on health, disease and treatment are holistic. Yoga has now become the icon of global health and many countries have started integrating it in their health care system. India has a rich heritage of medical wisdom derived from the Vedas that prevailed as Ayurveda. Under the department of AYUSH there are 3207 hospitals with 59783 beds in 28 states of India. Among all states, most of the hospitals are present in Uttar Pradesh having highest number of beds (i.e., 12416). There are 23373 dispensaries in all states and 776019 AYUSH practitioners registered, among them highest number of registered practitioners present in Bihar, whereas Bihar has only 26 AYUSH hospitals. AYUSH system is a substitute of the western medical system.

Table 1 to Table 8 describe the provision of health infrastructure for providing health care services in India. However, other health supporting staff such as nursing staff, laboratory technicians and pharmacists (see, Table 9) at different public health centers (see, Table 10).

Blood bank is also an important health infrastructure. Table 11 shows the available Blood Bank across India. Maximum Blood Bank is available in Tamil Nadu and minimum in Sikkim state, otherwise least Blood Bank is available in Dadra and Nagar Haveli.

Table 6. State wise government hospital and bed available in rural and urban areas in India (Per lakh population)

State	P.C. of Per Lakh Rural Hospital	P.C. of Bed Per Lakh Rural Population	P.C. of Per Lakh Urban Hospital	P.C. of Bed Per Lakh Urban Population
Andhra Pradesh	0.546	18.399	0.510	94.206
Arunachal Pradesh	4.876	121.910	4.726	118.159
Assam	4.059	27.993	1.114	133.612
Bihar	1.435	5.685	0.944	53.597
Chhattisgarh	2.122	7.762	3.722	176.833
Goa	3.081	289.453	1.764	188.683
Gujarat	0.865	28.607	0.342	69.850
Haryana	0.485	14.864	0.893	58.923
Himachal Pradesh	1.587	47.134	7.697	809.525
Jammu & Kashmir	15.393	37.637	16.515	113.304
Jharkhand	2.175	19.473	0.050	6.744
Karnataka	1.036	23.870	0.889	177.009
Kerala	6.496	100.709	0.904	125.642
Madhya Pradesh	0.635	19.065	0.468	81.163
Maharashtra	0.715	18.360	1.206	82.384
Manipur	1.138	36.109	0.839	83.558
Meghalaya	1.181	35.422	2.015	367.285
Mizoram	5.519	270.252	1.224	36.728
Nagaland	1.492	44.759	5.605	314.730
Odisha	4.744	20.300	1.299	136.843
Punjab	0.542	16.720	1.404	85.622
Rajasthan	5.144	63.976	2.868	79.956
Sikkim	5.252	56.893	5.860	846.475
Tamil Nadu	1.093	24.577	1.091	157.781
Tripura	0.774	46.452	2.184	240.781
Uttarakhand	9.464	53.233	0.951	138.358
Uttar Pradesh	0.332	9.947	0.778	91.997
West Bengal	2.046	31.647	1.011	201.110

Source: Authors Calculation

ANALYSIS

Now, we analyze these available data with basic statistical tools. We have selected some major variables for this analysis purpose. Figure 1 displays the matrix scatter diagram of major variables. Life expectancy at birth (LEB) and infant mortality rate (IMR) are strongly associated with number of trained health staff (THS) and number of hospital beds available per one lakh population.

Table 7. State wise health centre served per lakh population in India

State	Total Health Centre	Available Health Centre	Rank
Andhra Pradesh	14552	17.205	16
Arunachal Pradesh	455	32.882	3
Assam	5786	18.542	14
Bihar	11682	11.222	28
Chhattisgarh	6133	24.008	8
Goa	234	16.043	18
Gujarat	9630	15.933	19
Haryana	3139	12.382	26
Himachal Pradesh	2643	38.502	**2**
Jammu & Kashmir	2986	23.809	9
Jharkhand	4472	13.556	22
Karnataka	11823	19.352	12
Kerala	5624	16.835	17
Madhya Pradesh	10697	14.729	20
Maharashtra	12751	11.347	27
Manipur	523	18.314	15
Meghalaya	565	19.044	13
Mizoram	436	39.737	**1**
Nagaland	545	27.546	6
Odisha	8370	19.941	11
Punjab	3528	12.717	24
Rajasthan	17058	24.885	7
Sikkim	173	28.334	5
Tamil Nadu	10463	14.502	21
Tripura	1128	30.703	4
Uttar Pradesh	24791	12.407	25
Uttarakhand	2164	21.455	10
West Bengal	11613	12.723	23

Source: Authors Calculation

Figures 2 and 3 respectively show the relationship between NSDP and IMR, and NSDP and Life Expectancy in India during 2012-13. Infant mortality rate (IMR) is inversely related to income level (NSDP) while life expectancy at birth (LEB) is directly associated with NSDP that improves with economic development.

Table 12 demonstrates the pair wise Correlation among Life expectancy at birth, infant mortality outcomes and major health Infrastructure variables such as trained health staff, health centre, number of hospitals and beds available per one lakh population, and per capita state domestic product (NSDP). Available beds per lakh population are significantly correlated with LEB, IMR, THS, HC and NSDP.

Table 8. State wise number of AYUSH Hospitals functioning in India as on 1-4-2014

State Name	Hospitals	Beds	Dispensaries	Registered Practitioners
Andhra Pradesh	0.236	13.2891	21.7307	362.6
Arunachal Pradesh	8.672	97.5626	45.5292	93.9492
Assam	0.128	6.56934	14.6128	53.0033
Bihar	0.250	22.3344	6.09033	1601.06
Chhattisgarh	0.548	36.4061	57.5842	100.958
Goa	1.371	99.4141	10.9698	588.257
Gujarat	1.109	48.5112	12.558	576.327
Haryana	0.394	31.3591	20.5905	1072.05
Himachal Pradesh	4.516	94.2516	165.487	1293.74
Jammu & Kashmir	0.319	28.3065	47.0446	358.894
Jharkhand	0.091	7.33597	6.24467	799.136
Karnataka	2.897	171.159	10.901	550.255
Kerala	4.849	160.21	43.1359	848.499
Madhya Pradesh	0.688	37.6032	22.3471	866.774
Maharashtra	0.934	85.5355	4.42272	1000.18
Manipur	5.953	85.0902	84.74	0
Meghalaya	3.708	37.0759	17.1897	84.9375
Mizoram	12.760	127.597	11.8483	0
Nagaland	1.011	5.05433	102.603	1009.35
Odisha	0.334	21.5132	31.8529	197.74
Punjab	0.721	60.3388	23.429	361.132
Rajasthan	1.926	19.0085	56.3251	463.176
Sikkim	1.638	16.378	8.18898	9.82677
Tamil Nadu	3.992	47.6943	8.649	415.485
Tripura	0.544	8.16567	36.4733	40.8284
Uttar Pradesh	9.969	62.1383	9.83423	502.131
Uttarakhand	0.991	37.3775	52.844	213.26
West Bengal	0.186	12.4786	20.1257	541.916

Source: State Governments and concerned agencies, all the figures are given after normalization for each ten lakh population

NSDP are strongly correlated with life expectancy at birth and infant mortality rate. So, economic development is strongly associated with good health outcomes.

Life expectancy and IMR are crucial health outcome that depends on health infrastructure. Table 13 and Table 14 present the regression results of IMR and Life Expectancy at birth, respectively. Table 13 suggests that infant mortality rate declines with increasing available health facilities like health care centers and numbers of beds. IMR also reduces with increasing NSDP which is the indicator of economic development.

Table 9. State-wise nursing staff, laboratory technicians and pharmacists in India 2015

State Name	Nursing Staff	Laboratory Technicians	Pharmacists
Andhra Pradesh	2006	776	951
Arunachal Pradesh	319	74	97
Assam	3056	1225	1347
Bihar	1736	611	250
Chhattisgarh	1511	657	844
Goa	86	14	16
Gujarat	2705	1401	879
Haryana	1685	437	508
Himachal Pradesh	635	157	456
Jammu & Kashmir	1184	763	872
Jharkhand	1230	301	305
Karnataka	3176	1294	2521
Kerala	3969	365	1102
Madhya Pradesh	3629	892	1023
Maharashtra	2535	1387	2100
Manipur	433	96	146
Meghalaya	413	125	135
Mizoram	224	61	46
Nagaland	378	72	101
Odisha	1260	378	1499
Punjab	1907	482	806
Rajasthan	9250	1930	667
Sikkim	41	31	14
Tamil Nadu	7349	1314	1526
Telangana	1453	566	691
Tripura	421	67	131
Uttarakhand	456	157	100
Uttar Pradesh	4412	963	2883
West Bengal	7047	448	966

Source: Rural Health Statistics 2014-15

Table 10. State wise number of sub centre, public health centre and community health centres functioning in India as on 31st March, 2015

State/UT	Sub Centre	PHCs	CHCs
Andhra Pradesh	7659	1069	179
Arunachal Pradesh	286	117	52
Assam	4621	1014	151
Bihar	9729	1883	70
Chhattisgarh	5186	792	155
Goa	209	21	4
Gujarat	8063	1247	320
Haryana	2569	461	109
Himachal Pradesh	2065	500	78
Jammu & Kashmir	2265	637	84
Jharkhand	3957	327	188
Karnataka	9264	2353	206
Kerala[1]	4575	827	222
Madhya Pradesh	9192	1171	334
Maharashtra	10580	1811	360
Manipur##	421	85	17
Meghalaya	428	110	27
Mizoram	370	57	9
Nagaland	396	128	21
Odisha#	6688	1305	377
Punjab	2951	427	150
Rajasthan	14407	2083	568
Sikkim	147	24	2
Tamil Nadu	8706	1372	385
Telangana	4863	668	114
Tripura	1017	91	20
Uttarakhand	1848	257	59
Uttar Pradesh	20521	3497	773
West Bengal	10357	909	347

Source: Rural Health Statistics in India 2014-15

Note: # State informed that there are 79 other hospitals functioning which are equal to PHCs level facilities.

Table 11. State wise number of licensed blood bank in India till December 2015

State	Total No. of Blood Banks
Andhra Pradesh	140
Arunachal Pradesh	13
Assam	76
Bihar	84
Chandigarh	4
Chhattisgarh	49
Dadra and Nagar Haveli	1
Daman and Diu	2
Delhi (NCT)	72
Goa	5
Gujarat	136
Haryana	79
Himachal Pradesh	22
Jammu and Kashmir	31
Jharkhand	54
Karnataka	185
Kerala	172
Lakshadweep	1
Madhya Pradesh	144
Maharashtra	297
Manipur	5
Meghalaya	7
Mizoram	10
Nagaland	6
Odisha(Orissa)	91
Puducherry	18
Punjab	103
Rajasthan	102
Sikkim	3
Tamil Nadu	304
Telangana	151
Tripura	8
Uttar Pradesh	240
Uttarakhand	24
West Bengal	118

Source: Drug Controller General (I), MOHFW

Table 14 suggests that life expectancy at birth increases with rising per capita income level (NSDP) and numbers of hospitals and beds. Trained health staff is not statistically significant in IMR and Life expectancy at birth. It is true that Life expectancy at birth and IMR are inversely related, however, both LEB and IMR improve with economic development in India.

Overall our findings suggest that improvement of health infrastructure and economic development certainly improve the quality of life in India

CONCLUSION

This chapter has reviewed the health infrastructure available in India and analyses the factors which are responsible for main health outcomes like Life expectancy at birth and infant mortality rate. LEB and IMR certainly depend on available health facilities like hospitals, beds and health personals and also on economic development. Life expectancy in India has increased and IMR declines over the years, except few states like Bihar, Jharkhand, Madhya Pradesh, Uttar Pradesh. The Government should focus more on health infrastructure of these states.

India has achieved a considerable progress in providing health infrastructure and its access to health care services to the mass population. In last two decades, in India, the health infrastructure has increased and improved in manifolds. Basic Health Care is necessary for all and India has achieved it too some extend. However, distribution of health infrastructure is not proper. Especially, Uttar Pradesh and Bihar are under developed compared to rest of India and they need more attention to improve health infrastructure and distribution of health facilities.

Economic development has strong feedback to improve infrastructure, more specifically health facilities that certainly improves human health capital, and later it helps to improve overall human capital.

Figure 1. Matrix of scatter diagram of major variables

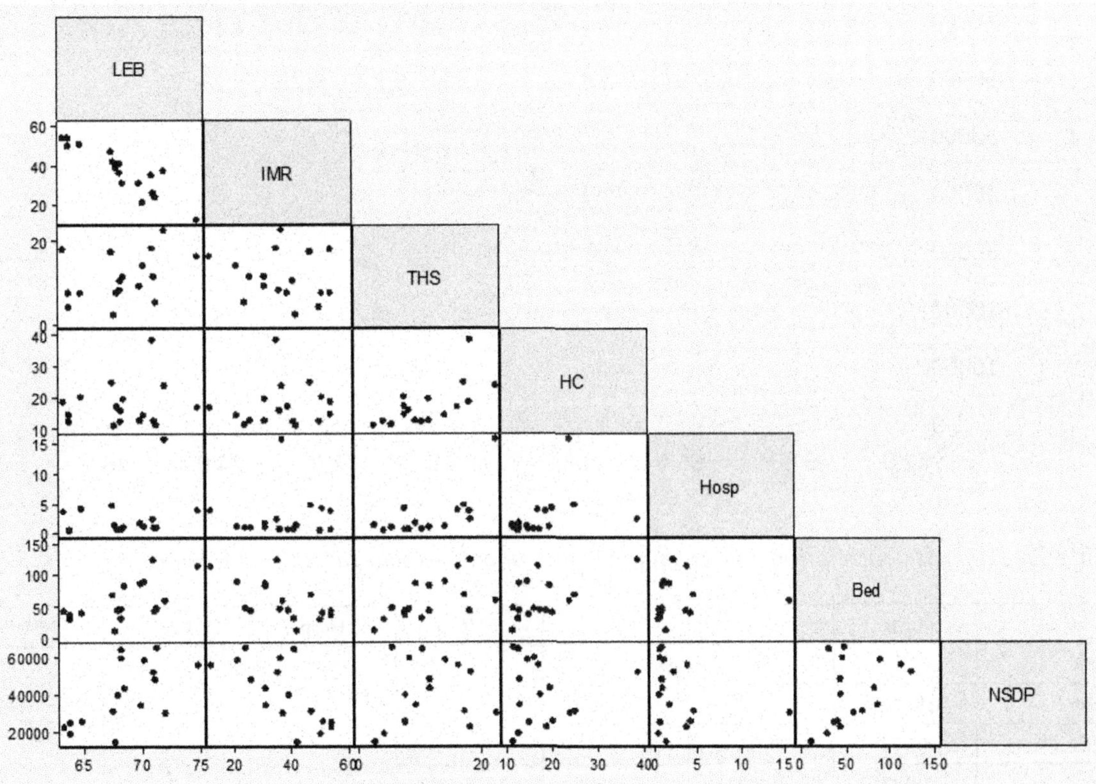

Figure 2. Relationship between NSDP and IMR

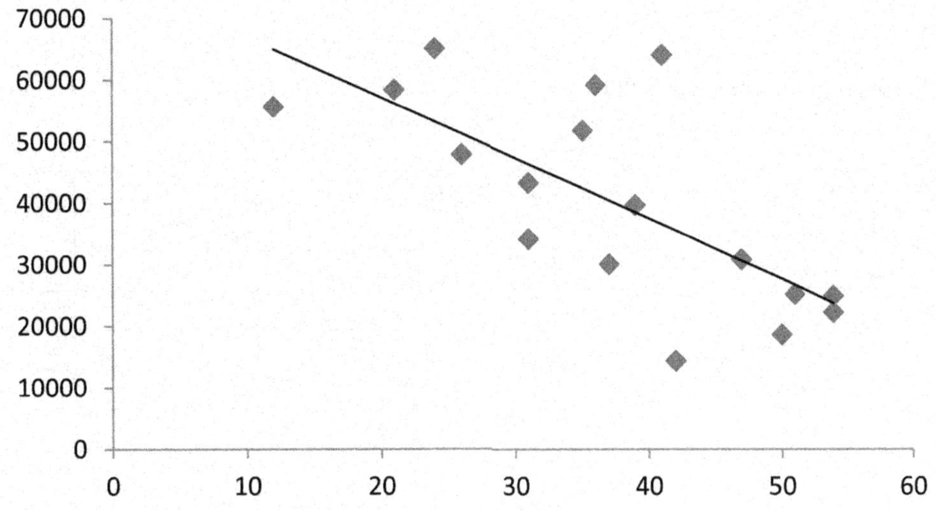

Figure 3. Relationship between NSDP and Life Expectancy at Birth

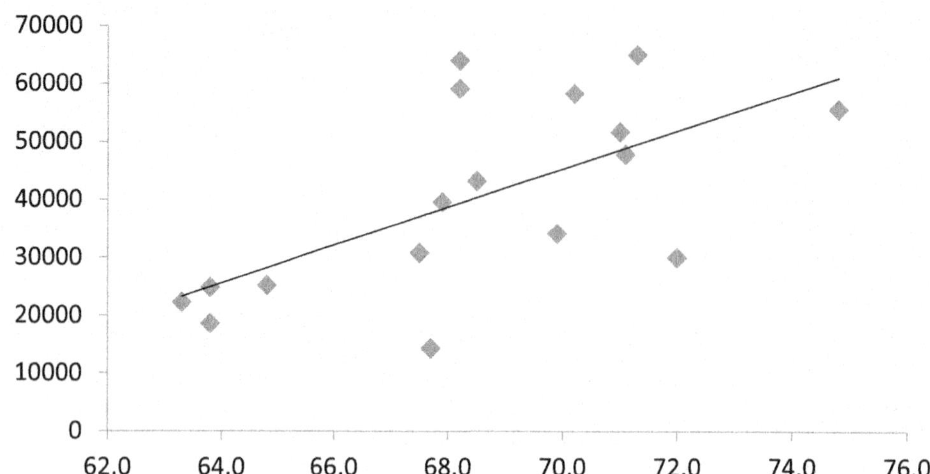

Table 12. Pair wise correlation among major health outcomes and Infrastructure variables

	LER	IMR	THS	HC	Hosp	Bed	NSDP
LER	1						
IMR	-0.903***	1					
THS	0.374	-0.169	1				
HC	0.147	0.102	0.658***	1			
Hosp	0.263	0.044	0.663***	0.39	1		
Bed	0.609***	-0.59**	0.6**	0.59**	0.125	1	
NSDP	0.633***	-0.71***	0.134	-0.002	-0.24	0.417*	1

Note: '***', '**' and '*' denote the statistical level of significance at 1%, 5% and 10%, respectively.

Table 13. Regression of IMR on health infrastructure

Variables	Coefficients	t-Value
THS	0.5875	1.12
HC	0.9886***	3.07
Hosp	-1.21287	-1.89
Bed	-0.3255***	-4.26
NSDP	-0.00035***	-3.22
Constant	49.4725***	8.77
R^2	0.8331	
Adj.R^2	0.7572	
Root MSE	5.954	
F(5, 11)	10.98***	

Note: '***', and '**' denote the statistical level of significance at 1%, and 5%, respectively.

Table 14. Regression of LEB and health infrastructure

Variables	Coefficients	t-Value
THS	-0.20826	-1.24
HC	-0.123	-1.20
Hosp	0.57776**	2.82
Bed	0.06886**	2.82
NSDP	0.0001***	3.10
Constant	63.11567***	35.06
R^2	0.7591	
Adj.R^2	0.6496	
Root MSE	1.8993	
F(5, 11)	6.93***	

Note: '***',and '**' denote the statistical level of significance at 1%, and 5%, respectively.

REFERENCES

Ademiluyi, I. A., & Aluko-Arowolo, S. O. (2009). Infrastructural Distribution of healthcare services in Nigeria: An overview. *Journal of Geography and Planning*, *2*(5), 104–110.

Banerjee,, A., Duflo, & Deaton, A. (2004). Health Care Delivery in Rural Rajasthan. *Economic and Political Weekly*, *39*(9), 944–949.

Bhandari L. & Dutta S. (2007). *Health Infrastructure in Rural India*. India Infrastructure Report 2007.

Binder, S., Adigun, L., Dusenbury, C., Greenspan, A., & Tanhuanpaa, P. (2008). National Public Health Institutes: Contributing to the Public Good. *Journal of Public Health Policy*, *29*(1), 3–21. doi:10.1057/palgrave.jphp.3200167 PMID:18368014

Choudhury, M., & Nageshwaran, S. (2011). Rigorous health infrastructure is needed. *British Medical Journal*, *342*(7798), 614.

Datta K. S. & Singh K. (2016). Analysis of child deprivation in India: Focus on health and educational perspectives. *Economic Analysis and Policy*, 120–130.

Dey, B., Mitra, A., Prakash, K., Basud, A., Raye, S., & Mitra, A. (2013). Gaps in Health Infrastructure in Indian Scenario: A Review. *Indo Global. Journal of Pharmaceutical Sciences*, *3*(2), 156–166.

James, C., Fried, Northridge, & Rosner, D. (2010). Schools of Public Health: Essential Infrastructure of a Responsible Society and a 21st-Century Health System. *Association of Schools of Public Health*, *125*(1), 8–14. PMID:20402192

Kumar, A., & Gupta, S. (2012). *Health Infrastructure in India: Critical Analysis of Policy Gaps in the Indian Healthcare Delivery*. Vivekananda International Foundation.

Lakshmi S. T. & Sahoo, D. (2013). Health Infrastructure and Health Indicators: The Case of Andhra Pradesh, India. *IOSR Journal of Humanities and Social Science, 6*, 22-29.

Lee Eva, K. (2009). Modeling and Optimizing the Public-Health Infrastructure for Emergency Response. *Interfaces*, *39*(5), 476–490. doi:10.1287/inte.1090.0463

Majumder, R. (2015). *Infrastructural Facilities in India: District Level Availability Index*. New Delhi: Central Statistical Office, Ministry of Statistics and Programme Implementation, Government of India.

Mavalankar, V. D., Ramani, V. K., Patel, A., & Sankar, P. (2005). *Building the Infrastructure to Reach and care for the Poor: Trends, Obstacles and Strategies to overcome them*. Ahmedabad: Center for Management of Health Service, Indian Institute of Management.

Ministry of Health and Family Welfare. (2005). *Rural Health Care System in India*. New Delhi: Ministry of Health and Family Welfare, Government of India.

Patil, V. A., Somasundaram, V. K., & Goyal, C. R. (2002). Current Health Scenario in Rural India. *The Australian Journal of Rural Health*, *10*(2), 129–135. doi:10.1111/j.1440-1584.2002.tb00022.x PMID:12047509

KEY TERMS AND DEFINITIONS

ANM and LHV Training School: Auxiliary Nurse Midwife health worker (Female) and Lady Health Assistant (Female) play vital role in Maternal & Child Health as well as in Family Welfare Service in the rural areas of India. It is therefore, crucial that the proper training to be given to them so that quality services be provided to the rural population.

AYUSH: The Ministry of AYUSH was formed with effect from 9th November 2014, is a Governmental body in India purposed with developing education and research In Ayurveda which is an Indian traditional medicine, Yoga, Naturopathy, Unani, Siddha, Homoeopathy and other alternative medicine systems.

Community Health Centre: Community Health Centres are being established and maintained by the State Government under Minimum Needs Programme (MNP) / Basic Minimum Service Programme (BMP). The Community Health Centres provide specialized medical care in the form of Surgeon, Physician, Gynecologist and Pediatrician supported by twenty-one paramedical and other staff. It has thirty in-door beds with OT, X-Ray, Labourroom and Laboratory facilities.

Health and Family Welfare Training Centre (HFWTC): In order to promote transparency and accountability in the working of every public authority and to empower the citizens to secure access to information under the control of each public authority, the Government of India has brought out an Act, namely, "The Right to Information Act, 2005", (RTI Act) which came into force on 15.6.2005. In accordance with the provisions of section 4(1)(b) of this Act, the Department of Health and Family Welfare, Government of India has brought out this manual for information and guidance of the stakeholders and the general public. The purpose of this manual is to inform the general public about this Department's organizational set-up, functions and duties of its officers and employees, records and documents available with the Department. This manual is aimed at the public in general and users of the services and provides information about the schemes, projects and programmes being implemented by the Department of Health and Family Welfare and the organizations under its administrative control.

IMR: Infant Mortality Rate (IMR) refers to the number of death per 1000 live birth in the first year of child's life. It measures the probability of a child during before attaining the age of one year. This is an important indicator of the quality of health services available to the people. The higher is the incidence of IMR poor is the level of health infrastructure and health care services and vice-versa.

Life Expectancy at Birth (LEB): Good health stands for a state of inclusive physical, mental and social wellbeing. Life expectancy at birth in that context works as the indicator of such state of health. It is a statistical measure of the average length of survival of human beings. Life expectancy of an individual is the number of years the person is expected to live, given the prevailing age-specific mortality rates of the population to which he/she belongs. A large number of factors which include the general health status and hygiene, the status of maternal and child health, the extent of coverage of public health care delivery services available to the poorest of the poor, the incidence of morbidity and disease and so on are likely to affect the life expectancy at birth.

MBBS: MBBS full form is Bachelor of Medicine and Bachelor of Surgery. It is the official undergraduate degree awarded to students who graduate from medical schools or universities to enter the medical profession.

Multipurpose Health Worker (M) Training Centre: The concept of Multipurpose Health Workers (Male and Female) was introduced in 1974 for the delivery of preventive and promotional health care services to the community at the level of Sub-Health Centres (SHCs). The Multipurpose Health Worker (Male) is the grass root health functionary for the control of communicable diseases including Malaria,

TB, Leprosy, Water Borne Diseases, as well as Environmental Sanitation, detection of disease outbreaks and their control, health education.

Public Health Centre: Primary Health Centres (PHC) is the contact point between village community and the medical officer. The PHC are established and maintained by the State Government under the Minimum Needs Programme (MNP) / Basic Minimum Service Programme (BMP). At present, a medical officer supported by fourteen paramedical and other staff is in charge of one PHC. It has four to six beds for in patients. It acts as a referral unit for six sub centres.

Sub Centre: The Sub Centre is the most essential and first contact point between the primary health care system and the community. One Auxiliary Nurse Midwife (ANM) and Lady Health worker manned every sub centre. One lady health worker is supervised of six sub centres. The sub centres are provided with basic drugs for taking care of essential health needs of men, women and children. In sub centre are provided promotive, preventive and curative primary health care service to the needed people.

Trained Health Staff: Nursing Staff, Laboratory Technicians and Pharmacists, etc., are considered, here, total trained health staff. This supporting staffs are essential in the health care service.

Chapter 7
Anatomy and Significance of Public Healthcare Expenditure and Economic Growth Nexus in India:
Its Implications for Public Health Infrastructure Thereof

Sovik Mukherjee
Jadavpur University, India

ABSTRACT

The objective of this chapter is to take a closer look at the liaison between the two focus variables viz. growth and public healthcare expenditure, and the associated implications for public health infrastructure development. Initially, a theoretical model has been proposed which brings out the link between the focus variables. Panel cointegration and causality are the techniques applied in a Vector Error Correction Mechanism (VECM) set-up using panel data from 1980-2015. Next, a health infrastructure index has been constructed using the Euclidean distance function approach for India for two time points i.e. 2005-06 and 2014-15, to evaluate the interstate performance in public healthcare infrastructure. The findings validate the existence of a cointegrated relationship between health expenditure and economic growth coupled with a bidirectional causality linking the focus variables in this model. It comes to a close by highlighting the policy implications and the future research possibilities in this regard.

INTRODUCTION

It is health that is real wealth and not pieces of gold and silver. — Mahatma Gandhi

In the quest for achieving economic development, development of infrastructure in terms of both quantity and quality is a must. It is suggested that infrastructure supports the processes of growth on which much

DOI: 10.4018/978-1-5225-2364-2.ch007

of poverty reduction depends and also assists the poor to have an access to the basic services which can improve their lives and the standard of living. There are several studies that establish the constructive impact of infrastructure on economic growth and productivity. For a systematic understanding of the healthcare policy and the associated welfare mechanisms, it becomes crucial to scrutinize the health infrastructure condition of an economy.

Now, coming to the notion of health infrastructure, it has been expressed as the basic support for the provision of public health services. It is one of the critical indicators for understanding the investment priorities with regards to the creation of health care facilities and welfare mechanisms in a country. By and large, the five components of health infrastructure can be categorized as – the percentage of competent workforce; an integrated electronic information system; number of public health organizations, material resources and ongoing research in the health arena (Novick & Mays, 2005). In the context of health infrastructure, the focus should not only be on the end results of healthcare policy but also on capacity building in the domain of public health delivery mechanisms. In India, the healthcare services are alienated into State List and Concurrent List. Some items like public hospitals come under the jurisdiction of the State List, while population control and family welfare, medical education, and quality control of drugs are included in the Concurrent List. The Union Ministry of Health and Family Welfare (UMHFW) function as the pivotal force for the implementation of various schemes in the field of family welfare, curative prevention, and control of major diseases.

Healthcare in India has been developed as a three-tier structure. The Sub-Centres form the lower tier of the structure followed by Primary Health Centres and Community Health Centres forming the middlemost and uppermost tiers respectively. Talking about the recent health infrastructure position in India, there exist 1 Sub-Centre per 5,000 populations in the general areas and 1 Sub- Centre per 3,000 populations in the tribal and hilly areas. For Primary Health Centres, the figure stands at 1 per 30,000 populations and 1 per 20,000 populations in the general and tribal areas respectively. One can locate 1 Community Health Centre per 1,20,000 populations in the general areas and 1 per 80,000 populations in the tribal and hilly areas. Coming to the overall position, there are 1,53,655 Sub-Centres (SCs), 25,308 Primary Health Centres (PHCs), 5,396 Community Health Centres (CHCs), 1022 Sub-divisional Hospitals (SDHs) and 763 District Hospitals (DH) in the country. There is an acute shortfall of 33145 SCs (20 per cent), 6556 PHCs (22 per cent) and 2316 CHCs (32 per cent) across the country as per the Rural Health Statistics of 2015. There needs to be a lot of improvement in this arena given the fact that India's total health expenditure is 4 per cent of GDP whereas public health expenditure stands at an all time low of 1 per cent of GDP. In this backdrop, this paper explores the impact of health expenditure on growth and also the position of the states with regards to the health infrastructure situation.

Although, studies about of the interaction between health and per-capita economic growth have been flourishing but panel data studies for any of the developing countries is a rare phenomenon. So, a modest attempt has been made in this regard. The rest of the paper has been organized as follows. To start with, a brief evaluation of the select literature on the liaison between healthcare expenditure and economic growth has been carried out in Section 2. In Section 3, a theoretical construct has been developed to draw out the relationship between the focus variables. Section 4 illustrates the methodology employed and puts forward the empirical results and the discussions thereof. Section 5 looks at the health infrastructure in India, in the light of healthcare expenditure It comes to a close by highlighting the policy implications and the future research possibilities in this regard.

REVIEW OF SELECTED LITERATURE

One of the essential issues in healthcare systems across the world is that what factors control the resources a country allocates to medical care. The share of health expenditures of GDP in the developing countries is often less as compared to the developed countries. The role of health care spending on stimulating economic growth was first suggested by Mushkin (1962). This is known as the "health-led growth hypothesis". According to Mushkin's hypothesis, "health is a capital, thus investment on health can increase income, hence lead to overall economic growth." In fact, health affects the growth prospects of a nation through its impact on human and physical capital accumulation. Since healthier people are much more productive, they have a strong incentive to develop their knowledge and skills because they want to savor the benefit over a longer period of time (Bloom & Canning, 2000). In contrast, poor health status has an unfavourable impact on productivity, thus it transpires to be a significant factor in explaining the under-development in many regions throughout the world.

On the other hand, economic growth can also liven up the health status of the population in two aspects:– Firstly, economic growth implies rising per-capita income and a part of this increased income goes into the consumption of a higher quantity of nourishing food. As a result, health improves. Secondly, economic growth is fueled by the technological health care expenditure and part of this progress is reflected in improvements in medical science. From the microeconomic perspective, when individual's income is low, demand for medical care also tends to be low. As a result, the marginal rate of return to invest in health through medical care investment is very high. Hence, a small percentage increase of income will strongly improve the health state. When an individual attains a very healthy condition, an additional income will not make this individual healthier, but stagnant. As a result, the effect of economic growth on the health status of a nation is concave and depends on the level of development (Preston, 1975).

The theoretical relations proposed by the two schools of thought have been summarized below. Following Halder and Mallik (2010), with the help of an implicit production function (standard assumptions are applicable):

$$Y = Y(K, N, H) \tag{1}$$

where, Y stands for the aggregate output, H stands for the stock of human capital i.e. investment on health and education and N stands for the aggregate employment in the economy. If health can be treated as an investment in human capital — an increase in the health expenditure must in due course lead to higher economic growth. Since better health leads to higher labour productivity, hence, that would pave the way for higher growth (Behrman & Deolalikar, 1988).

Totally differentiating equation (1), with respect to time t and then dividing throughout by Y, we have:

$$\frac{1}{Y}\left(\frac{\partial Y}{\partial t}\right) = \frac{1}{Y}\left(\frac{\partial Y}{\partial K}\right)\left(\frac{\partial K}{\partial t}\right) + \frac{1}{Y}\left(\frac{\partial Y}{\partial N}\right)\left(\frac{\partial N}{\partial t}\right) + \frac{1}{Y}\left(\frac{\partial Y}{\partial H}\right)\left(\frac{\partial H}{\partial t}\right)$$

This implies that,

$$y = MP_K \frac{I_K}{Y} + MP_N n \frac{N}{Y} + MP_H \frac{I_H}{Y} \tag{2}$$

Here,

$y = \left(\frac{\frac{\partial Y}{\partial t}}{Y} \right)$ = rate of growth of output; $n = \left(\frac{\frac{\partial N}{\partial t}}{N} \right)$ = rate of growth of employment; I_H stands for the investment in human capital which implies that $\left(\frac{\partial H}{\partial t} \right) = I_H$. Also, $\left(\frac{\partial Y}{\partial H} \right) = MP_H$ is nothing but marginal productivity of human capital and it is assumed to be greater than zero. Similar argument holds for investment in physical capital. Similarly, $\left(\frac{\partial Y}{\partial N} \right) = MP_N$ is nothing but the marginal productivity of labour and it is also positive given the standard assumptions. If one looks at the various components of equation (2), it is clear that the growth rate of output depends not only on the investment possibilities in physical capital but also in human capital. The more a country invests in health infrastructure, the more is the level of human capital, the greater will be the growth rate of output. So, from equation (2), it is clear that there exists a theoretical liaison between economic growth and health human capital.

Shifting the focus, a variety of empirical studies, based on time-series or cross-country data, have estimated the extent of the contribution of public expenditures to economic growth. Some studies try to associate levels of public expenditures to growth while others focus have focused on the relationship between certain expenditure components, such as public investment which includes education or health expenditures. Some studies (Devarajan, Swaroop & Zou 1996; De & Endow, 2008) have predicted a positive unidirectional relation between the focus variables while others (Baltagi & Moscone, 2010; Erdil & Yetkiner, 2009) have hit upon a positive bidirectional impact between health expenditure and income. The authors of Baltagi and Moscone (2010) examined the long run relationship between health expenditure and income growth in 20 OECD countries during 1971-2004. The study by Erdil and Yetkiner (2009) shows that the bidirectional causality between health expenditure and GDP growth depend on the type of countries *viz.* high, low and middle income countries. Their analysis brings to light that one-way causality runs from GDP to healthcare expenditure in the low and the middle income countries, whereas the reverse holds for high income countries. Initially, health expenditure acts as an investment in human capital, and given that human capital accumulation is an elemental source of economic growth, an increase in healthcare expenditure in due course leads to a higher level of GDP. Additionally, an increase in the healthcare expenditures associated with effective health intervention increases labour supply and productivity. This in turn increases the earnings of an individual which ultimately leads to a rise in GDP. Thus, all kinds of expenditure on health make a positive contribution to economic growth by developing the quality of human capital. Taking a walk down memory lane, the study by Sorkin (1978) can be regarded as one of the earliest studies of its kind to examine the impact of health on economic growth. Sorkin (1978) argues that a decline in the birth rate positively affects economic growth. Similar research papers such as Arora (2001) scrutinized the effect of health on economic growth for 10 industrialized countries. With a rise in the growth rate, health parameters have significantly improved. Bhargava et al. (2001) have studied the impact of health indicators for the period 1965-90 for developed and developing countries. The extent of increase in economic growth performance with the improvement in public health in developing countries is much more as compared to the developed countries. Going by Bloom et al. (2001), an annual improvement of 1 year in the life expectancy component makes an increase of growth to the tune of 4 per cent. Howitt (2005) highlighted the channels that influence the health of the country in the light of Schumpeterian growth theory. Some time series studies like Halder (2008), McCoskey and Selden (1998) have tried to focus on the direction of causality and issue of cointegration between health expenditure and growth. The empirical literature however brings in controversial results as research papers have come up with bidirectional, unidirectional or no causality results (Devlin & Hansen, 2001). Heading for a different issue, Aghion et al. (2011) portrays the relationship between health and growth in the light of modern endogenous growth theory and observed that in those OECD countries where mortality rates are less than 40 years have experienced increase in growth. In India, studies with regard to the trivariate analysis of growth, health infrastructure and health expenditure are very few. Ghei et al. (2010) found positive association between child immunization and availability of adequate healthcare infrastructure whereas Datar, Mukherji and Sood (2007) showed that the availability of healthcare infrastructure had only a modest effect on immunization coverage. These are a few studies that have dealt with this particular issue.

AN ILLUSTRATIVE MODEL

In this framework, the author has considered a three-equation model (at the individualistic level) comprising of health status, health expenditure and income earned by a person in a given period. To expand the concept of the inter-relationship between health expenditure and economic growth and how the dynamics have evolved, a framework of difference equations has been used. The difference of this model with the one proposed by Hurd and Kapteyn (2003) lies in the fact that it was developed in the context of a discrete time variable that is the time variable is only permitted to take integer values, as against a continuous time variable. The pattern of change of variables over a period of time must be described by the expected differences rather than by the derivatives or differentials. This structure is very much applicable given the fact that all the major variables in this framework can be considered at discrete time points. Before moving onto the structure of the model, the set of assumptions following Hurd and Kapteyn (2003) have been discussed below.

1. Healthcare spending depends on income but it varies across the population.
2. Health and its evolution depend on the amount of spending on healthcare facilities.
3. Healthcare spending includes spending on nutrition, housing, medical insurance and several other attributes that affect health.
4. Income growth at the current period depends on the current health status.

Let y_t be the earnings, h_t be the health status and s_t be the spending on healthcare at age t and be y_{t+1} the earnings, h_{t+1} be the health status and s_{t+1} be the spending on health at age $(t + 1)$. Then, consider this simple system of difference equations:

$$y_{t+1} = a + bh_t \tag{3}$$

$$h_{t+1} = c + ds_t \tag{4}$$

$$s_t = e + fy_t \tag{5}$$

Substituting equation (5) in (4), we get

$$h_{t+1} = c + d\left[e + fy_t\right] \tag{6}$$

or,

$$h_{t+1} = \left[c + de\right] + dfy_t$$

or,

$$h_{t+1} = g + ky_t$$

where,

$$g = c + de$$

and

$$k = df \,.$$

This is a system of simultaneous difference equations consisting of equation (3) and equation (6).

The generic solution of this system of difference equations is given by the 'particular solution' together with the complementary function.

In matrix notations, equation 6 shows,

$$\begin{pmatrix} 1 & 0 \\ 0 & 1 \end{pmatrix}\begin{pmatrix} y_{t+1} \\ h_{t+1} \end{pmatrix} + \begin{pmatrix} 0 & -b \\ -k & 0 \end{pmatrix}\begin{pmatrix} y_t \\ h_t \end{pmatrix} = \begin{pmatrix} a \\ g \end{pmatrix} \tag{7}$$

If stationary equilibrium exists, the particular solution can be expressed as $y_{t+1} = y_t = \bar{y}$ and $h_{t+1} = h_t = \bar{h}$. Substituting these values in the matrix form,

$$\bar{y} - b\bar{h} = a \tag{8}$$

$$\bar{h} - k\bar{y} = g \tag{9}$$

Solving (8) and (9) simultaneously, the particular solution is:

$$\bar{h} = \frac{ak+g}{1-bk} \text{ and } \bar{y} = \frac{a+bg}{1-bk}$$

The search for the complementary function, based on the trial solutions mr^t and nr^t, involves the reduced form of the matrix since $r^t \neq 0$

$$\begin{pmatrix} r & -b \\ -k & r \end{pmatrix}\begin{pmatrix} m \\ n \end{pmatrix} = \begin{pmatrix} 0 \\ 0 \end{pmatrix} \tag{10}$$

In order to avoid the trivial solutions, set

$$\begin{vmatrix} r & -b \\ -k & r \end{vmatrix} = 0$$

or,

$$r^2 - bk = 0$$

or,

$$r^2 = bk$$

or,

$$r = \pm\sqrt{bk}$$

Assuming only positive values or r (given both b and k to be positive), the solution is

$$y_t = m\left(\sqrt{bk}\right)^t + \left(\frac{a+bg}{1-bk}\right) \tag{11}$$

$$h_t = n\left(\sqrt{bk}\right)^t + \left(\frac{ak+g}{1-bk}\right) \tag{12}$$

Given the values at the initial level, one can definitize the value of m and n. The values of m and n are basically functions of the initial health and the income variables and the final solution of the model is:

$$y_t = \left[y_0 - \left(\frac{a+bg}{1-bk} \right) \right] \left(\sqrt{bk} \right)^t + \left(\frac{a+bg}{1-bk} \right) \tag{13}$$

$$h_t = \left[h_0 - \left(\frac{ak+g}{1-bk} \right) \right] \left(\sqrt{bk} \right)^t + \left(\frac{ak+g}{1-bk} \right) \tag{14}$$

Consequently, equation (13) has to be substituted in equation (5) to derive the time path of health expenditure.

For convergence of the time paths in case of equations (13) and (14), $\sqrt{bk}$ has to be less than 1 but the empirical dynamics of the convergence issue has been left for further research. The time paths demonstrate that an individual's income and health status will act in an analogous manner depending on the initial health status and income levels.

THE EMPIRICAL FRAMEWORK

The theoretical structure developed in the preceding section will motivate the empirical structure used in this segment. The idea is to generalize this micro model to a macro model empirically. Ideally, one should consider a simultaneous equation framework which enables the measurement of feedback effects and establishes the interdependence between economic growth and health expenditure. This has been represented in the following schematic diagram (Figure 1).

Data Description

This paper evaluated the causality and long-run relationship existence between economic growth (using Gross State Domestic Product, GSDP) and public healthcare expenditure (PHE) across 23 major states in India from 1980-2015 using Panel Cointegration method. The 23 major states on which this analysis has been carried out includes — Andhra Pradesh, Arunachal Pradesh, Assam, Bihar, Goa, Gujarat, Haryana, Himachal Pradesh, Jammu and Kashmir, Karnataka, Madhya Pradesh, Maharashtra, Manipur,

Figure 1. The Causal Nexus

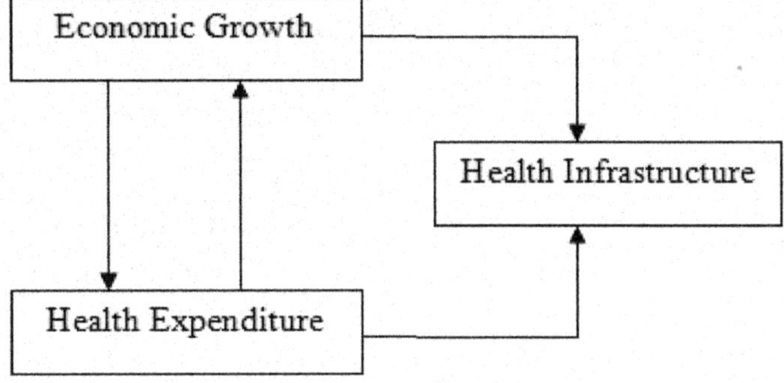

Meghalaya, Nagaland, Orissa, Punjab, Rajasthan, Sikkim, Tamil Nadu, Tripura, Uttar Pradesh and West Bengal. Uttarakhand was created out of Uttar Pradesh in 2000, so the data for Uttar Pradesh post 2000 includes the data of Uttar Pradesh plus Uttarakhand to maintain uniformity. Same is the case for Bihar and Madhya Pradesh which includes the data for Jharkhand and Chattisgarh post 2000. In the backward areas, private healthcare institutions are limited and to get an appropriate idea of the extent of public healthcare intervention, the spotlight has been only on public healthcare expenditure. Also, since the objective of this paper is to throw light on the public health infrastructural issues, private healthcare expenditure has not been taken into account. Annual data on the necessary components have been extracted from the Sample Registration System-Registrar General, Budget minutiae of the State Governments, the Reserve Bank of India Bulletin (several issues), Central Statistical Organization and the Ministry of Statistics and Programme Implementation (MOSPI), Government of India, New Delhi. Also, for extracting data on the per-capita state GDP at market prices, the website www.indiastat.com was visited. In order to avoid the scale effect, the author has considered state public healthcare expenditure as a percentage of the GSDP (both in real per-capita terms) coupled with real per-capita GSDP growth rate. It should be noted that the expenditure on health does not include fund allocation for water supply and sanitation.

Econometric Methodology

Before starting off with the panel unit root tests, the heteroskedasticity needs to be looked at. The Chi-Square value of 18.22 in Table 1 is low and lies within the confidence limits and the results undeniably confirm the absence of heteroskedasticity as the null hypothesis of "constant variance in the model" gets accepted. The foremost difference lies in the fact that in case of a panel data study, it is required to take into account the asymptotic behaviour of the time-series dimension *T* and cross-sectional dimension *N*.

Levin, Lin and Chu (LLC) unit root tests have been used in this study. The test is based on their model given below:

$$\Delta y_{it} = \alpha_i y_{it-1} + \sum_{j=1}^{p_j} \beta_{ij} \Delta y_{it-j} + x_{it}^{'}\delta + \varepsilon_{it}$$

Here, α_i is the error correction term and consequently, the null hypothesis of non-stationarity is as follows:

Tests hypotheses:

H$_0$: $\alpha_i = 0$ for all the cross section units, so the series is non-stationary and has a unit root.
H$_1$: $\alpha_i < 0$ for at least one cross section unit, so the series is trend stationary.

Table 1. Heteroskedasticity results

	Likelihood-Ratio Test	
H_0: Constant variance	LR Chi-Square value (χ^2)	Probability > Chi-Square (χ^2)
	18.22	0.98*

Notes: * denotes significance at 95 per cent level and calculation has been done by the author in Stata 12

When the probability value obtained from the test results is smaller than 0.05, H_0 is rejected and the stationarity of the series gets determined. LLC panel unit root test results that I have got are reported in Table 2. As Levin, Lin and Chu (2002) have pointed out; this test-statistic performs well when N lies between 10 and 250 and when T lies between 5 and 250. To determine whether a cointegrating relationship exists or not, the methodology proposed by Pedroni (1999) has been employed. Fundamentally, it employs four panel statistics and three group panel statistics to test the null hypothesis of no cointegration against the alternative hypothesis of cointegration. The first set is the within-dimension approach comprising of four statistics that are - panel v-statistic, panel ρ-statistic, panel PP-statistic and the panel ADF-statistic (Pedroni, 1999). This set pools the autoregressive coefficients across various members for the unit root tests to be carried out on the estimated residuals. The second set of statistics, centered on the between-dimensional approach, includes three statistics that are respectively the group ρ-statistic, group PP-statistic and group ADF-statistic. If the variables are not cointegrated it implies that the residuals are not I(0). These estimators are based on Monte Carlo simulations and the details for these calculations are given in the original paper (Refer to Pedroni, 1999). If the null hypothesis is rejected in the panel case, then the variables in question are cointegrated for all the 23 states considered. On the other hand, if the null is rejected in the group panel case, then cointegration among the relevant variables exists for at least one of the states. The VECM framework used has been given below.

$$\Delta GDP_{i,t} = \alpha_{1,i} + \varphi_{1,i} ECT_{i,t} + \sum_{j=1}^{k} \beta_{1,j,i} \Delta HE_{i,t-j} + \sum_{j=1}^{k} v_{1,j,i} \Delta GDP_{i,t-j} + \varepsilon_{1,i,t}$$

$$\Delta HE_{i,t} = \alpha_{2,i} + \varphi_{2,i} ECT_{i,t} + \sum_{j=1}^{k} \beta_{2,j,i} \Delta HE_{i,t-j} + \sum_{j=1}^{k} v_{2,j,i} \Delta GDP_{i,t-j} + \varepsilon_{2,i,t}$$

Where i (i = 1,…N) denotes the state, t (t = 1,...T) the period, j is the optimum lag considering the Akaike Information Criteria (AIC). ECT is the lagged error correction term derived from the long-run co-integrating relationship; the φ_1 and φ_2 are the adjustment coefficients and $\varepsilon_{1,i,t}$ and $\varepsilon_{2,i,t}$ are disturbance terms assumed to be white-noises and uncorrelated. The coefficients on the ECTs represent how fast the deviations from the long-run equilibrium are eliminated following a change in each of the variables. If the ECTs coefficients are zero ($\varphi_{1,i} = 0$, or $\varphi_{2,i} = 0$) for all i, then there is no error correction and thus there exists no contegration. But if ($\varphi_{1,i} < 0$, or $\varphi_{2,i} < 0$) then there exists error correction and consequently, we have cointegration. This paper examines the health expenditure and per-capita GDP growth rate relationship by taking advantage of the heterogeneous panel cointegration framework developed by Pedroni (1999) across the 23 major states in India. It should be noted that the first four statistics comply with the 'within-dimension' based terminology of panel data and the rest are 'between-dimension' based statistics. Now, I move on to the causality issue in case of panel data. Given that, this analysis is being carried out across the 29 states in India, the assumption that coefficients are different across cross-sections follows from Dumitrescu and Hurlin (2012), i.e:

$$\alpha_{0,i} \neq \alpha_{0,j}, \alpha_{1,i} \neq \alpha_{1,j}, \ldots \alpha_{p,i} \neq \alpha_{p,j},$$

$$\mu_{0,i} \neq \mu_{0,j}, \mu_{1,i} \neq \mu_{1,j}, \ldots \mu_{p,i} \neq \mu_{p,j}$$

and

$$\beta_{1,i} \neq \beta_{1,j}, \ldots \beta_{p,i} \neq \beta_{p,j}$$

and

$$\eta_{1,i} \neq \eta_{1,j}, \ldots \eta_{p,i} \neq \eta_{p,j}$$

for all i and j. Bivariate regressions in Dumitrescu and Hurlin (2012) take the form,

$$y_{i,t} = \alpha_{0,i} + \sum_{p=1}^{k} \alpha_{p,i} y_{i,t-p} + \sum_{p=1}^{k} \beta_{p,i} x_{i,t-p} + \varepsilon_{i,t}$$

$$x_{i,t} = \mu_{0,i} + \sum_{p=1}^{k} \mu_{p,i} x_{i,t-p} + \sum_{p=1}^{k} \eta_{p,i} y_{i,t-p} + e_{i,t}$$

where, t denotes the time period dimension of the panel, and i denotes the cross-sectional dimension and k is the number of lags. This assumption is applicable for India contrary to the assumption where the panel is treated as one large stacked data set. The intention is to perform Granger causality regressions for each and every individual cross-sectional unit. Subsequently, take the average of the Wald statistics derived from each cross section to get the W-bar statistic.

RESULTS AND DISCUSSION

Table 2 presents the results of the Levin, Lin, Chu (LLC) unit root tests. The results indicate that both variables are stationary after first differencing. In other word, both variables are integrated of order (1). Hence, we can apply the procedure of Pedroni (1999) to look into the cointegration possibility between the focus variables. In this study, given the AIC criteria, an optimum lag of 2 has been considered. The results in Table 3 designate the existence of a cointegrated relationship between health spending and per-capita economic growth in the long run. Under the alternative hypothesis, the panel-v statistic diverges to positive infinity $\left(\infty^{+}\right)$, and the right-hand tail of the standard normal distribution has been used to reject the null hypothesis. However, all the other panel cointegration test statistics diverge to negative infinity $\left(\infty^{-}\right)$. Therefore, the left-hand tail of the standard normal distribution is used to reject the null hypothesis. There is a strong evidence of panel cointegration as the test statistic values lie in the critical region (be it right-hand tail or left-hand tail) and the null hypothesis of 'no cointegration' gets resoundingly rejected.

Table 2. LLC Unit Root Test Results

Variables	Level	Probability	1st Difference	Probability	Result
GSDP	0.37	0.61	-3.40	0.00*	I(1)
PHE	-0.63	0.27	-4.62	0.00*	I(1)

Notes: * denotes significance at 95 per cent level and calculation has been done by the author in Eviews-7

Table 3. Panel Cointegration test

Test Procedure	Test statistic	Probability Value	Result
Panel v-statistic	3.19	0.00*	Cointegration
Panel rho-statistic	-2.35	0.00*	Cointegration
Panel PP-statistic	-3.08	0.00*	Cointegration
Panel ADF-statistic	-2.90	0.00*	Cointegration
Group rho-statistic	-4.72	0.00*	Cointegration
Group PP-statistic	-2.77	0.00*	Cointegration
Group ADF-statistic	-8.11	0.00*	Cointegration

Notes: * denotes significance at 95 per cent level and calculation has been done by the author in Eviews-7

This tests of whether GSDP and PHE follows a unit root process or not. At the level value, the approximate p-value for GSDP and PHE is 0.61 and 0.27 respectively. So, the null hypothesis of existence of unit root cannot be rejected. The next step is to carry out the first order differencing of the data and the results suggest that the both the GSDP and PHE series become stationary at the first order. The p-value of 0.00 implies that the null hypothesis of presence of unit root gets rejected. This helps in building up a model based on first order stationary data set. However, the presence of a cointegrating liaison does not give any clear idea regarding the causality between the concerned variables in this section. The results of the test for causality are reported in Table 4 below.

The author has found only one cointegrating vector. From the theoretical framework proposed by the author to the model given by Halder and Mallik (2010), theoretically, there exist the presence cointegration. This is justified because if investment on public health rises, it is bound to create a repercussion effect on income growth in the long run. Consequently, the policy formulations at the federal level should take into account this liaison but what happens to this relationship at the state level has been left for further research and is worth exploring. The Wbar statistic for both cases lies in the critical borough as suggested by the p-value and the null hypothesis of 'PHE does not Granger Cause GSDP' and 'GSDP does not Granger Cause PHE' gets rejected. Therefore, there exists a bilateral causality running between

Table 4. Results of Panel Causality test

Null Hypothesis	W-Bar Statistic	Probability
PHE does not Granger Cause GSDP	3.23	0.00*
GSDP does not Granger Cause PHE	4.59	0.00*

Notes: * denotes significance at 95 per cent level and calculation has been done by the author in Eviews-7

GSDP and PHE which is in harmony with the results obtained in Hurd and Kapteyn (2003). The higher is the healthcare expenditure, better are the infrastructural facilities and as people are able to avail these facilities, the burden of disease falls. Thus, labourers become more productive and are capable enough to bring in more income. A rise in income in the subsequent periods leads to growth. In contrast, if economic growth rises it means that citizens are better off. This in turn means that the citizens will be capable enough to demand high quality health infrastructure which in turn will put pressure on the Government to increase healthcare expenditure. These arguments can be seen in light of a negative perspective also. If healthcare expenditure is at its minimal level, quality of health infrastructure will be poor and labour productivity will fall. The quality of the healthcare infrastructure is actually poor for many states across India (Refer to Table 7). Consequently, economic growth peters out (Refer to Figure 3). When economic growth is low, this means that people are not capable enough to earn more, so demand for quality healthcare services will be less. This justifies the fact that healthcare expenditure will also be less. As a result, the bidirectional causal relation is justified in the Indian context.

PUBLIC HEALTH INFRASTRUCTURE AND HEALTH EXPENDITURE IN INDIA

This section primarily aims at constructing the health infrastructure index across 23 major states in India. As already mentioned, the idea is explore the link between public health infrastructure and health expenditure given the fact that public healthcare expenditure is cointegrated with per-capita growth rate of the states. To construct the index, two terminal points have been considered *viz.* 2005-06 and 2014-15. After the index construction, the position of the states with respect to this index will be discussed in the light of per-capita health expenditure of the concerned states. Before moving onto the index construction, the methodology needs to be discussed in detail.

The Key Dimensions

This paper considers five dimensions on the basis of which the index will be constructed. These include:

1. Number of Sub-Centres (SC).
2. Number of Primary Health Centres (PHC).
3. Number of Community Health Centres (CHC).
4. Number of District Hospitals (DH).
5. Percentage of SCs, PHCs and CHCs adequately equipped with supply of drugs, attendants, nurses, etc. (ADQ).

Coming to the problem of multicollinearity, the most widely-used marker for multicollinearity, is the variance inflation factor (VIF). It may be calculated for each predictor by performing a linear regression of that predictor on all the other predictors in the model (Table 5). VIF is defined as:

$$VIF = \frac{1}{1-R^2}$$

The rule of thumb is that VIFs over and above the value of 4 demand further investigation, while VIFs exceeding 10 gives an indication of severe multicollinearity and hence requires correction.

Each of the dimensions taken into account is assumed to be independent given that the value of VIF is below 4. One can include other indicators like number of beds, health assistants but these factors depend on the figures of SCs, PHCs, CHCs and the number of hospitals. Consequently, if these factors are included, the independence assumption will break down on account of very high correlation.

METHODOLOGY FOR CALCULATING THE INDEX

The following steps are to be followed for calculating the index.

Step 1: Normalizing the parameters

It is an aggregate index comprising of five parameters (already stated) so cannot be aggregated to derive the composite index as the parameters have different units of measurement.

As a result, each parameter is normalized by –

$$X_{iN} = \frac{(X_i - X_{\min})}{(X_{\max} - X_{\min})}$$

where, X_{iN} is the normalized value, X_{min} is the minimum value observed across the 23 states considered for some parameter, X_{max} is the maximum value observed across the 23 states for a particular parameter and X_i is the value a particular parameter for state i.

Normalization yields a value for every parameter for every state which lies between 0 and 1. The value '0' depicts the worst case and '1' depicts the best case scenario.

Step 2: Aggregation using the Weighted Euclidean Distance Method

Firstly, in this analysis the author has given equal weights to all the parameters given the fact that all the parameters are of equal importance in judging the quality of healthcare infrastructure. The five

Table 5. Results of VIF Test

Variables	VIF
(SC)	3.82
(PHC)	2.67
(CHC)	3.41
(DH)	1.39
(ADQ)	1.20
Mean Score VIF	2.49

Notes: Computed by the author in Stata 12

dimension-indices may be represented in a five-dimensional space with the value '0' being the minimum value and '1' as the ideally required value.

The Public Health Infrastructure Index (PHI) uses inverse of the weighted Euclidean distance from the ideal point of (1,1,1,1,1). So the PHI calculation for state i is given by:

$$PHI_i = 1 - \sqrt{\frac{\left[\left(1 - SC_i\right)^2 + \left(1 - PHC_i\right)^2 + \left(1 - CHC_i\right)^2 + \left(1 - DH_i\right)^2 + \left(1 - ADQ_i\right)^2\right]}{5}}$$

The numerator of the term within the square root gives the Euclidean distance of state i from the ideal point (1,1,1,1,1). The inverse distance has been calculated to show that higher is the value of PHI, better will be the public health infrastructure and higher will be the position of the state concerned among other states. As proposed by Nathan et al. (2008), this PHI index satisfies the properties of *NAMPUS* i.e. normalization, anonymity, monotonicity, proximity, uniformity and signaling. Moreover, this framework relaxes the assumption of a perfect substitutability among the five-dimension indices signifying that a decent performance taking into account one specific dimension does not make up for the bad performance with respect to another dimension.

The results reported in Table 7 provide us with the PHI scores (rounded up to 3 decimal places) and ranks for the 23 states. Though, data is available from 1980 onwards, for comparison of the current inter-state performance, time points 2005-06 and 2014-15 have been taken into account. The trends in public healthcare expenditure from 2001 onwards have been reported in Figure 2. Public healthcare expenditure has more or less hovered between 1.1 to 1.4 per cent of GDP in the Indian context. Now, the question is to what extent this has impacted health infrastructure.

The real per-capita public health expenditure data in Table 7 has also been normalized based on the normalization criteria (value lies between 0 (min) and 1 (max)) in the previous sub-section.

Figure 2. Trends in Central Public Health Expenditure (as a percentage of GDP) in India

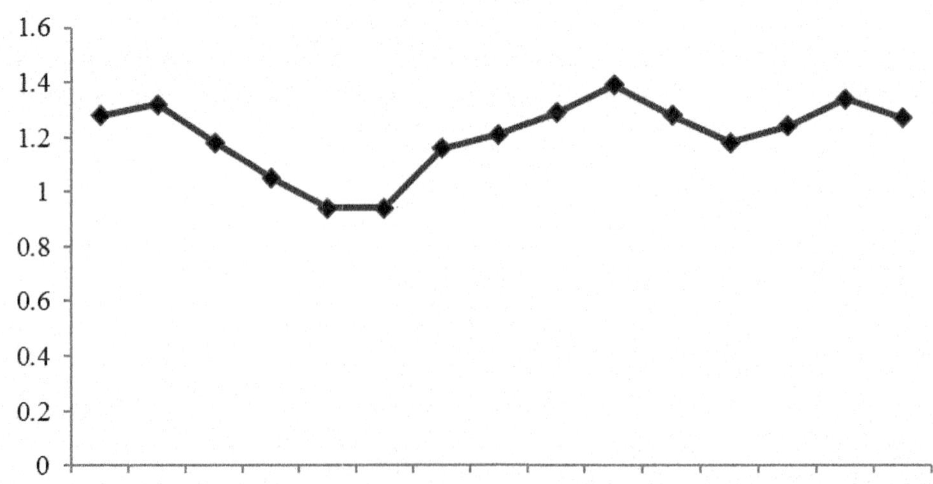

Table 6. Pattern of central allocation (Total vs Healthcare) (crore INR)

Plan Period	Total Planned Investment	Family Welfare Allocation	Total for Health Sector
Eighth Plan (1992-97)	434100	6500 (1.5%)	14102.2 (3.2%)
Ninth Plan (1997-2002)	859200	15120.2 (1.76%)	35204.95 (4.09%)
Tenth Plan (2002-07)	1484131.3	27125 (1.83%)	58920.3 (3.97%)
Eleventh Plan (2007-12)	2156571	136147.0 (6.31%)	140135 (6.49%)

Source: Compiled from Planning Commission of India (2011)

Table 7. PHI Scores

State	PHI Score (2014-15)	PHI Score (2005-06)	Rank (2014-15)	Rank (2005-06)	Real Per-Capita PHE (2005-06)	Real Per-Capita PHE (2014-15)
Andhra Pradesh	0.351	0.332	9	9	0.41	0.34
Arunachal Pradesh	0.313	0.309	12	12	0.55	0.36
Assam	0.217	0.191	16	17	0.56	0.38
Bihar	0.151	0.148	20	21	0.43	0.00
Goa	0.534	0.487	2	4	0.47	0.42
Gujarat	0.328	0.311	11	11	0.59	0.69
Haryana	0.410	0.370	8	7	0.42	0.35
Himachal Pradesh	0.414	0.387	6	6	0.73	0.67
Karnataka	0.331	0.330	10	10	0.63	0.58
Kerala	0.561	0.509	1	2	0.79	0.67
Madhya Pradesh	0.274	0.254	14	14	0.44	0.51
Maharashtra	0.431	0.427	5	5	0.46	0.39
Manipur	0.157	0.151	19	20	0.28	0.27
Meghalaya	0.143	0.122	22	23	0.36	0.35
Nagaland	0.142	0.131	23	22	0.00	0.24
Orissa	0.234	0.196	15	16	0.50	0.37
Punjab	0.519	0.489	4	3	1.00	1.00
Rajasthan	0.196	0.215	17	15	0.51	0.37
Sikkim	0.149	0.156	21	19	0.42	0.31
Tamil Nadu	0.520	0.512	3	1	0.53	0.58
Tripura	0.176	0.174	18	18	0.39	0.24
Uttar Pradesh	0.304	0.296	13	13	0.34	0.44
West Bengal	0.411	0.365	7	8	0.36	0.29

Notes: Computed by the author

The results in Table 7 help us to judge the position of the states with respect to public healthcare infrastructure in light of real per-capita GSDP. Table 8 is an extension of Table 7 in the sense that it gives us an idea about the average values of public healthcare infrastructure in the country, measures of dispersion and other distributional features of the health infrastructure. Before going on to the expla-

Table 8. Summary Statistics of PHI Scores of 2014-15 and 2005-06 – A Comparison

Observations	23	PHI_Scr_14_15	
		Percentiles	
1%	0.142	Mean	0.31591
25%	0.176	Standard Deviation	0.13910
50%	0.313	Variance	0.01935
75%	0.414	Skewness	0.28569
99%	0.561	Kurtosis	1.83167
		PHI_Scr_05_06	
		Percentiles	
1%	0.122	Mean	0.29835
25%	0.174	Standard Deviation	0.12940
50%	0.309	Variance	0.01675
75%	0.387	Skewness	0.25213
99%	0.512	Kurtosis	1.81361

Notes: Computed by the author in Stata 12

nation of Table 7, a snapshot analysis of Table 8 demonstrates that average value of the index hovers around 0.3 indicating that the overall position in terms of public healthcare infrastructure is not quite up to the mark. Between 2005-06 and 2014-15, there has not been any significant improvement in the health infrastructure index. The median value (50th percentile) has remained almost the same at 0.31. The value of kurtosis less than implies that the distribution of the PHI Scores has too thick tails and flat in the middle i.e. platykurtic in nature. The percentile values show the percentage of states having PHI Scores at or below the corresponding partition value. It is appalling to observe that 99 per cent of the values for PHI Scores lie below 0.56 in 2004-05. The figure has further deteriorated to 0.51 as the maximum value of the PHI Score has worsened. The value of variance in 2005-06 is 0.016 and in 2014-15 it has been 0.019. This gives an indication that the estimates have been highly consistent and that the predicted values are very close to the observed ones. This also validates the absence of hetero-skedasticity in the analysis. Another motivating feature is the measure of the skewness (i.e. positively skewed) which reflects that a majority of the states have performed disappointingly with regards to the public health infrastructure index.

Looking at Table 7, the top 5 performing states are Kerala, Punjab, Tamil Nadu, Maharashtra and Goa. As before, the position of Maharashtra has remained the same but the position of the other top performing states have changed but they have remained within the top 5 bracket. The highest score is 0.56, attained by Kerala, signifying that even the top performing state needs to improve a lot in terms of public health infrastructure development. Interestingly, the scores obtained by all the states have improved between this time span except for Rajasthan and Sikkim. For states like Goa and Maharashtra, in spite of spending somewhat less on real per-capita health, its position on the health infrastructure index is at the top indicating that a majority of health expenditure has been incurred on development of health infrastructure. On the contrary, the position of states like Rajasthan, Karnataka and Arunachal Pradesh on the index is not consistent to per-capita health expenditure. This draws our attention to the fact that per-capita health expenditure has not been incurred on the development of public health infrastructure *per se*.

Coming down to the final part of the analysis, the relation between the normalized value of real per-capita spending and health infrastructure index has been explored in Figure 3 and 4. Due to lack of data points (since I have considered health infrastructure at two points *viz.* 2005-06 and 2014-15), it was not possible to carry out a panel data analysis. As an alternative, a scatter plot analysis has been carried out (Refer to Figure 3 and 4).

There are exceptions where in spite of increase in healthcare spending, infrastructure position has deteriorated but in general the relation is clearly positive indicating that the increase in real per-capita health expenditure indeed influences the health infrastructure of the state concerned. The relationship has more or less remained the same between the time periods considered.

Figure 3. PHI scores and Real per-capita PHE Scatter plots for 2005-06

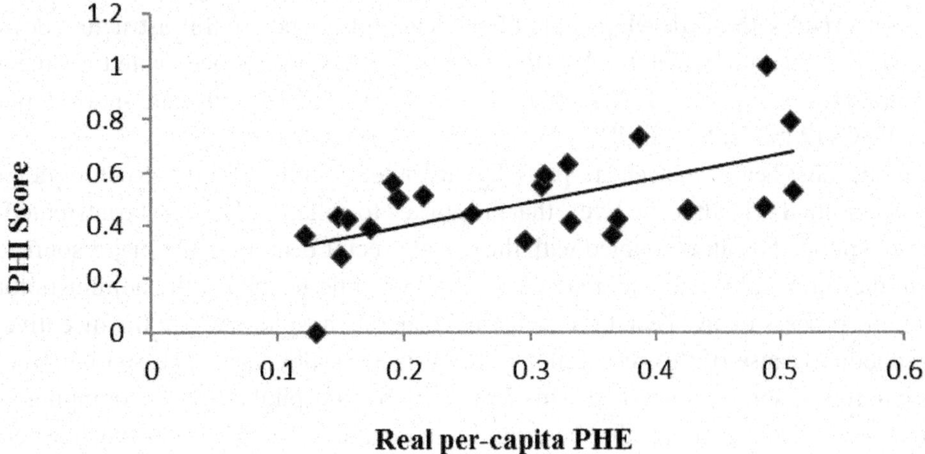

Figure 4. PHI Scores and Real per-capita PHE Scatter plots for 2014-15

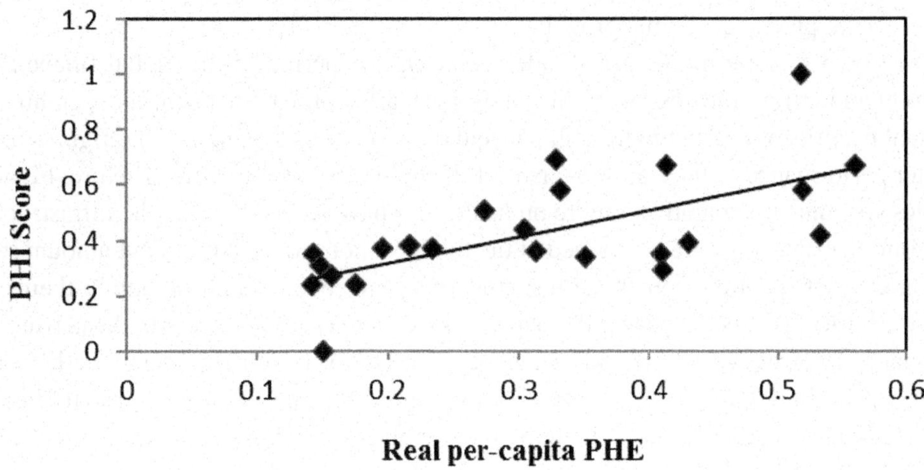

This issue of the triangular analysis of health expenditure, healthcare infrastructure and economic growth has cropped up on account of India's healthcare system primarily focusing on curative measures rather than preventive ones. Their focus has never been on health infrastructure *per se*. Therefore, both the central and the state governments have a critical role in the development of health infrastructure of the states concerned and the country in general. Figuring out the pattern of investments, sources of funding and proportion of allocation against the total allocation helps us to comprehend the health outcomes as regards to the healthcare expenditure. The data in Table 6 below table shows the percentage of allocation for the health sector alongside the total planned investment in the country by the centre. Figure 2 noticeably shows the decline in the total health sector allocation from 2001 onwards. It increased to some extent in the Eleventh Plan when the National Rural Health Mission (NRHM) schemes were started. There are several schemes under the umbrella of NRHM, which includes Facility Based Newborn and Child Care (FBNC), Janani Shishu Suraksha Karyakram (JSSK), Facility Based Integrated Management of Neonatal and Childhood Illness (F-IMNCI), Navjat Shishu Suraksha Karyakram (NSSK), etc but none of them are concerned with the development of healthcare infrastructure. Infrastructure development is a part of preventive measure which the Indian health sector has not yet been able to come to terms to. As per the Rural Health Statistics (RHS) reported on 31.3.2015, there is an acute shortfall of 33145 SCs (20%), 6556 PHCs (22%) and 2316 CHCs (32%) across the country.

Kerala's noticeable health indices are partially attributed to a health infrastructure developed by a government committed to healthcare. Even, that has started to collapse. This can be attributed to the poor condition of the public hospitals coupled with the private sector becoming the major source of curative healthcare in the rural and the urban areas. Precisely, in public hospitals, the administrators fight for funds and in this process many specialists switch to corporate hospitals where the incentives are much more. The economic cause of this resurgence of the private health sector is essentially the incentives they propose to the personnel concerned. This reduces public hospitals to sheer 'dumping grounds' for the unwanted cases. The question is that how can India maintain the growth prospects when the health infrastructure is in such a shambles? Interestingly, increase in real per-capita health expenditure does not always lead to a rise in the value of the infrastructure index. Health Infrastructure and per-capita spending on healthcare are more or less positively related except for a few cases so, given that health expenditure is related to economic growth so by the law of transitivity, public healthcare infrastructure indeed has a role to play in economic growth.

India has grown steadily in the last decade excluding the period of the global financial crisis i.e. (between 2009 and 2013). The results of this analysis clearly validate that health expenditure will motivate the dual benefits of health progress in particular and growth in general. The figures are a sign of the lackluster performance of the states in terms of the public healthcare infrastructure. Figure 3 shows that the states spending comparatively more on healthcare have scored high on the infrastructure index, *vice versa*. But, the states that are positioned at the top have not spent a significant amount so the question is that inspite of spending somewhat less how they have been able to maintain their position on the growth trajectory. This is the puzzle the paper talks about. The big players in the private healthcare sector like Narayana Hrudayalaya, Wockhardt, Fortis, MEDICA, Columbia Asia and others are making their presence increasingly felt across the states which in turn is pushing up the growth. Public healthcare infrastructure has taken a backseat with the private players taking their place. Actually, the private health sector is the missing link in this analysis.

CONCLUDING REMARKS AND FUTURE RESEARCH POSSIBILITIES

This paper shows that the North-Eastern states are the worst performers in terms of development of public healthcare infrastructure. Not only there is an acute shortage of health centres but also trained personnel including doctors, nurses, mid-wives and other health workers. In line with the "Look East" policy of the Government of India, various private healthcare providers are either setting up their amenities or formulating plans for exploiting the potential in the North-Eastern market. For example, only a few days back, Kolkata was the sole healthcare hub in Eastern India for catering to the requirements of the patients coming from all the North-Eastern states, Bihar, Orissa as well as from Bangladesh and Nepal. To lessen the burden on Kolkata and also for the purpose of decentralization of the health sector, recently three cities (*viz.* Asansol and Siliguri in West Bengal and Bhubaneswar in Odisha) have emerged as future healthcare hubs in the Eastern part of India. Given their performance, do the North-Eastern states have the potential to become the Mecca of healthcare on their own? It is my belief that the performance of the governments (at all levels) will go a long way in determining whether North East India gets to welcome the rising healthcare sun.

On the whole, India's public healthcare system is erratic, underfunded coupled with overcrowded hospitals and clinics, and lack of penetration in the rural areas. Cutting down on funding by the Government of India has been accredited for the celebrated failures on the part of the Ministry of Health and Family Welfare to use up its allocated budget wholly. Now, healthcare services are increasingly becoming unreachable because of the lack of government support and the growing penetration of private institutes in the medical sector. A question which warrants an immediate answer is concerned with the role of the current public healthcare system. Despite, the growth of public-private partnership (PPP) model, financial as well as logistical constraints still hinders the development of large scale undertakings under such a framework. The private sector is not only promising to be a major player in terms of service provision but is also trying to fill in the gaps left by the public sector. The speedy growth of the private health sector has resulted in a situation where these private players have become commercial units and the social-welfare goal has taken a backseat. This is of serious concern from the welfare perspective. Therefore, the twofold goals of both the centre and the state under such a situation should be to arrange for equitable access to healthcare services and preserving the standard of health infrastructure.

Summing up, this article has explored the causal liaison between real per-capita public healthcare expenditure and real per-capita GSDP growth across 23 major states in India over an interval of 35 years. It illustrates that the variables of interest are non-stationary, and that they are linked in the long run. The results reject the null hypothesis of 'no cointegration' in the panel cointegration test. Moreover, the "health-led growth hypothesis" gets validated in this study. Moving onto the health infrastructure index section, the calculation shows a positive relationship between health infrastructure position and health expenditure across the states in India. The variability in the index reveals the fallacy in the "one-size-fits-all" strategy which is followed for allocating funds across the states. Here, the focus is primarily on health so incorporating education expenditure as a percentage of GSDP would put in another dimension to this subject. Likewise, any researcher can use this framework to construct an educational infrastructure index. Hence, the impact of healthcare spending on economic growth coupled with the implications for health infrastructure endorses the requirement for governments' intervention. This can be productively carried out by implementing policies designed to develop a healthier and a productive India.

REFERENCES

Aghion, P., Howitt, P., & Murtin, F. (2010). *The relationship between health and growth: When Lucas meets Nelson-Phelps*. National Bureau of Economic Research.

Arora, S. (2001). Health Human Productivity and Long-Term Economic Growth. *The Journal of Economic History*, *61*(3), 699–749.

Baltagi, B. H., & Kao, C. (2000). *Nonstationary panels, cointegration in panels and dynamic panels: A survey.* Syracuse University Center for Policy Research Working Paper, (16).

Baltagi, B. H., & Moscone, F. (2010). Health care expenditure and income in the OECD reconsidered: Evidence from panel data. *Economic Modelling*, *27*(4), 804–881. doi:10.1016/j.econmod.2009.12.001

Behrman, J. R., & Deolikar, A. B. (1988). Health and nutrition. In Handbook of Development Economics (Vol. 1). Academic Press.

Bhandari, L., & Dutta, S. (2007). Health infrastructure in rural India. *India Infrastructure Report*, 265-271.

Bhargava, A., Jamison, D., Lau, L. J., & Murray, C. (2001). Modeling the effects of Health on Economic Growth. *Journal of Health Economics*, *20*(3), 423–440. doi:10.1016/S0167-6296(01)00073-X PMID:11373839

Bloom, D. E., & Canning, D. (2000). The health and wealth of nations. *Science*, *287*(5456), 1207–1209. doi:10.1126/science.287.5456.1207 PMID:10712155

Bloom, D. E., Canning, D., & Sevilla, J. (2001). *The effect of health on economic growth: Theory and evidence*. National Bureau of Economic Research.

Datar, A., Mukherji, A., & Sood, N. (2007). Health infrastructure & immunization coverage in rural India. *The Indian Journal of Medical Research*, *125*(1), 31.

De, A., & Endow, T. (2008). *Public expenditure on education in India: Recent trends and outcomes*. Academic Press.

Devarajan, S., Swaroop, V., & Zou, H. F. (1996). The composition of public expenditure and economic growth. *Journal of Monetary Economics*, *37*(2), 313–344. doi:10.1016/S0304-3932(96)90039-2

Devlin, N., & Hansen, P. (2001). Health care spending and economic output: Granger causality. *Applied Economics Letters*, *8*(8), 561–564. doi:10.1080/13504850010017357

Dumitrescu, E. I., & Hurlin, C. (2012). Testing for Granger non-causality in heterogeneous panels. *Economic Modelling*, *29*(4), 1450–1460. doi:10.1016/j.econmod.2012.02.014

Erdil, E., & Yetkiner, I. H. (2009). The Granger-causality between health care expenditure and output: A panel data approach. *Applied Economics*, *41*(4), 511–518. doi:10.1080/00036840601019083

Ghei, K., Agarwal, S., Subramanyam, M. A., & Subramanian, S. V. (2010). Association between child immunization and availability of health infrastructure in slums in India. *Archives of Pediatrics & Adolescent Medicine*, *164*(3), 243–249. doi:10.1001/archpediatrics.2009.277 PMID:20194257

Halder, S. (2008). Effect of Health Human Capital Expenditure on Economic Growth in India: A State Level Study. *Asia-Pacific Social Science Review, 8*(2).

Halder, S., & Mallik, G. (2010). Does human capital cause economic growth? A case study of India. *International Journal of Economic Sciences and Applied Research, 3*(1), 7–25.

Howitt, P. (2005). Health, human capital, and economic growth: A Schumpeterian perspective. *Health and economic growth: Findings and policy implications*, 19-40.

Hurd, M., & Kapteyn, A. (2003). Health, wealth, and the role of institutions. *The Journal of Human Resources, 38*(2), 386–415. doi:10.2307/1558749

Learning Planning Commission. (2011). *High level expert group report on universal health coverage for India.*

Levin, A., Lin, C. F., & Chu, C. S. J. (2002). Unit root tests in panel data: Asymptotic and finite- sample properties. *Journal of Econometrics, 108*(1), 1–24. doi:10.1016/S0304-4076(01)00098-7

McCoskey, S. K., & Selden, T. M. (1998). Health care expenditures and GDP: Panel data unit root test results. *Journal of Health Economics, 17*(3), 369–376. doi:10.1016/S0167-6296(97)00040-4 PMID:10180923

Mushkin, S. J. (1962). Health as an Investment. *Journal of Political Economy, 70*(5, Part 2), 129–157. doi:10.1086/258730

Nathan, H. S. K., Mishra, S., & Reddy, B. S. (2008). *An alternative approach to measure HDI.* Indira Gandhi Institute of Development Research (IGIDR), Working Paper, WP- 2008-001.

Novick, L. F., & Mays, G. P. (2005). *Public health administration: principles for population- based management.* Jones & Bartlett.

Pedroni, P. (1999). Critical values for cointegration tests in heterogeneous panels with multiple regressors, *Oxford Bulletin of Economics and Statistics, 61*(s 1), 653-670.

Preston, S. H. (1975). The changing relation between mortality and level of economic development. *Population Studies, 29*(2), 231–248. doi:10.1080/00324728.1975.10410201 PMID:11630494

Sorkin, A. (1978). Health manpower. *Health Care Management Review, 3*(1), 87–88. doi:10.1097/00004010-197824000-00011 PMID:10239260

ADDITIONAL READING

Akachi, Y., & Canning, D. (2010). Health trends in Sub-Saharan Africa: Conflicting evidence from infant mortality rates and adult heights. *Economics and Human Biology, 8*(2), 273–288. doi:10.1016/j.ehb.2010.05.015 PMID:20634153

Balarajan, Y., Selvaraj, S., & Subramanian, S. V. (2011). Health care and equity in India. *Lancet, 377*(9764), 505–515. doi:10.1016/S0140-6736(10)61894-6 PMID:21227492

Barrett, G., Sellman, D., & Thomas, J. (2005). *Interprofessional working in health and social care: professional perspectives*. Palgrave Macmillan.

Caselli, F., Esquivel, G., & Lefort, F. (1996). Reopening the convergence debate: A new look at cross-country growth empirics. *Journal of Economic Growth*, *1*(3), 363–389. doi:10.1007/BF00141044

Chakrabarti, A., & Rao, D. N. (2005). Variation in Health Expenditures: is it Just Income or Other Factors; Empirical Investigation Using a Panel of Indian States. *Empirical Investigation Using a Panel of Indian States*

Gerdtham, U. G., & Löthgren, M. (2000). On stationarity and cointegration of international health expenditure and GDP. *Journal of Health Economics*, *19*(4), 461–475. doi:10.1016/S0167-6296(99)00036-3 PMID:11010235

Gill, K. (2009). *A primary evaluation of service delivery under the National Rural Health Mission (NRHM): findings from a study in Andhra Pradesh*. Uttar Pradesh, Bihar and Rajasthan: Planning Commission of India, Government of India.

Goel, M. M., & Garg, I. (2011). Public expenditure on health and economic growth in Haryana: An Analysis'. *Indian Journal of Applied Research,/(3)*, 211-214.

Granger, C. W. (1981). Some properties of time series data and their use in econometric model specification. *Journal of Econometrics*, *16*(1), 121–130. doi:10.1016/0304-4076(81)90079-8

Hartwig, J. (2010). Is health capital formation good for long-term economic growth?–Panel Granger-causality evidence for OECD countries. *Journal of Macroeconomics*, *32*(1), 314–325. doi:10.1016/j.jmacro.2009.06.003

Holtz-Eakin, D., Newey, W., & Rosen, H. S. (1988). Estimating vector autoregressions with panel data. *Econometrica*, *56*(6), 1371–1395. doi:10.2307/1913103

Jørgensen, O. H. (2008). *Health, Endogenous Fertility and Economic Growth*. Syddansk Universitet.

Karatzas, G. (2000). On the determination of the US aggregate health care expenditure. *Applied Economics*, *32*(9), 1085–1099. doi:10.1080/000368400404236

Lopez-Casasnovas, G., Rivera, B., & Currais, L. (2005). Introduction: the role health plays in economic growth. *Health and economic growth: Findings and policy implications*, 1-16.

Morand, O. F. (2005). Economic growth, health, and longevity in the very long term: facts and mechanisms. *Health and economic growth: findings and policy implications, 74*(2).

Murthy, V. N., & Okunade, A. A. (2009). The core determinants of health expenditure in the African context: Some econometric evidence for policy. *Health Policy (Amsterdam)*, *91*(1), 57–62. doi:10.1016/j.healthpol.2008.10.001 PMID:19108929

Parkin, D., McGuire, A., & Yule, B. (1987). Aggregate health care expenditures and national income: Is health care a luxury good? *Journal of Health Economics*, *6*(2), 109–127. doi:10.1016/0167-6296(87)90002-6 PMID:10312163

Paul, V. K., Sachdev, H. S., Mavalankar, D., Ramachandran, P., Sankar, M. J., Bhandari, N., & Kirkwood, B. (2011). Reproductive health, and child health and nutrition in India: Meeting the challenge. *Lancet, 377*(9762), 332–349. doi:10.1016/S0140-6736(10)61492-4 PMID:21227494

Pradhan, R. P. (2011). Government spending and economic growth in SAARC: Evidence from panel cointegration. *International Journal of Economic Policy in Emerging Economies, 4*(1), 78–94. doi:10.1504/IJEPEE.2011.038874

Ramani, K. V., Mavalankar, D. V., & Govil, D. (Eds.). (2008). *Strategic issues and challenges in health management*. SAGE Publications India.

Reddy, K. N., & Selvaraju, V. (1994). *Health Care Expenditure by Government of India 1974-75 to 1990-91*. New Delhi: Seven Hills Publication.

Schultz, T. P. (1999). Health and schooling investments in Africa. *The Journal of Economic Perspectives, 13*(3), 67–88. doi:10.1257/jep.13.3.67 PMID:15179964

Wagstaff, A., & Van Doorslaer, E. (1993). Equity in the delivery of health care: methods and findings. *Equity in the finance and delivery of health care: An international perspective*, 49-86.

KEY TERMS AND DEFINITIONS

Cointegration: Cointegration is an econometric characteristic where a collection of time series variables (X_1, X_2, X_3, ….. X_k) being integrated of the same order (greater than zero i.e. non- stationary) can be combined to generate a linear combination from this collection of variables which is integrated of order zero (i.e. a stationary trend). Then the time series variables X_1, X_2, X_3, ….. X_k are said to be cointegrated.

Difference Equations: When time is permitted to take integer values only, the pattern of change of a variable say x, is described by the so-called 'differences' between the two consecutive time periods. In notational terms, the difference is characterized as: $\Delta y_t = y_{t+1} - y_t$ and a difference equation of the first order is like: $y_{t+1} - y_t = 2$.

Economic Growth: It can be defined as the increase in the capability of an economy to produce goods and services from one period to another. It can be measured either in nominal terms or in inflation adjusted real terms. Typically, GDP or GNP is taken as a measure of economic growth. In notational terms, GDP growth rate, g_t, $g_t = \frac{GDP_t - GDP_{t-1}}{GDP_{t-1}} \times 100$ where, *t* indicates the particular time point.

Euclidean Distance Function: The Euclidean Distance in Euclidean-n space is the distance (dist) between two vectors **a**, a = (a_1, a_2, … a_n) and **b**, b = (b_1, b_2, … b_n) is given by

$$dist(a,b) = dist(b,a) = \sqrt{\left(a_1 - b_1\right)^2 + \left(a_2 - b_2\right)^2 + \ldots\ldots\left(a_n - b_n\right)^2}.$$

Granger Causality: Granger Causality is a statistical hypothesis that asserts that a time series variable say X, is said to "Granger cause" another time series variable Y, if and only if the past values of X contain adequate information to predict Y.

Panel Data: Also called longitudinal data, represents cross-sectional time series data i.e. data on multi-dimensional cross-sections (comprising of individuals, firms and countries) over a period of time.

Public Health Infrastructure: This can be explained by the following: (i) A competent public healthcare workforce; (ii) Up to-date data and information systems; (iii) Evaluation of the machinery (consisting of health centres, doctors, nurses, attendants etc.), effectiveness, accessibility and quality of public health services.

Public Healthcare Expenditure: It includes public healthcare expenditures covering the entire gamut of provision of healthcare services (preventive and curative), family planning measures, nutritional requirements, reproductive and child health (RCH) and other problems pertaining to emergency aid in this arena.

Chapter 8
Sustainable Infrastructures:
A New Infrastructure Investment Strategy

Amir Manzoor
Bahria University, Pakistan

ABSTRACT

Infrastructure investments can have long term consequences for the economy and environment of a country. Some notable public infrastructure projects include energy, transportation, water, and waste disposal systems. There are strong financial, environmental, and social change drivers that are forcing immediate changes. We need to rethink our infrastructure investments and develop sustainable, resilient, and affordable infrastructure systems for vital services of our society. These systems will be able to support the healthy and prosperous communities in future. The objective of this chapter is to review the current state of sustainable infrastructures and provide suggestions to policy makers responsible for infrastructure development how to develop sustainable infrastructures.

INTRODUCTION

Infrastructure is essential for economic development and poverty reduction. To date, both developed and developing countries have been slow in expanding infrastructure access. Most of the time infrastructure is dominated by public sector and is often mismanaged. Private participation is important for infrastructure expansion. The flows of capital in the form of private participation in infrastructure (PPI) amounts has increased especially in developing world (World Bank, 2016b)

Infrastructure investments can have long term consequences for economy and environment of a country. Some notable public infrastructure projects include Energy, transportation, water, and waste disposal systems. There are strong financial, environmental, and social change drivers that are forcing immediate changes. We need to rethink our infrastructure investments and develop sustainable, resilient, and affordable infrastructures for critical services of our society. Extensive capital investments are needed to modernize the infrastructure for future society needs. It is estimated that around 6$60 trillion would be needed in global infrastructure investments during next two decades just to make sure that infrastructures are able to support the GDP growth. This investment requirement does not include the investments required for climate improvements and decrease greenhouse gases (Dobbs et al., 2015).

DOI: 10.4018/978-1-5225-2364-2.ch008

These infrastructure investments will be important for long-term well-being of the society and sustainability. Design of much of the existing infrastructures and the various types of activities (such as personal and commercial activities) they support have resulted in significant degradation of the environment. The infrastructure investment is not usually available especially in cases where the infrastructures have become very old and the demand they are fulfilling has increased many fold. These infrastructure deficits have long-term implications for national and global economy. According to a study (ASCE, 2011), the investment needed to fix the drinking and wastewater infrastructures in US alone would need $80 billion more than the estimated investment by 2020. The resulting deficit in infrastructure could result in an increased for economy of $ 206 billion (Roth, 2015).

This deficit of resources shows that the infrastructure managers will have a tough task in hand to ensure reliable operations of the existing aging infrastructures. The general public may appear insensitive to the urgency of this situation but infrastructure professionals have not only started to recognize the seriousness of the situation but also thinking about the remedies. They realize that innovative and creative approaches are the need of the time to inspire the required investment and generate public support. It is important given that infrastructure represents a crucial intergenerational legacy. It is a generation's long-term investment that shapes their choices of look, feel, and functionality of the built environment. The immediate infrastructure choices we make today will decide whether we achieve or distort our future vision of built environment.

INFRASTRUCTURE MATTERS

Infrastructure choices matter for economic growth, poverty reduction, and environmental sustainability.

Infrastructure and Growth

Modern economies cannot function without infrastructure. However, more infrastructure may not necessarily cause more growth. The effect of infrastructure may also vary as changes in the economy influence firms' ability to take advantage of it. Infrastructure can affect growth through many channels and is likely to affect the costs of investment adjustment, the durability of private capital, and both demand for and supply of health and education services (Agénor & Moreno-Dodson, 2006). Both infrastructure quantity and quality are significant influences on growth (Calderón & Servén, 2010), a doubling of infrastructure capital raises GDP by roughly 10 percent (Easterly & Servén, 2003).

Infrastructure and Poverty Reduction

The implications of limited access or low quality infrastructure are substantial (Fay et al. 2005). Limited infrastructure access can impact the poor's productivity. Electricity access positively impacts educational outcome and access to reliable transportation determines access to job and markets to sell goods. Increased infrastructure quantity and quality reduces inequality (Calderón & Servén, 2010).

Infrastructure and Environmental Sustainability

There exist inadequate pollution control measures and emissions from power plants and factories continue to negatively impact air quality. Deteriorating air quality is producing adverse effects on human health and environment. If levels of contamination are high, these effects can be severe. The emission levels differ across countries. Figure 1-2 shows top countries/regions responsible for harmful emissions (CO2, and GHG) in developing and developed world. Infrastructure improvements can provide significant economic development benefits and can also help facilitate more sustainable development. Management and maintenance of infrastructure can improve both the quality of service and environmental consequences of its use.

The objective of this chapter is to explore how some of the forces pressuring infrastructure decision-makers to reconsider their investment strategies for infrastructure development, and what are some key challenges facing the shift towards sustainable infrastructures. After introduction, section 2 explores the current state of sustainable infrastructures and some key challenges. Section 3 provides some guidelines for sustainable infrastructure innovation. Section 4 provides some policy guidelines for future infrastructure development. Concluding remarks are provided in section 5.

Current State of Flexible Infrastructures and Key Challenges

The progress to date is in expanding infrastructure availability. Slow progress affects households particularly those in poor countries. More than 16% of world population have no access to electricity (Figure 4). Access to water has improved still around 9% of world population don't have access to improved

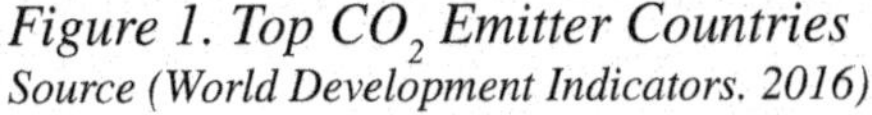

Figure 1. Top CO_2 Emitter Countries
Source (World Development Indicators. 2016)

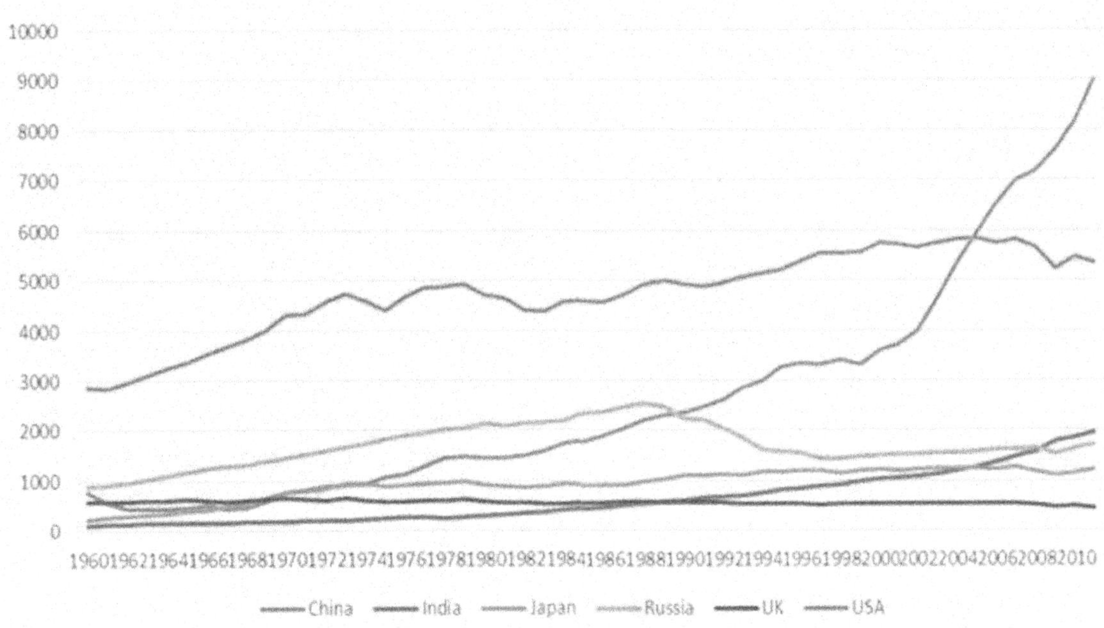

Figure 2. GHG Emissions
Source (World Development Indicators. 2016)

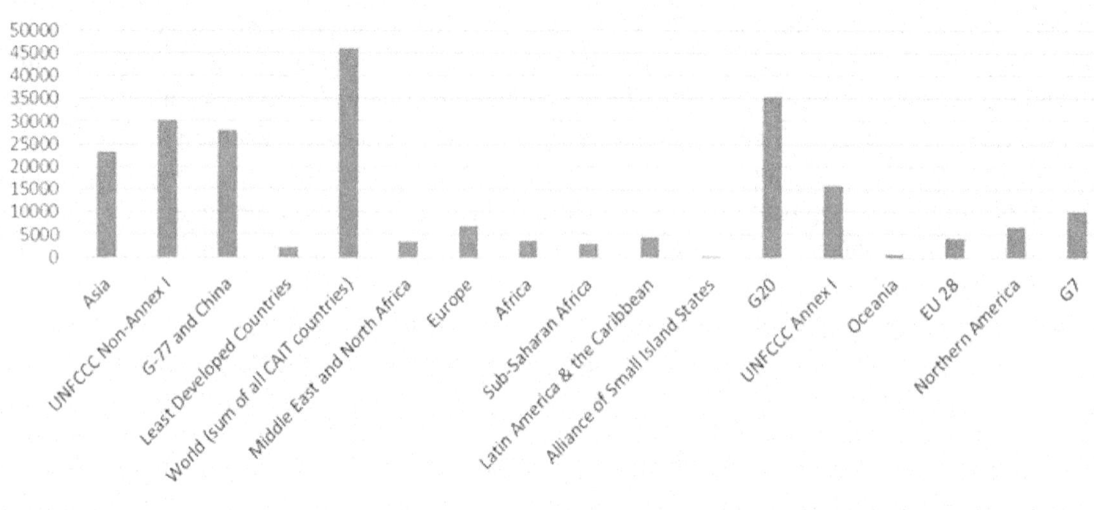

water resource (Figure 3) and 32% of world population is without access to improved sanitation (Figure 5). Figure 3, 4, and 5 shows percentage of world population having access to water, electricity, and improved sanitation respectively.

There are several reasons for this generally disappointing infrastructure situation. Infrastructure is expensive and as much as 15% of GDP may be needed to achieve even relatively modest improvements (Fay, Toman, Benitez, & Csordas, 2011). Infrastructure spending is often inefficient and suffers from many

Figure 3. % of World Population with Access to Water
Source (World Development Indicators. 2016)

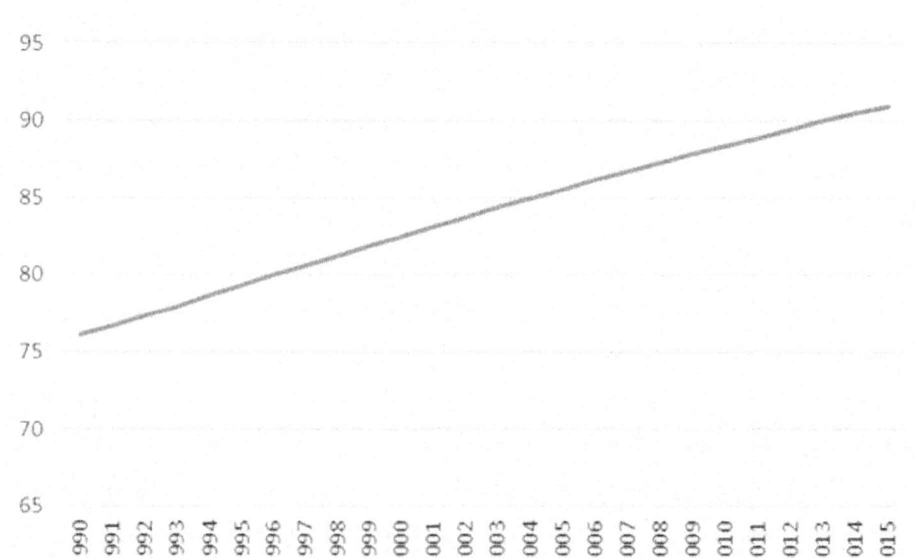

Figure 4. % of Population with Access to Electricity
Source (World Development Indicators. 2016)

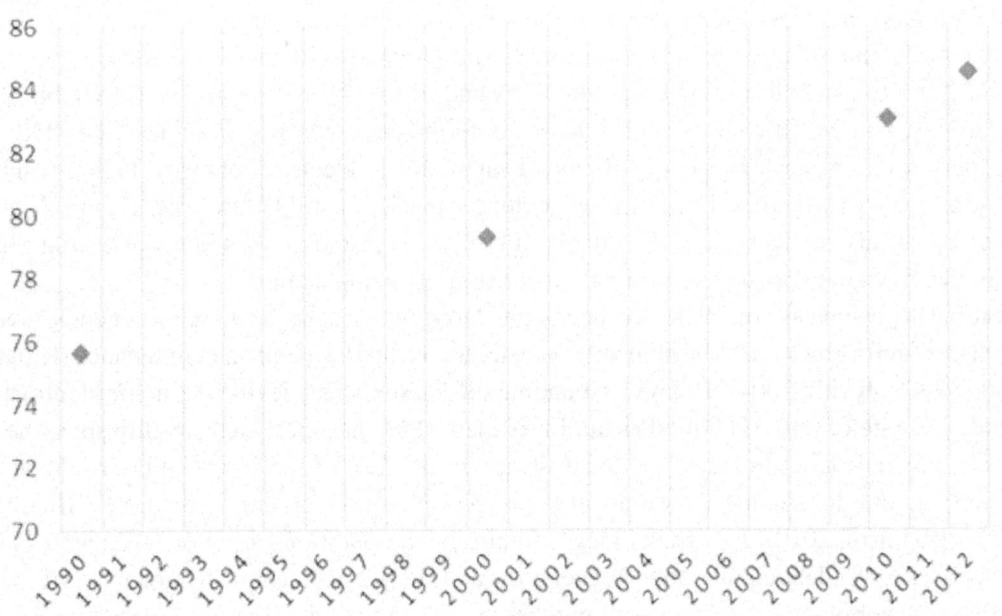

Figure 5. % of World Population with Access to Improved Sanitation Facilities
Source (World Development Indicators, 2016)

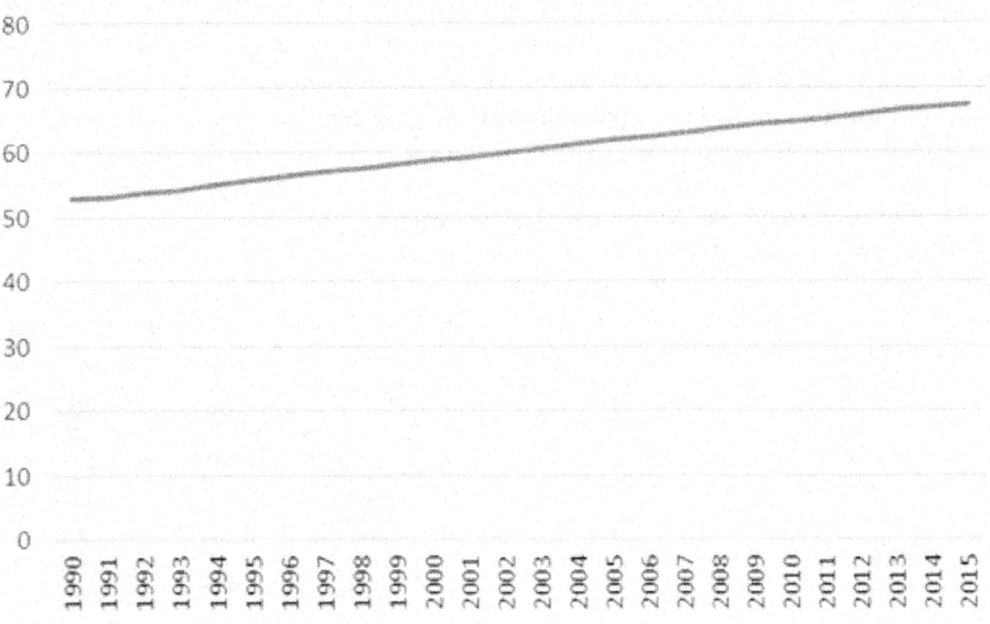

shortcomings of public management. The private sector through PPP's helping to increase efficiency of and access to infrastructure. However, private sector cannot be an alternative to public investment and financing. Limited data is available to monitor spending and its effectiveness and to assess the condition of infrastructure. This situation reduces the motivation to improve upon the status quo.

The infrastructure deficit also affects productivity and firms' ability to compete. Unreliability affects the bottom line, with significant amount of losses in terms of percentage of annual sales. Developing region experienced greater losses (as % of annual sales) due to electrical outages. Figure 6 shows the losses due to electrical outages. Electricity generating capacity is still below 70%. Figure 7 shows the worldwide electricity production by all sources. It took a long time to get a new connection. Figure 8 shows number of days to obtain an electrical connection upon application.

According to estimates, maintenance needs are large, particularly within low-income countries. Maintenance of infrastructure is essential but countries tend to underspend on maintenance (Rioja, 2003; Kalaitzidakis & Kalyvitis, 2004). This underspending substantially reduces the useful life of infrastructure assets and their rate of return. Public-Private Investment (PPI) has increased steadily since the 1990s. Overall PPI volumes have remained relatively steady in the face of the financial crisis. However, the selective investments have reduced the number of projects. New projects are facing more difficult market conditions (Izaguirre, 2010). Deals take longer to close and conditions are more stringent. Financing usually involves lower debt/equity ratios, higher costs and shorter debt tenors. Sector-wise, PPI has been concentrated in energy sector and most PPI projects are concentrated in Latin American region (Figure 9). PPI has also been concentrated geographically. Figure 9 and 10 shows the distribution of PPI projects region wise and category wise respectively. The concentration of PPI flows developing countries has increased. Table 1 shows the number of PPI projects region wise.

In order to develop smarter, affordable, sustainable, and resilient systems, we need to change our spending and investment priorities for infrastructure projects. Still, sustainable infrastructure has not become the standard in infrastructure development. There are many reasons for this. One reason is the typical bidding approach that favors the construction of the infrastructure by the contractor who could develop the infrastructure in the lowest possible costs. This system does not incentivize the contractor

Figure 6. Losses due to electrical outages (% of annual sales)
Source (www.enterprisesurveys.org, 2016)

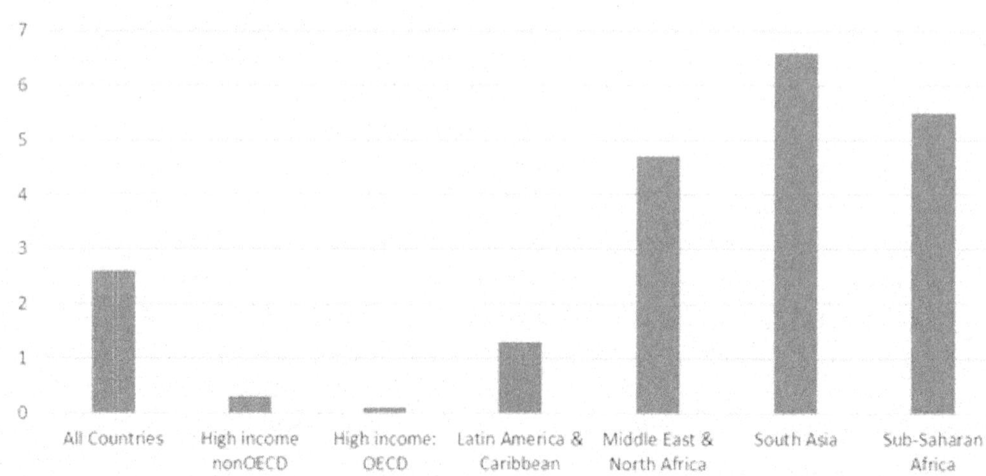

Figure 7. Electricity production from oil, gas and coal sources (% of total)
Source (www.enterprisesurveys.org, 2016)

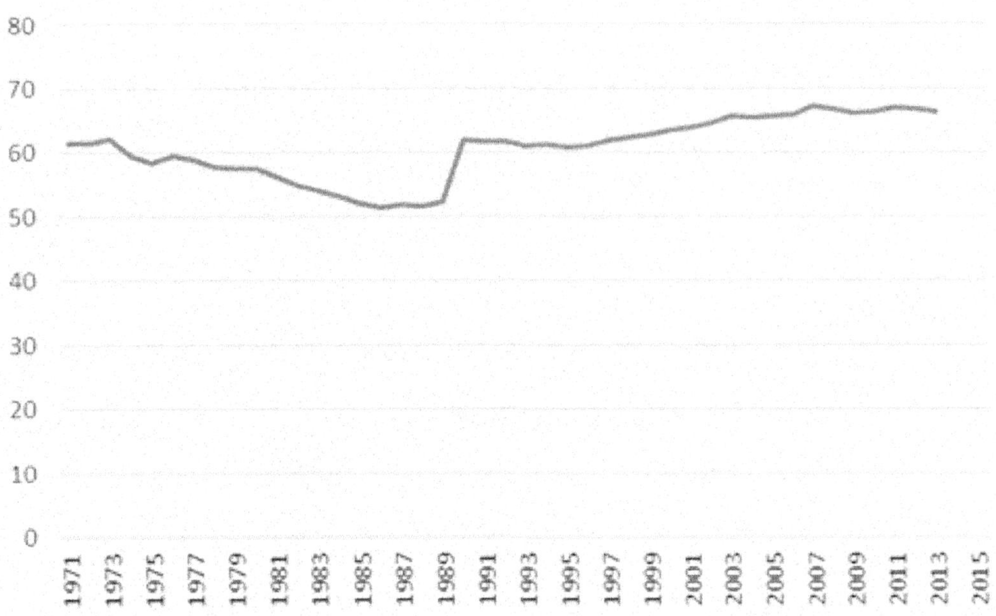

Figure 8. Days to obtain an electrical connection (upon application)
Source (www.enterprisesurveys.org, 2016)

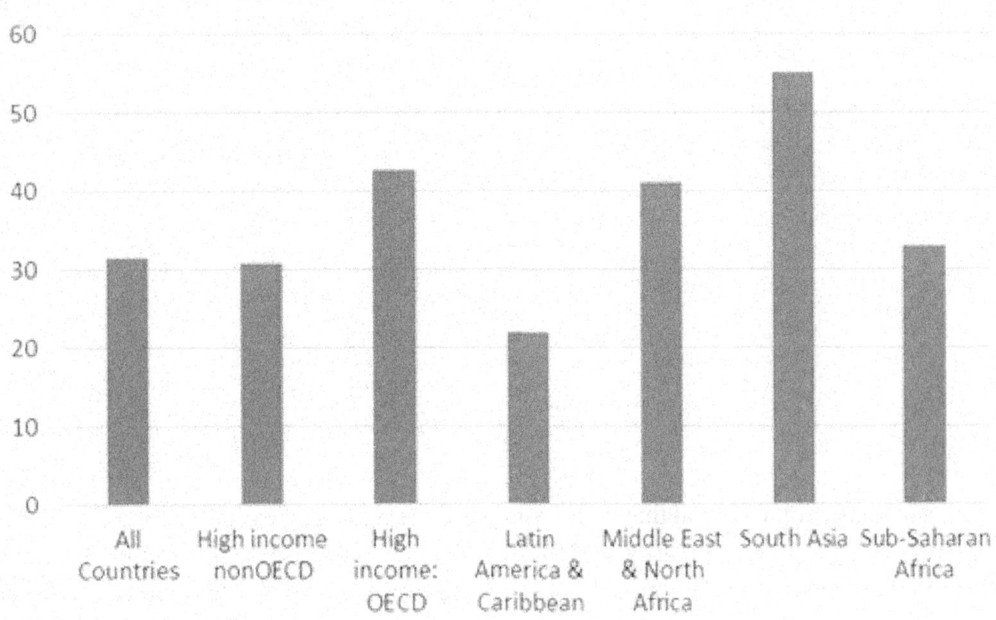

Figure 9. PPI Projects Distribution, Region Wise
Source (ppi.worldbank.org, *2016)*

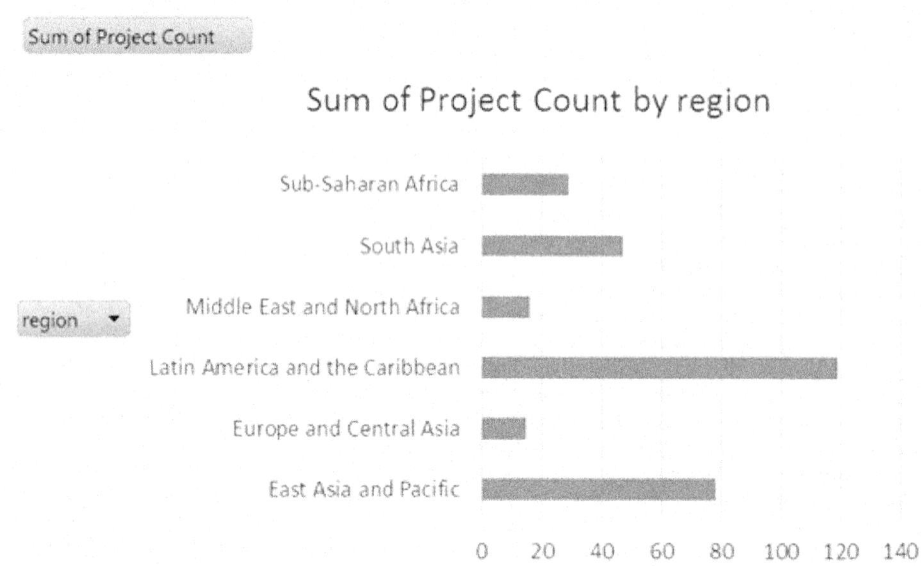

Figure 10. PPI Projects Distribution, Category Wise
Source (ppi.worldbank.org, *2016)*

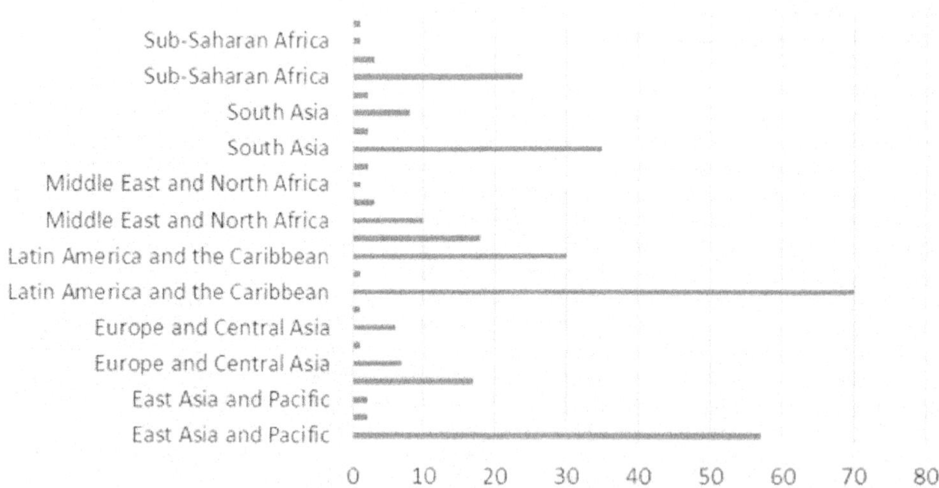

respond with a construction proposal that could minimize the operating expenses for a long time (Roth, 2015). This approach does not necessarily work for construction projects that large, complex, and require innovative thinking. One reason traditional procurement practices used for such projects is that all cost overruns are covered by tax money and public owner of the project bears a significant portion of total risk. In building sustainable infrastructures, the primary responsibility of controlling long-term design, construction, and performance costs and risks lies with the contractor. These risks discourage innovative thinking by the contractors and favor long-proven methodologies, even if the innovative solution might

Table 1. Number of PPI Projects (Region-wise)

Region	Primary sector	Project Count
East Asia and Pacific	Energy	57
East Asia and Pacific	Information and communication technology (ICT)	2
East Asia and Pacific	Transport	2
East Asia and Pacific	Water and sewerage	17
Europe and Central Asia	Energy	7
Europe and Central Asia	Information and communication technology (ICT)	1
Europe and Central Asia	Transport	6
Europe and Central Asia	Water and sewerage	1
Latin America and the Caribbean	Energy	70
Latin America and the Caribbean	Information and communication technology (ICT)	1
Latin America and the Caribbean	Transport	30
Latin America and the Caribbean	Water and sewerage	18
Middle East and North Africa	Energy	10
Middle East and North Africa	Information and communication technology (ICT)	3
Middle East and North Africa	Transport	1
Middle East and North Africa	Water and sewerage	2
South Asia	Energy	35
South Asia	Information and communication technology (ICT)	2
South Asia	Transport	8
South Asia	Water and sewerage	2
Sub-Saharan Africa	Energy	24
Sub-Saharan Africa	Information and communication technology (ICT)	3
Sub-Saharan Africa	Transport	1
Sub-Saharan Africa	Water and sewerage	1

Source (ppi.worldbank.org, 2016)

provide an infrastructure that provides far better performance. In public sector, risk aversion tends to be high among senior government officials that fears things could go wrong if non-traditional approaches are used. They fear a high-profile failure can be politically detrimental for them (Choguill, 1996; Ostrom, Schroeder & Wynne, 1993).

It appears that civil engineering culture favors standard practices over innovative approaches (Jowitt, 2004). This situation is especially true in public sector infrastructure projects where political stakes are involved. As such, infrastructure managers are under pressure not take any risk of anything going wrong if they use some innovative approach. These infrastructures are designed to be redundant and big enough to handle any future scenarios (Roth, 2015). The infrastructure managers of these projects are not incentivized for developing systems approaches (George Town University, 2016). Politicians and contractors also influence the infrastructure development to develop mega projects that are under-cost. Many studies found that huge infrastructure projects consistently go over budget (Edwards & Kaeding, 2015). Highway development projects, in particular, lack strategic thinking (McKinsey, 2013). One reason for this is the lack of transparent processes and accountability mechanisms that could check the over budgeting of the project. The basic business model used to fund utilities and infrastructure agencies may pose a fundamental barrier to innovation. In many infrastructure projects (such as gas, electricity, and water), the revenues to build and operate the infrastructure are derived from sales volumes. As such, the infrastructure managers have no incentive to fully investing in affordable and sustainable infrastructure solutions. This area requires attention of policy makers responsible for developing infrastructure development policies (Lenferink, Tillema, & Arts, 2013).

Lack of out-of-the-box thinking by civil engineers is one big issue but the bigger issues is the wave of retirements of experienced civil engineers that pose a significant threat of drain of critical knowledge required to build and maintain infrastructures (Roth, 2015). Infrastructure agencies worldwide have experienced engineers that are a source of very valuable institutional and professional knowledge. When these people retire, this knowledge base is lost and there are not enough suitable people to replace them. The situation gets severe in countries where infrastructure agencies in different parts of the country is facing the same situation and the schools are not graduating enough qualified persons (Boyle et al., 2010).

Institutional silos are another key challenge. In conventional infrastructure projects, the design occurs within its silo and infrastructure managers do not look for opportunities to optimize between systems. For example, the project of shifting conventional vehicles into electrical vehicles project may not look into an opportunity to collaborate with electrical industry to develop some innovative ideas. Cross-silo communication is challenging given that people may have different perspective and backgrounds and can speak very different languages. Segregation of duties can leave people with no interest to develop integrated strategies for optimizing the system as a whole. Another reason there may be no comprehensively rethinking of infrastructure systems is that the governments may have limited funding for infrastructure projects and limited capacity to provide necessary and direction for the infrastructure projects (Kevern, 2010).

Another challenge is the shortsightedness of infrastructure managers and decision makers in the predesign phase (or planning phase) where it is decided which projects are the right ones. This phase of infrastructure projects is critically underfunded. Meanwhile, infrastructure managers tend to defer vital infrastructure maintenance due to various budget constraints. Depending on the type of infrastructure asset, this deferred maintenance can increase total maintenance cost by a factor of two to four. Infrastructure managers do not usually have access to adequate tools that could help them assess the economics and pay for infrastructure systems. The available tools also do not provide comprehensive coverage of the environmental costs and benefits associated with various types of infrastructures. One example is lack of carbon pricing (Roth, 2015). This external cost must be reflected on the economic balance sheet of today's infrastructure projects. Similarly, the currently available economic assessment tools to infrastructure managers cannot provide assessment of health benefits of sustainable infrastructures and healthy natural systems (such as cleaner air and water). The correct valuation of these benefits can help obtain required financing for protection and enhancement of these natural systems. The current accounting rules are not customized to account for sustainable infrastructure. These rules need changes in order realize the true value of these infrastructures on the balance sheet (Hunt & Rogers, 2005).

GUIDELINES FOR SUSTAINABLE INFRASTRUCTURE INNOVATION

Looking at the current landscape of sustainable infrastructures and the key challenges, the following are some suggested guidelines that infrastructure managers, government officials, and community planners in both developing and developed countries can use to develop innovative sustainable infrastructures.

Resilience, Sustainability, and Fiscal Strength

The sustainable infrastructures can help fill the existing infrastructure deficit if they are designed to provide three key benefits. First, they should be able to attract adequate finances to deal with increasing costs of operation. Second, these infrastructures should offer quick recovery in natural disasters and emergencies. Third, their design should provide great environmental performance.

Broad Alternatives

Public infrastructure decision-makers should compare the best available innovations thoroughly to achieve maximum benefits out of sustainable infrastructures.

Remove Organizational Silos

There are multiple communities involved when it comes to investing in multiple infrastructure (such as water, sewerage, and electricity). In many situations, planning and investment for these systems is distributed among various departments. With increase in their size, these departments become compartmentalized. This can result in result in reduced multiple benefits and reduced overall value. Removing these organizations can improve synergy among different departments and contribute to increase the overall value.

A Better Business Case

When short-listing their options for infrastructure development, infrastructure planners should thoroughly analyze the life-cycle costs and benefits of each option. These life-cycle costs would include the construction as well as operations and maintenance costs. This cost-benefit analysis should not be limited to a single government entity tasked with managing a particular infrastructure. This analysis should include accrued benefits for all stakeholders (i.e. all departments, government, and the community). This would help save money and provide better risk management. A key here is the simultaneous consideration of capital and operating budgets. A well-documented good business case should be prepared supported by a careful evaluation of alternatives so that a wise investment decision can be made (Roth, 2015).

Education, Engagement, and Inspiration of People

Unarguably, infrastructures are the most expensive and long-term assets of any country. With limited ability of governments to finance infrastructure projects, the importance of public support for needed investment is increasing. To gain this support, effective communication and public engagement is needed supported by a convincing vision of what is to be achieved from the infrastructure and why it is important.

Prosperity of Community

Since investment from public is used to fund the development of infrastructures, it is important that infrastructure should work to develop prosper communities. Infrastructure planners should evaluate community's strategies for infrastructure keeping in view the community's economic development goals. This evaluation can reveal how the infrastructure development can be structured to maximize the economic benefits for the community.

Build Infrastructure for a Changing World

Mega infrastructure projects are developed over many years and can be operational after a long time since the start of their development. Infrastructure planners should ensure that infrastructure systems are well-adapted to future changes such as technology revolutions, environmental changes, shifting living patterns, and changing lifestyles (Roth, 2015).

ICT Integration

Today, people carry mobile electronic gadgets everywhere. People use these gadgets for a wide variety of tasks. Use of these devices in infrastructure systems can provide low-cost monitoring and real-time management. This way infrastructure systems can not only improve their services but also reduce their operational costs.

Integrate Nature

People enjoy the most when they see a combination of natural sceneries and beautiful structures. Infrastructure planners should not rely solely on traditional infrastructure approaches. Investment in natural systems can result in increased functionality savings. Even when use of traditional approach is necessary, the design of Infrastructure should be elegant and eye-catching.

Sophistication and Expertise

Developing sustainable Infrastructures require sophisticated and expert human resources. Without these resources, it is very difficult to extract long-term cost savings and desired outcomes out of a sustainable Infrastructure. Infrastructure planners should have access to data, tools, and knowledge bases that can help them develop the best design (Roth, 2015). Instead of a low-bid war, new procurement strategies should be sought to hire the most economical contractor and incentivize the contractor for innovation and sustainability. New approaches are needed to reduce risk of cost overrun and developing rewards for quality performance. A redesign of job descriptions and performance metrics may be needed to incorporate the new vision into the daily priorities of the staff.

Best Practices Repository

New and aspiring infrastructure professionals need access to modern tools and techniques to master new approaches of infrastructure development. There is a need to develop new toolkits for infrastructure planners. Best practices and case studies should be developed that identify the evolving needs of infrastructures. This research is very important given that this field is still in its nascent stages and rapidly developing. New standards and templates should also be developed. These standards and templates would help infrastructure professionals and planners reduce risk in infrastructure planning. Governments should provide their infrastructure decision makers the skills needed so that they could understand and practice different infrastructure development approaches being used worldwide. Well-known professionals in sustainable infrastructures field should be asked to develop curriculum and training programs for infrastructure professionals. These professionals should also be consulted to help public sector infrastructure decision makers in redesign of their strategies of infrastructure planning, management, and investment (Roth, 2015).

Partnership with Academic Institutions

There is a large number of highly experienced professionals that retire every year. Their retirement brings a drain of critical knowledge and understanding of infrastructures. It is important that a new generation of infrastructure professionals is inspired and educated to compensate for this knowledge drain. Infrastructure planners and decision makers can develop mutually beneficial relationships with universities to utilize the students' infrastructure research projects. Universities can benefit by doing joint projects with the industry in which their faculty and students participate and gain practical knowledge (Walz, 2007).

Communication, Communication, Communication

Today, many infrastructures have become old and under stress. There are serious constraints on the government funding. As such, public support for needed infrastructure investment is essential. Infrastructure planners should develop a persuasive message for all stakeholders (Roth, 2015). This message should enable Infrastructure planners educate public and elected officials to understand what sustainable infrastructures are all about and encourage them to invest in these infrastructures.

Policy Environment

For modern infrastructure development, infrastructure policies must encourage sustainable, resilient, and affordable systems. There is a need to develop a compelling shared vision that could overcome the problems inherent in the current infrastructure policy development process. Communities of Infrastructure professionals should assemble the best policy examples being implemented around the globe to help policymakers take targeted measures for effective advancement of the vision.

In order to comprehensively implement the guidelines provided following are some recommendations. Infrastructure is at the core of the future of a community. Better infrastructures can boost economy and provide good quality of life. Community leaders should develop a long-term strategic plan for various infrastructure needs. Such plan can help align implementation efforts and different community plans. Different department and agencies, responsible for developing the infrastructures can use this plan to harmonize their plans with the community's goals and aspirations (Sarté, 2010). Sustainable Asset Management approach can provide two additional but vital elements to traditional asset management approach: integrated strategies and 'Triple Bottom Line' metrics. Triple bottom line metrics include financial as well as social and environmental metrics to provide a holistic picture of the infrastructure performance. Infrastructure planners should acknowledge and explicitly plan to allow certain level of tolerance against failure when running pilot projects of using state-of-the art approaches and innovations. A redesign of institutions would be needed to transform their current infrastructure management practices and implement the innovative infrastructure approaches. Infrastructure planners should be cautious and strike a balance between small scale and mega infrastructure projects. Governments should support programs of higher education designed to inspire and educate the next generation of sustainability oriented infrastructure professionals (Roth, 2015).

Use of Market Mechanisms

There is a need to use market mechanisms to stimulate Innovation and adoption. Governments should implement a comprehensive water pricing system and carbon pricing system and the generated revenues should be devoted to sustainable infrastructure investments.

Innovative Financing Alternatives

With respect to financing infrastructure, governments only really have two options – taxes or user fees. As a result, governments are increasingly seeking new approaches to financing. Given the financial pressures that most governments are now facing, private financing for project development has become ever more important.

Innovative financing alternatives are key for developing sustainable infrastructures. Innovative private-sector financing of infrastructure investment in support of sustainable communities is a necessity. The cost to renew present infrastructure is too high to be covered only through taxes. Private sector financing, offered through private-public partnerships (PPP), provides a significant alternative source of funds as well as a range of techniques. The private sector financing can also stimulate infrastructure innovation. Governments should implement programs to enhance the knowledge and use of alternative financing techniques, such as PPP. Public Private Partnerships (PPP) can mobilize untapped resources from the local, regional or international private sector. The private funds acts as leverage for increased and better social services. Governments can than redirect their limited funds towards other important projects. PPP can two to three projects with the same amount of financial resource.

Governments should encourage the wide-spread use of energy performance contracting to finance improvements in energy and water use of buildings. Such contracts should include provision for any savings generated to be reinvested towards the implementation of more sustainable infrastructure. Governments should encourage the use of on-gas bill financing to support energy improvements within smaller buildings and businesses. In this arrangement, a gas-utility company provides funds to its customers to finance energy-improvement investments, and takes repayments through an agreed-upon surcharge on energy bills.

Governments should also consider the use of Built-Own-Operate-Transfer under PPP to finance sustainable larger infrastructure investments. These partnerships should consider longer-term planning to ensure public safety and prudence. Governments should investigate different project delivery mechanisms including Built-Own-Operate-Transfer as alternatives for financing and implementing projects. A comprehensive review of experience with these alternatives should be undertaken to assess their pros and cons and to recommend ways to improve upon the potential failures of these project delivery mechanisms. Multilateral and Bilateral Financial Institutions (e.g. the Asian Development Bank) can also provide low-cost, long-tenor financing for infrastructure projects. They can also provide global best practices and experience in project development and financing.

Risk Reduction

The choice of infrastructure is critical in achieving sustainable community development and success in achieving sustainability can be attainable by using state-of-the-art technologies. These technologies carry with them significant uncertainties and risks. Governments should lead and broker partnerships for a comprehensive program of pilot projects where these technologies are used. Where appropriate, the universities could be used for pilot projects especially in PPP projects. That mechanisms could be helpful to alleviate risks associated with the implementation of state-of-the-art technologies.

Congruence and Alignment Of Policies

Policies and standards for sustainable infrastructure development vary enormously across and between governments, and often are simply inconsistent. Often, planning is disconnected from actual implementation and is undertaken without regard for higher level consequences or impacts. Governments should identify policy inconsistencies and begin comprehensive policy congruence and realignment among different levels of government.

Comprehensive Planning Techniques

Comprehensive long term planning for sustainability is not common and rarely linked to decision-making bodies and applicable governance structures. Governments should implement programs to accelerate the dissemination of knowledge, sustainable infrastructure innovations and planning techniques required to realize sustainable infrastructure development. This should also include techniques to enhance the sociological and economic and environmental attributes of sustainability.

Accountability

Issues of accountability and ownership can dilute the impact of infrastructure investment and delivery. Often, accountability for infrastructure is fractured between multiple government departments and agencies and lose sight of the broader, more strategic, objective of infrastructure development. Coordinating infrastructure development across multiple levels of government can often be a massive challenge and jurisdictional disagreements can often delay even the most critical infrastructure projects. Governments should create infrastructure agencies with the power and accountability to coordinate spend and planning.

POLICY GUIDELINES FOR FUTURE INFRASTRUCTURE DEVELOPMENT

Following are some policy guidelines that infrastructure planners in both developing and developed countries can use to develop sustainable infrastructures in future.

Physical Design of Infrastructure

Cross-Sector Integration of Infrastructures

Integration across infrastructure categories, where technically feasible, can provide many potential efficiencies and benefits. However, this integration can increase project complexity and provide conflicting objectives of stakeholders. Therefore, at least some state policy support is needed to provide such cross-integration (Roth, 2015).

New Business Models

There are emerging trends toward decentralization of infrastructure services. There are many advantages of this decentralization such as greater flexibility and resiliency, optimal size of infrastructure, and cost savings (Yigitcanlar, & Dur, 2010).

Incorporate Nature in Infrastructure Design

Investment should be made to incorporate natural system functions to augment infrastructure systems. There are additional co-benefits to this approach such as biodiversity, and community amenities (Roth, 2015).

Mixed-Use Development

Urban land development policy makers should ensure that their policies promote mixed-use development. Mixed-use development is a type of urban development that blends residential, commercial, cultural, institutional, or industrial uses, where those functions are physically and functionally integrated, and that provides pedestrian connections. Mixed-use development is very cost-effective and can serve all types of infrastructures.

Infrastructure Security

Infrastructure security should be considered a priority of public policy. A focus on infrastructure security could transform current views of the core features of infrastructure system planning and design (such as sustainability).

INFRASTRUCTURE FINANCING

Private Investment

Public investment is a vital opportunity to address the infrastructure funding gap. Private sector's more active roles (such as appropriate risk-sharing and public-private partnerships) is important here. The ownership of infrastructure remains with the public sector but the active role of private sector can help generate new innovative ideas for infrastructure development (Panayotou, 1998).

Incentive for Savings

Today, citizens' taxation is the major source of funding to support infrastructure projects. This tax collection is based on sales volume. The shift toward sustainable infrastructure encourage conservation. There is a need to design new revenue systems based on the amount of services provided rather than sales volume (Roth, 2015).

Life-Cycle Costs

Current infrastructure projects face significant issues of funding to support ongoing infrastructure operation and maintenance (O&M) costs. One way to handle this problem is to factor these costs in initial estimation of infrastructure life-cycle costs. Besides this, these costs should be analyzed in detail to understand their associated benefits and risks.

Reform Procurement Strategies

Public procurement rules and regulation should encourage broader project scopes and more flexible criteria in PPP projects where a private partner is actively involved in ongoing infrastructure management. It also helps finance life-cycle costs of infrastructure project.

Carbon Pricing

Carbon pricing can be a strong initiative to reduce carbon emissions and promote a healthy natural environment. Carbon pricing may come in the form of a carbon tax and provide market forces a strong incentive to reduce carbon emissions. A carbon price may also provide new revenue for infrastructure (Roth, 2015).

Up Gradation of Municipal Bond Rating Methods

The worth of improved environment is a significant benefit that is not accounted for while establishing the rating of municipal bonds. These bonds are used to finance the infrastructure projects. If their rating mechanism accounts for healthy environment, investors looking for investment opportunities that give priority to safe environment, can be attracted to buy these bonds.

Analysis of Infrastructure Projects

There is a need to improve analysis stage in the development of infrastructure planning. Some key enhancement should be accounting relevant life-cycle costs and benefits (such as costs of total capital), consideration of environmental and equity outcomes, asset management, and use of triple bottom. These steps should preferentially be included in the earliest stages of planning. Optimal infrastructure solutions provide long-term benefits to a country. The infrastructure policies should have some built-in incentives that promote developing infrastructures that provide multiple benefits to all the stakeholders.

CONCLUSION

Infrastructure investments are long-term investments that provide benefits to many generations of human beings. The current financial, social, and environmental landscape is pressurizing the infrastructure planners to plan, design, and invest in sustainable infrastructure. These infrastructures are expected to play a vital role in the future economic and social development of a country. This chapter highlighted the urgent need of these new and smart infrastructures in order to meet the critical infrastructure challenges countries facing today. It is recommended that infrastructure planners should realize the critical significance of these infrastructures for providing greater financial, social and economic benefits and plan ahead to develop these infrastructures in a manner that benefits all stakeholders.

REFERENCES

ASCE. (2011). *Water & Wastewater Report | ASCE*. Retrieved February 26, 2016, from http://www.asce.org/water_and_wastewater_report/

Boyle, C., Mudd, G., Mihelcic, J. R., Anastas, P., Collins, T., Culligan, P., & Handy, S. (2010). Delivering sustainable infrastructure that supports the urban built environment. *Environmental Science & Technology*, *44*(13), 4836–4840. doi:10.1021/es903749d PMID:20583825

Calderón, C., Easterly, W., & Servén, L. (2003). Infrastructure compression and public sector solvency in Latin America.The Limits of Stabilization: Infrastructure, Public Deficits, and Growth in Latin America. Stanford University Press and the World Bank.

Choguill, C. L. (1996). Ten steps to sustainable infrastructure. *Habitat International*, *20*(3), 389–404. doi:10.1016/0197-3975(96)00013-6

Dobbs, R., Pohl, H., Lin, D.-Y., Mischke, J., Garemo, N., Hexter, J., …Nanavatty, R. (2015). *Infrastructure productivity: How to save $1 trillion a year | McKinsey & Company*. Retrieved February 26, 2016, from http://www.mckinsey.com/industries/infrastructure/our-insights/infrastructure-productivity

Edwards, C., & Kaeding, N. (2015, September). *Federal Government Cost Overruns*. Retrieved from https://www.heartland.org/sites/default/files/cato_cost_overruns.pdf

Enterprise Surveys. (2016). *Enterprise Surveys - What Businesses Experience - World Bank Group*. Retrieved September 6, 2016, from http://www.enterprisesurveys.org/

Fay, M., Toman, M., Benitez, D., & Csordas, S. (2011). *Infrastructure and sustainable development.* Postcrisis Growth and Development: A Development Agenda for the G 20.

George Town University. (2016, May 20). *Performance-based infrastructure: An Acceleration Agenda for the United States Recommendations to the Build America Investment Initiative*. Retrieved from http://beeckcenter.georgetown.edu/wp-content/uploads/2016/04/Performance-Based-Infrastructure_Working-Paper_BeeckCenter_5.20.2016.pdf

Hunt, D. V., & Rogers, C. D. (2005). Barriers to sustainable infrastructure in urban regeneration. In *Proceedings of the Institution of Civil Engineers, Engineering Sustainability* (Vol. 158, pp. 67–81). doi:10.1680/ensu.2005.158.2.67

Jowitt, P. W. (2004). Systems and sustainability: sustainable development, civil engineering and the formation of the civil engineer. In *Proceedings of the institution of civil engineers, Engineering Sustainability* (Vol. 157, pp. 1–11).

Kevern, J. T. (2010). Green building and sustainable infrastructure: Sustainability education for civil engineers. *Journal of Professional Issues in Engineering Education and Practice*, *137*(2), 107–112. doi:10.1061/(ASCE)EI.1943-5541.0000048

Lenferink, S., Tillema, T., & Arts, J. (2013). Towards sustainable infrastructure development through integrated contracts: Experiences with inclusiveness in Dutch infrastructure projects. *International Journal of Project Management*, *31*(4), 615–627. doi:10.1016/j.ijproman.2012.09.014

McKinsey. (2013, November). *A risk-management approach to a successful infrastructure project Initiation, financing, and execution*. Retrieved from http://www.mckinsey.com/~/media/McKinsey/dotcom/client_service/Risk/Working%20papers/52_A_risk-management_approach_to_a_successful_infrastructure_project.ashx

Ostrom, E., Schroeder, L., & Wynne, S. (1993). Institutional incentives and sustainable development: Infrastructure policies in perspective. Boulder, CO: Westview Press

Panayotou, T. (1998). *The role of the private sector in sustainable infrastructure development*. Citeseer. Retrieved from environment.yale.edu/publication-series/documents/downloads/0.../101panayotou.pdf

Sarté, S. B. (2010). *Sustainable infrastructure: The guide to green engineering and design*. John Wiley & Sons.

Walz, R. (2007). The role of regulation for sustainable infrastructure innovations: The case of wind energy. *International Journal of Public Policy*, *2*(1-2), 57–88. doi:10.1504/IJPP.2007.012276

World Bank. (2016). *Private Participation in Infrastructure (PPI) Project Database - World Bank Group*. Retrieved September 6, 2016, from http://ppi.worldbank.org/

World Bank. (2016). *World Development Indicators | Data*. Retrieved September 6, 2016, from http://data.worldbank.org/data-catalog/world-development-indicators

Yigitcanlar, T., & Dur, F. (2010). Developing a sustainability assessment model: The sustainable infrastructure, land-use, environment and transport model. *Sustainability*, *2*(1), 321–340. doi:10.3390/su2010321

KEY TERMS AND DEFINITIONS

Citizens: A citizen is an inhabitant of a particular town or city.

CO_2: Its full form is carbon di oxide which is one of the worst pollutants in air causing greenhouse gases to increase and the leader in global warming problem.

Development: Development refers to the process of developing or being developed.

Government: Government refers to the group of people with the authority to govern a country or state.

Infrastructures: Infrastructure refers to the basic physical and organizational structures and facilities needed for the operation of a society or enterprise.

Strategy: It is a method or plan chosen to bring about a desired future, such as achievement of a goal or solution to a problem with the resources for their most efficient and effective use.

Sustainability: Sustainability refers to the ability to sustain.

Chapter 9
Energy Challenges and Infrastructure Development in South Asia

Sudhakar Patra
Berhampur University, India

ABSTRACT

The present chapter seeks to analyze the trend and growth of energy production, supply, growth, consumption and trade in South Asian countries based on data from 1971 to 2011 collected from World Bank data base, South Asia Development reports, Energy Outlook, ADB database. While India, Pakistan, and Bangladesh account for the major natural gas and coal resources, Bhutan and Nepal have large hydro-power resources. The study suggests that South Asian countries need enhanced regional energy transfer to leverage economies of scale through a more vibrant intra and inter regional energy trade structure. Mobilizing financial resources to develop the necessary energy infrastructure is a major challenge to enhance energy security in the region. Therefore, South Asian countries need to develop policies that will attract investment in the region.

INTRODUCTION

Energy and its resources lie at the heart of the future prosperity of the South Asian region and the well-being of its large population. South Asia houses nearly 1.4 billion people which are around 25% of the world's population and it has a sizeable energy deficit that is filled up by imports. South Asian nations are faced with rapidly rising energy demand coupled with increasingly insufficient energy supplies. Most of South Asia is already grappling with energy shortfalls, typically in the form of recurrent, costly, and widespread electricity outages. In India alone, the current electricity supply/demand deficit is around 8%, with a peak demand deficit of about 12%; yet a large part of the population is not yet connected to the electricity grid. Improving the supply of energy, particularly the supply of electricity, is an important priority of national and local governments emphasizing the firm belief that development and energy use go hand in hand. The term, 'energy access' has a dual meaning in South Asia; on one hand it implies an open access regime in which the urban, middle class consumers are offered a choice of energy to

DOI: 10.4018/978-1-5225-2364-2.ch009

select from, and on the other it implies the enormous task of creating access for the large number of poor people who are still dependent on traditional energy sources. It is these poor who will be a factor in infrastructure development and the eventual energy future of South Asia. Looking at the current energy scenario in South Asia, we see a remarkable contrast — great demand and huge absolute consumption with extremely low per capita consumption; it is this South Asian situation that has been described as the 'Asian energy pattern'. Although the South Asian region is a repository of the poorest people in the world, with more people without adequate access to energy than South Asia's commercial energy mix in 2012 (South Asia Energy Report, 2014) was 46% coal, 34% petroleum, 12% natural gas, 6% hydro-electricity, 1% nuclear and 0.3% 'other'. There are significant variations within the region reflecting the nature of indigenous energy resources and amount of fuel that has to be imported. Bangladesh's energy mix is dominated by natural gas (66.4%), while India relies heavily on coal (54.5%). Sri Lanka and the Maldives are overwhelmingly dependent on petroleum (82% and 100%, respectively); Pakistan is diversified among petroleum (42.7%), natural gas (42.2%), and hydroelectricity (10%). The Himalayan countries of Bhutan and Nepal have the highest shares of hydroelectric power in their energy consumption mix at 80% and 31%, respectively. All these data discount the 'non-commercial' or 'traditional' sources of energy including animal waste, wood, and other biomass, which except for India and Pakistan form the dominant source of energy.

The low per capita energy consumption in South Asia, achieving targets such as electricity for entire populations; the 'Power for All' policy that India has adopted would be a gigantic task for the region. Besides economic growth, energy demand will increase from improved standards of living of the population, as more and more people enter the commercial energy market. As the population becomes urbanized and as standards of living improve, the changes in the nature of energy consumption, popularly known as energy transition also assumes great importance. Much of the energy demand comes from the rising urban centres and the new industries. South Asia is experiencing rapid urbanization; it has a large number of million-plus cities, including 10 million plus mega-cities that create a great energy demand. Yet, the vast majority of the population living in rural areas still depends on traditional (or non-commercial) energy sources, but gradually changing over to commercial fuels. Nearly 680 million people in rural areas and 110 million in urban areas of South Asia are without access to electricity (IEA, 2002). Providing energy to these poor, enabling them to switch over from traditional to modern sources, will be at the centre of sustained economic growth and improved well-being of South Asian nations.

South Asian countries are aiming at diversifying their energy baskets, and are promoting foreign investment for energy infrastructure development, attempting to improve energy efficiency, undertaking reform and privatizing their energy sectors, and endorsing and expanding intra and cross regional energy trade and investment. Procuring an energy secure future for South Asia would involve pressing environmental and ecological issues such as deforestation, soil erosion, desertification, air and water pollution, carbon emissions, water shortages in cities, climatic vagaries such as severe tropical storms, droughts, floods and flash floods. Above all, energy security for South Asia would involve a heightened level of geopolitical cooperation between the nations, and between South Asia and other regions, especially other parts of Asia. South Asian regions are going to play an increasingly important role in the global economic matters and energy markets. Given that these Asian regions are among the fastest growing regions in the world, they will require increasing energy supplies to fuel their rapid pace of economic expansion. Reliable supply of energy is also crucial for meeting the social and developmental objectives of these nations. The region's energy demand is characterized by a rapidly growing demand for electricity and increasing motorization. Another characteristic feature of the energy sector here is that these regions are becoming increasingly reliant on energy imports. Hence, energy security is one of the biggest challenges that these economies face.

LITERATURE REVIEW

There is plethora of literature on energy consumption in India and abroad. Few important and relevant literatures on energy are reviewed in this section.

Nicholas and James (2009) utilize U.S. annual data from 1949 to 2006 to examine the casual relationship between energy consumption and real GDP of USA using aggregate and sectoral primary energy consumption measures within a multivariate framework. The long run causality tests reveal that the relationship between energy consumption and the real GDP is not uniform across sectors. The results suggest that prudent energy and environmental policies should recognize the differences in the relationship between energy consumption and real GDP by sector.

Stela (2009) investigates the casual relationship between aggregated and disaggregated levels of energy consumption and economic growth for Greece for the period 1960- 2006 through the application of a later development in the methodology of time series proposed by To-do and Yamamoto. At aggregated levels of energy consumption empirical findings suggest the presence of a uni-directional casual relationship running from total energy consumption to real GDP. At disaggregated levels empirical evidence suggests that there is a bidirectional casual relationship between industrial and residential energy consumption to real GDP but this is not the case for the transport energy consumption with casual relationship being identified in neither direction. The importance of these finding lie on their policy implications and their adoption on structural policies affecting energy consumption in Greece suggesting that in order to address energy import dependence and environmental concerns without hindering economic growth emphasis should be put on the demand side and energy efficiency improvements.

Paul (1984), in his study, examines the state of energy demand analysis and develops recommendations for improving it. Despite the value of modelling, serious gaps in theory and empirical knowledge have led existing models to systematically overlook important factors affecting energy demand. It is suggested that both energy demand analysis and the policy choices it supports can benefit from improved data collection and from a more balanced reliance on a variety of analytic methods. The study distinguished the formal modelling approach to energy demand analyses. Advantages of formal models over informal judgments for answering such questions are that they can ensure that all parts of energy demand are included in the analysis and that their construction requires that the assumption on which they are based are in quantitative form.

Pan (2002) studied the rural energy patterns in China and explained that commercial energy consumption by rural is disproportionately lower than that of their urban counterparts. Wide variation in energy consumption by rural and urban people is due to difference in income, access to energy use, local economy and climatic condition. There are significant variations in rural energy consumption. The reasons behind the variations are attributable to a number of reasons, but mainly to policy discrimination, low income, and high cost of commercial energy. Improvement in energy efficiency and environmental considerations particularly in rural areas, household energy consumption has been largely reliant on non commercial traditional biological matters such a crop residues, fuel wood, and biogas.

Foysal (2012) made a case study on "Household consumption pattern areas of Bangladesh." They explained that energy is the important determinant of the quality of life in human settlements. They have explained revealed that households use fire wood, cow dung, leaves and twigs, branches, straw and rice husk as biomass energy mainly for cooking is 98.3 percent. This study is helpful to formulate polices support tools to take into account the future challenges for demand fuel resources, their sustainable utilization, promotion, and development. Half of the world population lives in rural areas, which depend mostly on biomass for their energy supply and have no access to modern form of energy (Demirbas & Demirbas, 2007). In many developing countries like Nepal and Bangladesh, the rural household energy consumption constitutes over 70 percent to the national energy use (ADB, 1998; Koopmans, 2005). The use of energy varies between rural and urban population, between high and low income groups with in a country. Energy use variations not only subsists in rural and urban regions, but also varied in lower and higher earner groups, between national and international levels (Pachuari, 2004).

Drunkenly, Knapp and Glatt (1981) made a study on "factors affecting the consumption of energy use in developing country." They explained that when income raises agriculture sector and industrial sector get more mechanized resulting to the growth of urban population and they use more electrical devices which gave rise to increase in demand of electricity. They also stated that in 1973 around 11 percent of primary electricity was used. From my field study it was found that in urban areas when income increases the demand for electricity do not rise because they already have all the electrical devices. Thus, the increase in income do not necessarily increase any use of electrical devices, hence the consumption of electricity do not increase when the income of household rises though only negligibly. However, in the case of rural areas when income increases they used to buy electrical devices like cooler, fan, TV, cell phone and their demand of electricity also increases.

The study of Sahu (2008) is an attempt to find out the trend of total energy consumption in Indian economy from 1980 to 2005. It examined the structural stability of the regression model and a strong one way / two way casual relationship between energy demand and GDP.From the trend analysis as well as the regression it is now clear that there is positive relationship between total primary energy consumption to GDP, population and per capita energy consumption; however a negative relationship do exist between the energy use and the production of the energy resources in case of India. He summarized that total primary energy use is one of the key component of the GDP. Population is an important factor for the total energy consumption and one of the major contributors for the demand of more energy resources. The findings also suggests in the same way, as increase in GDP, population, per capita consumption leads to more demand of energy resources.

Rodriguez, Charap, and Silva (2013) stated that, a panel of cross country data explores the responsiveness of energy consumption to changes in energy prices and the implications of findings for the debate on energy subsidy reform. The use of cross country data provides key sources of heterogeneity to estimate income and price elasticities of energy demand, as countries differ widely in their energy consumption, income per capita and energy prices. The findings indicate a long term price elasticity of energy demand between -0.3 and -0.5 and income elasticity in between 0.7 to 0.8 which suggest that countries can reap significant long term benefits from the reform of energy subsidies.

ENERGY CONSUMPTION IN SOUTH ASIA

Economic and population growth in South Asia has resulted into rapid increases in energy consumption in recent years, well above rates seen in other developed countries. However, more than half of the total energy consumption in South Asia is still contributed by non-commercial energy sources like animal waste, wood, or other biomass. The Energy Information Administration (EIA) estimates that South Asia's commercial energy consumption showed an increase of nearly 59 per cent between 1992 and 2013, thereby growing at an annual rate of 4.2 per cent. In 2013, South Asia accounted for approximately 4 per cent of world commercial energy consumption, up from about 2.8 per cent in 1990. Despite this growth in energy demand, South Asia continues to average among the lowest levels of per capita energy consumption in the world. It can be seen that the South Asian countries are far below the world average. For instance, Nepal is just 3.7 per cent of the world average of 66.7 million (British Thermal Units) per person, followed by Bangladesh, which is 6.3 per cent. India's per capita energy consumption is almost 20 per cent of the world average. The South Asian reserves are around 105 billion short tons (11 per cent of world's total). Similarly, for India as well the coal import market is coming into sharper focus with imports projected to grow from around 7 per cent of total coal requirement in 2001 to 71 per cent by 2031/32. This trend raises concerns not only with regard to the magnitude of imports and its impact on monetary outflows, but also regarding the sources from which coal could be imported, as well as the infrastructure requirements including handling facilities for such volumes of imports, and further transportation networks.

In the face of growing oil demand, several South Asian countries have responded with plans to expand their refining and transportation capacities.. India, at present is importing over 70 per cent of its crude requirement and its import dependency is projected to go up to 91 per cent by 2030. While there is no prospect for Pakistan to reach self-sufficiency in oil, the government has encouraged private (including foreign) firms to develop domestic production capacity. World Energy Outlook projects that the South Asian oil import dependency will increase from 72 per cent in 2000 to 95 per cent in 2030. Hence, almost

Table 1. Energy use (kg of oil equivalent per capita)

Year	Bangladesh	India	Nepal	Pakistan	Sri Lanka
1971	84.08	275.56	309.81	280.04	299.28
1972	85.45	275.70	311.63	279.73	314.56
1973	91.08	276.80	314.27	285.66	315.79
1974	92.57	281.87	313.74	294.17	295.66
1975	93.09	285.63	312.75	298.58	304.46
1976	96.76	290.57	311.52	293.00	301.56
1977	96.53	291.77	312.49	296.08	293.84
1978	97.12	286.15	312.43	298.64	304.49
1979	98.15	292.70	315.74	305.64	309.98
1980	101.85	293.51	317.12	309.56	307.51
1981	101.15	302.09	315.28	320.77	311.51
1982	104.03	307.12	316.57	328.37	322.00
1983	103.74	310.30	319.45	334.69	318.98

continued on following page

Table 1. Continued

Year	Bangladesh	India	Nepal	Pakistan	Sri Lanka
1984	102.49	316.71	320.02	334.31	324.69
1985	105.52	325.93	315.63	340.43	315.34
1986	110.00	330.82	318.93	343.61	320.02
1987	105.42	336.40	317.69	365.28	327.41
1988	112.84	347.09	317.86	371.33	327.58
1989	115.46	356.52	314.69	380.30	324.19
1990	118.60	364.54	319.65	385.79	324.20
1991	114.22	371.74	321.86	385.10	324.30
1992	117.88	379.12	321.37	399.33	329.73
1993	121.76	380.48	321.40	409.16	343.29
1994	124.49	387.93	324.28	415.22	325.14
1995	132.62	402.05	326.01	422.59	328.04
1996	130.64	407.63	325.50	433.13	366.52
1997	133.70	416.18	327.77	432.96	375.08
1998	136.53	419.01	328.27	430.91	376.91
1999	135.77	437.40	338.48	443.84	396.75
2000	140.44	438.66	349.71	445.43	435.90
2001	150.10	438.42	354.03	443.23	428.24
2002	151.49	443.52	351.30	439.40	433.30
2003	156.00	447.53	355.02	450.69	452.82
2004	159.69	467.45	354.41	474.25	452.69
2005	166.75	478.54	361.05	482.54	458.20
2006	174.86	496.10	356.21	493.12	457.41
2007	181.80	521.67	358.71	509.60	462.17
2008	188.37	538.84	367.03	491.27	442.30
2009	194.85	586.79	376.20	489.12	444.11
2010	203.51	600.31	380.63	486.93	476.66
2011	204.72	613.72	382.64	481.62	499.34

Source- Compiled from World Bank database.

all of the incremental oil demand in the future will have to be met by imports. The primary source of the region's imports is the Middle East. Natural Gas around 67.57 Tcf of these reserves are in the South Asian region (approximately1 per cent of the total world's reserves). India, Pakistan and Bangladesh are the other countries in this region which have gas reserves (around 30.14, 26.83 and 10.6 Tcf, respectively). The Energy use (kg of oil equivalent per capita) in five major south Asian countries is shown in Table 1.

In 1971 Nepal had higher per capita energy use followed by Sri Lanka, Pakistan, and India. It was very low in Bangladesh. Over the time per capita energy consumption in India increased substantially and it was highest in 2011 in India followed by Sri Lanka, Pakistan and Nepal. Bangladesh continues to

Table 2. Descriptive statistics of energy use (kg of oil equivalent per capita)

	Bangladesh	India	Nepal	Pakistan	Sri Lanka
Mean	127.71	385.87	331.44	387.94	362.73
Standard Error	5.31	14.89	3.38	11.42	9.93
Median	117.88	371.74	321.37	385.79	327.41
Standard Deviation	34.00	95.35	21.62	73.15	63.60
Sample Variance	1155.77	9090.69	467.32	5351.35	4045.12
Kurtosis	-0.24	-0.12	-0.21	-1.40	-1.06
Skewness	0.87	0.81	1.05	0.01	0.75
Range	120.64	338.16	72.83	229.87	205.50
Minimum	84.08	275.56	309.81	279.73	293.84
Maximum	204.72	613.72	382.64	509.60	499.34
Sum	5236.12	15820.87	13589.15	15905.42	14871.95
Count	41.00	41.00	41.00	41.00	41.00

Source- Compiled by the author

Figure 1. Trend of Energy Use (Kg of Oil Per Capita)

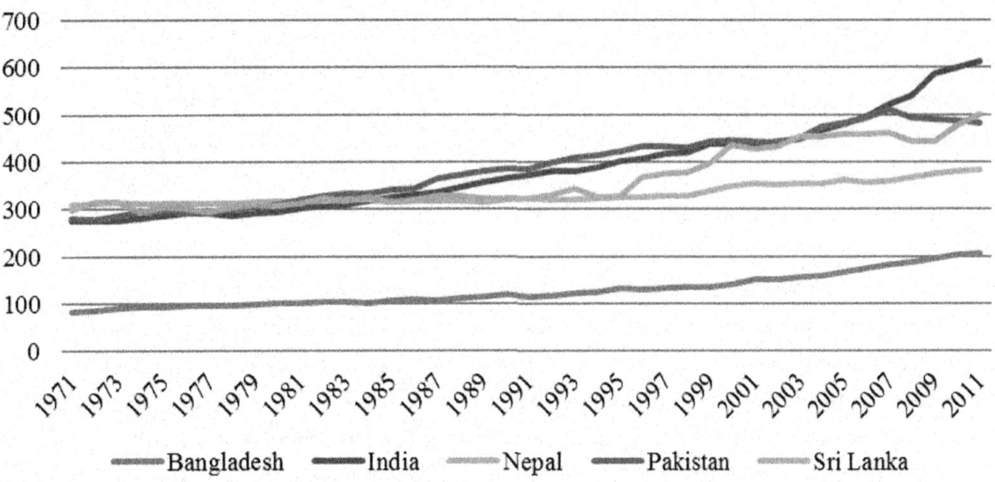

be energy poor country in South Asian Region. The descriptive statistics given in Table 2 shows more year wise fluctuation in India as standard deviation is 95.35.

The trend of per capita energy use from 1971 to 2011 is shown in Figure 1. The trend line of Bangladesh remained low throughout the period but line of India increased substantially.

The commercial energy mix of South Asia is 46 per cent coal, 34 per cent petroleum, 12 per cent natural gas, 6 per cent hydroelectricity, 1 per cent nuclear and 0.3 per cent ‘other’. However, there are significant variations within the region. The commercial energy consumption in South Asian countries is given in Table 3.

Table 3. Commercial energy consumption in South Asia in 2013

Total Consumption		Petroleum	Coal	Hydroelectric	Nuclear	Others	Natural Gas
	(Quadrillion Btu)	(%)	(%)	(%)	(%)	(%)	
Bangladesh	0.61	29.02	2.48	1.86	0.00	0.00	67.45
India	14.03	34.28	51.89	5.00	1.41	0.31	7.05
Nepal	0.06	51.67	14.25	37.81	0.00	0.00	0.00
Pakistan	1.91	38.22	5.56	14.00	1.01	0.00	21.99
Sri Lanka	0.19	84.21	0.02	15.85	0.00	0.02	0.00

Source: EIA website

India is the fourth largest energy consumer in the world after the United States, China, and Russia. In recent years, India's energy consumption has been increasing at a relatively fast rate due to population growth and economic development. Rapid urbanization and improving standards of living for millions of Indian households, the demand is likely to grow significantly. In order to sustain the production, industries have opted for inefficient diesel-fueled backup power. India's energy planning, which is based on the twin objectives of high economic growth and providing electricity to all, is failing to meet either. The domestic power demand of India was 918 billion units in 2012. It is expected that at 9.8% annual growth the demand will reach 1,640 billion units by 2020. At this pace, India will require 390 GW in the next eight years which is almost double its current installed capacity of 210 giga watts (GW). The large increases in energy consumption that have accompanied rising population and economic growth in India have been shaped by a variety of environmental factors and policy choices.

The per capita primary energy consumption in India is a low 305 kg against the world average of 1,487 kg (World Energy Statistics, 2015). Accordingly, with a total primary energy consumption of 314.7 million metric tones of oil equivalent (MMTOE), India accounts for just 3.4% of the total world primary energy consumption. However, at this stage, the point to note is that while the consumption of primary energy in the world grew at a low compounded annual growth rate (CAGR) of 1.1% during 1991-2001, it experienced a higher growth of 4.3% in India. The world primary energy consumption showed a higher growth rate of 3.1% per annum during the 1970s before declining to the current level. These efficiency gains are apparent in items as diverse as automobiles, airplanes, household electrical goods, power plants and manufacturing equipment. Oil, gas, hydroelectricity, nuclear power and coal are the five constituents of primary energy. Oil and gas account for 62.2% of the total world primary energy consumption. In India, coal is the principal source of energy accounting for over 55% of the total primary energy consumption. However, the share of oil & gas has increased from 34.8% in 1999 to the current level of 38.4%. The reasons for the growing importance of oil and gas are to be found in their multiple, varied and cost-effective applications. As in the case of per capita primary energy consumption, the per capita consumption of oil & gas in India is also a low 117 kg against the world average of 925 kg. Thus, the growth in primary energy consumption, the increasing share of oil & gas in the primary energy consumption, and the low per capita consumption of oil & gas are indicative of an enormous potential for growth in the demand for oil & gas in India.

The commercial energy constitutes a higher proportion of total primary energy compared to non-commercial energy as shown in Table 6. The share of primary energy consumption is projected to increase from 550 MTOE in 2006-07 to 2043MTOE in 2031-32 and the share will increase from 72.2%

Table 4. Total primary energy requirement

Year	Total Primary Energy (MTOE)	Share of Primary Commercial Energy (%)	Share of Non-Commercial Energy (%)
2006-07	550	72.2	27.8
2011-12	715	76.4	23.6
Projected Total Primary Energy Requirement			
2021-22	1192	84.8	15.2
2031-32	2043	90.4	9.1
Com. Annual Growth Rate	5.4	6.37	0.76

Source: Planning Commission, Government of India

to 90.4% during the same period. The share of non-commercial energy will significantly reduce to 9.1% in 2031-32. The projected compound annual growth rate of total primary energy requirement from 2006 to 2032 is 5.4% where as it is only 0.76% in case of Non-commercial Energy (Table 4).

The projections, growth rates and GDP elasticity of total energy requirements are essential for an inclusive growth of Indian economy at the GDP growth rate of 8% per year. During fifteen-year period from 1995 to 2010, the compound growth rate of total primary energy is 2.9% and for total primary commercial energy is 4.9%. The compound growth rate of gross generation of electricity is 5.8% and it is for final use of electricity is 4.6% as shown in Table 5. It is clear that electricity is generated at higher rate than its use. The GDP elasticity is an important indicator of energy equity and sustainable development. This elasticity is 0.54 for total primary energy, 0.56 for final energy and 0.99 for gross generation of electricity.

ENERGY PRODUCTION IN SOUTH ASIA

To match energy demand, energy production in South Asia must increase significantly. Energy production depends on water. It is used in power generation, primarily for cooling thermal power plants; in the extraction, transport and processing of fuels; and, increasingly, in irrigation to grow biomass feedstock crops. Energy is also vital to providing freshwater, needed to power systems that collect, transport, distribute and treat it. Each resource faces rising demands and constraints in many regions as a consequence of economic and population growth and climate change, which will amplify their vulnerability to one

Table 5. Growth Rates and GDP elasticity of Energy use in India

Type of Energy	Period	Compound Growth Rate	GDP Elasticity
Total Primary Energy	1995-2010	2.9	0.54
Total Primary Commercial Energy	1995-2010	4.9	0.79
Final Energy	1995-2010	3.4	0.56
Gross generation of Electricity	1995-2010	5.8	0.99
Final use of Electricity	1995-2010	4.6	0.75

Source: Author's calculation based on data

another. For the energy sector, constraints on water can challenge the reliability of existing operations as well as the physical, economic and environmental viability of future projects. Water constraints can occur naturally, as in the case of droughts and heat waves, or be human-induced, as a result of growing competition among users or regulations that limit access to water. The primary Production of energy is shown in Table 6.

India has 4 percent of World's and 14 percent of Asia's total energy production. Over the years India's share has increased marginally in Asia and World.

Table 6. Total primary production (mtoe) of energy

Year	India	Asia	World	% of India to World	% of India to Asia
1990	281	1693	8817	3.19	16.62
1991	291	1737	8831	3.29	16.72
1992	295	1765	8884	3.32	16.71
1993	297	1815	8919	3.33	16.38
1994	309	1903	9057	3.41	16.25
1995	323	1995	9244	3.49	16.19
1996	329	2051	9475	3.47	16.04
1997	339	2071	9592	3.53	16.36
1998	339	2086	9715	3.49	16.27
1999	345	2107	9719	3.55	16.35
2000	351	2202	10027	3.50	15.94
2001	359	2271	10186	3.52	15.80
2002	368	2355	10273	3.58	15.63
2003	379	2539	10694	3.54	14.93
2004	392	2789	11244	3.48	14.05
2005	404	3011	11626	3.47	13.41
2006	417	3173	11937	3.49	13.14
2007	430	3318	12143	3.54	12.97
2008	445	3395	12387	3.59	13.11
2009	480	3527	12263	3.91	13.61
2010	496	3739	12794	3.88	13.27
2011	504	3959	13165	3.83	12.74
2012	513	3994	13342	3.85	12.85
2013	523	4111	13592	3.85	12.73
2014	550	4202	13779	3.99	13.09
2015	593	4219	13887	4.27	14.06

Source- Energy Data, Internet

Electricity Production

In the South Asian region, the level of electrification is very poor particularly in rural areas. The access to electricity in India (in 2001/2) was around 46 per cent, while it was 30 per cent for Bangladesh. Only 11 per cent of Bhutan's population has access to electricity and for Nepal, it was around 15 per cent (SASEC Issue paper). Countries, like Nepal and Bhutan with substantial hydropower potential have not been able to harness it fully. Nepal which has a huge hydropower potential has a per capita electricity consumption of about 42 kWh, among the lowest in the world. Domestic supplies have not been able to meet local demand. Nepal also imports electricity from India. Despite having a high potential of exportable power and a large market in India, Nepal has not been to utilize this fully. One of the reasons for this is the high power generation costs. The poor level of progress in developing the hydropower potential is due to lack of financial resources and poor development of infrastructure. India too has an unutilized hydropower potential of more than 150,000 MW. India accounts for more than 80 per cent generation in the South Asian region. This is followed by Pakistan (11 per cent), Bangladesh (3 per cent) and Sri Lanka (1 per cent). China is the second largest producer of electricity in the world. Top ten energy producing countries are given in Table 7.

Figure 2 shows ten highest energy producing countries with USA in first rank.

Electricity production from oil, gas and coal sources (% of total) in five South Asian Countries are given in Table 8.

The electricity production is 88 percent of total energy production in Bangladesh where as it is 72% in India, 55% in Pakistan, 26% in Sri Lanka and only 5% in Nepal (refer to Table 9 and Figure 3). In Sri Lanka there is significant rise in electricity production from coal and oil in 1984 and 1996 to 46.4 percent and 28.21 percent.

Table 7. Ten Highest Energy Producing Countries in the World

Sl No	Country	Energy Production(Mtoe)
1	United States	2012
2	Russia	1341
3	Saudi Arabia	650
4	India	593
5	Canada	456
6	Indonesia	401
7	Australia	355
8	Iran	289
9	Brazil	280
10	Nigeria	259

Source- Energy Data

Figure 2. Energy production (mtoe)

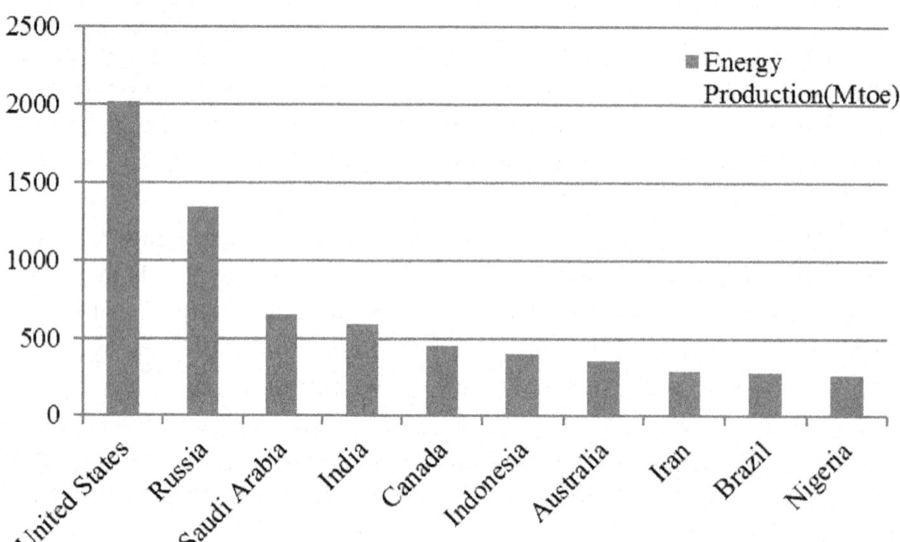

Table 8. Electricity production from oil, gas and coal sources (% of total)

Year	Bangladesh	India	Nepal	Pakistan	Sri Lanka
1971	83.01	55.98	22.09	50.04	7.33
1972	83.01	59.82	21.50	50.04	13.97
1973	76.42	56.90	22.12	44.38	31.33
1974	84.31	60.76	14.29	49.21	7.23
1975	73.20	58.18	14.77	50.07	4.09
1976	72.07	60.16	9.79	41.41	5.66
1977	77.40	59.27	11.46	48.46	3.65
1978	77.20	54.65	12.07	38.00	1.37
1979	75.56	57.13	11.92	41.17	4.20
1980	75.22	58.45	6.45	41.79	11.33
1981	76.52	59.88	3.95	42.77	16.03
1982	82.77	64.07	1.54	45.12	22.17
1983	80.72	64.56	0.84	41.14	42.43
1984	77.38	65.70	1.04	39.88	7.52
1985	83.68	69.45	0.70	45.28	2.80
1986	90.63	70.75	0.18	44.37	0.26
1987	90.75	76.03	1.06	45.12	19.58
1988	89.68	73.60	3.77	48.80	7.22
1989	87.07	75.15	0.14	50.87	1.96
1990	88.57	73.11	0.11	54.30	0.16
1991	89.87	75.18	3.43	54.50	7.73
1992	91.05	76.95	5.30	55.55	18.08

continued on following page

Table 8. Continued

Year	Bangladesh	India	Nepal	Pakistan	Sri Lanka
1993	93.40	78.68	6.65	60.64	4.60
1994	91.34	77.02	8.02	56.36	6.79
1995	96.56	80.58	3.09	58.41	7.29
1996	93.56	81.93	3.28	64.14	28.21
1997	93.94	81.58	9.15	63.90	33.00
1998	93.29	80.67	9.52	65.25	31.11
1999	94.24	82.00	4.53	70.07	32.52
2000	95.25	83.18	1.63	71.83	54.20
2001	94.29	83.23	0.96	70.69	53.99
2002	95.99	85.26	0.19	68.18	61.82
2003	96.20	84.45	0.18	64.49	57.10
2004	96.97	83.78	0.58	66.78	63.86
2005	97.17	81.78	0.63	64.46	62.77
2006	97.46	80.85	0.47	65.18	51.00
2007	97.58	79.86	0.32	66.78	59.93
2008	97.23	81.65	0.32	67.91	55.03
2009	98.88	82.23	0.42	67.52	60.35
2010	98.25	80.90	0.09	62.70	46.71
2011	98.02	79.42	0.09	64.54	59.11

Source- World Bank database.

Table 9. Descriptive statistics of electricity production from oil, gas and coal sources (% of total)

	Bangladesh	India	Nepal	Pakistan	Sri Lanka
Mean	88.43	72.56	5.33	55.17	25.99
Standard Error	1.31	1.59	1.01	1.64	3.56
Median	90.75	76.03	3.09	54.50	18.08
S.D	8.38	10.15	6.44	10.50	22.78
Variance	70.23	103.02	41.42	110.20	519.12
Kurtosis	-1.14	-1.40	1.13	-1.49	-1.42
Skewness	-0.53	-0.48	1.38	-0.01	0.48
Range	26.81	30.61	22.03	33.83	63.70
Minimum	72.07	54.65	0.09	38.00	0.16
Maximum	98.88	85.26	22.12	71.83	63.86
Sum	3625.71	2974.78	218.64	2262.10	1065.49
Count	41.00	41.00	41.00	41.00	41.00

Source- Computed by the Author

Figure 3. Trend of electricity production from oil, gas and coal sources (% of total)

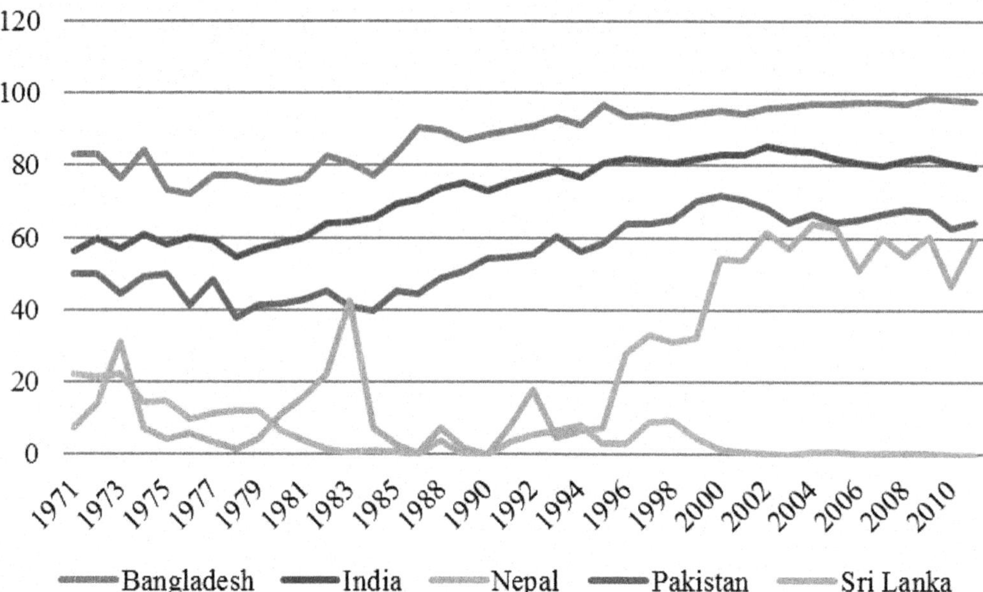

INEFFICIENCY IN ENERGY PRODUCTION, CONSUMPTION AND ENERGY INTENSITY

Inefficiency is a major strain on volume needs in most of Asia. One of the reasons for the low level of efficiency in energy production in this region is the high level of technical losses. The power sector, for instance, faces problems of high technical losses. These are due to poor quality transmission lines, pilferage, unmetered connections as well as low plant load factors due to aging generators and poor maintenance of equipment at existing plants (plus low-quality coal in many cases). Transmission and distribution (T&D) losses of electricity are very high in the region. For instance, the T&D losses as a percentage of availability for India in 2002-03 were around 38 per cent (TERI 2004) and in some areas of Pakistan, transmission losses were approximately 30 per cent. An integrated national grid for India is still evolving. This has led to a situation where, despite the national shortage of generating capacity, there are some locations which still have surplus capacity, but lack of transmission capacity to move it to areas with a capacity shortage. Highly prevalent energy subsidies are a major reason for inefficiency in energy consumption. These subsidies end up giving wrong signals to consumers creating distortions in the energy markets and promoting unnecessary wastage of resources. They also impose a heavy burden on the supply system as well as government tax revenues. In many of the South and East Asian countries, electricity rates are widely subsidized. The state electricity companies are faced with the challenge of incurring higher cost of generation or having to pay independent power plants their asking price while providing lower rates to their customers. Further, subsidies are made in a non- transparent manner and are not properly accounted for. Also, subsidies in a number of cases are provided through elaborate systems of cross-subsidization, which provide wrong kind of signals. An analysis carried out by the International Energy Agency revealed that the distortion in energy prices in China and India were around 11 per cent and 14 per cent. The phasing out of energy subsidies could imply energy saving potential of 7–9 per cent for these two countries (IEA 1999). However, progress has been quite slow in phasing out subsidies in the region due to entrenched interest and political resistance. In India, for instance, despite reforms in the power sector and commitment to gradually remove subsidies, the commercial and industrial sector continue to cross-subsidize agricultural and domestic sectors. This is unlike most industrial countries, where the cost of supplying electricity to household consumers is on average 50 per cent higher than to industrial consumers (UNEP 2004). While agricultural sector tariffs have been increased in some states, power is still underpriced for the agricultural sector in a few states. The gross subsidy for states (for agriculture and domestic sector) in the year 2004/5 is estimated to be in the range of Rs 34,311 million. There was an uncovered subsidy of Rs175, 200 million. In addition to under pricing of energy (Electricity), subsidies also stem from poor recovery of revenues, largely due to inadequate metering, poor credit control and theft. Another energy sub-sector where subsidies are widespread is petroleum and petroleum products. In India, the Government has historically maintained heavy subsidies through the public distribution system on the two principal household fuels, LPG and kerosene. During the process of dismantling Administered Pricing Mechanism (APM) in 2002, the Government had committed to remove subsidies in a period of 3 years. However, the two fuels continue to be subsidized. In fact the increase in the international product prices have severely dented the profitability of public sector oil marketing companies who have not been able to raise the domestic retail price in line with international prices. Indonesia, which has recently turned importer for oil, is crippled with subsidies with fuel prices less than half the import cost. Subsidies account for up to one-quarter of the state budget. While one cannot expect subsidies to be phased out completely, effective targeting of the beneficiary group(s) might actually add to national welfare. Subsidy reform is a pre-requisite for attracting private sector investment.

Though the per capita energy consumption figures are quite low for South Asian countries, they have among the highest levels of energy consumption per unit of GDP. Even within these countries there are significant variations in the energy intensity values. For instance, the highest numbers are recorded by India, followed by Pakistan. The energy intensity values for the other South Asian countries like Bangladesh, Nepal and Sri Lanka are comparatively much lower. However, these countries have recorded increasing energy intensities, with the highest growth occurring in Nepal (6 per cent), followed by Bangladesh (2.1 per cent) and Sri Lanka (0.7 per cent). The reason for this is primarily inefficient use of energy in these countries. Pakistan has recorded a modest growth rate in its energy intensity at 0.2 per cent. India on the other hand has witnessed a decline in its energy intensity between 1990 and 2013.

COMMERCIAL ENERGY MIX AND ENERGY DEMAND FORECASTS

The energy demand forecast estimates for the South Asian countries. It can be seen that between 2003–4 and 2019–20, electricity consumption will rise at the fastest pace in Bangladesh and Nepal. Demand for natural gas is projected to grow at the fastest pace in Bangladesh and India followed by Pakistan. Nepal, which is a major hydropower, will see significant increase in the demand for coal, along with Pakistan. Demand for oil will be very fast growing in almost all of the countries. (Table 10)

ENERGY IMPORT IN SOUTH ASIA

According to the World Bank net energy Imports are estimated as energy use less production, both measured in oil equivalents. A negative value indicates that the country is a net exporter. Energy use

Table 10. Energy demand forecast in South Asia (2019–20)

Fuels	Unit	Bangladesh	India	Nepal	Pakistan	Sri Lanka
Electricity (total)	BkWh	72.7	1756	8.08	251.06	23.8
Growth rate	(%)	8.2	7.1	8	7.5	7.2
Oil products	Mtoe	11.6	246.9	1.61	30.9	7.8
Growth rate	(%)	7.3	4.8	4.9	4.5	6.2
Natural gas	Mtoe	44.03	101.8	0	72.7	0
Growth rate	(%)	11	8	0	6.2	0
Coal	Mtoe	0.9	447.6	0.78	13.9	7
Growth rate	(%)	3.7	6.2	10	9.4	–

Source: Pragya Jaswal and Mitali Das Gupta (2006) on Asia

Table 11. Energy imports, net (% of energy use)

Year	Bangladesh	India	Nepal	Pakistan	Sri Lanka
1971	14.73	9.53	1.66	15.74	26.01
1972	14.27	8.91	2.18	15.26	30.49
1973	15.90	9.42	2.99	15.14	31.11
1974	16.55	8.67	2.77	15.79	26.35
1975	18.91	6.80	2.48	16.06	24.07
1976	19.17	8.22	1.96	15.71	23.54
1977	17.77	8.45	2.21	15.00	25.40
1978	18.50	7.03	2.15	15.17	27.41
1979	18.70	9.55	3.13	16.25	28.81
1980	19.72	8.91	3.48	15.50	29.24
1981	19.78	7.39	3.02	16.83	28.65
1982	19.07	6.21	3.47	17.85	30.11
1983	16.11	4.59	4.48	18.95	30.48
1984	15.27	3.74	4.79	20.29	26.46
1985	15.41	6.04	3.57	19.41	24.43
1986	15.99	4.97	4.52	18.30	24.14
1987	16.28	5.60	4.25	18.30	25.70
1988	14.76	5.68	4.43	19.21	24.57
1989	15.47	7.26	3.43	19.30	23.31
1990	15.53	7.87	4.98	20.25	24.02
1991	13.61	8.47	5.97	17.77	25.00
1992	14.24	10.63	6.34	19.46	24.68
1993	14.54	11.59	6.77	20.87	29.68
1994	14.77	11.81	7.95	22.90	31.29
1995	19.63	12.62	8.54	23.34	32.40

continued on following page

Table 11. Continued

Year	Bangladesh	India	Nepal	Pakistan	Sri Lanka
1996	18.96	13.72	8.74	25.49	37.45
1997	21.60	14.35	9.83	27.02	37.59
1998	21.30	16.65	10.13	26.68	39.00
1999	18.19	19.83	12.66	27.70	39.85
2000	18.54	19.86	11.96	26.80	42.98
2001	19.90	19.37	12.38	24.92	43.31
2002	19.37	19.66	10.04	24.25	44.58
2003	19.22	19.03	10.49	20.10	46.38
2004	18.44	21.04	9.77	20.83	45.84
2005	19.27	21.42	10.73	20.34	45.34
2006	16.71	22.42	8.94	23.07	43.25
2007	17.48	23.79	8.86	24.31	45.19
2008	16.67	24.51	10.07	24.23	43.28
2009	15.88	26.36	11.44	23.50	43.76
2010	16.24	26.59	13.12	23.73	43.68
2011	16.63	27.82	13.02	23.31	48.86

Source- World Bank Data Base(Development Indicators)

refers to use of primary energy before transformation to other end-use fuels, which is equal to indigenous production plus imports and stock changes, minus exports and fuels supplied to ships and aircraft engaged in international transport. Table 11 shows Energy imports, net (% of energy use) in South Asian Countries. Sri Lanka has highest percent import compared to other countries.

Table 12. Descriptive statistics of energy imports as % of total

	Bangladesh	India	Nepal	Pakistan	Sri Lanka
Mean	17.29	13.08	6.68	20.36	33.36
Standard Error	0.33	1.11	0.58	0.60	1.32
Median	16.71	9.55	5.97	20.10	30.48
S.D	2.09	7.14	3.72	3.86	8.46
Variance	4.36	50.93	13.85	14.94	71.58
Kurtosis	-1.02	-0.95	-1.41	-1.12	-1.46
Skewness	0.12	0.64	0.28	0.25	0.42
Range	7.99	24.08	11.46	12.70	25.55
Minimum	13.61	3.74	1.66	15.00	23.31
Maximum	21.60	27.82	13.12	27.70	48.86
Sum	709.08	536.38	273.70	834.93	1367.69
Count	41.00	41.00	41.00	41.00	41.00

Source- Computed by the Author

Figure 4. Energy import, net % of total

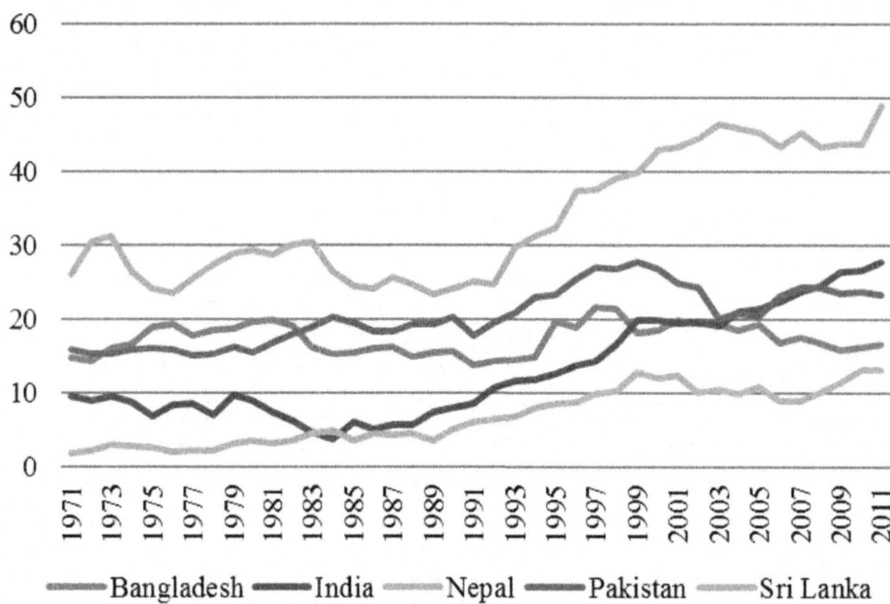

Table 12 shows that energy import is highest 33.36% in Sri Lanka followed by Pakistan, Bangladesh, India and Nepal.

Figure 4 shows that import of all South Asian countries as percent of total energy is increasing over time. There is growing energy inequity between rural and urban areas and also between the developed and developing states. There are millions who are yet to be benefited from electricity in rural India. The scarcity of electricity in rural areas in comparison to urban areas seems to be biased in delivery through the centralized system. While the urban-rural difference in energy supply could be reduced through renewable energy, it is more complex to overcome the widening gap between developed and not so developed states. Current centralized energy planning of India is dependent on coal and fossil fuel sources. The main concern arises on how to protect the fossil fuel for our coming generation with simultaneously utilizing the different resources of energy for high and sustained economic growth. Pressure to increase its energy supplies and the consequent negative environmental impact of fossil fuels has led India to conscious policy toward renewable sources. Energy is a vital input for social and economic development of any nation. With increasing agricultural and industrial activities in the country, the demand for energy is also increasing. Formulation of an energy model will help in the proper allocation of widely available renewable energy sources such as solar, wind, bio energy and small hydropower in meeting the future energy demand in India. During the last decade several new concepts of energy planning and management such as decentralized planning, energy conservation through improved technologies, waste recycling, integrated energy planning, introduction of renewable energy sources and energy forecasting have emerged. There is also essential to improve the efficiency levels, for this one has to understand past trends in energy use and assess the factors that contribute to changes in energy consumption and measure the performance of energy related policies (Deb, 2015). Basically, energy require for development increasing day by day. The Literature showed that non-renewable energy easy to produce than former energy and there has been a tendency to produce and use of non-renewable energy but from the sustainable development point of view such rain pant use of non-renewable resources like coal, petroleum etc are the sources of unsustainable development and alternative sources of energy has to be explored. Renewable sources of energy such as wind, solar, geothermal, biogas, hydro, tidal can be alternative of formal energy.

CHALLENGES IN THE ENERGY SECTOR

With the growing demand of energy and constraints in the domestic resource availability, the South and East Asian countries face a number of challenges in terms of provision of energy services. The energy demand is going to grow rapidly. Some of the important challenges are as follows:

1. **Increasing Supplies and Investment:** Given the energy demand supply gap, a major challenge for the region is to increase the supply of energy. This entails finding new energy sources as well as investing in infrastructure. Developing countries will require almost half of global investment in the energy sector which amounts to about US$8 trillion. Capital needs will be almost as big in the rest of Asia including India. Energy sector projects are characterized by high capital intensity involving large initial investments before production/supply can begin. For instance, the electricity sector requires two to three times as much investment as manufacturing industries. The financial markets in South Asia are not well developed. This limits access to capital, especially long-term capital and imposes an important constraint on the level of funds available. Access to international credit will also be limited by the exchange-rate risk, deficiencies in the legal and regulatory systems and fears of economic and political instability. The private sector will have to play an increasingly important role. However, the private sector will be constrained by the poor financial situation of energy sub-sectors, particularly the electricity sector.
2. **Inadequate Regulatory and Institutional Framework in South Asia:** The energy sector of many of the countries in South Asian region faces problems relating to regulatory regimes and institutional frameworks. The power sector in this region suffers from inadequacies in their regulatory structure, generating companies and own management practices. Energy utilities in most of South Asia are operated to a large extent at the public sector level. In most of the cases, the public sector operates in a commercially unviable manner. Revenue from sale of energy does not realize the full costs of supply. As a result, most of the power utilities are faced with poor financial health and consequent deterioration of service delivery. In India, while in the past few years, the rate of return of State Electricity Boards (SEBs) has improved, it continues to be negative. One of the major implications of the inadequacies in the regulatory and institutional frameworks is the constraint it imposes in terms of attracting private sector participation. With the growing realization of the important role that the private sector will have to play in the development of energy sector, providing the right kind of framework for stimulating and sustaining private sector participation is an important challenge that these countries face.
3. **Environmental Concerns and Policy Response:** Energy processing and generation is one of the major sources of air pollution in the region. There are many energy-related environment problems, including urban and transboundary pollution and global climate change. While coal is the fuel of comparative advantage for this region, there is a whole set of concerns in the coal using nations of this region which relate to the need to address the environmental impact of the heavy coal use in

Indian industries. Coal-fired power plants with outdated pollution control equipment, using poor quality coal, have increased the frequency of acid rain, particularly in India. In India, the management of fly ash has been a source of environmental concerns with over 60 per cent power generating being coal-based and power grade coal containing on an average over 40 per cent ash.

4. **Development of Alternative Sources of Energy:** The South Asian region has a great potential in renewable energy forms, which has not been explored to a substantial extent. Experience in South Asia indicates that the main initiative for promotion of commercialization of renewable energy technologies has to come from governments. International and regional organizations should continue to enhance their catalytic role, particularly in terms of capacity building and promoting regional and sub-regional cooperation. However, some activities on renewable energy technologies have already been started in these countries.
5. **Regional Cooperation:** Regional cooperation in energy is intended to offset discontinuities imposed by national frontiers and thus increasing trade within the region thereby stimulating production and providing enhanced investment opportunities. The richly endowed natural resources such as water potential of Nepal, Bhutan, India and Pakistan, the natural gas of Bangladesh and Pakistan, and the coal of India are in abundance for the generation of power (energy), which can be of tremendous benefits to the region. To fulfill such an initiative, creation of an apex energy institution of South Asia comprising companies like Petrobangla of Bangladesh, ONGC and Coal India Limited of India, Sui Gas of Pakistan and Ceylon Petroleum Corporation of Sri Lanka could be a right step. This apex body may join hands for a comprehensive resource assessment of material, manpower and technology in the region, joint R&D, consultancy and HRD activities and sharing of experiences for mutual benefit. There can also be substantial gains derived from the collective promotion of non- conventional sources of energy. Hence there is a further need for a firm commitment and understanding among the countries in the region to reap benefits from energy cooperation.

SUGGESTIONS

The South Asian countries need to intensify efforts towards:

1. More rigorous reforms in the energy sub-sectors, especially cost-reflective pricing and improved collection in the electricity sector.
2. Development and exploration of new energy sources and supplies.
3. Diversification of the energy mix and promotion of alternative fuel sources particularly renewable energy.
4. Facilitating energy efficiency and conservation.
5. Promoting technological development in the energy sector especially for utilising existing hydrocarbon base (particularly for exploiting the rich coal base of the region) in an environmentally friendly manner.
6. Enhancing emergency response coordination and preparedness in the event of energy supply disruptions.
7. Promoting regional cooperation not only to better utilize the energy resources within the region but also to tackle competition and confrontation over energy resources, which are emerging between Asian countries especially between Japan, China and India.

CONCLUSION

It is concluded from the study that the electricity production is 88 percent of total energy production in Bangladesh where as it is 72% in India, 55% in Pakistan, 26% in Sri Lanka and only 5% in Nepal Energy import is highest 33.36% in Sri Lanka followed by Pakistan, Bangladesh, India and Nepal. Energy is a prerequisite to economic development and in turn the prosperity that economic development brings stimulates the demand for more and better energy services. The energy and growth inter-linkage is well understood. There is absence of holistic energy policies as well as the lack of effective leadership and political will. Hence the desired outcomes for India have not yet been realized as far as energy and sustainable development is concerned. It is essential to supply to the poor people in the form of clean fuel which is our primary concern. More focus should be on supply of subsistence level of energy. India has to grow its primary energy and electricity supply manifold to ensure sustained GDP growth. India must explore and invest in new energy technologies like gas hydrates, coal to liquid, Coal Bed Methane (CBM) etc. India should make use of novel technologies to extract coal efficiently which is economically viable and sustainable. India will also need to seek new and clean coal technologies so as to tap its existing coal reserves which are at present difficult to extract economically using the available conventional technologies. Adequate technologies and allocation of funds for energy related R&D needs to be promoted for developing indigenous solutions which are typical to India. Energy conservation and sustainable energy use can also be directly improved by government policies. Energy loss during transmission can also be brought down by decentralizing energy production and distribution. These two imperatives, energy security and energy transition, would be the major drivers of South Asia. The private sector can play an important role in this regard but given the volatile nature of South Asian politics, the private sector may be reluctant to invest in mega projects without the necessary legal regimes to protect investments. There is absence of holistic energy policies as well as the lack of effective leadership and political will. Hence the desired outcomes for South Asian Countries have not yet been realized as far as energy and sustainable development is concerned. It is essential to supply to the poor people in the form of clean fuel which is the primary concern. More focus should be on supply of subsistence level of energy. South Asia has to grow its primary energy and electricity supply manifold to ensure sustained GDP growth. Adequate technologies and allocation of funds for energy related R&D needs to be promoted for developing indigenous solutions which are typical to South Asia. Energy conservation and sustainable energy use can also be directly improved by government policies. Energy loss during transmission can also be brought down by decentralizing energy production and distribution.

REFERENCES

Ailawadi, V. S., & Bhattacharyya, S. C. (2006). Access to energy services by the poor in India: Current situation and need for alternative strategies. *Natural Resources Forum*, *30*(1), 2–14. doi:10.1111/j.1477-8947.2006.00153.x

Bhattacharyya, S. (2005). *Our coal, our future*. Working Paper, Department of Fuel and Mineral Engineering, Indian School of Mines, Dhanbad.

Birol, F. (2007). Energy economics: A place for Energy poverty in the Agenda. *The Energy Journal (Cambridge, Mass.)*, *28*(3). doi:10.5547/ISSN0195-6574-EJ-Vol28-No3-1

Cecelski, E. (2000). *Enabling equitable access to rural electrification: Current thinking on energy, poverty and gender, Briefing Paper, Asia Alternative Energy Policy and Project Development Support.* Washington, DC: The World Bank.

Chakraborty, A. (2005). *Status of gas in India's fuel basket.* London: Council.

Dunkerley, J., Knapp, G., & Glatt, S. (1981). *Factors Affecting the Composition of Energy Use in Developing Countries Discussion Paper D-73C 4.* Energy Policy Research Resources For The Future.

Foysal, M. A. (2012). *Household Energy Consumption Pattern in Rural Areas of Bangladesh.* Retrieved from https://www.researchgate.net/publication/258248028

Gupta, V. (2005). Climate change and domestic mitigation efforts. *Economic and Political Weekly, 5*(March), 981–987.

Kelkar, G., & Nathan, D. (2002). *Gender relations and the energy transition in rural Asia, Collaborative Research Group on Gender and Energy, ENERGIA International Network on Gender and Sustainable Energy Use, DFID International Energy Agency (2012).* World Energy Outlook.

Kumar, N., Sen, R., & Asher, M. (Eds.). (2006). *India-ASEAN Economic Relations: Meeting the challenges of globalisation.* New Delhi: ISEAS, Singapore, and RIS.

Lahiri-Dutt, K., & Williams, D. (2005). *The coal cycle: A small part of the illegal supply of coal in eastern India.* New Delhi: Resources, Environment and Development.

Mattoo, A. (2005, August 27). Striking a balance. *Economic and Political Weekly*, 3815–18.

Mehta, J. K. (2005). *India: Facing up to the future, The World Energy Book.* London: World Energy Council.

Nicholas, B., & Payne, J. E. (2009). The causal relationship between U.S. energy consumption and real output: A disaggregated analysis. *Journal of Policy Modeling, 31*(2), 180–188. doi:10.1016/j.jpolmod.2008.09.001

Pan, J. (2002). *Rural Energy Patterns in China: A preliminary assessment from available data sources.* Retrieved from https://pesd.fsi.stanford.edu/sites/default/files/evnts/media//PAN_paper.pdf

Paul, L. J. (1984). Energy Policies and Their Consequences after 25 Years. *The Energy Journal (Cambridge, Mass.), 24*(4).

Raza, H. (2005). *Co-operation fuels development, The World Energy Book.* World Energy Institute.

Reddy, B.S. & P. Balachandra (2002, December 28). A sustainable energy strategy for India revisited. *Economic and Political Weekly*, 5264–73.

Rodriguez, C., & Silva, A. R. (2013). *Energy Subsidies and Energy Consumption — A Cross-Country Analysis.* IMF Working Paper No. 13/112.

Roy, A. K. (2003). Disinvestment and outsourcing in coal. *Economic and Political Weekly*, (December): 6.

Sagar, A. (2002, September 21). India's energy R and D landscape. *Economic and Political Weekly*, 3925–34.

Sahu, S. (2008). *Trend and patterns of energy consumption in India.* Available at http://mpra.ub.uni-muenchen.de/16753/

Sajal, G. (2002). *Electricity Consumption and Economic Growth.* Elsevier Energy Policy.

Srinivasan, M.R., Grover, R.B., & Bharadwaj, S.A. (2005, December 3). Nuclear power in India: Winds of change. *Economic and Political Weekly*, 5183–88.

Stela, Z. T. (2010). Energy consumption and economic growth: A causality analysis for Greece. *Energy Economics*, *32*(3), 582–590. doi:10.1016/j.eneco.2009.09.007

KEY TERMS AND DEFINITIONS

Coal: It is a black or dark-brown combustible mineral substance consisting of carbonized vegetable matter, used as a fuel.

Consumption: It is the process in which the substance of a thing is completely destroyed, used up, or incorporated or transformed into something else.

Demand: It refers desire and willingness of a consumer to pay a price for a specific good or service.

Electricity: It is a form of energy that is carried through wires and is used to operate machines, lights, etc.

Energy: It is power derived from the utilization of physical or chemical resources, especially to provide light and heat or to work machines.

Infrastructure: It is the basic physical and organizational structures and facilities (e.g. buildings, roads, power supplies) needed for the operation of a society or enterprise.

Security: It means safety, as well as the measures taken to be safe or protected.

Supply: It refers to the total amount of a product (good or service) available for purchase at any specified price.

Chapter 10
Public-Sector Project Abandonment Decision:
A Test of the Ricardian Equivalence Theory on the Failed Lagos Metroline in Nigeria

Kehinde Adekunle Adetiloye
Covenant University, Nigeria

Patrick Omoruyi Eke
Covenant University, Nigeria

Joseph Niyan Taiwo
Covenant University, Nigeria

ABSTRACT

This chapter examines the implications of projects abandonment with test of the Ricardian Equivalence on the failed Lagos metro line project in Nigeria as case study. The main variables used are Rail and Pipeline Output, Budget Deficit, Interest Rate, Corruption Index, Savings and some others. The study results on the Ricardian Equivalence hypothesis on deficit financing of projects using Vector auto-regression model from 1980-2012 indicate that no causal influence holds in Nigeria. Results show that poor planning, corruption, political factors, poor support infrastructures, poor quality of local resources, etc. were attributable. The results of the Impulse Response tests reveal that Rail and Pipeline output and a few others responded positively to shocks in the short run (years 1-2), and negatively to others. The result affirms that Government should privatize the railway system, legislate against project abandonment and ensure that projects are adequately planned, funded, insured and insulated against corruption.

INTRODUCTION

One of the fundamental challenges facing developing economies globally is the need to fill huge infrastructural gaps limiting the transformation of their economies and ensure sustainable development. Lofty social and economic policies and planned goals to improve living standards are handicapped due to lack of disciplined use of development capital. Public capital investment remains strategic policy deci-

DOI: 10.4018/978-1-5225-2364-2.ch010

sion that falls within the purview or domain of the highest government authority. Hall and Jones (1997) argue that differences in economic successes across countries are attributed to institutions, government policies and infrastructure that shape the economic environment in which people produce and transact. A government that engages in fund raising from investors for the purpose of capital investment decision must ensure that optimal social returns are obtained on the funds. Dwivedi (2008) regards investment as committing money, time and labour to create assets that can generate income for the long-term or which enhance returns on the existing asset. When technical, financial and political feasibilities are shoddy, project failure or abandonment becomes inevitable. Dean (1951) suggested that capital project should be examined in terms of economic behaviour rather than in terms of "accounting convention". Public projects are usually of social dimension for development and improvement in the living standard of the people.

Capital project decisions are normally irreversible, with expectation of immense future benefits over a reasonable long period in the future; otherwise it could result in time, capital and social welfare loss. Projects benefits may be pecuniary, non-monetary or partially monetary. Olowe (2011) identified the following as critical to a successful capital investment decision process: identifying possible investment project; identifying possible alternatives to the projects being evaluated; acquiring relevant data to the project under consideration; evaluating the project from the date assembled; project selection; project execution; and project monitoring and control. Before implementing these criteria, it is assumed that probable funding obstacles and other reasons that could result in abandonment would have been taken care of *ex ante*. Yescombe (2014) defines project abandonment as when the sponsor fails to continue construction or project operations; arguing that project abandonment clearly exposes the lender and the investors to much higher risk, such that there may not be real market upon a sale decision. Meir and Sepe (1989) argued the valuation effects of abandonment on the entity: that abandonment can be by termination or by sell-off. In a sell-off, the project assets are sold to outsiders, while in a termination assets remain with the firm. However, this chapter sees it as discontinuance of project with direct loss of capital, non-optimization of economic resources, and with indirect negative implications on outputs, employment, tax, and human welfare, etc. Thus the chapter examines the implications of public-sector project abandonment.

Lagos and the Metro-Line Project of 1981: The Case Study

Lagos state is the smallest state in the Nigerian federation and yet the most populous, being a coastal city. The current estimated population figure is put at 18 million and increasing at 3.2% per annum (*Businessdayonline*, 2014). Lagos's share of Nigeria's urban population is also a hefty 27.4%.As a result of overpopulation, the city is however severely challenged with poor infrastructure, particularly in the area of public transport. As at 2010, the size of the Lagos economy was estimated at ₦12.091 trillion ($80.61 billion), accounting for 35% of Nigeria's GDP (Lagos State GDP Report, 2010).

Lagos had been the political and commercial capital of Nigeria since the colonial years up to 1990 when the administrative capital moved to Abuja. The city is characterized by perennial transportation problem, dominated by inefficient land transit resources. On the average the city daily witnesses broken down trucks, a major means of movement of goods and people. Though an oil producing economy, over 80% of refined petroleum are imported through its two main seaports and hauled by road through the city to other parts of the country. According to the project publication on the ill-fated transport system, the Lagos State Ministry of Public Transportation (LSMPT) Final Report (1981) Phase 1 on the failed Lagos Metroline project, the rapid growth in population of Lagos metropolitan area, then estimated at four (4) million in 1979, was to be thirteen (13) million by 2000, required higher capacity transport system beyond what the then road infrastructure could sustain. The Lagos master plan of the Federal government had recommended intensification of intergraded road and rail transport system, one of which is the Lagos metro-line (LML). The recommendation was to make the Lagos metro-line a pioneer, and to be extended to Africa.

Despite the importance of rail infrastructure to economic development, Nigeria's rail infrastructure tracks as at 2012 was 3,528kilometres, while the population per kilometre track was 49. It consists of only two (2) main routes, linking the seaports of Lagos and Port-Harcourt with the hinterland, extending to Kano (northwest) and Maiduguri (northeast) respectively. In comparison with selected peers (Table 1), Nigeria rail infrastructure can be assessed as abysmally poor.

The successes achieved by Brazil and Mexico may be attributable to appropriate economic policy formulation and implementations, institutions, and systems, which otherwise may have been responsible for Nigeria's poor performance. It may therefore be imperative to consider advancing public-private investment policy options, and progressing to full privatisation of the Nigerian rail sector.

Objectives of the Metroline Project

A major objective was to alleviate the congestion on road usage which at peak periods reduced available speed movement. The LSMPT (1981) report had analysed that while the average operating speed of an average bus was estimated at 18km per hour, the master plan estimated the peak operating speed at less than 10 km per hour. Another objective was the need to alleviate the air pollution problems of the period and the future Lagos. The success of the scheme was not expected to drastically reduce vehicular traffic largely, however the operational condition of the vehicles on the road was supposed to be improved by the reduction of road traffic demand and concentration on the major road section. Further, the construction of the scheme and its extension was expected to attract a sizeable number of old and new passengers, thereby bringing in a large part of the steadily increasing traffic demand and volume by private vehicles on the highway system.

Immediate cause and financial consequence of metro-line project failure: The ex-governor Kayode Jakande (1979-1983) who initiated the project in 1981 blamed the failure and abandonment on the administration of the then President, Shehu Shagari (1979-1983) inferring that his administration's action defied logic. Thus the cause of the failure was entirely political, as the rivalry between the ruling defunct National Party of Nigeria (NPN) at the Federal level and the ruling Unity Party of Nigeria (UPN) in Lagos state stalled the release of the initial ₦70 million ($50.7million) (estimated at ₦14,837.4 billion

Table 1. Rail length of selected African and other MINT Countries as at 2012

Countries	Nigeria	S Africa	Egypt	Algeria	Brazil	Mexico	Indonesia	Turkey
Rail (Km)	3,528	20,500	6,700	4,691	29,817	26,704	8,529	12,000
Popu. per Km track	49	3	12	8	7	5	29	6
Status	Nationalized	Nationalized	Nationalized	Nationlized/priv.	Private	Private	Nationalized	Nationlized

Sources: The World Bank, data.worldbank.org; International Union of Railway(IUR), World Population 2012, www.unpopulation.org, population per kilometre was computed by author, accessed May 15 and 18, 2015.

at 2014 inflation adjusted Naira) by the Central Bank of Nigeria to the Japanese and French consortium of contractors as mobilisation payment. In the court case instituted by the foreign consortium following the failure of the project, Nigeria had no legal representation. The judgment was severe on the country with financial claim by the contractors in excess of $600 million. This subsequently became part of the Paris Club debt with the Federal government as guarantor of the debt, the state had to pay from its monthly statutory allocations.

Report of Abandoned Projects in Nigeria

The Presidential Projects Assessment Committee (PPAC) that was set up identified 11,886 total uncompleted (on-going or abandoned) Federal Government projects all over the country, resulting in loss of capital and social welfare to the economy costing over ₦7.78trillion (El-Rufai, 2012; Omotosho, 2012). Multi-billion dollar abandoned projects in Nigeria included the multibillion dollar Ajaokuta steel complex project. If projects abandoned by state governments were added to the list, the figure would be higher. The reasons for this sad state of affairs are many, the most immediate being insufficient planning for the projects. Then there is the factor of inadequate budgetary provision to compete them from onset. Moreover delays in funding, sometimes deliberately done to increase the mark-up fees for corrupt officials, add to the costs of execution, causing frequent reviews of the original contract terms.

Secondly, many projects are corruption-driven. Consequently, there is a rush to come up with as many projects as possible even when there is no money to execute them. Government officials and legislators are often inundated with proposals from contractors proposing one project or the other regardless of whether or not such projects are beneficial to the country. Contractors and government officials tend to conjure projects, not with the public interest in mind, but, as a conduit for looting. By colluding with contractors, government officials compromise themselves and are unable to contractually deal with contractors when they fail to perform their obligations. Many projects are listed every year in annual budgets, with little to show on the ground each year though sums were advanced.

Thirdly, it has become routine for contractors to collect mobilisation fees, often in amount almost equal to the full cost of contract, and thereafter abscond and go scot-free, a reflection of the pervasive culture of impunity in the country. Unless those responsible for saddling the country with abandoned projects are prosecuted, there may be no end to the problem.

Fourthly, lack of quality products manufactured locally for the construction industry also affects the execution of contracts; so do the inadequate supply of electricity, water, etc., which add to the costs of construction. Other reasons include inadequate planning, inadequate finance inflation, delayed payment and political factor, incompetent project manager, wrong estimate, faulty designs and inadequate cost control.

Abandonment and Failure Decision: Remote Causes and Events

Failure and abandonment of a project can occur in several ways. Ubani and Ononuju (2013) believe that project failure occurs when it cannot meet up with the scope, time, quality and cost goals. Also, projects fail when they do not meet or satisfy the customer/sponsor main objective coupled with no concerted effort to resuscitate the project. Schwable (2006) however sees the potential conflict between intents of the project manager and the project sponsor as responsible for failure asserting that good project managers should assume same definition of project success with the sponsor. Corroborating this claim, Okoroafor

(2004) as cited in Ubani and Ononuju (2013) contend that while the private entrepreneur sees project work from the profit maximization perspective, the public administrator thinks in terms of social cost or benefit. Elinwa and Joshua (2001) claim that in Nigeria, cost and time overrun are most responsible for most public projects abandonment.

Generally, the following are the reasons for project failures. First, an inflationary economy distorts capital budgeting decisions, with the presence of inflation resulting in lower real rate of project returns and less incentive for business to undertake capital projects.In estimating cash flows for a project, it is important that government take anticipated inflation into consideration. Often there is tendency to assume that price level will be unchanged through the life of the project. Secondly, information to analyse fundamental acquisition for capital projects is vital. Capital and technological equipment for a capital projects are not necessarily generally internal sourced, requiring detail information of the sources of all prospective facilities for the project as construction progress. Thirdly, one of the constraints state governments in Nigeria have always faced in their effort at raising long term funds is their inability to service such loans comfortably. It is suggested that such loans and bonds should be limited to projects that can pay back from future cash flows derived there from. Information from the failed metro-line project is that the Lagos state government is currently subjected to first charge from the federation account, to pay the external creditors, as the debt was converted to foreign loan account. Fourthly, the absorptive capacity for any type project: with respect to the Lagos metro-line, a past governor, added that government realized that the initiative then failed because it did not have the capacity to provide the kind of results desired in terms of sustainability for the vehicles that it would be managing.

REVIEW OF THEORETICAL LITERATURE

Theoretical issues on project failures and abandonment are widely documented in project development literature. Studies by Kerzner (2004), Telsang (2004), and Stephenson (2007) cited in Ubani and Ononuju (2013) discuss the systemic approach to project management and success factors. The authors see project failure from dysfunctions or lack of effective management of the dynamic interrelationship among subsystems on the project success chain such as planning, finance, control, procurement/purchasing, operations and implementation units. Meir and Sepe (1989) argue the normative and behavioural approaches to project abandonment claiming that projects can be abandoned if the expected present value of cash flow given abandonment today is greater than the expected present value of cash flow given that the project is continued for at least one additional period, bearing sunk costs. Odufalu and Loto (2008) argue that a fundamental obstacle to rapid economic development in developing countries is paucity of well-prepared and analysed projects, as many projects often turned white elephants because of improper planning, analysis and appraisal. Several obstacles to project success in Nigeria are as follows: lack of pre-investment studies; wrong location; over-ambitious projects; manpower constraints; financial constraints; feeder stock problem; inadequate support infrastructure; political instability and institutional challenges. Evidently, Diji (2004) provided ample analyses for the failure and sub-optimal operations of the Nigerian iron and steel companies (Aladja and Delta Steel and the Jos, Oshogbo and Katsina steel rolling mills) to politically motivated choice of location, inappropriate technology and wrong investment layout. Yescombe (2014) examined project failures and argued for solutions on early sign of project failure that can be dealt with by deductions or penalties rather than termination such as compensation for the contracting authority; 'walk away' by the off taker/contracting authority; transferring the project to the off taker/contracting authority without payment of any termination sum; payment of termination sum equal to the outstanding debt by the off taker/contracting authority; sale of the project with its project agreement in the open market; payment by the off taker/contracting authority of the termination sum based on the estimated value that would be achieved by a market sale.

Similarly, problems of unquantifiable uncertainties of contracts prompts input suppliers to terminate input-supply contracts that impact negatively on the project. Such events are failure by the project company to pay for supplies; signs of abandonment of the project; and insolvency of the project company or when its debt keeps accelerating. Otherwise, termination might arise from the project company itself arising from failure of input supplier to make delivery; insolvency of input supplier; and where there arise default by a guarantor of the input supplier. Another cause for concern is principle of 'optimism bias'. Yescombe (2014) argued that project *force majeure* event is usually a possibility, with the need that insurance contract be taken to cover project companies and lenders against unexpected losses. This key success factor in project contracting is however often neglected in project development and may result in underestimation of the project cost and a lack of guarantee against failure. Substantial evidence exists between corruption and project abandonment in Nigeria. Ingwe *et al.,* (2012) believes that project abandonment was encouraged by many administrations starting with Yakubu Gowon (1966-1975) with the practice of sharing unspent budgeted capital funds among top government functionaries of the respective Ministries, Departments and Agencies (MDAs) at every fiscal year end. This was discouraged by the Yar' Adua administration in 2007 policy measures towards curbing corruption when it began the practice returning unspent budgeted funds back to the nation's treasury.

EMPIRICAL REVIEW OF LITERATURE

Bangsung *et al.* (1997) assessed the private and public economic impacts of railroad abandonment in the rural economies of North Dakota in the United States, using input- output quantitative measure. Specifically, the study examined the cost of moving freights by truck compared to cost by rail, cost of increased traffic on local road system, and the consequences of local property tax revenue of rail line abandonment. The outcome of the variables included increased transport cost. It was also discovered that other media compared to rail-shipping, highway and local road cost, reduction in business and workers' income; employment implication, tax revenue reduction and general economic downturn.

Citkara (2006) studied project failure and abandonment in India and attributed the causes to the following: inadequate project formulation such as poor field investigation, inadequate project information, poor cost estimation, lack of experience, poor investment decision; poor planning and implementation, lack of project management experience during execution, *etc*. Ubani and Ononuju (2013) used 'opinion and judgmental sampling' method to capture the key factors responsible for civil project abandonment in Nigeria. Analytical tools used on the primary data are the Severity Index (SI) and Spearman rank correlation. The study reveals that most critical factors for project abandonment and failure include frequent change of government and political power, deficient financing methods and non-payment for completed work, including influence of political contracting. Ingwe *et al.,* (2012), examined project abandonment, corruption, and recovery of unspent budgeted public funds in Nigeria. The study noted abandonment consequences of project resources waste in time, human skills, and development opportunity cost. The paper used sampled survey and descriptive methods and found that a high rate of project delay and abandonments were discovered in critical sectors of the economy – power supply, road construction, petroleum, oil and natural gas development and in service sectors- education, health, representing huge opportunity costs with abundant spin-off impact on economy. The paper also found that the project management culture is defective, partly arising from inadequate human management.

Garrett (2004) studied the pros and cons of metro-line and light rail project in the United States. The paper advanced the argument that rail transit system transforms the well-being of the people, increases income by boosting property value, reduce health risks of pollution, traffic congestion and improve the income base of the poor. However, Garrett (2004) claims that excessive cost of the rail system greatly annoying to the economy and that citizens generally have preference and more value for automobile to rail as it grants personal space and a sense of independence, including the freedom in the time to commute. Apanisile and Akinlo (2013) studied the link between rail transportation and economic growth in Nigeria between 1970-2011 using error correction mechanisms (ECM). The study discovered long run relationship with correct negative signing of the ECM coefficient, the relationship between rail output and economic growth was negative. This significantly provides empirical evidence that the non-development of the rail transport system has been inimical to Nigerian economic growth.

Musgrave and Musgrave (2004) contend that under certain circumstances the market mechanism is sometimes better placed to produce social goods rather than evolving budgetary process, particularly where there is attributes of 'non-rivalry in consumption' but 'exclusion' is possible, e.g. education. It is the case that private supplier may provide the good to various consumers at differentiated prices, exacting from successive units the maximum amount each consumer is willing to pay. While the supplier appropriates the consumer surplus, derived by the buyer, an efficient outcome however ensues, since at the margin, the price paid equals the benefit derived (Musgrave & Musgrave, 2004).

Due to market failure attributes, pure public projects are generally provided by governments. Varian (2002: 644) reveals that public good possess troublesome kind of externality; with a particular kind of consumption externality, where everyone must consume the same amount. For example, people cannot purchase different amount of public defence. In this light, Musgrave and Musgrave (2004) contend that the theory of social/public good provides rationale for the allocation function of budgetary policy. The demand for pure public good cannot therefore be determined via the market system. Odufalu and Loto (2008) argue that a discussion of the need rather than the demand of these services, while the volume of the services placed at the disposal of the users are determined by the decision of general government policy. Be that as it may, the level of service that the government can comfortably place at the disposal of the consumers is generally a function of budgetary constraints and the competing requirements for public expenditure.

In practice, where the service is of direct benefit to the consumer (e.g. hospitals and education) a market analysis is a crucial step in the preparation, analysis and appraisal of projects. The analysis is crucial to determining the size and location of the project, and dictates the sales effort and sales budget. Odufalu and Loto (2008: 90) provide quantitative approximate estimation process for possible future demand for a public project to establish the probable level of need.

Funding Public Projects

Although, taxation is the commonest source of public project financing for most sub-units of a country, other alternatives are: statutory allocations; the use of debt; equity project finance; donations; user charges; and government–run enterprises such as state lotteries. Debt project finance has wide range of financing features of various packages. The essence of debt and equity project finance is to bring in private sector participation (in a public –private partnership), hence establish robust financing structure. Merna and Al-Thani (2008) argue that a common feature in project finance is that financing is not primarily dependent on the credit support of the sponsors or value of the physical assets being undertaking. Thus most road infrastructure is provided by the government at least in most developing countries fall into one of these categories.

Hellewel (2001) argues that transport is a lubricant of commerce, adding value to goods: the greater the economic activities the greater the demand for movement by all modes; while traffic congestion is symptom of failure of investments to keep up demand. An efficient transport system minimizes four time elements in the transport chain: access, waiting, in-vehicle, and egress. Kavanagh et al., (2005) argue that "traffic is a leading source of air pollution", requiring that initiatives which reduce traffic volume would have potential benefits to environmental health.

Economic Burden of Public Project Abandonment

The efficient functioning of any economy could be weakened by project abandonment, as loss of multiplier proportion on capital and by implication on welfare. The economics of financing public sector projects through taxation and debt is highly consequential to the consumption and savings power of the citizen. Although the theories in the literature of inter-generational equity of deficit and tax financing for public project is highly controversial, a theory of public-sector financing says that government merely acquire the right to private resources as individuals are made to give-up their rights over resource use in order for the government to provide goods and services (Hyman, 2002).

It is a requirement as acceptance criterion for financial evaluation of projects to compare the internal rate of return with a required (the hurdle) rate of return, and therefore to accept a project on the condition that the IRR exceeds the required return. However, Miller (1988) cited in Van Horne and Dhamija (2012) reasons that for capital-expanding projects such as Metrorail line which is highly related to the level of the nation's economic activity and capable of producing cash flows as the economy become prosperous require that such capacity-expanding investment projects adopt different return in line with prevailing systematic risks. Besides, since output values of social infrastructural projects are rather difficult to evaluate, knowledge from cost effectiveness and cost utility analyses reveal the measuring and valuation mechanism of public projects. At best, it is the relative net present costs of various options and interventions that may be accurate while benefits and outcomes are arrived at often through non-monetary criteria such as a defined quality adjusted life year of the citizens - a combination of the duration of life and health related quality of life. Jhingan (2007) also reasons that in developing countries the knowledge of factors which influence demand and supply of capital is imperfect, hence in a mixed economy, the price of inputs such as capital in development planning and project evaluation can better be determined in accordance with shadow prices.

In either way of financing (by tax and debt), citizens would be forced to reduce their consumption and saving (investment) power. For debt financing of huge capital project, the burden of capital and interest repayment is postponed to future period and paid for from future taxation- an inter-generational transfer of burden. All things being equal, the increased tax revenues necessary to pay interest and principal in future redistribute income from the taxpayer to the holders of public debt. A prudent use of debt however, would mean government taxing its citizen as the facility is being constructed and after completion during use. If facilities are however, financed immediately by taxation, individuals would be forced to forgo

Table 2. Trend in Nigeria's Economic indicators (1980-2013)

Yrs	1980	1985	1990	1995	2000	2005	2010	2013
BD(₦'b)	1.97	3.04	22.1	0.0	103.8	161.0	1,105.4	266.2
INRT (%)	9.0	11.75	27.7	20.79	21.55	19.49	21.51	24.75
SVN(₦' b)	5.7	12.5	29.6	108.5	385.2	1,317.0	5,954.3	8,659
Infl.(%)	10	5.5	7.5	72.8	6.9	17.9	11.8	8.0
HDI	0.19	0.22	0.28	0.31	0.40	0.43	0.46	0.47

Source: National Bureau of Statistics: Legend Budget deficit (*BD*), Interest rate (*INRT*); Gross Private savings (*SVN*); Inflation rate (*INFL*); Human development Index (*HDI*)

consumption and savings opportunities equivalent to the entire capital cost of the facility, without any benefits accruing until the facility was fully constructed and functioning. Therefore, to Hyman (2002) where debt finance is prudentially and efficiently deployed, it can improve the economics of scarce resources by linking cost of public investments to the streams of benefits produced by those investments.

When capital project is abandoned, the welfare and well-being impact is enormous on the future generation paying the debt. The economic effects of debt repayment consequent upon abandoned project also affect interest rates, national savings and investment. The inter-generational equity to this implies that budget deficit increases national debt and thus increases the future interest costs, which affects welfare, as it denies provision of goods and service to the citizens.

OBJECTIVES OF THE STUDY

The basic objective of this chapter is to test the Ricardian Equivalence Hypothesis on public sector abandonment decision on public projects using the Lagos Metroline that failed project in 1982 as a result of the politics between Lagos State and the Federal Government of Nigeria as case study by showing the impacts of the important direct variables on development factors.

THEORETICAL FRAMEWORK AND METHODOLOGY

This study follows the models developed by Ubani and Ononuju (2013); Apanisile and Akinlo (2013) with some modifications. Following Ubani and Ononuju (2013) study on the failure and abandonment of civil engineering projects in the public sector in Nigeria which the authors concluded to have resulted in sizeable waste of scarce resources, with adverse implications on environmental degradation, unemployment, aggravated deterioration and decay of road and infrastructure, ravaging flood, displacement of homes, destruction of buildings and other settlements, etc. Clunies-Ross *et al.*, (2009) argue that economic appraisal of projects follows similar logic to financial appraisal, in which the net benefits is estimated per period of the project's prospective life rather than the net cash flows; they are then discounted for time, with the result summed up to give expected net present value(NPV). This study intuitively establishes a link between public projects abandonment and worsening macroeconomic variables. The discounted economic benefits and costs of the project to the society are usually arrived at as follows:

$$NPV = \sum_{t=0}^{n} \left[(B_t - C_t) / (1+i)^t \right] \tag{1}$$

Where: NPV is the net-present value of the project; $t = 0, 1, 2..., n$ is the number of years from the original investment; n is the lifetime of the project in years; i per year is the discount-rate for time; B_t and C_t are the society's benefits and costs respectively in year t.

However, for efficient management of capital resources, periodic reappraisal for continuity, termination, or sell-off decisions is appropriate using the present value of cash flow (PVCF) approach. A modified form of Ubani and Ononuju's (2013) framework is presented here:

$$PVCF = \sum_{n=1}^{T} \frac{NC_n}{(1+i)^n} + \frac{SV_T}{(1+i)^T} \tag{2}$$

Where T is the estimated remaining life of the project; NC_n is the new forecast net cash flows reassessed periodically; SV is salvage value in time T. Decision rule suggest that a project could be abandoned (termination or see-off) when the net present value of cash flows associated with it is higher than for continuity. Deficit budgets for capital projects are financed by borrowings from domestic and global financial markets. When projects are abandoned, capital is wasted but borrowed fund must be repaid contractually. Analytically, subsequent interest rates in the economy could be affected, resulting in adverse consequences on national growth.

The theory of Ricardian equivalence claims that should interest rate remain stable overtime when capital projects are financed either by debt or taxation it will have no future effect on the economy and no impact on future economic growth. Hyman (2002) states that when government increases borrowing, it invites increased savings by forward-looking tax payers and hence keep the level of interest rates in the economy fixed. Given the Ricardian equivalence, the associated variables to the theory can be tested using the restricted VAR model for want of degree of freedom, with each variable treated symmetrically. Popularized by Sims (1980), it proposes that linear interdependent relationship exist among variables such that all variables in a model can be treated as endogenous plus their lags. Asteriou and Hall (2011: 321) reveal that a unique merit of the VAR model is that forecasts obtainable are better than those of simultaneous equation models.

In a simple form by Maddala and Kim (1998), the VAR model is a multiple time series generalization of the AR model, whose matrix specification can be presented as follows:

$$Y_t = A_1 Y_{t-1} + ... + A_p Y_{t-p} + U_t \tag{3}$$

Where $Y_t' = (y_{1t}, y_{2t}, ..., y_{kt})$ and $A_{1,} A_2, ..., A_p$ and k x k matrices. U_t represents k-dimensional vector white noise process, that $E(ut) = 0$, $E(u_{tk}, u_{sk}) = 0 \ for \ t \neq s$, $E(u_t, u_t') = \Omega \ for \ k$ x k positive semi-definite matrix, and $\sum$ is positive definite. L as lag operator, the model can be compactly represented as:

$$Y_t = A(L)Y_t + U_t \tag{4}$$

In the VAR (1) model specification of variables, Rail and pipeline output (*RPO*),economic growth (*GDP*), interest rate (*INRT*), budget deficit (BD), private savings (*SVN*), corruption index (*CDX*),and Human development index (*HDI*) are treated symmetrically as follows:

$$\begin{aligned} lGdp_t = \alpha_t + \beta_i lRpo_{t-1} + \gamma_i lBd_{t-1} + \tau_i lInrt_{t-1} + \xi_i lSvn_{t-1} \\ + \zeta_i lCdx_{t-1} + \psi_i lHdi_{t-1} + \omega_i lGdp_{t-1} + u_{t1} \end{aligned} \tag{5}$$

$$\begin{aligned} lRpo_t = \alpha_t + \beta_i lRpo_{t-1} + \gamma_i lBd_{t-1} + \tau_i Inrt_{t-1} + \xi_i lSvn_{t-1} \\ + \zeta_i lCdx_{t-1} + \psi_i lHdi_{t-1} + \omega_i lGdp_{t-1} + u_{t2} \end{aligned} \tag{6}$$

$$\begin{aligned} lBd_t = \alpha_t + \beta_i lRpo_{t-1} + \gamma_i lBd_{t-1} + \tau_i Inrt_{t-1} + \xi_i lSvn_{t-1} \\ + \zeta_i lCdx_{t-1} + \psi_i lHdi_{t-1} + \omega_i lGdp_{t-1} + u_{t3} \end{aligned} \tag{7}$$

$$\begin{aligned} Int_t = \alpha_{it} + \beta_i lRpo_{t-1} + \gamma_i lBd_{t-1} + \tau_i Inrt_{t-1} + \xi_i lSvn_{t-1} \\ + \zeta_i lCdx_{t-1} + \psi_i lHdi_{t-1} + \omega_i lGdp_{t-1} + u_{t4} \end{aligned} \tag{8}$$

$$\begin{aligned} lSvn_t = \alpha_{it} + \beta_i lRpo_{t-1} + \gamma_i lBd_{t-1} + \tau_i Inrt_{t-1} + \xi_i lSvn_{t-1} \\ + \zeta_i Cdx_{t-1} + \psi_i lHdi_{t-1} + \omega_i lGdp_{t-1} + u_{t5} \end{aligned} \tag{9}$$

$$\begin{aligned} lCdx_t = \alpha_{it} + \beta_i lRpo_{t-1} + \gamma_i lBd_{t-1} + \tau_i Inrt_{t-1} + \xi_i lSvn_{t-1} \\ + \zeta_i Cdx_{t-1} + \psi_i lHdi_{t-1} + \omega_i lGdp_{t-1} + u_{t6} \end{aligned} \tag{10}$$

$$\begin{aligned} Hdi_t = \alpha_{it} + \beta_i lRpo_{t-1} + \gamma_i lBd_{t-1} + \tau_i Inrt_{t-1} + \xi_i lSvn_{t-1} \\ + \zeta_i Cdx_{t-1} + \psi_i lHdi_{t-1} + \omega_i lGdp_{t-1} + u_{t7} \end{aligned} \tag{11}$$

Where $\beta, \gamma, \tau, \xi, \zeta, \psi, \omega$ are parameters, α is constant term, while $u's$ is the stochastic error. *GDP, RPO, BD, INRT, SVN, CDX* and *HDI* are transformed into log form values. They are as earlier defined. The estimation technique assesses how shocks in the model variables reverberate through the entire system.

RESULTS AND DISCUSSIONS

Data and Descriptive Statistics

Data for 32 years (1981-2012) were sourced from the National Bureau of Statistics (NBS) and the Central Bank of Nigeria (CBN) Statistical Bulletin. The data for gross domestic product (*GDP*), Budget deficits (*BD*), Rail and Pipeline output (*RPO*) were sourced from the NBS; total private savings (*SVN*) and nominal interest rate (*INRT*) were sourced from CBN. Data on corruption index (*CDX*) was sourced from Transparency International (*TI*) organization. The TI index sums up the perceptions of the degree of corruption as seen by business people and country analyst, and range between zero (0) representing highest corrupt, and ten (10), which is least corrupt (Transparency International, 2014). The *HDI* is sourced from United Nations Development Programme (UNDP).

Descriptive Statistics

The descriptive statistics are presented in Table 3 revealing the first to fourth moment statistics and the test of normality of individual variable's residuals. *GDP's* highest and lowest values were achieved in 2012 (₦4.54 tn) and 1981(₦47.6 bn) respectively. *RPO*'s highest and lowest values were achieved in 1986 (₦138.5Bn) and 1995 (₦2.4bn) respectively; while *BD*'s highest and lowest values were achieved in 2011(₦1.2tn) and 1995(₦1bn) respectively. On the *RPO*, it implies the subsector started dwindling in contribution to national productivity in 1986 up to 1995 when it started improving. Interest rates highest and lowest statistics occurred in 1993 (36%) and 1981 (10%) respectively. *SVN* and *HDI* highest and lowest values were achieved in 2012 and 1981 respectively; Corruption's highest value occurred in 2009, 2012, while the lowest value occurred in 1981, implying that corruption is progressive in Nigeria.

Since the value of the $\chi^2 crit.$is higher than the Jarque-Bera (J.B) statistics in each variable, at this instance, we cannot reject the null hypothesis that their residuals are normally distributed. In addition,

Table 3. Descriptive statistics of Variables

	LGDP	LRPO	LBD	LINRT	LSVN	LCDX	LHDI
Mean	14.23143	2.860043	10.72512	2.990581	12.11056	0.316677	-1.128608
Median	14.81082	2.351457	10.92526	3.041178	11.94845	0.222343	-1.001463
Maximum	17.51790	4.930870	13.96265	3.586016	15.90278	0.993252	-0.761426
Minimum	10.77100	0.875469	6.907755	2.302585	8.789142	-0.356675	-1.619488
Std.Dev.	2.309684	1.408641	1.963758	0.307502	2.256140	0.369540	0.311486
Skewness	-0.157251	0.234699	-0.087299	-0.58791	0.193389	0.280858	-0.216368
Kurtosis	1.629590	1.448957	2.012521	2.942483	1.800867	2.206527	1.349518
J.Bera	2.635913	3.501426	1.340799	1.847816	2.116691	1.260166	3.881802
Probability	0.267682	0.173650	0.511504	0.396965	0.347029	0.532548	0.143575
Sum	455.4059	91.52137	343.2038	95.69859	387.5378	10.13365	-36.11545
SSq.D.	165.3738	61.51235	119.5468	2.931286	157.7951	4.233358	3.007725

Source: Authors' estimation from Data

the p-values are higher than the 5% chosen level of significance, which also concludes that we cannot reject the null hypothesis of normality.

The unit root test examines the extent of stationarity of the data employed using the Augmented Dickey Fuller (ADF) processes. While *GDP* and *BD* were stationary at level $I(0)$; *RPO,INRT, SVN, CDX* and *HDI* were stationary at first difference $I(1)$, all with constant term and drift parameter, and significant at 5% and 1% respectively (Table 4). As a necessary precondition to testing for co-integration, it implies that being stationery at level and $I(1)$ the variables might be suitable for co-integration test.

The Granger causality test was applied to the model as inference test requiring dropping variables that are insignificant. It examined the standard VAR model that expresses both unidirectional bi-directional and no-directional feedback relationship between two variables Y_t and X_t estimated (Granger 1969, Sims, 1980).The results of the short run predictive and causal mechanism of variables are presented in Table 5 which suggest that we reject the hypothesis that bi-directional or feedback relations were found to exist between *HDI* and *GDP*. Similarly, we also reject the null hypothesis to suggest that unidirectional causal relations run as follows *RPO*to*GDP; INRT*to*GDP; GDP*to*CDX; RPO*to*BD; INRT*to*RPO; RPO*to*HDI; SVN*to*BD; CDX*to*BD; HDI*to*BD; INRT*to*HDI, SVN*to*CDX* and *CDX* to*HDI.*

RESULTS AND DISCUSSION OF FINDINGS

Impulse Response Function (IRF)

The *IRF* is the vector moving average (VMA) representation of each equation, which provides information on the time part of various shocks on the variables in the VAR system. It is an essential and categorical tool in empirical causal analysis for testing policy effectiveness. It visually represents the behaviour of the variables followings various innovations. From equation 1(Table 6 and 7 and Figure 1) *GDP's* response is positive to its own shock in the ten periods (years) examined. On *RPO*'s impulse, *GDP*'s response was negative in years 2 and 3, and zero (0) level reactions through the remaining innovation periods; and to *BD*'s innovation, no obvious effect occurred as *GDP* remain steady at zero level and negative the very long run. On interest rate *(INRT)* innovation, *GDP*'s reaction is zero and negative it returns to

Table 4. Unit Root Test Results

Variables	ADF test: Level and First difference (Intercept and Trend)	Remark: Order of Integration	% Level of Significance
LGDP	-3.5807	I(0)	5
LRPO	-5.67148	I(1)	1
LBD	-4.58879	I(0)	1
LSNR	-3.99726	I(1)	5
LINRT	-6.23162	I(1)	1
LHDI	-4.49368	I(1)	1
LCdx	-5.38663	I(1)	1

Source: Authors' output estimates; MacKinnon (1996) one-sided p-value. Note: variable critical values at 1 and 5 percent are -4.296729 and -3.568379 respectively.

Table 5. Granger Causality Test

Pairwise Granger Causality Tests			
Lags: 2			
Null Hypothesis:	Obs	F-Statistic	Prob.
LRPO does not Granger Cause LGDP	**30**	**6.95855**	**0.0040**
LGDP does not Granger Cause LRPO		0.02921	0.9712
LINRT does not Granger Cause LGDP	**30**	**5.39636**	**0.0113**
LGDP does not Granger Cause LINRT		0.00816	0.9919
LCDX does not Granger Cause LGDP	30	0.72055	0.4963
LGDP does not Granger Cause LCDX		**3.95506**	**0.0322**
LHDI does not Granger Cause LGDP	**30**	**3.65976**	**0.0404**
LGDP does not Granger Cause LHDI		**3.52972**	**0.0446**
LBD does not Granger Cause LRPO	30	0.27205	0.7640
LRPO does not Granger Cause LBD		**11.0812**	**0.0004**
LINRT does not Granger Cause LRPO	**30**	**5.83619**	**0.0083**
LRPO does not Granger Cause LINRT		0.00037	0.9996
LHDI does not Granger Cause LRPO	30	0.41663	0.6638
LRPO does not Granger Cause LHDI		**8.75616**	**0.0013**
LSVN does not Granger Cause LBD	**30**	**3.34922**	**0.0514**
LBD does not Granger Cause LSVN		0.00934	0.9907
LCDX does not Granger Cause LBD	**30**	**6.42885**	**0.0056**
LBD does not Granger Cause LCDX		2.39578	0.1117
LHDI does not Granger Cause LBD	**30**	**5.04687**	**0.0144**
LBD does not Granger Cause LHDI		0.30062	0.7430
LHDI does not Granger Cause LINRT	30	0.36632	0.6969
LINRT does not Granger Cause LHDI		**3.56151**	**0.0436**
LCDX does not Granger Cause LSVN	30	0.66042	0.5254
LSVN does not Granger Cause LCDX		**3.93496**	**0.0327**
LHDI does not Granger Cause LCDX	**30**	**3.25246**	**0.0555**
LCDX does not Granger Cause LHDI		0.69206	0.5099

Source: Author's estimation using Eviews 7.0

positive in long run (years 7 to 9).On *SVN* impulse, *GDP* responds remain at zero level through to period 6 and negative in the long run. Its response to *CDX* is zero in the first 3 years, negative in years 4 and 5 and thereafter remained at zero level in the long run. Its response to *HDI*'s innovation was of negative impact in the entire 10 year period. The entire equation's summary is that the economy is positively driven largely by its own shocks.

The Rail and pipeline output (*RPO*) response positively to its own innovation in the short run and thereafter negative through years 4 to 10. Its response to innovations from *GDP, BD* and *INRT* are revealing. On *GDP*, except in year short run (year 2), it responded negatively to *GDP*'s shock through the

Figure 1. Impulse Response Function
Source: Author's Estimation Using Eview 7.0

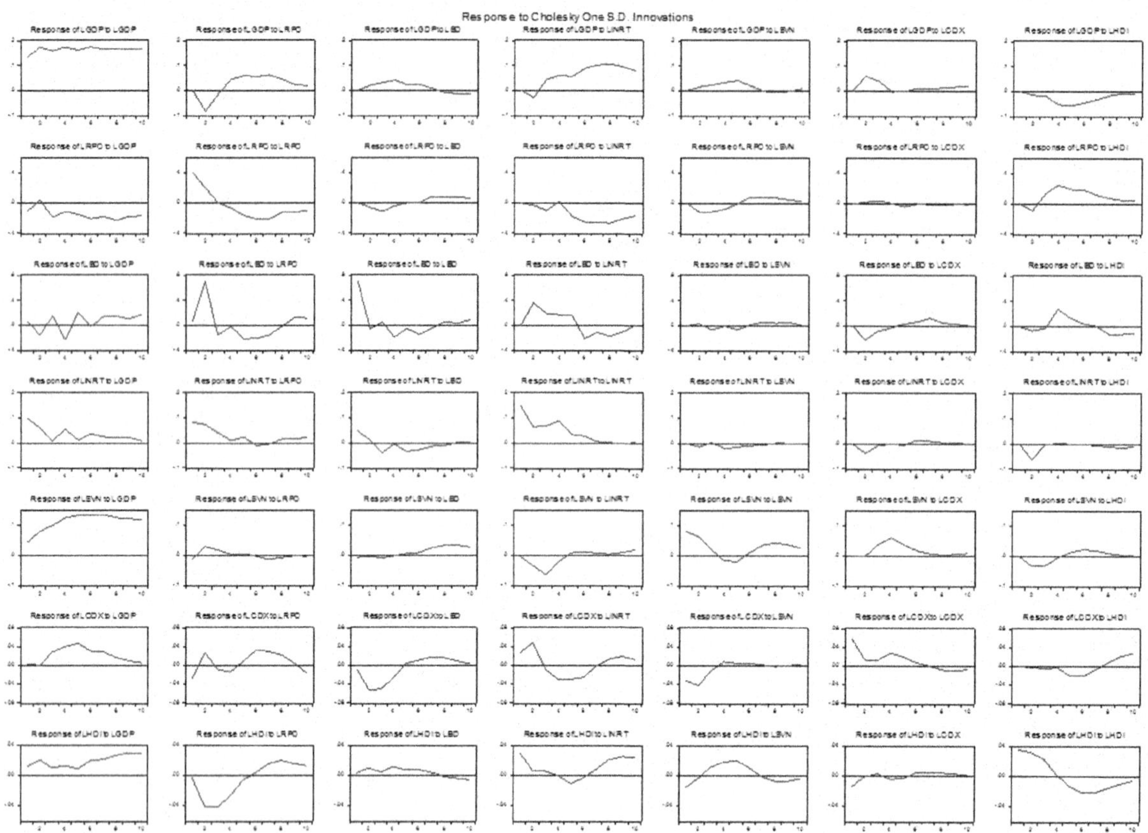

Table 6. Impulse Response Function

Response of LGDP: Period	LGDP	LRPO	LBD	LINRT	LSVN	LCDX	LHDI
1	0.133623	0.000000	0.000000	0.000000	0.000000	0.000000	0.000000
2	0.171495	-0.083596	0.020499	-0.028775	0.015171	0.059961	-0.016589
3	0.158549	-0.015085	0.031576	0.043850	0.022950	0.038764	-0.018916
4	0.172150	0.043872	0.040091	0.059310	0.032272	-0.003701	-0.053221
5	0.161470	0.058760	0.021544	0.055141	0.040250	-0.001913	-0.057798
6	0.174216	0.055418	0.022596	0.088796	0.018246	0.010113	-0.046591
7	0.164152	0.062416	0.006840	0.102759	-0.002317	0.007502	-0.033061
8	0.167246	0.044560	-0.010427	0.106760	-0.006590	0.012024	-0.017560
9	0.168031	0.022817	-0.014101	0.095407	-0.002114	0.016015	-0.008970
10	0.163440	0.018716	-0.013684	0.077838	0.007350	0.016705	-0.009258

continued on following page

Table 6. Continued

Response of LRPO: Period	LGDP	LRPO	LBD	LINRT	LSVN	LCDX	LHDI
1	-0.112362	0.411905	0.000000	0.000000	0.000000	0.000000	0.000000
2	0.036054	0.203785	-0.064300	-0.033288	-0.125620	0.018881	-0.087305
3	-0.192759	0.001003	-0.113969	-0.101273	-0.112550	0.039376	0.142679
4	-0.109476	-0.067555	-0.040433	0.015898	-0.075569	0.004776	0.254020
5	-0.150307	-0.166055	-0.003111	-0.176623	-8.24E-05	-0.037154	0.195499
6	-0.209880	-0.215933	0.001316	-0.251909	0.083677	-0.003783	0.186768
7	-0.181150	-0.209547	0.086696	-0.254829	0.079451	-0.004788	0.122995
8	-0.228807	-0.128236	0.074883	-0.270712	0.074063	-0.018966	0.075629
9	-0.180154	-0.123582	0.078193	-0.211963	0.050514	-0.002331	0.052921
10	-0.170974	-0.102217	0.067791	-0.164177	0.027549	-0.006023	0.047181
Response of LBD: Period	**LGDP**	**LRPO**	**LBD**	**LINRT**	**LSVN**	**LCDX**	**LHDI**
1	0.069460	0.059891	0.715444	0.000000	0.000000	0.000000	0.000000
2	-0.157352	0.696192	-0.055989	0.362227	0.032785	-0.215849	-0.067389
3	0.157022	-0.158934	0.055308	0.192341	-0.065340	-0.076749	-0.030842
4	-0.237045	-0.018778	-0.193059	0.172182	-0.001893	-0.025922	0.278826
5	0.212644	-0.217522	-0.049335	0.168808	-0.061998	0.038757	0.129925
6	-0.018478	-0.206937	-0.142003	-0.205740	0.021694	0.069909	0.043664
7	0.140992	-0.159181	-0.049303	-0.107622	0.060636	0.127258	0.002970
8	0.144534	-0.011746	0.060851	-0.168559	0.044483	0.054676	-0.121302
9	0.106524	0.129483	0.035821	-0.106117	0.059451	0.032164	-0.122276
10	0.172336	0.119267	0.095828	0.017720	0.007879	0.015409	-0.103720
Response of LINRT: Period	**LGDP**	**LRPO**	**LBD**	**LINRT**	**LSVN**	**LCDX**	**LHDI**
1	0.099146	0.082305	0.047564	0.148471	0.000000	0.000000	0.000000
2	0.059713	0.073908	0.012854	0.064691	-0.014224	-0.037583	-0.062850
3	0.008288	0.040944	-0.039598	0.067569	0.004441	-0.007241	-0.002999
4	0.056050	0.010139	-0.003352	0.089102	-0.020676	-0.001121	0.003137
5	0.011886	0.023340	-0.033349	0.034300	-0.014969	-0.005138	0.000186
6	0.036996	-0.009483	-0.027306	0.027479	-0.008646	0.014846	0.000717
7	0.024049	-0.003275	-0.012942	0.006043	-0.006037	0.010346	-0.005933
8	0.019540	0.015912	-0.009907	0.001612	0.001267	0.005323	-0.010686
9	0.022422	0.014827	0.002243	-0.002166	0.000606	0.003456	-0.016195
10	0.008683	0.022608	0.002422	0.002885	-0.000585	-0.000288	-0.009094

continued on following page

Table 6. Continued

Response of LSVN: Period	LGDP	LRPO	LBD	LINRT	LSVN	LCDX	LHDI
1	0.042552	-0.013140	-0.006802	-0.003777	0.080806	0.000000	0.000000
2	0.079863	0.029156	-0.003025	-0.034093	0.062405	-0.001676	-0.031321
3	0.099244	0.018390	-0.008603	-0.063953	0.021108	0.038220	-0.032600
4	0.124193	0.004494	-0.002252	-0.021474	-0.016119	0.059945	-0.005223
5	0.133681	0.004725	0.005710	0.008886	-0.018916	0.039026	0.013288
6	0.134690	-0.002905	0.009280	0.012637	0.011015	0.017941	0.022207
7	0.136066	-0.013879	0.024982	0.008006	0.035896	0.008472	0.018680
8	0.125028	-0.006487	0.033199	0.004309	0.043386	0.003860	0.010365
9	0.121173	-0.001566	0.033172	0.010149	0.036411	0.005803	0.004077
10	0.119186	-0.002888	0.026678	0.019751	0.025402	0.009827	0.004223
Response of LCDX: Period	**LGDP**	**LRPO**	**LBD**	**LINRT**	**LSVN**	**LCDX**	**LHDI**
1	0.002651	-0.028113	-0.008722	0.026944	-0.031964	0.058451	0.000000
2	0.000445	0.027883	-0.052484	0.049155	-0.041757	0.013565	-0.002469
3	0.029002	-0.008944	-0.049584	-0.008984	-0.011265	0.012753	-0.004515
4	0.039602	-0.013857	-0.027025	-0.029823	0.008686	0.027845	-0.003485
5	0.047662	0.009448	0.004888	-0.029235	0.005359	0.019993	-0.019407
6	0.030574	0.033102	0.010604	-0.025141	0.005052	0.007066	-0.020517
7	0.029154	0.030019	0.017594	-0.000977	0.001652	0.000396	-0.007575
8	0.017029	0.022324	0.016525	0.013693	-0.001187	-0.008368	0.008494
9	0.009670	0.005497	0.008885	0.019808	0.000354	-0.010658	0.022140
10	0.005818	-0.016171	0.003847	0.013277	0.003185	-0.007528	0.027794
Response of LHDI: Period	**LGDP**	**LRPO**	**LBD**	**LINRT**	**LSVN**	**LCDX**	**LHDI**
1	0.011281	-0.002491	0.003480	0.030189	-0.015465	-0.014092	0.035662
2	0.020699	-0.041006	0.009900	0.006766	-0.003585	-0.000865	0.031773
3	0.010332	-0.041760	0.004512	0.005527	0.011540	0.002918	0.023204
4	0.013006	-0.027313	0.011608	-0.000307	0.018249	-0.003932	0.002430
5	0.008852	-0.005654	0.006910	-0.010675	0.020560	-0.003163	-0.013573
6	0.019854	0.003724	0.007870	-0.002960	0.010468	0.004528	-0.021966
7	0.021167	0.015685	0.004060	0.008222	-0.001431	0.005548	-0.021422
8	0.026627	0.019680	-0.001416	0.021300	-0.007135	0.004441	-0.015651
9	0.030044	0.015724	-0.004018	0.025715	-0.007118	0.002697	-0.010067
10	0.029541	0.012701	-0.005648	0.025115	-0.003594	0.001438	-0.005648

Source: Author's estimation using Eview 7.0

Table 7. Variance Decomposition

Variance Decomposition of LGDP: Period	S.E.	LGDP	LRPO	LBD	LINRT	LSVN	LCDX	LHDI
1	0.133623	100.0000	0.000000	0.000000	0.000000	0.000000	0.000000	0.000000
2	0.244137	79.30110	11.72465	0.705019	1.389237	0.386168	6.032105	0.461715
3	0.300458	80.20306	7.993109	1.569931	3.047202	0.838378	5.647137	0.701183
4	0.361729	77.98282	6.985628	2.311506	4.790665	1.374381	3.906560	2.648444
5	0.410904	75.87644	7.458633	2.066238	5.513429	2.024602	3.029640	4.031020
6	0.461808	74.30290	7.345061	1.875240	8.062109	1.758974	2.446512	4.209208
7	0.505835	72.46244	7.644677	1.581295	10.84667	1.468199	2.061158	3.935564
8	0.545736	71.64530	7.234339	1.395017	13.14545	1.275936	1.819320	3.484633
9	0.579850	71.86068	6.563000	1.294839	14.35148	1.131550	1.687833	3.110611
10	0.608238	72.52988	6.059359	1.227405	14.68079	1.042991	1.609385	2.850195
Variance Decomposition of LRPO Period	**S.E.**	**LGDP**	**LRPO**	**LBD**	**LINRT**	**LSVN**	**LCDX**	**LHDI**
1	0.426955	6.925844	93.07416	0.000000	0.000000	0.000000	0.000000	0.000000
2	0.504104	5.479715	83.10771	1.626999	0.436037	6.209818	0.140283	2.999441
3	0.590845	14.63231	60.49730	4.905048	3.255320	8.149008	0.546248	8.014767
4	0.661660	14.40542	49.28313	4.284720	2.653536	7.802444	0.440790	21.12996
5	0.747507	15.32990	43.54822	3.358815	7.662021	6.113225	0.592408	23.39542
6	0.868793	17.18440	38.41537	2.486701	14.07932	5.453145	0.440445	21.94063
7	0.962000	17.56166	36.07670	2.840345	18.50020	5.129737	0.361709	19.52965
8	1.041488	19.80973	32.29601	2.940286	22.54028	4.882299	0.341765	17.18963
9	1.090333	20.80466	30.75190	3.197045	24.34522	4.669304	0.312287	15.91958
10	1.123867	21.89600	29.77133	3.372949	25.04805	4.454902	0.296801	15.15997
Variance Decomposition of LBD: Period	**S.E.**	**LGDP**	**LRPO**	**LBD**	**LINRT**	**LSVN**	**LCDX**	**LHDI**
1	0.721299	0.927353	0.689438	98.38321	0.000000	0.000000	0.000000	0.000000
2	1.102844	2.432400	40.14507	42.34234	10.78781	0.088374	3.830635	0.373374
3	1.147757	4.117389	38.98220	39.32559	12.76836	0.405681	3.983850	0.416934
4	1.232569	7.268853	33.82530	36.55319	13.02309	0.352009	3.498690	5.478862
5	1.290317	9.348681	33.70732	33.50078	13.59507	0.552072	3.282755	6.013324
6	1.333356	8.774088	33.97505	32.50715	15.11247	0.543477	3.349147	5.738618
7	1.362700	9.470795	33.89215	31.25317	15.09238	0.718325	4.078566	5.494614
8	1.389164	10.19590	32.62028	30.26562	15.99513	0.793755	4.079564	6.049742
9	1.410657	10.45780	32.47635	29.41485	16.07730	0.947365	4.008181	6.618141
10	1.433329	11.57523	32.14946	28.93865	15.58800	0.920654	3.893942	6.934066

continued on following page

Table 7. Continued

Variance Decomposition of LINRT: Period	S.E.	LGDP	LRPO	LBD	LINRT	LSVN	LCDX	LHDI
1	0.202262	24.02814	16.55880	5.529939	53.88312	0.000000	0.000000	0.000000
2	0.244649	22.38064	20.44432	4.055784	43.82147	0.338049	2.359945	6.599790
3	0.260409	19.85490	20.51664	5.891978	45.41042	0.327456	2.160246	5.838369
4	0.281862	20.90186	17.64174	5.043350	48.75410	0.817615	1.845501	4.995835
5	0.287527	20.25732	17.61242	6.191882	48.27521	1.056754	1.805437	4.800978
6	0.293132	21.08284	17.04988	6.825088	47.32521	1.103724	1.993553	4.619706
7	0.294785	21.51263	16.87155	6.941521	46.83799	1.133321	2.094441	4.608549
8	0.296274	21.73197	16.99087	6.983750	46.37144	1.123789	2.105730	4.692453
9	0.297968	22.05176	17.04578	6.910214	45.85084	1.111458	2.095302	4.934647
10	0.299114	21.96748	17.48676	6.863955	45.50971	1.103346	2.079381	4.989373
Variance Decomposition of LSVN: Period	**S.E.**	**LGDP**	**LRPO**	**LBD**	**LINRT**	**LSVN**	**LCDX**	**LHDI**
1	0.092593	21.11983	2.013734	0.539645	0.166349	76.16044	0.000000	0.000000
2	0.147822	37.47523	4.680356	0.253613	5.384381	47.70422	0.012855	4.489343
3	0.197919	46.04882	3.474194	0.330405	13.44458	27.74835	3.736288	5.217365
4	0.242823	56.75137	2.342336	0.228107	9.713993	18.87530	8.576468	3.512436
5	0.281113	64.95788	1.775948	0.211462	7.347840	14.53625	8.326439	2.844171
6	0.313619	70.63489	1.435466	0.257463	6.065994	11.80252	7.017136	2.786536
7	0.345631	73.65446	1.343114	0.734400	5.048023	10.79607	5.837565	2.586361
8	0.371833	74.94572	1.190926	1.431729	4.375066	10.68956	5.054603	2.312396
9	0.394366	76.06685	1.060299	1.980335	3.955620	10.35536	4.515150	2.066387
10	0.414246	77.21921	0.965832	2.209582	3.812402	9.761313	4.148459	1.883202
Variance Decomposition of LCDX: Period	**S.E.**	**LGDP**	**LRPO**	**LBD**	**LINRT**	**LSVN**	**LCDX**	**LHDI**
1	0.077702	0.116368	13.09051	1.259877	12.02393	16.92260	56.58671	0.000000
2	0.117982	0.051896	11.26313	20.33514	22.57352	19.86657	25.86596	0.043784
3	0.133004	4.795543	9.314776	29.89907	18.21869	16.34968	21.27255	0.149696
4	0.148098	11.01817	8.388248	27.44499	18.74935	13.53078	20.69234	0.176127
5	0.161176	18.04752	7.425845	23.26385	19.12024	11.53463	19.00935	1.598560
6	0.171024	19.22483	10.34152	21.04631	19.14266	10.33177	17.05392	2.858987
7	0.177119	20.63389	12.51465	20.60947	17.85091	9.641637	15.90091	2.848539
8	0.181007	20.64198	13.50384	20.56699	17.66454	9.236158	15.43881	2.947687
9	0.184289	20.18861	13.11610	20.07341	18.19622	8.910478	15.22826	4.286922
10	0.187851	19.52605	13.36438	19.36118	18.01217	8.604452	14.81672	6.315038

continued on following page

Table 7. Continued

Variance Decomposition of LHDI: Period	S.E.	LGDP	LRPO	LBD	LINRT	LSVN	LCDX	LHDI
1	0.052597	4.599815	0.224300	0.437654	32.94391	8.645661	7.178591	45.97007
2	0.077739	9.195533	27.92700	1.821977	15.83828	4.170458	3.298535	37.74822
3	0.092871	7.680643	39.78715	1.512618	11.45165	4.466206	2.409916	32.69181
4	0.100147	8.291787	41.65409	2.644329	9.849045	7.161215	2.226604	28.17293
5	0.104492	8.334294	38.55530	2.866373	10.09083	10.44982	2.136937	27.56644
6	0.109589	10.85904	35.16738	3.121575	9.246874	10.41261	2.113512	29.07902
7	0.115237	13.19465	33.65703	2.947205	8.871698	9.432328	2.143153	29.75393
8	0.123074	16.24862	32.06420	2.597068	10.77301	8.605424	2.009104	27.70258
9	0.130896	19.63282	29.78961	2.390165	13.38337	7.903381	1.818603	25.08205
10	0.137395	22.44224	27.89280	2.338370	15.48869	7.241842	1.661586	22.93447

Source: Author's estimation using Eview 7.0

remaining 9 years. Similarly, it responded negatively to *BD* in the short run and zero impact from year 6 on; and to *INRT*'s shocks, zero level impact occurred in year 1 and 4, the rest 8years periods witness negative impacts. Savings innovation generated negative impulse in the first half period while the rest half of the period resulted in zero response. *CDX* innovation has zero impact in the short run while the long run was of negative impact. *HDI*'s impulse resulted in positive response from year 3 through to the 7th year, while the 8th to 10[th]year produces zero response. The summary of the output is that while its performance is weakened by its history, other macroeconomic variables like *GDP*, *INRT,* and *SVN*do not drive the rail system while *CDX* impacts negatively on it.

BD's response to shocks in *GDP, RPO, INRT, SVN, CDX, HDI* and itself result in fluctuations from positive value to zero level and negative values. On to itself, negative outcome occurs within years 2 and 7 while the rest of the periods are of negative consequence. On *GDP* shock, *BD* response is negative in years 2, 4 and 6, while the long run is of positive outcomes. On *INRT* shock, the response is mixed through the innovation period, with positive response in the short run but negative in the long run. On saving, the response was zero in year 1 and 2; negative in years 3-5 and zero in the long run. It implies that the saving rate is not encouraging for deficit financing. The shock from *CDX* induces negative impact in the short run and zero level impact in the long run, short of period 7 with positive impact. On *HDI* shock, except for period 4 and 5 with positive impact the rest innovation periods are of negative ad zero impacts. On *RPO* shock, *BD* records high positive response in year 2, low positive response in year 9 and 10, the rest periods are of negative response. In summary, the equation's outcome is that GDP's shock significantly drives *BD*, while *INRT* enhances it in the short run.

The interest rate (*INRT*) responses to the model's innovations were also unique. On shock from *GDP, INRT* maintained zero response through the entire 10 year period. On *RPO* and *BD's* impulses, it is largely zero level response in the short run and negative in the long run. Its responds to its own shock is positive in year 1 to year 4, but maintain zero level response thereafter while from *SVN* and *HDI* negative responses are revealed, an apparent weakness of the Ricardian hypothesis. In summary, *INRT*'s response to variables in the model is weak; Ricardian hypothesis did not hold between *SVN* and *INRT*.

SVN responds positively to *GDP*'s impulse in the entire ten innovation period. Its response to innovations from *RPO, BD* and *HDI* fluctuate around zero level in the entire 10 year period. Its response to *INRT* is negative in the years 1 to 5, and thereafter remains negative through the long run. Its response to self-innovation is negative in year4 and 5 thereafter assume zero state to the 10th period. Its response to *CDX*'s shock remains of zero response in the entire period. In summary, *SVN* is driven by *GDP*'s innovation and not to *BD* as Ricardian hypothesis claims.

CDX's responses to shocks in all the variables in the model were negative and zero level in short and long run period. Given the context of estimating the corruption index, it suggests that corruption is encouraged by the variables as *CDX* responded negatively to short run shocks in *RPO, BD, INRT* and *HDI*; and zero level response in the long run.

Similarly, *HDI*'s responses to innovations were of zero impact from itself and BD in the short-run, and for GDP in the 10 years period. It responded negatively in the short run to shock in RPO and *CDX,* while the long run period experienced zero level response. This suggests that given level of innovations in the studied variables the living standards might remain at same level in the short run and deteriorate further in the long run.

Variance Decomposition (VD)

The decomposition of Cholesky's standard deviation in *GDP, RPO, BD, INRT, SVN, CDX* and *HDI* (see *table 9*) produced interesting revelations. The *GDP*'s forecast error is largely attributed to itself, *INRT* and *RPO*. While *GDP* generated average of 64% of the forecast error in the 10 year period, both *INRT* and *RPO* accounted, on average for 14% and 7% of the errors respectively. The Statistics of the *RPO*'s forecast error variance show that it is attributed to self in the short run by about 70%; while the long run forecast error is attributed to self (33%), *INRT* (22%), *HDI* and *GDP* (18%) respectively. The forecast error for *BD* is attributed to itself by 98% in year 1 and thereafter from years 2 to 10 by 53%; *RPO*(34%) and *INRT*(20%) respectively. The rest variables produced marginal influence to the forecast error.

The decomposition of the *INRT* error in the 10 year forecasts is generally patterned as follows: to self, 45%, *GDP* 21% and Rpo18%, implying that high interest rate problem is both self and economy wide induced. The *SVN*'s forecast terror is attributed to itself by 90% and 62% in years 1 and 2 respectively while *GDP* absorbed average of72% of the error from year's 3 to 10 innovation period, implying that long term ability to grow saving is a function of the economy. Corruption's forecast error is due to self by 56% in year 1 declining marginally to 14% in year 10. From years 5 to 10 the pattern on average is as follows: *BD* 22%, GDP 19% and *INRT*, 15%.The *HDI*'s forecast error is attributed to itself, *RPO* and *INRT* by average of 30% in the short run, while in the long-run itself and *RPO* absorbed the larger of the forecast error more than any other variable in the model.

Policy Implications and Recommendations

The result of Granger causality test that Rail and Pipeline output (RPO) significantly predicts GDP, indicate that economic growth can be influenced by RPO, if the sector is appropriately managed. Government investment in rail and pipeline transport can ignite rapid growth, giving its linkage effect on growth inspired sectors such as agriculture and industrial transportation. Full privatization should be the lasting solution to a sound rail industry as practiced in Brazil and Mexico. Interest rate also significantly granger causes GDP implying that interest rate regime can be managed to create favourable credit economy and thus a pointer to high economic growth.

That *HDI* and *GDP* is bi-directly causal is accordance with economic growth theories which postulates that indices of standard of living-per capita income, knowledge economy, and life expectancy are potent determinants of economic growth. Hence, investments in *HDI* indicators and *GDP* are bound to produce symmetrical growth in the average citizen and the country. Interest rate granger causes *RPO* means that the interest rate as an investment instrument can effectively improve the fortunes of the rail and pipeline sector investment and hence boost productivity.

CDX granger causes *BD* implies that budget deficit (*BD*) policies might not be growth induced but borne to advance corrupt practices. *HDI* granger causing *CDX* may partly be attributed to poverty induced corruption. However, the non-significance of *CDX* and *RPO* imply that corruption might not be responsible for poor state *RPO*.

RPO significantly granger causes *HDI* indicating influence of rail and pipeline output in poverty reduction. Developed rail and pipeline transport produces cheaper, efficient and effective transportation of goods and services which increases access of the rural and urban poor to cheaper mode of transportation (Bangsund *et al.*, 1997). The result also shows that *SVN* significantly granger causes *BD* indicating that improved savings can reduce Budget deficit. The non-causal influence from *BD* to *SVN* suggests that the Ricardian hypothesis does not suffice in the Nigerian case. The non- causality from *SVN* to *INRT* further put doubt on the efficacy of the Ricardian hypothesis in Nigeria fiscal system.

Interest rate granger causes *HDI* implies that interest rate influences standards of living. Nigeria's relative experience of high interest rate regimes (persistence of availability and cost doctrine) makes credit accessible only at high cost, easily transmitted to inflation, hence a deterrent to improved living standard. Government through the Central Bank can improve the credit system by lowering its monetary rate below 5%, boost credit towards the productive sector.

The Impulse Response function (*IRF*) results show that *GDP* maintains improved positive growth behaviour following improvements in the economy's growth variables generally. On the *RPO*'s innovation *GDP* maintenance of zero response in the greater part of the innovation period, shows the weak link in *RPO* and growth, indicating that the rail and pipeline sector needs more investments inputs for it to impact *GDP*.

RPO's negative response to *GDP*, *BD*, *SVN* and *INRT* in the innovation period shows that the sector was adversely affected by the economy's growth trend. *BD* financing should be directly invested in critical infrastructures like the rail and pipeline sector as catalysts, generating reproductive investment mechanism that permeates all sectors of the economy. The savings and interest rate shock to which *RPO* responds negatively indicates weak policies that are counterproductive to rapid rail and pipeline growth process.

The negative responses in years 1 to 5 on *SVN* for innovation from *BD* while other years are of zero impact suggests weakness of the Ricardian hypothesis in Nigerian case, as *BD* does not positively invite savings. It implies that the theory of savings on account of *BD* does not hold in Nigeria in the context of study. Impulses from *RPO, GDP, BD, INRT* on *HDI* and *CDX* were both of zero and negative response suggesting that living standards and corruption matters are not being encouraged by these variables. Government should review its policies dealing with *BD, RPO, INRT* and growth to positively impact *HDI* and reduce *CDX*.

The dynamic decomposition of forecast error variance produces implications as follows: the *LGDP* forecast error is attributed to itself and exogenous shocks in BD and INRT. For future improvement in *GDP, BD* and *INRT* mechanism and process might need to often examine for greater impact on the economic growth potential. Similarly, the *RPO*'s forecast error from year 4 to 10 is attributed to external shocks from *LBD, INRT and HDI*, indicating strong relationship between Rail and pipeline growth, budget deficit, interest rate and living standard. Government should regularly re-examine its policies on budget deficit and interest rate to impact on rail output growth.

Budget deficit (*BD*) forecast error is highly absorbed by external shock from interest rate and *RPO*. Government's fiscal and monetary policies should be increasingly examined towards low interest rate regime. The *BD* should be strictly applied to productive infrastructure such as the *RPO*, since the quantity of *BD* often crowd out the private sector credit, which impacts on high lending rate, and inflation in the economy. This *BD* result is symmetrical to the forecast error variance of interest rate which is highly attributed to external shocks from *RPO* and *BD*.

Real Options in Public Capital Investments

It is normal practice for investors to make changes that affect subsequent cash flows over the life of the project (Van Horne & Dhamija, 2012). The presence of real options enhances the worth of an investment project. It's worth becomes the net present value (NPV) originally computed plus the value of the option. Real option can be of three important types: the option to vary output; the option to abandon; option to postpone. Option to vary entails either to expand production if conditions turn favourable, otherwise called growth option and to contract production if condition turn bad, which involve shutting down. Option to abandon would be viable if the project has abandonment value which effectively represents a put option to the option writer. Option to postpone, also known as investment timing option evolves from the option that the project should wait to obtain new information (Van Horne & Dhamija, 2012). Abandonment option may be preferred when the project goes awry, necessitating selling the assets. However, selling the assets may not be best option to realizing abandonment value as the asset may simply be employed in another area. In either case the abandonment value should be estimated.

Financial Lessons learned

First, information from interviews with senior members of the State Ministry of Transport reveals that the state had to pay penalty due from judgment debt on the contract cancellation totalling over ₦600 million as cost and penalty to the foreign consortium. Secondly, the non-availability of rail transport as envisioned by the government since the failure in the early 1980s has increased the average cost of transportation, freight and passengers in the state, impacting negatively on citizens' health and welfare; reduced the productive time for business and productivity and the nation's GDP. Ochonma (2015) estimated at ₦500 billion the annual losses due to lack of functional freight rail services that would have assisted in transporting goods from the country's two busiest seaports to other parts of Nigeria. Thirdly, the financial cost (on litigations and demolishing physical structures) to reclaim the original routes for reconstruction, having been encroached on, as promised by current Governor would be enormous.

CONCLUSION

The economics of abandoning a project needs to be considered seriously as part of the project planning process. Successful project requires careful and elaborate planning from inception. Decisions must be taken upon information supplied by competent professionals, not only on the technical, economic, commercial viability of the project but on the political feasibility. Prompt payment for work done, inflation financing should be effectively managed while changes in government should not affect on-going project. Legal instruments should be put in place as a policy to avoid project abandonment or flimsy excuse of not continuing with inherited projects. Project insurance should be considered as part of any successful project to cover project companies and lenders against unpredictable losses.

The study used VAR model to examine the behaviour of *GDP, RPO, BD, INRT, SVN, CDX* and *HDI* as proposed by theory and literature. The responses of *RPO* from shocks in *GDP, BD, INRT* and *SVN* are either zero (0) or negative, suggesting that the variables do not impact *RPO* growth. Similarly, *CDX* innovation has zero impact in the short run while the long run was of negative impact. *HD*I's impulse however resulted in positive response from year 3 through to the 7th year, while the 8th to 10th year produces zero response. The summary of the equation's output is that while *RPO*'s performance is weakened by its history, other macroeconomic variables like *GDP, INRT* and *SVN* do not drive the rail system while *CDX* impacts negatively on it. Since *RPO* is highly significant in the tests carried out, its abandonment speaks of possible the negative impact the GDP and other variables of importance would suffer.

The Ricardian hypothesis tested reveal that it does not hold as *BD* did not granger cause *SVN*, while *SVN* also failed to granger cause *INRT* as the theory suggests. The variance decomposition result of *RPO*'s forecast error variance show that it's variance is attributed to self in the short run by about 80%, *GDP* (10%) and *HDI*(5%); while the long run forecast error is attributed to self (33%), *INRT* (22%), *HDI* and *GDP* (18%) respectively. Apart from the impact of *RPO* on the major macroeconomic variables, project abandonment economic implications are enormous if the benefit to be derived by investment in is taken into account. Such investment becomes sunk are consequently cost in addition to the incalculable loss in welfare effects on the populace generally.

Government investment in rail and pipeline transport can ignite rapid growth, giving its linkage effect on growth stimulating sectors such as agriculture and industrial transportation. Full privatization would be the lasting solution to a sound rail transport industry as practiced in Brazil and Mexico and elsewhere.

ACKNOWLEDGMENT

The authors acknowledge and are indebted to Mr. Salaam, Director of Transport Policy, Lagos State Ministry of Transport, Ikeja, Lagos, Nigeria; Prof. A. Omotayo, Dean, Faculty of Social Sciences, Lagos State University, Ojo, Lagos; Dr (Mrs.) Sangosanya, Head of Dept. of Geography and Planning, Lagos State University, Lagos- for the supply of vital information, support and encouragement in writing this report and for their useful and insightful comments and suggestions.

REFERENCES

Apanisile, O. T., & Akinlo, T. (2013). Rail transport and economic growth in Nigeria (1970-2011). *Australian Journal of Business and Management Research, 3*(5), 18–24.

Asteriou, D., & Hall, S. G. (2011). *Applied Econometrics* (2nd ed.). Palgrave Macmillan.

Bangsund, D. A., Leistritz, F. L., & Honeyman, J. S. (1997). *Assessing Economic impacts of Railroad Abandonment on Rural Communities*. Retrieved from www.handystevenson.com

Bashir, O. K. (2013). Growth-Effects of Macroeconomic Stability Factors: Empirical Evidence from Nigeria. *Developing Country Studies*, *3*(14), 47–55.

Chitkara, K. K. (2006). *Construction Project Management: Planning, Scheduling and Controlling*. New Delhi: Tata McGraw-Hill Publishing Company.

Clunies-Ross, A., Forsyth, D., & Hug, M. (2009). *Development Economics* (1st ed.). McGraw-Hill Higher Education.

Dean, J. (1951). *Capital Budgeting*. New York: Columbia University Press.

Dickey, D. A., & Fuller, W. A. (1979). Distribution of the Estimators for Autoregressive Time Series with a Unit Root. *Journal of the American Statistical Association*, *74*, 427–431.

Diji, C. J. (2004). Constraints to Industrialization: An Ex-Post Evaluation of the Iron and Steel Industry in Nigeria. *Challenges of Nigerian Industrialization: a Pathway to Nigeria Becoming a Highly Industrialized Country in the Year 2015, Selected papers for 2004 Annual Conference of the Nigerian Economic Society*, 493-519.

Dwivedi, D. N. (2008). *Managerial Economics* (7th ed.). Vikas Publishing House PVT Ltd.

El-Rufai, N. A. (2012). *The Tragedy of Abandoned Projects*. Retrieved from www.nigeriaintel.com

Elinwa, A. U., & Joshua, M. (2001). Time-Overrun Factors in Nigeria Construction Industry. *Journal of Construction Engineering and Management*, *127*(5), 419–425. doi:10.1061/(ASCE)0733-9364(2001)127:5(419)

Garrett, A. T. (2004). *Light-Rail Transit in America Policy Issues and Prospects for Economic Development.* Federal Reserve Bank of St. Louis.

Granger, C. W. J. (1969). Investigating Causal Relations by Econometric Models and Cross Spectral Methods. *Econometrica*, *35*(3), 424–438. doi:10.2307/1912791

Granger, C. W. J. (1986). Development in the Study of Co-integrated economic variables. *Oxford Bulletin of Economics and Statistics*, *48*, 3.

Hall, R. E. & Jones C. I. (1997). Level of Economic Activities Across countries. *American Economic Review*, *87*(2), 173-177.

Hellewel, D. S. (2001). Toward the year 2000 Transport for our cities. In Global Issues (vol. 3). I.B. Tauris Publishers.

Hyman, D. N. (2002). *Public Finance: A Contemporary Application of Theory to Policy* (7th ed.). Harcourt College Publishers.

Ingwe, R., Mbato, W. A., & Ebong, E. (2012). *Project Abandonment, corruption, and Recovery of Unspent Budgeted Public Funds in Nigeria*. Retrieved from www.revecon.ro/articles/2012-1/2012-1-2.pdf

Interstate Commerce Commission, Rail Services Planning Office. (1975). *Rail Service Continuation Subsidy Decisions: Intent to Establish Criteria.* Academic Press.

Jhingan, M. L. (2007). The Economics of Development and Planning (39th ed.). Vrinda Publications.

Kavanagh, P., Doyle, C., & Metcalfe, O. (2005). *Health impacts of Transport: A Review*. Institute of Public Health in Ireland.

Kerzner, H. (2004). *Production Management: A system Approach to planning, scheduling and controlling* (2nd ed.). CBS Publishers and Distribution.

Lagos State G. D. P. Survey. (2010). *Lagos State Gross Domestic Product (GDP) Survey: 2010.* Lagos State Bureau of Statistic, Ministry of Economic Planning and Budget, Alausa, Ikeja. Retrieved from www.lagosstate.gov.ng

Lagos State Government (LSG). (1981). Ministry of Public Transportation (LSMPT). Lagos Metro Line Project Phase 1 Final Report (1981). The Japanese Consortium.

LAMATA. (2015). *Lagos Rail Mass Transit*. Retrieved from www.lamata-ng.com

Maddala, G. S., & Kim, I. (1998). Unit Roots, Co-integration and Structural Change. Cambridge University Press.

Meir, S., & Sepe, J. F. (1989). Project termination announcements and the market value of the firm. *Financial Management*, *18*(4), 74–81. doi:10.2307/3665799

Merna, T., & Al-Thani, F. F. (2008). *Corporate Risk Management* (2nd ed.). John Wiley Sons, Ltd.

Miller, M. E. (1988). On the Systematic Risk of Expansion Investment. *The Quarterly Review of Economics and Business*, *28*(Autumn), 66–77.

Musgrave, R. A., & Musgrave, P. B. (2004). Public Finance in Theory and Practice (5th ed.). Tata McGraw Hill Education Private Ltd.

Nairaland Forum. (2014). *Lagos, emerging cities hold promise of 50% world growth*. Retrieved from www.businessdayonline.com

National Bureau of Statistics. (2014). *Nigerian Gross Domestic Product Report, Quarter four*. National Bureau of Statistics. Retrieved from www.nigerianstat.gov.ng

Ochonma, M. (2015). *Nigeria loses ₦500bn yearly to failed freight rail service*. Retrieved from www.businessdayonline.com

Odufalu, O., & Loto, M. A. (2008). *Project Analysis and Evaluation Principles and Techniques* (3rd ed.). Concept Publications.

OECD. (2012). *Debt and Macroeconomic Stability*. OECD Economics Department Policy Notes, No. 16.

Okorafor, G. F. (2004). *Impact Analysis of Federal Highways on the Local Economy- A case of selected highways in Nigeria* (Unpublished PhD Thesis). Federal University of Technology Owerri.

Olowe, R. A. (2011). *Financial Management, Concepts, Financial System and Business Finance* (3rd ed.). Lagos: Brierly Jones Nigeria Ltd.

Omotosho, K. (2012). *About 12,000 federal projects abandoned across Nigeria*. Retrieved from http://www.premiumtimesng.com/news/108450-about-12000-federal-projects-abandoned-across-nigeria.html

Rojas-Rueda, D., Nazelle, A., Teixidó, O., & Nieuwenhuijsen, M. J. (2013). Health impact assessment of increasing public transport and cycling use in Barcelona: A morbidity and burden of disease approach. Preventive Medicine, 57(5), 573-579.

Schwable, K. (2006). *Introduction to Project Management.* Thomson Course Technology. Retrieved from www.thomsonrights.com

Sims, C. (1980). Macroeconomics and Reality. *Econometrica*, *48*(Jan), 1–49. doi:10.2307/1912017

Stevenson, W. J. (2007). Operations Management (9th ed.). McGraw-Hill Irwin. Retrieved from www.mhhe.com

Telsang, M. (2004). *Industrial Engineering and Production Management*. S. Chand and Company Ltd.

Ubani, E. C., & Ononuju, C. N. (2013). A study of failure and abandonment of public sector-driven civil engineering projects in Nigeria: An empirical review. *American Journal of Scientific and Industrial Research*, *4*(1), 75–82. doi:10.5251/ajsir.2013.4.1.75.82

Van Horne, J. C., & Dhamija, S. (2012). Financial Management and Policy (12th ed.). Pearson.

Varian, R. H. (2002). *Intermediate Microeconomics A modern Approach* (6th ed.). New York: W.W. Norton & Company.

Vittas, D. (1999). *Pension Reform and Financial Markets*. Harvard Institute for International Development, Harvard University.

Yescombe, E. R. (2014). Principles of Project Finance (2nd ed.). Elsevier.

KEY TERMS AND DEFINITIONS

Abandonment Decision: Any option to discontinue projects that have earlier been appraised and undertaken by an investor, usually after difficult and impossible conditions force the investor to discontinue such projects. Since most projects are capital intensive, the losses can be substantial.

Capital Projects: These are the type of projects that are proposed to be revenue and return yielding, either by the private or public sector. Appraisals of these types of projects are technical.

Lagos: The former capital city of Nigeria, noted for its bustling economic activities and population congestion.

Metroline: The type of railways services that is built to serve the public in cities and metropolitan centres.

Public-Sector Project: Public sector projects are the type of capital projects that are to be executed for the benefit of the public either for the people to derive benefits or to save costs. Capital projects in the public sector is not necessarily to yield revenue for the government.

Ricardian Equivalence: A theory that shows how the people internalise the budgets deficits caused by a high expenditure on public sector project by possible surpluses in the future since the expenditure was incurred for the people's benefits today.

Chapter 11
Electric Power Transmission, Distribution Losses, and Economic Growth in Ghana

Samuel Adams
Ghana Institute of Management and Public Administration, Ghana

Edem Kwame Mensah Klobodu
Ghana Institute of Management and Public Administration, Ghana

Richmond Odartey Lamptey
Ghana Institute of Management and Public Administration, Ghana

ABSTRACT

This study examined the effect of electric power transmission and distribution losses (ETL) on economic growth over the period of 1971 to 2012 in Ghana. Using bounds testing approach to cointegration and Bai-Perron test in ordinary least squares framework, we find long-run relationship between ETL, gross capital formation, inflation, trade openness and economic growth. Secondly, while ETL do not have robust impact on economic growth, trade openness exerts a positive impact on economic growth in the long-run. Inflation and gross capital formation, however, have mixed relationships with economic growth. Furthermore, ETL yield a threshold value of 2.07. Finally, controlling for the urban population reveals that ETL moderates the relationship between urbanization and economic growth; higher ETL associates with an increasing negative effect on GDP per capita.

INTRODUCTION

Development experts and practitioners all over the world agree that infrastructure is a key driver of economic growth. The infrastructure deficit in many developing countries is what Romer (1993) refers to as the object gap. The World Bank (2010) study shows that doubling infrastructure capital raises output by approximately 10 percent. Improved infrastructure quality accounted for 30 percent of growth attributed to infrastructure in developing countries. In recent times, infrastructure investment is known

DOI: 10.4018/978-1-5225-2364-2.ch011

to have contributed immensely to the commendable GDP growth rates observed in numerous African countries (KPMG, 2016). The KPMG report notes that investments in energy infrastructure, particularly in energy generation could catapult the Sub-Saharan Africa (SSA) to a new growth frontier to lift the mass of citizenry out of poverty. This is in light of the fact that the African continent lacks adequate energy infrastructure, and severely underperforms in the provision of power. East Africa's most developed economy, Kenya, as well as Ghana on the West Coast of Africa perform commendably in terms of electricity generation in an African context. However, with an estimated annual per capita electricity usage of 150 kWh in Kenya and 342 kWh in Ghana, the countries perform very poorly when considered against the estimated global average annual figure of 2,550 kWh. According to the International Renewable Energy Agency (IRENA) (2012), Africa currently has 147 GW of installed capacity, a level comparable to the capacity that China installs in one to two years. In addition, average per capita electricity consumption in sub-Saharan Africa (when excluding South Africa) is just 153 kWh/year, which is roughly 6% that of the global average.

Although the consumption of energy is increasing in Africa, it is still the region with the highest energy poverty level. Africa is home to 15% of the world's population, but it consumes just 3% of the world's energy output, and generates less than 50% of the 74,000 MW of current peak demand requirement. Moreover, electrification rates are low with only 25% of the region's population having access to power compared to the developing countries average of 72% (Ecobank, 2014). The International Energy Agency (IEA) recounts that energy use in SSA increased by approximately 45% to over 600 GW over the period 2000-2012 (IEA, 2014). The big problem, however, is that even when it produces or generates energy, so much of it is lost during the transmission and distribution process such that the benefits are minimal. The gap between generation and consumption, equivalent to nearly 12% of total generation, is an indication of wastages due to inefficient transmission and distribution systems (KPMG, 2015). Though the quality differential between SSA and other regions of the world has reduced in the last decade, losses attributed to transmission and distributions are still significant. Research conducted by Ecobank (2014) shows that transmission and distribution losses in SSA continue to occur between sources of supply and points of distribution, and the cost of these inefficiencies is approximately $5bn annually. The report further notes that utilities across the region actually lose up to 25% of power consumed as a result of these inefficiencies, compared to the global average of 10%. Similarly, there are startling statistics in Latin America and Caribbean (LAC) area of the world. Jimenez, Seberisky and Mercado (2014) find that each year 17% of electricity generated is lost in LAC higher than the loss levels of OECD countries (6%) or low-income countries (15%). In putting the losses in proper context and appreciation, it is further suggested that 33.3 percent of the World electricity losses occur in LAC which is the equivalent of two times the annual electricity consumption of Peru. Further, the authors pointed out that 20 of 26 LAC countries have losses above 10 percent of total electricity output while 12 of the 26 LAC countries have losses above 17%. As noted in the case of SSA where high losses occur in transmission and distribution, it is no different in LAC. It is estimated that 80% electricity losses in LAC occur in distribution subsector (Jimenez, Serebrisky & Mercado, 2014). In terms of comparison, LAC loses about 3 percentage points more than Africa as at 2012 (Ecobank 2014; KPMG, 2015; Jimenez, Serebrisky & Mercado, 2014).

In this chapter, we describe electric power transmission and distribution losses to include losses in transmission between sources of supply and points of distribution and in the distribution to consumers, including pilferage (World Bank, 2015). The losses of electricity that occur along the entire chain of a power system serve as a key measure of its efficiency. Broadly speaking, such losses account for the difference between the electricity available for use and what is paid by end-users.

The value for Electric power transmission and distribution losses (kWh) in Ghana was 180 thousand as of 1971, but decreased to its minimum value of 59 thousand kWh in 1984 and greatest loss of about 2 billion in 2011. With the 2011 value, Ghana was ranked 78th out of 135 countries ranked by the International Energy Agency. It is of interest to note that only four other countries (South Africa, Nigeria Zambia, and Zimbabwe) in SSA had higher losses than Ghana in 2011. These losses in Ghana represent 6.22% of GDP in 1971, but decreased to 3.22% in 1984 and increased again to a peak of 23.73% in 2004 and reduced slightly to 18.38% in 2011. The least value of electricity transmission and distribution loss occurred in 1999 at 1.99% of GDP. The descriptive data provided suggests that while the transmission and distributional losses have increased 11 fold in absolute terms, the loss per GDP increased just about three fold over the past 40 years. The big issue is whether the electricity infrastructure is having any effect on the growth of the economy. This is the question the study seeks to examine. The objective of this study therefore is to examine how the electricity infrastructure in terms of quality per the losses in transmission and distribution are affecting the economic growth of Ghana.

The study contributes to the literature in three main ways. First, despite the important economic consequences of electricity losses, there is currently no systematic monitoring of the losses and their impact. In filling the gap in the literature, it will serve as input and complement efforts by various stakeholders to quantify, monitor, and deal with the challenges of electricity transmission and distribution losses to improve Ghana's energy infrastructure. The findings of the study should provide the impetus to establish proper regulatory and governance schemes that offer adequate signals to promote reduction in losses. Second, we identify threshold effects, if any, to determine the level beyond which any losses could be detrimental to economic growth. This is consistent with the view that there is a minimum level of technical losses that is acceptable. Obviously, this level is dependent on many actors (both technical and commercial or nontechnical) which are country specific. Our study examines the case of Ghana using annual series data for the period 1971-2012. The Economic Intelligence Unit (2014) notes that the ratio of electricity losses in high-income countries ranged from 6 to 9 percent over the last three decades, 17% in Latin America and the Caribbean, and about 14% in SSA.

Finally, we contribute to the literature by controlling for the level of urbanization. To the knowledge of the authors, this is one of the first studies which considers the impact of rural-urban divide in the energy loss and economic growth relationship. Obviously, this is important in light of the fact many reports do suggest that distance from the source as well as the demographic characteristics of the end market partially determine the degree of loss and the cost of delivery (Jiménez, Serebrisky & Mercado, 2014; KPMG, 2015). To answer the research question appropriately, we employ robust techniques; bounds testing approach to co-integration and Bai-Perron test in ordinary least squares framework (i.e. for detecting multiple breakpoints) over the period 1971-2013.

BRIEF BACKGROUND OF ENERGY SECTOR IN GHANA

Ghana's power sector is managed through the activities of three main public institutions which include Volta River Authority (VRA), Ghana Grid Company Limited (GRIDCo) and the Electricity Company of Ghana (ECG). The VRA is responsible for generation, GRIDCo is in charge of transmission and ECG handles the distribution to consumers. In the last decade, the power sector in Ghana has gone through two major energy challenges in terms of power deficit occurring in the periods 2006-2007 and 2014-2015. The power crisis in 2006–7 is estimated to have cost the country nearly 1% in lost growth of gross domestic product during those years (World Bank, 2013a). The report further notes that in the past 15 years, Ghana added about 1,000 megawatts (MW) of thermal generation capacity. As a result, Ghana's current generation capacity of 2,125 MW was made up of about 50% hydro and 50% thermal plants. Nevertheless, inadequate and unreliable power supply remains a major constraint to future economic growth. The report identified various challenges in the power sector focusing the three key institutions and recommended appropriate remedies for Government implementation. Nevertheless, the country was engulfed in huge power outages and rationing that affected individuals, businesses and institutions for the period 2014-2015.

Power transmission and distribution (T&D) losses in sub-Saharan Africa (SSA) often occur between sources of sources supply and points of distribution, and the cost of this inefficiency is approximately $5bn annually (Ecobank, 2014). The T&D losses in Ghana are estimated at 27% as at 2011 above the SSA average of 25% and global average of 10%. ECG's distribution losses were very high; they were 27% in the second quarter of 2012. ECG had to pay for "lost" energy it buys from VRA, but does not earn any revenue on it. The financial losses associated with these operational deficiencies of ECG had climbed to $331 million by 2009. Overall, the hidden costs associated with Ghana's power sector were a staggering 6.3 percent of GDP in 2009. Reducing these losses by 10% would save ECG US$85 million per year (World Bank, 2013a).

In 2014, the World Bank and IEA estimated that the duration of electricity outages and sales lost annually in Ghana were 400 hours and 5% respectively. The total hidden cost of electricity arising from transmission and distribution losses in the late 2000's was 118.5 percent of revenues compared to middle income countries average of 3.5 percent. It is obvious that electricity transmission and distribution losses negatively have serious repercussions on economic growth in Ghana (Pokharel, 2010; Wijayatunga and Jayalath, 2004). For instance, the GDP growth has slowed to just 3.4% in 2015 as energy rationing, high inflation and on-going fiscal consolidation continue to weigh on economic activity (World Bank, 2016).

In relation to electricity availability through improvement in T&D, the World Bank Report (2015) on Poverty Reductions in Ghana notes that sustained and inclusive growth in the last twenty years has allowed Ghana to reduce its poverty rate by more than half from 52.6% to 21.4% between 1991 and 2012. Furthermore, the report highlights that the impact of rapid growth on poverty has been far stronger in Ghana than elsewhere in Sub-Saharan Africa. For instance until 2005 for every 1% increase in GDP in Ghana, the incidence of poverty fell by 2.5%, which is far above the Sub-Saharan average of 1.6%. However, the report further notes that for sustainability of the poverty reduction progress a continued commitment to expanding access to public services, including health and education, and productive infrastructure, particularly electricity, as well as increasing the quality of these services are pre-requisites for development (World Bank, 2015)

Access to electricity has improved across all city size groups in both urban and rural areas. The proportion of households using electricity for lighting increased from around 30 percent in small towns (class 7 and others) to almost 70 percent between 2000 and 2010. In Accra, 86–92 percent of households in peri-urban areas had access to electricity by 2010, compared to 60–75 percent in 2000 (World Bank, 2014). Prior reports of the World Bank (2013b), notes that there are high losses due to old and overloaded networks in many areas, combined with problems of metering, billing, electricity theft, and inadequate revenue collection.

The role of urbanization in the transmission and distribution losses are obvious since service delivery pressure is increasingly placed on cities due to urbanization trends – largely driven by higher access to power rates than what is found in rural areas, which in certain countries are as low as 2 percent. The development of slums in urban areas due to migration causes the dwellers to engage in illegal connections resulting in huge transmission and distribution losses. Thus, the rural-urban divide in terms of access to electricity is further compounded by such nefarious activities prevalent in densely populated urban cities. King and Amponsah (2012) revealed that the slum dwellers' illegitimate access to electricity contribute significantly to electricity transmission losses in Ghana. Furthermore, the rural-urban divide in terms of transmission losses is due to the unavailability of transmission lines in the rural areas for connection to the national grid.

LITERATURE REVIEW

Infrastructure is a heterogeneous term, including physical structures of various types used by many industries as inputs to the production of goods and services (Chan, Forwood, Roper, & Sayers, 2009). It could be both "social infrastructure" such as hospitals and schools as well as "economic infrastructure" (e.g. Network of utilities). It is variously measured in terms of physical stocks, spending flows, or capital stocks constructed accumulating the latter.

In reference to the concept of electricity systems, three sub-systems constitute the whole electricity or power system. In fact, across the entire chain of a power system represented by the sub-systems, losses do occur because of the efficiency of respective sub-system (Jimenez, Serebrisky & Mercado, 2014). The first sub-system is the power generation plants that transform the various sources of fuel (i.e. Hydro, thermal, biofuel, coal, renewables and gas) into electric power for transmission. In total the IEA (2012) estimates that losses from power transformation and auto consumption of electricity by generation plants account for approximately two-thirds of total input. However the per cent of losses are influence by factors such as the size of the plant, its age, and its capacity utilization, and efficiency depends heavily on the electricity mix (Jimenez, Serebrisky, & Mercado, 2014). The transmission system is the second part of the power system after generation. The transmission sub-system receives output from the generation system, which is usually composed of high- and medium voltage networks (100 KV). These transmission lines are also connected with transformers that step down the high voltage power transmission to lower voltage for distribution. It is sufficient to say that, determinants of transmission losses are mainly as a result of technical factors, climatological events, and specific geographic conditions (Jimenez, Serebrisky & Mercado, 2014). Finally, the distribution system ensures that domestic, commercial and other industrial users have access to electricity. The distribution system (including commercialization) involves several steps in addition to transporting electricity, connecting, metering, and charging for service. As a matter of emphasis, once power enters distribution systems that deliver electricity to end-users, losses are a result of both technical and non-technical factors unlike transmission system with losses caused by technical losses only (Jimenez, Serebrisky & Mercado, 2014). Whereas transmission losses offer a direct measure of the technical efficiency of the system, nontechnical factors resulting in losses, reflect the operational efficiency of the utilities (KPMG, 2012; IEA, 2014)

Conceptually, infrastructure may affect aggregate output in two main ways: firstly, directly, considering the sector contribution to GDP formation and as an additional input in the production process of other sectors; and secondly indirectly, raising total factor productivity by reducing transaction and other costs thus allowing a more efficient use of conventional productive inputs (Straub, 2011). It is worth noting that infrastructure investment is complementary to other investment. It means insufficient infrastructure investment stifles other investment and excessive adds no value. In view of this, suboptimal infrastructure investment constrains other investment and therefore lowering of economic growth (Newbery, 2012). To further expatiate on the infrastructure-growth nexus, the causality between infrastructure and economic growth stems from the fact that infrastructure systems are intricately intertwined with economies and some research show bi-directional relationship. Thus, infrastructure can increase connectivity, facilitate productivity, create jobs and stimulate trade which is key enablers of economic growth. On the other hand, economic growth can be a key enabler of increased investment and funding for infrastructure implying that economies with stronger growth prospects tend to attract more investment for infrastructure than those with poor or no growth prospects (Canning 2004; KPMG, 2015).

Neoclassical growth theory assumes that investment responds automatically to the changes in rates of return. To this end, if the interconnection between rates of return and investment in the economy is constrained, the anticipated growth per the neoclassical model will be unachievable. The key assumption of the Solow (1956) model is that technology is free; it is publicly available as a non-excludable, non-rival good. In view of certain shortcomings, basic changes in the neoclassical growth model were made to incorporate an analysis of imperfect competition. Such imperfections include Government regulations, market power and externalities (Vellutini & Walters, 2008) which ought to be considered in ensuring that prices of infrastructure services represent the cost of input or marginal social value. The additions to the theory finally occurred after Romer's research in the late 1980s. Notable differences in the infrastructure investment and long term growth across countries are partially explained by the neoclassical growth model (Barro and Sala-i-Martin, 2005).

Endogenous growth theory anticipate instances where aggregate economy exhibit increasing returns to scale irrespective of the presence of diminishing or constant returns to individual factors (Aghion & Howitt, 1998; Barro & Sala-i-Martin, 2005). The endogenous growth model built on the earlier works of Arrows (1962) by Romer (1986), Lucas (1988) and Rebelo (1991) did not initially include the theory of technological change. This framework assumes that long-term growth rate depends on governmental actions, such as taxation, maintenance of law and order, provision of infrastructure services, protection of intellectual property rights, and regulations of international trade, financial markets, and other aspects of the economy (Barro & Sala-i-Martin, 2005). In effect, infrastructure stock play significant role in these economies of scale and as such determine long-run growth. As such governments play a major role in facilitating infrastructural investments to increase growth.

In support of causality in the infrastructure-growth nexus, Esfahani and Ramirez (2003) adopted a structural model of infrastructure and growth to investigate 75 countries. The authors show that the impact of infrastructure on GDP growth was substantial, subject to the role of institutional and economic characteristics. Similarly, Canning (2004), using panel co-integration technique to investigate relationship between infrastructure and growth show a bi-directional causality in both short run and long run. Herranz-Loncan (2007) studied the effects of infrastructure investment on Spanish economic growth using VAR system. The author finds a positive and significant effect of local infrastructure on economic growth for the period 1850 to 1935. Kumo (2012) analyzed data on South Africa for the period 1960-2009 using bivariate vector autoregressive (VAR). Additionally, the author conducted a pairwise Granger causality tests between economic growth, economic infrastructure investment, and employment. The results indicate a strong causality between economic infrastructure investment and GDP growth that runs in both directions.

Another dimension of the infrastructure-growth nexus is the effectiveness of infrastructure usage to promote growth. According to Markard (2009), infrastructure usage effectiveness has many dimensions which are difficult to model. He further asserted that infrastructure facilities are usually public goods organized in capital- intensive networks (e.g. railroads, air and water transportation, electricity generation and distribution, telecommunications). The efficiency of any segment of the infrastructure will depend on size and configuration of the whole network. Thus, the possibilities of complementarities and substitutes will exist between and within segments of the network. In view of the productive/ usage efficiency of unique infrastructure types in relation to growth, recent researches have focused on a more detailed understanding of infrastructure and they estimate the effect of different infrastructure sub-sectors and try to find the dependence between several variables (Snieska&Simkunaite, 2009). Agénor and Moreno-Dodson (2006) focused on infrastructure sub-sectors to include transport, water supply and sanitation, information and technology (ICT) and energy. Seethepalli, Bramati and Veredas (2008) and Straub (2011) analyze telecom (number of phones lines, number of mobile subscribers), electricity (electric power consumption), roads (kilometers of paved roads, percentage of paved roads), sanitation (percentage of population with access to improved sanitation facilities) and water (percentage of population with access to improved water source) as physical indicators of infrastructure. Some researchers analyze physical infrastructure indicators from three different sectors – telecom, energy and transport: the main telephone lines or number of telephones, electricity generating capacity, rail route length or paved road length (Grubesic, 2009; Yeaple & Golub, 2007; Canning & Pedroni, 2008).

The empirical literature on infrastructure and growth is far from unanimous but most studies find a positive long-run effect of infrastructure on output, productivity, or their growth rate (Calderon, 2008). Some of the studies focus on quantifying the impact of infrastructure on aggregate performance, and silent about the specific channels through which the impact occurs. Another strand of the empirical literature focuses on the poverty effects of specific infrastructure and market development.

The relationship between energy consumption and economic growth, however, shows mixed results (Adams, Klobodu, & Opoku, 2016; Ahmad, Hayat, Hamad, & Lugman, 2012; Kouakou, 2010; Ouadraogo, 2013). For instance, Adams, Klobodu, and Opoku (2016) found a feedback effect between for energy consumption and growth by employing a panel vector autoregressive model. Ahmad, Hayat, Hamad, & Lugman (2012) investigated the relationship between energy consumption and economic growth in Pakistan for the period of 1973-2006 and found a positive relationship with a unidirectional causality from GDP to energy consumption. Earlier, Kouakou (2010) show bi-directional relationship between per capita electricity consumption and per capita GDP in Cote d'Ivoire over the period 1971-2008. Similarly, a study by Ouadraogo (2013) for 15 countries of ECOWAS from 1980-2008 using a panel co-integration technique found GDP and energy consumption as well as GDP and electricity to exhibit a long-run co-integrating relationship.

In expanding the research to focus on cross-country analysis, Bildirici (2013) investigates the relationship between electricity consumption and economic growth by using the Autoregressive Distributed Lag (ARDL) bounds testing approach and vector error-correction models (VECM) in Ghana and other nine African countries for the period 1970-2010. The author finds that there exists a bi-directional causality between economic growth and electricity consumption in Ghana. Similarly, Ackah and Adu (2014) examine the impact of energy consumption on economic growth for ten oil producing countries in Africa including Ghana for the period 1971 to 2011. Using the fixed effect estimation with a disaggregation of energy consumption into renewal and non-renewable the authors conclude that the effect on economic growth was significant. The empirical review of the above literature indicates that most of the global and country specific studies have focused on the energy-growth nexus. Additionally, environment-growth nexus has been examined in some of the reviewed literature. However, the effect of electricity T&D losses and growth appear not to have caught the attention of researchers. This gap in literature therefore makes this study unique.

DATA AND METHODOLOGY

This study relies on the production function in explaining the relationship between electric power transmission and distribution losses and economic growth. Following Hulten (1996) and Straub, Vellutini & Warlters (2008), we input electric power transmission and distribution losses (a measure of infrastructure) as an additional factor of production in the model. This approach allows us to capture the direct effect of electric power transmission and distribution losses on economic growth. Thus, the base model is specified as follows:

$$\begin{aligned}\ln GDPPC_t &= \beta_1 + \beta_2 \ln GCF_t + \beta_3 \ln CPI_t + \\ &\beta_4 \ln TR_t + \beta_5 \ln POP_t + \beta_6 \ln ETL_t + \varepsilon_t\end{aligned} \tag{1}$$

Afterwards, we model threshold effect of ETL by including a square term of ETL in equation (1). This relationship is given as:

$$\begin{aligned}\ln GDPPC_t &= \beta_1 + \beta_2 \ln GCF_t + \beta_3 \ln CPI_t + \beta_4 \ln TR_t + \\ &\beta_5 \ln POP_t + \beta_6 \ln ETL_t + \beta_7 \ln ETL_T^2 + \varepsilon_t\end{aligned} \tag{2}$$

Finally, controlling for the level of urbanization in the base equation (1) we obtain:

$$\begin{aligned}\ln GDPPC_t &= \beta_1 + \beta_2 \ln GCF_t + \beta_3 \ln CPI_t + \beta_4 \ln TR_t \\ &+ \beta_5 \ln POP_t + \beta_6 \ln ETL_t + \beta_7 \ln URB_t + \beta_8 \ln ETL_t * \ln URB_t + \varepsilon_t\end{aligned} \tag{3}$$

where GDPPC is real GDP per capita; GCF is gross capital formation as a share of GDP; CPI (consumer price index) measures inflation; TR measures trade openness as a share of GDP; POP captures total population; ETL is electric power transmission and distribution losses (as a percentage of output); ETL^2 is the square term of electric power transmission and distribution losses (as a percentage of output); URB measures urban population (% of total); $\beta 's$ represent the coefficients of variables; and ε_t is the error. The variables constitute annual data from World Bank's (2015) World Development Indicators over the period 1971-2012 and have all been expressed as natural logarithms (ln) in order to able achieve stationary variance. Table 1 presents the descriptive statistics as well as the pairwise correlation among the variables. According to the descriptive statistics whereas GDP per capita (6%), gross capital formation (3%) and population (16%) grow at an impressive rate, inflation (measure by CPI) grows at an alarming rate (3%). Pairwise correlations over the study period 1971-2012 reveal very high correlations between trade and gross capital formation (0.980), population and urban population (0.993), urban population and gross capital formation (0.826) and finally between population and gross capital formation (0.795).

Table 1. Descriptive Statistics and Correlation Matrix

Variables	lnGDPPC	lnGCF	lnCPI	lnTR	lnPOP	lnETL	lnURB
Mean	6.086	2.642	3.188	3.815	16.527	1.909	3.636
Median	6.056	2.718	3.208	3.827	16.540	1.596	3.625
Maximum	6.583	3.490	4.811	4.754	17.056	3.362	3.953
Minimum	5.771	1.217	2.166	1.844	15.993	0.687	3.373
SD	0.185	0.609	0.732	0.694	0.323	0.897	0.192
Skewness	0.683	-0.673	0.552	-0.873	-0.030	0.445	0.156
Kurtosis	3.180	2.454	2.532	3.283	1.743	1.587	1.573
N	42	42	42	42	42	42	42
lnGDPPC	1.000						
lnGCF	0.599	1.000					
lnCPI	-0.566	-0.538	1.000				
lnTR	0.567	0.980	-0.536	1.000			
lnPOP	0.535	0.795	-0.454	0.751	1.000		
lnETL	0.625	0.480	-0.432	0.517	0.648	1.000	
lnURB	0.611	0.826	-0.487	0.788	0.993	0.672	1.000

The high correlations in the data suggest the possibility of multicollinearity in our regressions and also a plausible relationship amongst our variables of interest. As a result, we re-specify the equations to avoid multicollinearity as follows:

$$\ln GDPPC_t = \beta_1 + \beta_2 \ln GCF_t + \beta_3 \ln CPI_t + \beta_4 \ln TR_t + \beta_5 \ln ETL_t + \varepsilon_t \tag{1a}$$

$$\begin{aligned}\ln GDPPC_t &= \beta_1 + \beta_2 \ln GCF_t + \beta_3 \ln CPI_t + \\ &\beta_4 \ln TR_t + \beta_5 \ln ETL_t + \beta_6 \ln ETL_T^2 + \varepsilon_t\end{aligned} \tag{2a}$$

$$\begin{aligned}\ln GDPPC_t &= \beta_1 + \beta_2 \ln CPI_t + \beta_3 \ln TR_t + \\ &\beta_4 \ln ETL_t + \beta_5 \ln URB_t + \beta_6 \ln ETL_t * \ln URB_t + \varepsilon_t\end{aligned} \tag{3a}$$

Consequently, eliminating population due to its very high growth rate (i.e. indicated by its mean) and strong correlation with urban population is deemed fit due to the implementation of a cointegration framework (i.e. Bounds test). A cointegration framework controls for omitted variable bias and specification problem. Once cointegration is established, it implies that no relevant integrated variable is omitted (see Chintrakarn & Herzer, 2012; Herzer & Vollmer, 2012).

Prior to estimating equations, we test for stationarity in the variables to avoid issues of spurious regression (a perquisite in time series analysis) and also to determine the order integration which enables us to apply the appropriate estimation technique. We test for the stationarity by using Dickey Fuller-Generalized Least Squares (DF-GLS) test by Elliott, Rothenberg and Stock (1996), Phillips-Perron (PP) test and

The Kwiatkowski, Phillips, Schmidt, and Shin (KPSS) test. Whereas DF-GLS and PP assume series to be non-stationary (i.e. have unit root) under the null hypothesis, KPSS assumes series to be stationary (i.e. have no unit root). Based on DF-GLS, PP and KPSS tests there is strong evidence that most of the variables are non-stationary (i.e. have unit root) at levels but are stationary at first difference (Table 2).

The next step involves investigating cointegration among the variables. The presence of cointegration implies that short-term disturbances that occur will not distort the long-run equilibrium relation that exists among variables. Due to the presence of a mixed series (I(0) and I(1)), we employ the Bounds testing approach to cointegration developed by Pesaran and Shin (1999) and Pesaran, Shin, and Smith (2001). This framework has a number of advantages over traditional cointegration models (such as Engle and Granger (1987) and Johansen and Juselius (1990)) some of which include; (1) appropriate for modeling limited data, (2) applicability in data with a mixture of series and (3) ease of interpretation.

The F-statistic is employed to ''bounds testing'' for the existence of a long-run relationship. The null hypothesis of the bounds test is the non-existence of a long run relationship. According to Pesaran, Shin, and Smith's (2001) critical values for F statistic, lower bound values assume all variables are I(0) while the upper bound values assume all variables are I(1). A calculated F statistic greater than the upper bound indicates significant long run relationship (i.e. rejecting the null hypothesis of no cointegration) otherwise we fail to reject the null hypothesis. However, if the F statistic falls within their respective bounds, inference would be inconclusive and requires in-depth knowledge about time series properties of the variables before reaching any conclusion. It is worth mentioning that we read Narayan's critical

Table 2. Unit root tests

	Deterministic Terms	DF-GLS	PP	KPSS
Levels				
lnGDPPC	Constant, Trend	-0.628	-0.257	0.207**
lnGCF	Constant, Trend	-2.344	-2.925	0.092
lnCPI	Constant, Trend	-3.568**	-4.204***	0.111
lnTR	Constant, Trend	-2.452	-1.873	0.101
lnPOP	Constant, Trend	-1.606	-1.822	0.102
lnETL	Constant, Trend	-2.354	-2.536	0.135**
lnURB	Constant, Trend	-3.384**	-2.552	0.146
$lnURB^2$	Constant, Trend	-3.298**	-2.695	0.161
First Differences				
ΔlnGDPPC	Constant	-3.463***	-3.945***	0.803***
ΔlnGCF	Constant	-0.811	-7.421***	0.177
ΔlnCPI	Constant	-8.790***	-10.023***	0.243
ΔlnTR	Constant	-4.255***	-4.002***	0.151
ΔlnPOP	Constant	-0.986	-2.408	0.083
ΔlnETL	Constant	-7.707***	-7.625***	0.087
ΔlnURB	Constant	-1.469	-1.616	0.322
$\Delta lnURB^2$	Constant	-1.363	-1.606	0.388*

Note: ***, **,* denote significance at 1%, 5% and 10% respectively

values instead of Pesaran, Shin, and Smith's (2001) table to correct for small sample bias which we encounter in our study. An F-statistic of 6.2815 and 5.7477 indicates long run relationship or cointegration among the variables (Table 3, Panel A). As shown in Table 3, panel B, the Bounds test passes all the diagnostic tests against serial correlation, non-normality, serial correlation and heteroscedasticity.

Although, the bounds test gives an indication of a long-run relationship among variables, it does not provide long-run estimates of individual variables (in equations (1) and (2)). Accordingly, we control for structural breaks using the Bai-Perron (1998) technique in an ordinary least square (OLS) framework so as to obtain long-run estimates. Unlike standard linear regression that assumes parameters to be stable over time, the Bai-Perron (1998) technique captures structural change or breaks in time series data which enables unbiased coefficients as well as enables us to draw accurate inferences. Additionally, what makes

Table 4. Multiple Breakpoint test

Break Test [Break dates]	F-Statistic	Scaled F-Statistic	Bai-Perron (2003) Critical Values
0 vs. 1 *	7.4752	29.9007	16.19
1 vs. 2*	3.9532	15.8126	18.11
Breaks: 1986			

Note: * denote significance at 5%; Bai-Perron test of L+1 vs. L sequentially determined breaks; Trimming 0.15, Max. breaks 5.

Table 3. Bounds Test for level relationship

Panel A: Bounds Test F-statistic					
99% Critical Values		95% Critical Values		90% Critical Values	
I(0)	I(1)	I(0)	I(1)	I(0)	I(1)
3.892	5.173	2.850	3.905	2.402	3.345
$F_{\ln GDPPC}(\text{lnGDPPC} \mid \text{lnGCF}, \text{lnCPI}, \text{lnTR}, \text{lnETL}) = 6.2815$					
$F_{\ln GDPPC}(\text{lnGDPPC} \mid \text{lnCPI}, \text{lnTR}, \text{lnETL}, \text{lnURB}) = 5.7477$					
Panel B: Diagnostic tests					
Breusch-Godfrey Serial Correlation LM Test			F-statistic = 0.3730 (0.6926)		
Jarque-Bera Normality Test			χ^2 (1) = 0.1856 (0.9114)		
ARCH LM Test			F-statistic = 0.1712 (0.6815)		
Ramsey REST Test			F-statistic = 3.0279 (0.0941)		
Breusch-Godfrey Serial Correlation LM Test			F-statistic = 1.941 (0.1685)		
Jarque-Bera Normality Test			χ^2 (1) = 1.096 (0.5782)		
ARCH LM Test			F-statistic = 1.8778 (0.1793)		
Ramsey REST Test			F-statistic = 0.4479 (0.6586)		

Note: I(0) denote lower bound and I(1) denote upper bound Narayan (2005) critical values, lag length k=4; p-values in parenthesis

Table 5. Multiple Breakpoint test

Break Test [Break dates]	F-statistic	Scaled F-statistic	Bai-Perron (2003) Critical Values
0 vs. 1 *	121.7322	365.1966	13.98
1 vs. 2*	18.663	55.989	15.72
2 vs. 3	3.1102	9.3306	16.83
Breaks: 1982,2007			

Note: * denote significance at 5%; Bai-Perron test of L+1 vs. L sequentially determined breaks; Trimming 0.15, Max. breaks 5

this methodology appealing is breakpoints are identified endogenously. The Bai-Perron (1998) test shows break at 1986 (for equation 1a and 2a, see Table 4).

Applying the test to equation (3a) reveal multiple breaks at 1982 and 2007 (Table 5).

RESULTS AND DISCUSSION

Empirical analysis

Results from Table 6 reveal that electric power transmission and distribution losses (ETL) do not have robust impact on economic growth. While ETL exhibit a positive and significant elasticity in over the period 1971-1985, it is insignificant in the latter years. This is consistent with conventional knowledge that losses are detrimental to growth. Moreover, Hulten's (1996) assertion that inefficient infrastructure use in low and middle income economies yields a low growth dividend is confirmed. The low growth dividend the Ghanaian economy experiences can also be attributed to the upward trending ETL (with the greatest loss of 2 billion in 2011 representing about 22% of output). Trade openness, however, has positive and significant effect on growth over the period 1971-2012. This suggests that trade policies undertaken during the Economic Recovery Programme (post 1983), have been beneficial to economic growth. Like ETL coefficients, gross capital formation and inflation are sensitive to structural breaks. For instance, prior to 1986 gross capital formation displayed a negative coefficient and a positive coefficient after 1985.

Afterwards, the square term of ETL was added to the equation (1) to investigate the threshold effects of ETL (see Table 7).

Strikingly, ETL^2exhibit a negative coefficient over the entire period 1971-2012 while ETL exhibit a positive and significant coefficient in both periods (1971-1985 and 1986-2012).A percentage increase in ETL^2 results in a 0.7119% decrease in economic growth, ceteris paribus. More importantly, the presence of $\beta_{ETL^2} < 0$ and $\beta_{ETL} > 0$ provides sufficient evidence of a threshold effect of ETL which is computed by finding the maximum value $V_{\max} = -\left(\beta_{urb} / 2\beta_{urb^2}\right)$. Thus, computing $V_{\max}$ we conclude that ETL and GDP per capita coefficients are peaked at the approximately 2.07 threshold level (see Figure 1); this implies that when ETL exceeds 2.07 growth declines steadily.

Next, recognizing the prominence of the rural-urban divide in the energy loss growth nexus we examine the interaction effect of URB and ETL. Table 8 reveals that the interaction effect between URB and ETL is negative. The effect of URB on the GDP per capita, when one considers the interaction term, is as follows:

Table 6. Long run estimates

PERIOD 1: 1971-1985			
DV:lnGDPPC	**C**	**t-stat**	**Prob.**
lnGCF	-0.2172	-0.3742	0.7106
lnCPI	0.5358	5.5212***	0.0000
lnTR	1.1415	2.6554**	0.0120
lnETL	0.6821	2.0408**	0.0491
PERIOD 2: 1986-2012			
	C	**t-stat**	**Prob.**
lnGCF	0.3025	0.5276	0.6012
lnCPI	0.2868	1.6216	0.1141
lnTR	1.0086	2.0346**	0.0497
lnETL	0.0376	0.3254	0.7469

Note: ***, **,* denote significance at 1%, 5% and 10% respectively; DV stands for dependent variable

Table 7. Long run estimates

PERIOD 1: 1971-1985			
DV:lnGDPPC	**C**	**t-stat**	**Prob.**
lnGCF	-0.0521	-0.1191	0.9060
lnCPI	0.3464	4.2457***	0.0002
lnTR	0.7544	2.2731**	0.0297
lnETL	2.8385	5.8537***	0.0000
PERIOD 2: 1986-2012			
	C	**t-stat**	**Prob.**
lnGCF	1.0459	2.3013**	0.0278
lnCPI	-0.1874	-1.1617	0.2537
lnTR	0.3106	0.7834	0.4390
lnETL	2.8899	5.2049***	0.0000
Non-Breaking Variables			
	C	t-stat	Prob.
$\ln ETL^2$	-0.7119	-5.2013***	0.0000

Note: ***, **,* denote significance at 1%, 5% and 10% respectively; DV stands for dependent variable

$$\frac{\partial GDP_{it}}{\partial URB_{it}} = 1.7297 - 0.2010 * \mathrm{ETL}_{it} \text{ Where } 0.687 < ETL_{it} < 3.362$$

Thus, when $ETL_{it} = 0.687$ the effect is 1.5916 and when $ETL_{it} = 3.362$ the effect equals 1.0539. As a result, urbanization has a larger positive effect (i.e. 1.5916) on GDP per capita in the presence of low ETL. In other words, higher ETL associates with an increasing negative effect on GDP per capita.

Figure 1. Relationship between GDP per capita and electric power transmission and distribution losses

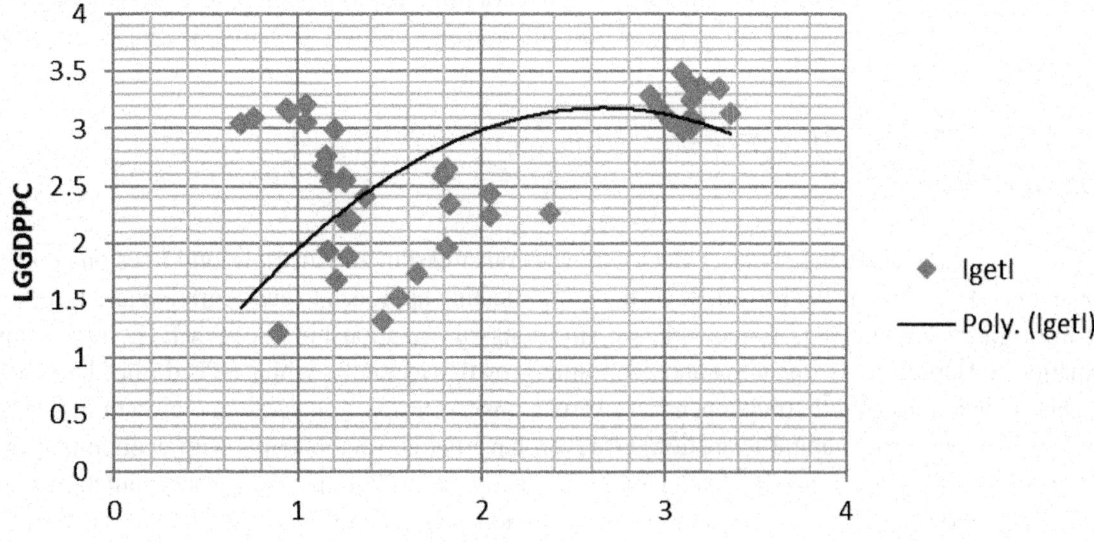

Table 8. Long run estimates

PERIOD 1: 1971-1981			
DV:lnGDPPC	**C**	**t-stat**	**Prob.**
lnCPI	-0.0760	-6.9581***	0.0000
lnTR	0.1239	6.6654***	0.0000
lnETL	0.7302	5.4897***	0.0000
PERIOD 2: 1982-2006			
	C	**t-stat**	**Prob.**
lnCPI	-0.0010	-0.7958	0.4322
lnTR	-0.0847	-5.5730***	0.0000
lnETL	0.7574	5.4909***	0.0000
PERIOD 2: 1987-2012			
	C	**t-stat**	**Prob.**
lnCPI	-0.0149	-0.2501	0.8041
lnTR	0.5021	4.1709	0.0002
lnETL	-0.0094	-0.0411	0.9675
Non-Breaking Variables			
	C	**t-stat**	**Prob.**
lnURB	1.7297	81.6497***	0.0000
lnURB*lnETL	-0.2010	-5.5624***	0.0000

Note: ***, **,* denote significance at 1%, 5% and 10% respectively; DV stands for dependent variable

Precisely, when ETL is greater than or equal to 8.43, more urbanization leads to lower GDP per capita. In simple terms, the degree of ETL moderates the effect of urbanization on economic growth; our results suggest that the degree of losses in electricity transmission and losses deters urbanization from promoting growth.

CONCLUSION

In this study we examine the effect of electric power transmission and distribution losses on economic growth over the period of 1971 to 2012. Using bounds testing approach to cointegration and Bai-Perron test in ordinary least squares framework, we find long-run relationship between ETL, gross capital formation, inflation, trade openness and economic growth. Secondly, while ETL do not have robust impact on economic growth, trade openness exerts a positive impact on economic growth in the long-run. Inflation and gross capital formation, however, have mixed relationships with economic growth. Furthermore, ETL yield a threshold value of 2.07. Finally, controlling for the urban population reveals that ETL moderates the relationship between urbanization and economic growth; higher ETL associates with an increasing negative effect on GDP per capita. These results suggest that although Ghana has not reached the threshold where electric power transmission and distribution losses significantly deter economic growth, the distance from the source as well as the demographic characteristics of the end market (rural-urban divide) determines the degree of loss and the cost of delivery of electricity which in turn impedes economic growth in the long-run.

In Ghana urbanization is an inevitable process- urban population in Ghana is growing at 4.4 percent annually, and, rising from under 4 million in 1984 to nearly 14 million people in 2013- therefore governments and policy makers need to put measures in place to make transmission lines in the rural areas available for connection to the national grid.

REFERENCES

Ackah, I., & Adu, F. (2014). The Impact of Energy Consumption and Total Factor Productivity on Economic Growth Oil Producing African Countries. *Bulletin of Energy Economics*, *2*(2), 28–40.

Adams, S., Klobodu, E. K. M., & Opoku, E. E. O. (2016). Energy consumption, political regime and economic growth in sub-Saharan Africa. *Energy Policy*, *96*, 36–44. doi:10.1016/j.enpol.2016.05.029

Agénor, P. R., & Moreno-Dodson, B. (2006). *Public Infrastructure and Growth: New Channels and Policy Implications* (World Bank Policy Research Working Paper 4064). Washington, DC: World Bank.

Ahmad, N., Hayat, M. F., Hamad, N., & Luqman, M. (2012). Energy consumption and economic growth: Evidence from Pakistan. *Australian Journal of Business and Management Research*, *2*(6), 9–14.

Barro, R., & Sala-i-Martin, X. (2005). *Growth Theory*. Cambridge, MA: MIT Press.

Bildirici, M. E. (2013). The analysis of relationship between economic growth and electricity consumption in Africa by ARDL method. *Energy Economics Letters*, *1*(1), 1–14.

Calderón, C., & Servén, L. (2008). *Infrastructure and economic development in Sub-Saharan Africa* (World Bank Policy Research Working Paper No. 4712). Washington, DC: World Bank.

Canning, D., & Pedroni, P. (2008). Infrastructure, long-run economic growth and causality tests for cointegrated panels. *The Manchester School*, *76*(5), 504–527. doi:10.1111/j.1467-9957.2008.01073.x

Chan, C., Forwood, D., Roper, H., & Sayers, C. (2009). *Public Infrastructure Financing: An International Perspective* (Productivity Commission Staff Working Paper). Retrieved from http://www.pc.gov.au/research/supporting/public-infrastructure-financing

Chintrakarn, P., & Herzer, D. (2012). More inequality, more crime? A panel cointegration analysis for the United States. *Economics Letters*, *116*(3), 389–391. doi:10.1016/j.econlet.2012.04.014

Ecobank. (2014). *Middle Africa Insight Series, Power*. Ecobank Research Division.

Esfahani, H. S., & Ramírez, M. T. (2003). Institutions, infrastructure, and economic growth. *Journal of Development Economics*, *70*(2), 443–477. doi:10.1016/S0304-3878(02)00105-0

Grubesic, T. H. (2009). The Management and Measurement of Infrastructure: Performance, Efficiency and Innovation. Growth and Change, 40(1), 184-187.

Herranz-Loncán, A. (2007). Infrastructure investment and Spanish economic growth, 1850–1935. *Explorations in Economic History*, *44*(3), 452–468. doi:10.1016/j.eeh.2006.06.002

Herzer, D., & Vollmer, S. (2012). Inequality and growth: Evidence from panel cointegration. *The Journal of Economic Inequality*, *10*(4), 489–503. doi:10.1007/s10888-011-9171-6

Hulten, C. R. (1996). *Infrastructure capital and economic growth: How well you use it may be more important than how much you have* (NBER Working Paper No. 5847). Cambridge, MA: National Bureau of Economic Research.

International Energy Agency (IEA). (2012). *World Energy Outlook 2012*. Retrieved from http://www.worldenergyoutlook.org/weo2014/

International Energy Agency (IEA). (2014). *World Energy Outlook 2014*. Retrieved from http://www.worldenergyoutlook.org/weo2014/

International Renewable Energy Agency (IRENA). (2012). *Prospects for the African Power Sector*. Abu Dhabi: IRENA. Retrieved from http://www.irena.org/menu/index.aspx?mnu=Subcat&PriMenuID=36&CatID=141&SubcatID=244

Jiménez, R., Serebrisky, T., & Mercado, J. (2014). Power lost: sizing electricity losses in transmission and distribution systems in Latin America and the Caribbean (Inter-American Development Bank (IDB) Monograph; 241). Washington, DC: IDB.

King, R. S., & Amponsah, O. (2012). The Role of City Authorities in Contributing to the Development of Urban Slums in Ghana. *Journal of Construction Project Management and Innovation*, *2*(1), 285–313.

Kouakou, A. K. (2011). Economic growth and electricity consumption in Cote dIvoire: Evidence from time series analysis. *Energy Policy*, *39*(6), 3638–3644. doi:10.1016/j.enpol.2011.03.069

KPMG. (2015). *Sector Report: Power in Africa.* Retrieved from http;//www. kpmg.com/africa

Kumo, W. L. (2012). *Infrastructure Investment and Economic Growth in South Africa: A Granger Causality Analysis* (African development Bank Group Working Paper Series 160). Tunis, Tunisia: African Development Bank.

Markard, J. (2009, September). *Characteristics of infrastructure sectors and implications for innovation processes* (Discussion Paper for the Workshop on Environmental Innovation in Infrastructure Sectors). Retrieved from http://citeseerx.ist.psu.edu/viewdoc/download?doi=10.1.1.476.1015&rep=rep1&type=pdf

Newbery, D. (2012). *Energy and infrastructure* (Submission to the LSE Growth Commission). Retrieved from http://tinyurl.com/c8qtahl

Ouedraogo, N. S. (2013). Energy consumption and economic growth: Evidence from the economic community of West African States (ECOWAS). *Energy Economics*, *36*, 637–647. doi:10.1016/j.eneco.2012.11.011

Pesaran, M. H., Shin, Y., & Smith, R. J. (2001). Bounds testing approaches to the analysis of level relationships. *Journal of Applied Econometrics*, *16*(3), 289–326. doi:10.1002/jae.616

Pokharel, B. (2010). *Power Shortage, its impacts and the Hydropower Sustainability Assessment Protocol: In the context of South Asia* (Master's Thesis). Retrieved from http://lnweb90.worldbank.org/exteu/SharePapers.nsf/(ID)/9FC30006ED600CA08525785E00780506/$File/nrsc_616_project_paper_bipin_pokharel.pdf

Romer, P. (1993). Idea gaps and object gaps in economic development. *Journal of Monetary Economics*, *32*(3), 543–573. doi:10.1016/0304-3932(93)90029-F

Seethepalli, K., Bramati, M. C., & Veredas, D. (2008). *How relevant is infrastructure to growth in East Asia?* (World Bank Policy Research Working Paper No. 4597). Washington, DC: World Bank.

Snieska, V., &Simkunaite, I. (2015). Socio-economic impact of infrastructure investments. *Engineering Economics, 63*(4), 16-25.

Straub, S. (2011). Infrastructure and development: A critical appraisal of the macro-level literature. *The Journal of Development Studies*, *47*(5), 683–708. doi:10.1080/00220388.2010.509785

Straub, S., Vellutini, C., & Warlters, M. (2008). *Infrastructure and economic growth in East Asia* (World Bank Policy Research Working Paper No. 4589). Washington, DC: World Bank.

World Bank. (2010). *Infrastructure and Growth.* Retrieved from http://go.worldbank.org/TQMEWOD650

World Bank. (2013a). *Energizing Economic Growth in Ghana: Making the Power and Petroleum Sectors Rise to the Challenge* (Report No. 79656). Washington, DC: World Bank.

World Bank. (2013b). *Energizing Economic Growth in Ghana: Making the Power and Petroleum Sectors Rise to the Challenge.* Retrieved from http://documents.worldbank.org/curated/en/485911468029951116/text/796560WP0P13140Box0377384B00PUBLIC0.txt

World Bank. (2015). *World Development Indicators 2015*. Washington, DC: World Bank.

World Bank. (2016). *Ghana Overview*. Retrieved from http://www.worldbank.org/en/country/ghana/overview

Yeaple, S. R., & Golub, S. S. (2007). International productivity differences, infrastructure, and comparative advantage. *Review of International Economics*, *15*(2), 223–242. doi:10.1111/j.1467-9396.2007.00667.x

KEY TERMS AND DEFINITIONS

Bai-Perron Test: It is an econometric technique used for identifying multiple structural breaks in time series data.

Bounds Test: Bounds testing approach to cointegration: An econometric methodology proposed by Pesaran, Shin and Smith (2001) used to assess long-run relationship between variables.

Cointegration: It is a process whereby linear combination of nonstationary time series results in a stationary linear combination.

Economic Growth: It is an increase in a country's productive capacity or output.

Electric Power Transmission and Distribution Losses: Electric power transmission and distribution losses to include losses in transmission between sources of supply and points of distribution and in the distribution to consumers, including pilferage.

Ordinary Least Squares: It is a technique for estimating unknown regression parameters by minimizing the sum of square the errors.

Threshold Value: The point or value that must be exceeded to begin producing a given effect.

Urbanization: It is a population shifts from rural to urban areas. In other words it is the gradual surge in the proportion of people living in urban areas.

Chapter 12
An Assessment of Infrastructural Facilities in the Dryland Areas of West Bengal

Nilendu Chatterjee
Rabindra Bharati University, India

ABSTRACT

The present chapter focuses on the importance of infrastructure in the dryland areas of West Bengal, India, covering four districts, namely, Purulia, Bankura, West Midnapore and Birbhum. The importance and necessity of having good infrastructure is a well-known phenomenon but it carries a special significance for the drylands, where good infrastructure can open various avenues of earning, communication, better life standard as well as management and nourishment of all types of natural resources in these areas. Sustainable use of natural resources occur utmost importance because it is the only source of livelihood for the people of these areas. Through this study, we have tried to make an assessment of the existing infrastructure scenarios in these four districts for the period 2003-04 to 2012-13. Doing the SWOT analysis amongst the districts, the results show that West Midnapur and Bankura are in a better position than Purulia and Birbhum, although, Birbhum is in a good position in few indicators.

INTRODUCTION

Infrastructure may be defined as the basic equipments and structures that are needed for a country or region for its upliftment. So, the basic physical and organizational structures and facilities needed for the operation of a society or enterprise may be termed as infrastructure. It includes transport facilities like roads, bridges, etc; water supply facilities, health facilities, education facilities and various other sectors needed for smooth running of life. The importance of infrastructure in economic development and welfare has been recognized and talked about over the last four decades. After the Second World War, especially, after the formation and independence of many poor third world countries, it was thought and modeled that the government should invest in economies for creating a conducive environment for private sector to grow. Gradually, this view has been represented as – infrastructure and its development is the sole

DOI: 10.4018/978-1-5225-2364-2.ch012

responsibility of the government, especially in the third world nations. Later, it has been realized that infrastructure needs to be divided into two parts- public works (mainly construction of infrastructure) and public service delivery (provision of utilities such as electricity and water).

In the era of inflation, public sector loss and global financial crisis, governments have been finding it tough to continue invest in infrastructure, especially in third world economies where such investments do not generate any revenue for the governments. This has resulted in cancellation of many projects. Governments, now-a-days are trying to change the mode of investment in infrastructure by involving private sector in it through public- private- partnership (PPP) and corporate social responsibility (CSR) models. However, these types of models have also fallen short of meeting the challenge. In spite of welcoming private entities in this field, broadly speaking, infrastructure development has remained as a public sector duty in several nations, including India, where after the initiation of market economy in 1991, social sector development has become one of the primary as well as basic areas for the government to focus.

If we look at drylands, we will see that the drylands make up over 40% of the earth's surface; around 2.3 billion people live in the drylands. Over one billion people from the developing world depend on the drylands' natural resources for their livelihoods; the majority of whom are at constant risk of food insecurity and poverty. The Drylands are home to the worlds poorest and most marginalized people, they are plagued with recurrent droughts and aridity, insufficient infrastructure and limited investment, the lowest level of renewable water supply and the highest population growth. Without the development of people residing in drylands, it is virtually impossible to achieve any development goals by any government. Development of infrastructure is the primary task for development of drylands. Poverty is the greatest threat of drylands. Investment in drylands has occurred in high potential areas. Along with poverty, drylands are cursed with multifarious infrastructure shortages such as lack of water, lack of irrigation, land degradation, food crisis, lack of roads, lack of markets, and lack of access to information and communication technologies. So, in short, people in the drylands have been living almost being separated from the rest of the world, or even from the nearby developed regions.

As a developing country, India is also faced with infrastructure issues which can be categorized into broad headings of quantity, quality, efficiency, delivery and financing. Inter-and intra-regional inequalities exist in access to even basic infrastructure facilities like water supply, electricity, road, housing, etc.

Most of the drought-prone areas are found in arid, semi-arid, and sub-humid regions of the country, which experience less than average annual rainfall. Broadly, the drought-affected areas in India can be divided into two tracts. The first tract comprising the desert and the semi-arid regions covers an area of 0.6 million sq. km. It is rectangle shaped area whose one side extends from Ahmedabad to Kanpur and the other from Kanpur to Jullundur. In this region, rainfall is less than 750mm and at some places it is even less than 400 mm. The second tract comprises the regions east of the Western Ghats up to a distance of about 300 km from coast. This area is known as the "rain shadow area" of the Western Ghats, rainfall in this region is less than 750mm and is highly erratic. This region is thickly populated and periodic droughts cause considerable suffering and distress.

Besides these two tracts of scarcity, there are many pockets of drought in India. Some of these are: Tirunelveli district, south of Vaigai River in Tamil Nadu, Coimbatore area in Kerala, Saurashtra and Kutch regions in Gujarat, Mirzapur plateau and Palamu regions in Uttar Pradesh, Purulia district of West Bengal.[1]

On the basis of the document regarding "State Agriculture Plan for West Bengal" [2]Bankura, Birbhum and West Midnapore districts have been identified as the districts containing red laterite soils which are coarse in texture, highly drained with honeycomb type of ferruginous concentration at a depth of 15cm to 30cm. Soils are acidic in nature and poor nutrient status limit crop productivity. The district of Purulia which is mostly a plateau, like the three other districts mentioned above, soils are acidic in nature and crop productivity is poor due to high slopes. Entire district of Purulia and parts of three other states can be combined together as "red laterite soil region" in West Bengal and here crop productivity is limited. The State Plan of West Bengal referred to the four districts together as "dryland areas of West Bengal" based on their nature of soil. Out of these dryland areas, Purulia is considered as arid zone and three other districts are considered as semi arid. The Dryland areas are evident if we have a look into the map of West Bengal showing its various agro-climatic sub regions as mentioned below. FAO's classification for categories of dryland areas are on the basis of P/PET ratio and also on the basis of rainfall (in mm.). The State Plan of West Bengal has considered FAO's classification. Additionally, the plan has classified agro-climatic region on the basis of soil contents.

These areas also constitute a part of 'Chhotonagpur plateau'.[3] These four districts are faced with more or less similar problems. Purulia, being in the arid zone, has severe water crisis but it has huge area under forestry. Other districts can be termed as semi arid for the nature of their soil and parts of them showing features of aridity.

These areas are blessed with forests which has been the primary source of livelihood of people in this part of the world but lack of accessibility with other parts of Bengal due to lack of proper infrastructural facilities has been holding them back. Everyone has accepted that investment in infrastructure for the development of drylands must be given utmost priority to provide them some sort of relief from their unviewable conditions. The problems of people residing in dryland areas are manifold. Due to scarcity of rainfall and dryness of atmosphere, people cannot depend on agriculture for their livelihood, like other parts of Bengal. Here, people mainly depend on forest and to some extent on wood works or stone works. Here, forest is also protected by the government and Joint Forest Management (JFM) groups. So, it cannot be used as wished, for the sake of its sustainability. So, people tend to go to nearby agro-based districts for getting seasonal employment. This does not serve their purpose. Lacks of irrigational facilities, lack of ground water availability, aridity and hardness of soil have contributed to lower agricultural facility here. All these have forced them to be forest dependent. There is lack of natural resources in these areas, but the existing ones have not been properly utilised owing to poor education, lack of awareness and confidence. These have caused many government sponsored development scheme to go wasted. Rain water could be stored to solve the problem to some extent, but that has not been done for so long, only recently started. Watersheds have not been maintained properly and manifold use of watersheds has led to depletion of water at the time of needs. About 80-85% of the livestock population of these areas is unproductive due to the lack of knowledge and aridity of soil, causing immense pressure on forest resources, while more than 85% of the rural population is underemployed. It is possible to make sustainable use of these natural resources through application of appropriate technology and use of idle labour force by enforcing various employment generation programmes. For ensuring success, it is necessary to support the beneficiaries with an appropriate technology package with critical inputs and build a strong infrastructure at various levels to provide necessary services. Development projects are often launched without proper planning. In the absence of an integrated approach to solve these multidimensional inter-related problems, sectoral development activities may not deliver desired outcomes. Apart from integration of various sectors, many of these projects also lack proper resource mobilization. In the absence of industries, rural development projects are not implemented on sound management principles taking into consideration the required inputs, technologies, human skills. To solve these problems, a strong development of infrastructure is needed at various levels. An ideal connection at all levels amongst various organization associated with development is badly needed to overcome these manifold problems of drylands. Apart from mobilizing people, infrastructure is also necessary to organize input supply, finance, and post production processing, sustainable use of soil; forests, water bodies and marketing of the produce. There is good scope of developing markets for selling the products produced here. The lack of proper infrastructural facilities make it very tough for the people of these areas to reach nearby markets with their products, or even development of market is hindered because of lack of infrastructure. Several attempts, programmes have been taken, both nationally as well as regionally, and many more are going on at present for improving the infrastructural situation of these areas. It cannot be denied that the conditions have improved to some extent but again, they are far below than the required levels, given the extreme poverty-stricken condition of people of these areas.

MOTIVATION OF THE CHAPTER

The motivation of our work generates from the above discussion. Dryland areas suffer from several problems that need to be addressed. Problem of availability of natural resources along with lack of availability of infrastructure makes it even tougher for people of these areas to earn their livelihoods. Development of infrastructure can open several income opportunities, but, in drylands, the absence of proper infrastructure limits that chance. To quote famous economist Dr. V.K.R.V. Rao, "the link between infrastructure and development is not a once for all affair. It is a continuous process and progress in development has to be preceded accompanied and followed by progress in infrastructure, if we are to fulfill our declared objectives of a self-accelerating process of economic development". Through this paper, we shall try to investigate how far infrastructure has developed in these four districts over the years. Development of infrastructure can solve many problems as seen from the history of development economics. Most of the existing studies have only focused on the importance and use of infrastructure but what role it can play in the development of dryland areas and contribute to the efficient use of the natural resources and thereby increase income opportunities in those areas that has been neglected. No work has focused on the infrastructure scenario of drylands of West Bengal and how it can play a role in the development of these areas. This chapter tries to throw light on that and fill that lacuna

DATA AND METHODOLOGY

In our entire work, we have used secondary data from different sources. For all-India data, we have used the source of planning commission as well as that of RBI for using different and changing definitions of Infrastructure in India. For analyzing the condition of infrastructure in the dryland areas of West Bengal, we have used the secondary data provided by the Bureau of Applied Economics and Statistics. Only for analyzing the condition of various angles of infrastructure related to irrigation, we have used the data for the time-period 1998-99 to 2012-13. But, for the rest of the analysis, on various other types of infrastructure, we have used the data for 2003-04 to 2012-13, covering 10 years.

We have adopted a very simple methodology of only describing and analyzing the data on various types of infrastructure. This should help in understanding the real situation of infrastructure in the dryland areas of West Bengal.

REVIEW OF RELATED LITERATURE

We, for the sake of simplicity, have divided the literature survey segment into two streams- one emphasizes on the literatures on India and the other section reviews the literature of the rest of the world.

Indian Evidence

Lall (2006) has taken a pooled dataset of Indian states and shown that the spending on transport and communications infrastructure are significant determinants of regional growth. There are also positive externalities from investments by local and neighbouring states.

Agarwalla (2011) has shown the importance and necessity of infrastructure investment for removing regional disparities and inequalities in India. She has shown how infrastructure plays a vital role in contributing to the growth of productivity in Indian states. She has done her analysis by using data from 25 states covering two decades and found a positive relation between infrastructure investment and regional productivity growth.

Taqvi (2013) has also emphasized on the importance of investment on infrastructure in India. His work tells that if India properly invests in the development of infrastructure, especially in urban infrastructure since the pressure of urban economy is very high, then it can certainly become one of the dominating forces in the world by fully utilizing its resources. But, that is not happening as the supply of infrastructure investment is far below than its demand at present.

Nanda (2015) has shown the role of public-private partnership in the development of infrastructure. He has highlighted the concept and status of PPP model in this nation by analyzing various infrastructural projects and plans that are presently going on as well as those emerging areas where this model can be applied.

Panigrahi and Beura (2013) have made a study on infrastructure financing in India. Their work is exploratory in nature. They have viewed infrastructure as a crucial pillar for development in this nation by its twin effects- attracting FDI and reducing poverty. The authors have identified resource constraint as the crucial factor for deficit of infrastructure in India. They have pointed out that stable exchange rate, mild inflation, clarity of taxation rules, fiscal discipline & sustainability of economic policy create investment climate in India. They believe that public-private-partnership (PPP) model is the best for financing infrastructure in India but the success of that depends upon the effectiveness of bond market as well as pricing policy of infrastructure. They have also recommended that inadequate allocation of fuel to the power stations, delay in environment clearances, issues in the land acquisition, absence of credible dispute resolution mechanism are the technical barriers of investment in infrastructure. Finally, they have suggested setting up an infrastructure fund for those infrastructure sectors in which private participation is negligible along with amendment of company act 2013 for more participation of corporate sector in infrastructure development.

World Evidence

In the year 1994 The World Bank has provided a new dynamics about infrastructure from the point of view of availability, efficiency and financing. They had defined infrastructure as a combination of both public services (comprising of water, energy and electricity) and public works (such as rail, roads, etc).

Aschauer (1998) has commented that large public investments are not the sufficient condition for economic growth. He has done his work on Mexico. He has referred that public investment in infrastructure must be accompanied by proper policies regarding use and financing of infrastructural goods.

Devarajan, Swaroop and Zhou (1996) have found a negative and significant relationship between economic growth and transport and communications expenditures-to-total expenditures ratio in their sample of countries, and contributed this to the possibility that over investment in transport and communications makes such expenditures relatively unproductive.

Canning and Pedroni, in 2008, have analyzed a panel data set of various nations covering the time period from 1950-1992. They have shown that there is no long-run relationship between infrastructure and economic growth. But, this result also varied across nations, as they have found infrastructure is undersupplied in few nations but oversupplied in others.

Straub, Vellutini and Warlters (2008) have shown, for East Asia, that the failure to find a significant link between infrastructure, productivity and growth may arise because investments in infrastructure were made to relieve constraints and bottlenecks (where they existed) rather than to directly encourage growth.

In their time-series analysis in 2006, Nketiah-Amponsah has shown that government expenditure resulted negatively on economic growth in Ghana from 1970-2004. But, in short run, health and infrastructure expenditures positively influenced growth, but education expenditure did the opposite.

Rioja (2001) did his computable general equilibrium analysis on Brazil, Peru and Mexico. He found that these nations under invested in infrastructure in the decade of 1970's. He has found that infrastructure can have a positive influence on growth, welfare and private investment.

Dissou and Didic (2011) have shown that the crowding out effects of public infrastructure is sensitive to the mode of financing selected by the government. Overall, their findings have shown that public investment in infrastructure can support private investment and sustain capital accumulation. The positive impact of public investment on private investment can be explained through the infrastructure financing channels such as public private partnerships and subcontracting which in turn tend to crowd-in private investment.

Ramirez (2004) have questioned stabilization policies in developing countries which disproportionately reduce public infrastructure spending in order to comply with reductions in fiscal deficits, because of terms of trade shocks owing to globalization.

Dodonov et al (2002) have done his analysis on transitional countries. They have shown that infrastructure reform in these nations must be complemented with tax reforms. A failure to do so may lead to a fall in infrastructure by both public and private sectors.

Ehlers (2014) has identified few important obstacles for greater and better infrastructure investment and finance. He believes this is important as infrastructure investment is being hold back even though long run real interest rates are low and potential long term supply of money is ample. One such obstacle is the lack of investable projects. Often, projects are not properly designed and contractual arrangements imply a distribution of risks and returns that create the wrong incentives among the various partners. He thinks involving private sector and proper designing of infrastructural projects can remove such problems. A pipeline of investable projects would allow large investors to commit a greater share of their financial resources to infrastructure. Tapping the vast resources of capital markets, could significantly boost infrastructure finance. A greater variety of financial instruments for infrastructure finance would help to make infrastructure more attractive for a broader group of investors and would allow a better diversification of risks.

STATE OF INFRASTRUCTURE IN INDIA AND WEST BENGAL

The Harmonized Master List of 29 infrastructure sub-sectors was notified by the Government of India on 27th March, 2012 and was subsequently updated vide its Gazette Notifications dated April 5, 2013 and May 9, 2013. RBI further expanded the definition on September 18, 2013. As per the expanded definition of infrastructure, it comprises of following categories: a) Energy, b) Communication, c) Transport, d) Water & Sanitation, e) mining, exploration and refining, and f) Social & Commercial infrastructure and various infrastructure subsectors are included within each category. On 6th January, 2014, this definition was further expanded to include 'Maintenance, Repairs and Overhaul' (MRO) as a part of airport infrastructure.[4]

In India, the state or condition of infrastructure is still far below than what is required. Apart from few metropolitan cities, the status of infrastructure is lagging behind even in small towns and especially in villages. The effort has been going on to improve the scenario through various government and PPP model projects but they are falling short of expectations because in a developing nation like this, the need for better infrastructural facilities has always been rising and this trend will continue.

The government of India has published several "Infrastructure Development Report" starting from 2001, but every time focusing on different sub-sector of the item. For example, the first report in 2001 was on "Issues in Regulation and Market Structure", in 2006, it was on "Urban Infrastructure", the next year's (2007) report was on "Rural Infrastructure", the areas of Education and Health were given priority in the report in 2012 and 2013 respectively. If we look from the world standard, we will see that according to the Global Competitiveness Reports, India has shown signs of improvement in 2015-16 by getting the rank of 55 (out of 140 countries), with a total score of 4.3 out of 7, jumping from the rank 71 of the previous year's report. But, this rank in 2012-13 and 2013-14 was 59 and 60 respectively. So, one can see a ray of hope through this ranking improvement, after two successive years of drop in ranks. But, the rank of infrastructure, considered as the 2nd pillar of development by the report, is still 71 with a score of only 4.0. This is a matter of great worry for all of us. Within infrastructure, the ranks of few sub-sectors are as follows- Quality of roads (61), Quality of railroad infrastructure (29), Quality of port infrastructure (60), Quality of air-transport infrastructure (71), Quality of electricity supply (98).[5]

If we look at the investment pattern on infrastructure in India over the plan periods, we will see that it has always increased. Most of it has been by the public sector, as up to 1991, the nation was almost entirely dominated by the government. Private sector was there but there role was very insignificant. After the initiation of globalization process in 1991, the role of private sector became prominent and started to become visible in infrastructure development. Very recently, over the last decade or so, the PPP model of infrastructural projects started to take place. This has paced up the investment in infrastructure but they have fallen short of expectation. Table 1 gives the pattern of investment in infrastructure in India, since 1951, the beginning of First Five Years' plan.

We have presented the data of last three plans, that is, 10th plan, 11th plan and ongoing 12th plan separately because from the beginning of 2000, private sector started to take significant part in infrastructure.

The following tables and figures describe the investment of private and public sectors in the last three plans. These figures would help us to understand how private sector has been coming up, gradually but surely.

The following table (Table-2) shows that not only private sector is growing up but also growing up by leaps and bounds. It has helped the total investment plan to increase more than six times over the

Table 1. Investment in Infrastructure, as a percentage of total plan outlay, in India over the planning periods

Items	1st FYP	2nd FYP	3rd FYP	4th FYP	5th FYP	6th FYP	7th FYP	8th FYP	9th FYP
Irrigation	16%	9.2%	7.8%	8.6%	9.8%	10.0%	7.6%	7.5%	7.42%
Power	13%	9.7%	14.6%	18.6%	18.8%	28.1%	28.1%	26.6%	26.47%
Transport & Communication	27%	27%	24.6%	19.5%	17.4%	16.2%	17.4%	18.4%	21.3%
Social services & Others	23%	18.3%	17.4%	18.9%	17.3%	15.4%	16.7%	18.2%	23.84%

Source: Planning Commission[6]

Table 2. Investment by Centre, States and Private Sectors in the last three Plans (figures in the brackets indicate percentage share of total investment in infrastructure)

	10th Plan (Actual)	11th Plan (Anticipated)	12th Plan (Projected)
Centre	$68 billion (42%)	$165 billion (35%)	$308 billion (29%)
States	$57 billion (36%)	$131 billion (28%)	$248 billion (23%)
Private	$36 billion (22%)	$171 billion (37%)	$516 billion (48%)
Total	$161 billion	$466 billion	$1072 billion

Source: Planning Commission

last decade and private sector is sharing the responsibility of infrastructure development almost equally with central and state governments by investing 48% of the total investment in the ongoing 12th plan.

Table 3 depicts sector wise investment in infrastructure in the 12th plan (2012-17). The data do show the signs of improvements but the bulk of the investment by private sector has been in the profit earning areas, that is, not in the unproductive areas like rural infrastructure. This is supported by the Figure 1.

Table 3. Investment in different sectors of infrastructure in the 12th plan

Sectors	Investment amount (Rs. Crore)	Share (%)
Electricity	1820292	32.7%
Roads & Bridges	914536	16.4%
Telecommunications	943899	16.9%
Railways	643379	11.5%
Irrigation (including watershed)	504371	9.0%
Water supply& sanitation	255319	4.6%
Ports	197781	3.5%
Airports	87714	1.6%
Storage	148933	2.7%
Oil & Gas pipeline	58441	1.0%
Grand Total	5574663	100%

Source: Planning Commission

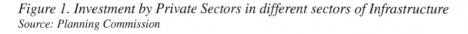

Figure 1. Investment by Private Sectors in different sectors of Infrastructure
Source: Planning Commission

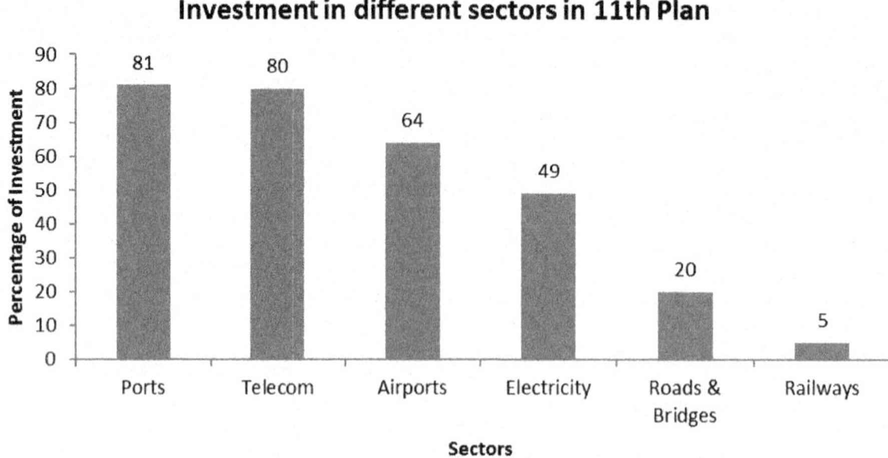

This is very interesting because if this trend of growth of investment by private sector continues, then it will benefit the richer section of the society as well as the investors as they will get good profit in return, but the backward areas and the people living there will become deprived of basic amenities and become more poorer.

If we look at West Bengal, we will see that it still has half of the rural population under poverty and in our study area this number is even higher. Lack of infrastructure and depriviation from the basic amenities of life for people living here is a well-known story world over. Their depriviation has led to many agitations that has forced all types of organisational bodies to draw attention to them. Over the last few years there have been few signs of improvements like establishing watersheds, building roads, schools, etc. The role of few ongoing industrial parks (two plastic and steel industrial projects in Barjora; Bankura, three projects on Steel, power and cement in West Medinipur) can also be important. But, these are not enough for the very poor people of these areas. They need more of these as the dryness of these areas coupled with lack of variety of natural resources has forced them to highly depend on forest resource only.

ASSESSMENT OF INFRASTRUCTURAL FACILITIES IN THE DRYLANDS OF WEST BENGAL

In this section, we shall look at the available infrastructure facilities of the four districts constituting the dryland areas, namely, Purulia, Bankura, West Midnapore and Birbhum one by one.

Infrastructure of Bankura

Table 4 gives a description about the areas irrigated by different sources in this district from 1998-99 to 2012-13, covering 15 years time span. This should give us a good idea about agricultural facilities.

In Table 5, we have shown the number of these sources of irrigation in Bankura district. STW and ODW hold the respective highest numbers in irrigation component in the district.

Table 4. Irrigation of land from different sources in Bankura (in thousand Hectares) from 1998-99 to 2012-13

Year	Govt. canal	Tank	HDTW	MDTW	LDTW	STW	RLI	ODW	OTHERS	TOTAL
1998-99	187.00	44.70	1.79	1.22	14.10	94.06	5.32	4.60	16.81	369.60
1999-2000	205.20	44.60	1.51	1.41	16.20	93.65	5.40	6.10	17.93	392.00
2000-01	151.00	39.50	1.51	1.56	17.40	93.06	5.83	4.30	18.62	332.78
2001-02	183.60	36.20	1.52	1.68	20.30	87.69	5.94	5.20	9.97	352.10
2002-03	152.73	40.46	1.53	1.84	18.96	98.10	3.81	5.86	8.84	332.13
2003-04	109.02	26.74	1.02	1.36	7.49	44.25	4.18	2.66	5.96	202.68
2004-05	109.89	32.35	0.50	1.45	0.68	47.98	7.28	2.17	6.32	208.62
2005-06	176.29	33.11	0.47	1.46	0.70	47.43	5.38	2.52	6.20	273.55
2006-07	180.35	33.47	0.53	1.49	1.35	45.91	5.08	2.49	6.28	276.94
2007-08	195.93	32.76	0.76	2.50	1.14	48.71	9.67	3.36	6.21	301.04
2008-09	180.60	35.18	0.95	2.50	1.14	55.32	11.57	3.58	6.68	297.52
2009-10	152.04	35.02	0.95	2.50	1.14	56.45	10.30	3.43	5.20	267.03
2010-11	26.36	19.29	1.03	2.54	1.16	50.80	6.24	2.01	5.77	115.20
2011-12	183.21	27.80	0.80	2.94	1.42	54.49	8.88	2.42	6.33	288.29
2012-13	153.32	29.19	0.80	2.94	1.42	53.18	19.04	2.37	6.59	268.85

Source: Bureau of Applied Economics and Statistics, West Bengal[7]

Table 5. Irrigation of land from different sources in Bankura (in Numbers)

Year	Tank	HDTW	MDTW	LDTW	STW	RLI	ODW	OTHERS
1998-99	22328	41	76	118	130	197	1479	6859
1999-00	22438	42	77	147	153	224	1479	3702
2000-01	21351	42	75	171	148	232	1479	751
2001-02	21391	41	85	164	151	232	1479	912
2002-03	21392	38	102	1065[8]	25930[9]	236	7379[10]	969
2003-04	20716	38	104	173	27445	281	6765	791
2004-05	20952	38	104	173	27754	353	7049	1065
2005-06	20957	38	104	173	27785	354	7084	1179
2006-07	20977	38	104	173	27798	355	7106	1190
2007-08	21006	38	125	190	28700	386	7257	1191
2008-09	21006	38	125	190	28870	434	7257	1195
2009-10	21011	38	125	190	28890	436	7272	1191
2010-11	21293	41	127	194	29634	438	6089	1676
2011-12	21343	32	147	237	29700	438	6101	1681
2012-13	21409	32	147	237	29887	473	6119	1736

Source: Bureau of Applied Economics and Statistics, West Bengal

The Table 4 shows that irrigation (in hectares) has shown up and down during times, if we look at the sources separately. The down swing is due to severe droughts; this proves that droughts occur very frequently. Figure 2 present the shape of the total irrigation in Bankura over years. It has a downward trend up to the period 2010-11 and then it took the upward movement.

The data of numbers of sources also show the same trend, what is interesting to see is that the private efforts to irrigate have been much more visible than that by the government. The numbers of sources have remained almost constant or shown slight increase. Whenever the private numbers are taken together, it has shown significant increase in numbers. So, the governments' effort towards investment in improvement of infrastructure related to irrigational or agricultural development have not been that good so far.

The improvement of transportation is one of the main indicators for infrastructural development.

Table 6 shows that there has been significant rise in the roads maintained by gram panchayats and PMGSY scheme but Zilla Parishads have not performed their tasks well enough, leading to a fall in the kilometers of roads maintained by them. The fall in the roads maintained by P.W.D has started to fall after 2011-12 because of the transfer of authority of maintenance to other agencies.

Forestry is an important aspect of Bankura. Its development and revenue earned from forestry is also important for the sustainable development of forestry. A part of revenue earned from forestry is distributed by government to Joint Forest Management (J.F.M.) committees for development of infrastructure in the forests and nearby forest villages. All these elements are described in the following table. (Table 7).

From Table 7, it is apparent that expenditure is much higher than revenue earned. So, here forestry runs in subsidies. Also, the production of Non-timber is very high compared to that of timber. There is absence of private bodies in forest-owner category. So, from these figures it is appearing that there is scope for developing forests in these areas and the government has been doing that by providing subsidies.

Figure 2. Total irrigation in Bankura

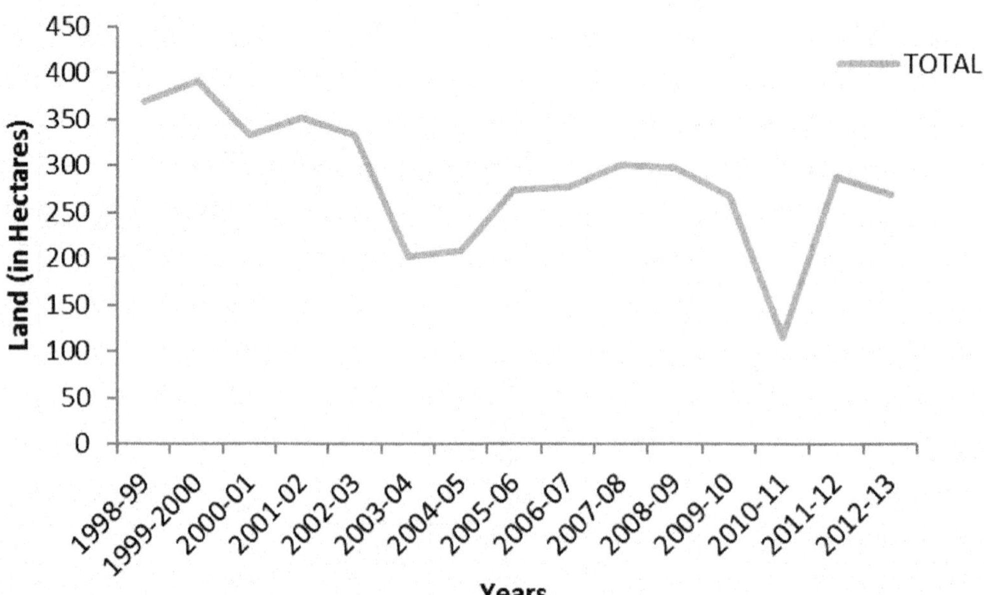

Table 6. Length of Roads Maintained by Public Works Department (P.W.D), Zilla Parishad and Panchayat in Bankura (in Kilometers) from 2003-04 to 2012-13

Year	P.W.D			Zilla Parishad			Gram Panchayats			P.M.G.S.Y[11]		
	Surfaced	Unsurfaced	Total	Surfaced	Unsurfaced	Total	Surfaced	Unsurfaced	Total	Surfaced	Unsurfaced	Total
03-04	1164.00	22.00	1186.00	549.90	690.70	1240.60	94.16	6360.32	6454.48	..	-	..
04-05	1164.00	22.00	1186.00	571.70	732.75	1304.45	133.16	6680.00	6813.16	..	-	..
05-06	1170.00	16.00	1186.00	573.70	742.00	1315.70	147.16	6949.00	7096.16	..	-	..
06-07	1177.00	15.00	1192.00	578.70	699.88	1278.58	186.56	7078.00	7264.56	51.22	-	51.22
07-08	1183.00	14.00	1197.00	582.95	539.18	1122.13	202.48	7255.00	7457.48	207.67	-	207.67
08-09	1184.00	15.00	1199.00	590.35	532.78	1123.13	202.48	7377.00	7579.48	672.39	-	672.39
09-10	1186.00	16.00	1202.00	635.91	493.96	1129.87	224.23	7487.00	7711.23	727.98	-	727.98
10-11	1189.00	15.00	1204.00	651.95	478.02	1129.97	242.23	7629.00	7871.23	830.20	-	830.20
11-12	1160.00	-	1160.00	714.54	449.98	1164.52	246.15	8007.00	8253.15	876.71	-	876.71
12-13	..	..	..	719.23	398.02	1117.25	267.95	8250.00	8517.95	946.17	-	946.17

Source: Bureau of Applied Economics and Statistics, West Bengal

Infrastructure of Purulia

We shall, now, see the condition of infrastructure in Purulia by the help of same parameters as in the case of Bankura (see Table 8).

Table 9 gives the numbers of the above sources of irrigation for Purulia district. The table makes one thing clear, that is, the situation of irrigational infrastructure is really very poor in Purulia. The unavailability of ground water has caused the absence of tubewells. The numbers of sources are also very low. Only positive thing is that after 2004-05, there has been an upsurge in the total irrigated land, except in 2010-11 because of severe drought.

Now, we look at the transport infrastructure of Purulia district. Table 10 depicts the same. Here the numbers are quite satisfactory to some extent, except the role of Zilla Parishads and Gram panchayats who have performed quite poorly for few years in succession. But, the role of P.M.G.S.Y scheme is being performed well enough.

Forestry, the most important aspect of natural resource of Purulia, does have an important impact on the lives of people living here. Forest Department does play a vital role in the development of this district. Table 11 describes the condition of forestry in this district.

Like Bankura, here also the forestry sector is running under huge subsidy. So, there is effort, on part of the government, to improve forestry. What is interesting is that there was existence of private ownership of forest in Purulia but it is no longer in existence.

Table 7. Forest Area, Forest Produce, Revenue and Expenditure from Forestry in Bankura from (2003-04 to 2012-13)

Item	Unit	03-04	04-05	05-06	06-07	07-08	08-09	09-10	10-11	11-12	12-13
Reserved Forest	Hectare	8004	3889	3889	3889	4449	4449	4449	4572	4572	4572
Protected Forest	,,	131119	131199	131199	131199	132002	132002	132002	136230	136230	136230
Unclasse-d State Forest	,,	9054	7756	7756	7756	2713	2713	2713	2238	2238	2238
Khas Forest	,,	-	-	-	-	-	-	-	-	-	-
Vested Waste Land	,,	-	-	-	-	-	-	-	-	-	-
Forest owned by Corporates	,,	-	-	-	-	-	-	-	-	-	-
Forest owned by Individuals	,,	-	-	-	-	-	-	-	-	-	-
Total	,,	**148177**	**142844**	**142844**	**142844**	**139164**	**139164**	**139164**	**143040**	**143040**	**143040**
Forest produce	Thousand cubic meters										
Timber	,,	4.89	6.287	5.546	5.56	5.011	5.38	4918.41	546.63	840.44	765.51
Non-timber	,,	51.723	46.760	44.686	21.684	6.965	13.99	8945.43	950.23	3597.23	2532.54
Revenue earned	Thousand Rs	15032	14378	30823	30619	59207	68491	148972	170799	181725	210569
Expenditure	,,	70318	60958	105286	142740	203087	182203	543342	631482	487296	158652

Source: Bureau of applied Economics and Statistics, West Bengal

Infrastructure of West Midnapore

Now, we shall move towards West Midnapore to see its infrastructural conditions. Like other districts, we first look at the irrigational condition. Table 12 presents the results. Keeping aside the extreme drought of 2010-11, this district has performed fairly well regarding irrigation, although there were few years of poor performance in between good seasons, like other two districts.

Let us check the numbers of sources of irrigation in Table 13. We can see that the number of sources of irrigation has varied over the years but the number of tanks has gone down consistently, but, that of other sources have fluctuated year by year, showing ups and downs.

Next, we shall focus on transport condition of this district. Table 14 presents the data. The roles of various organizations have been quite satisfying as seen from the table. All the bodies have consistently done well.

Next we shall focus on forestry, as forest covers a huge area in this district and it is one of the main available natural resources of this district. From Table 15, we observe that the district shows good figures regarding the forest area, its produce and revenue generation. Like other districts, discussed earlier, a huge subsidy is given by the governments to run forestry sector, indicating the scope and effort for further improvement.

Table 8. Irrigation of land from different sources in Bankura (in thousand Hectares) from 1998-99 to 2012-13

Year	Govt. canal	Tank	HDTW	MDTW	LDTW	STW	RLI	ODW	OTHERS	TOTAL
1998-99	28.38	32.09	--	--	--	--	1.98	11.17	11.21	84.83
1999-2000	29.45	28.95	--	--	--	--	5.09	5.16	13.38	82.03
2000-01	27.33	27.81	--	--	--	--	1.39	1.02	12.71	70.26
2001-02	23.76	22.44	--	--	--	--	1.04	1.09	3.01	51.34
2002-03	23.76	22.80	--	--	--	--	1.43	1.02	2.96	51.97
2003-04	29.06	27.14	-	-	-	-	1.12	3.99	4.59	65.90
2004-05	29.82	27.76	-	-	-	-	0.93	4.05	3.19	65.75
2005-06	30.29	28.31	-	-	-	-	1.32	3.42	8.79	72.13
2006-07	28.83	28.85	-	-	-	-	0.97	3.44	9.04	71.13
2007-08	28.87	37.60	-	-	-	-	0.91	3.44	9.22	80.04
2008-09	30.36	46.86	-	-	-	-	0.70	3.45	10.02	91.39
2009-10	27.66	53.16	-	-	-	-	0.73	3.45	10.84	95.84
2010-11	8.90	60.21	-	-	-	-	1.14	3.45	12.13	85.83
2011-12	30.79	70.75	-	-	-	-	8.12	3.45	13.48	126.59
2012-13	31.85	82.22	-	-	-	-	0.92	3.45	15.31	133.75

Source: Bureau of Applied Economics and Statistics, West Bengal

Table 9. Irrigation of land from different sources in Purulia (in Numbers)

Year	Tank	HDTW	MDTW	LDTW	STW	RLI	ODW	OTHERS
1998-99	9225	--	--	--	--	135	7088	405
1999-00	9201	--	--	--	--	135	7120	518
2000-01	9203	--	--	--	--	132	7125	521
2001-02	9273	--	--	--	--	147	4218	577
2002-03	9273	--	--	--	--	135	4490	579
2003-04	9279	-	-	-	-	135	4218	596
2004-05	9404	-	-	-	-	135	4218	583
2005-06	9470	-	-	-	-	217	4294	650
2006-07	9540	-	-	-	-	135	4294	719
2007-08	9593	-	-	-	-	135	4306	723
2008-09	9772	-	-	-	-	135	4312	736
2009-10	9963	-	-	-	-	135	4312	750
2010-11	9972	-	-	-	-	135	4312	772
2011-12	10190	-	-	-	-	135	4312	802
2012-13	10441	-	-	-	-	135	4312	835

Source: Bureau of Applied Economics and Statistics, West Bengal

Table 10. Length of Roads Maintained by Public Works Department (P.W.D), Zilla Parishad and Panchayat in Purulia (in Kilometers) from 2003-04 to 2012-13

Year	P.W.D			Zilla Parishad			Gram Panchayats			P.M.G.S.Y		
	Surfaced	Unsurfaced	Total	Surfaced	Unsurfaced	Total	Surfaced	Unsurfaced	Total	Surfaced	Unsurfaced	Total
03-04	847.00	2.00	849.00	803.20	815.59	1618.79	694.00	3361.00	4055.00	..	-	..
04-05	847.00	2.00	849.00	884.20	734.59	1618.79	694.00	3361.00	4055.00	..	-	..
05-06	847.00	2.00	849.00	986.20	649.92	1636.12	697.00	3378.00	4075.00	..	-	..
06-07	849.00	4.00	853.00	940.73	535.09	1475.82	697.00	3378.00	4075.00	162.50	-	162.50
07-08	854.00	3.00	857.00	833.23	527.09	1360.32	702.00	3397.00	4099.00	278.00	-	278.00
08-09	855.00	4.00	859.00	852.98	430.69	1283.67	711.00	3363.99	4074.99	384.66	-	384.66
09-10	856.00	5.00	861.00	881.48	388.44	1269.92	716.00	3147.24	3863.24	472.96	-	472.96
10-11	857.00	6.00	863.00	889.48	424.31	1313.79	716.00	3147.24	3863.24	561.26	-	561.26
11-12	883.00	-	883.00	897.48	416.31	1313.79	789.17	3189.07	3978.24	642.42	-	642.42
12-13	..	..	..	897.48	416.31	1313.79	1065.79	3929.55	4995.34	706.28	-	706.28

Source: Bureau of Applied Economics and Statistics, West Bengal

Table 11. Forest Area, Forest Produce, Revenue and Expenditure from Forestry in Purulia from (2003-04 to 2012-13)

Item	Unit	03-04	04-05	05-06	06-07	07-08	08-09	09-10	10-11	11-12	12-13
Reserved Forest	Hectare	10435.62	10435.62	10435.62	10435.62	10435.62	10435.62	10435.62	10435.62	10435.62	10435.62
Protected Forest	,,	56184.66	56184.66	56264.66	56264.66	56184.66	56264.00	56264.00	56264.66	56264.66	56264.66
Unclasse-d State Forest	,,	26427.07	26427.07	26438.67	26602.71	26602.71	26602.65	26596.65	26441.40	26441.40	26441.40
Khas Forest	,,	22274.59	22274.99	22274.99	22274.59	22274.99	22274.99	22274.99	34191.05	34191.05	34191.05
Vested Waste Land	,,	-	-	-	-	-	-	-	175.64	175.64	175.64
Forest owned by Corporates	,,	-	-	2.00	2.00	-	-	-	-	-	-
Forest owned by Individuals	,,	790.00	4500.00	4500.00	..	2020.00	2530.00	1660.00	-	-	-
Total	,,	**116111.94**	**119822.34**	**119915.94**	**115579.58**	**117517.98**	**118107.26**	**117231.26**	**127508.37**	**127508.37**	**127508.37**
Forest produce	Thousand cubic meters										
Timber	,,	0.625	0.508	0.744	0.351	0.360	0.300	0.332	0.069	0.066	0.623
Non-timber	,,	4.877	4.226	10.651	6.759	6.386	2.062	11.659	2.217	1.526	4.719
Revenue earned	Thousand Rs	6110	4160	3720	4809	4259	5589	7227	9653	15162	4192
Expenditure	,,	34196	108031	106698	121298	172528	215539	326512	502559	258205	104791

Source: Bureau of Applied Economics and Statistics, West Bengal

Table 12. Irrigation of land from different sources in West Midnapur (in thousand Hectares) from 2000-01 to 2012-13[12]

Year	Govt. Canal	Tank	HDTW	MDTW	LDTW	STW	RLI	ODW	OTHERS	TOTAL
2000-01	133.31	33.46	9.78	@	@[13]	116.01	14.13	#[14]	50.15	356.84
2001-02	142.15	26.38	8.26	20.71	$[15]	114.60	14.00	8.35	47.02	381.47
2002-03	108.28	22.09	8.11	18.52	0.52	132.39	16.52	9.64	29.24	345.31
2003-04	90.71	24.70	8.59	22.97	0.59	112.93	15.69	9.91	37.70	323.79
2004-05	66.11	24.70	8.59	22.97	0.59	112.93	15.69	9.91	37.70	299.19
2005-06	153.87	24.70	8.59	22.97	0.59	113.07	15.69	9.85	42.45	391.78
2006-07	160.70	25.31	8.18	31.76	0.54	133.37	15.94	10.57	41.75	428.12
2007-08	163.73	25.31	7.88	31.70	0.54	123.37	16.24	10.57	41.75	421.09
2008-09	137.10	40.11	8.18	31.70	0.54	108.57	15.94	10.57	41.75	394.46
2009-10	121.22	26.38	9.10	48.20	1.72	105.16	17.81	8.94	18.68	357.21
2010-11	19.02	26.51	9.63	66.19	2.28	103.69	14.81	6.47	19.32	267.92
2011-12	118.45	25.92	9.87	75.41	4.90	104.33	13.06	6.26	19.93	378.13
2012-13	105.55	25.04	9.47	81.26	5.09	104.39	13.98	5.33	19.61	369.72

Source: Bureau of Applied Economics and Statistics, West Bengal

Table 13. Irrigation of land from different sources in West Midnapur (in Numbers)

Year	Tank	HDTW	MDTW	LDTW	STW	RLI	ODW	OTHERS
2000-01	46192	660	#[16]	#	44067	450	@[17]	12925
2001-02	40480	324	2731	$$[18]	48417	385	5190	7808
2002-03	39797	313	2819	34	52713	388	11411	960
2003-04	40245	311	2988	29	47629	393	13279	1249
2004-05	40245	311	2988	29	47629	393	13279	1252
2005-06	40245	311	2989	29	47664	393	13279	1697
2006-07	40401	344	3738	36	46861	384	14226	1650
2007-08	35409	344	3788	36	47861	395	14226	1840
2008-09	36754	344	3783	36	47861	395	14226	1840
2009-10	31948	349	5874	217	45928	462	12159	2797
2010-11	31814	339	7213	243	43836	446	12184	4746
2011-12	32300	422	7702	439	42172	449	11827	4705
2012-13	31749	352	8548	509	38604	406	12189	3456

Source: Bureau of Applied Economics and Statistics, West Bengal

Table 14. Length of Roads Maintained by Public Works Department (P.W.D), Zilla Parishad and Panchayat in West Medinipur (in Kilometers) from 2003-04 to 2012-13

Year	P.W.D			Zilla Parishad			Gram Panchayats			P.M.G.S.Y		
	Surfaced	Unsurfaced	Total	Surfaced	Unsurfaced	Total	Surfaced	Unsurfaced	Total	Surfaced	Unsurfaced	Total
03-04	1311	48	1359	997	135	1132	6653	7861	14514	..	-	..
04-05	1373	48	1421	673	419	1092	2810	12765	15575	..	-	..
05-06	1464	25	1489	873	224	1097	4727	14166	18893	..	-	..
06-07	1454	32	1486	955	239	1194	4736	15991	20727	513	-	513
07-08	1473	32	1505	1111	200	1311	5827	15114	20941	606	-	606
08-09	1218	-	1218	1181	240	1421	6239	14421	20660	660	-	660
09-10	1218	-	1218	1497	204	1701	4786	13499	18285	707	-	707
10-11	1250	-	1250	1538	160	1698	4902	17871	22773	876	-	876
11-12	1250	-	1250	1592	166	1758	5062	18386	23448	915	-	915
12-13	..	..	..	1631	367	1998	5098	19368	24466	1019	-	1019

Source: Bureau of Applied Economics and Statistics, West Bengal

Infrastructure of Birbhum

In the infrastructure of Birbhum, we shall again look at the infrastructure on irrigation first. Table 16 present the data.

Again, the figures of 2010-11 show the effect of drought, but overall the condition of irrigation has been quite good, in spite of few bad seasons in between.

The number of sources is also supporting the above figures as given below (refer to Table 17).

What is astonishing from the above figures is that in spite of presence of HDTW in this district, there was no irrigation from this source until 2007-08. Same can be said about LDTW for the time periods 2003-04 to 2007-08. The figure of Tanks also registered a huge fall but then seems to have recovered quite nicely since 2008-09. But, the figures of STW have continuously fallen. Other sources of irrigation have not been that much significant in this district, becoming obsolete from time to time. Tanks and STW are the two prime sources of irrigation in this district.

Next, we shall look at the condition of road infrastructure of this district. Table 18 shows the data.

Here the role played by all the organizational bodies are quite satisfying, except that of Zilla Parishad. Road maintained by this body have gone down since 2008-09. Other bodies have performed well.

Last, we shall look at the forestry sector. Although the area under forestry is the lowest among the four districts of our study but being in the dryland, forest is an important resource of this district, its development is significant (refer to Table 19).

Table 15. Forest Area, Forest Produce, Revenue and Expenditure from Forestry in West Midnapur from (2003-04 to 2012-13)

Item	Unit	03-04	04-05	05-06	06-07	07-08	08-09	09-10	10-11	11-12	12-13
Reserved Forest	Hectare	6127.71	6211.79	6211.79	6211.79	6182.34	6182.42	6182.00	6192.17	6192.17	6192.17
Protected Forest	,,	148989.96	148819.66	146494.07	146494.07	160179.30	160150.15	160150.15	159487.53	159487.53	160173.48
Unclasse-d State Forest	,,	20178.87	19730.74	21800.77	21801.42	8777.18	8774.36	8774.36	8647.04	8647.04	8774.37
Khas Forest	,,	-	-	0.65	-	-	-	-	-	-	-
Vested Waste Land	,,	-	-	-	-	-	-	-	3733.43	3733.43	3733.43
Forest owned by Corporates	,,	-	-	-	-	-	-	-	1577.75	1577.75	1577.75
Forest owned by Individuals	,,	-	-	-	-	-	-	-	-	-	-
Total	,,	**175296.54**	**174762.19**	**174507.28**	**174507.28**	**175138.82**	**175106.93**	**175106.51**	**179637.92**	**179637.92**	**180451.20**
Forest produce	Thousand cubic meters										
Timber	,,	2.54	2.82	2.92	3.05	1.83	2.68	1.69	2.32	3.79	2.01
Non-timber	,,	93.66	51.00	65.01	41.24	56.14	50.38	26.02	12.17	10.03	31.72
Revenue earned	Thousand Rs	23127.47	55944.10	35221.26	35129.00	53337.00	104580.00	126769.00	87526.41	92791.60	164285.92
Expenditure	,,	195009.64	146133.00	159897.03	275638.00	302563.00	257456.00	348200.00	573474.89	664467.68	337140.68

Source: Bureau of applied Economics and Statistics, West Bengal

Figures are describing a story of low production, low revenue generation and high subsidy. In a way, these trends are similar with other districts, but the values are really low compared to others.

Next we shall make an inter-district comparison by the help of SWOT[19] analysis, while doing this; we shall have a look at the condition of infrastructure within these districts at block level as well.

SWOT ANALYSIS

At the beginning if we look at the land utilization statistics of the four districts, we will then go for the SWOT analysis for them (refer to Table 20).

For comparing with other districts, it is necessary to have their values as well in this regard. Table 21, 22 and 23 respectively present the results for Purulia, West Midnapore and Birbhum districts.

If we go for a comparison, we will see that in Bankura around 50% of the area is sown over the years, but the irrigated area is much lower than that. It has varied from 16.75% in 2010-11 to more than 87% in 2007-08. In Purulia, the conditions are entirely different. Here, the area sown is around 45% to 50% of the area but the irrigation has spread over only 19% to 41% of the sown area. In West Midnapur and Birbhum, more than 50% of the area is sown along with good proportion of land being irrigated. So, Birbhum is in the first place, followed by West Midnapur, Bankura and Purulia respectively as far as

Table 16. Irrigation of land from different sources in Birbhum (in thousand Hectares) from 1998-99 to 2012-13

Year	Govt. Canal	Tank	HDTW	MDTW	LDTW	STW	RLI	ODW	OTHERS	TOTAL
1998-99	183.63	41	---	0.90	0.86	39.35	2.13	0.35	9.13	277.35
1999-2000	182.98	41	---	0.70	0.69	39.00	2.00	3.80	1.40	271.57
2000-01	185.66	41	---	0.75	0.82	40.15	2.05	3.00	0.35	273.78
2001-02	155.88	40.75	---	0.90	0.88	40.75	2.15	2.10	3.20	276.39
2002-03	169.23	40.50	---	0.90	0.88	40.75	2.15	2.00	3.20	259.61
2003-04	192.64	25.40	---	3.89	---	45.68	2.15	0.60	54.95	325.31
2004-05	184.02	25.40	---	3.74	---	45.68	2.15	0.60	54.95	316.54
2005-06	159.89	25.28	---	3.72	---	45.68	2.08	0.64	54.53	291.82
2006-07	184.66	25.28	---	3.71	---	45.68	2.07	0.62	54.53	316.55
2007-08	196.65	24.47	---	8.23	---	44.25	2.07	0.51	52.36	328.54
2008-09	179.78	25.90	1.40	15.30	7.90	25.10	4.70	0.50	2.30	262.88
2009-10	158.38	26.30	1.40	16.40	11.40	19.90	4.40	0.90	2.30	241.38
2010-11	93.17	31.30	1.21	18.08	24.63	15.02	5.53	0.51	3.02	192.47
2011-12	152.17	31.42	1.21	22.10	23.65	16.59	5.63	0.62	2.61	256.00
2012-13	163.73	27.02	0.87	28.47	21.97	14.90	4.51	0.38	7.05	268.90

Source: Bureau of Applied Economics and Statistics, West Bengal

Table 17. Irrigation of land from different sources in Birbhum (in Numbers)

Year	Tank	HDTW	MDTW	LDTW	STW	RLI	ODW	OTHERS
1998-99	31580	41	43	59	20151	115	950	---
1999-00	31580	39	46	69	21151	110	6250	---
2000-01	31580	35	64	69	21230	112	6550	---
2001-02	31560	32	82	87	21230	158	6550	1886
2002-03	31560	--	34	69	21230	108	6550	1886
2003-04	14681	36	95	153	17461	170	950	..
2004-05	14681	34	93	189	17461	188	950	..
2005-06	14681	34	95	189	17461	213	950	..
2006-07	14681	34	95	189	17461	226	950	..
2007-08	14681	34	95	189	17461	226	950	15983
2008-09	26697	47	2480	2050	11528	123	581	412
2009-10	26982	46	2616	3900	9181	111	524	417
2010-11	27494	51	2687	5654	6583	139	580	423
2011-12	27514	50	3297	5501	6159	142	598	290
2012-13	27052	45	12721	3611	7841	141	554	1694

Source: Bureau of Applied Economics and Statistics, West Bengal

Table 18. Length of Roads Maintained by Public Works Department (P.W.D), Zilla Parishad and Panchayat in Birbhum (in Kilometers) from 2003-04 to 2012-13

Year	P.W.D			Zilla Parishad			Gram Panchayats			P.M.G.S.Y		
	Surfaced	Unsurfaced	Total	Surfaced	Unsurfaced	Total	Surfaced	Unsurfaced	Total	Surfaced	Unsurfaced	Total
03-04	1166.00	11.00	1177.00	1009.00	849.00	1858.00	80.00	4021.00	4101.00	..	-	..
04-05	1166.00	11.00	1177.00	1009.00	849.00	1858.00	90.00	4027.00	4117.00	..	-	..
05-06	1168.00	9.00	1177.00	1009.00	849.00	1858.00	98.00	4169.00	4267.00	..	-	..
06-07	1176.00	11.00	1187.00	1009.00	849.00	1858.00	98.00	4169.00	4267.00	281.00	-	281.00
07-08	1183.00	10.00	1193.00	1009.00	849.00	1858.00	98.00	4169.00	4267.00	397.62	-	397.62
08-09	1185.00	10.00	1195.00	208.37	-	208.37	1541.00	4629.00	6170.00	650.00	-	650.00
09-10	1188.00	11.00	1199.00	235.25	-	235.25	2684.78	4768.47	7453.25	650.00	-	650.00
10-11	1188.00	11.00	1199.00	259.96	-	259.96	3549.19	4914.17	8463.36	661.39	-	661.39
11-12	1230.00	-	1230.00	264.57	-	264.57	4727.38	5232.87	9960.25	707.95	-	707.95
12-13	..	..	..	284.77	-	284.77	4969.23	5582.94	10552.17	822.36	-	822.36

Source: Bureau of Applied Economics and Statistics, West Bengal

Table 19. Forest Area, Forest Produce, Revenue and Expenditure from Forestry in Birbhum from (2003-04 to 2012-13)

Item	Unit	03-04	04-05	05-06	06-07	07-08	08-09	09-10	10-11	11-12	12-13
Reserved Forest	Hectare	2848.79	2848.79	2848.79	2848.79	2848.79	2978.60	2978.60	2848.79	2978.60	2978.60
Protected Forest	,,	6242.30	6242.30	6242.30	6242.30	6242.30	5629.75	5629.75	6242.30	5629.75	5629.80
Unclasse-d State Forest	,,	6835.49	6835.49	6835.49	6835.49	6835.49	7318.06	7318.06	6835.49	7318.06	7318.10
Khas Forest	,,	-	-	-	-	-	-	-	-	-	-
Vested Waste Land	,,	-	-	-	-	-	-	-	-	-	-
Forest owned by Corporates	,,	-	-	-	-	-	-	-	-	-	-
Forest owned by Individuals	,,	-	-	-	-	-	-	-	-	-	-
Total	,,	**15926.58**	**15926.58**	**15926.58**	**15926.58**	**15926.58**	**15926.41**	**15926.41**	**15926.58**	**15926.41**	**15926.50**
Forest produce	Thousand cubic meters										
Timber	,,	1.36	0.71	0.19	0.22	0.15	0.30	1.90	79.17	0.06	0.12
Non-timber	,,	2.14	1.32	1.30	0.02	0.02	1.68	2.80	11.13	0.01	0.05
Revenue earned	Thousand Rs	2214	2258	1953	2378	338	401	540	3378	450	342
Expenditure	,,	195009.64	146133.00	159897.03	275638.00	302563.00	357456.00	248200.00	573474.89	164467.68	237140.68

Source: Bureau of applied Economics and Statistics, West Bengal

Table 20. Land Use pattern of Bankura (area in thousand hectares) (2003-04-2012-13)

Year	Reporting Area	Forest Area	Area Under Non-Agricultural Use	Net Area Sown	Irrigated Area
2003-04	688.10	147.70	142.18	348.13	202.68
2004-05	688.00	148.93	143.99	338.18	208.62
2005-06	687.99	148.93	146.55	335.58	273.55
2006-07	688.01	149.17	146.66	344.66	276.94
2007-08	688.00	148.93	147.97	345.39	301.04
2008-09	688.00	148.93	146.19	346.87	297.52
2009-10	688.00	148.93	147.00	350.15	267.03
2010-11	688.00	148.93	148.48	264.09	115.20
2011-12	688.00	148.93	156.02	329.29	288.29
2012-13	688.00	148.93	158.52	331.19	268.85

Source: Bureau of Applied Economics and Statistics, West Bengal

Table 21. Land Use pattern of Purulia (area in thousand hectares) (2003-04-2012-13)

Year	Reporting Area	Forest Area	Area Under Non-Agricultural Use	Net Area Sown	Irrigated Area
2003-04	625.48	75.05	84.75	339.14	65.90
2004-05	625.48	75.05	100.87	331.79	65.75
2005-06	625.65	75.05	103.47	308.64	72.13
2006-07	625.65	75.05	99.90	310.24	71.13
2007-08	625.65	75.05	100.23	312.92	80.04
2008-09	625.65	75.05	104.33	317.09	91.39
2009-10	625.65	75.05	104.48	319.41	95.84
2010-11	625.65	75.05	105.72	226.13	85.83
2011-12	625.65	75.05	109.06	295.40	126.59
2012-13	625.65	75.05	109.97	298.60	133.75

Source: Bureau of Applied Economics and Statistics, West Bengal

Table 22. Land Use pattern of West Midnapore (area in thousand hectare) (2003-04-2012-13)

Year	Reporting Area	Forest Area	Area Under Non-Agricultural Use	Net Area Sown	Irrigated Area
2003-04	928.58	169.69	146.07	565.28	323.79
2004-05	928.58	171.93	158.46	552.12	299.19
2005-06	928.58	171.93	154.32	551.72	391.78
2006-07	928.58	171.93	156.93	555.62	428.12
2007-08	928.58	171.93	157.55	558.70	421.09
2008-09	928.58	171.94	158.90	560.36	394.46
2009-10	928.58	171.94	159.37	564.39	357.21
2010-11	928.58	171.94	156.59	486.20	267.92
2011-12	928.58	171.94	157.07	511.38	378.13
2012-13	928.58	171.94	158.87	512.70	369.72

Source: Bureau of Applied Economics and Statistics, West Bengal

Table 23. Land Use pattern of Birbhum (area in thousand hectare) (2003-04-2012-13)

Year	Reporting Area	Forest Area	Area Under Non-Agricultural Use	Net Area Sown	Irrigated Area
2003-04	451.12	15.85	90.81	311.45	325.31
2004-05	451.12	15.85	91.77	320.61	316.54
2005-06	451.12	15.85	96.38	319.96	291.82
2006-07	451.12	15.85	94.57	317.67	316.55
2007-08	451.12	15.85	96.81	318.54	328.54
2008-09	451.12	15.85	98.16	320.08	262.88
2009-10	451.12	15.85	98.35	322.23	241.38
2010-11	451.12	15.85	101.19	319.96	192.47
2011-12	451.12	15.85	99.84	325.39	256.00
2012-13	451.12	15.85	100.67	326.02	268.90

Source: Bureau of Applied Economics and Statistics, West Bengal

agriculture and irrigation is concerned. If we go through the numbers of sources of irrigation, then by combining all sources of irrigation together, West Midnapur is in the first place, whereas Purulia is in the last place. Birbhum and Purulia are in 2nd and 3rd place respectively.

If we look at the condition of transportation, then we will see that West Midnapur should get the first place, followed by Bankura, Birbhum and Purulia,[20] respectively.

In forestry sector, Bankura has the highest proportion of land in the forestry, followed by West Midnapore, Purulia and Birbhum. In the revenue generating case, West Midnapur has the highest rank, followed by Bankura, Purulia and Birbhum. This should be a matter of concern for the government. But again, one can say that revenue is generated from selling of timber and non-timber produce and the felling or cutting of trees is completely performed in planned manner by the officials.

Next, we shall see how far the fishery sector is developed in these four districts. For that, we have done block-level analysis of each district, in two-time periods- 2007-08 and 2012-13. This will help us in understanding the condition and progress of infrastructure of fisheries. This should help us to understand which part of the district is more developed than the others. Table 24 to 31 present the data for the block levels in each of these four districts for the periods 2007-08 and 2012-13.

From the tables, if we go for a comparison over time, within a district, then we will see that Bankura has done quite well in 2012-13, compared to what it did in 2007-08. Then Purulia has shown a slight downfall, both in government schemes as well as in production, over time. In West Medinipur, number of government schemes has fallen in few blocks but increased in few as well in 2012-13 than in 2007-08 but the production has increased in most of the blocks, which is good. But, Birbhum has performed really badly over time; here government schemes as well as production of both items have considerably fallen. But, in Purulia, more persons are engaged in this profession in comparison to other districts.

We know that health and education are the two most important indicators for the development of human-capital, which in turn, helps in development, management and and proper utilization of social infrastructure. Over the next four tables (Table 32 to Table 35), we shall have a look at the development of health infrastructure in our study area. Then we shall focus on the condition of education.

Table 24. Fisheries in the Blocks of Bankura in 2007-08

Name of Block	No. of Govt. Schemes	Net Area Under Pisciculture (hect.)	Net Area Under Effective Pisciculture (hect.)	No. of Persons in Profession	Approx Annual Production (In Quintal)
Bankura-I	3	1221	1020	5284	22160
Bankura-II	3	1206	1047	4941	26160
Chhatna	2	2234	2085	5546	49390
Saltora	3	985	783	2933	16540
Mejia	2	526	485	3394	13480
Gangajal Ghati	2	2258	1866	3844	41200
Barjora	2	1441	1245	4855	27490
Onda	4	3068	2526	8330	64840
Indpur	3	1520	1482	3833	28100
Khatra	1	476	435	5189	17300
Hirbandh	1	362	303	4811	7170
Ranibandh	4	619	569	3404	13470
Taldangra	2	487	465	5333	11010
Simlapal	3	998	910	4877	21550
Raipur	3	967	773	4269	18310
Sarenga	2	435	343	4188	8120
Bishnupur	3	1126	1000	6600	23690
Joypur	3	742	685	5856	16220
Kotulpur	3	2187	1975	6918	46780
Sonamukhi	2	1309	1170	6297	27710
Patrasayer	2	923	830	6607	19660
Indus	2	723	658	7269	15580

Source: Bureau of Applied Economics and Statistics, West Bengal

Table 25. Fisheries in the Blocks of Bankura in 2012-13

Name of Block	No. of Govt. Schemes	Net Area Under Pisciculture (hect.)	Net Area Under Effective Pisciculture (hect.)	No. of Persons in Profession	Approx Annual Production (In Quintal)
Bankura-I	6	1221	1020	4590	16270
Bankura-II	6	1206	1047	4712	15550
Chhatna	7	2234	2085	4795	30910
Saltora	6	985	783	1957	13080
Mejia	3	526	485	3360	8870
Gangajalghati	6	2258	1866	3420	27760
Barjora	8	1441	1295	4860	35580
Onda	8	3068	2526	8060	71520
Indpur	5	1520	1482	3680	23590

continued on following page

Table 25. Continued

Name of Block	No. of Govt. Schemes	Net Area Under Pisciculture (hect.)	Net Area Under Effective Pisciculture (hect.)	No. of Persons in Profession	Approx Annual Production (In Quintal)
Khatra	7	476	435	5385	9460
Hirbandh	5	362	303	4590	5790
Ranibandh	8	619	569	3460	6490
Taldangra	3	487	465	5230	10800
Simlapal	8	998	910	4975	12560
Raipur	7	967	773	4385	13190
Sarenga	7	435	343	4120	8660
Bishnupur	8	1126	1000	6780	30860
Joypur	7	742	685	6020	23650
Kotulpur	7	2187	1975	7420	60020
Sonamukhi	8	1309	1170	5680	37230
Patrasayer	8	923	830	5370	25930
Indus	7	723	658	6875	23280

Source: Bureau of Applied Economics and Statistics, West Bengal

Table 26. Fisheries in the Blocks of Purulia in 2007-08

Name of Block	No. of Govt. Schemes	Net Area Under Pisciculture (hect.)	Net Area Under Effective Pisciculture (hect.)	No. of Persons in Profession	Approx Annual Production (In Quintal)
Arsha	6	1274	1101	7763	26802
Baghmundi	8	725	695	4566	16888
Balarampur	6	1124	915	7039	22646
Barabazar	6	1646	1417	9813	34858
Jaypur	7	879	749	5877	18725
Jhalda-I	6	625	539	4279	13205
Jhalda-II	7	916	796	9391	19741
Bandowan	8	281	219	1753	5344
Hura	9	1219	1088	7613	26982
Manbazar-I	6	779	693	5493	17672
Manbazar-II	8	470	412	2917	10135
Puncha	4	994	796	6416	19582
Purulia-I	7	881	753	5719	18448
Purulia-II	6	1236	1098	7653	26846
Kashipur	6	1176	1059	8544	26422
Neturia	5	609	511	3863	12468
Para	6	1273	1161	8049	28677

continued on following page

Table 26. Continued

Name of Block	No. of Govt. Schemes	Net Area Under Pisciculture (hect.)	Net Area Under Effective Pisciculture (hect.)	No. of Persons in Profession	Approx Annual Production (In Quintal)
Raghunathpur-I	6	956	885	6923	21948
Raghunathpur-II	5	896	771	6217	19082
Santuri	6	619	556	4303	13678

Source: Bureau of Applied Economics and Statistics, West Bengal

Table 27. Fisheries in the Blocks of Purulia in 2012-13

Name of Block	No. of Govt. Schemes	Net Area Under Pisciculture (hect.)	Net Area Under Effective Pisciculture (hect.)	No. of Persons in Profession	Approx Annual Production (In Quintal)
Arsha	4	1274	1101	14552	25403
Baghmundi	5	725	695	6920	18227
Balarampur	4	1124	915	8016	21758
Barabazar	4	1646	1417	9976	7689
Jaypur	4	879	749	6116	18305
Jhalda-I	4	625	539	5314	14225
Jhalda-II	4	916	796	10412	19858
Bandowan	4	281	219	4521	31862
Hura	5	1219	1088	8507	25245
Manbazar-I	5	779	693	6012	17211
Manbazar-II	4	470	412	3015	11555
Puncha	5	994	796	7132	19680
Purulia-I	5	881	753	6436	19541
Purulia-II	4	1236	1098	8240	24900
Kashipur	5	1176	1059	9120	24602
Neturia	4	609	511	4200	13850
Para	5	1273	1161	9042	26490
Raghunathpur-I	4	956	885	7112	20987
Raghunathpur-II	5	896	771	4314	18502
Santuri	4	619	556	4108	14350

Source: Bureau of Applied Economics and Statistics, West Bengal

The health-infrastructural situation is really worrying in all these districts. West medinipur is in a better position than others, while Purulia has the worst health facilities available. Number of hospitals, primary health centre, doctors all should increase. NGOs have been playing good role, in recent past, in all these districts to uplift the health scenario. But, the governments' role should develop for the development of human health condition which is an integral part of infrastructure. But, overall, the health sector is not showing signs of hope or conditions for development of human-capital.

Table 28. Fisheries in the Blocks of West Midnapore in 2007-08

Name of Block	No. of Govt. Schemes	Net Area Under Pisciculture (hect.)	Net Area Under Effective Pisciculture (hect.)	No. of Persons in Profession	Approx Annual Production (In Quintal)
Jhargram	5	522.67	144.39	802	4741.98
Binpur-I	3	228.50	140.77	1013	4623.23
Binpur-II	4	324.70	162.86	426	5348.66
Jamboni	4	605.50	177.51	651	5829.63
Nayagram	4	120.60	109.34	534	3590.98
Sankrail	5	853.90	358.66	4735	11779.00
Gopiballavpur-I	4	874.17	103.35	272	3394.29
Gopiballavpur-II	3	311.00	138.86	393	4560.54
Salboni	3	396.88	330.07	1832	10839.96
Keshpur	4	1077.50	1022.90	9355	50932.20
Garbeta-I	4	277.87	133.48	4830	4383.75
Garbeta-II	3	727.60	439.87	345	14445.87
Garbeta-III	4	253.00	187.22	1305	6148.72
Medinipur	5	568.70	458.39	2064	15054.20
Debra	5	1300.60	923.08	1326	45962.04
Pingla	4	820.70	549.42	841	27356.75
Keshiary	4	699.40	604.71	399	12859.54
Dantan-I	4	747.10	655.71	924	21534.63
Dantan-II	4	1219.25	889.56	3277	44292.92
Narayangarh	4	1733.60	1373.66	931	68397.42
Mohanpur	3	740.76	547.79	1269	17990.41
Sabong	4	2311.30	1646.54	15459	81984.77
Kharagpur-I	4	381.25	223.70	2089	7346.82
Kharagpur-II	4	1069.20	690.20	2308	22667.38
Chandrakona-I	3	1089.00	939.30	2110	30848.10
Chandrakona-II	3	587.22	426.75	829	14014.99
Ghatal	5	1532.00	888.21	1316	29170.36
Daspur-I	4	928.10	587.95	732	19309.25
Daspur-II	5	867.50	847.59	579	27836.26

Source: Bureau of Applied Economics and Statistics, West Bengal

One more parameter of developing human-capital is development of education. In the following tables (Table 36 to Table 39), we shall see the condition of that as well.

From the four tables, we get to see the numbers of educational institutes in the four districts. In all these districts, Anganwadi centres[21] have played a huge role in the expansion of education, in few years; their numbers are more than that of primary school. These two are the most dominant forms of institutes in all districts. The growth of numbers of degree colleges should improve. The absence of any special

Table 29. Fisheries in the Blocks of West Midnapur in 2012-13

Name of Block	No. of Govt. Schemes	Net Area Under Pisciculture (hect.)	Net Area Under Effective Pisciculture (hect.)	No. of Persons in Profession	Approx Annual Production (In Quintal)
Jhargram	3	364.23	364.23	853	5047
Binpur-I	3	356.18	353.27	1081	1917
Binpur-II	3	450.08	446.49	456	5692
Jamboni	3	605.50	514.02	702	6191
Nayagram	3	250.60	238.27	571	3820
Sankrail	3	853.90	711.43	5080	12516
Gopiballavpur-I	3	874.17	214.00	296	3612
Gopiballavpur-II	3	440.00	404.36	428	485
Salboni	3	397.90	336.29	1932	11511
Keshpur	3	1077.50	1071.17	9853	54080
Garbeta-I	4	277.87	206.39	5090	4662
Garbeta-II	4	727.60	425.77	377	15357
Garbeta-III	3	260.30	197.67	1387	6528
Medinipur	3	468.70	472.28	2234	15994
Debra	6	1300.60	1151.91	1408	48797
Pingla	5	820.70	575.21	887	29418
Keshiary	4	699.40	623.07	449	21095
Dantan-I	2	747.10	677.61	1000	22879
Dantan-II	3	1219.25	1017.47	3458	47019
Narayangarh	4	1733.60	1515.30	367	72609
Mohanpur	3	740.76	564.39	1346	19115
Sabong	5	2311.30	1778.16	16269	57386
Kharagpur-I	5	381.25	232.46	2224	7813
Kharagpur-II	7	1069.20	711.10	2428	24068
Chandrakona-I	3	1039.00	979.90	2234	32843
Chandrakona-II	4	587.22	444.70	887	14890
Ghatal	5	1532.00	915.14	1408	30977
Daspur-I	6	928.10	706.70	785	20501
Daspur-II	5	868.00	873.27	418	29548

Source: Bureau of Applied Economics and Statistics, West Bengal

institute for nurturing and managing of natural resources, like agriculture or forest research centres is somewhat surprising and worrying. This type of institute is badly needed in these areas. All the four districts have one (1) university each; Bankura and Purulia have the recent ones. Here also, Bankura and West Medinipur are in a better position than the other two districts but their conditions are also not that bad.

Table 30. Fisheries in the Blocks of Birbhum in 2007-08

Name of Block	No. of Govt. Schemes	Net Area Under Pisciculture (hect.)	Net Area Under Effective Pisciculture (hect.)	No. of Persons in Profession	Approx Annual Production (In Quintal)
Nalhati-I	4	5.8	5.8	18	209.6
Nalhati-II	4	11.1	11.1	19	400.4
Murarai-I	2	4.1	4.1	7	148.4
Murarai-II	2	1.9	1.9	7	68.4
Mayureswar-I	2	6.1	6.1	9	220.8
Mayureswar-II	2	5.5	5.5	14	198.4
Rampurhat-I	2	3.5	3.5	11	128.2
Rampurhat-II	4	1.9	1.9	5	70.2
Md.Bazar	2	2.7	2.7	6	99.2
Sainthia	2	3.5	3.5	7	126.0
Dubrajpur	2	8.3	8.3	8	300.5
Rajnagar	2	1.0	1.0	2	36.2
Suri-I	3	2.6	2.6	5	94.1
Suri-II	2	7.9	7.9	15	284.2
Khoyrasol	2	2.2	2.2	3	77.8
Bolpur-Srinikitan	2	11.5	11.5	18	415.6
Labhpur	2	7.1	7.1	11	255.2
Nanoor	3	8.2	8.2	8	296.8
Illambazar	2	5.3	5.3	6	192.2

Source: Bureau of Applied Economics and Statistics, West Bengal

Table 31. Fisheries in the Blocks of Birbhum in 2012-13

Name of Block	No. of Govt. Schemes	Net Area Under Pisciculture (hect.)	Net Area Under Effective Pisciculture (hect.)	No. of Persons in Profession	Approx Annual Production (In Quintal)
Nalhati-I	1	950.72	454.08	1	18007.55
Nalhati-II	1	465.20	399.61	1	14612.05
Murarai-I	1	736.00	389.68	7	14077.98
Murarai-II	1	690.00	400.40	6	15187.62
Mayureswar-I	1	1752.09	448.89	5	15956.31
Mayureswar-II	1	1225.75	550.66	1	17607.37
Rampurhat-I	1	1192.19	573.10	1	21174.91
Rampurhat-II	1	1127.42	434.19	5	16129.92
Md.Bazar	1	1086.59	378.18	5	14999.41
Sainthia	1	1660.00	989.08	7	31310.82
Dubrajpur	1	1703.58	632.14	2	25574.62

continued on following page

Table 31. Continued

Name of Block	No. of Govt. Schemes	Net Area Under Pisciculture (hect.)	Net Area Under Effective Pisciculture (hect.)	No. of Persons in Profession	Approx Annual Production (In Quintal)
Rajnagar	1	649.85	283.49	1	11916.83
Suri-I	1	810.19	353.52	1	14600.23
Suri-II	1	694.30	307.94	6	12993.38
Khoyrasol	1	952.00	474.63	13	19043.58
Bolpur-Srinikitan	1	1874.92	688.70	2	26384.66
Labhpur	1	1477.33	812.42	7	30987.88
Nanoor	1	1246.74	474.15	6	19532.64
Illambazar	1	1082.00	536.31	1	20164.59

Source: Bureau of Applied Economics and Statistics, West Bengal

Table 32. No. of Health Institutions in Bankura

Year	Health and Family Welfare Dept, WB				Other Departments of Govt. of West Bengal including State Govt. Undertaking	Local Bodies	Govt. of India including Central Govt. Undertaking	N.G.O / Private Bodies (Nursing Homes)	Total	Total No. of beds	Total No. of Doctors
	Hospitals	Rural Hospitals	Block Primary Health Centres	Primary Health Centres							
2004	5	5	17	70	3	-	1	2	103	3040	330
2005	4	5	17	70	3	-	1	2	102	3125	271
2006	4	5	16	70	2	-	1	36	134	3508	286
2007	4	5	17	70	2	-	1	38	137	3441	286
2008	4	5	17	70	2	-	1	39	138	3536	470
2009	4	5	17	70	2	-	1	39	138	3536	418
2010	4	5	17	70	2	-	2	46	146	3821	460
2011	4	5	17	70	2	-	2	46	146	3821	487
2012	4	5	17	70	3	-	2	46	147	3900	326
2013	4	5	17	69	3	-	2	46	146	3920	362

Source: Bureau of Applied Economics and Statistics, West Bengal

CONCLUSION AND SUGGESTIONS

In our concluding comments, we can say that the process of developing various types of infrastructure has been going on in the dryland areas of West Bengal. Still, they are far away from what is needed. This should provide all sorts of benefits in early and fruit-full completion of government projects and proper management and use of natural resources of these backward districts. It appears from the figures that West Midnapur and Bankura are in a better position than the other two districts, that is, Purulia and Birbhum, although, Birbhum is in a good position in few indicators. But, overall, their position is not that well, if the condition of the rest of the Bengal as well as their needs and backwardness are taken

Table 33. No. of Health Institutions in Purulia

Year	Health and Family Welfare Dept, WB				Other Departments of Govt. of West Bengal including State Govt. Undertaking	Local Bodies	Govt. of India including Central Govt. Undertaking	N.G.O / Private Bodies (Nursing Homes)	Total	Total No. of beds	Total No. of Doctors
	Hospitals	Rural Hospitals	Block Primary Health Centres	Primary Health Centres							
2004	3	5	15	53	3	-	1	7	87	2461	266
2005	3	5	15	53	3	-	1	7	87	2451	312
2006	3	5	15	53	3	-	1	11	91	2346	332
2007	3	5	15	53	3	-	1	11	91	2402	326
2008	3	5	15	53	3	-	1	12	92	2405	331
2009	3	5	15	53	3	-	1	12	92	2535	341
2010	3	5	15	53	3	-	1	12	92	2535	355
2011	3	5	15	53	3	-	1	12	92	2579	283
2012	3	5	15	53	3	-	1	12	92	2491	253
2013	3	5	15	53	3	-	1	13	93	2601	279

Source: Bureau of Applied Economics and Statistics, West Bengal

Table 34. No. of Health Institutions in West Medinipur

Year	Health and Family Welfare Dept, WB				Other Departments of Govt. of West Bengal including State Govt. Undertaking	Local Bodies	Govt. of India including Central Govt. Undertaking	N.G.O / Private Bodies (Nursing Homes)	Total	Total No. of beds	Total No. of Doctors
	Hospitals	Rural Hospitals	Block Primary Health Centres	Primary Health Centres							
2004	5	9	20	84	5	-	3	21	128	3435	526
2005	5	9	20	84	5	-	3	21	128	3435	595
2006	5	9	20	84	4	-	3	134	259	4815	605
2007	5	9	20	82	6	-	3	119	244	4782	467
2008	5	9	20	82	6	-	3	119	244	5055	484
2009	5	9	20	82	6	-	3	123	248	5142	442
2010	5	9	20	82	6	-	3	123	248	5102	696
2011	5	23	6	82	6	-	3	122	247	5164	628
2012	5	23	6	82	6	-	3	124	249	5243	903
2013	6	23	6	82	5	1	3	133	259	5480	790

Source: Bureau of Applied Economics and Statistics, West Bengal

Table 35. No. of Health Institutions in Birbhum

Year	Health and Family Welfare Dept, WB				Other Departments of Govt. of West Bengal including State Govt. Undertaking	Local Bodies	Govt. of India including Central Govt. Undertaking	N.G.O / Private Bodies (Nursing Homes)	Total	Total No. of beds	Total No. of Doctors
	Hospitals	Rural Hospitals	Block Primary Health Centres	Primary Health Centres							
2004	4	4	15	58	3	-	2	1	87	2271	244
2005	4	4	15	58	3	-	2	1	87	2200	226
2006	4	4	15	58	3	-	1	39	124	2611	244
2007	4	4	15	58	3	-	2	38	124	2611	307
2008	4	4	15	58	3	-	2	38	124	2743	248
2009	4	4	15	58	3	-	2	38	124	2743	253
2010	4	4	15	58	3	-	2	44	130	2912	288
2011	4	4	15	58	3	-	2	44	130	2977	253
2012	4	4	15	58	3	-	2	44	130	2977	256
2013	4	4	15	58	3	-	2	44	130	2985	251

Source: Bureau of Applied Economics and Statistics, West Bengal

Table 36. No. of Educational Institutes in Bankura

Type of Institutions	Year									
	2003-04	2004-05	2005-06	2006-07	2007-08	2008-09	2009-10	2010-11	2011-12	2012-13
1. General Recognised Schools	3930	3934	3936	3935	3940	4080	4161	4267	4376	4381
1.A. Primary Schools	3472	3473	3473	3472	3475	3478	3475	3533	3556	3551
1.B. Middle Schools	119	122	116	71	43	179	201	260	345	353
1.C.High Schools	217	208	202	247	249	250	278	262	223	193
1.D. Higher Secondary Schools	122	131	145	145	173	173	207	212	252	284
2.Degree Colleges	14	14	14	18	18	18	18	18	18	21
3. Technical Schools	12	16	16	20	21	21	23	23	23	22
4. Technical Colleges	8	9	9	11	12	13	14	15	16	15
5. Anganwadi (education) Centres under I.C.D.S.	2781	2796	2808	2920	4099	4100	5331	5319	5332	5331

Source: Bureau of Applied Economics and Statistics

Table 37. No. of Educational Institutes in Purulia

Type of Institutions	Year									
	2003-04	2004-05	2005-06	2006-07	2007-08	2008-09	2009-10	2010-11	2011-12	2012-13
1. General Recognised Schools	3316	3318	3318	3324	3323	3338	3437	3529	3580	3636
1.A. Primary Schools	2975	2975	2975	2981	2981	2995	2999	2998	2999	2999
1.B. Middle Schools	97	92	73	69	67	23	112	197	244	299
1.C.High Schools	139	139	148	141	133	174	178	163	163	80
1.D. Higher Secondary Schools	105	112	122	133	142	146	148	171	174	258
2.Degree Colleges	11	11	11	11	12	14	16	17	18	19
3. Technical Schools	8	9	9	9	9	9	9	9	9	10
4. Technical Colleges	3	3	4	4	5	8	8	9	8	8
5. Anganwadi (education) Centres under I.C.D.S.	2415	2438	2447	2548	3879	4020	4427	4691	4715	4845

Source: Bureau of Applied Economics and Statistics

Table 38. No. of Educational Institutes in West Medinipur

Type of Institutions	Year									
	2003-04	2004-05	2005-06	2006-07	2007-08	2008-09	2009-10	2010-11	2011-12	2012-13
1. General Recognised Schools	5403	5432	5434	5431	5436	5437	5446	5459	5746	5751
1.A. Primary Schools	4635	4666	4671	4668	4673	4674	4681	4691	4691	4692
1.B. Middle Schools	228	214	136	110	105	9	11	12	297	300
1.C.High Schools	326	318	384	389	394	486	468	440	322	288
1.D. Higher Secondary Schools	214	234	243	264	264	268	286	316	436	471
2.Degree Colleges	18	18	18	21	21	24	24	24	24	24
3. Technical Schools	15	20	20	19	21	20	22	22	21	21
4. Technical Colleges	9	11	12	16	17	18	15	15	16	21
5. Anganwadi (education) Centres under I.C.D.S.	4557	4379	4498	4771	6524	6996	8720	8720	8720	9009

Source: Bureau of Applied Economics and Statistics

Table 39. No. of Educational Institutes in Birbhum

Type of Institutions	Year									
	2003-04	2004-05	2005-06	2006-07	2007-08	2008-09	2009-10	2010-11	2011-12	2012-13
1. General Recognised Schools	2794	2795	2794	2796	2799	2789	2789	2803	2992	3091
1.A. Primary Schools	2382	2383	2381	2382	2382	2372	2372	2379	2395	2428
1.B. Middle Schools	81	81	80	80	48	48	48	48	220	286
1.C.High Schools	219	219	220	221	231	231	211	210	210	207
1.D. Higher Secondary Schools	112	112	113	113	138	138	158	166	167	170
2.Degree Colleges	12	12	12	14	15	14	14	14	17	18
3. Technical Schools	7	9	9	11	16	15	15	29	38	42
4. Technical Colleges	8	8	10	11	11	10	10	10	12	14
5. Anganwadi (education) Centres under I.C.D.S.	2407	2404	2404	3084	3816	3816	3816	4796	4796	4796

Source: Bureau of Applied Economics and Statistics

into consideration. Urge for fast and rapid development of infrastructure of these areas for the sake of their overall development is a century long demand. There is no doubt that the process has started and some sort of improvement has occurred over the last decade or so but the pace needs to be fastened even more. Natural resources and their uses have been the main source of livelihood in these areas that can be sustainably guided through improvement of various types of infrastructure only. It can also open more avenues for earning livelihood in the dryland areas, resulting in a fall in the over-usage and over-dependency of natural resources and help in their sustainable use.

REFERENCES

Agarwalla, A. (2011). *Estimating the Contribution of Infrastructure in Regional Productivity Growth in India*. Working Paper No. 2011-05-01. IIM, Ahmedabad.

Aschauer, D. A. (1989). Is Public Expenditure Productive? *Journal of Monetary Economics*, *23*(2), 177–200. doi:10.1016/0304-3932(89)90047-0

Canning, D., & Pedroni, P. L. (2008). Infrastructure, Long-Run Economic Growth and Causality Tests for Cointegrated Panels. *Manchester School*, *76*(5), 504–527. doi:10.1111/j.1467-9957.2008.01073.x

Dissou, Y., & Didic, S. (2011). *Public Infrastructure and Economic Growth*. Working Paper, Department of Economics, University of Ottawa.

Dodonov, B., Von Hirschhausen, C., Opitz, P., & Sugolov, P. (2002). Efficiency Infrastructure Supply for Economic Development in Transition Countries: The Case of Ukraine. *Post-Communist Economies*, *14*(2), 149–167. doi:10.1080/14631370220139909

Ehlers, T. (2014). *Understanding the Challenges for Infrastructure Finance*. BIS Working Papers No.54.

Lall, S. V. (2006). Infrastructure and Regional Growth, Growth Dynamics and Policy Relevance for India. *The Annals of Regional Science*, *41*(3), 581–599. doi:10.1007/s00168-006-0112-4

Nanda, S. S. (2015). Infrastructure Development in India: The role of public-private partnership. *International Journal of Core Engineering & Management*, *2*(6), 60–70.

Nketiah-Amponsah, E. (2009). Public Spending and Economic Growth: Evidence from Ghana (19702004). *Development Southern Africa*, *26*(3), 477–497. doi:10.1080/03768350903086846

Panigrahi, S., & Beura, D. (2013). An Exploratory Study on Infrastructure Financing in India. *International Journal of Science and Research*, *4*(3), 405–408.

Ramirez, M. D. (2004). Is Public Infrastructure Spending Productive in the Mexican Case? A Vector Error Correction Analysis. *The Journal of International Trade & Economic Development*, *13*(2), 159–178. doi:10.1080/0963819042000218700

Rioja, F. K. (2001). Growth, Welfare, and Public Infrastructure: A General Equilibrium Analysis of Latin American Economies. *Journal of Economic Development*, *26*(2), 119–130.

Straub, S., Vellutini, C., & Warlters, M. (2008). *Infrastructure and Economic Growth in East Asia*. Policy Research Working Paper 4589. World Bank.

Taqvi, S. M. A. (2013). Emerging Trends in Infrastructure Development in India. *Indian Journal of Applied Research*, *3*(4), 257–259. doi:10.15373/2249555X/APR2013/87

KEY TERMS AND DEFINITIONS

Assessment: The process of making a judgment about something.

Drylands: Areas suffering from the lack of rainfall and aridity of soil, here Precipitation is counter balanced by evapotranspiration and evaporation.

Infrastructure: Structures, facilities, system, institutions needed for smooth economic functioning of a city, a region or a society.

Livelihood: A means of securing the necessities of life.

Natural Resources: Substances or goods occurring in nature and can be used for economic and social gain.

SWOT Analysis: The process followed to identify strength, weakness, opportunities and threats of an area or region.

West Bengal: A state in eastern India and the nation's fourth most populous state. This state has the four districts, namely, Purulia, Bankura, West Medinipur and Birbhum, that together has been named as 'drylands'.

ENDNOTES

1 www.nih.ernet.in/rbis/india_information/draught.htm
2 Prepared by NABARD Consultancy Services Pvt Ltd (NABCONS), West Bengal
3 Major part of Chhotonagpur Plateau lies in Jharkhand.
4 See www.rbi.org.in for details.
5 The numbers in the brackets denoting the ranks of those categories.
6 From 6th plan onwards, data on Power sector shows data of whole Energy Sector.
7 HDTW- High Capacity Deep Tubewell, MDTW- Middle Capacity Deep Tubewell, LDTW- Low Capacity Deep Tubewell, STW- Shallow Tubewell, RLI-Riverlift Irrigation, ODW- Open Dug Well.
8 Including Private LDTW
9 Including Private STW from here onwards
10 Including Private ODW from here onwards
11 Pradhan Mantri gram Sadak Yojona
12 This district was created by dividing Midnapore in two parts, namely East Midnapore and West Midnappore in 2000-01, so, we have used the data from that year only.
13 @ stands for included with HDTW
14 # stands for included with Other Sources
15 $ stands for included with MDTW
16 Included with HDTW
17 Included with Other Sources
18 Included with MDTW
19 Strength, Weakness, Opportunities, Threats (SWOT)
20 Considering total length of road being maintained by various authorities together.
21 It is a form of non-formal educational institute

Chapter 13
Infrastructure Development and Changing Market Penetration of Consumer Durables in Rural India:
An Empirical Investigation

Debabrata Mukhopadhyay
West Bengal State University, India

Arun Kumar Mandal
West Bengal State University, India

ABSTRACT

In recent years, Indian rural market has been gaining increasing attention from researchers in view of its growing importance in huge potential marketing for various consumer durables such as white goods, brown goods and consumer electronics. India has a vast rural market, which consists of around 833 million potential consumers constituting 68.84% of the total population spread over 6.40 Lac villages. Rural India is now exhibiting changing living standard with higher income, modern education and infrastructure development. This is leading to higher demand for several consumer durables such as colour television, refrigerator, two wheelers etc. The urban consumer's durable market is growing annually 10% to 20%. The corresponding rural market is zooming ahead 20% to 40% annually. Thus, this chapter attempts to investigate the changing market penetration of consumer durables in rural India during 1995-96 to 2009-10. This work also finds out the role of per capita income, rural infrastructure in market penetration of consumer durables.

DOI: 10.4018/978-1-5225-2364-2.ch013

INTRODUCTION

After the opening up of the Indian economy in 1991 by the government of India, there has been some improvement in the purchasing power of rural people as agriculture the main livelihood of the rural community, has witnessed a phenomenal change during this period through the introduction of market mechanism, export outlook etc. Apart from this institutional change, the major technological change also has taken place in Indian agriculture in the early 1960's which is popularly known as 'Green Revaluation' through Varity(HYV) of seeds, fertilizers, water resources, pesticides, better quality seeds, modern farm equipments and methods of farming have changed the village far better. As a result the rural economy has witnessed increased per capita income and development in basic infrastructure. This overall change in the rural economy has important implications for rural consumption pattern in particular; consumer durables are exhibiting tremendous growth for the rural areas.

Consumer durable is a category of consumer products that is not purchased frequently as it lasts for an extended period of time. Penetration of consumer durables in rural market is generating huge demand for first time buyer and not the replacement market. Improving rural infrastructure, agricultural reforms and power availability are boosting this growth of rural consumer durables, in which durables manufacturers are looking to strengthen their presence in rural India to leverage their opportunity. Rural India is now witnessing higher income with changing demographic pattern including higher literacy rate. Rapid proliferation of communication technology has also changed the consumer awareness and the overall aspirations of the millions of rural people living in India which is leading to higher penetration of consumer durables in rural market which is changing more rapidly compared to urban market.

The perception about the rural consumer is now changing. Now rural consumers are choosy in their purchase, they are not sticking only to essential items. Apart from food and consumable items, they are now interested in buying consumer durables like radio, TV set, Two wheelers, mostly bicycles and motorcycles, wrist watches, Table fan and ceiling fan, refrigerators etc. For this change in purchasing behavior, consumer durables market in rural India is growing very fast. Consumer durable market players like LG, Sony, Samsung, and Whirlpool are having the major share in rural and suburban market. Rural infrastructure development is the key component of rural development as well as marketing improvement. Proper rural development improves rural economy, poverty reduction, quality of life. It promotes better productivity, increase agricultural income, adequate employment and so on and forth. Various infrastructure projects like irrigation, rural road, rural housing, rural water supply, rural electrification, rural telecommunication & Internet etc. under Bharat Nirman have become lifeline to new income, new market, new business and new opportunities for all things. Since the two and half decades of economic liberalization India has focusing on foreign direct investments(FDI) with the recent campaign of 'Make in India' program. Under this backdrop it is very interesting and pertinent to investigate the penetration of the consumer durables in rural market for the overall manufacturing sector growth of the Indian economy.

LITERATURE REVIEW AND RESEARCH GAP

There are many studies carried out in India concerned in terms of rural marketing. Joshi (2011) had explained about rural marketing strategies. Kumar (2013) did his work on challenges and opportunities to the marketers. Studies on rural consumer brand awareness were carried out by Suganthi (2015). Again some research was done on prospects and problems on Indian rural marketing by Kotni (2012). Kalotra (2013) explained about rural market potential in Indian economy. Pathak and Pathak (2013) carried out a study upon information technology and pointed out bridging between Urban and Rural marketing. Bhatnagar (2000) presented Information and communication Technology in rural India in terms of telephony, internet and other electronic media. Sharma (2012) did his work about BSNL leading telecommunication services provided in rural India and analyzed their various marketing strategies. Vilas (2012) explained about Indian rural marketing environment of Demographic, Physical, Economic, Socio-culture, Political and Technological Environment. Most of these studies are concerned with various issues related to rural marketing. But little work has been done on consumer durables marketing in rural India except few for example, Sharma (2013) examined some marketing of consumer durable in eastern Rajasthan, Kishor (2014) and Laddh (2015) worked on consumer behavior and brand awareness of consumer durables. No comprehensive study on penetration of consumer durables has been conducted so far considering overall Indian rural market. The paper is organized as follows. First we have presented some issues relevant to rural marketing thereafter presented data and methodology, empirical results, summary and conclusions.

Rural Area and Rural Marketing

According to National Sample Survey Organization (NSSO), Rural is an area with a population density of up to 400 per square kilometer, villages with clear surveyed boundaries but no municipal board and A minimum of 75% of male working population involved in agriculture and allied activities.

- **Marketing:** Identifying the needs of consumers and potential of consumers, providing products & services that satisfy the needs of customers and developing efficient process or systems to deliver your product & service to the market when, where, and how consumer want it.
- **Rural Marketing:** "Rural marketing is defined as a function that manage all activities involved in assessing stimulating and converting the purchasing power of rural consumers into an effective demand for specific products & services and moving these product & services to the people in rural areas to create satisfaction and better stander of living and thereby achieving organizational goal"(Iyer, 2010).

Consumer Durable Products

Consumer durables are a category of consumer products that do not have to be purchased frequently because they are made to last for an extended period of time (typically more than three years).

The consumer durables industry can be broadly classified into two segments: Consumer Electronics and Consumer Appliances. Consumer Appliances can be further categorized into Brown Goods and White Goods.

Consumer appliances are electrical or mechanical machines which accomplish some household functions. Electrical devices take the energy of electric current and transform it in simple ways into some other form of energy, most likely light, heat, or motion. Consumer electronics includes specialized circuitry which makes the device much more complicated and sophisticated. Such devices would contain circuits to provide signal control (such as amplifiers, radio and TV tuners, music players, etc.) or logic functions (such as computers, digital clocks, and printers).

Box 1.

White Goods	Brown Goods /Kitchen Appliance	Consumer Electronics
• Air conditioners • Refrigerators • Washing machines • Sewing machines • Watches and clocks • Cleaning equipments •Other domestic appliances	• Cooking Products • Chimneys • Mixers • Grinders • Electronics Fans • Irons • Microwave Ovens	• Televisions • Audio and video systems • Electronics accessories • Personal Computers • Mobile phones • Digital cameras • DVD,VCD,MP3 • Camcorders

Share in the Consumer Durables Market in India

Share of Urban market was 67% and rural market was 33% of the total revenue in the consumer durables sector in India in FY-2015. The rural consumer durables market is growing at the Compound Annual Growth Rate (CAGR) of 25%. (IBEF, n.d.).

Notable Trends in the Consumer Durables Sector in India

1. Consumer durable market is valued at USD9.7 billion in FY15, and expected to reach USD20.6 billion by 2020. India is expected to have the fifth largest consumer durables market by 2025 in the world.
2. India is one of the largest growing electronics market in the world.
3. By 2020, the electronics market in India is expected to increase to USD400 billion from USD94.2 billion in 2015.
4. By 2025, India would rise from the twelfth to the fifth largest position in the consumer durables markets in the word, the market estimated to reach USD12.5 billion in 2016. (IBEF, n.d.)

Organized Retail Market Penetration

1. The organized retail market penetration in India is low (8%) compared with that in other countries, such as the US (85%). This indicates strong growth potential for organized retail in India.
2. The Indian retail market is in its growing stage, organized retail market penetration would reach 8% during 2013.
3. In 2019, it is estimated that organized retail penetration share would be reach 13% and unorganized penetration would hold a major share of 87%.
4. Organized retail market penetration is expected to account for 24% of the overall retail market by 2020. (IBEF, n.d.) *Source: ibef.org*

Government Initiatives

A different initiative is being taken by the government of India such as i. Bharat Nirman Program (rural infrastructure development of irrigation, drinking water, electrification, roads, Housing and rural tele-communication). ii. Poverty alleviation programmes, iii. Rurban Mission (creating smart villages) iv.

Make a 'Digital India' initiative. v. The Pradhan Mantri Krishi Sinchaee Yojana (PMKSY) (to provide irrigation to every village in India). vi. NavKalpanaKosh' (aims to improve rural areas at various levels, such as governance, agriculture and hygiene). vii. Export promotion capital goods (EPCG) scheme allows import of capital goods for pre-production, production and post production at zero customs duty. viii.100% FDI is permitted in electronics hardware-manufacturing through automatic route. (IBEF, n.d.).

DETERMINANTS AND INFRASTRUCTURE OF CONSUMER DURABLES MARKET IN RURAL INDIA

1. **Large Rural Population:** 833 million potential consumers which constituted 68.84% of the total population reside in 6, 40,867 villages (census 2011).The size of rural market offers great opportunities for the marketers.
2. **Rural Literacy Rate:** The rural literacy rate increase from 24% in 1971 to 59% in 2001.

Table 1 shows literacy rates across genders. An improvement in female literacy rate is more than male in rural areas according to census of 2011. Literacy rate increased to 68.9% in 2011 from 58.7% in 2001.

3. **New Employment Opportunities in Rural Areas:** Government scheme like IRDP (Integrated Rural Development Programmers) JRY (Jawarhar Rozgar Yojana) JGSY (Jawarhar Grambriddhi Yojana), SGSY (Swarnajoyanti Gram Swarojgar Yojana), *MGNREGS* (Mahatma Gandhi National Rural Employment Guarantee Scheme) at least 100 days of guaranteed employment, TRYSEM (Training of Rural Youth for Self-Employment) has created new Employment opportunities in rural areas.
4. **Increasing Disposable Income:** Since Green Revaluation and various Agricultural development programs of the Government have helped to increase income in the agricultural sector. These created greater purchasing power in rural market.
5. **Improved Lifestyle:** In this modern era, the consumption basket of rural people is not limited to agricultural and traditional products; they are keen on buying modern products that can raise their stander of living.
6. **Increased in Percentage Composition Expenditure of Durable Goods:** The rural consumption expenditure has increased 19.55% per annum where in urban it has increased only 14.58% per annum during last twelve years (Table 2).

Table 1. The improvement in literacy rate in rural area is two times more than that in urban India from 2001 to 2011

		2001	2011	Difference
Rural	Male	70.7	78.6	+7.9
	Female	46.1	58.8	+12.7
	Persons	58.7	68.9	+10.2
Urban		79.9	85	+5.1

Source: Census India, 2011

Table 2. Percentage composition expenditure of durable goods

	1993-94	1999-2000	2004-05	2009-10	2011-12
Rural	2.7	2.6	3.4	4.8	6.1
Urban	3.3	3.6	4.1	6.7	6.3

Source: NSSO, 68th Round

7. **Increasing Rural Tele-Density:** Rural tele-density has been increasing 5.18% annually (Table 3). Maximum increase has happened from 2009 to 2011.
8. **Rural Electrification:** Rural electrification has been increasing significantly during five year plane period (Table 4). Starting from 1500 villages in 1947, the year of independence, rural electrification has now covered over 57 lacs villages in 2015.
9. **Road:** The road network has been increased from 3, 54,530 km in 1971 to 24, 50,559 km in 2008. The rural surfaced road coverage is just 33% of the total rural road network in India.
10. **Internet:** The Internet mobile Association of India (IAMAI) states that there are going to be 371 million mobile internet users in India by June 2016. It adds that the country had 306 million mobile internet users in December 2015, of which 87 million were from rural India, up by 93% year over year.
11. **Other Determinants:** Government policies, Globalization, Better Credit Facility through Bank, Media, Accessibility of Markets, and IT Penetration in rural India

DATA AND METHODOLOGY

This study examines the penetration of the consumer durables market in India for the period 1995-96 to 2009-10 covering twenty one Indian states. It covers market information survey of rural consumer in India from these states. This study is carried out based on secondary data which have been collected from the various sources such as research papers, websites, books, journals, magazines, newspapers, library, and reports of certain government agencies such as National Council of Applied Economic

Table 3. Rural tele-density

Year	31.03.2009	28.02.2011	31.10.11	31.10.12	31.10.13	31.10.14	31.10.15	31.03.16
Tele-density%	15.11	32.99	36.76	40.61	42.00	45.39	49.37	51.37%

Source: www.tari.gov.in (Press Release)

Table 4. Rural electrification over years

Year	1947	1st 1956	2nd 1961	3rd 1966	4th 1974	5th 1979	6th 1985	7th 1990	8th 1997	11th 2012	12th Plan 2015
No. of villages electrified(Cum.)	1500	7294	21754	45148	156729	216863	370332	470838	498836	557439	578957

Source: GOI, Ministry of Power, Central Electricity Authority, Annual Report 2014-15

Research (NCAER), Census Report in India 2011, National Sampling Survey (NSS), Reserve Bank of India, Central Statistical Organization (CSO), Planning Commission of India, Rural Marketing Books / Magazine / Journal etc. Main data has been collected from "The Great Indian Market"- National Council of Applied Economic Research (NCAER).

We have followed the exploratory analysis for this study using the statistical diagrams and Graphs. We have also carried out some exercises to understand the determinants of this market penetration by multiple linear regressions. In this context, we have followed a static panel regression for determining the penetration of consumer durables with per capita State Domestic product and tele density as explanatory variables, where latter is used as an indicator of rural infrastructure.

EMPIRICAL RESULTS

Demand Situation of Consumer Durables

First of all, we have presented in Table 5 below a comparison of rural and urban growth in major consumer durables in two time points namely, 1995-96 and 2009-10 and found that for majority of the items the rural consumption growth has exceeded urban growth indicating rapid growth for Indian rural market. Demand for several items such as motor car, motor cycle, small colour TV, regular colour TV, VCR/VCPs/, Refrigerators, Air Conditioner, Washing Machines, Pressure Cooker, Transistors, Wrist Watches, Electric Irons, Table Fan and Ceiling Fan are increasing at a higher rate in rural areas compared to urban areas. Some items such as Black and White TV, Scooter, mopeds etc. are decreasing in both urban and rural areas.

Changing Rural Market Penetration of Some Consumer Durables

We now discuss the market penetration of major consumer durables in rural and urban India during the year 1995-96 to 2009-10 for the selected items (A) Ceiling Fan from low cost goods, (B) Motorcycle from Automotive sectors, (C) Refrigerators from White goods and (D) Colour TVs (large) from Television. This analysis is conducted in three stages: first we figure out the growth of market penetration of these items in rural and urban areas, second we figure out state wise growth and last we figure out zone wise growth of these consumer durables in rural area.

Ceiling Fans

From the Figure 1 and Table 6, the results show that market penetration for ceiling fan has grown steadily in rural areas compared to that of urban areas. It has increased 19.9% per annum in rural area and 9.92% p.a. in urban areas. This indicates that the Indian rural market of consumer durables is expanding mass market today.

From the Figure 2 and Table 7 we got the highest growth of market penetration of Ceiling Fans as in Bihar. It increased 36.52% p.a. during this period. In this term Madhya Pradesh was second (35.26%), Maharashtra was third, Uttar Pradesh was fourth, Rajasthan was fifth, Assam sixth, Karnataka comes seventh, next was Pondicherry, Tamil Nadu, Delhi and so on.

Table 5. Demand scenario for major consumer durables

Demand Decreasing: (Figure in'000)								
Name of Consumer Durables	Rural				Urban			
	1995-96	2009-10			1995-96	2009-10		
	Total Sale	Total Sale	Total Change	% Change	Total Sale	Total Sale	Total Change	% Change
Scooters	368	311	-57	-15.49	743	468	-275	-37.01
Mopeds'	283	141	-142	-50.18	253	103	-150	-59.29
Small B&W TVs	3237	1285	-1952	-60.3	1922	323	-1599	-83.19
Regular B&W TVs	1020	328	-692	-67.84	724	153	-571	-78.87
Demand Increasing: (Figure in'000)								
Name of Consumer Durables	Rural				Urban			
	1995-96	2009-10			1995-96	2009-10		
	Total Sale	Total Sale	Total Change	% Change	Total Sale	Total Sale	Total Change	% Change
Cars/Jeeps	6	376	370	6166.67	270	3090	2820	1044.44
Motor Cycles	359	4045	3686	1026.74	401	4325	3924	978.55
Small Color TVs	72	1891	1819	2526.39	221	3521	3300	1493.21
Regular Color TVs	523	4208	3685	704.59	1262	5749	4487	355.55
VCR/VCPs	89	188	99	111.24	218	462	244	**111.93**
Refrigerators	583	2201	1618	277.53	1266	4573	3307	261.22
Air Condition	4	24	20	500	216	763	547	253.24
Washing Machines	144	681	537	372.92	969	3708	2739	282.66
Pressure Cookers	3094	12747	9653	311.99	3473	11765	8292	238.76
Transistors	6744	18773	12029	178.37	2141	4334	2193	102.43
Wrist Watches	9313	20644	11331	121.67	10368	23818	13450	**129.73**
Electric Irons	1638	6337	4699	286.87	2527	7810	5283	209.06
Table Fans	2711	9913	7202	265.66	1654	4619	2965	179.26
Ceiling Fans	4339	22648	18309	421.96	5404	20266	14862	275.02

Source: The Great Indian Market, National Council of Applied Economic Research, (Base year-1995-96)

Table 6. Growth of market penetration of Ceiling Fans (Total penetration per'000households)

Areas	1995-96	1998-99		2001-02		2005-06		2009-10	
	Total	Total	% Change	Total	% Change	Total	% Change	Total	% Change
Rural	190.48	280.29	47.14	347.47	82.42	485.20	154.71	699.69	267.33
Urban	813.93	933.44	14.68	1078.45	32.50	1402.61	72.33	1878.83	138.83

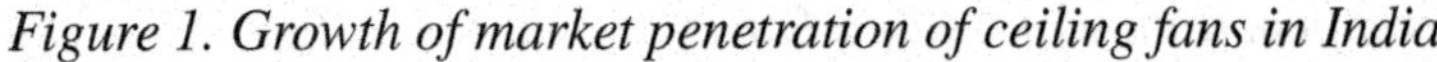

Figure 1. Growth of market penetration of ceiling fans in India

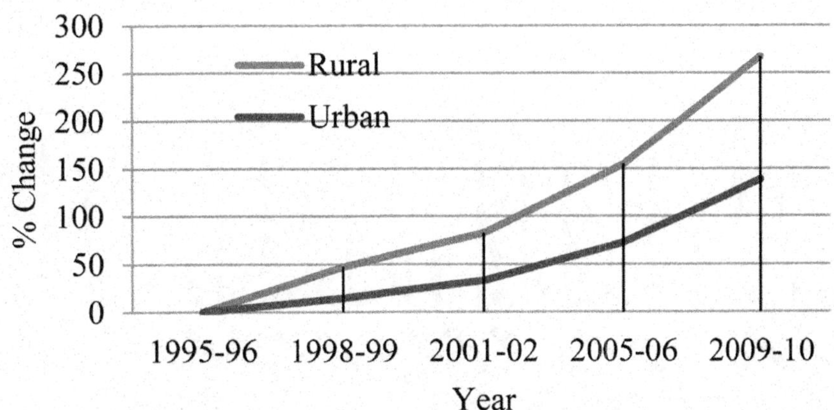

Table 7. State-Wise market penetration of Ceiling Fans in rural India (Total penetration per'000 households)

States	1995-96	1998-99		2001-02		2005-06		2009-10	
	Total	Total	%Ch.	Total	%Ch	Total	%Ch	Total	%Ch
Haryana	436.01	529.86	21.52	631.73	44.89	881.53	102.18	1195.04	174.1
Himachal Pradesh	74.24	102.51	38.08	127.43	71.65	184.98	149.16	258.01	247.5
Madhya Pradesh	111.67	197.19	76.58	266.01	38.21	425.32	280.87	662.84	493.6
Punjab	773.87	994.96	28.57	1156.2	49.4	1567.9	102.61	2051.20	165.1
Uttar Pradesh	71.78	116.18	61.86	152.46	12.4	234.10	226.14	352.77	384.7
Chandigarh	211.04	229.22	8.61	263.13	24.68	352.46	67.01	455.09	115.6
Delhi	415.28	610.14	44.24	774.59	80.21	1165.4	180.64	1719.29	314.0
Andhra Pradesh	224.10	332.75	48.48	437.62	95.28	591.27	163.84	846.16	277.6
Karnataka	125.71	203.80	62.12	276.25	119.8	386.98	207.84	578.51	360.2
Kerala	779.45	1017.3	30.52	1195.3	53.36	1428.3	83.24	1797.40	130.6
Tamil Nadu	256.03	394.88	54.23	526.67	105.7	728.86	184.68	1071.68	318.6
Pondicherry	185.14	435.97	135.4	518.70	180.2	626.95	238.64	799.23	331.7
Assam	109.77	177.48	61.68	223.25	103.6	326.67	197.59	509.54	364.2
Bihar	51.22	92.74	81.06	120.99	136.2	185.74	262.63	313.07	511.2
Meghalaya	25.23	43.91	74.04	49.03	94.33	62.94	149.46	85.68	239.6
Orissa	202.35	293.68	45.13	323.15	59.7	406.42	100.85	542.76	168.2
West Bengal	145.81	198.34	36.03	217.01	48.83	271.02	85.87	359.56	146.6
Gujarat	315.15	400.69	27.14	509.47	61.66	767.57	143.56	1110.75	252.5
Maharashtra	181.24	311.17	71.69	398.98	120.1	611.70	237.51	891.55	391.9
Rajasthan	202.66	343.94	69.71	439.70	116.9	669.21	230.21	968.77	378.0
Goa	269.60	368.26	36.59	441.83	63.88	628.33	133.06	849.78	215.2

Source: The Great Indian Market, NCAER, (% change calculate on the base year1995-96)

Figure 2. State-wise growth of rural market penetration of Ceiling Fans

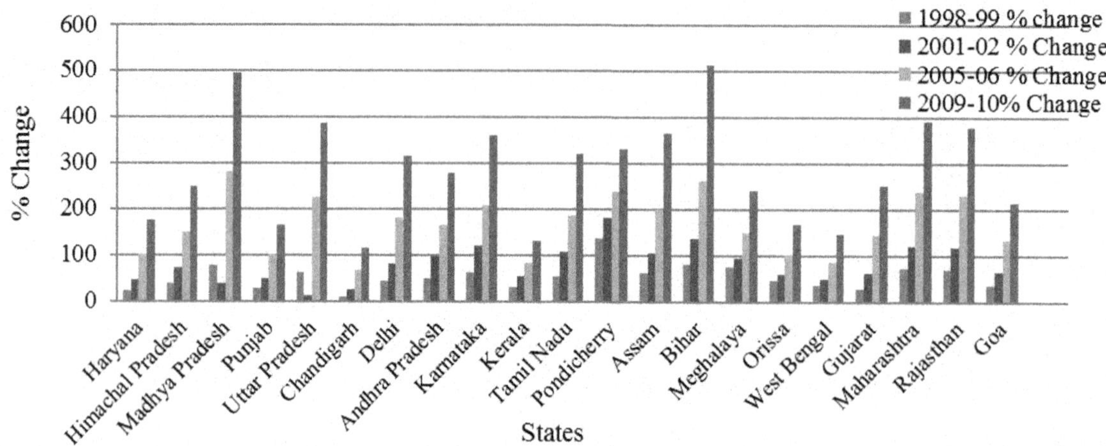

Figure 3. Zone-wise rural market penetration of Ceiling Fans

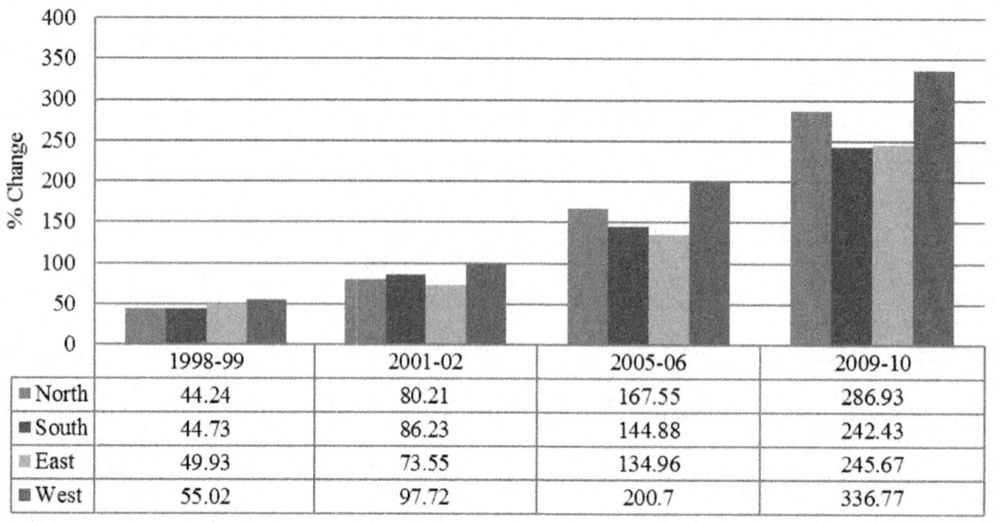

	1998-99	2001-02	2005-06	2009-10
North	44.24	80.21	167.55	286.93
South	44.73	86.23	144.88	242.43
East	49.93	73.55	134.96	245.67
West	55.02	97.72	200.7	336.77

We find the result from the Figure 3 that, highest growth of market penetration of Ceiling Fans came from Western Zone. It increased 24.06% annually during that period. Northern Indian households are the second highest. It increased 20.50% p.a. during this period. Eastern Zone is the third. It increased 17.55% p.a. and southern zone is the fourth which has increased 17.32% annually.

Motorcycle

We get result from the Figure 4 and Table 8 that the market penetration of Motorcycle in rural India has been increasing more than urban India. It has been growing 82.42 percent annually. In urban market it has been growing only 44.44% annually. Thus we can say that market penetration of Motorcycle in rural market is growing faster in compression to urban market.

Figure 4. Growth of market penetration of Motorcycle in rural and urban India

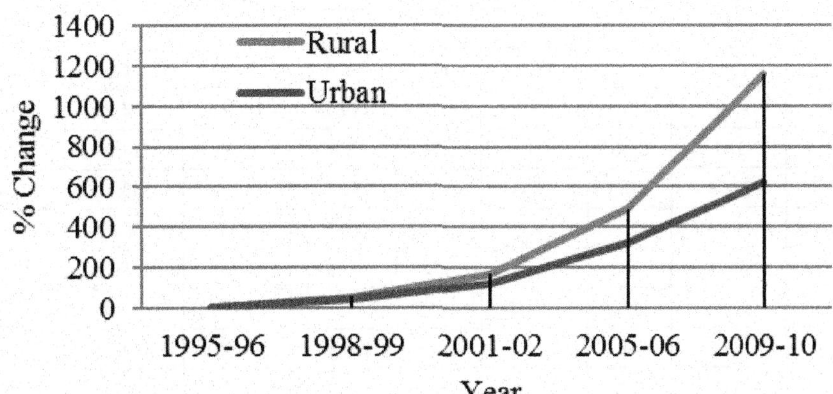

Table 8. Growth of market penetration of Motorcycle in India (Total penetration per'000 households)

Areas	1995-96	1998-99		2001-02		2005-06		2009-10	
	Total	Total	% Change	Total	% Change	Total	% Change	Total	% Change
Rural	18.70	28.3	50.42	49.81	166.36	109.78	487.10	227.34	1153.94
Urban	56.03	77.20	37.78	123.57	120	236.63	322.32	404.63	622.17

From Figure 5 and Table 9 we show that, Chandigarh had highest market penetration during this period. It has changed 297.52% on average per year during this period. Kerala was second, Punjab was third, Tamil Nadu was fourth, Rajasthan was fifth and Himachal Pradesh had lowest growth rate of market penetration of motorcycle in rural India.

Figure 5. State-wise growth of rural market penetration of Motorcycle

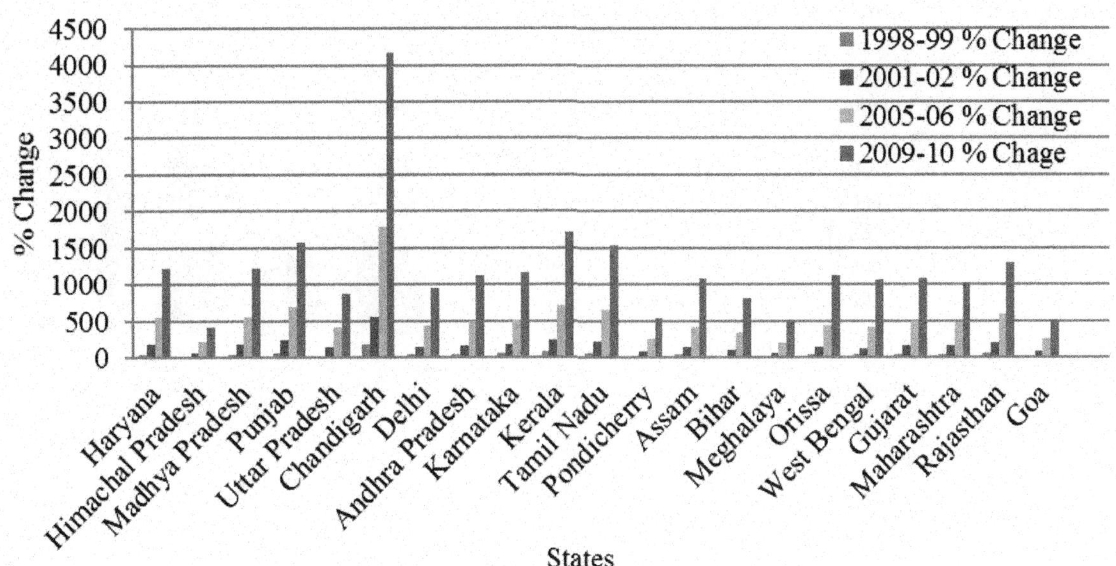

Table 9. State-wise rural market penetration of Motorcycles (Total penetration per'000 households)

States	1995-96	1998-99		2001-02		2005-06		2009-10	
	Total	Total	%Ch.	Total	%Ch.	Total	%Ch.	Total	%Ch.
Haryana	27.63	43.02	55.7	80.05	189.72	180.86	554.58	364.03	1217.52
Himachal Pradesh	3.41	3.46	1.47	5.56	63.05	10.71	214.08	18.04	429.03
Madhya Pradesh	22.54	34.71	53.99	64.31	185.31	146.38	549.42	297.03	1217.8
Punjab	19.96	34.78	74.25	67.18	236.57	159.73	700.25	334.54	1576.05
Uttar Pradesh	16.31	22.19	36.05	39.45	141.88	84.14	415.88	158.57	872.23
Chandigarh	11.52	33.03	186.72	75.56	555.9	218.82	1799.48	595.05	4165.36
Delhi	53.05	74.97	41.32	134.8	154.16	291.40	449.29	561.09	957.66
Andhra Pradesh	13.68	20.98	53.36	37.19	171.86	80.74	490.2	167.91	1127.41
Karnataka	22.81	36.02	57.31	64.51	182.81	139.89	513.28	288.42	1164.45
Kerala	23.93	43.91	83.49	82.81	246.05	194.12	711.2	434.31	1714.92
Tamil Nadu	17.10	30.08	75.91	55.94	227.13	128.84	653.45	279.07	1531.99
Pondicherry	61.93	71.29	15.02	114.7	85.23	221.72	258.02	397.91	542.52
Assam	7.29	10.72	47.05	17.41	138.82	37.99	421.12	86.70	1089.3
Bihar	11.71	15.58	33.05	24.55	109.65	50.83	334.07	107.66	819.39
Meghalaya	32.28	35.22	9.11	51.84	60.59	99.85	209.32	196.83	509.76
Orissa	12.68	19.21	51.5	31.55	148.82	69.07	444.72	154.45	1118.06
West Bengal	6.08	8.94	47.04	14.56	128.97	31.54	418.75	71.38	1074.01
Gujarat	28.27	41.70	47.51	75.35	166.54	170.02	501.41	334.45	1083.06
Maharashtra	35.22	50.42	43.16	90.38	156.61	202.01	473.57	398.25	1030.75
Rajasthan	28.35	45.58	60.78	84.96	199.68	196.75	594	395.40	1294.71
Goa	180.41	197.5	9.5	323.1	79.11	648.72	259.58	1126.8	524.57

Source: The Great Indian Market, NCAER, (% change calculate on the base year1995-96)

Figure 6. Zone-wise rural market penetration of Motorcycle

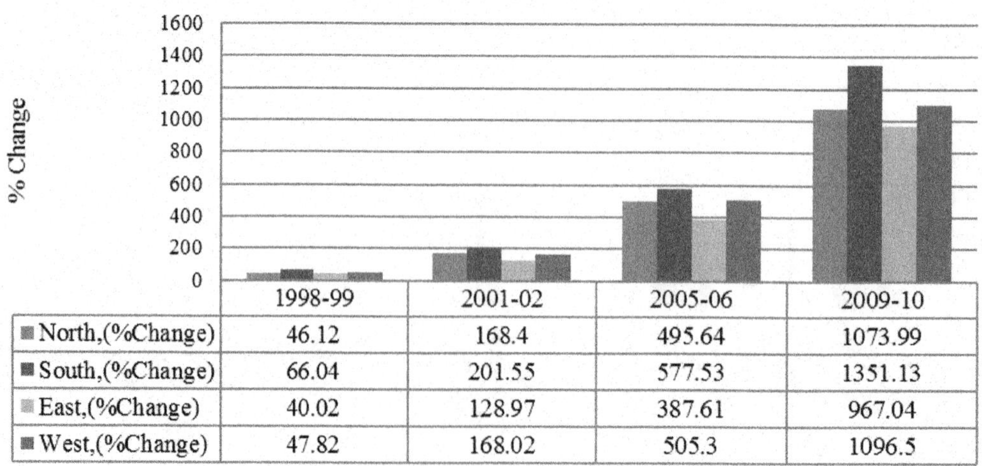

% Change
1600
1400
1200
1000
800
600
400
200
0
1998-99
2001-02
2005-06
2009-10
North,(%Change) 46.12 168.4 495.64 1073.99
South,(%Change) 66.04 201.55 577.53 1351.13
East,(%Change) 40.02 128.97 387.61 967.04
West,(%Change) 47.82 168.02 505.3 1096.5

From Figure 6 we get that Southern Zone is the largest market penetration zone in rural India in all the phases. Annual growth in this zone is 96.51%. Western Indian homes are the second largest. It has changed 78.32% per year during this period. Northern India was third, and Eastern zone was with lowest growth rate for market penetration of motorcycle.

Refrigerators

We get the result from Figure 7 and Table 10 that the growth of market penetration of refrigerators in rural areas has been increasing more than urban area. It has been increasing 18.08% annually on average. In urban market it has increased only 8.79% every year. This indicates that Indian rural market of refrigerators has vast potential to the marketers.

From the Figure 8 and Table 11 we get that the highest growth of market penetration of Refrigerators comes from Tamil Nadu. It has increased 107.50% annually. Madhya Pradesh was second. It has grown 67.27% per annum during this period. Bihar was third; Pondicherry was fourth, Goa was fifth, Maharashtra was sixth, and Karnataka was seventh and so on.

We get the result from the Figure 9 that, the highest growth of market penetration of refrigerators has been coming from Western Zone in all the phases. It has been increasing 25.46% per annum. Northern zone takes place the second. It has increased 20.80% p.a. Eastern zone was third and Southern zone was last.

Figure 7. Growth of rural and urban market penetration of Refrigerators

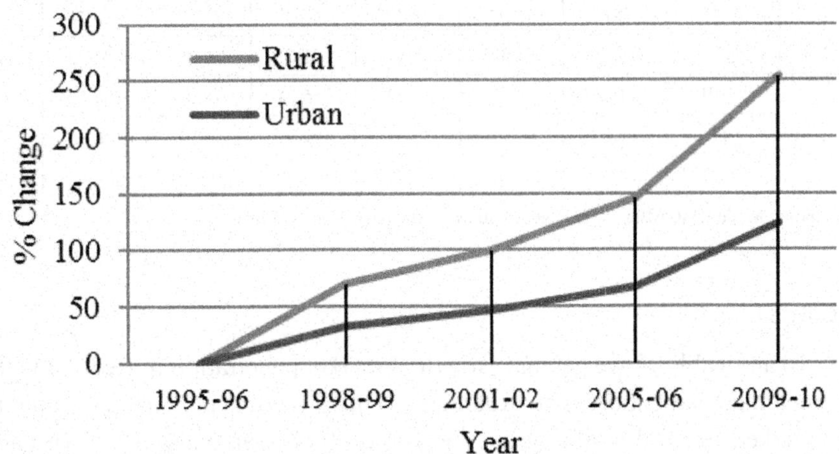

Table 10. Growth of market penetration of Refrigerators in India

Areas	1995-96	1998-99		2001-02		2005-06		2009-10	
	Total	Total	% Change	Total	% Change	Total	% Change	Total	% Change
Rural	20.37	34.55	69.61	40.54	99	49.97	145.31	71.94	253.16
Urban	252.25	334.97	32.80	369.49	46.48	421.70	67.17	562.46	123

Table 11. State-Wise rural market penetration of Refrigerators (Total penetration per'000 households)

	1995-96	1998-99		2001-02		2005-06		2009-10	
States	Total	Total	%Ch.	Total	%Ch.	Total	%Ch.	Total	%Ch.
Haryana	33.88	63.27	86.75	75.75	123.58	93.79	176.83	129.91	283.44
Himachal Pradesh	10.16	14.81	45.77	16.28	60.24	18.33	80.41	22.93	125.69
Madhya Pradesh	5.87	12.75	117.21	20.27	245.32	32.56	454.68	61.15	941.74
Punjab	88.81	135.78	52.89	151.37	70.55	173.15	94.97	222.35	150.37
Uttar Pradesh	9.61	18.95	97.19	23.05	139.85	28.98	201.56	41.72	334.13
Chandigarh	231.68	267.84	15.61	272.07	17.43	277.85	19.93	314.07	35.56
Delhi	264.88	398.31	50.37	453.31	71.14	517.25	95.28	653.16	146.59
Andhra Pradesh	29.84	48.08	61.17	56.24	88.47	65.87	120.74	88.02	194.97
Karnataka	13.89	29.23	110.44	37.57	170.48	48.26	247.44	69.43	399.86
Kerala	144.18	198.23	37.49	219.63	52.33	244.26	69.41	305.68	112.01
Tamil Nadu	2.42	8.50	251.24	12.90	433.05	20.66	753.72	38.84	1504.9
Pondicherry	16.48	35.48	115.29	45.85	178.22	60.96	269.9	91.50	455.23
Assam	8.48	14.81	74.65	16.34	92.69	19.63	121.49	28.52	236.32
Bihar	2.74	6.47	136.13	7.85	186.5	10.40	279.46	16.98	519.71
Meghalaya	14.06	14.84	5.55	13.77	-2.06	13.82	-1.71	16.62	18.21
Orissa	14.82	23.15	56.21	24.54	65.58	28.43	91.84	39.72	168.02
West Bengal	10.56	17.11	62.03	18.39	74.15	21.57	104.26	30.61	189.87
Gujarat	43.22	78.39	81.37	95.52	121.01	126.52	192.73	180.75	318.21
Maharashtra	22.19	44.83	102.03	56.63	155.21	78.67	254.53	118.78	435.29
Rajasthan	6.62	11.24	69.79	13.41	102.57	17.27	160.88	23.90	261.03
Goa	58.94	120.82	104.99	152.76	159.18	213.99	163.06	321.44	445.37

Source: The Great Indian Market, NCAER, (% change calculate on the base year1995-96)

Colour TVs (Large)

From the Figure 10 and Table 12 we get that growth of market penetration of Regular Colour TVs in the rural areas has been increasing more than urban area. This growth is near about double in rural market from the urban market. In rural market it has increased 40.88% annually. But in urban market it has increased only 17.05% annually. This depicts that marketing of large colour TVs in rural India is now zooming ahead vast potential to the marketers.

We observe from Figure 11 and Table 13 that the highest growth of market penetration of Colour TVs is in Rajasthan for all the phases. It has increased 375.85% annually during this period. Haryana was second. It increased 205.56% annually. Madhya Pradesh was third, Orissa was fourth, Pondicherry was fifth and Kerala was the lowest.

We observe from the results presented in Figure 12 that the highest growth of market penetration of refrigerators was in Northern zone in all the periods. It has increased 73.17% per annum during this period. Eastern Zone was second, Western zone was third and Southern zone was the lowest for the rank of market penetration of refrigerators.

Figure 8. State-wise growth of rural market penetration of Refrigerators

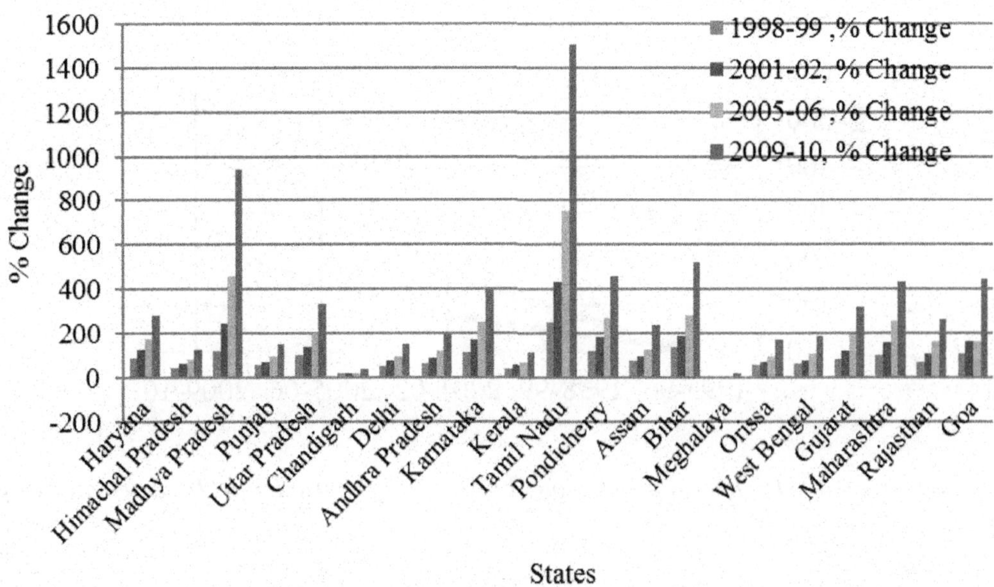

Figure 9. Zone wise rural market penetration of Refrigerators

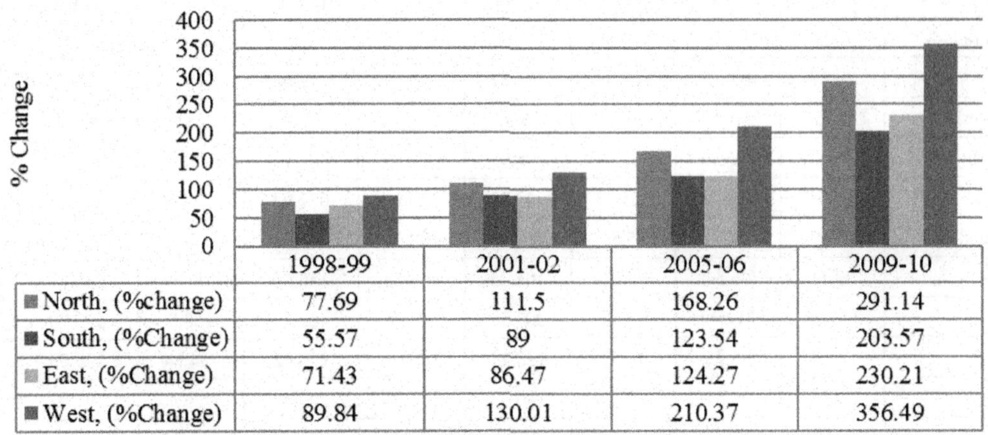

	1998-99	2001-02	2005-06	2009-10
North, (%change)	77.69	111.5	168.26	291.14
South, (%Change)	55.57	89	123.54	203.57
East, (%Change)	71.43	86.47	124.27	230.21
West, (%Change)	89.84	130.01	210.37	356.49

Table 12. Growth of market penetration of Colour TVs (Large) in India

Areas	1995-96	1998-99		2001-02		2005-06		2009-10	
	Total	Total	% Change	Total	% Change	Total	% Change	Total	% Change
Rural	23.40	42.13	80	64.42	175.30	99.48	325.12	157.31	572.26
Urban	194.82	267.77	37.44	350.09	79.70	480.52	146.45	659.89	238.72

Source: *The Great Indian Market, NCAER, (% change calculate on the base year1995-96)*

Figure 10. Growth of rural and urban market penetration of Large Colour TVs

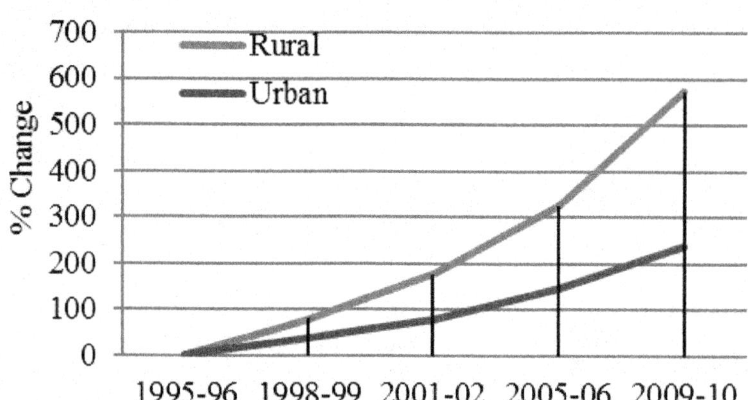

Table 13. State-wise market penetration of Colour TVs (Large) in rural India (Total penetration per'000 households)

States	1995-96	1998-99		2001-02		2005-06		2009-10	
	Total	Total	%Ch.	Total	%Ch.	Total	%Ch.	Total	%Ch.
Haryana	8.83	31.06	251.76	58.93	567.38	122.95	1292.4	262.94	2877.8
Himachal Pradesh	32.63	55.26	69.35	81.39	149.43	128.12	292.64	196.51	502.24
Madhya Pradesh	4.09	13.03	218.58	23.74	480.44	46.90	1046.7	92.63	2164.8
Punjab	29.67	63.64	114.49	101.81	243.14	172.68	482	285.39	861.88
Uttar Pradesh	5.78	10.99	90.14	16.87	191.87	27.86	382	46.11	697.75
Chandigarh	56.12	226.15	302.97	295.97	427.39	405.72	622.95	543.53	868.51
Delhi	131.8	336.53	155.33	449.33	240.91	632.04	379.54	866.97	557.79
Andhra Pradesh	17.97	33.35	85.59	53.58	198.16	81.98	356.2	128.91	617.36
Karnataka	39.11	66.54	70.01	104.26	166.58	156.66	400.56	233.71	497.57
Kerala	157.06	212.72	35.44	307.50	95.79	422.19	168.8	590.70	276.1
Tamil Nadu	51.04	85.45	67.42	133.17	160.91	196.42	284.84	293.03	474.12
Pondicherry	19.58	93.51	377.58	140.43	617.21	200.97	926.4	295.02	1406.7
Assam	6.69	17.23	157.55	26.32	293.42	41.47	519.88	70.29	950.67
Bihar	7.82	14.37	83.76	19.60	150.64	27.76	254.99	42.82	447.57
Meghalaya	22.61	43.47	92.26	60.02	165.46	84.94	275.67	130.65	477.84
Orissa	8.02	25.34	215.96	41.32	415.21	72.64	805.74	143.12	1684.5
West Bengal	5.55	13.82	149.01	20.77	274.23	33.31	500.18	57.62	938.2
Gujarat	45.50	75.37	65.65	114.56	151.78	169.35	272.2	230.62	406.86
Maharashtra	43.66	87.00	99.27	140.50	221.8	224.96	415.25	331.36	658.96
Rajasthan	3.49	17.56	403.15	38.62	1006.6	88.43	2433.8	187.13	5261.9
Goa	115.19	223.37	93.91	293.54	154.83	375.56	226.04	437.36	279.69

Source: The Great Indian Market, NCEAR, (% change calculate on the base year1995-96)

Figure 11. State- wise growth of rural market penetration of large Colour TVs

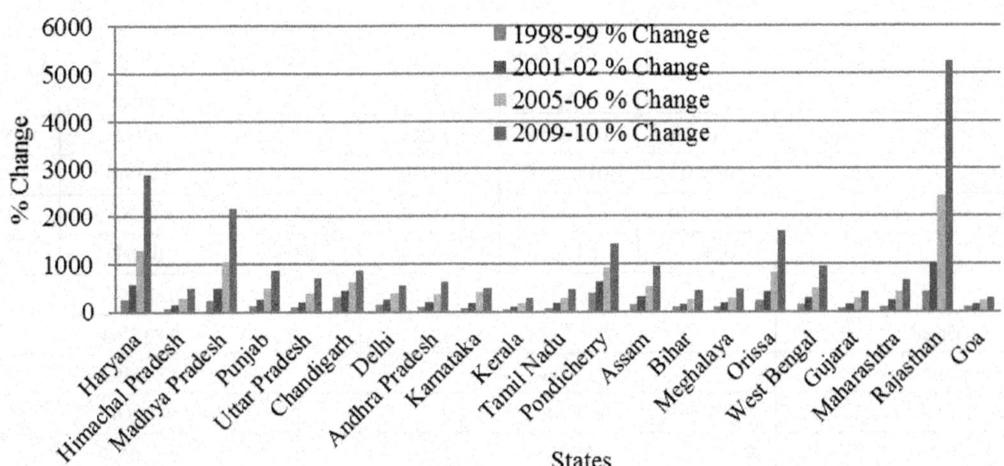

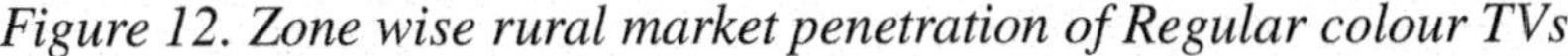

Figure 12. Zone wise rural market penetration of Regular colour TVs

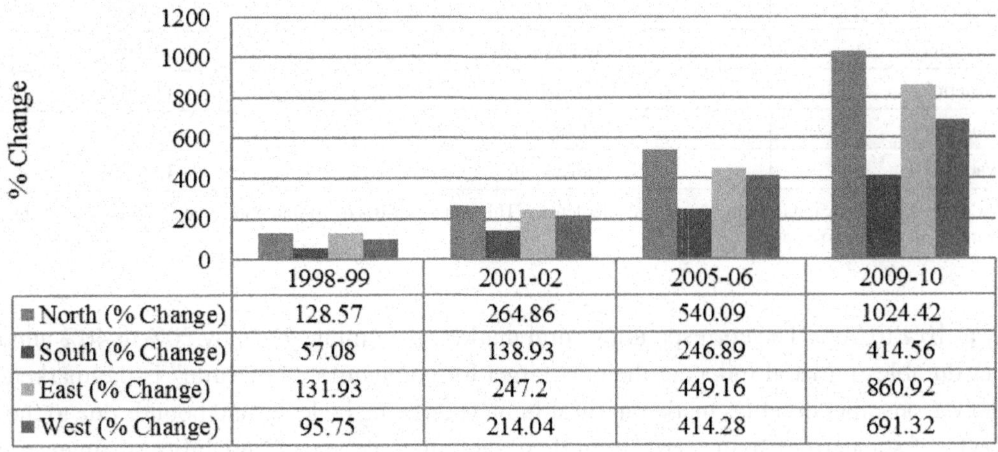

	1998-99	2001-02	2005-06	2009-10
North (% Change)	128.57	264.86	540.09	1024.42
South (% Change)	57.08	138.93	246.89	414.56
East (% Change)	131.93	247.2	449.16	860.92
West (% Change)	95.75	214.04	414.28	691.32

We have presented the panel regression results in Table 14 and Table 15. The static panel regression on penetration of ceiling fan and motorcycle are presented in Table 14. These results show that state level per capita income and tele-density are statistically significant in explaining penetration of above consumer durables. We have also obtained similar results for the penetration of two other consumer durables as shown in Table 15.

CONCLUSION

Today penetration of consumer durables market in rural India is changing rapidly rather than urban markets. Total share of penetration is low in rural areas compared to urban areas but the growth of penetration change in rural area is higher than urban area. The urban consumer durables market is growing

Table 14. Panel regression on consumer durables

	Dependent Variable: Rural Penetration of Ceiling Fan			Dependent Variable: Rural Penetration of Motorcycle		
	C	X_1	X_2	C	X_1	X_2
Coefficient	216.8118	0.013558	5.032249	-54.91783	0.006267	2.516605
Std. Error	50.74042	0.002207	2.177501	26.59811	0.001198	1.153029
t-Statistic	4.272960	6.143497	2.311020	-2.064727	5.232050	2.182604
Prob.	0.0002	0.0000	0.0279	0.0477	0.0000	0.0370
R-squared	0.971489			0.894849		
Adjusted R-squared	0.955333			0.835264		
S.E. of regression	94.94112			47.41892		
Sum squared resid	270414.5			67456.62		
Log likelihood	-275.3853			-242.0620		
F-statistic	60.13105			15.01792		
Prob(F-statistic)	0.000000			0.000000		
Mean dependent var	628.7375			137.6998		
S.D. dependent var	449.2213			116.8307		
Akaike info criterion	12.22439			10.83592		
Schwarz criterion	12.92609			11.53762		
Hannan-Quinn criter.	12.48956			11.10109		
Durbin-Watson stat	**1.575347**			**1.567239**		

Note: C: Constant, X_1=Per-capita income, X_2=Rural tele-density. This panel consists of 16 states and 3 years. This panel regression has been conducted by using the fixed-effect model.

annually at 10% to 20%. The corresponding rural market is zooming ahead by 20% to 40% annually, so consumer durables for rural India are the next target for companies. “Go Rural” is the marketer’s new slogan now. Consumer durables market in rural India is growing by leaps and bounds due to the significant growth of standard of living, growth in disposable income, easy availability of finance, increase in consumer awareness, growth of media, improvements in technology, increase in education, power availability, improving rural infrastructure, agricultural reforms and various government policies for rural development & minimum amenities. The urban market is a replacement and up gradation market where, rural market is an untapped vest potential market with large population generating huge demand for first time buyer. The demand for consumer durables in the urban market often follows a cyclical but the rural market it is steady. Consumer durables market has been transformed by the introduction of new brands. The demand for consumer durables market in rural India has increased significantly due to increasing competition which results in the decrease in price. Purchase behavior of rural household has been dramatically increased due to the influence of the rural youth. They insist their family members to buy products which are trendy. They are not sticking only to essential items, they are now interested to buying consumer durables. The penetration level of consumer durables is very low in India compared to other countries. This translates into vast unrealized potential market in rural India. Today consumer durables market in rural India is growing at a faster pace, which is looking for a better opportunity to the marketers.

Table 15. Panel regression on consumer durables

	Dependent Variable: Rural Penetration of Refrigerators			Dependent Variable: Rural Penetration of Colour TV		
	C	X_1	X_2	C	X_1	X_2
Coefficient	42.76681	0.001208	0.050535	4.506289	0.004319	1.557043
Std. Error	35.78488	0.001485	0.605556	17.13609	0.000696	0.417986
t-Statistic	1.195109	0.813330	0.083452	0.262971	6.202784	3.725110
Prob.	0.2519	0.4296	0.9347	0.7944	0.0000	0.0008
R-squared	0.879331			0.973142		
Adjusted R-squared	0.732805			0.957922		
S.E. of regression	40.66206			24.13163		
Sum squared resid	23147.65			17470.07		
Log likelihood	-150.7486			-209.6381		
F-statistic	6.001183			63.94024		
Prob(F-statistic)	0.000768			0.000000		
Mean dependent var	75.05281			135.1981		
S.D. dependent var	78.66385			117.6417		
Akaike info criterion	10.54679			9.484920		
Schwarz criterion	11.37127			10.18662		
Hannan-Quinn criter.	10.82008			9.750094		
Durbin-Watson stat	3.764706			1.610756		

Note: C: Constant, X_1=Per-capita income, X_2=Rural tele-density. This panel consists of 16 states and 3 years. This panel regression has been conducted by using the fixed-effect model.

REFERENCES

Ahamed, A. (2013). Rural marketing Strategies for Selling Products &Services: Issue and Challenge. *Journal of Business Management &Social Sciences Research, 2*(1), 55-60.

Badi, R. V., & Badi, N. V. (2011). *Rural Marketing*. Himalaya Publishing House.

Banerjee, B. (1995). *Financial Policy and Management Accounting*. Kolkata: World Press Pvt. Ltd.

Gangopadhyay, P. (1992). *Business Organization & Principal of Management*. Retrieved from: www.ibef.org

Kalotra, A. (2013). Rural marketing Potential in India. *International Journal of Advance Research in Computer Science and Software Engineering, 3*(1), 1-10.

Karti, R. & Valarmati, S. (2015). Aggressive Business Expansion in Rural markets through understanding Indian consumers. *International Journal of Scientific and Research Publication, 5*.

Kaur, B. (2015). Rural Marketing-A Concept of Marketing Management. *IOSR Journal of Business and Management*, 40-45.

Kishor, N.R. (2014). Rural Consumer Behavior towards Consumer Durable goods in India. *International Journal of Advance Research in Computer Science and Management Studies, 2*, 1-13.

Konti, V.V.D.P. (2012). Prospect and Problems of Indian rural market. *ZENITH International Journal of Business Economics & Management, 2*(3), 200-213.

Kumar, K.R. (2010). Consumer durable Industry in India-A Bird's Eye View. *Asian Journal of Management, 1*(2), 61-64.

Kumar, P. (2013). Challenge and Opportunity of Indian Rural Market. *International Journal of Marketing Studies, 5*(3), 161-173.

Kumar, P., & Dangi, N. (2013). Rural Marketing in India: Challenges and Opportunities. *International Journal of Management & Social Science Research, 2*, 34–56.

Laddha, S. (2015). Rural Consumer Buying Behavior and Brand Awareness of Consumer Durables. *NBR E-Journal, 1*(1), 1-9.

Panicker, P., & Warrier, A. (2013). Rural Marketing –Profitability in Rural Sales. *International Journal of Scientific and Research*, 1359-1361.

Patel, S. K. (2013). The challenges and Strategies of marketing in Rural India. *Asia Pacific Journal of Marketing & Management Review, 2*(7), 38-43.

Pathak, R. & Pathak, N. (2013). Information Technology: Bridging the gap between urban and rural marketing. *Scholars World-IRMJCR, 1*(3), 102-111.

Peddada, K. (2014). Growth of Financial Infrastructure in Rural India. *Kurukshetra' Ministry of Rural Development, Monthly Journal, 62*(5), 52.

Rajnani, R.C. (2014). Rural Infrastructure key to inclusive growth. *Kurukshetra' Ministry of Rural Development, Monthly Journal, 62*(5).

Rani, M. (2013). Rural Market: The Core of Indian Market. *G.J.C.M.P. (Global Institute for Research & Management), 2*(6), 123-125.

Ray Chowdhury, N. C. (1992). *Business Management*. Kolkata: Modern Book Agency Pvt. Ltd.

Sing, P., & Sharma, A. (2012). The Changing Face of Rural Marketing in Indian Economy. *A Journal of Economics and Management, 1*(7), 47-60.

Siras, M. K. (2012). Potentials and strategies for durables-A Study in Ghaziabad District. *International journal of Trade and Commerce, 1*(1), 60-69.

Sivanesan, R. (2014).Problem of Rural Marketing in India. *International Journal of Research in Business and Management, 1*, 1–7.

Suganthi, V. (2015).Rural consumer brand awareness. *International Journal of Multidisciplinary Research and Development, 2*, 145–152.

Thakur, C. (2013). A Study of purchaser Institution about Consumer Durable Goods. *International Global Researches Analysis*, *2*(3), 107-108.

Tripati, K.K, (2014). Review of Rural Infrastructure under Bharat Nirman. *'Kurukshetra' Ministry of Rural Development, Monthly Journal*, *62*(5), 52.

Vilas, G. D. (2012). Rural Marketing Environment in India. *International Referred Multidisciplinary Online Research Journal*, *1*(VI), 1–35.

KEY TERMS AND DEFINITIONS

Brown Goods: Relatively light electronic consumer durables such as TVs, radios, digital media players and computers are called brown goods.

Changing Market Penetration: One of the four alternative growth strategies (Ref. Ansoff Matrix). Which is (a) Retain or increase your product's market share, (b) Dominate growth markets (c) Drive out your competitors and (d) Increase existing customers usage.A market penetration strategy involves focusing on selling your existing products or services into your existing markets to gain a higher market share.

Consumer Durables: Consumer durables are a category of consumer household used products that do not have to be purchased frequently because they are made to last for an extended period of time (typically more than three years).

Consumer Electronics: Consumer electronics refers to any device containing an electronic circuit board that is intended for everyday use by individuals.

Disposable Income: Income remaining after deduction of taxes and social security charges, available to be spent or saved as one wishes.

Marketing Strategies: A marketing strategy is a process or model to allow a company or organization to focus limited resources on the best opportunities to increase sales and thereby achieve a sustainable competitive advantage.

Rural Marketing: Rural marketing is a process of developing, pricing, promoting, and distributing rural specific goods and services leading to desired exchange with rural customers to satisfy their needs and wants, and also to achieve organizational objectives.

White Goods: Heavy consumer durables such as air conditioners, refrigerators, stoves etc, which used to be painted only white enamel finish. Despite their availability in varied colors now, they are called white goods.

Chapter 14
Importance of Sustainable Rural Development through Agrarian Reforms:
An Indian Scenario

Partha Mukhopadhyay
National Institute of Technology Durgapur, India

Madhabendra Sinha
National Institute of Technology Durgapur, India

Partha Pratim Sengupta
National Institute of Technology Durgapur, India

ABSTRACT

The chapter tries to find out the relationship between public expenditures on infrastructure related to agriculture and allied factors and agricultural sustainability in Indian context. India has been suffering from appalling chronic poverty and to reduce the same, we need to focus on rural development, particularly in agriculture as it is unavoidable relation with economic development. Gini index of India is 33.9 (2011) i.e. asymmetrical wealth distribution exists. India is being burdened with a population of 1.2 billion as in 2015. The reciprocal relationship between agrarian reform and democratic development is pronounced. Agrarian reform was one of the focal points around which social mobilization occurred. Sustainable rural development could be achieved by a new balance as we find from some econometric model, which is being sought between agriculture and public expenditure and also export of agricultural produce. Adopting bottom-up agricultural development approaches which emphasize the involvement of the rural people in the implementations of different development programmes may escalate agrarian reforms.

DOI: 10.4018/978-1-5225-2364-2.ch014

INTRODUCTION

Development is a concept construing changes in the conditions of well being of the people irrespective of income level. It is generally evaluated in terms of changes in aesthetic qualities of the community, i.e. demographics, housing, employment, income, market effects, public services etc. Of late India shows as one of the fastest growing economies in the world. This chapter brushes one more stroke the emerging relationship of infrastructure availability and productivity growth. This analysis relies on both qualitative and quantitative measures of impacts.

Infrastructure, no doubt, is the backbone of any society. Infrastructure development is a *sine qua non* for accelerating progress of the quality of human life. Though infrastructure projects, involve huge initial capital investments, high incremental capital output ratio, high risk with long gestation periods, and low rate of returns on investments but infrastructure development particularly, rural infrastructure encompass economic development of the country. Rural infrastructure has a direct and strong relationship with farmers. Rural infrastructure development is supposed to be a benchmark to transform the existing traditional agriculture or subsistence farming into a most modern, commercial and dynamic farming system so that India could oust the surplus labourers to any other productive jobs. We can group infrastructure under some categories as given in Table 1.

Role of Agriculture in Infrastructure Development

Agriculture ensures supply of food to industrial sector (Lewis, 1954) and hence it is a driving force of overall economic development (Mellor, 1966; Schultz, 1964). Technology spillovers also increase in productivity of Land and labour and as a result income of farmers increase which enhance their purchasing powers. A number of empirical studies (Hazell & Roel, 1983; Hammer & Hazel, 1991; Delgado, 1998; Zhang, 2002) ensured that multiplier effects of agricultural growth are greater than two.

Several studies explain the elasticity of poverty reduction with respect to agricultural productivity is significant ((Thirtle, Lin & Piesse, 2003). Some econometric studies (Binswanger & Rosenzweig, 1993;

Table 1. Categorization of infrastructure

Based	Resources	Rural Sector	Urban Sector
Input Based	-	Agricultural input like Seed, Fertilizer, Pesticides, Farm equipment and machinery etc.	-
Resource Based:	Water	Irrigation and Drinking	Drinking
	Electricity	Pump and Household	Household and Industrial Purpose
Physical Infrastructure:	Telecommunication, Road connectivity, Transport, storage (including Cold storage), processing, preservation, and Sanitation etc.	Required all Resources	Required all Resources
Institutional Infrastructure:	Education, research, information & communication services, financial services, market, etc.	Required all Resources	Required all Resources

Source: Authors' Own Observation

Butzer, 2002; Zhang, 2004) estimated that there is a positive significant relationship between agricultural output and infrastructure investment.

Agricultural sector has also played an important role as foreign exchange earner too. Agricultural exports accounted for 44 percent of India's total merchandise export during 1960-61and in 2013-14 it is more than 17 percent of export earnings of India.

There is a positive correlation between GDP and Public Expenditure on Agriculture (0.98) and similarly, GDP to export of Agricultural and allied product (0.96). So, agricultural infrastructural growth plays a significant role to the economic development in the context of India in particular.

A Brief Discussion on Indian Agriculture

Agriculture is consistently losing its importance in India's economic growth. According to CIA Factbook-2014, agriculture sector contributes 17.9 percent of India's Gross Domestic Product (GDP), and in 2015, in the Budget it is reported that more than 50 percent of the population is still dependent on it. The farm sector, including forestry and fishing, grew by 3.2 percent in the quarter ending September, as compared o 3.8 percent in previous quarter and 4.7 percent in 2013-14. For the entire financial year, it was 1.4 percent. Backed by continued technological innovations in the sector, India's food grain production has more than doubled over the decades to a record 264 million tons in 2014, but the same is not being capitalized to increase the profit margins and revenue of farmers. There is still a large dependency on rainfall and other climatic conditions for good yield, and post-harvest logistics remains an area of concern.

Figure 1. Role of Infrastructure in Agricultural Development

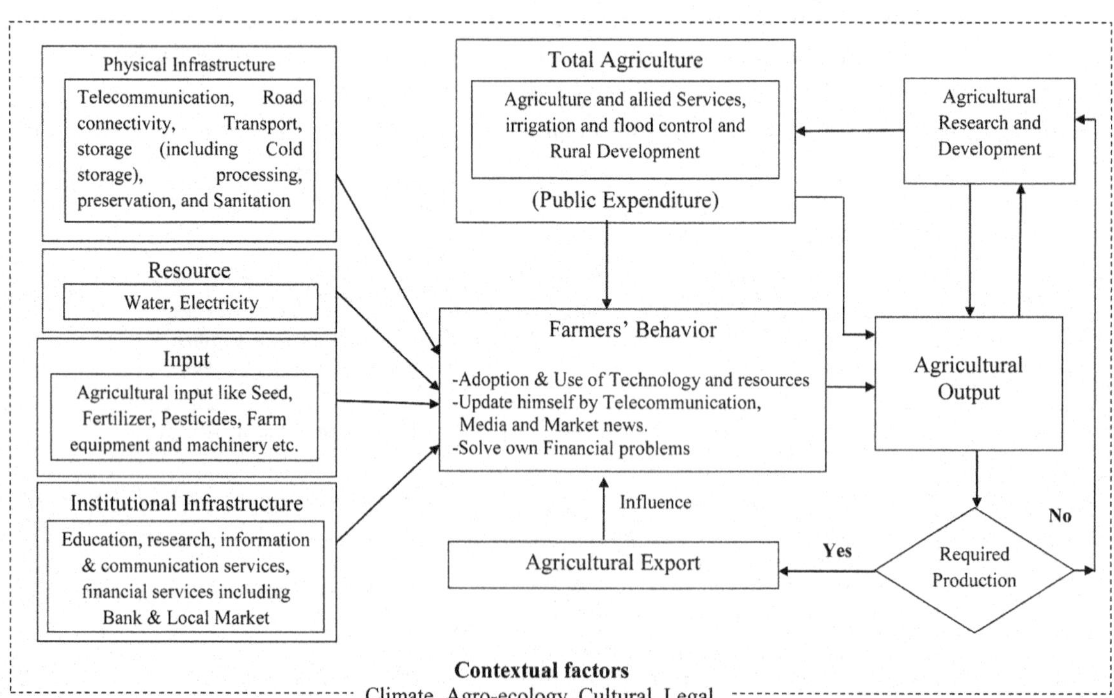

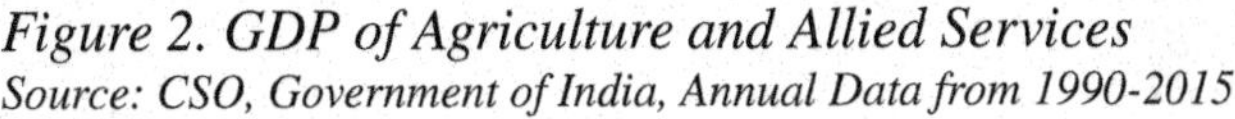

Figure 2. GDP of Agriculture and Allied Services
Source: CSO, Government of India, Annual Data from 1990-2015

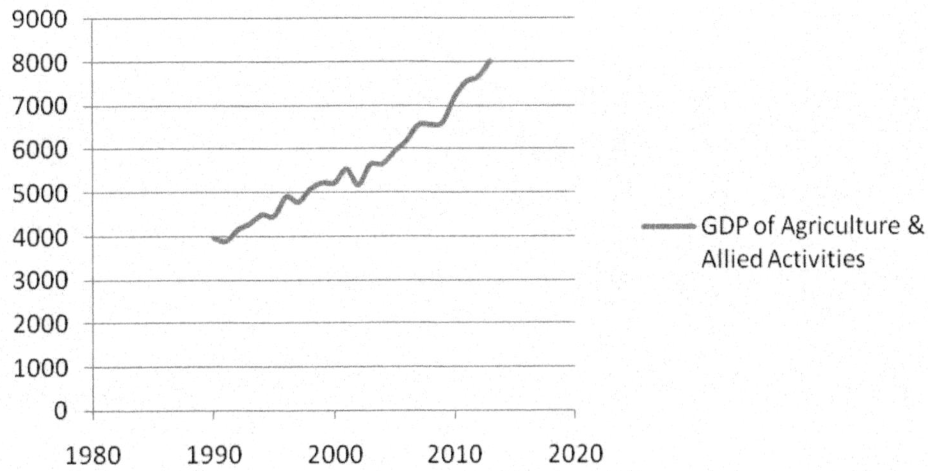

In the post-1990s period, there has been a continuous decline in government support in the form of declining investments in agriculture. The withdrawal of the State has led to a much greater dependence of farmers on private sources. Very unfortunate to say that there has also been an upward trend in the cases of farmer suicides over the years and the victims have largely been marginal and small farmers. Increasing costs of cultivation leading to higher indebtedness, crop failures, inability to face price rise with greater liberalization of the agricultural sector and profile of gobbling up of lion's share of profit margin by the marketing middleman have forced farmers to take this extreme step a death trap to speak of.

A report was published by zee news exclusive of union budget-2015 that it's a fact in India; farmers are receiving only around 25 to 30 percent of the price paid by the consumers. The loss appears not due to their inefficiencies but also for unwanted role of middlemen. Farmers in developed economies of Europe and the United States, in contrast, receive around 75 percent of the price that consumers pay. The wide gap between ultimate sellers of agricultural goods and the ultimate purchasers of the same makes the system vulnerable in view of sustainability when market is treated as an institution in the age of globalization. The entire system is likely to be changed without any more delay. The growth performance of the agriculture sector has been fluctuating across the time periods 1990 to 2015.

Inflationary trend of food items has got a close link with the supply crunch, triggered by the international market. To deal with this type of vulnerability, there is also a need to make long-term plan. India is still dependent on the other Countries for some commodities such as edible oil (mostly palm oil) and pulses, despite the prevailing agriculture-intensity profile of India. India imports more than 50 percent of its cooking oil. Long-term approach in trade policy and lack of consistency make us dependable for these commodities on overseas market. Government of India generally reduces the import duty of a particular commodity to tame price rise but in the long run escalates the inflow of that commodity in the domestic market and increase our dependability. While taking a decision on duty, the government should take into account the concerns of all stakeholders related to that commodity, mainly producers, exporters and consumers too. When the government reduces import duty, it impacts all stakeholders simultaneously. Cutting of import duty makes the same domestic commodity uncompetitive. But con-

Figure 3. Pattern of growth of GDP and GDP of agriculture
Source: CSO, Government of India, Annual Data from 1990-2015

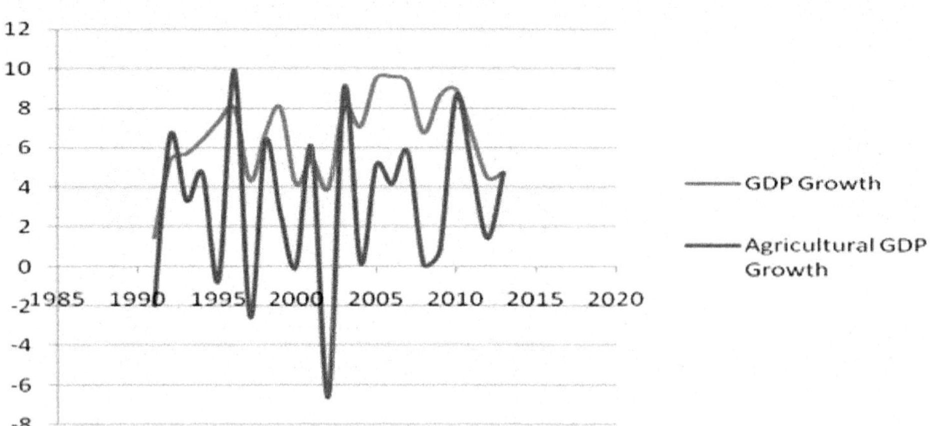

sumers get that international commodity at a lower price. When government decides to increase import duty, the same impact appears. In that situation, at the best competitive price, the produce for which import duty is increased minimizes the only option for consumers to get same international commodity.

As export is one of components of GDP the growth by export led hypothesis postulates that export expansion is one of the main determinants of growth. India's export performance is fluctuating in nature from 1990-2015. In 1997, for the first time after liberalization, India's exports registered with negative growth of 2.33 because of the East Asian Crisis. Since the ASEAN countries and Japan were most acutely affected by the crisis, their respective currencies lost value, which also meant that the Indian rupee appreciated against these currencies (due to interest rate differentials). Agricultural export of India faces the impact of negative growth in the year 1999-2000 than previous year. The next major setback for India's exports was the global crisis of 2008. India's trade deficit dampened in 2009-10 with a negative import growth (-0.78 percent) were also impacted with a negative growth rate of 2.9 percent in 2008-09 than previous years. India has been following overall an increasing path in agricultural exports throughout the period from1990 to 2015 except the years 1999-2000 and 2009-2010.

Figure 4. Agricultural export as a share of agricultural GDP
Source: DGCIS and CSO, Government of India, Annual Data from 1990-2015

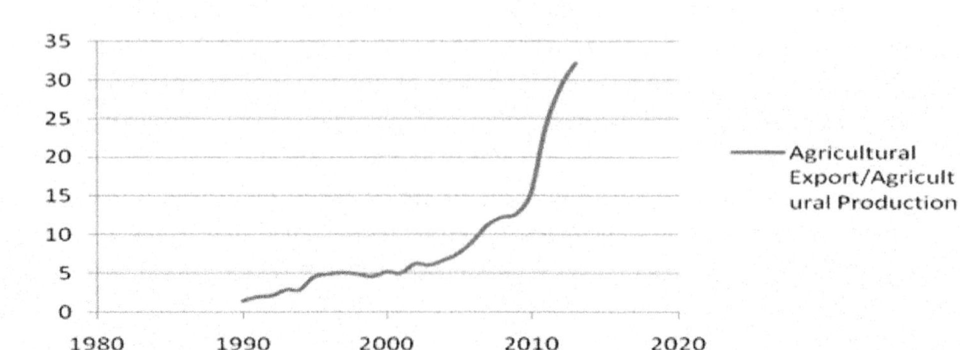

Some commodities such as wheat, sugar, cotton, edible oil, rubber etc are directly related to the government's trade decisions and control. It is observed that in the past few years, the government's approach to deal with the trade of the commodities has been widely exposed. Indian Government has to adopt bottom-up agricultural approaches which emphasize the involvement of the rural people and first prioritize the concerns of our own farmers. Composition of exports means goods that we are selling to other countries. At the time of Independence, exports of India were consisted of agricultural products like tea, spices, tobacco and other raw materials etc. We were also exporting cotton textiles and jute products in large quantities. We are now exporting large quantities of items such as machinery and transport equipment, chemicals allied products, marine products, and handicrafts, however export of items such as fish, cotton, fabric, tea, Jute, manufactures spices etc.

Rural Infrastructure

Rural infrastructure is a major bottleneck in achieving the potential growth-path under globalization. In a Study, (Oshikoya & Hussain, 2002) it is revealed that better rural infrastructure improves price-competitiveness and attracting Foreign Direct Investment (FDI).

In their studies (Wheeler & Ashoka, 1992; Asiedu & Donald, 2004) they found that status of domestic infrastructure is an important determinant of the magnitude of private capital inflow such as FDI. Efficient transportation system with modern telecommunication facilities, reliable energy supply and access to safe water are the essential conditions for attracting investments from outside the country.

Market

Market integration over space and time requires sound infrastructure with all other facilities. Market integration is assumed to be poor in India resulting in drastic drops in local prices and restricted access to commercial finance. We are suffering from poor transport, storage capacity and weak form of communication infrastructure. Rule of law hardly works due low quality of governance; effective competition among the markets is absent. Hence market transaction is highly non-transparent in India. So, development of transparent rules and regulations is essential for infrastructure development as everything is hanging together. As the economic environment becomes adverse, then global financial crisis arises (J.N. Verma, W.P. No. 2009-02-06).

Despite the bottleneck of agrarian crisis, India's food grain production has more than doubled over the decades to a record 264 million tonnes in 2014 because of technological spillover and other factors too, whereas the wellbeing of the growth of output is not transmitted to the farmers with a same rate, a gross inequality. There is still a large dependency on rainfall and other climatic conditions for better yield and post-harvest logistics remains an area of concern. Over the years, marginal and small farmers' suicidal upward trend is observed due to increasing costs of cultivation, higher indebtedness, crop failures and inability to get adequate price.

Problem Background

Does investment in "Infrastructure" is beneficial? Govt. of India invests Rs. 12810.22 billion in 2013-14 Union Budget and Rs. 4845.33 Billion in 2014-15 Union Budget for total Infrastructure Development.

Figure 5. Infrastructure as a base of overall development including agricultural development
Source: Authors' Own Observation

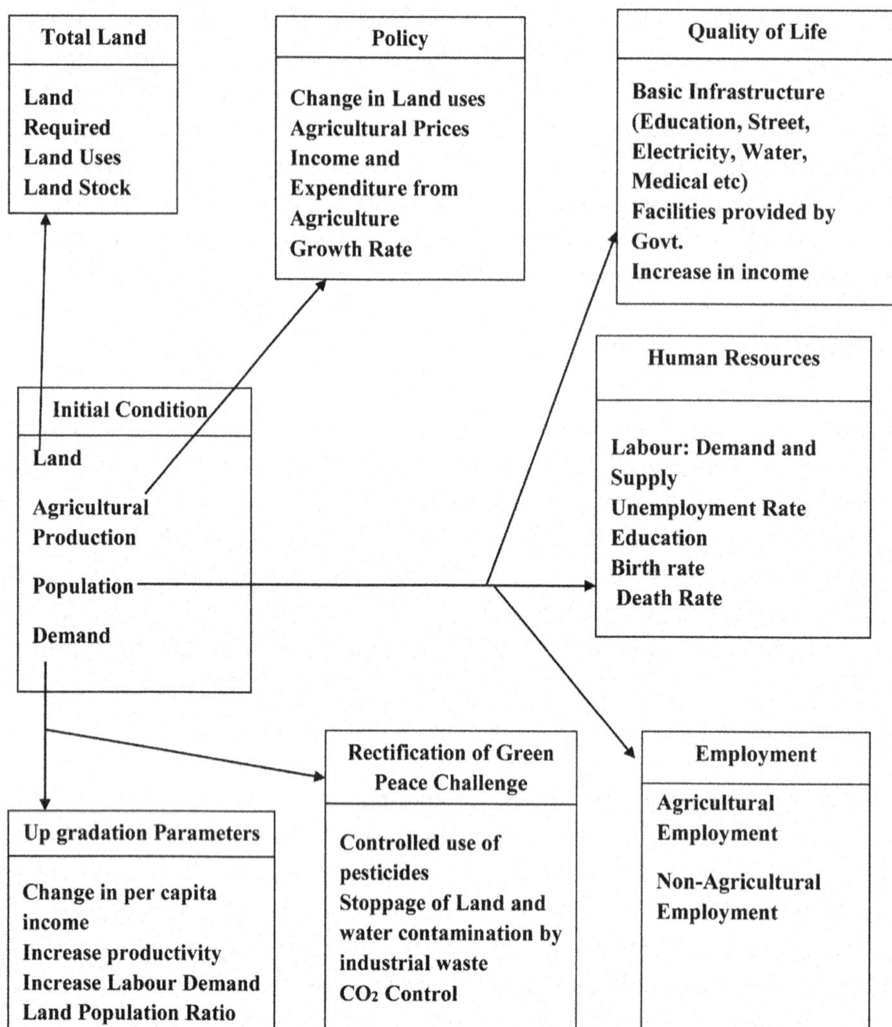

Only a few researches are available in investment in infrastructure. Bennathan and Canning (2000) indicate that investments in electricity generating and paved roads are more profitable than other public investments. But the question is why the investment is low?

In the view of agrarian crisis, India's food grain production has more than doubled over the decades to a record 264 million tonnes in 2014 backed by Technological spillover, but the same is not being capitalized to increase the revenue and profit margins of farmers. There is still a large dependency on rainfall and other climatic conditions for good yield and post-harvest logistics remains an area of concern. Farmers are greater dependence on private sources led by withdrawal of state. Over the years, marginal and small farmers' suicidal upward trend is observed due to increasing costs of cultivation, higher indebtedness, crop failures and inability to get adequate price.

REVIEW OF LITERATURE

Tripathi (2008) examined the performance of agricultural productivity in India during the last 37 years, and found stagnation of TFP growth in Indian agriculture. Using the time series data for the period from 1970 to 2005, Shombe (2005) investigated causal relationships among agriculture, manufacturing and exports in Tanzania. The empirical results show that the evidence of Granger causality but agriculture causes both exports and manufacturing. It is really an interesting study where scenario of exports and manufacturing sector become better off with the progress of agricultural activities in developing nation. Khalafalla and Webb (2000) empirically tested the growth hypothesis of export leading for Malaysian economy undergoing major structural changes. Khalafalla and Webb also investigated the relationship between the exports and economic growth in Malaysia using the quarterly data from 1965-1996. Bashir (2003) studied the Pakistan's impacts of economic reforms and trade liberalization on agricultural export performance. He suggested that economic reforms affected the agricultural export performance which is more sensitive to the domestic factors. Shirazi and Manap (2004) re-investigate the exports-economic growth nexus, using the data from 1960 to 2003 period and the results strongly support a long-run relationship among the three variables (imports, export and output). As far as the causality between the exports and output growth is concerned, exports cause output growth, but converse is not true. Khan *et. al.* (1995) investigated the export- growth and economic growth using the granger causality test and co-integration methods and found stable long-run two way relationship between total exports and output while one way relationship between output and primary exports. In their findings, there is a bi-directional causality between total exports growth and economic growth exclude. Huges and Penson (1985) have shown a marked increase in volume of agricultural exports over the years. The authors measured the effects of GDP movements on agriculture. In his research, Chandra (2000) found the bi-directional causal relationship between the growth of exports and GDP growth; short run causal relation is pronounced, because co-integration between GDP growth and growth of exports was not found. Sharma and Panagiotidis (2005) test the export-led growth hypothesis in the Indian context, and the results strengthen the arguments against the export-led growth hypothesis in the context of India. Raju and Kurien (2005) analyzed the relationship between exports and economic growth in India over the period of pre-liberalization (1960-1992), and found strong support for unidirectional causality from exports to economic growth. They have use Granger causality regressions based on stationary variables, with and without an error-correction term. The causal relationship between growth of exports and economic growth in India for the post-liberalization period 1992-2007, analyzed by Dash (2009) ; the results indicate that there exists a long-run relationship between output and exports, and it is unidirectional from growth of exports to output growth.

RESEARCH OBJECTIVE

We are estimating the relationship between public expenditures on infrastructure related to agriculture and allied factors and agricultural sustainability measured in terms of production and export for a given period.

It is an attempt to provide the emerging relationship of infrastructure availability and productivity growth. By measuring the impact of availability of different type of infrastructural facilities on growth of total factor productivity in state economies in India we may conclude whether the trend is sustainable or not.

HYPOTHESES

On the basis of introductory background, following two null hypotheses are to be tested for achieving the above mentioned objective of the study. They are categorized as following:

H1: Public expenditure on agriculture does not cause output of agriculture in terms of market value.
H2: Public expenditure on agriculture does not have any impact on agricultural export.

DATA SOURCES

The study relies on secondary data compiled from various published sources such as RBI Handbook, World Bank Data etc. The other major sources for the collection of the information are found to be available literature as, journals, books, and news of Government of India and states Governments related to the agriculture, energy, transport, education etc. For trend analysis, we are collecting data from the year 1970-71 to 2014-15. GDP data and export of agriculture and allied product data of same time span are collected for comparing the trend also.

RESEARCH METHODOLOGY

A large number of methods or econometric tools are used in the literature to study the relationship, including infrastructural growth, agricultural-export and GDP. The independent variables used, as a proxy for infrastructure is either some measure of investment or a physical indicator (Straub, 2008).

We know that time series data on any quantitative character or variable may contain either deterministic trend or stochastic trend or both. But implications are obviously different in nature. The time series with deterministic trend follows trend stationary process (TSP), while a non-stationary time series showing stochastic trend is a difference stationary process (DSP). The issue whether a macroeconomic time series is of DSP or TSP is extremely important because the dynamic properties of the two processes are different (Nelson & Plosser, 1982). While the former is predictable, the latter is completely unpredictable. In a series following TSP, cyclical fluctuations are temporary around a stable trend, while for DSP any random shock to the series has a permanent effect. The cyclical components of a TSP originate from the residuals of a regression of the series on the variable time, and a DSP involves regression of a series on its own lagged values and time. A TSP has a trend in the mean but no trend in the variance, but a DSP has a trend in the variance with or without trend in the mean and here it should be mentioned that a random walk without drift has no trend in the mean values of the variable.

The most widely used model to take over stochastic trend is autoregressive of order p [AR(p)]:

$$X_t = \alpha + \beta_1 X_{t-1} + \beta_2 X_{t-2} + \beta_3 X_{t-3} + \dots\dots\dots\dots + \beta_p X_{t-p} + \varepsilon_t \quad (1)$$

X_t gives values in log form in time t and ε_t is a stationary series with mean zero and variance σ^2.

This model can generate the trend behaviour of macroeconomic time series and the randomly fluctuating behaviour of their growth rates. If, for example, X_t is generated by the model:

$$X_t = \alpha + X_{t-1} + \varepsilon_t \quad (2)$$

Equation (2) is AR (1) with β_1=1, accumulating X_t starting with an initial value X_0 we get,

$$X_t = X_0 + \alpha t + \sum_{j=1}^{t} \varepsilon_j \quad (3)$$

The Equation (3) has the same form as the conventional log-linear trend equation, excepting for the fact that the disturbance is not stationary.

One important property of time series data, not usually present in cross-sectional data, is the existence of correlation across observations. Income today, for example, is highly correlated with income of the last year. Thus X_t tends to exhibit trend behaviour and to be highly correlated over time. The non-stationary time series containing a unit root will give a stochastic trend. If β_1 = 1 for the AR(1) model, then X_t has a unit root and exhibit trend behaviour, especially when $\alpha \neq 0$. Unit root series contain a so called stochastic trend.

The Augmented Dickey-Fuller (ADF) test is performed for unit root hypothesis. The more appropriate model for testing a unit root is the AR(p) with deterministic trend:

$$\Delta X_t = \alpha + \rho X_{t-1} + \eta_1 \Delta X_{t-1} + \eta_2 \Delta X_{t-2} + \dots\dots\dots\dots + \eta_{p-1} \Delta X_{t-p+1} + \delta t + \varepsilon_t, \quad (4)$$

A series belongs to the class DSP exhibiting stochastic trend if ρ =0, δ=0, and the TSP class if ρ < 0. If ρ = 0, then X_t contains a unit root. In this case we cannot perform hypothesis testing by utilising the usual distributions appropriate for least square. Thus we have to follow ADF test. If the t-statistics on ρ are less negative than the Dickey-Fuller critical value, we conclude that the series X_t has a unit root.

To test whether the series has a unit root, we have to choose lag length (p). Many sophisticated statistical criteria and testing methods are available to determine the appropriate lag length in an AR(p) model. But we have performed a simple route by choosing a maximum lag length and then sequentially drop lag lengths if the relevant coefficients are insignificant. The maximum lag length is chosen by following Schwert (1989) rule:

P_{max} = integer part of $[12(T/100)^{.25}]$. (5)

AIC is also used for selecting the appropriate lag length. By following such criteria, the maximum lag length is found to be 1. Thus our model would be:

$$\Delta X_t = \alpha + \rho X_{t-1} + \eta_1 \Delta X_{t-1} + \delta t + \varepsilon_t, \tag{6}$$

The stochastic properties of the time series data in this study have been examined by carrying out Augmented Dickey Fuller (ADF) and Phillips-Perron (PP) unit root tests. Both the intercept and trend components have been incorporated in the ADF estimated relation as following:

$$\Delta X_t = \varphi_0 + \beta t + \rho X_{t-1} + \sum_{i=1}^{P} \gamma_i \Delta X_{t-1} + \varepsilon_t \tag{7}$$

The ADF statistic is the t-value associated with the estimated coefficient of ρ, the probability distribution of which is a functional of the Weiner process, the process used in explaining Brownian motion of a particle with large number of molecular shocks (Maddala & Kim, 1998). The PP test is the non-parametric extension of the DF unit root test by adding a correction factor to the DF t statistic. The tests have been performed for all the logarithmic series and their first differences. The choice of lag length is very much crucial at this stage and the number of lags used in the ADF regressions is selected by the Akaike (1969) Information Criterion (AIC).

We have applied cointegration theory developed in Engle and Granger (1987) by utilizing the methodology developed by Johansen and Juselius (1990). The concept of cointegration, first developed in Granger (1981), is relevant to the problem of the determination of long-run equilibrium relationships in economics in a sense that the variables move together over time so that short-term disturbances from the long-term trend will be corrected (Manning & Andrianacos, 1993).

Engle and Granger (1987) have shown that if two time series are cointegrated there will be a causal relation in at least one direction. Furthermore, the Granger Representation Theorem demonstrates how to model cointegrated I(1) series in the form of vector autoregression (VAR). In particular, the VAR can be constructed either in terms of the levels (logarithmic values) of the data, the I(1) variables; or in terms of their first differences, the I(0) variables, with the addition of an error correction mechanism (ECM, which is first used by Sargan (1984) and later popularized by Engle and Granger (1987)) to capture the short-run dynamics. If the data are I(1) but not cointegrated, causality tests cannot accurately be performed unless the data series are transformed into stationary series.

For two variables Y and X, the model can be presented either of the following form:

$$\ln X_t = \theta + \sum_{i=1}^{p} \pi_i \ln X_{t-i} + \sum_{j=1}^{r} \varphi_j \ln Y_{t-j} + v_t \tag{8}$$

$$\ln Y_t = \alpha + \sum_{i=1}^{m} \beta_i \ln X_{t-i} + \sum_{j=1}^{n} \gamma_j \ln Y_{t-j} + u_t \tag{9}$$

or,

$$\Delta \ln X_t = \theta + \sum_{i=1}^{p} \pi_i \Delta \ln X_{t-i} + \sum_{j=1}^{r} \varphi_j \Delta \ln Y_{t-j} + \lambda ECM_{t-1} + v_t \qquad (8.a)$$

$$\Delta \ln Y_t = \alpha + \sum_{i=1}^{m} \beta_i \Delta \ln X_{t-i} + \sum_{j=1}^{n} \gamma_j \Delta \ln Y_{t-j} + \delta ECM_{t-1} + u_t \qquad (9.a)$$

Where u_t and v_t are zero-mean, serially uncorrelated, random disturbances, error-correction mechanism is denoted by *ECM*. If the data are I(1) but not cointegrated, valid tests may be done by using the first differences without the error correction term:

$$\Delta \ln X_t = \theta + \sum_{i=1}^{p} \pi_i \Delta \ln X_{t-i} + \sum_{j=1}^{r} \varphi_j \Delta \ln Y_{t-j} + v_t \qquad (10)$$

$$\Delta \ln Y_t = \alpha + \sum_{i=1}^{m} \beta_i \Delta \ln X_{t-i} + \sum_{j=1}^{n} \gamma_j \Delta \ln Y_{t-j} + u_t \qquad (11)$$

RESULTS AND DISCUSSION

We present our results of unit root test on the basis of methodology taken in our study as mentioned in earlier.

Unit Root Test

Table 2 represents the ADF and PP test statistics for testing unit roots of all the series. Unlike most of the time series analysis, here the null hypothesis of the presence of unit roots is rejected in the original series indicating that all the series are stationary at level in case of both ADF and PP test.

To find the dynamic relationships between agricultural export and different measures of India's public expenditure on agriculture as mentioned above we have used cointegration theory developed in Engle and Granger (1987). The ADF and PP unit root tests suggest that the all the series of the variables are

Table 2. Estimated Statistics of Unit Root Tests

Series	Augmented Dickey-Fuller Test Statistics		Phillips Perron Test Statistics	
	Level	First Difference	Level	First Difference
GDPAGR	0.05	-2.04***	-0.33	-4.78***
PEAGRT	0.31	-5.15***	0.29	-5.15***
EXAGR	-0.07	-4.14***	-0.11	-4.15***
Note: ***, ** and * denote the level of significance at 1%, 5%, and 10%, respectively				

Source: Authors' own estimation by using data from HBSIE, RBI database, in E-views 7

integrated of order one I(1). All the stationary variables at same order of integration may have a common trend and it is reasonable to search for a possible cointegrating relationship among them. In this context we plan for co-integration test. We can also argue that agricultural exports from India continuously follow a time trend.

Cointegration Test

The estimated results of Johansen's cointegration tests have been shown by Table 3. Both the trace or LR test statistic and the eigenvalues are used for testing the hypothesis of presence of cointegrating relation, against the alternative hypothesis of full rank. Findings suggest that are three cointegrating equations as trace statistic reports at 5 percent level. But maximum eigenvalue test indicates no cointegration at the 5 percent level, also denotes the rejection of the hypothesis in case of at most two hypothesized number of cointegrating equations. So we think there may have a long run relationship between India's agricultural export and India's public expenditure on agriculture.

Now we have to test the long run dynamic relationship among the variables by utilizing the structure of vector error correction mechanism (VECM) by incorporating two period lag as suggested by the minimum AIC rule

If a set of variables have one or more cointegrating vectors then a suitable estimation technique is a VECM (Vector Error Correction Model). VECM adjusts to both short run changes in variables and deviations from equilibrium. The vector error correction model (VECM) is a special case of the VAR for variables that are stationary in their differences (i.e., I(1)). The VEC can also take into account any co-integrating relationships among the variables.

Table 4 shows the estimation of coefficients with corresponding t statistics in [] from the mechanism of vector error correction. Results indicate that only the GDP growth of India is significantly determined by the India's Agricultural export with one period lag.

Table 3. Estimated statistics of Johansen Cointegration Test

Unrestricted Cointegration Rank Test					
Tests	**Hypothesized No. of CE(s)**	**Eigenvalue**	**Statistic**	**5% Critical Value**	**Prob.****
Trace	None *	0.588955	31.39727	29.79707	0.0324
	At most 1 *	0.299622	9.170966	15.49471	0.3498
	At most 2 *	0.010646	0.267572	3.841466	0.605
Maximum Eigenvalue	None*	0.588955	22.22631	21.13162	0.035
	At most 1*	0.299622	8.903394	14.2646	0.2943
	At most 2 *	0.010646	0.267572	3.841466	0.605
Trace test indicates 3 cointegrating eqn(s) at the 0.05 level					
Max-eigenvalue test indicates 3 cointegrating eqn(s) at the 0.05 level					
* denotes rejection of the hypothesis at the 0.05 level					
**MacKinnon-Haug-Michelis (1999) p-values					

Source: Authors' own estimation by using data from HBSIE, RBI database in E-views 7

CONCLUSION AND POLICY SUGGESTION

The chapter tried to contribute a new dimension to the study of sustainable rural development through agrarian reforms by investigating the impact of public expenditure on agriculture in terms of production and export empirically in India for a long period from 1970-71 to 2014-15. Our findings, by applying Johansen cointegration tests on the basis of unit root test results, imply that there is at least one co-integrating equation as suggested by both trace and maximum eigen value statistics. So there may have a long run equilibrium relationship among variables. The results of vector error correction mechanism model to find the long run dynamics show that growth of agricultural output is significantly influenced by public expenditures on agricultural and allied sectors with one period lag.

Low productivity with high cost of production and absenteeism of labour are the important barriers to the Indian agriculture. To develop agricultural market, value addition in the current infrastructure, such as more number of cold storage, roads, green mandi are urgently required. Currently India is facing some problems in productivity gain and in lowering cost of production. FAO suggested that the unit cost must be reduced through productivity gain.

Table 4. Results of Vector Error Correction Model

Error Correction:	D(GDPAGR)	D(PEAGRT)	D(EXAGR)
CointEq1	-0.71822	-1.17944	2.661093
	[-2.76333]	[-1.61121]	[2.62920]
D(GDPAGR(-1))	0.52214	0.928719	-1.00734
	[2.46658]	[1.25972]	[-0.98822]
D(GDPAGR(-2))	-0.06179	0.085089	0.342979
	[-0.35720]	[0.17465]	[0.50915]
D(PEAGRT(-1))	-0.16023	-0.92865	0.314009
	[-1.92889]	[-3.96931]	[0.97071]
D(PEAGRT(-2))	0.866918	-0.61785	0.225633
	[3.77236]	[-2.53196]	[0.66876]
D(EXAGR(-1))	-0.25396	-0.53041	0.411644
	[-2.34835]	[-1.74146]	[0.97748]
D(EXAGR(-2))	-0.26477	-0.45654	0.288386
	[-3.36582]	[-2.06067]	[0.94144]
C	0.001782	0.006193	-0.005
	[0.22709]	[0.28027]	[-0.16366]
R-squared	0.814224	0.584802	0.517655
Adj. R-squared	0.727529	0.391043	0.29256
Sum sq. resids	0.020508	0.162677	0.310994
S.E. equation	0.036976	0.10414	0.143989
F-statistic	9.391802	3.018194	2.299723
Log likelihood	48.12225	24.3065	16.85439

Source: Authors' own estimation by using data from HBSIE, RBI database in E-views 7

It is most challenging time for introduction of energy and cost effective technology and equipment so that long-term strategy with a good infrastructure only pays the agricultural sustainability. There is also a huge scope to carry forward this research study further by looking at the aspects of long run relationship with direction of causality between agricultural performance and private investment in Indian agriculture in India. This would ensure more robust results and much more meaningful analysis which could be helpful for the policymakers as well as researchers in India to frame an Infrastructure led growth policies in the years to come.

REFERENCES

Ahmad, S. (1966). On the theory of induced innovation. *The Economic Journal*, *76*(302), 344–357. doi:10.2307/2229720

Alston, J. M., George, W. N., & Philip, G. P. (1995). *Science under Scarcity: Principles and Practice for Agricultural Research Evaluation and Priority Setting*. Ithaca, NY: Cornell University Press.

Antle, J. M., & Capalbo, S. M. (1988). An Introduction to Recent Developments in Production Theory and Productivity Measurement. Agricultural Productivity: Measurement and Explanation. Washington, DC: Resources for the Future.

Arnade, C. (1998). Using a Programming Approach to Measure International Agricultural Efficiency and Productivity. *Journal of Agricultural Economics*, *49*(1), 67–84. doi:10.1111/j.1477-9552.1998.tb01252.x

Bashir, Z. (2003). The Impacts of Economic Reforms and Trade Liberalisation on Agricultural Export Performance in Pakistan. *Pakistan Development Review*, *42*(4), 941–959.

Bhaumik, S. K. (2015). *Principles of Econometrics: A Modern Approach using E-views*. Oxford University Press.

Bhushan, S. (2005). Total Factor Productivity Growth of Wheat in India: A Malmquist Approach. *Indian Journal of Agricultural Economics*, *60*(1).

Binswanger, H. P., & Ruttan, V. W. (1978). *Induced Innovation: Technology, Institutions and Development, Baltomore and London*. The John Hopkins University Press.

Bradshaw, G., & Orden, D. (1990). Granger Causality from the Exchange Rate to Agricultural Prices and Export Sales. *Western Journal of Agricultural Economics*, *15*(1), 100–110.

Chambers, R. G., & Just, R. E. (1991). Effects of Exchange Rate Changes on U.S. Agriculture. *American Journal of Agricultural Economics*, *73*, 33–43.

Chandra, R. (2000). *The Impact of Trade Policy on Growth in India* (Unpublished PhD Thesis). Department of Economics, University of Strathclyde, Glasgow, UK.

Chandra, R. (2002). Export Growth and Economic Growth: An Investigation of Causality in India. *The Indian Economic Journal*, *49*, 64–73.

Dickey, D. A., & Fuller, W. A. (1979). Distribution of the Estimators for Autoregressive Time Series with a Unit Root. *Journal of the American Statistical Association*, *74*, 427–431.

Engle, R. F., & Granger, C. W. J. (1987). Co-integration and Error Correction Representation: Estimation and Testing. *Econometrica*, *55*(2), 251–276. doi:10.2307/1913236

Fan, S., Hazell, P., & Thorat, S. (1999). *Linkages Between Government Spending, Growth, and Poverty in Rural India. Research Report 110*. Washington, DC: International Food Policy Research Institute.

Fischer, A., Petersen, L., Feldkötter, C., & Huppert, W. (2007). Sustainable Governance of Natural Resources and Institutional Change: An Analytical Framework. *Public Administration and Development*, *27*(2), 123–137. doi:10.1002/pad.442

Government of India. (2015). *Agricultural Statistics at a Glance, Directorate of Economics and Statistics*. New Delhi: Ministry of Agriculture.

Gujrati, D. N. (2003). Basic Econometrics. *McGraw Hill Education*, *4*, 696–702.

Hughes, D. W., & Penson, J. B. (1985). Effects of Selected Macroeconomic Policies on Agriculture: 1984-1990. *Agricultural Financial Review*, *45*, 81–91.

Johnson, P. R., Grennes, T., & Thursby, M. (1977). Devaluation, Foreign Trade Control, and Domestic Wheat Prices. *American Journal of Agricultural Economics*, *59*(4), 619–627. doi:10.2307/1239389

Khalafalla, K. Y., & Webb, A. J. (2001). Export-led Growth and Structural Change: Evidence from Malaysia. *Applied Economics*, *33*(13), 1703–1715. doi:10.1080/00036840010015066

Mellor, J. W. (1966). *The Economics of Agricultural Development*. New York: Cornell University Press.

Oshikoya, W. T., & Hussain, M. N. (2002). Infrastructure for Economic Development in Africa. In J. B. de Macedo & O. Kabbaj (Eds.), *Regional Integration in Africa*. OECD.

Pindyck, R. S. (1998). Irreversible Investment, Capacity Choice, and the Value of the Firm. *The American Economic Review*, *78*, 969–985.

Pinstrup-Andersen, P. (2002). Food and Agricultural Policy for a Globalizing World: Preparing for the Future. *American Journal of Agricultural Economics*, *84*(5), 1201–1214. doi:10.1111/1467-8276.00381

Pinstrup-Andersen, P., & Shimokawa, S. (2002). *Rural Infrastructure and Agricultural development* (pp. 185–203). Rethinking Infrastructure for Development.

Rao, K. S. C., & Dhar, B. (2011). *India's FDI Inflows- Trend and Concepts*. Working Paper No. 01. Institute for Studies in Industrial Development.

Razin, O., & Collins, S. M. (1997). Real Exchange Rate Misalignments and Growth. In *The Economics of Globalization: Policy Perspectives from Public Economics*. Cambridge, UK: Cambridge University Press.

RBI handbook data for GDP growth, export and total public expenditure on agriculture. (n.d.). Retrieved from https://rbi.org.in/Scripts/AnnualPublications.aspx?head=Handbook%20of%20Statistics%20on%20Indian%20Economy

Schultz, T. W. (1964). *Transforming Traditional Agriculture*. New Haven, CT: Yale University Press.

Sinha, M., & Sengupta, P. P. (2016). *Post Reform Trends in India's Foreign Exchange Rate: Testing the Role of Agricultural Exports*. Presented at National Symposium on Statistics for Sustainable Agricultural Development, Kolkata, India.

Tripathi, A., & Prasad, A. R. (2008). *An Overview of Agrarian Economy in India: Then Performance and Determinant*. Retrieved from http://blogs.wsj.com/indiarealtime/2013/08/26/where-are-the-onions/

Zee News. (2015). *Exclusive Union Budget*. Available at: http://zeenews.india.com/exclusive/budget-2015-the-need-for-an-overhaul-in-indian-agriculture-sector_1541831.html

KEY TERMS AND DEFINITIONS

Agrarian Reform: Agrarian reform is government-initiated or government-backed redistribution of agricultural land.

Agricultural Development: Agricultural development includes providing assistance, employing latest techniques, controlling pests and facilitating diversity to the crop producers with the help of various agricultural resources.

Agriculture: Agriculture is the cultivation of plants and animals for food, fiber, bio fuel, medicine and other products which are used to sustain and enhance human life.

Econometric Model: Econometric models are based on statistical models used in econometrics which specifies the statistical relationship to hold among the various economic quantities pertaining to a particular economic phenomenon under study.

Economic Development: Economic development is the efforts that seek to improve the economic well-being and improve quality of life for a community by creating jobs and supporting or growing incomes and the tax base.

Implementation: The process of execution of a decision or plan into effect.

Infrastructure Development: For economic development and prosperity of a country, infrastructure development is essential. Infrastructure includes the basic physical systems of a nation communication, transportation, sewage, water and electric systems etc.

Policy: A course or principle of action adopted or proposed by an individual or organization.

Public Expenditure: When spending is made by the government of a country based on collective needs and wants such as pension, provision, infrastructure, etc.

Rural Development: Rural development is the process of improving the quality of life and economic well-being of people living in sparsely populated areas.

Social Mobilization: Social mobilization is the primary step of community development for awareness and to organize and initiate action for their recovery with their own initiative and creativity to protect from disasters etc.

Chapter 15
Point of View of Economical Organization at Manzanillo's Harbor

José G. Vargas-Hernández
University of Guadalajara, Mexico

Gabriela Muratalla-Bautista
Technological Institute of Morelia Valley, Mexico

Irving Daniel Austin Cruz
University of Guadalajara, Mexico

ABSTRACT

The objective of this research is to analyze Manzanillo's harbor from the perspective of theories based on the Industry, the Dynamic Resources and Institutions, around the Mexican port system based on a review into an updated literature about the port's status and its global environment. The port's competitiveness is based on its resources VRIO, its generic strategies and how it has handled the institutions that affect the port and commercial operation of the port at local, national and international level.

INTRODUCTION

Globalization has become as a trigger for international trade due to its role as integrator of the world economy and social standardization in a technological, cultural and universal knowledge, that allow free access to resources with a minimum effort. The free trade agreements (FTAs) have allowed countries to reduce their barriers to imports of goods, allowing the consumption of products and services from foreign countries at competitive prices at their local markets. The free trade agreements (FTAs) have allowed countries to reduce their barriers to imports of goods, allowing the consumption of products and services from foreign countries at competitive prices at their local markets. The evolution of international trade and technological innovations have brought about changes inherent in other areas such as international shipping, which hits into two groups, the size, depth and nature of vessels and therefore the port infrastructure to serve them.

DOI: 10.4018/978-1-5225-2364-2.ch015

It's well known at the context of international trade, that the ports serve as key development for their regions where they're settled. In a peculiar sense the Mexican port with the greatest international impact is the Manzanillo's harbor, located on the Pacific Mexican coast. This port has become the number one in containers movement. In this respect, Reyes, Guizar, Gutierrez and Rubio (2014, P. 697) they mentioned that "the cargo moving via containers in Mexican ports are the most important worldwide movement of cargo containers, and all of this becomes the transport's instrument which has revolutionized global logistics". Regarding the analysis on the first point, it can be seen as an historical background of international trade and shipping, and its development and implications in the port environment. At the second point defines the problem based on the Manzanillo's port as height harbor nationally. In the third chapter, it delves justification and the review of relevant literature to analyze the port of Manzanillo versus others Mexican ports. The fourth mentions the objective of the chapter. The fifth point is methodology. The sixth point is the analysis of results. The last chapter shows those conclusions and recommendations on this investigation.

BACKGROUND OF THE PROBLEM

Trade is:

an activity as old as humanity itself. As soon as an individual, the human being had control or possession of something that someone else wanted or needed, were initiated the exchange relationships (Portales, 2012, p. 12).

Around it can be inferred that the trade began as the exchange of goods or services for a payment, usually receiving money between individuals with the skills to interchange. Meanwhile, international trade is one that occurs between individuals of different nations. International trade has become as the input key to the world's economies to create an atmosphere of interchange of effective goods and services, same services that are necessary for economic, social and cultural development, which help to welfare of countries in the world. No doubt, the international trade's hand is globalization, a process according to Lamy (2006, SP) defines it as

a historical phase of accelerated expansion of the market capitalism. It is a fundamental transformation of the society, due to the recent technological revolution leading to a restructuring of the economic and social forces on a new territorial dimension.

But Loyola, and Schettino (1994, pp. 4-5) mention on globalization that

the process of globalization makes an increasing in the relationship between the production network units of different regions and therefore the relationship between different economies, modifies substantially the structure of the world economy.

As the authors say, globalization has brought fundamental changes into the way: how nations conduct their economies, thereby showing greater international openness, giving rise to a more dynamic world trade and putting through clearer rules and a more fair play.

The moving on rules in international trade, by the year 1947 was signed the Act of the General Agreement on Tariffs and Trade, GATT in English. This before the need to create a regulatory mechanism of protectionist tariffs and regulations that countries had begun to spread because of the wars, the Second World War had been the most devastating to the international trade; but the GATT was not enough for international trade malfunction, and acted only as an instrument and not as an organization that would be able to regulate those irregularities that appeared on tariffs. As a result of this in the year 1995 the WTO, World Trade Organization emerges in Geneva, Switzerland. The WTO is the only international organization dealing with the rules governing trade between countries. The goal is to help producers of goods and services, exporters and importers to conduct their business (WTO, 2015). There are 161 member countries at WTO, the last country to be member and access in 2015, at the international organization was Seychelles.

Globalization has become a catalyst for international trade and as a result has been increasing interchange of goods between one nation and another, and thus has brought immediate results in the creation of new media to deliver the goods from their point of origin to their final destination, as well as the adaptation and innovation in processes that exist already. In a broader context, the media and types of transport have had a latent development since the industrial revolution, which was the most fruitful period in this area until today with globalization and technological advances.

As was mentioned previously, the means and modes of transport have been developing according to the needs of international trade demands. Portales (2012, p. 14) makes a clear distinction between these two concepts. "Types of transport are the ways that can be done, i.e., water, land, etc., transportation modes are the physical rides made to carry and transport, such as airplane, boat, etc.".

On this basis can classify the types of international transportation into 4 main groups 1) Air transport, 2) Water Transport, which are divided into river, sea and lake. 3) Ground transportation, which can be motor transport and rail and 4) multimodal transportation, which is a combination of three types of previous transport. These four groups belong to a conventional type of driving; however, there is a group that is a response to technology and innovations in this field.The special driving in which can make getting from one place to another, it's not necessarily physical, what is required this type of transport is just a medium to pass the information, energy, gas files, software, etc

Focusing exclusively on maritime transport, it has been one of the most dynamic transports that exists, whose evolution has faithfully gone hand in hand with the growth of international trade. It can be concluded that is the means of transport of foreign trade by excellence, because it allows a lot of load volumes to long distances, at low rates, it connects and transports continents with enhanced security. Surely this transport, it's the main as the core of international logistics.

The growth of shipping and world trade is explained by Musso, Gonzalez Cariou and Barros (2004, p. 11) sustaining that "port traffic depends on the level of industrial production, geographical organization, and the resulting entity of world trade and maritime transits". The same authors refer to this in recent decade and the harbor industry has been changed mainly by four factors:

1. The globalization trend of world economies entails the relocation of industrial, commercial and social activities, thereby increasing international trade, today it is easy to produce a good in Japan and be available to an individual in Brazil.
2. The organizational and technological innovations, especially those related to maritime transport and hence seaports.

3. Innovations in ICT (Information and Communication technologies), that is in those areas that complement the port-maritime, such as better roads, bridges or paths.
4. The new institutional, organizational and management models the transport industry. One example, the addition of China to the WTO, brought in less than 10 years 9 of the 10 largest ports in the world are of such country.

These changes have brought new port models, new ways of assessing port competitiveness and restructuring in the way of conceiving the demand for port services (Musso, Gonzalez, Cariou, and Barros, 2004). Shipping is one of the oldest and its influence on transport is reflected in terms and nomenclature used in the environment. According to Portales (2012), currently 85% of international trade in goods is by this means of transport. So much importance is that this is divided into two: Height which is the inter-oceanic and coastal routing same coastline. With this, ports also receive this classification based on vessel traffic they have.

The agency responsible for regulating the safety and maritime regulations is the International Maritime Organization or IMO by its acronym in English. The ports are to be more than a logistical link between international trade bodies. Today, the ports have become the key to development and economic growth of countries that boast of having port infrastructure. According to De Larrucea, Mari, and Mallofré, (2014, p. 93) a port

is a place on the coast where ships can find shelter, loading and unloading goods. It originated in the existence of navigation, which inherent and inseparable element became, evolving with the characteristics of the boats.

The Ports Act, SCT (1993) defines port as the place of the shore or bank qualified as such by the Federal Executive for the reception, shelter and care of ships, comprising the port area, the development zone, access and areas of internal navigation and operation. This, as discussed above, proves to be a very basic concept, since the ports currently function more as a detonator of the economy of a country than just pier merchandise.

Ports fulfill their function in terms of infrastructure as influencing a particular economic environment of the country in which it is found, However, a port is of great value to the nation according to its area of influence, the greater it is, the greater the impact of the port and its importance and economic interest in the country. De Larrucea, et al. (2014) classified this area into two terms according to the management to be given:

1. **Hinterland (Hinterland):** The direct area of influence of the port, where shipped goods come from and where they disembark the goods destined.
2. **Foreland:** Turns out to be the opposite of a hinterland, where they come from goods landed and destination of the goods being shipped.

There are different types of port management, this according to the origin of capital or authority thereof. According to the origin of capital may be a) Private management: One whose capital is from private sources, companies seeking infrastructure efficiency and customer satisfaction. b) Governance: It is the government who has the control and management of them, and seeks to work more in infrastructure efficiency. c) Mixed Management: Where there is private capital and government regulatory body remains the same. An example is the Mexican APIs meaning Integral Port Administration. According to its authority can be centralized and decentralized, the first under a hierarchy and vertical integration, while under decentralized authority, there is coordination in decision-making.

The ports have different types of classifications depending on the area to be analyzed, i.e., by maritime traffic or navigation can be high and cabotage. On this regard, Mexican regulation through the Ports Act, SCT (1993) defines as follows: a) high, in attending vessels, people and goods between ports or sailing national and international points, b) cabotage, when only attend boats, people and goods in shipping between ports or national points.

Another classification of great importance is the type of infrastructure that the port has in this sense is divided into four main groups: a) Commercial: is dedicated to the handling of goods and / or people. b) Industrial: It is dedicated to the management of related industries established in the port area goods. c) Fishing: It is dedicated to boat handling and products fishing industry, d): Touristic: When engaged in tourist activity and sea cruises, this according to the Ports Act (SCT, 1993).

For the year 2011 according to statistics from the American Association of Port Authorities or AAPA by its acronym in English, 9 of the world's major ports in general cargo were Asian, with only one belonging to Europe. This is a clear example on how technological change makes it more efficient port infrastructure. This comes up because it makes it no less than a decade the main ports in the world belonged to the old continent and these were references for quintessential port cities and the great adventures of merchant sailors. It is worth remembering the Silk Road from Venice.

Now for movements of containers in TEU (Twenty-foot Equivalent Unit) the same AAPA accurate statistics of 2011, where it can be observed a similar pattern to the movement of general cargo. The importance of being measured in TEUs is that the containers have become the most secure and accurate packaging for movement of goods through maritime transport. According to De Larrucea, et al. (2014) in 2010 the movement of containerized goods reached 576 million TEUs, and the forecast for 2020 is 1,002 million.

In this environment, the Mexican ports are not yet included in degree of importance even that Mexico is one of the countries with more free trade agreements and treaties signed to benefit from international trade. In Mexico the authority to regulate and license enabling ports in Mexico is the Communications and Transport Secretary (SCT by its acronymic in Spanish), who through the Directorate General of Ports performs the control and management thereof. The port operations according to Mexican Ports Act should be through APIs (Integral Port Authority) on the basis of concessions granted by the SCT. According to data from the SCT (2015) there are 16 ports of Height, which in addition to handling general cargo also are handling bulk containers. The main ports according to their locations are:

1. **Pacific:** Ensenada, BC; Guaymas, Sonora; Mazatlan,Sinaloa; Manzanillo, Colima; Lazaro Cardenas, Michoacanand finallySalinaCruz, Oaxaca.
2. **Gulf of Mexico:** Altamira andTampico, Tamaulipas; Tuxpan, Veracruz, Coatzacoalcos, Veracruz; Dos Bocas, Tabasco; PuertoProgreso,Yucatan andPuertoMorelos, and Quintana Roo.

According to dataofthe Secretary of Communications and Transport (SCT)in themainMexicanportsaccordingto the general movementofgeneral cargo andalso accordingto the movement ofTEUsin 2014, the Mexican busiest portofbothcontainerizedgeneralmerchandiseper tonne, is the Port ofManzanillo, Colima, accordingtothe sameprojectionsportcarries atrendgrowthover therest of theports.

DEFINITION OF THE PROBLEM

Manzanillo port has become the most dynamic port in Mexico, not only for its annual cargo movement in recent years that has been growing, but also for its area of national and international influence, becoming the gateway merchandise to Asian, South American and US origin to the center and shoal (Bajio) country.

Manzanillo's Port, according to the Port Authority of Manzanillo (2015) is located in the State of Colima, on the Pacific Ocean coast. It is distinguished by its security and social peace, which allows them attract mostly private national and foreign investments, increasing its installed capacity. The harbor's location is strategic as a competitive advantage, it allows to have a larger area of influence, since 67% of national GDP is concentrated in the center and country shoal area, also lies about 55% of the total population. 46% of the containers entering the country, it is by this Mexican Pacific port and all of this make it as the number one category nationwide. In Figure 1, it can be seen the Hinterland and Foreland port of Manzanillo.

JUSTIFICATION

Manzanillo consolidates it as one of the most dynamic American Pacific ports and greater growth prospects in the movement of containers according not only to its strategic location,being the link with US and Canadian products from Asia, but also by economic agreements that Mexico has signed with over 50 countries around the world thus increase trade between it and its trading partners. Based on data from SCT, the Manzanillo's port is number one in container movement in Mexico. For its part, the Economic Commission for Latin America ECLAC in 2013, Manzanillo is the 4th port in Latin America, below ports like Colon, Panama; Santos, Brazil and Balboa, Panama.

Likewise, the AAPA in 2011 in its statistics placed the port of Manzanillo at number 71 of the annual ranking for container movement (See Figure 2). However, considering that each port of the world is manifested as an individual agent and trader and whose competence is not only international but also

Figure 1. Hinterland and Foreland of Manzanillo's Port

Hinterland del puerto de Manzanillo	Zona de influencia	Foreland
-Aguascalientes. -Coahuila. -Colima. -Distrito Federal. -Durango. -Estado de México. -Guanajuato. -Hidalgo -Jalisco -Michoacán -Morelos. -Nayarit. -Nuevo León -Querétaro. -San Luis Potosí -Tamaulipas. -Zacatecas.		-E.U.A. -Canadá. -Guatemala. -Colombia. -Ecuador. -Chile. -Japón. -China. -Taiwán. -Corea. -Indonesia. -Malasia. -Singapur. -Filipinas. -España. -Rusia. -Alemania. Oceanía, Australia Nueva Zelanda y Sudáfrica.

Figure 2. Behavior of load rate movements seen at the Port of Manzanillo (2011-2016)
Source: own calculations based on data at the Port Authority of Manzanillo
** Data for the period from January to July*

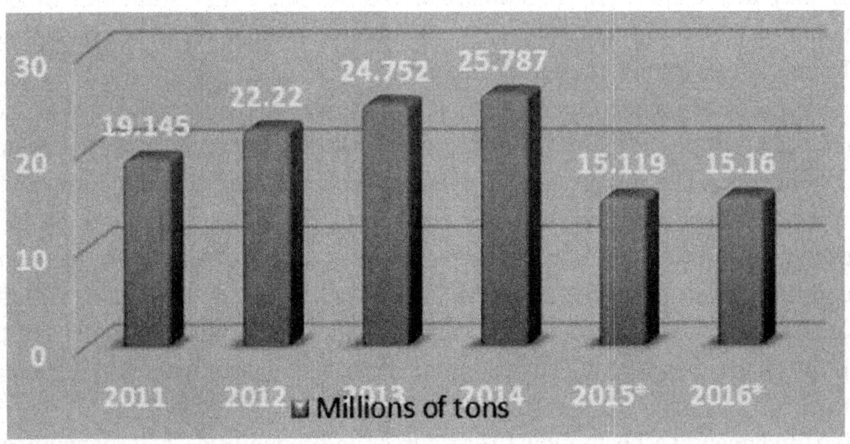

naional. It is not surprising that the Port of Manzanillo also has this premise, for this reason it is considered as an organization represented through its authorized administrator, the API Manzanillo.

As it is possible to observe in the Figure 2 there have increased the movements of the type of load to that from 2011 to 2016 attend in the Port of Tree of the included period. In the year 2012 there exists an increase of 16% with regard to 2011, of the year 2012 to 2013 there is increased 12% that are 2,532,000 tons approximately. In the year 2015 and 2016 the information corresponds exclusively to the period from January to July where it is possible to observe that the same behavior is kept in conformity with the quantity attended tons.

With information from the preceding paragraphs is that the economy, organizations theories come into play, especially 3 of the most important in strategic management: the theory based on Dynamic Resource, based theory of industry and the theory based on the institutions.The port of Manzanillo has to cope with a constant competition with two Mexican ports, Lazaro Cardenas and Veracruz. Manzanillo should in turn consider appropriate to take advantage of its natural and human resources strategies and meet those changes in Mexican institutions that are constantly changing, such as the restructuring of the port system

REVIEW OF RELEVANT LITERATURE

Resource-Based Theory and Dynamic Capabilities

The behavior of the organization and his internal interaction for the achievement of the raised aims propitiates a nature, which has interaction with an internal and external context, nevertheless, it is of vital attention to know the internal dynamism with which his elements demonstrate and which in turn they allow the development of " dynamic capacities ", it refers not to the changes that happen in the context in the one that produces, the company, but to the modifications that take place in the organizational capacities of the same one... " (Zahra, Sapienza and Davidsson, 2006, p. 921). Hereby it is that the organizations can confront external changeable contexts, that guarantee his permanency.

The theory of dynamic resource tries to explain those internal behaviors of the organization, namely that related to resources that companies have to set their strategies to the market. The importance of resources is that they are the guts of the organizations and with them their strategies fail or are a success; everything depends on the good relationship that exists between them. It can be conceptualized as based on the strengths and threats that the company has focus.

According to Vargas-Hernandez, Guerra-Garcia, Bojorquez, and Bojorquez, (2014), the point of view based on resources focuses on the use of resources and capabilities of enterprises to develop an effective strategy by the companies.The importance of dynamic resources impacts the competitive advantages that companies can have and must on the other hand focus on conservation and use strategically. On the other hand, the capabilities that may prove particularly useful in enterprise environments are the operational flexibility and strategic flexibility Mahoney (2010), i.e., operational flexibility can be seen as the way in which resources adapted to the changes as the operating environment of the company's strategic flexibility as they respond to changes in the industrial environment and resources are adapted to be competitive.

There are two fundamental aspects about the resources and capabilities, heterogeneity and immobility of resources. Heterogeneity in turn refers to companies to be different. Even in the same industry have different resource and depend on each one uses, while the immobility of resources refers to that some resources are expensive to use and are more apt to give them up to potentiate them (Barney, 2008). It is the same Barney, who complements that resources have a potential value and how they can be detected through a value chain, which is defined "as a set of business activities in which it develops produces and markets products and services" (Barney, 2008, p. 81).

A term of great importance in this regard is the resource, for that Peng (2012) defines them "as real or tangible or intangible assets using a firm to choose and implement their strategies". However, he also gave a differentiation between each of them. The tangible are those that can be seen and easily quantified while intangibles are those that are difficult to see or quantify. Examples of tangible resources are financial, physical and organizations while intangible are such as human beings, innovation and reputation (Vargas-Hernández, et al., 2014).

Returning with the added value and competitive advantage that resources provide to organizations in an industry it can be found under VRIO that stands for Value, Rarity, Imitation and Organization. Value: One resource that adds value and competitive advantage to the company. Rarity: A resource that is not common in the industry. Imitation: The resources that happen to be difficult to imitate. Organization: Resources must be well organized and thus will contribute to competitive advantage (Peng, 2012).

The impact of the organization's resources is on limiting the management and growth of the same when they are not aimed at the target that was raised as part of the company strategy to achieve generic goals. In this same vein is important to distinguish the resources aside from being tangible or intangible can be considered as physical and human (Penrose, 1959). On the other hand, some of the factors limiting the growth of enterprises according to Vargas-Hernández (2014, p. 116) are as follows: The ability of management: a) the conditions within the company. b) The markets of products or factors: "the conditions outside the company. c) Uncertainty and risk: a combination of internal attitudes and external conditions".

Theory Based on Industry

The theory based on the industry makes the assumption of all those needs that the company has to cope with the competition that belongs to the same commercial or industrial sector. Their greatest authors in basic theories and concepts are Michael Porter and Mike Peng. Based on the definition of industry, it is said the industry is a group of firms or companies that produce goods and / or services similar to each other (Peng, 2012). This industry can be conceptualized as companies engaged in production or service same or similar to meet the same group needs.

According to Saloner, Shepard and Podoly (2001) the objective to study the industry is to provide the tools for the management of the firm, it is necessary to answer two questions. What characteristics of the context are important market and determinants of the profitability of the firm? What strategically actions can be taken to improve the performance of my business? In the context of industry, the strategies are based on the framework of the five forces or diamond by Porter, same as they were introduced and propagated by Porter (1980). These forces are:

1. **Intensity of Rivalry Among Competitors:** The number of competitors is important because the greater the number of companies in most industries is the possibility of income and the market is vast and sufficient for all.
2. **The Threat of Potential Entries:** Holding companies seek ways to prevent new companies from entering to be competitive, there is no small enemy and because of this define barriers to entry, which can be defined by input costs or scale production that makes it more difficult for new competitors. It can also attack potential inflows through product diversification, thus the competition will be even greater for companies seeking to join the market.
3. **The Bargaining Power of Suppliers:** Here suppliers can make use of their power to tax and increase prices or lower the quality of inputs.
4. **The Bargaining Power of Buyers:** This affects mainly industry where competition is between few buyers, or the products are not being of quality that buyers expect.
5. **The Threat of Substitutes:** Here come those products from the focal industry and without direct competition can affect industry of company product.

Porter on the other hand also speaks of three generic strategies that reinforce the model previously explained it. These strategies are cost leadership, differentiation and focus, (Peng, 2012). While the former refers to the low costs that can have for being sometimes leaders or pioneers in the production of a product, differentiation is focused on what happens to be the know-how of the company, how does feel special the customer and finally the approach that is concerned with niche market to which is intended its product or service.

Theory Based in Institutions

North (1990, p. 3) defines institutions as "the rules of the game in a society or, more formally, are the humanly devised constraints that shape human interaction". This leads to realize that are the institutions that define modes of social interaction, i.e., they make the informal language in which societies have evolved economically, politically and socially.

On the other hand, part of the functions of the institutions is to reduce uncertainty by creating structures to this day by day societies. That is, the institutions provide certainty of what and how to act every day, since there are institutions for all that as an individual within a society do. This is aimed to make the most practical way of living. Institutions have their rules and ways of working and thus as the individual must return his behavior, according to the activity to perform, which is why certainty of action in society is created. As commented, are the institutions that create the language of social behavior.

But to give a clearer picture of what are the institutions, in the same way North (1990, p. 4) says that "the institutions include any form of constraint that human beings design to shape human interaction". In this way, it is delimited such as formal and informal, defining formal organizations and the rules that humans invent, while informal institutions such as conventions and codes of conduct.

Likewise, it is mentioned that institutions are looking to put rules and these regulations have as objectives to define the rules of the game, i.e. the daily act, how and what to do. But going at the end of organizations, they seek to win the game all forms, often bypassing the rules, leaving aside formal institutions to move to the informal corruption. For a company to win the game in an environment of formal rules, it should be considered a combination of skills, strategies, individuals and a sublime combination of these.

But what kind of organizations are there? North (1990, p. 2) also makes a classification of them:

Organizations include political bodies (political parties, the Senate, a city council, a regulatory agency), economic bodies (firms, trade unions, family farms cooperatives), the bodies (churches, clubs, sports social associations) and educational institutions (schools, universities, vocational training centers).

As can be seen, organizations, citing again into North, are groups of individuals bound by some purpose of achieving common goals.

To understand an institution or an organization, it is important first to understand the behavior of its individuals, i.e. their informal institutions and culture that are defined as behaviors to be processed. Institutions evolve alongside the individual, from the organizations formed by feudal chiefs and slavery to new forms of work organizations that coexist. A new organizational theory based on the behavior of workers leads to a change and with it an evolution in organizations.

People who work in the institutions seek to meet and discuss topics such as

the rules, procedures and formal organizations of a system of government (...) and aims to explain the one hand, the relationship between the structure and democracy and on the other, how the rules, procedures and formal organizations determine whether or not the political behavior (Marsh and Stoker. 1997. p.65).

The CROM

Regional Confederation of Mexican Workers or CROM as it is known in a Mexican organization that has the membership of the Mexican workers and laborers. It was founded in 1918 and serves as a representative of the rights of workers under the statute of the Union. Today is who manages and controls the unionized personnel working in the loading and unloading operations in the Mexican ports. In the port of Manzanillo it is represented by the Longshoremen and Laborers Union of the Pacific.

Custom's Agencies

Customs officers are the legal representatives of Mexican importers and exporters authorized by law to do their transactions in foreign trade to Customs. The Customs Law (SHCP, 1995) includes this legal figure within its responsibilities, which stipulates and specifies what those responsibilities are and obligations that the customers officers have towards their represented. The Customs Law defines the figure of the broker as Customs Agent is the physical person authorized by the Tax Administration Service, through a patent, employed to promote the release of goods in different customs regimes under this Act.

The importance of customs agent is representing the importer and exporter in all those processes that customs clearance of merchandise bearing. This is who through a custom conferred plays "owner" of the goods before the departments and private companies in the port area.Nationally, there is a confederation of Customs Agents, whose role is to create synergy between all members of the same interests and ensure the CAAAREM (2015), which according to its website is defined as the Confederation of Customs Agents of Mexican Republic, is a body that represents and defends the professional interests of specialists in foreign trade. The Customs Brokers on the case of the Manzanillo's harbor are represented by the AAAPUMAC, the Association of Customs Agents Port Manzanillo.

Shipping Lines

According to Castro (2015) a shipping company is understood to be the natural or legal person, using its own or other merchant ships, and is dedicated to exploit them. Another definition according to the Mexican Navigation Law (2006) is a natural or legal person having under its ownership or possession one or more vessels or naval craft to perform the following functions: Equip, victual, provision, provide crew, keep seaworthy, operate with it and operate vessels. In the port slang, a Line is a shipping company that owns the vessel, while a shipping agency is a company that conducts its representative in ports. According to the directory API Manzanillo there are 30 shipping companies in the Port of Manzanillo.

Port Community

It is understood by the port community to all parties involved in the handling and clearance of goods at the port of Manzanillo, without being a formal organization has created the figure in order to expedite customs and port procedures. The community is made up of the following companies and government agencies:

Manzanillo Customs, SAGARPA, INAMI, OISA SENASICA, API Manzanillo CROM, Harbor, AAAPUMAC, AMANAC, CLAA, ANIERM Manzanillo, occupy, TIMSA, SSA Mexico, Haulers Association, FERROMEX, Multimodal Corporation, FRIMAN, Comercializadora La Junta, Granelera Manzanillo, USG, APASCO, Arcelor Mittal, CEMEX, ATREP, Grupo TMM, SSM, Union pilots of the Port of Manzanillo, Almacont Group Terminal Company Manzanillo Manzanillo City Hall H, Federal Police, Traffic and roads, Boatmen's Union.

OBJECTIVE OF THE CHAPTER

The objective of the present chapter is to analyze the port of Manzanillo from the perspective of the economics of organizations, especially based on the theories of Dynamic Resources, Industry and institutionalism.

METHODOLGY

As it was mentioned in the paragraphs of precedents, definition of the problem and the justification, the Manzanillo's port has turned into one of the most dynamic and competitive harbors of Mexico, this is to a great extent to the signature of international agreements for the imports and exports of the products that are generated in the Mexican territory. The method used for this investigation is qualitative and descriptive, primarily a review of the literature was affected, as well as the principal contributions of the three theories, to describe the behavior of the comparative information about the agreement to the criteria of evaluation of the ports that are established worldwide.

ANALYSIS OF RESULTS

As objective of this chapter is mentioned analyze Manzanillo's port from the perspective of the economics of organizations, especially based on the theories of Dynamic Resources, Industry and institutionalism. Therefore the analysis results according to the contributions of the above theories are discussed.

The Port of Manzanillo from the Point of View of Dynamic Resources

As he mentioned in paragraph review of relevant literature the resourceshave a potentialvalue andhow theycan be detectedthrougha value chain, which is defined "as a set of business activitiesin whichit devel-opsproduces andmarkets productsand services"(Barney, 2008, p. 81). That is why the port of Manzanillo has privileged natural resources, particularly its geographic location and its vast hinterland, not only nationally, connecting it to the main industrial centers of the country with the largest economies in the world. The port of Manzanillo accounts with a static capacity of 49.069 TEU and dynamic capacity of 2'132,667 Teu's without causing complications of saturation in their yards (API, 2015).

The added value and competitive advantage provide resources to organizations in an industry that can be found around the framework VRIO (Peng, 2012), is presented below these aspects:

1. **Value:** The Port of Manzanillo has a natural formation in its location within the bay, its access channel and docks ciaboga have a draft of 16 meters, without dredging. This gives rise to ships deep draft Post-Panamax can dock in the port docks. Create a competitive advantage over other ports on two fronts, the first such large-capacity vessels are transportation of containers and the second does not need constant dredging to maintain its depths. Another competitive advantage is the convergence of 30 shipping companies at the port that gives dynamism to maritime transport.
2. **Rarity:** The port of Manzanillo has a peculiarity regarding various ports of Mexico. It has only one point of access to it by sea, on top of that size is too small and does not give rise to growth in infrastructure (docks, patios, etc.). However, it has become a multimodal port connection, since converge in the trucking, rail and sea.
3. **Imitation:** In imitation enters the process of coordination of operations and port authority's communications system, creating an informal institution called Community port responsible for reviewing the strategies that need for their daily work. The experience in customs clearance is one of human resources with whom the port customs brokers account and those that streamline foreign trade procedures.

4. **Organization:** As previously mentioned the small size of the port could be a disadvantage that it has, but the joint work of all entities has resulted in shipments of containers lower to two days, giving an average of offices 3 days.

The Harbor of Manzanillo from the Industry Point of View

Michael Porter and Mike Peng author's theories based on industry makes the assumption of all the needs that the company has to face competition belonging to the same industrial or commercial sector. Peng (2012) defines the industry as a group of companies or companies producing goods and / or services similar to each other.

Based on the preceding paragraph port individually it serves as a great company which is represented by the Integral Port Authority, API, to which it belongs. So it is that this analysis is routed from that perspective. The industry then there are all those ports of the Republic who are in the same range of navigation, or cabotage height, and load levels allow it to be an important competition. All ports even without being in the same geographical area of the country pose a direct competition with each other, because the geographic location of Mexico creates a connection between two oceans and makes more agile the connection between the two ends of the country and the center of same.

The port of Manzanillo is the main port of Mexico with a cargo movement of 2.36 million TEUs last year, followed by the Port of Lazaro Cardenas with 996.654, its main domestic competition in the field of containers, and the port of Veracruz with 847.370. These three ports had played in past years the title of Mexico's main port, but in recent years has shown that the rightful place is for the Colima's port.

Based on the three generic strategies of Porter, is intended to present an analysis of the Port of Manzanillo in abstract revealing the strategies that the port carries and differs from other ports.

1. **Cost Leadership:** As a figure API cannot implement a different rate for use of infrastructure, but as part of its dealers it is possible. This is to say that its private companies realize it. The constant competition between tendered companies that specialize in container handling in the port (OCUPAS, TIMSA, SSA and CONTECON) work third shift leaving costs of a first turn maneuvers. With this services are not hurt as to costs for customers. With regard to other ports specializing in Cruise Terminal, Manzanillo handles a coupon rate of 25% on all services and port infrastructure, giving with it an advantage over other ports in tourist height as Acapulco, Puerto Vallarta and others.
2. **Differentiation:** The port of Manzanillo has the greatest diversification in terms ofports in Mexico. It hasspecialized terminals in Cruiseand Petroleumin the polygon1, while the polygon 2 is made up of container terminals, general cargo fisheries, refrigerators, cars, bulk seed and bulk industry. On the other hand, most cargo movement is in containers, which have become specialized in the management of packaging, coupled with this complementary means of transportrailway and motor transport are less than 15minutes awayin terms of location.
3. **Focus:** The port ofManzanillo is optingto specialize incontainer handlingmorethan other typesofpackaging, as this is the best wayto handle largequantities ofgoodsover long distancesandsafeway.

Michael Porter and Mike Peng author's theories based on industry makes the assumption of all the needs that the company has to face competition belonging to the same industrial or commercial sector. Peng (2012) defines the industry as a group of companies or companies producing goods and / or services similar to each other.

Based on the preceding paragraph port individually it serves as a great company which is represented by the Integral Port Authority, API, to which it belongs. So it is that this analysis is routed from that perspective. The industry then there are all those ports of the Republic who are in the same range of navigation, or cabotage height, and load levels allow it to be an important competition. All ports even without being in the same geographical area of the country pose a direct competition with each other, because the geographic location of Mexico creates a connection between two oceans and makes more agile the connection between the two ends of the country and the center of same.

The port of Manzanillo is the main port of Mexico with a cargo movement of 2.36 million TEUs last year, followed by the Port of Lazaro Cardenas with 996.654, its main domestic competition in the field of containers, and the port of Veracruz with 847.370. These three ports had played in past years the title of Mexico's main port, but in recent years has shown that the rightful place is for the Colima's port.

Based on the three generic strategies of Porter, is intended to present an analysis of the Port of Manzanillo in abstract revealing the strategies that the port carries and differs from other ports.

1. **Cost Leadership:** As a figure API cannot implement a different rate for use of infrastructure, but as part of its dealers it is possible. This is to say that its private companies realize it. The constant competition between tendered companies that specialize in container handling in the port (OCUPAS, TIMSA, SSA and CONTECON) work third shift leaving costs of a first turn maneuvers. With this services are not hurt as to costs for customers. With regard to other ports specializing in Cruise Terminal, Manzanillo handles a coupon rate of 25% on all services and port infrastructure, giving with it an advantage over other ports in tourist height as Acapulco, Puerto Vallarta and others.
2. **Differentiation:** The port of Manzanillo has the greatest diversification in terms of ports in Mexico. It hasspecialized terminals in Cruiseand Petroleumin the polygon1, while the polygon2 is made up of container terminals, general cargo fisheries, refrigerators, cars, bulk seed and bulk industry. On the other hand, most cargo movement is in containers, which have becomes ecialized in the management of packaging, coupled with this complementary means of transport rail way and motor transport are less than 15minutes awayin terms of location.
3. **Focus:** The port of Manzanillo is opting to specialize in container handling more than other types of packaging, as this is the best wayto handle largequantities ofgoodsover long distancesandsafeway.

The Port of Manzanillo from the Point of View of the Institutions

As defined North (1990) the rules of the game in a society or, more formally, are the humanly devised constraints that shape human interaction, it is because of that Port of Manzanillo is regulated by various authorities and laws, from the field of Foreign Trade, Customs, Ports, Navigation and social. From the point of view of foreign trade are the Foreign Trade and Customs Act governing the processes and procedures for foreign trade and customs clearance, Customs and authority regulates the handling and use of goods at the port found either deposited or in transit; from the port area the Ports Act is one of its top in structure, order and handling. The SCT as the authority in charge of regulating port infrastructure and therefore to allocate concessions to the API's for a period of 50 years.

Port harbormaster in Navigation and respective Navigation law governing shipping and navigation processes in an international legal environment. Finally, the same API plays the role of manager and regulator of private operating companies that have a bid assigned by the same, with a term of 20 years for the management, control and protection of goods.

An institution that certainly affects the action of the port is the CROM, since as the role of union seeks to ensure the welfare of its workers. However, this creates for the port a number of problems, since the laborer staff does not receive training as members of their union, work demands are too high, and the costs increase year after year with a "negotiation" that is disadvantageous for all port operators, the damage caused by crane operators, chassis, forklift or any other union personnel are covered by the companies that hire them. As seen is this institution that defines the rules regarding port operations personnel, making more expensive the end customer prices and operating times.

The API as state owned company (parastatal company) is governed by the SCT and its time as part of its commitments acquired is the offer in infrastructure in communications not only port ones, but also those who support and rectified the collateral damage caused by the impact of the port within a city. This is the reason why it is that within its port development plans also includes investments in road infrastructure projects and remodeling the city. Note that the polygon 1 is located in the very historical city center of the city of Manzanillo thereby enabling a tourist boardwalk between the cruise terminal and oil terminal of PEMEX, while the polygon 2 is found among the colonies of San Pedrito, Tapeixtles and Brisas, hindering access in and out of the area, and it is committed to creating alternative access through road construction and remodeling.

CONCLUSION AND RECOMMENDATIONS

What can be concluded after having conducted the analysis of the Port of Manzanillo based on the theories of Dynamic Resources, Industry and institutionalism, is the next: The development of dynamic capabilities implies the awareness of the company in an internal and external interaction. That is why the Port of Manzanillo has a dynamic capability that allows management of up to 2.13 million tue's with smooth saturation, while its strategic location gives it a catchment area to the most important industrial centers of the country and the most important economies in the world (China, Japan, USA, South Korea, etc.), its natural and human resources allow flexibility in foreign trade offices as part of their competitive advantage against other ports of the country.

In the specific case of Manzanillo, is the star port today in the national port area and other ports should be turned to him and see those strategies that the port is performing an industry to make its relevance adjustments, to analyze if possible based on the specific resources that make imitations or to structure similar strategies.

Mexican height ports have a constant management of the Port Authority who in turn is regulated by the SCT, who work together on issues of interest in the ports to be competitive. In the area of institutions it shows that the ports are regulated or restricted by various institutions that benefit or hinder the way the international competitiveness of a port. Manzanillo despite all those factors that has, against the institutional sphere has shown that teamwork is the answer to these rules of the game port.

The port of Manzanillo is Mexico's number one port and trends of economic, development and logistical growth confirms their status not only nationally but also internationally.Some general recommendations on the subject of industry and resources are directed towards care for their VRIO resources of the port of Manzanillo, since its closest competition is the Port of Lazaro Cardenas, who although currently handles a third of containerized cargo, a future in the short term can absorb part of the cargo arriving at Colima port, and displace it. It should be noted that the Michoacan port also has a strategic location that will allow achieving these results due to the aforementioned reasons.

REFERENCES

AAPA Surveys. (2015). Retrieved from: http://aapa.files.cms-plus.com/PDFs/WORLD%20PORT%20 RANKINGS%202011.pdf

Administración Portuaria Integral de Manzanillo. (2015). Retrieved from: http://www.puertomanzanillo.com.mx/esps/0020202/ubicacion-y-zona-de-influencia

Administración Portuaria Integral de Manzanillo. (2016). Retrieved from http://www.puertomanzanillo.com.mx/esps/0000209/estadisticas

Barney, J. (2008). *Strategy Management and competitive advantages*. Pearson.

CAAAREM. (2015). *¿Qué es la CAAAREM?* Retrieved from: http://www.caaarem.mx/

CEPPAL. (2015). *Movimiento contenerizado de América Latina y el Caribe, Ranking 2013*. retrieved from: http://www.cepal.org/cgi-bin/getProd.asp?xml=/Transporte/noticias/noticias/2/53122/P53122.xml&xsl=/Transporte/tpl/p1f.xsl&base=/Transporte/tpl/top-bottom.xsl

De Larrucea, J., Marí, R., & Mallofré, J. (2014). *Transporte en contenedor.* Alfaomega Grupo Editor, S.A. de C.V.

Lamy, P. (2006). *Conferencia Humanizando la globalización*. Santiago, Chile: Academic Press.

Loyola, J., & Schettino. (1994). *Estrategias Empresariales en una economía global*. Instituto Mexicano de Ejecutivos de Finanzas.

Mahoney, J. (2010). *Resource-basedtheory, dinamyccapabilities, and real options. In Economic Foundations of Strategy*. Thousand Oaks, CA: Sage.

Marsh, D., & Stoker, G. (1997). Teoría y métodos de la Ciencia Política. Alianza.

Musso, E., González, F., Cariou, P., & Barros, E. (2004). *Gestión portuaria y tráficos marítimos*. La Coruña: Netbiblo.

North, D. (1990). *Institutions, Institutional Change, and Economic Performance*. New York: Cambridge University Press. doi:10.1017/CBO9780511808678

OMC. (2015). *¿Qué es la OMC?* Retrieved from: https://www.wto.org/spanish/thewto_s/whatis_s/whatis_s.htm

Peng, M. (2012). *Global Strategy*. Cincinnati, OH: Thomson South-Western.

Penrose, E. (1959). *The Theory of the Growth of the Firm*. New York: JonhWilwy&Sons.

Portales, G. (2012). *Transportación internacional*. Trillas.

PromPerú. La consolidación de carga. (2015). Retrieved from: http://www.prompex.gob.pe/Miercoles/Portal/MME/descargar.aspx?archivo=99121C8D-4B6B-46E5-8577-BD1C2FD4FD3A.PDF

Reyes, O., Guizar, A., Gutiérrez, A., & Rubio, M. (2014). Afectaciones por el servicio de consolidación y desconsolidación de carga de los recintos fiscalizados del puerto de Manzanillo, Colima, México. *Global Conference on Business and Finance Proceedings*, *9*(1).

Saloner, G., Shepard, A., & Podony, J. (2001). Strategic management. California University.

SCT. (1993). *Ley de Puertos*. SCT.

SCT. (2006). *Ley de Navegación*. SCT.

SCT. (2015). Retrieved from: http://www.sct.gob.mx/index.php?id=171

SCT. (2015). *Informe Estadístico mensual movimiento de carga, buques y pasajeros*. Retrieved from: http://www.sct.gob.mx/fileadmin/CGPMM/U_DGP/estadisticas/2014/Mensuales/12_diciembre_2014.pdf

SHCP. (1995). *Ley Aduanera*. SHCP.

Vargas-Hernández, J., Guerra, E., Bojórquez, A., & Bojórquez, F. (2014). *Gestión estratégica de organizaciones*. Ediciones Insumisos Latinos.

Zahra, A., Sapienza, J., & Davidsson, P. (2006). Entrepreneurship and Dynamic Capabilities: A Review, Model and Research Agenda. *Journal of Management Studies*, *43*(4), 917–955. doi:10.1111/j.1467-6486.2006.00616.x

KEY TERMS AND DEFINITIONS

Economy of Organizations: It is a field of applied economics that studies the economic transactions occurring at micro level within individual companies. The analysis is opposed to the transactions at macro that occur at a macro level within the market.

Industry-Based Theory: A strategic perspective for an analysis of industrial competition using different tools such as the dynamic framework of Porter's five forces.

Instituionalism: An approach to economic analysis, especially regarding the role of political sciences, history, social organizations and international relations in determining the impact of formal and informal institutions on economic phenomena and the variables of the sociopolitical environment in which individuals and organizations make their decisions.

Institutions: Are defined as the rules of the game operating in one society and cultural, ethical and property rights restrictions imposed by humans to structure human interactions.

International Trade: The exchange of goods, services, capital and investments involving activities of business, government and individuals, along and across international borders of countries that allows for a greater competition in their domestic markets. The international trade results in an increasing gross domestic product (GDP) and more affordable products for the consumer. The international trade also affects the market supply and demand of goods and services of better quality and right pricing obtainable and available to consumers globally.

Manzanillo's Port: The Port of Manzanillo has positioned itself as the main Pacific gateway for cargo handling at the International Trade Center and the shoal areas of Mexico, which in turn represent more than 67% of the country's GDP and where 55% of the national population lies. The Port is situated in the State of Colima, in the Republic of Mexico, at the geographic coordinates: North Latitude 19º03'30'' y 104º18'30".

The Resource-Based View (RBV): A theoretical approach to assess the effectiveness and efficient application of the available assets in terms of the amount of tangible and intangible resources to determine the competitive advantage of the business strategy.

Compilation of References

AAPA Surveys. (2015). Retrieved from: http://aapa.files.cms-plus.com/PDFs/WORLD%20PORT%20RANKINGS%20 2011.pdf

Aboudou, M. T. (2011). Infrastructure Development and Economic Growth in Togo. *International Journal of Economics and Finance, 3*(3). Retrieved from www.ccsenet.org/ijef

Acemoglu, D., & Johnson, S. (2007). Disease and Development: The Effect of Life Expectancy on Economic Growth. *Journal of Political Economy, 115*(6), 699–749. doi:10.1086/529000

Ackah, I., & Adu, F. (2014). The Impact of Energy Consumption and Total Factor Productivity on Economic Growth Oil Producing African Countries. *Bulletin of Energy Economics*, *2*(2), 28–40.

Adams, S., Klobodu, E. K. M., & Opoku, E. E. O. (2016). Energy consumption, political regime and economic growth in sub-Saharan Africa. *Energy Policy*, *96*, 36–44. doi:10.1016/j.enpol.2016.05.029

Ademiluyi, I. A., & Aluko-Arowolo, S. O. (2009). Infrastructural Distribution of healthcare services in Nigeria: An overview. *Journal of Geography and Planning*, *2*(5), 104–110.

Administración Portuaria Integral de Manzanillo. (2015). Retrieved from: http://www.puertomanzanillo.com.mx/esps/0020202/ubicacion-y-zona-de-influencia

Administración Portuaria Integral de Manzanillo. (2016). Retrieved from http://www.puertomanzanillo.com.mx/esps/0000209/estadisticas

Agarwalla, A. (2011). *Estimating the Contribution of Infrastructure in Regional Productivity Growth in India*. Working Paper No. 2011-05-01. IIM, Ahmedabad.

Agénor, P. R., & Moreno-Dodson, B. (2006). *Public Infrastructure and Growth: New Channels and Policy Implications* (World Bank Policy Research Working Paper 4064). Washington, DC: World Bank.

Aghion, P., Howitt, P., & Murtin, F. (2010). *The relationship between health and growth: When Lucas meets Nelson-Phelps*. National Bureau of Economic Research.

Ahamed, A. (2013). Rural marketing Strategies for Selling Products &Services: Issue and Challenge. *Journal of Business Management &Social Sciences Research, 2*(1), 55-60.

Ahmad, N., Hayat, M. F., Hamad, N., & Luqman, M. (2012). Energy consumption and economic growth: Evidence from Pakistan. *Australian Journal of Business and Management Research*, *2*(6), 9–14.

Ahmad, S. (1966). On the theory of induced innovation. *The Economic Journal*, *76*(302), 344–357. doi:10.2307/2229720

Ailawadi, V. S., & Bhattacharyya, S. C. (2006). Access to energy services by the poor in India: Current situation and need for alternative strategies. *Natural Resources Forum*, *30*(1), 2–14. doi:10.1111/j.1477-8947.2006.00153.x

Almada, C., Gonzalez, L. B., Eason, P., & Fullerton, T. M. Jr. (2006). Econometric Evidence Regarding Education and Border Income Performance. *Mountains Plains Journal of Business and Economics*, *7*, 11–24.

Alsan, M., Bloom, D. E., Canning, D., & Jamison, D. (2006). The consequences of population health for economic performance. In S. Mills, L. Gibson & A. Mills (Eds.), Health, Economic Development and Household Poverty (pp. 21–39). Oxford, UK: Routledge.

Alston, J. M., George, W. N., & Philip, G. P. (1995). *Science under Scarcity: Principles and Practice for Agricultural Research Evaluation and Priority Setting*. Ithaca, NY: Cornell University Press.

Antle, J. M., & Capalbo, S. M. (1988). An Introduction to Recent Developments in Production Theory and Productivity Measurement. Agricultural Productivity: Measurement and Explanation. Washington, DC: Resources for the Future.

Apanisile, O. T., & Akinlo, T. (2013). Rail transport and economic growth in Nigeria (1970-2011). *Australian Journal of Business and Management Research*, *3*(5), 18–24.

Arnade, C. (1998). Using a Programming Approach to Measure International Agricultural Efficiency and Productivity. *Journal of Agricultural Economics*, *49*(1), 67–84. doi:10.1111/j.1477-9552.1998.tb01252.x

Arora, S. (2001). Health Human Productivity and Long-Term Economic Growth. *The Journal of Economic History*, *61*(3), 699–749.

Arora, S. (2001). Health, human productivity, and long-term economic growth. *The Journal of Economic History*, *61*(03), 699–749.

ASCE. (2011). *Water & Wastewater Report | ASCE*. Retrieved February 26, 2016, from http://www.asce.org/water_and_wastewater_report/

Aschauer, D. A. (1989). Is Public Expenditure Productive? *Journal of Monetary Economics*, *23*(2), 177–200. doi:10.1016/0304-3932(89)90047-0

Ashraf, Q. H., Lester, A., & Weil, D. N. (2008). *When does improving health raise GDP?* (NBER Working Paper No. 14449). Cambridge, MA: National Bureau of Economic Research.

Asteriou, D., & Hall, S. G. (2011). *Applied Econometrics* (2nd ed.). Palgrave Macmillan.

Badi, R. V., & Badi, N. V. (2011). *Rural Marketing*. Himalaya Publishing House.

Baltagi, B. H., & Kao, C. (2000). *Nonstationary panels, cointegration in panels and dynamic panels: A survey*. Syracuse University Center for Policy Research Working Paper, (16).

Baltagi, B. H., & Moscone, F. (2010). Health care expenditure and income in the OECD reconsidered: Evidence from panel data. *Economic Modelling*, *27*(4), 804–881. doi:10.1016/j.econmod.2009.12.001

Banerjee,, A., Duflo, & Deaton, A. (2004). Health Care Delivery in Rural Rajasthan. *Economic and Political Weekly*, *39*(9), 944–949.

Banerjee, B. (1995). *Financial Policy and Management Accounting*. Kolkata: World Press Pvt. Ltd.

Banerjee, N. (2002). Between the Devil and Deep Sea - Shrinking Options for Women in Contemporary India. In K. Kapadia (Ed.), *The Violence of Development: The Politics of Identity - Gender and Social Inequalities in India*. New Delhi: Kali for Women.

Bangsund, D. A., Leistritz, F. L., & Honeyman, J. S. (1997). *Assessing Economic impacts of Railroad Abandonment on Rural Communities*. Retrieved from www.handystevenson.com

Barney, J. (2008). *Strategy Management and competitive advantages*. Pearson.

Barrett, M. (1980). *Women"s Oppression Today*. London: Verso.

Barro, R., & Sala-i-Martin, X. (2005). *Growth Theory*. Cambridge, MA: MIT Press.

Bashir, O. K. (2013). Growth-Effects of Macroeconomic Stability Factors: Empirical Evidence from Nigeria. *Developing Country Studies*, *3*(14), 47–55.

Bashir, Z. (2003). The Impacts of Economic Reforms and Trade Liberalisation on Agricultural Export Performance in Pakistan. *Pakistan Development Review*, *42*(4), 941–959.

Bayer, C., & Hanck, C. (2013). Combining non-cointegration tests. *Journal of Time Series Analysis*, *34*(1), 83–95. doi:10.1111/j.1467-9892.2012.00814.x

Behrman, J. R., & Deolikar, A. B. (1988). Health and nutrition. In Handbook of Development Economics (Vol. 1). Academic Press.

Beltrao, G. (2013). *Urban Planning and Land Management for Promoting Inclusive Cities. Inclusive urban Planning*. Oxford University Press.

Bhaduri, A., & Skarstein, R. (2003). Effective demand and the terms of trade in a dual economy: A Kaldorian perspective. *Cambridge Journal of Economics*, *27*(4), 583–595. doi:10.1093/cje/27.4.583

Bhandari L. & Dutta S. (2007). *Health Infrastructure in Rural India*. India Infrastructure Report 2007.

Bhandari, L., & Dutta, S. (2007). Health infrastructure in rural India. *India Infrastructure Report*, 265-271.

Bhandari, L., & Dutta, S. (2007). Health Infrastructure in Rural India. In P. Kalra & A. Rastogi (Eds.), *India Infrastructure Report* (pp. 265–285). New Delhi: Oxford University Press.

Bhandari, L., & Gupta, S. (2011). *The Indicus Handbook 2011: Indian Economy, Markets and Consumers*. Pearson.

Bhargava, A., Jamison, D. T., Lau, L. J., & Murray, C. J. (2001). Modeling the effects of health on economic growth. *Journal of Health Economics*, *20*(3), 423–440. doi:10.1016/S0167-6296(01)00073-X PMID:11373839

Bhattacharyya, S. (2005). *Our coal, our future*. Working Paper, Department of Fuel and Mineral Engineering, Indian School of Mines, Dhanbad.

Bhaumik, S. K. (2015). *Principles of Econometrics: A Modern Approach using E-views*. Oxford University Press.

Bhushan, S. (2005). Total Factor Productivity Growth of Wheat in India: A Malmquist Approach. *Indian Journal of Agricultural Economics*, *60*(1).

Bildirici, M. E. (2013). The analysis of relationship between economic growth and electricity consumption in Africa by ARDL method. *Energy Economics Letters*, *1*(1), 1–14.

Binder, S., Adigun, L., Dusenbury, C., Greenspan, A., & Tanhuanpaa, P. (2008). National Public Health Institutes: Contributing to the Public Good. *Journal of Public Health Policy*, *29*(1), 3–21. doi:10.1057/palgrave.jphp.3200167 PMID:18368014

Binswanger, H. P., & Ruttan, V. W. (1978). *Induced Innovation: Technology, Institutions and Development, Baltomore and London*. The John Hopkins University Press.

Birol, F. (2007). Energy economics: A place for Energy poverty in the Agenda. *The Energy Journal (Cambridge, Mass.), 28*(3). doi:10.5547/ISSN0195-6574-EJ-Vol28-No3-1

Black, S. E., & Spitz-Oener, A. (2010). Explaining Women's Success: Technological Change and Skill Content of Women's Work. *The Review of Economics and Statistics*, 92.

Bloom, D. E. (2014). *The world has come a long way, but still has a long way to go*. Retrieved from http://www.imf.org/external/pubs/ft/fandd/2014/12/bloom.htm

Bloom, D. E., & Canning, D. (2008). Population Health and Economic Growth. In M. Spence & M. A. Lewis (Eds.), Health and Growth (pp. 53-75). Washington, DC: World Bank.

Bloom, D. E., & Canning, D. (2000). The health and wealth of nations. *Science, 287*(5456), 1207–1209. doi:10.1126/science.287.5456.1207 PMID:10712155

Bloom, D. E., Canning, D., & Graham, B. (2003). Longevity and life-cycle savings. *The Scandinavian Journal of Economics, 105*(3), 319–338. doi:10.1111/1467-9442.t01-1-00001

Bloom, D. E., Canning, D., & Sevilla, J. (2001). *The effect of health on economic growth: Theory and evidence*. National Bureau of Economic Research.

Bloom, D. E., Canning, D., & Sevilla, J. (2004). The effect of health on economic growth: A production function approach. *World Development, 32*(1), 1–13. doi:10.1016/j.worlddev.2003.07.002

Bouddha, C., Dhote, K. K., & Sharma, A. (2014). Slum Redevelopment Strategy: A Way forward to Urban Environment Management through Inclusive Approach: Evidence from a review paper. *Research Journal of Engineering Sciences, 3*(7), 28–37.

Boyle, C., Mudd, G., Mihelcic, J. R., Anastas, P., Collins, T., Culligan, P., & Handy, S. (2010). Delivering sustainable infrastructure that supports the urban built environment. *Environmental Science & Technology, 44*(13), 4836–4840. doi:10.1021/es903749d PMID:20583825

Bradshaw, G., & Orden, D. (1990). Granger Causality from the Exchange Rate to Agricultural Prices and Export Sales. *Western Journal of Agricultural Economics, 15*(1), 100–110.

Buckley, R.M., et al. (2007). Strategizing Slum Improvement in India: A Method to Monitor and Refocus Slum Development Programs. *Global Urban Development Magazine, 3*(1), 3.

CAAAREM. (2015). *¿Qué es la CAAAREM?* Retrieved from: http://www.caaarem.mx/

Calderón, C., & Servén, L. (2008). *Infrastructure and economic development in Sub-Saharan Africa* (World Bank Policy Research Working Paper No. 4712). Washington, DC: World Bank.

Calderón, C., Easterly, W., & Servén, L. (2003). Infrastructure compression and public sector solvency in Latin America. The Limits of Stabilization: Infrastructure, Public Deficits, and Growth in Latin America. Stanford University Press and the World Bank.

Canning, D., & Pedroni, P. (2008). Infrastructure, long-run economic growth and causality tests for cointegrated panels. *The Manchester School, 76*(5), 504–527. doi:10.1111/j.1467-9957.2008.01073.x

Cassano, G. (Ed.). (2009). Class Struggle on the Home Front: Work, Conflict and Exploitation in the Household. Palgrave-Macmillan.

Cecelski, E. (2000). *Enabling equitable access to rural electrification: Current thinking on energy, poverty and gender, Briefing Paper, Asia Alternative Energy Policy and Project Development Support*. Washington, DC: The World Bank.

CEPPAL. (2015). *Movimiento contenerizado de América Latina y el Caribe, Ranking 2013*. retrieved from: http://www.cepal.org/cgi-bin/getProd.asp?xml=/Transporte/noticias/noticias/2/53122/P53122.xml&xsl=/Transporte/tpl/p1f.xsl&base=/Transporte/tpl/top-bottom.xsl

Chakrabarti, A., Dhar, A., & Cullenberg, S. (2012). *World of the Third and Global Capitalism*. Delhi: Worldview Publications.

Chakrabarti, S. (2011). A macroeconomic structure of employment: Rural-urban conflict in a Kaleckian framework. *The Review of Radical Political Economics*, *43*(2), 172–197. doi:10.1177/0486613410391404

Chakrabarti, S. (2014). Agriculture-industry relation and the question of 'home market': Towards closing a centuries old debate. *Indian Journal of Agricultural Economics*, *69*(2), 183–210.

Chakrabarti, S., & Mukherjee, A. (2013). National Rural Employment Guarantee Scheme of India: Some Conceptual Problem. *International Critical Thought*, *3*(1), 1–19. doi:10.1080/21598282.2013.761441

Chakraborty, A. (2005). *Status of gas in India's fuel basket*. London: Council.

Chakravarti, U. (2009). Gendering Caste - Through a Feminist Lens. STREE.

Chakravarti, U. (1993). Conceptualizing Brahminical Patriarchy in Early India, Gender, Caste, Class and State. *Economic and Political Weekly*, *28*(14), 3.

Chambers, R. G., & Just, R. E. (1991). Effects of Exchange Rate Changes on U.S. Agriculture. *American Journal of Agricultural Economics*, *73*, 33–43.

Chan, C., Forwood, D., Roper, H., & Sayers, C. (2009). *Public Infrastructure Financing: An International Perspective* (Productivity Commission Staff Working Paper). Retrieved from http://www.pc.gov.au/research/supporting/public-infrastructure-financing

Chandra, R. (2000). *The Impact of Trade Policy on Growth in India* (Unpublished PhD Thesis). Department of Economics, University of Strathclyde, Glasgow, UK.

Chandra, R. (2002). Export Growth and Economic Growth: An Investigation of Causality in India. *The Indian Economic Journal*, *49*, 64–73.

Chandrashekhar, S. (2005). *Growth of Slums, Availability of Infrastructure and Demographic Outcomes in Slums: Evidence from India*. Paper to be presented during the session on urbanization in developing countries at population association of America*Annual Meeting*, Philadelphia, PA.

Chintrakarn, P., & Herzer, D. (2012). More inequality, more crime? A panel cointegration analysis for the United States. *Economics Letters*, *116*(3), 389–391. doi:10.1016/j.econlet.2012.04.014

Chitkara, K. K. (2006). *Construction Project Management: Planning, Scheduling and Controlling*. New Delhi: Tata McGraw-Hill Publishing Company.

Choguill, C. L. (1996). Ten steps to sustainable infrastructure. *Habitat International*, *20*(3), 389–404. doi:10.1016/0197-3975(96)00013-6

Choudhury, M., & Nageshwaran, S. (2011). Rigorous health infrastructure is needed. *British Medical Journal*, *342*(7798), 614.

Clunies-Ross, A., Forsyth, D., & Hug, M. (2009). *Development Economics* (1st ed.). McGraw-Hill Higher Education.

Comfort, K., & Dada, J. (2009). 'Rural Women's Use of Cell Phones to Meet Their Communication Needs: A Study from Northern Nigeria. In I. Buskens & A. Webb (Eds.), *African Women and ICTs: Investigating Technology, gender and Empowerment*. London: Zed Books.

Conditions of Urban Slums. NSS 58th Round July- December, 2002; NSSO Report no. 486 by Government of India.

Cooray, A. (2013). Does health capital have differential effects on economic growth? *Applied Economics Letters*, *20*(3), 244–249. doi:10.1080/13504851.2012.690844

Dalberg Group. (2015). *From Response to Recovery in the Ebola Crisis. Revitalizing Health Systems And Economies, Ebola Report*. Retrieved fromhttp://www.dalberg.com/wp-content/uploads/2015/04/Dalberg_Ebola_Report.pdf

Das, D., & Mahnta, R. (2012). Role of Infrastructure in Developing Countries: A Case Study of Assam. In R. P. Pradhan (Ed.), *Inclusive Financial Infrastructure*. Blumsbury.

Datar, A., Mukherji, A., & Sood, N. (2007). Health infrastructure & immunization coverage in rural India. *The Indian Journal of Medical Research*, *125*(1), 31.

Datta K. S. & Singh K. (2016). Analysis of child deprivation in India: Focus on health and educational perspectives. *Economic Analysis and Policy*, 120–130.

David, E., & Ellis, P. (2013). *Urban Planning and Land Management for Promoting Inclusive Cities, Inclusive urban Planning*. Oxford University Press.

Davis, M. (2004). The Planets of Slums. *New Left Review*.

De Larrucea, J., Marí, R., & Mallofré, J. (2014). *Transporte en contenedor.* Alfaomega Grupo Editor, S.A. de C.V.

De, A., & Endow, T. (2008). *Public expenditure on education in India: Recent trends and outcomes*. Academic Press.

Dean, J. (1951). *Capital Budgeting*. New York: Columbia University Press.

De, P. (2008). Infrastructure Development in India. In N. Kumar (Ed.), *International Infrastructure Development in East Asia – Towards Balanced Regional Development and Integration, ERIA Research Project Report 2007-2* (pp. 105–130). Chiba: IDE-JETRO.

Devarajan, S., Swaroop, V., & Zou, H. F. (1996). The composition of public expenditure and economic growth. *Journal of Monetary Economics*, *37*(2), 313–344. doi:10.1016/S0304-3932(96)90039-2

Devlin, N., & Hansen, P. (2001). Health care spending and economic output: Granger causality. *Applied Economics Letters*, *8*(8), 561–564. doi:10.1080/13504850010017357

Dev, S. M. (2006). Policies and programmes for employment. *Economic and Political Weekly*, (April): 1511–1516.

Dey, B., Mitra, A., Prakash, K., Basud, A., Raye, S., & Mitra, A. (2013). Gaps in Health Infrastructure in Indian Scenario: A Review. *Indo Global. Journal of Pharmaceutical Sciences*, *3*(2), 156–166.

Dickey, D. A., & Fuller, W. A. (1979). Distribution of the Estimators for Autoregressive Time Series with a Unit Root. *Journal of the American Statistical Association*, *74*, 427–431.

Diji, C. J. (2004). Constraints to Industrialization: An Ex-Post Evaluation of the Iron and Steel Industry in Nigeria. *Challenges of Nigerian Industrialization: a Pathway to Nigeria Becoming a Highly Industrialized Country in the Year 2015, Selected papers for 2004 Annual Conference of the Nigerian Economic Society*, 493-519.

Dissou, Y., & Didic, S. (2011). *Public Infrastructure and Economic Growth*. Working Paper, Department of Economics, University of Ottawa.

Dobbs, R., Pohl, H., Lin, D.-Y., Mischke, J., Garemo, N., Hexter, J., ...Nanavatty, R. (2015). *Infrastructure productivity: How to save $1 trillion a year | McKinsey & Company*. Retrieved February 26, 2016, from http://www.mckinsey.com/industries/infrastructure/our-insights/infrastructure-productivity

Dodonov, B., Von Hirschhausen, C., Opitz, P., & Sugolov, P. (2002). Efficiency Infrastructure Supply for Economic Development in Transition Countries: The Case of Ukraine. *Post-Communist Economies*, *14*(2), 149–167. doi:10.1080/14631370220139909

Dreze, J. (2004, November 22). Employment as a social responsibility. *The Hindu*. Retrieved from http://www.hindu.com/ 2004/11/22/stories/2004112205071000.htm

Dreze, J., & Sen, A. A. (1989). Hunger and public action. Oxford, UK: Oxford University Press.

Dube, L. (1986). *Seed and Earth: Symbolism of Biological Reproduction and Sexual Relations of Production. In Visibility and Power: Essays on Women in Society and Development*. Delhi: Oxford University Press.

Dumitrescu, E. I., & Hurlin, C. (2012). Testing for Granger non-causality in heterogeneous panels. *Economic Modelling*, *29*(4), 1450–1460. doi:10.1016/j.econmod.2012.02.014

Dunkerley, J., Knapp, G., & Glatt, S. (1981). *Factors Affecting the Composition of Energy Use in Developing Countries Discussion Paper D-73C 4*. Energy Policy Research Resources For The Future.

Dutt, A. K. (2001). Demand and wage-goods constraints in agriculture-industry interaction in less-developed countries: a theoretical analysis. In A. Bose, D. Ray, & A. Sarkar (Eds.), *Contemporary Macroeconomics*. New Delhi: Oxford University Press.

Dwivedi, D. N. (2008). *Managerial Economics* (7th ed.). Vikas Publishing House PVT Ltd.

Eberhardt, M., & Teal, F. (2010). *Productivity analysis in global manufacturing production* (Discussion Paper Number 515). Oxford, UK: University of Oxford, Department of Economics.

Ecobank. (2014). *Middle Africa Insight Series, Power*. Ecobank Research Division.

Edwards, C., & Kaeding, N. (2015, September). *Federal Government Cost Overruns*. Retrieved from https://www.heartland.org/sites/default/files/cato_cost_overruns.pdf

Ehlers, T. (2014). *Understanding the Challenges for Infrastructure Finance*. BIS Working Papers No.54.

Elinwa, A. U., & Joshua, M. (2001). Time-Overrun Factors in Nigeria Construction Industry. *Journal of Construction Engineering and Management*, *127*(5), 419–425. doi:10.1061/(ASCE)0733-9364(2001)127:5(419)

El-Rufai, N. A. (2012). *The Tragedy of Abandoned Projects*. Retrieved from www.nigeriaintel.com

Engle, R. F., & Granger, C. W. J. (1987). Co-integration and Error Correction Representation: Estimation and Testing. *Econometrica*, *55*(2), 251–276. doi:10.2307/1913236

Enterprise Surveys. (2016). *Enterprise Surveys - What Businesses Experience - World Bank Group*. Retrieved September 6, 2016, from http://www.enterprisesurveys.org/

Erdil, E., & Yetkiner, I. H. (2009). The Granger-causality between health care expenditure and output: A panel data approach. *Applied Economics*, *41*(4), 511–518. doi:10.1080/00036840601019083

ESED. (2014). *Success and failure in MGNREGA implementation in India* (Briefing No. 1). Retrieved from www.effective-states.org

Esfahani, H. S., & Ramírez, M. T. (2003). Institutions, infrastructure, and economic growth. *Journal of Development Economics*, *70*(2), 443–477. doi:10.1016/S0304-3878(02)00105-0

Estache, A. & Grégoire, G. (2012). The Impact of Infrastructure on growth in developing countries. *IFC Economic Notes*, 2012.

Fan, S., Hazell, P., & Thorat, S. (1999). *Linkages Between Government Spending, Growth, and Poverty in Rural India. Research Report 110*. Washington, DC: International Food Policy Research Institute.

Fay, M., Toman, M., Benitez, D., & Csordas, S. (2011). *Infrastructure and sustainable development*. Postcrisis Growth and Development: A Development Agenda for the G 20.

Fischer, A., Petersen, L., Feldkötter, C., & Huppert, W. (2007). Sustainable Governance of Natural Resources and Institutional Change: An Analytical Framework. *Public Administration and Development*, *27*(2), 123–137. doi:10.1002/pad.442

Foysal, M. A. (2012). *Household Energy Consumption Pattern in Rural Areas of Bangladesh*. Retrieved from https://www.researchgate.net/publication/258248028

Fraad, H., Resnick, S. A., & Wolff, R. D. (2009). For Every Knight in Shining Armour, There's a Castle Waiting to be Cleaned. In Class Struggle on the Home Front: Work, Conflict and Exploitation in the Household. Palgrave-Macmillan.

Fullerton, T. Jr, Licerio, E., & Wangmo, P. (2010). Education, infrastructure, and regional income performance in Arkansas. *Regional and Sectoral Economic Studies*, *10*(1), 5–22.

Gangopadhyay, P. (1992). *Business Organization & Principal of Management*. Retrieved from: www.ibef.org

Garrett, A. T. (2004). *Light-Rail Transit in America Policy Issues and Prospects for Economic Development*. Federal Reserve Bank of St. Louis.

George Town University. (2016, May 20). *Performance-based infrastructure: An Acceleration Agenda for the United States Recommendations to the Build America Investment Initiative*. Retrieved from http://beeckcenter.georgetown.edu/wp-content/uploads/2016/04/Performance-Based-Infrastructure_Working-Paper_BeeckCenter_5.20.2016.pdf

Ghei, K., Agarwal, S., Subramanyam, M. A., & Subramanian, S. V. (2010). Association between child immunization and availability of health infrastructure in slums in India. *Archives of Pediatrics & Adolescent Medicine*, *164*(3), 243–249. doi:10.1001/archpediatrics.2009.277 PMID:20194257

Ghose, A. (2011). *Addressing the employment challenge: India's MGNREGA* (Employment Sector Employment Working Paper No. 105). International Labour Office (ILO).

Ghosh, B., & De, P. (2004). How do Different Categories of Infrastructure affect Development? Evidence from Indian States. *EPW*, *39*(42), 4645–4657.

Gong, L., Li, H., & Wang, D. (2012). Health investment, physical capital accumulation, and economic growth. *China Economic Review*, *23*(4), 1104–1119. doi:10.1016/j.chieco.2012.07.002

Government of India. (2012). *Statistics of School Education, 2011-12*. Ministry of Human Resource Development, Govt. of India.

Government of India. (2013). *Annual Report, 2012-13*. Department of Telecommunications, Ministry of Communication & Information Technology, Govt. of India. Retrieved from www.mospi.nic.in

Government of India. (2014a). *Annual Survey of Industries, 2011-12*. Ministry of Statistics and Programme Implementation, Govt. of India.

Government of India. (2014b). *Educational Statistics at a Glance*. MHRD, Govt. of India.

Government of India. (2015). *Agricultural Statistics at a Glance, Directorate of Economics and Statistics*. New Delhi: Ministry of Agriculture.

Government of India. (2015). *Annual Report, Indian Post, 2014-15*. Department of Post, Ministry of Communications and Information Technology, Govt. of India.

Government of India. (2016). National family health survey, 2015-2016. In *Ministry of Health and Family welfare*. New Delhi: Author.

Granger, C. W. J. (1969). Investigating Causal Relations by Econometric Models and Cross Spectral Methods. *Econometrica, 35*(3), 424–438. doi:10.2307/1912791

Granger, C. W. J. (1986). Development in the Study of Co-integrated economic variables. *Oxford Bulletin of Economics and Statistics*, *48*, 3.

Grubesic, T. H. (2009). The Management and Measurement of Infrastructure: Performance, Efficiency and Innovation. Growth and Change, 40(1), 184-187.

GSMA Development Fund. (2010). *Women and Mobile: A Global Opportunity: A study on the Mobile Phone Gender Gap in Low and Middle Income Countries*. London: GSMA and the Cherie Blair Foundation for Women.

Gujrati, D. N. (2003). Basic Econometrics. *McGraw Hill Education*, *4*, 696–702.

Gupta, V. (2005). Climate change and domestic mitigation efforts. *Economic and Political Weekly*, *5*(March), 981–987.

Gyimah-Brempong, K., & Wilson, M. (2004). Health human capital and economic growth in Sub-Saharan African and OECD countries. *The Quarterly Review of Economics and Finance*, *44*(2), 296–320. doi:10.1016/j.qref.2003.07.002

Halder, S. (2008). Effect of Health Human Capital Expenditure on Economic Growth in India: A State Level Study. *Asia-Pacific Social Science Review, 8*(2).

Halder, S., & Mallik, G. (2010). Does human capital cause economic growth? A case study of India. *International Journal of Economic Sciences and Applied Research*, *3*(1), 7–25.

Hall, R. E. & Jones C. I. (1997). Level of Economic Activities Across countries. *American Economic Review*, *87*(2), 173-177.

Hall, R. E., & Jones, C. I. (1999). Why Do Some Countries Produce So Much More Output per Worker than Others. *The Quarterly Journal of Economics*, *114*(1), 83–116. doi:10.1162/003355399555954

Harvey, D. (2008). The Right to the City. *New Left Review, 53*.

Hati, K. K., & Majumder, R. (2013). *Health Infrastructure, Health Outcome and Economic Wellbeing- A District Level Study in India*. Retrieved from https://mpra.ub.uni-muenchen.de/53363/

Hellewel, D. S. (2001). Toward the year 2000 Transport for our cities. In Global Issues (vol. 3). I.B. Tauris Publishers.

Herranz-Loncán, A. (2007). Infrastructure investment and Spanish economic growth, 1850–1935. *Explorations in Economic History*, *44*(3), 452–468. doi:10.1016/j.eeh.2006.06.002

Herzer, D., & Vollmer, S. (2012). Inequality and growth: Evidence from panel cointegration. *The Journal of Economic Inequality*, *10*(4), 489–503. doi:10.1007/s10888-011-9171-6

Hoddinott, J., Alderman, H., & Behrman, J. (2005). Nutrition, Malnutrition and Economic Growth. In G. López-Casasnovas, B. Rivera, & L. Currais (Eds.), *Health and Economic Growth: Findings and Policy Implications* (pp. 164–194). Cambridge, MA: MIT Press.

Howitt, P. (2005). Health, human capital, and economic growth: A Schumpeterian perspective. *Health and economic growth: Findings and policy implications*, 19-40.

Hughes, D. W., & Penson, J. B. (1985). Effects of Selected Macroeconomic Policies on Agriculture: 1984-1990. *Agricultural Financial Review*, *45*, 81–91.

Hulten, C. R. (1996). *Infrastructure capital and economic growth: How well you use it may be more important than how much you have* (NBER Working Paper No. 5847). Cambridge, MA: National Bureau of Economic Research.

Hunt, D. V., & Rogers, C. D. (2005). Barriers to sustainable infrastructure in urban regeneration. In *Proceedings of the Institution of Civil Engineers, Engineering Sustainability* (Vol. 158, pp. 67–81). doi:10.1680/ensu.2005.158.2.67

Hurd, M., & Kapteyn, A. (2003). Health, wealth, and the role of institutions. *The Journal of Human Resources*, *38*(2), 386–415. doi:10.2307/1558749

Hyman, D. N. (2002). *Public Finance: A Contemporary Application of Theory to Policy* (7th ed.). Harcourt College Publishers.

ILO. (2011). Women and labour market in Asia-Rebalancing for gender equality. International Labour Organisation and Asian Development Bank.

Ingwe, R., Mbato, W. A., & Ebong, E. (2012). *Project Abandonment, corruption, and Recovery of Unspent Budgeted Public Funds in Nigeria*. Retrieved from www.revecon.ro/articles/2012-1/2012-1-2.pdf

International Energy Agency (IEA). (2012). *World Energy Outlook 2012*. Retrieved from http://www.worldenergyoutlook.org/weo2014/

International Energy Agency (IEA). (2014). *World Energy Outlook 2014*. Retrieved from http://www.worldenergyoutlook.org/weo2014/

International Finance Corporation (IFC). (2007). *The Business of Health in Africa; Partnering with the Private Sector to Improve People's Lives*. Washington, DC: IFC.

International Renewable Energy Agency (IRENA). (2012). *Prospects for the African Power Sector*. Abu Dhabi: IRENA. Retrieved from http://www.irena.org/menu/index.aspx?mnu=Subcat&PriMenuID=36&CatID=141&SubcatID=244

Interstate Commerce Commission, Rail Services Planning Office. (1975). *Rail Service Continuation Subsidy Decisions: Intent to Establish Criteria*. Academic Press.

James, C., Fried, Northridge, & Rosner, D. (2010). Schools of Public Health: Essential Infrastructure of a Responsible Society and a 21st-Century Health System. *Association of Schools of Public Health*, *125*(1), 8–14. PMID:20402192

Jamison, D. T., Lau, L. J., & Wang, J. (2005). Health's Contribution to Economic Growth in an Environment of Partially Endogenous Technical Progress. In G. López-Casasnovas, B. Rivera, & L. Currais (Eds.), *Health and Economic Growth: Findings and Policy Implications* (pp. 67–91). Cambridge, MA: MIT Press.

Jana, S. K., Palanisami, K. & Das, A. (2012). A Study on Tank Irrigation in the Dry Zones of West Bengal. *Indian Journal of Agricultural Economics*, *67*(2).

Jana, S. K. (2014). *Tank Irrigation in the Dry Zones in India*. New Delhi: Concept Publishing Co.

Jensen, R., & Lleras-Muney, A. (2012). Does staying in school (and not working) prevent teen smoking and drinking? *Journal of Health Economics*, *31*(4), 644–657.

Jhingan, M. L. (2007). The Economics of Development and Planning (39th ed.). Vrinda Publications.

Jiménez, R., Serebrisky, T., & Mercado, J. (2014). Power lost: sizing electricity losses in transmission and distribution systems in Latin America and the Caribbean (Inter-American Development Bank (IDB) Monograph; 241). Washington, DC: IDB.

Jingan, M. L. (2009). The Economics of Development and Planning (39th ed.). Vrinda Publications.

Johnson, P. R., Grennes, T., & Thursby, M. (1977). Devaluation, Foreign Trade Control, and Domestic Wheat Prices. *American Journal of Agricultural Economics*, *59*(4), 619–627. doi:10.2307/1239389

Jowitt, P. W. (2004). Systems and sustainability: sustainable development, civil engineering and the formation of the civil engineer. In *Proceedings of the institution of civil engineers, Engineering Sustainability* (Vol. 157, pp. 1–11).

Kabeer, N. (1996). Agency, Well-Being & Inequality: Reflections on the Gender Dimensions of Poverty. IDS Bulletin, 27(1), 11-21.

Kaboub, F. (2007). *Employment Guarantee Programs: A Survey of Theories and Policy Experiences*. Working Paper No. 498. Annandale-on-Hudson, NY: The Levy Economics Institute of Bard College.

Kaldor, N. (1976). Inflation and recession in the world economy. *The Economic Journal*, *86*(December), 703–714. doi:10.2307/2231447

Kaldor, N. (1984). The problem of inter sectoral balance. In *Causes of growth and stagnation in the world economy*. Cambridge, UK: Cambridge University Press.

Kalecki, M. (1971). On foreign trade and domestic exports. In *Selected essays on the dynamics of the capitalist economy*. Cambridge, UK: Cambridge University Press. (Original work published 1934)

Kalecki, M. (1993). The problem of financing economic development. In J. Osiatynski (Ed.), *Collected works of Michał Kalecki* (Vol. 5). Oxford, UK: Clarendon Press. (Original work published 1954)

Kalotra, A. (2013). Rural marketing Potential in India. *International Journal of Advance Research in Computer Science and Software Engineering, 3*(1), 1-10.

Karti, R. & Valarmati, S. (2015). Aggressive Business Expansion in Rural markets through understanding Indian consumers. *International Journal of Scientific and Research Publication, 5*.

Kaur, B. (2015). Rural Marketing-A Concept of Marketing Management. *IOSR Journal of Business and Management*, 40-45.

Kavanagh, P., Doyle, C., & Metcalfe, O. (2005). *Health impacts of Transport: A Review*. Institute of Public Health in Ireland.

Kelkar, G., & Nathan, D. (2002). *Gender relations and the energy transition in rural Asia, Collaborative Research Group on Gender and Energy, ENERGIA International Network on Gender and Sustainable Energy Use, DFID International Energy Agency (2012)*. World Energy Outlook.

Kelley, E., & Hurst, J. (2006). *Health care quality indicators project. Conceptual framework paper* (OECD Health Working Papers No. 23). Paris: Organisation for Economic Co-operation and Development.

Kerzner, H. (2004). *Production Management: A system Approach to planning, scheduling and controlling* (2nd ed.). CBS Publishers and Distribution.

Kevern, J. T. (2010). Green building and sustainable infrastructure: Sustainability education for civil engineers. *Journal of Professional Issues in Engineering Education and Practice*, *137*(2), 107–112. doi:10.1061/(ASCE)EI.1943-5541.0000048

Khalafalla, K. Y., & Webb, A. J. (2001). Export-led Growth and Structural Change: Evidence from Malaysia. *Applied Economics*, *33*(13), 1703–1715. doi:10.1080/00036840010015066

King, R. S., & Amponsah, O. (2012). The Role of City Authorities in Contributing to the Development of Urban Slums in Ghana. *Journal of Construction Project Management and Innovation*, *2*(1), 285–313.

Kishor, N.R. (2014). Rural Consumer Behavior towards Consumer Durable goods in India. *International Journal of Advance Research in Computer Science and Management Studies, 2*, 1-13.

Kolkata Study Report. (2014). Society for Participatory Research in Asia.

Konti, V.V.D.P. (2012). Prospect and Problems of Indian rural market. *ZENITH International Journal of Business Economics & Management*, *2*(3), 200-213.

Kostzer, D. (2008). *Argentina: A Case Study on the Plan Jefes y Jefas de Hogar Desocupados, or the Employment Road to Economic Recovery*. The Levy Economics Institute of Bard College, Working Paper No. 534.

Kouakou, A. K. (2011). Economic growth and electricity consumption in Cote dIvoire: Evidence from time series analysis. *Energy Policy*, *39*(6), 3638–3644. doi:10.1016/j.enpol.2011.03.069

KPMG. (2012). *The State of Health Care in Africa*. Retrieved from https://www.kpmg.com/Africa/en/IssuesAndInsights/Articles-Publications/Documents/The-State-of-Healthcare-in-Africa.pdf

KPMG. (2015). *Sector Report: Power in Africa*. Retrieved from http;//www. kpmg.com/africa

Kumar, K.R. (2010). Consumer durable Industry in India-A Bird's Eye View. *Asian Journal of Management*, *1*(2), 61-64.

Kumar, P. (2013). Challenge and Opportunity of Indian Rural Market. *International Journal of Marketing Studies*, *5*(3), 161-173.

Kumar, A., & Gupta, S. (2012). *Health Infrastructure in India: Critical Analysis of Policy Gaps in the Indian Healthcare Delivery*. Vivekananda International Foundation.

Kumari, R., & Raman, R. (2011). Inter- District Disparity in Health Care Facility and Education: A Case of Uttar Pradesh. *Journal of Education and Practice*, *2*(1), 38–56.

Kumar, N., Sen, R., & Asher, M. (Eds.). (2006). *India-ASEAN Economic Relations: Meeting the challenges of globalisation*. New Delhi: ISEAS, Singapore, and RIS.

Kumar, P., & Dangi, N. (2013). Rural Marketing in India: Challenges and Opportunities. *International Journal of Management & Social Science Research*, *2*, 34–56.

Kumo, W. L. (2012). *Infrastructure Investment and Economic Growth in South Africa: A Granger Causality Analysis* (African development Bank Group Working Paper Series 160). Tunis, Tunisia: African Development Bank.

Laddha, S. (2015). Rural Consumer Buying Behavior and Brand Awareness of Consumer Durables. *NBR E-Journal*, *1*(1), 1-9.

Lagos State G. D. P. Survey. (2010). *Lagos State Gross Domestic Product (GDP) Survey: 2010*. Lagos State Bureau of Statistic, Ministry of Economic Planning and Budget, Alausa, Ikeja. Retrieved from www.lagosstate.gov.ng

Lagos State Government (LSG). (1981). Ministry of Public Transportation (LSMPT). Lagos Metro Line Project Phase 1 Final Report (1981). The Japanese Consortium.

Lahiri-Dutt, K., & Williams, D. (2005). *The coal cycle: A small part of the illegal supply of coal in eastern India*. New Delhi: Resources, Environment and Development.

Lakshmi S. T. & Sahoo, D. (2013). Health Infrastructure and Health Indicators: The Case of Andhra Pradesh, India. *IOSR Journal of Humanities and Social Science, 6*, 22-29.

Lall, S. V. (2006). Infrastructure and Regional Growth, Growth Dynamics and Policy Relevance for India. *The Annals of Regional Science*, *41*(3), 581–599. doi:10.1007/s00168-006-0112-4

LAMATA. (2015). *Lagos Rail Mass Transit*. Retrieved from www.lamata-ng.com

Lamy, P. (2006). *Conferencia Humanizando la globalización*. Santiago, Chile: Academic Press.

Lasara, M. L. (2015). Inter-State Variations in Rural Healthcare Infrastructure in North-East India. *The NEHU Journal, 13*(2), 31-48.

Learning Planning Commission. (2011). *High level expert group report on universal health coverage for India.*

Lee Eva, K. (2009). Modeling and Optimizing the Public-Health Infrastructure for Emergency Response. *Interfaces*, *39*(5), 476–490. doi:10.1287/inte.1090.0463

Lenferink, S., Tillema, T., & Arts, J. (2013). Towards sustainable infrastructure development through integrated contracts: Experiences with inclusiveness in Dutch infrastructure projects. *International Journal of Project Management*, *31*(4), 615–627. doi:10.1016/j.ijproman.2012.09.014

Levin, A., Lin, C. F., & Chu, C. S. J. (2002). Unit root tests in panel data: Asymptotic and finite- sample properties. *Journal of Econometrics*, *108*(1), 1–24. doi:10.1016/S0304-4076(01)00098-7

Lleras-Muney, A., & Jayachandran, S. (2009). Longevity and human capital investments: Evidence from maternal mortality declines in Sri Lanka. *The Quarterly Journal of Economics*, *124*(1), 349–397.

Lorentzen, P., McMillan, J., & Wacziarg, R. (2008). Death and development. *Journal of Economic Growth*, *13*(2), 81–124. doi:10.1007/s10887-008-9029-3

Loyola, J., & Schettino. (1994). *Estrategias Empresariales en una economía global*. Instituto Mexicano de Ejecutivos de Finanzas.

Lucas, R. E. Jr. (1988). On the mechanics of economic development. *Journal of Monetary Economics*, *22*(1), 3–42. doi:10.1016/0304-3932(88)90168-7

Maddala, G. S., & Kim, I. (1998). Unit Roots, Co-integration and Structural Change. Cambridge University Press.

Mahoney, J. (2010). *Resource-basedtheory, dinamyccapabilities, and real options. In Economic Foundations of Strategy*. Thousand Oaks, CA: Sage.

Majumder, R. (2015). *Infrastructural Facilities in India: District Level Availability Index*. New Delhi: Central Statistical Office, Ministry of Statistics and Programme Implementation, Government of India.

Mandal, K. (2012). *Gender and Empowerment- A comparative Analysis of India and USA*. Levant Book.

Marjit, S., & Maiti, D. S. (2007). Politics and contemporary macro economy of India. In *India macroeconomics annual 2006*. Sage.

Markard, J. (2009, September). *Characteristics of infrastructure sectors and implications for innovation processes* (Discussion Paper for the Workshop on Environmental Innovation in Infrastructure Sectors). Retrieved from http://citeseerx.ist.psu.edu/viewdoc/download?doi=10.1.1.476.1015&rep=rep1&type=pdf

Marsh, D., & Stoker, G. (1997). Teoría y métodos de la Ciencia Política. Alianza.

Marx, B., Stoker, T., & Suri, T. (2013). The Economics of Slums in the Developing World. *The Journal of Economic Perspectives*, *27*(4), 187–210. doi:10.1257/jep.27.4.187

Mattoo, A. (2005, August 27). Striking a balance. *Economic and Political Weekly*, 3815–18.

Mavalankar, V. D., Ramani, V. K., Patel, A., & Sankar, P. (2005). *Building the Infrastructure to Reach and care for the Poor: Trends, Obstacles and Strategies to overcome them.* Ahmedabad: Center for Management of Health Service, Indian Institute of Management.

McCoskey, S. K., & Selden, T. M. (1998). Health care expenditures and GDP: Panel data unit root test results. *Journal of Health Economics*, *17*(3), 369–376. doi:10.1016/S0167-6296(97)00040-4 PMID:10180923

McDonald, S., & Roberts, J. (2006). AIDS and economic growth: A human capital approach. *Journal of Development Economics*, *80*(1), 228–250. doi:10.1016/j.jdeveco.2005.01.004

McKinsey. (2013, November). *A risk-management approach to a successful infrastructure project Initiation, financing, and execution.* Retrieved from http://www.mckinsey.com/~/media/McKinsey/dotcom/client_service/Risk/Working%20papers/52_A_risk-management_approach_to_a_successful_infrastructure_project.ashx

Mehta, J. K. (2005). *India: Facing up to the future, The World Energy Book.* London: World Energy Council.

Meir, S., & Sepe, J. F. (1989). Project termination announcements and the market value of the firm. *Financial Management*, *18*(4), 74–81. doi:10.2307/3665799

Mellor, J. W. (1966). *The Economics of Agricultural Development.* New York: Cornell University Press.

Merna, T., & Al-Thani, F. F. (2008). *Corporate Risk Management* (2nd ed.). John Wiley Sons, Ltd.

Miguel, E., & Kremer, M. (2004). Worms: Identifying impacts on education and health in the presence of treatment externalities. *Econometrica*, *72*(1), 159–217. doi:10.1111/j.1468-0262.2004.00481.x

Miller, M. E. (1988). On the Systematic Risk of Expansion Investment. *The Quarterly Review of Economics and Business*, *28*(Autumn), 66–77.

Ministry of Health and Family Welfare. (2005). *Rural Health Care System in India.* New Delhi: Ministry of Health and Family Welfare, Government of India.

Minsky, H. P. (1965). The Role of Employment Policy. In M. S. Gordon (Ed.), *Poverty in America.* Chandler.

Mitchell, W. (1998). The Buffer Stock Employment Model and the NAIRU: The Path to Full Employment. *Journal of Economic Issues*, *39*(1), 235–244. doi:10.1080/00213624.2005.11506788

Mitra, I. (2015). *Sustainable Slum Improvement Models, Terra Green, Planning Sustainable Cities.* Earth Scan Publications UN-Habitat, Ltd.

MNREGA Sameeksha-II. (2015). *An Anthology of Research Studies.* UNDP India.

Mohan, R. (2016). *Infrastructure and Economic Development - A Conceptual Clarification.* Accessed on July 7, 2016. http://shodhganga.inflibnet.ac.in/bitstream/10603/8497/12/12_chapter%202.pdf

Mohan, R. (2003). Infrastructure Development in India: Emerging Challenges. *World Bank Annual Bank Conference on Development Economics*, Bangalore, India.

Montgomery, E. (2008). *Infrastructure in India: A vast land of construction opportunity.* Available to download at www.pwc.com

Murgai, R., & Ravallion, M. (2005). Employment guarantee in rural India. *Economic and Political Weekly*, (July): 3, 450–455.

Musgrave, R. A., & Musgrave, P. B. (2004). Public Finance in Theory and Practice (5th ed.). Tata McGraw Hill Education Private Ltd.

Mushkin, S. J. (1962). Health as an Investment. *Journal of Political Economy*, *70*(5, Part 2), 129–157. doi:10.1086/258730

Musso, E., González, F., Cariou, P., & Barros, E. (2004). *Gestión portuaria y tráficos marítimos*. La Coruña: Netbiblo.

Nairaland Forum. (2014). *Lagos, emerging cities hold promise of 50% world growth*. Retrieved from www.businessdayonline.com

Nanda, S. S. (2015). Infrastructure Development in India: The role of public-private partnership. *International Journal of Core Engineering & Management*, *2*(6), 60–70.

Naoyuki, Y., & Nakahigashi, M. (2000). *The Role of Infrastructure in Economic Development*. Retrieved from http://econ.keio.ac.jp/staff/dikamiya/pdf00/seminar/1205.pdf

Nathan, H. S. K., Mishra, S., & Reddy, B. S. (2008). *An alternative approach to measure HDI.* Indira Gandhi Institute of Development Research (IGIDR), Working Paper, WP- 2008-001.

National Bureau of Statistics. (2014). *Nigerian Gross Domestic Product Report, Quarter four*. National Bureau of Statistics. Retrieved from www.nigerianstat.gov.ng

Ndulu, B. J., & OConnell, S. A. (1999). Governance and growth in sub-Saharan Africa. *The Journal of Economic Perspectives*, *13*(3), 41–66. doi:10.1257/jep.13.3.41

Newbery, D. (2012). *Energy and infrastructure* (Submission to the LSE Growth Commission). Retrieved from http://tinyurl.com/c8qtahl

Nicholas, B., & Payne, J. E. (2009). The causal relationship between U.S. energy consumption and real output: A disaggregated analysis. *Journal of Policy Modeling*, *31*(2), 180–188. doi:10.1016/j.jpolmod.2008.09.001

Nketiah-Amponsah, E. (2009). Public Spending and Economic Growth: Evidence from Ghana (19702004). *Development Southern Africa*, *26*(3), 477–497. doi:10.1080/03768350903086846

North, D. (1990). *Institutions, Institutional Change, and Economic Performance*. New York: Cambridge University Press. doi:10.1017/CBO9780511808678

Novianti, T., Amzul, R., Dian, V. P., & Retno, W. (2014). The Infrastructure's Influence on the ASEAN Countries' Economic Growth. *Journal of Economics and Development Studies*, *2*(4).

Novick, L. F., & Mays, G. P. (2005). *Public health administration: principles for population- based management*. Jones & Bartlett.

Ochonma, M. (2015). *Nigeria loses ₦500bn yearly to failed freight rail service*. Retrieved from www.businessdayonline.com

Odufalu, O., & Loto, M. A. (2008). *Project Analysis and Evaluation Principles and Techniques* (3rd ed.). Concept Publications.

OECD. (2012). *Debt and Macroeconomic Stability.* OECD Economics Department Policy Notes, No. 16.

Okorafor, G. F. (2004). *Impact Analysis of Federal Highways on the Local Economy- A case of selected highways in Nigeria* (Unpublished PhD Thesis). Federal University of Technology Owerri.

Olowe, R. A. (2011). *Financial Management, Concepts, Financial System and Business Finance* (3rd ed.). Lagos: Brierly Jones Nigeria Ltd.

OMC. (2015). *¿Qué es la OMC?* Retrieved from: https://www.wto.org/spanish/thewto_s/whatis_s/whatis_s.htm

Omotosho, K. (2012). *About 12,000 federal projects abandoned across Nigeria.* Retrieved from http://www.premiumtimesng.com/news/108450-about-12000-federal-projects-abandoned-across-nigeria.html

Organisation for Economic Co-operation and Development (OECD). (2015). *Health at a Glance 2015: OECD Indicators.* Paris: OECD Publishing.

Oshikoya, W. T., & Hussain, M. N. (2002). Infrastructure for Economic Development in Africa. In J. B. de Macedo & O. Kabbaj (Eds.), *Regional Integration in Africa.* OECD.

Ostrom, E., Schroeder, L., & Wynne, S. (1993). Institutional incentives and sustainable development: Infrastructure policies in perspective. Boulder, CO: Westview Press

Ouedraogo, N. S. (2013). Energy consumption and economic growth: Evidence from the economic community of West African States (ECOWAS). *Energy Economics, 36*, 637–647. doi:10.1016/j.eneco.2012.11.011

Owolabi-Merus, O. (2015). Infrastructure Development and Economic Growth Nexus in Nigeria. *International Journal of Academic Research in Business and Social Sciences, 5*(1).

Pan, J. (2002). *Rural Energy Patterns in China: A preliminary assessment from available data sources.* Retrieved from https://pesd.fsi.stanford.edu/sites/default/files/evnts/media//PAN_paper.pdf

Panayotou, T. (1998). *The role of the private sector in sustainable infrastructure development.* Citeseer. Retrieved from environment.yale.edu/publication-series/documents/downloads/0.../101panayotou.pdf

Panicker, P., & Warrier, A. (2013). Rural Marketing –Profitability in Rural Sales. *International Journal of Scientific and Research*, 1359-1361.

Panigrahi, S., & Beura, D. (2013). An Exploratory Study on Infrastructure Financing in India. *International Journal of Science and Research, 4*(3), 405–408.

Papadimitriou, D. B. (2008). *Promoting Equality Through an Employment of Last Resort Policy.* Working papers, The Levy Economics Institute, No. 545. Available at www.econstor.eu

Patel, S. K. (2013). The challenges and Strategies of marketing in Rural India. *Asia Pacific Journal of Marketing & Management Review, 2*(7), 38-43.

Pathak, R. & Pathak, N. (2013). Information Technology: Bridging the gap between urban and rural marketing. *Scholars World-IRMJCR, 1*(3), 102-111.

Patil, V. A., Somasundaram, V. K., & Goyal, C. R. (2002). Current Health Scenario in Rural India. *The Australian Journal of Rural Health, 10*(2), 129–135. doi:10.1111/j.1440-1584.2002.tb00022.x PMID:12047509

Patnaik, P. (2005). On the need for providing employment guarantee. *Economic and Political Weekly*, 203-7. Retrieved from http://www.censusindia.gov.in/Census_Data_2001/Census_Data_Online/CensusDataOnline_Login.aspx

Paul, L. J. (1984). Energy Policies and Their Consequences after 25 Years. *The Energy Journal (Cambridge, Mass.), 24*(4).

Peddada, K. (2014). Growth of Financial Infrastructure in Rural India. *Kurukshetra' Ministry of Rural Development, Monthly Journal, 62*(5), 52.

Pedroni, P. (1999). Critical values for cointegration tests in heterogeneous panels with multiple regressors, *Oxford Bulletin of Economics and Statistics, 61*(s 1), 653-670.

Peng, M. (2012). *Global Strategy*. Cincinnati, OH: Thomson South-Western.

Penrose, E. (1959). *The Theory of the Growth of the Firm*. New York: JonhWilwy&Sons.

Pesaran, M. H. (2004). *General Diagnostic Tests for Cross Section Dependence in Panels* (IZA Discussion Paper No. 1240). Bonn: IZA.

Pesaran, M. H. (2006). Estimation and inference in large heterogeneous panels with a multifactor error structure. *Econometrica, 74*(4), 967–1012. doi:10.1111/j.1468-0262.2006.00692.x

Pesaran, M. H., Shin, Y., & Smith, R. J. (2001). Bounds testing approaches to the analysis of level relationships. *Journal of Applied Econometrics, 16*(3), 289–326. doi:10.1002/jae.616

Pesaran, M. H., & Smith, R. (1995). Estimating long-run relationships from dynamic heterogeneous panels. *Journal of Econometrics, 68*(1), 79–113. doi:10.1016/0304-4076(94)01644-F

Pindyck, R. S. (1998). Irreversible Investment, Capacity Choice, and the Value of the Firm. *The American Economic Review, 78*, 969–985.

Pinstrup-Andersen, P. (2002). Food and Agricultural Policy for a Globalizing World: Preparing for the Future. *American Journal of Agricultural Economics, 84*(5), 1201–1214. doi:10.1111/1467-8276.00381

Pinstrup-Andersen, P., & Shimokawa, S. (2002). *Rural Infrastructure and Agricultural development* (pp. 185–203). Rethinking Infrastructure for Development.

Pokharel, B. (2010). *Power Shortage, its impacts and the Hydropower Sustainability Assessment Protocol: In the context of South Asia* (Master's Thesis). Retrieved from http://lnweb90.worldbank.org/exteu/SharePapers.nsf/(ID)/9FC30006ED600CA08525785E00780506/$File/nrsc_616_project_paper_bipin_pokharel.pdf

Population, Slum population, Literacy rate, slum literacy rate, WPR, Slum WPR from Census 2001. (n. d.). Retrieved from http://www.censusindia.gov.in/Census_Data_2001/Census_Data_Online/CensusDataOnline_Login.aspx

Population, Slum population, Literacy rate, slum literacy rate, WPR, Slum WPR from Census 2011. (n. d.). Retrieved from http://www.censusindia.gov.in/2011census/population_enumeration.html

Portales, G. (2012). *Transportación internacional*. Trillas.

Powles, J., & Comim, F. (2003). Public health infrastructure and knowledge. *Global public health goods for health: Health economics and public health perspectives*, 159-176.

Preston, S. H. (1975). The changing relation between mortality and level of economic development. *Population Studies, 29*(2), 231–248. doi:10.1080/00324728.1975.10410201 PMID:11630494

PromPerú. La consolidación de carga. (2015). Retrieved from: http://www.prompex.gob.pe/Miercoles/Portal/MME/descargar.aspx?archivo=99121C8D-4B6B-46E5-8577-BD1C2FD4FD3A.PDF

Rajnani, R.C. (2014). Rural Infrastructure key to inclusive growth. *Kurukshetra' Ministry of Rural Development, Monthly Journal, 62*(5).

Ramirez, M. D. (2004). Is Public Infrastructure Spending Productive in the Mexican Case? A Vector Error Correction Analysis. *The Journal of International Trade & Economic Development, 13*(2), 159–178. doi:10.1080/0963819042000218700

Rani, M. (2013). Rural Market: The Core of Indian Market. *G.J.C.M.P. (Global Institute for Research & Management), 2(6)*, 123-125.

Rao, K. S. C., & Dhar, B. (2011). *India's FDI Inflows- Trend and Concepts*. Working Paper No. 01. Institute for Studies in Industrial Development.

Ray Chowdhury, N. C. (1992). *Business Management*. Kolkata: Modern Book Agency Pvt. Ltd.

Raza, H. (2005). *Co-operation fuels development, The World Energy Book*. World Energy Institute.

Razin, O., & Collins, S. M. (1997). Real Exchange Rate Misalignments and Growth. In *The Economics of Globalization: Policy Perspectives from Public Economics*. Cambridge, UK: Cambridge University Press.

RBI handbook data for GDP growth, export and total public expenditure on agriculture. (n.d.). Retrieved from https://rbi.org.in/Scripts/AnnualPublications.aspx?head=Handbook%20of%20Statistics%20on%20Indian%20Economy

Reddy, B.S. & P. Balachandra (2002, December 28). A sustainable energy strategy for India revisited. *Economic and Political Weekly*, 5264–73.

Resnick, S. A., & Wolff, R. D. (1987). *Knowledge and Class: A Marxist Critique of Political Economy*. Chicago: University of Chicago Press.

Reyes, O., Guizar, A., Gutiérrez, A., & Rubio, M. (2014). Afectaciones por el servicio de consolidación y desconsolidación de carga de los recintos fiscalizados del puerto de Manzanillo, Colima, México.*Global Conference on Business and Finance Proceedings*, *9*(1).

Rioja, F. K. (2001). Growth, Welfare, and Public Infrastructure: A General Equilibrium Analysis of Latin American Economies. *Journal of Economic Development*, *26*(2), 119–130.

Rivera, I. V. B. IV, & Currais, L. (1999). Economic growth and health: Direct impact or reverse causation? *Applied Economics Letters*, *6*(11), 761–764. doi:10.1080/135048599352367

Rodriguez, C., & Silva, A. R. (2013). *Energy Subsidies and Energy Consumption — A Cross-Country Analysis*. IMF Working Paper No. 13/112.

Rodrik, D., & Wacziarg, R. (2005). Do democratic transitions produce bad economic outcomes? *The American Economic Review*, *95*(2), 50–55. doi:10.1257/000282805774670059

Rojas-Rueda, D., Nazelle, A., Teixidó, O., & Nieuwenhuijsen, M. J. (2013). Health impact assessment of increasing public transport and cycling use in Barcelona: A morbidity and burden of disease approach. Preventive Medicine, 57(5), 573-579.

Romer, P. (1993). Idea gaps and object gaps in economic development. *Journal of Monetary Economics*, *32*(3), 543–573. doi:10.1016/0304-3932(93)90029-F

Romer, P. M. (1986). Increasing returns and long-run growth. *Journal of Political Economy*, *94*(5), 1002–1037. doi:10.1086/261420

Roy, A. K. (2003). Disinvestment and outsourcing in coal. *Economic and Political Weekly*, (December): 6.

Rusling, S (2010). *Approaches to Basic Service Delivery for the Working Poor: Assessing the Impact of Mahila Housing Trust's Parivartan Slum Upgrading Programme in Ahmedabad, India*. WIEGO Policy Brief (Urban Policies) No.1.

Rutherford, D. (2002). *Routledge Dictionary of Economics*. London: Routledge. doi:10.4324/9780203000540

Sagar, A. (2002, September 21). India's energy R and D landscape. *Economic and Political Weekly*, 3925–34.

Sahu, S. (2008). *Trend and patterns of energy consumption in India*. Available at http://mpra.ub.uni-muenchen.de/16753/

Sajal, G. (2002). *Electricity Consumption and Economic Growth*. Elsevier Energy Policy.

Saloner, G., Shepard, A., & Podony, J. (2001). Strategic management. California University.

Sanyal, K., & Bhattacharyya, R. (2009). Beyond the Factory: Globalisation, Informalisation of Production and the New Locations of Labour. Economic and Political Weekly, 44(22).

Sanyal, K. (2007). *Rethinking capitalist development: Primitive accumulation, governmentality and post colonial capitalism*. New Delhi: Routledge.

Sarté, S. B. (2010). *Sustainable infrastructure: The guide to green engineering and design*. John Wiley & Sons.

Sawada, Y. (2015). *The Impacts of Infrastructure in Development: A Selective Survey*. ADBI Working Paper Series, No. 511.

Schultz, T. W. (1959). Investment in man: An economists view. *The Social Service Review*, *33*(2), 109–117. doi:10.1086/640656

Schultz, T. W. (1964). *Transforming Traditional Agriculture*. New Haven, CT: Yale University Press.

Schwable, K. (2006). *Introduction to Project Management*. Thomson Course Technology. Retrieved from www.thomsonrights.com

SCT. (1993). *Ley de Puertos*. SCT.

SCT. (2006). *Ley de Navegación*. SCT.

SCT. (2015). *Informe Estadístico mensual movimiento de carga, buques y pasajeros*. Retrieved from: http://www.sct.gob.mx/fileadmin/CGPMM/U_DGP/estadisticas/2014/Mensuales/12_diciembre_2014.pdf

SCT. (2015). Retrieved from: http://www.sct.gob.mx/index.php?id=171

Seethepalli, K., Bramati, M. C., & Veredas, D. (2008). *How relevant is infrastructure to growth in East Asia?* (World Bank Policy Research Working Paper No. 4597). Washington, DC: World Bank.

Şen, H., Kaya, A., & Alpaslan, B. (2015). *Education, Health, and Economic Growth Nexus: A Bootstrap Panel Granger Causality Analysis for Developing Countries* (The University of Manchester, Discussion Paper Series EDP-1502). Manchester, UK: The University of Manchester.

Sharma, R. N. (1989). *Principles of Sociology*. Bombay: Media Promoters & Publishers Private Limited.

SHCP. (1995). *Ley Aduanera*. SHCP.

Sims, C. (1980). Macroeconomics and Reality. *Econometrica*, *48*(Jan), 1–49. doi:10.2307/1912017

Sing, P., & Sharma, A. (2012). The Changing Face of Rural Marketing in Indian Economy. *A Journal of Economics and Management, 1*(7), 47-60.

Sinha, M., & Sengupta, P. P. (2016). *Post Reform Trends in India's Foreign Exchange Rate: Testing the Role of Agricultural Exports*. Presented at National Symposium on Statistics for Sustainable Agricultural Development, Kolkata, India.

Siras, M. K. (2012). Potentials and strategies for durables-A Study in Ghaziabad District. *International journal of Trade and Commerce, 1*(1), 60-69.

Sivanesan, R. (2014).Problem of Rural Marketing in India. *International Journal of Research in Business and Management, 1*, 1–7.

Sjoblom, D., & Farrington, J. (2008). *The Indian national rural employment guarantee act.* Retrieved from http://www.odi.org.uk

Slums in India. NSS 49th Round January- June 1993; NSSO Report no. 417. Government of India State of Slums in India, A Statistical Compendium. (2013). MoHUPA, Government of India.

Snieska, V., &Simkunaite, I. (2015). Socio-economic impact of infrastructure investments. *Engineering Economics, 63*(4), 16-25.

Soares, R. R. (2006). The effect of longevity on schooling and fertility: Evidence from the Brazilian Demographic and Health Survey. *Journal of Population Economics, 19*(1), 71–97. doi:10.1007/s00148-005-0018-y

Solow, R. M. (1956). A contribution to the theory of economic growth. *The Quarterly Journal of Economics, 70*(1), 65–94. doi:10.2307/1884513

Sorkin, A. (1978). Health manpower. *Health Care Management Review, 3*(1), 87–88. doi:10.1097/00004010-197824000-00011 PMID:10239260

Srinivasan, M.R., Grover, R.B., & Bharadwaj, S.A. (2005, December 3). Nuclear power in India: Winds of change. *Economic and Political Weekly*, 5183–88.

State of the World's Cities. (2012). UN-Habitat.

Stela, Z. T. (2010). Energy consumption and economic growth: A causality analysis for Greece. *Energy Economics, 32*(3), 582–590. doi:10.1016/j.eneco.2009.09.007

Stevenson, W. J. (2007). Operations Management (9th ed.). McGraw-Hill Irwin. Retrieved from www.mhhe.com

Stewart, R., & Moslares, C. (2014). Regional Disparities Across Indian States: Are the Trends Reversing? *Journal of Economics, 2*(3), 95–111.

Straub, S., Vellutini, C., & Warlters, M. (2008). *Infrastructure and economic growth in East Asia* (World Bank Policy Research Working Paper No. 4589). Washington, DC: World Bank.

Straub, S., Vellutini, C., & Warlters, M. (2008). *Infrastructure and Economic Growth in East Asia*. Policy Research Working Paper 4589. World Bank.

Straub, S. (2011). Infrastructure and development: A critical appraisal of the macro-level literature. *The Journal of Development Studies, 47*(5), 683–708. doi:10.1080/00220388.2010.509785

Strauss, J., & Thomas, D. (1998). Health, nutrition, and economic development. *Journal of Economic Literature, 36*(2), 766–817.

Suganthi, V. (2015).Rural consumer brand awareness. *International Journal of Multidisciplinary Research and Development, 2*, 145–152.

Tang, C. F. (2013). A Note on the Health-Growth Nexus in Malaysia. *Journal of Health Management, 15*(3), 345–352. doi:10.1177/0972063413491872

Taqvi, S. M. A. (2013). Emerging Trends in Infrastructure Development in India. *Indian Journal of Applied Research, 3*(4), 257–259. doi:10.15373/2249555X/APR2013/87

Taylor, L. (1983). *Structuralist Macroeconomics*. New York: Basic Books.

Telsang, M. (2004). *Industrial Engineering and Production Management*. S. Chand and Company Ltd.

Thakur, C. (2013). A Study of purchaser Institution about Consumer Durable Goods. *International Global Researches Analysis*, *2*(3), 107-108.

The Challenges of Slums: Earth Scan. (2003). UN-Habitat, Ltd.

The Economist Intelligence Unit (EIU). (2012). *The future of healthcare in Africa*. Switzerland: EIU.

Tripathi, A., & Prasad, A. R. (2008). *An Overview of Agrarian Economy in India: Then Performance and Determinant.* Retrieved from http://blogs.wsj.com/indiarealtime/2013/08/26/where-are-the-onions/

Tripati, K.K, (2014). Review of Rural Infrastructure under Bharat Nirman. *'Kurukshetra' Ministry of Rural Development, Monthly Journal*, *62*(5), 52.

Ubani, E. C., & Ononuju, C. N. (2013). A study of failure and abandonment of public sector-driven civil engineering projects in Nigeria: An empirical review. *American Journal of Scientific and Industrial Research*, *4*(1), 75–82. doi:10.5251/ajsir.2013.4.1.75.82

UNAIDS. (2004). *Report on the Global AIDS Epidemic*. Geneva: UNAIDS.

United Nations (UN). (2005). The Millennium Development Goals Report 2005. New York: United Nations.

Urban Infrastructure in India. (2011). FICCI.

Usman, H. M., Muktarb, M., & Inuwaa, N. (2015). Health Outcomes and Economic Growth Nexus: Testing for Long Run Relationship and Causal Links in Nigeria. *International Journal of Economics and Empirical Research*, *3*(4), 176–183.

Van Horne, J. C., & Dhamija, S. (2012). Financial Management and Policy (12th ed.). Pearson.

Vargas-Hernández, J., Guerra, E., Bojórquez, A., & Bojórquez, F. (2014). *Gestión estratégica de organizaciones*. Ediciones Insumisos Latinos.

Varian, R. H. (2002). *Intermediate Microeconomics A modern Approach* (6th ed.). New York: W.W. Norton & Company.

Vilas, G. D. (2012). Rural Marketing Environment in India. *International Referred Multidisciplinary Online Research Journal*, *1*(VI), 1–35.

Vittas, D. (1999). *Pension Reform and Financial Markets*. Harvard Institute for International Development, Harvard University.

Walke, A., Thomas, G., Fullerton, M. Jr, & Martha, P. (2015, December). An Empirical Analysis of Education, Infrastructure, and Regional Growth in Mexico. *Journal of Economics and Development Studies*, *3*(4), 1–12. doi:10.15640/jeds.v3n4a1

Walz, R. (2007). The role of regulation for sustainable infrastructure innovations: The case of wind energy. *International Journal of Public Policy*, *2*(1-2), 57–88. doi:10.1504/IJPP.2007.012276

Wang, X., & Taniguchi, K. (2003). *Does better nutrition enhance economic growth? The economic cost of hunger.* Retrieved from http://www.fao.org/3/a-y4850e/y4850e04.htm

Wang, E. C. (2002). Public Infrastructure and Economic Growth: A New Applied to East Asian Economies. *Journal of Policy Modeling*, 24.

Weil, D. N. (2007). Accounting for the Effect of Health on Economic Growth. *The Quarterly Journal of Economics*, *122*(3), 1265–1305. doi:10.1162/qjec.122.3.1265

Wieczorek-Zuel & Heidemaria. (2009). IDA 16 and Gender Equality: Is a Breakthrough Possible? Gender Equality as Smart Economics: A World Bank Group Action Plan Newsletter.

World Bank. (2010). *Infrastructure and Growth.* Retrieved from http://go.worldbank.org/TQMEWOD650

World Bank. (2013a). *Energizing Economic Growth in Ghana: Making the Power and Petroleum Sectors Rise to the Challenge* (Report No. 79656). Washington, DC: World Bank.

World Bank. (2013b). *Energizing Economic Growth in Ghana: Making the Power and Petroleum Sectors Rise to the Challenge.* Retrieved from http://documents.worldbank.org/curated/en/485911468029951116/text/796560WP0P13140Box0377384B00PUBLIC0.txt

World Bank. (2015). *Global Economic Prospects.* Washington, DC: World Bank.

World Bank. (2015). *World Development Indicators 2015.* Washington, DC: World Bank.

World Bank. (2016). *Ghana Overview.* Retrieved from http://www.worldbank.org/en/country/ghana/overview

World Bank. (2016). *Private Participation in Infrastructure (PPI) Project Database - World Bank Group.* Retrieved September 6, 2016, from http://ppi.worldbank.org/

World Bank. (2016). *World Development Indicators | Data.* Retrieved September 6, 2016, from http://data.worldbank.org/data-catalog/world-development-indicators

World Bank. (2016). *World Development Indicators 2016.* Washington, DC: World Bank.

World Health Organization. (2007). *World Health Statistics 2007.* Geneva: World Health Organization.

Yeaple, S. R., & Golub, S. S. (2007). International productivity differences, infrastructure, and comparative advantage. *Review of International Economics, 15*(2), 223–242. doi:10.1111/j.1467-9396.2007.00667.x

Yescombe, E. R. (2014). Principles of Project Finance (2nd ed.). Elsevier.

Yigitcanlar, T., & Dur, F. (2010). Developing a sustainability assessment model: The sustainable infrastructure, land-use, environment and transport model. *Sustainability, 2*(1), 321–340. doi:10.3390/su2010321

Zahra, A., Sapienza, J., & Davidsson, P. (2006). Entrepreneurship and Dynamic Capabilities: A Review, Model and Research Agenda. *Journal of Management Studies, 43*(4), 917–955. doi:10.1111/j.1467-6486.2006.00616.x

Zee News. (2015). *Exclusive Union Budget.* Available at: http://zeenews.india.com/exclusive/budget-2015-the-need-for-an-overhaul-in-indian-agriculture-sector_1541831.html

Zhang, J., Zhang, J., & Lee, R. (2003). Rising longevity, education, savings, and growth. *Journal of Development Economics, 70*(1), 83–101. doi:10.1016/S0304-3878(02)00088-3

About the Contributors

Ramesh Chandra Das is currently Associate Professor of Economics at Katwa College, West Bengal, India with seventeen years of teaching and research experience in different fields of the subject. He has obtained Masters, M. Phil and Ph. D Degree in Economics from the University of Calcutta. Dr. Das has contributed several research papers to national and international journals with reputations along with completions of three minor research projects sponsored by UGC, India. He has written one text book on Microeconomics for different fields of students and academicians and edited Handbook of Research on Globalization, Investment and Growth-Implications of Confidence and Governance, and Handbook of Research on Global Indicators of Economic and Political Convergence, published by IGI Global, USA. He has been acting as editor-in-chief in Asian Journal of Research in Business Economics and Management and one of the editorial advisory board members of Society for the Study on Business and Finance.

* * *

Samuel Adams is Professor and Dean of the School of Governance at the Ghana Institute of Management and Public Administration (GIMPA), where he teaches Public Administration, Public Policy, Research methods and Strategic Management. Professor Adams has published articles in many refereed journals including Journal of Policy Modelling, Energy Policy, Environmental Science and Pollution Research, Economic Analysis and Policy, Social Science Quarterly, Public Organization Review, Third World Studies Journal, and the Journal of Social, Economic, and Political Studies.

Indrani Basu is presently Assistant Professor in Economics, Berhampore College, under the University of Kalyani, India. She has thirteen years of experience in teaching and research. She was awarded M. Phil and Ph. D by the University of Kalyani. She has published a number of research papers in peer reviewed journals and books. She has acted as 'external monitoring officer' in a project seeking the evaluation of 'Pulse-Polio Immunization programme' financed by Government of India and World Health Organization during 2003 – 2006 in West Bengal. Apart from this, her areas of interest to do something for the women, who serve the world a lot, but get very meager recognition from the society.

Saumya Chakrabarti teaches Economics at Visva-Bharati, Santiniketan, India. He has also taught at St Xavier's College, Kolkata; University of Calcutta; and at Presidency University. He has been a visiting fellow at Brown University, USA; and an honorary director at Agro-Economic Research Centre, Santiniketan. He has published in journals like Cambridge Journal of Economics, Review of Radical Political Economics, Economic and Political Weekly, Indian Journal of Agricultural Economics, Indian

Journal of Labour Economics, etc. He has written books published by Prentice Hall and Oxford University Press. He has presented papers at different institutions of North America, Latin America, Europe and Australia.

Nilendu Chatterjee had taught Economics in Panihati College during 2012-2014. Also he has been teaching Economics in Kingston College of Science since 2012. Presently he is the faculty member of Economics in Rabindra Bharati University (R.B.U), Kolkata, India. He has completed M. Phil. in Economics with specialization in International Economics and the dissertation was on "Green Capital and Environment in General Equilibrium Trade Models" from R.B.U. He is currently pursuing Ph. D. on Environmental Economics under R.B.U. His areas of research interests are General Equilibrium, Microeconomics, Macroeconomics, Game Theory, and Dynamic Optimization.

Irving Daniel Agustín Cruz, Ph. D., is a Research Assistant in Graduate Business and economic studies, University Center for Economic and Administrative Sciences, University of Guadalajara, Mexico.

Pratip Kumar Datta teaches Economics and Mathematics at Rajatpur Indranarayan Vidyapith (H.S.), Bolpur, India. Apart from teaching, he is engaged in serious research work till today. He had secured his M.Sc. degree in economics from University of Calcutta in the year 1997. He also secured his B.Ed degree from the same university in the year 2006. He has published papers in journals like Merit Research Journals (www.meritresearchjournals.org), Researcher's Tandem etc. He has presented papers at different institutes and universities of India like Burdwan University, Rabindra Bharati University, West Bengal State University, Centre for Studies in International Relations and Development, etc.

Soumyananda Dinda is a Professor at the Department of Economics, The University of Burdwan, West Bengal, India. Dr. Dinda taught at CIMP, MSE Chennai, Bath University, UK; and SRF College; and as a guest faculty in Presidency College and Calcutta University. He worked as economic affair officer at Trade and Investment Division, UN ESCAP, Bangkok. Dr. Dinda published one book "*Environment and Development Trajectory: A Freshlook on Theory and Empirics*", 2009, Nova Science Inc., New York. He has published papers in journals such as *Ecological Economics; Economics and Human Biology; Journal of Socio-Economics; and Journal of Public Economic Theory*. He served as Guest Editor for IJGEnvIs Special Issue on *EKC and Sustainable Development*.

Patrick Omoruyi Eke is a professionally qualified chartered accountant and a faculty of the Lagos State University in Nigeria where he teaches finance and other related courses. He is currently doctoral student in the Department of Finance at Covenant University. He has authored a number of books dealing in financial markets. His articles have appeared in both national and international journals.

Dibyendu Ghosh has completed his M.A. degree in Economics from Department of Economics, The University of Burdwan, West Bengal, India. Previously he was working as a Project Fellow of UGC DRS (PHASE-I) project entitled "Rural Livelihood: Vulnerability and Opportunities" in Burdwan University. Now He is working as a project fellow of UGC DRS (PHASE-II), project entitled "Inclusive and Sustainable Development: with special reference to West Bengal". He has published articles like

"Analysis of Motivation Issues and Link with Profitability: Case Study of Entrepreneurial Firms in a Rural Cluster in West Bengal, India" *Business and Economics Journal*, September 15, 2016, another entitled "A Search for Backward Blocks in Burdwan District, West Bengal: An Application of Composite Development Index".

Somenath Ghosh is a Ph. D scholar in Economics in Visva-Bharati University, India and currently working on the thesis *"Changing condition of Slums in India: an analysis of demographic socio-economic and infrastructural aspects"*. He has completed M. Phil. and M.A. in Economics with specialization in Statistics and Econometrics. Currently, he is engaged as Research Officer in a reputed NGO working on health issues in West Bengal and previously, worked as Researcher in multiple state level projects in Agro-Economic Research Centre (an institute sponsored by Ministry of Agriculture) for two years.

Sebak Kumar Jana is currently Professor in Economics and Head of the Department of Economics with Rural Development, Vidyasagar University, India. Dr. Jana was graduated from Presidency College, Kolkata and obtained M.Sc. degree in Economics from University of Calcutta in India. He obtained M. Phil and Ph. D degree in Economics from Jadavpur University, Kolkata. His area of research includes environmental and resource economics and economics of education. He has about thirty peer reviewed publications in national and international Journals and has also authored five books in different areas of Economics. He has completed three research projects funded by UGC, ICSSR.

Asim Kumar Karmakar is Assistant Professor, Department of Economics, Jadavpur University, India. He is presently the Executive Member of both the Indian Economic Association (IEA) and The Indian Econometric Society (TIES); formerly the Managing Editor (2011-2014) of the Quarterly Referred Journal Artha Beekshan of Bengal Economic Association. He has completed three minor research projects sponsored by the CAS, Jadavpur University and the UGC. He has contributed many research papers in reputed journals at home and abroad, and written books on different fields of economics; titles include Balance of Payments Theory and Policy: The Indian Experience, Capital Account Convertibility in India, Analytical Issues in Trade, Development and Finance.

Adekunle Adetiloye Kehinde teaches International Finance at Covenant University, Ota Nigeria where he obtained his Ph. D. Before venturing into academics he was a banker in the mortgage industry in Nigeria where he spent considerable time. He teaches other finance courses such as International Finance and Financial Systems, Real Estate Finance and Investments and others. He also performs other functions in the Department of Banking and Finance at Covenant University. He has published a number of articles in both national and international journals. He is the winner of the Best Paper Award of IAABD conference in 2012.

Edem Kwame Mensah Klobodu holds an M. Sc Finance degree from the Ghana Institute of Management and Public Administration (GIMPA) Business School where he is a research assistant. Additionally, he holds a Bachelor's degree in Statistics and Computer Science from the University of Ghana. His research focuses on financial markets, the flow of financial capital (FDI, debt, aid, portfolio equities, and remittances), income inequality and general economic growth and development. Mr. Mensah has published in journals like Journal of African Business, International Review of Applied Economics, Energy Policy and International Area Studies Review.

Richmond Odartey Lamptey is achievement-oriented Commercial & Corporate Banking professional and an academic. He is experienced with diversified working knowledge in business support, banking operations, corporate relationship, business valuation and SME funding. Mr. Lamptey holds an M. Sc Finance degree from GIMPA and EMBA in Entrepreneurship Management from the University of Ghana, Legon. Besides, he holds a B. Sc Degree in Administration (Banking and Finance) from the University of Ghana, Legon. His area of research includes economics, finance, entrepreneurship management and impact investing.

Arun Kumar Mandal is Ph.D. Research Scholar of Economics Department of West Bengal State University. He is an Assistant teacher of commerce in Baluhati High School (H.S.), Howrah, India. He has been teaching for the last ten years (Accountancy and Business Economics). His area of interest are Marketing, Consumer durables goods, rural development, Marketing management, Personal Management, Management Accounting, Financial accounting, e-commerce and Business Environment.

Amir Manzoor is a senior faculty member in MIS/Finance area at Bahria University, Karachi, Pakistan. He did MBA in General Management from Lahore University of Management Sciences (LUMS), Pakistan and an MBA in Finance from Bangor University, UK. He has more than 10 years of corporate experience and seven years of teaching experience. His research papers and book chapters have been published in reputed journals (like SAGE Open) and by publishers (like IGI Global). Dr. Amir has authored six books three of them adopted as reference texts in various reputable universities around the world. His research interests are in the areas of technology use for competitive advantage, quantitative analysis, management of academic institutions, and financial modeling.

Sovik Mukherjee is presently a research scholar in the Department of Economics, Jadavpur University, Kolkata, India. Mr. Mukherjee has a B.A (Hons.) degree in Economics from Jadavpur University (2013) and was awarded the Ujjayini Memorial Gold Centred Silver Medal, an M.A degree in Economics from Jadavpur University (2015). His research interests lie in the area of public economics and taxation, applied game theory, environmental economics and issues related to economics of climate change, health economics, international economics and the econometric analysis of financial crises. He has completed a consultancy research project sponsored by the State Bank of India, LHO, Kolkata, India.

Debabrata Mukhopadhyay is presently Associate Professor in Economics at West Bengal State University, Kolkata, India and has more than fifteen years of teaching experience. He did his Ph.D. in Quantitative Economics from the Indian Statistical Institute. His research interests are time series analysis, applied financial econometrics and applied development economics. He has published a number of research articles in several international journals namely *Applied Financial Economics, Emerging Markets Finance and Trade, International Econometric Review, Keio Economic Studies, Sankhya,* etc.

Partha Mukhopadhyay is a part time Ph. D Scholar at Department of Humanities and Social Sciences, National Institute of Technology Durgapur, India. He has been working in Durgapur Steel Plant, Steel Authority of India Limited since 1993. Having the degree of MBA (Finance), he has also completed a post graduate degree in Human Resource area. Till date he has published and presented more than fifteen research papers in national and international level journals, seminars and conferences.

Gabriela Muratalla-Bautista is the professor at the Department of Science and Economic Management of Technology Valley Morelia and Head of the Academic Management and Innovation of Enterprises and Institutions and Research Line Economy of Enterprises and Institutions, Morelia. Her specialization is in Auditing and Certified Public Accountant in the UMSNH.

Sudhakar Patra is presently Professor of Economics at Berhampur University, Odisha, India. He was Head of the Department of Economics of Ravenshaw University, India. He has done his masters from the Utkal University and obtained M. Phil Degree from Jawaharlal Nehru University, New Delhi. He has been conferred the Ph. D Degree by the Utkal University in the year 1993. He has about twenty-five years of teaching and research experiences in his credit. His areas of research are environmental economics and rural developments. He has many publications in national and international journals. He has carried out several research projects sponsored by the UGC, India and SANDEE, Nepal.

Partha Pratim Sengupta is Professor of Economics, Department of Humanities and Social Sciences, National Institute of Technology Durgapur, India. He has teaching experience of thirty four years, out of which twenty years of teaching at PG level and Research. Till now more than twenty students have been awarded Ph.D. degree under his supervision. He published more than one hundred research papers in national and international level peer reviewed journals. He has been invited to present papers at several conferences in India and abroad. Over and above he has received several national and international academic awards. His areas of research include International Economics, Business Economics, Development Economics, Operation research and Management.

Madhabendra Sinha is currently a Research Fellow in Economics at Department of Humanities and Social Sciences, National Institute of Technology Durgapur, India. He obtained the degree of M.Sc. and M. Phil. in Economics from University of Calcutta. His research interests include International Economics, Time Series Econometrics, Open Economy Macroeconomics, Development Economics and Applied Econometrics etc. Till now he has published and presented more than twenty-five research papers in national and international level journals, seminars and conferences.

Joseph Taiwo is an erudite former central banker who has varied experience in the different types (central, development and commercial) of banking in Nigeria before finally settling down to academic life in the Department of Banking and Finance where he now devotes his time to teaching and service. He was a former Registrar of Covenant University Nigeria. He has authored a number of articles that appeared in international and local journals.

Harsha Tiwary is a Ph. D scholar in Economics in Visva Bharati, Santiniketan, India and is working on the thesis Evaluating MGNREGS Performance. She has completed M. Phil in Economics in the year 2014. She has presented the paper on MGNREGS in seminar of Rabindra Bharati University, West Bengal State University and NIRD Hyderabad. She had worked as guest lecturer in Savitri Girls College in Kolkata.

José G. Vargas-Hernández, M.B.A, Ph. D, is a member of the National System of Researchers of Mexico and a research professor at University Center for Economic and Managerial Sciences, University of Guadalajara. Professor Vargas-Hernández has a Ph. D. in Public Administration and a Ph.D. in Organizational Economics. He has undertaken studies in Organizational Behavior and has a Master of Business Administration, published four books and more than 200 papers in international journals and reviews (some translated to English, French, German, Portuguese, Farsi, Chinese, etc.) and more than 300 essays in national journals and reviews. He has obtained several international Awards and recognition.

Index

F

G

H

I

L

M

N

O

P

R

S

T

U

W

CPSIA information can be obtained
at www.ICGtesting.com
Printed in the USA
BVOW04*0323261017
498557BV00009B/105/P

9 781522 523642